Footprint **Laos**

Jock O'Tailan
5th edition

The refuge of the last dreamers, the last loved ones, the last troubadours.

Marthe Bassenne, *Siam and Laos*

Laos Highlights

See colour maps at back of book

1 That Luang
Symbol of Lao nationhood and the country's holiest site, page 53.

2 Vang Vieng
Adventure capital en route to Luang Prabang, with caves, rafting and elephant trekking, page 86.

3 Kwang Si Falls
Popular getaway from Luang Prabang with the prospect of a cooling dip, page 118.

4 Luang Prabang
Perfectly formed little city with UNESCO World Heritage status, page 98.

5 Pak Ou Caves
4000 images of the Buddha crammed into cliff-side caves with a river view, page 117.

6 Phongsali
An upland town surrounded by stunning scenery, page 135.

7 Muang Sing
Attractive base for trekking and for visiting minorities, page 146.

8 The Mekong
Take a slow boat along the mother river of Southeast Asia, page 148.

CHINA

MYANMAR (BURMA)

Phongsali 6

Muang 7
Sing

Luang
Namtha

Udomxai

Xam !

Houei Xai

8 Mekong River

Luang 4
Prabang

5

3

Phonsavanh

Sayaboury

Plain of Jars 9

Vang Vieng 2

Nam Ngum
Reservoir

Phonhong

Paks

VIENTIANE 1

THAILAND

N

50 km
50 miles

CHINA

VIETNAM

Gulf of Tonkin

Annamite Range

⑪

Mahaxai

⑫

Thakhek

Mekong River

Savannakhet

Salavan

⑬
Tad Lo

Sekong

Pakse

⑭

Boloven Plateau

Attapeu

Mekong River

⑮

⑯

CAMBODIA

Wat Xieng Thong
The back of the temple is encrusted with a glass mosaic depicting a boddhi tree.

Contents

Southern Laos

Background

Footnotes

Inside front cover

Overview
Sleeping and eating
price codes

Akha village
The gates are sacred and must not be defiled; visitors must not touch them and should avoid going through them if they do not intend to enter a house in the village.

Xieng Khuan
Reinforced concrete sculptures of Vishnu, Buddha, Siva and various other assorted deities and near-deities adorn Buddha Park, near Vientiane

A foot in the door

Laos is fast becoming the darling of Southeast Asia, satisfying all the romantic images of perfumed frangipani trees, saffron-robed monks, rusty old bicycles and golden temples, all set amongst a rich tapestry of tropical river islands, ethnic minority villages, cascading waterfalls and vivid green rice paddies, and bound together by the mighty Mekong River, the country's lifeline. The vernacular architecture that other countries have swept away in a maelstrom of redevelopment survives in Laos. Simple wooden village homes, colonial-era brick-and-stucco shophouses and gently mouldering monasteries mark Laos out as different. Traditional customs are also firmly intact: incense wafts out of streetside wats, monks collect alms at daybreak and the clickety-clack of looms weaving richly coloured silk can be heard in most villages.

As compelling as these sights and sounds are, the lasting impression for most visitors is of the people and their overwhelming friendliness. Many believe the best thing about Laos is the constant chime of 'sabaidee' ringing out from schoolchildren, monks and other passers-by, extending an invitation to join their meal. This is a land that endures the terrible legacy of being the most bombed country per capita in the world, yet its people transform bomb casings into flower pots and bomb craters into fish ponds. Regardless of their history and their poverty, people here radiate a sunny, happy disposition.

Life is simple in Laos but the people share with their former French colonists an infectious *joie de vivre* that ensures that good food and great company are the pinnacle of enjoyment. If you're seeking a relaxed lifestyle and a warm welcome, you've come to the right place.

10 Contemporary Laos

The most frequently used epithet to describe Laos is 'forgotten', owing to its disengagement from the world political scene for two decades. From 1975, when the Pathet Lao government seized power, until the 1990s, the country was isolated from the West and, thus, insulated against many of the negative effects of rapid modernization associated with its near neighbours. Known affectionately by its citizens as 'Laos Please Don't Rush' (PDR), the country continues to exude a timeless, mellow, languorous air and is millennia away from becoming the next up-and-coming Asian giant.

However, a decade since first opening up to visitors, Laos is finally rousing. Incremental changes are noticeable, especially in the country's famously low-key capital, Vientiane: hammer-and-sickle flags adorn computerized ten-pin bowling galleries; cash machines have been installed on street corners – although some have human cashiers to dole out the kip; a couple of traffic lights command the dribble of tuk-tuks and bicycles; women meet for outdoor aerobics sessions, and the local chicken farmer can text the price of eggs to your mobile phone.

Xieng Khouang Province
Old bomb casings are used for everything from cattle troughs and fences, to stilts for houses and water-carriers.

In the countryside, though, home to 80% of the population, life remains relatively unchanged. The odd motorbike, maybe, a Metallica T-shirt, a mobile phone or a television antenna are the only concessions to 21st-century living. The scores of different ethnic groups scattered across the country are still heavily reliant on the land and on traditional ways of farming or hunting. They live in remote villages of wooden or thatched houses, with no proper infrastructure and, therefore, no easy access to markets where they could sell their produce.

For years cynics have warned that it is only a matter of time before Laos becomes a generic Asian country. But, for now, it remains unique because its gradual development has not been at the cost of its culture. The government may have brought in new liberalizing economic policies but, on the ground, bargaining power is still determined by your ability to tell a good joke and friendships are cemented for life by a decent karaoke performance and a bottle of Beer Lao. *Bopenyang*, meaning 'no problem', is one of the country's most commonly used phrases and encapsulates a culture that remains among the most laid-back on earth.

Plain of Jars
Hundreds of these ancient and mysterious jars still dot the landscape of Xieng Khouang Province, despite intensive bombing during the Secret War.

1 *Rice, the staple food crop, accounts for about a quarter of the country's GDP.* ▶▶ *See page 298.*

2 *Catch a golden crab at Tham Poukham and you'll be blessed with a lifetime of good fortune, so they say.* ▶▶ *See page 87.*

3 *The far north of Laos has some stunning mountainous landscape and is especially geared up for trekking.* ▶▶ *See page 21.*

4 *Tubing for 3 km down the Nam Song River at Vang Vieng is a is a great way to take in the scenery.* ▶▶ *See page 93.*

5 *Lanten women wear their hair back and pluck their eyebrows; their clothes are black, with coloured borders, and they wear delicate silver jewellery.* ▶▶ *See page 143.*

6 *Cookery classes can be arranged covering everything from purchasing the fresh ingredients at the market to preparing and eating a Lao meal.* ▶▶ *See page 30.*

7 *The Royal Palace at Luang Prabang contains* Pra Bang, *the Golden Buddha, from which the city derives its name.* ▶▶ *See page 103.*

8 *The Mekong and its tributaries are home to around a thousand species of fresh-water fish, including the world's largest, a giant 300-kg catfish.* ▶▶ *See page 254.*

9 *Laos was formerly known as Lane Xang or 'Land of a million elephants'. Visitors today can enjoy elephant trekking around Luang Prabang, Xe Pian Wetlands and Tad Lo.* ▶▶ *See page 23.*

10 *Brightly coloured tuk-tuks are ubiquitous and a great way to explore towns and outlying attractions.* ▶▶ *See page 29.*

11 *The romantic ruins of Wat Phou, the most significant Khmer archaeological site in Laos, conform to the Western ideal of the lost city.* ▶▶ *See page 223.*

12 *Idyllic palm-fringed Don Deth, a popular backpacker hangout, is a good place to relax, walk under frangipani trees, watch the sunsets and swim.* ▶▶ *See page 256.*

A lower case capital

In 1827, Siamese King Rama III ransacked Vieng Chan, the capital of Lane Xang, in retaliation for King Chou Anou's failed and foolhardy attempt to defeat the Siamese army. The city lay in ruins until the French took over and the result is that Vientiane is more of a French colonial outpost than an Asian city. It is a low-key place, restrained and understated, with simple shophouses, French villas and a great position on the Mekong. Old and new, East and West meet here. Baguettes and cafés coexist with spicy papaya salad and incense-filled pagodas, all watched over by glistening That Luang, the country's most important Buddhist monument.

A jewel in the crown

Luang Prabang is Laos' single greatest draw: a UNESCO World Heritage Site and a former royal capital. Anchored at the confluence of the Mekong and Nam Khan rivers and surrounded by a crown of mountains, its position alone makes it worth the journey. When you add a plethora of gilded temples and French colonial buildings, strung together by ancient cobbled paths, it becomes a place that should be at the top of every traveller's itinerary. Luang Prabang shows the merit of missed opportunities: starved of funds for 40 years from the French withdrawal through to 1990, its eclectic mix of 16th-century monasteries and late 19th- and 20th-century shophouses has survived with scarcely a pimple of redevelopment. UNESCO's recognition of the town's World Heritage status should mean that the core of Luang Prabang, including the incomparable Wat Xieng Thong, is protected for future generations. What's more, Luang Prabang has great little guesthouses, excellent

The Gothic-style limestone scenery riddled with caves make Laos an ideal destination for rock climbing, although this is still a relatively new activity.

Very early in the morning monks collect alms from crouching women and girls (rarely men).

restaurants and numerous opportunities for rewarding forays into the surrounding countryside, from the 4000 Buddhas of the Pak Ou caves to the waterfalls at Kwang Si.

Head for the hills

Laos has probably the richest forests, the cleanest rivers and the freshest air of all the countries in Southeast Asia. Rafting, trekking, caving and climbing are increasingly popular activities, particularly around Vang Vieng, with its honeycomb of limestone caves and riverside position, but other areas also have enormous potential. Northern Laos is like a Sung Dynasty painting, with jagged mountains, topped by misty cloud formations. Nestled against the border with China are the lofty provinces of Luang Namtha and Phongsali, where brilliant trekking opportunities abound. And, with the opening up of Laos' wild areas has come easier access to the country's minorities. The dominant cultural group in Laos are the Lao: lowland-living, wet-rice cultivating Theravada Buddhists, but more than half the population comprises an array of hill peoples each with their own traditions, beliefs and practices.

Bombed back to the Stone Age

Xieng Khouang in the northeast was unfortunate to lie at the epicentre of one of the war in Indochina's nastier 'sideshows'. It was bombed to bits – something that is still all too evident from the crater-pocked landscape. The war may be over but, day by day, the number of maimed and killed rises, as farmers plough up unexploded bombs and young children play with the detritus of war. Another tragedy was the total destruction of Xieng Khouang town, bombed so thoroughly that not a single building of the original settlement survived. All examples of one of the country's three religious architectural styles were obliterated in the process. However, Xieng Khouang's mysterious giant stone jars did survive – some 300 of them are still littered over the Plain of Jars. Archaeologists argue over their purpose and providence, but the Lao have always known the answer: the jars were left by King Khoon Chuong and his troops after they had used them to brew prodigious quantities of *lao-lao* to lubricate a stupendous victory celebration.

Southern secrets

One of the least explored but arguably most magnificent parts of the country are the central provinces, where imposing, Gothic-style limestone scenery is riddled with elaborate cave systems, including the massive river cave at Kong Lor. Further south, Champasak Province is home to raging waterfalls, coffee plantations and the romantic ruins of ancient, pre-Angkorian Wat Phou.

This fabulous concoction of pavilions, causeways and sanctuaries dates from the 12th century and belongs to another people: the Khmer, whose empire of Angkor extended its power and influence over southern Laos, as well as large areas of central and northeast Thailand. Wat Phou is ample evidence of the economic might and artistic prowess of the Khmer, conveniently left in Laos for another people to exploit.

Finally, right at the southern tip of Laos, the Mekong – the country's defining thread – unravels into a tangle of channels and cascades, surrounding the idyllic, palm-fringed Mekong islands of Siphandon.

In Vientiane, Pi Mai (Lao New Year) is celebrated with three days of festivities and a water fight.

⦂ Footprint features

Planning your trip

Where to go

Laos may not be on the travel itineraries of most international tourists or in the brochures of many tour companies, but it is a priceless country with a great deal to offer the discerning traveller. Notwithstanding the country's poverty and lack of development, it is civilized and refined, with elegant towns, sophisticated cuisine, a leisurely pace of life and a population which is probably the most welcoming and relaxed in Asia. Laos has style.

Certainly the former royal capital of Luang Prabang – designated a World Heritage Site by UNESCO – is a fabulous little city. Today's capital Vientiane, as well as the other Mekong towns of Pakse, Savannakhet and Thakhek, is also elegant with its French architectural heritage largely intact. Wat Phou, an outlier of the former Cambodian kingdom of Angkor, is highly satisfying too, and some visitors enjoy the war history and enigmatic stone urns that litter the Plain of Jars. The Mekong islands in the far south are a great place to relax and read at leisure. Laos has also firmly established itself as the region's premier ecotourism destination, with a wide range of eco-activities ranging from treks to kayaking. But what visitors tend to remember best of all is the warmth of the people and the pleasure that comes from visiting a country which has so far managed to keep the more lurid and gauche aspects of the modern world at bay.

Timetabling a visit Because travelling in Laos can be a bit of a lottery, it is strongly recommended that you allow some leeway in your schedule. Assuming, for example, that it will be possible to catch a flight from Phonsavanh to Vientiane to connect with another from Vientiane to Bangkok, and from there to the US or Europe, is – to say the least – risky. The same goes for road transport, especially during the wet season. Those on organized tours have some distinct advantages in this regard. They will have the services of a local tour guide to apply pressure and secure seats on overbooked planes. Local guides are also much more aware of when problems are likely to arise. A lone traveller, with no Lao, may be left floundering on the tarmac.

Nonetheless, a three- to four-week visit to Laos is sufficient to see much of the country – or at least that fraction of the country that it is possible to see. The main issue, perhaps, is how to couple a visit to the north with a trip to the south where Pakse, Champasak, Wat Phou and the Mekong islands are to be found. Vientiane to Pakse is a journey of around 750 km and many people (because they have booked a flight into and out of Vientiane) have then to retrace those 750 km to catch their plane out. By air this is bearable; by public bus it may test your patience, although now air-conditioned overnight buses make the journey in about 10 hours. The alternative is to enter and exit at different ends of the country. It is now possible to enter at Chiang Khong/Houei Xai in the far north, travel south, and then exit at Pakse/Chongmek. Alternatively, you can enter from Cambodia through the Siphandon area at Don Kralor and exit to Vietnam via Vieng Xai at Na Maew (though visas will be required in advance). ►► *See the box on border crossings on page 27.*

One to two weeks

A one-week trip will require careful planning and prioritizing. If you fly into **Vientiane**, head north to wonderfully preserved **Luang Prabang** via **Vang Vieng**. Or fly from Vientiane to **Luang Namtha** to access the interesting trekking region in the

! Packing for Laos

It is possible to buy most toiletries, as well as things like photographic supplies and peanut butter, in Vientiane. Luang Prabang, Savannakhet and Pakse also stock most basic items. Outside these cities little is available beyond such items as soap, washing powder, batteries, shampoo, and the like. Suitcases are not appropriate if you are intending to travel overland by bus. A backpack, or even better a travelpack (where the straps can be zipped out of sight), is recommended. In terms of clothing, most people in Laos dress tidily and modestly in Laos is relatively casual and suits are not necessary. Don't pack too may clothes; laundry services are cheap, and the turnaround is rapid.

You may want to pack antacid tablets for indigestion; antibiotics for travellers diarrhoea (eg Ciproxin/ Ciprofloxacin); antiseptic ointment (eg Cetrimide); anti-malarials (see page 38); mosquito repellents; travel sickness tablets; painkillers; condoms/ contraceptives; tampons/sanitary towels; high-factor sun screen and a sun hat and a blow-up pillow.

For longer trips involving jungle treks take a clean needle pack, clean dental pack and water filtration devices. However, be wary of carrying disposable needles as customs officials may find them suspicious. If you are a popular target for insect bites or develop lumps quite soon after being bitten, carry an Aspivenin kit. This syringe suction device is available from many chemists and draws out some of the allergic materials and provides quick relief.

Make sure your passport is valid for at least six months and take photocopies of essential documents, passport ID and visa pages and student ID card. Spare passport photos are useful when applying for permits or in case of loss or theft.

Other useful items include a digital camera memory card; bumbag/ money belt; cotton or silk sheet sleeping bag; earplugs; mosquito net; padlock; sun glasses; Swiss Army knife; torch; travel wash; umbrella; wet wipes.

north before overlanding it back to Luang Prabang. Alternatively, after visiting Luang Prabang, fly back to Vientiane and on to Pakse for a trip to the tranquil, laid-back **Siphandon** (4000 islands) in the south.

With an extra week, you could build on the one-week options and fly to **Pakse** for **Wat Phou**, the sublime **Tad Lo** and **Tad Fan falls** and **Siphandon**, or to **Vientiane** to access northern Laos.

Three to four weeks

With one month it is better to start at the extreme north or the south of Laos to cover as much territory as possible. You could travel overland to **Siphandon** in southern Laos via Don Kralor. Before heading north take a side trip to the interesting **Boloven Plateau** with its stunning coffee plantations and ubiquitous falls. Overland it to **Thakhek** and do the motorcycle loop around the limestone scenery of central Laos, visiting the **Kong Lor** river cave en route. Or fly direct to **Vientiane** in order to catch a flight to **Phonsavanh** and explore the mysterious **Plain of Jars**, then continue to **Xam Neua** to see the ancient rock formations at **Suan Hin** and the Pathet Lao caves at **Vieng Xai**. A long but interesting overland route will take you west from here via increasingly popular **Nong Khiaw** to **Luang Prabang**, from where you can head north to the trekking areas of **Luang Namtha, Muang Sing** and **Phongsali**, or catch a boat up the Mekong towards the Thai border. A flight from Vientiane to Xam Neua will save two days' travel and from Vientiane to Phongsali will save four days' travel.

When to go

Best time to visit The best time to travel is during the relatively cool and dry winter months from November to March. Not only is the weather more pleasant at this time of year but roads are also in better shape. However, temperatures in upland areas like the Plain of Jars, the Boloven Plateau and some towns in the north of the country can be extraordinarily cold. From April onwards, temperatures can exceed 40°C in many lowland areas, although it remains dry through to May. From June or July, as the wet season wears on, so unsurfaced roads begin to deteriorate and overland transport in some areas becomes slower and more difficult. In the north, the months from March through to the first rains in May or June can be very hazy as smoke from burning off the secondary forest hangs in the air. On the worst days this can cause itchiness of the eyes. What's more, it means that views are restricted and sometimes flights are cancelled. See page 320 for more details on climate. For daily weather reports for Champasak, Pak Lai, Pakbeng, Pakse, Phongsali, Savannakhet, Vientiane, Xam Neua and Xepon, see www.wunderground.com.

Activities and tours

Laos is starting to garner a reputation for itself as one of the prime adventure and ecotourism destinations in the region. The pleasure of floating lazily down the Nam Song, stopping every so often to get out of your inner tube and explore a cave or two, is indisputable, and people come back for more time and again. Kayaking is also an option, but gear yourself up for a pleasant, rather tame day out rather than a foam-flecked white-knuckle ride. There are also wonderful trekking opportunities through stunning mountainous landscape, home to a variety of ethnic groups. Other activities, such as rafting, kayaking, rock climbing and cycling, are fairly recently established or slowly emerging and are not as developed as they are in a place like Thailand. Safety is always an issue when participating in adventurous sports: make sure you are fully covered by your travel insurance; check the credentials of operators offering adventure activities; and make sure that vehicles and safety equipment are in a good condition. Note that medical care in Laos is very limited, see page 38.

Caving

Laos has some of the most extensive and largest caves in the region. Some of the best can be found around Vang Vieng, where caving tourism has been developed. Another highlight is the amazing Kong Lor river cave in the centre of the country. There are hundreds of caves around Vieng Xai but only a few open to tourists; for those interested in history these caves should be a first stop.

★ Head for ...
Vang Vieng, page 86; **Muang Sui**, page 170; **Tham Kong Lor**, page 189. ⓘ **Green Discovery**, Vang Vieng, T023-511230, www.greendiscoverylaos.com.

Cycling and mountain biking

In Laos, cycling is offered by several tour agencies; Luang Namtha is a popular place to start, and **Green Discovery** run excellent cycling tours. Many cyclists prefer to bring their own all-terrain or racing bikes but it's also possible to rent them from tour operators. Most cities and small towns have guesthouses that rent bicycles (for US$1-2 per day), though these bikes generally aren't suitable for riding around the country. You will also need to bring a proper helmet as they aren't available in Laos. Traffic is quite light but often speeds along the highways, particularly the southern roads. Most major roads are sealed now and for the most part traverse quite hilly areas.

⁑ The best wildlife experiences

→ Look for wild elephants while trekking through the stunning wilderness of Phou Khao Khouay National Park, www.trekkingcentrallaos.com, page 84.
→ Visit a camp 15 km out of Luang Prabang, set up by Tiger Trails for the rehabilitation of elephants previously employed in the logging trade, www.tigertrail-laos.com, page 111.
→ Catch a glimpse of the rare, black-cheeked crested gibbons chortling out soprano tunes from the jungle's canopy, with the Gibbon Experience, T084-212-021, jf@clemastecs.net, page 158.
→ See the beautiful, rare freshwater dolphins in Siphandon, page 257.

★ **Head for ...**
Luang Namtha, page 142.
ⓘ **Green Discovery**, Vang Vieng, T023-511230, www.greendiscoverylaos.com.
Symbiosis, www.symbiosis-travel.com.

Kayaking and rafting

Laos is criss-crossed by fantastic rivers, which carve their way through pristine wilderness and stunning mountain scenery. Kayaking/rafting is offered around the country. Before undertaking a trip ensure that the boats are in good condition and that you are supplied with safety equipment, such as helmets and life-jackets. Most kayaking and rafting trips will need to be organized from a provincial capital or Vientiane.

★ **Head for ...**
Nam Song, at Vang Vieng, page 86, hosts a variety of water-borne tours suitable to most travellers' tastes. See also **Luang Prabang**, page 128, **Luang Namtha**, page 157, and **Pakse**, page 230. There is also excellent kayaking around the **Boloven Plateau**, page 233.
ⓘ **Green Discovery**, www.green discoverylaos.com.
Paddle Asia, www.laosadventure.com.
Xplore-Asia, www.xplore-asia.com.

Rock climbing

Laos has stunning karst rock formations, caves and cliffs and is an ideal destination for rock climbers. However, rock climbing is still relatively new to Laos and the only area which has really developed facilities is Vang Vieng. It is expected that over the next few years this adventure sport will be established in other areas around the country. You can pick up a copy of the *Rock Climbing – Vang Vieng Guide*, by Dr Volker Schoeffl (2005) for US$5 at all **Green Discovery** offices.

★ **Head for ...**
Vang Vieng, page 86.
ⓘ **Green Discovery**, Vang Vieng, T023-511230, www.greendiscoverylaos.com.

Spas

There are only a handful of authentic spas in Laos. Luang Prabang is the place to go for a range of wonderful spas.
For extreme indulgence try the Spa at La Residence Phou Vao. For a cheaper luxury alternative the Spa Garden, T071-212325, spagardenlpb@hotmail.com. offers a wide selection of massage and beauty treatments.

★ **Head for ...**
Luang Prabang, page 128. For extreme indulgence try **The Spa at La Résidence Phou Vao**, page 128. For a cheaper luxury alternative the **Spa Garden**, page 128, which offers a wide selection of massage and beauty treatments.

Trekking

Treks are offered in abundance and the most northerly parts of the country are especially geared up for this sort of activity. When trekking in Laos, it is imperative that visitors abide by local rules and customs in order to support the country's efforts to keep tourism sustainable and as low impact

Essentials Planning your trip

Wildlife conservation

The opportunity to buy or consume wildlife will probably present itself throughout your travels in Laos . However, while the Government of Lao PDR permits subsistence hunting for local rural villagers, the sale and purchase of any wildlife is illegal in the country, and is damaging to biodiversity and local livelihoods.

You may see live wild animals for sale as meat or pets in rural areas and cities. Some travellers buy these live animals out of pity, and then release them. Please do not be tempted to do this, as the vendors do not know your motivation and the sale simply increases the demand for wildlife. Also, by this stage the animal could be sick, and could infect other wild animals if released.

You may also encounter rat snakes, soft-shelled turtles, mouse deer, sambar deer, squirrel, bamboo rat, muntjac and pangolins as food in markets and on the menus of Lao and Chinese restaurants in Vientiane, Luang Prabang and in the provinces. Some French restaurants in Vientiane and Luang Prabang serve deer – usually this is muntjac, a wild animal from the forest. Many of these species are either endangered themselves or are a prey source for endangered species, such as the Indochinese tiger.

Neither should travellers be tempted to purchase stuffed wild animals, animal products such as bags and wallets or insects in framed boxes (eg butterflies and beetles). Also to be avoided are animal teeth sold as rings and necklaces – sellers often state this is buffalo bone but it may be bear or wild pig bone. Do not buy bottles of alcohol with snakes, birds or insects inside. Though widely sold, all these items are illegal in Laos, and most travellers will find that their purchases are confiscated by customs in their home country (particularly in Australia and America). Only products with a CITES-certified label are legal to buy in Laos and take home.

As a part of many festivals and temple visits in Laos, Buddhists release small birds to gain merit. You are likely to see these tiny birds, frequently native munias and swallows, in small rattan cages outside temples. The Wildlife Conservation Society-Lao PDR Program, is working with the Lao Buddhist Association to discourage this practice. The birds, weakened by being caged, probably perish shortly after release. Please don't participate in buying and releasing birds.

For many species of wildlife in Laos, populations are at critically low levels. The Wildlife Conservation Society-Lao PDR Program is collaborating with the Vientiane Capital City government to monitor and control wildlife trade. Government staff patrol restaurants, markets and households with suspected trade or captured species, and confiscate the wildlife. Live wildlife is released or euthanized; dead wildlife is periodically burnt in ceremonial public fires (for project transparency and to raise awareness). The Wildlife Conservation Society (WCS) appreciates the support of all visitors and residents in Laos to help conserve wildlife. For more information visit www.wcs.org/international/Asia/laos.
Dr Renae Stenhouse, Wildlife Conservation Society.

as possible. For a different perspective on the landscape, **elephant trekking** is possible around Luang Prabang, Xe Pian Wetlands and Tad Lo.

★ **Head for ...**
Phou Hin Poun National Protected Area, page 83, **Vang Vieng**, page 86, **Luang**

Prabang, page 128, **Luang Namtha**, page 142, **Phongsali**, page 134, **Muang Sing**, page 146, **Bokeo Nature Reserve**, page 149, **Vieng Phouka**, page 157, **Xe Pian National** Protected Area, page 226, **Tad Lo**, page 235.
ⓘ **National Tourism Administration of Lao PDR**, T021-212251, www.trekkingcentrallaos.com.

Taking a tour

Numerous operators offer organized trips to this region, ranging from a whistle-stop tour of the highlights to specialist trips that focus on a specific destination or activity. The advantage of travelling with a reputable operator is that your transport, accommodation and activities are all arranged for you in advance – particularly valuable if you only have limited time in the region. By travelling independently, however, you can be much more flexible and spontaneous about where you go and what you do. You will be able to explore less-visited areas and you will save money, if you budget carefully. A list of specialist tour operators can be found in Essentials A-Z, page 42.

Local customs and laws

Bargaining/haggling

While bargaining is common in Laos – in the market or in negotiating a trip on a *saamlor* or tuk-tuk, for example – it is not heavy-duty haggling. The Lao are extremely laid back and it is rare to be fleeced; don't bargain hard with them, it may force them to lose face and reduce prices well below their profit margin. For most things, you won't even really need to bargain. Having said that, beware of the tuk-tuk drivers (where possible, try to flag down tuk-tuks rather than taking those waiting on street corners). Approach bargaining with a sense of fun; a smile or joke always helps.

Clothing

Informal, lightweight clothing is all that is needed, although a sweater is vital for the highlands in the winter months (November to March). An umbrella is useful during the rainy season (June and July). Sleeveless shirts and singlets, very short shorts and skirts are not ideal. When visiting monasteries (wats) women should keep their shoulders covered and take their shoes off. One of the main reasons for the tight controls on tourism in Laos is because of the perceived corrosive effects that badly dressed tourists were having on Lao culture. The assumption was that scruffy dress was a reflection of character. Today, 'scruffy' travellers are still frowned upon and officials are getting fed up with people wandering around skimpily clad, particularly in Vang Vieng and Siphandon. If you are bathing in public, particularly in rural areas, you should try to bathe with a sarong. It is expected that people will take their shoes off before entering a Lao home.

Conduct

Wats Monks are revered, don't touch their robes. If talking to a monk your head should be lower than his. Avoid visiting a wat around 1100 as this is when the monks have their morning meal. It is considerate to ask the abbot's permission to enter the *sim* and shoes should be removed before entry. When sitting down, feet should point away from the altar and main image. Arms and legs should be fully covered when visiting wats. A small donation is often appropriate (kneel when putting it into the box).
Forms of address Lao people are addressed by their first name, not their family name, even when a title is used.

Greeting The *nop* or *wai* – with palms together below your chin and head bowed, as if in prayer – remains the traditional form of greeting. Shaking hands, though, is very widespread – more so than in neighbouring Thailand. This can be put down to the influence of the French during the colonial period (whereas Thailand was never colonized). '*Sabaidee*' (hello) is also a good way to greet. Avoid hugging and kissing to greet Lao people, as they tend to get embarrassed.

In private homes Remove your shoes. When seated on the floor you should tuck your feet behind you.

Eating etiquette In Laos, who eats when is important. At a meal, a guest should not begin eating until the host has invited him or her to do so. Nor should the guest continue eating after everyone else has finished. It is also customary for guests to leave a small amount of food on their plate; to do otherwise would imply that the guest was still hungry and that the host had not provided sufficient food for the meal. Sharing is a big thing at meal times, where plates of food are ordered and shared amongst everyone. Lao people often invite tourists to eat with them or share on buses, and it is a nice gesture if this is reciprocated (though Lao people tend to be shy so don't take any refusal as a rejection). Most Lao are very tolerant of other cultures and don't expect things such as eating etiquette to be strictly adhered to.

General Pointing with the index finger is considered rude. If you want to call someone over, gesture with your palm facing the ground and fingers waving towards you (as opposed to the other direction). In Lao your head is considered 'high' and feet are considered 'low'. So try to keep your feet low, don't point them at people or touch people with your feet. Don't pat children on the head (or touch people's heads in general) , as it is the considered the most sacred part of the body.

Lao people have a passive nature. Yelling or boisterous people tend to completely freak them out and they go into panic mode. If a dispute arises, a smile and a few jokes will do the trick every time. Likewise for bargaining, keep a sense of humour, and the funnier you are, the more likely you are to get your desired price.

The Lao are proud people and begging is just not the done thing, so don't hand out money (or medicine) to local villagers. If you want to give a gift or a donation to someone, it is best to channel it through the village elder.

Responsible tourism

Since the early 1990s there has been a phenomenal growth in 'ecotourism', which promotes and supports the conservation of natural environments and is also fair and equitable to local communities. While the authenticity of some ecotourism operators needs to be interpreted with care, there is clearly both a huge demand for this type of activity and also significant opportunities to support worthwhile conservation and social development initiatives by this means. **Green Globe** ① T020-77304428, *www.greenglobe21.com*, and the **Centre for Environmentally Sustainable Tourism (CERT)** ① T01268-795772, *www.c-e-r-t.org*, now offer advice for travellers on selecting destinations and sites that aim to achieve certain commitments to conservation and sustainable development.

❧ *Particular rules apply when visiting minority villages, for details, see page 25.*

In addition, the **Eco-Tourism Society** ① T1-802-447 2121, *www.ecotourism.org*, **Tourism Concern** ① T020-7753 3330, *www.tourismconcern.org.uk*, and **Planeta** ① *www.planeta.com*, develop and promote ecotourism projects in destinations all over the world and their websites provide details for initiatives throughout Southeast Asia. For opportunities to participate directly in scientific research and development

*(margin, vertical)* Essentials Local customs & laws

How big is your footprint?

The benefits of international travel are self-evident for both hosts and travellers: employment, increased understanding of different cultures, business and leisure opportunities. At the same time there is clearly a downside to the industry. Where visitor pressure is high or poorly regulated, adverse impacts to society and the natural environment may occur. In order to ensure your contribution to the host nation is a positive one, follow these guidelines, taken from the Tourism Concern website, www.tourismconcern.org.uk.

→ Learn about the country you're visiting. Start enjoying your travels before you leave by tapping into as many sources of information as you can.

→ Think about where your money goes – be fair and realistic about how cheaply you travel. Try and put money into local people's hands; drink local beer or fruit juice rather than imported brands, and stay in locally-owned accommodation.

→ Open your mind to new cultures and traditions. It can transform your holiday experience and you'll earn respect and be more readily welcomed by local people.

→ Think about what happens to your rubbish: take biodegradable products and a water filter bottle. Be sensitive to limited resources like water, fuel and electricity.

→ Help preserve local wildlife and habitats by respecting rules and regulations, such as sticking to footpaths, not standing on coral and not buying products made from endangered plants or animals.

→ Use your guidebook as a starting point, not the only source of information. Talk to local people, then discover your own adventure!

→ Don't treat people as part of the landscape; they may not want their picture taken. Put yourself in their shoes, ask first and respect their wishes. See also Visiting minority villages below.

Essentials Responsible tourism

projects, contact **Earthwatch** ① *in the US and Canada 1-800-7760188, in the UK To1865-311601, www.earthwatch.org*), **Discovery International** ① *To20-7229 9881, www.discoveryinitiatives.com*, and the **Nautilus Institute** ① *www.nautilus.org*, which focuses on issues specifically connected with the environment and sustainability in the Asia-Pacific region. See also How big is your footprint?, above.

Visiting minority villages It is becoming increasingly popular for travellers to Laos to visit minority villages. This raises a whole series of questions about conduct which cannot be covered in a general discussion because of cultural differences between the many different ethnic peoples. There is certainly a case for advising that visitors, where possible, employ the services of a local guide. Just as was the case in northern Thailand when trekking became popularized there, the actions of a few are tarring the reputation of the many. In more than a few cases, visitors have no idea how to behave with minority people. Many seek to buy drugs, female travellers potter around scantily clad, they have little notion of local customs, where not to go, what not to bring (many bring sweets), and so on. Because the numbers of travellers visiting minority villages has exploded in recent years this has become quite a serious problem.

Getting there

Air

The easiest – and cheapest – way to access the region is via **Bangkok** or **Hong Kong**. Most major airlines have direct flights from Europe, North America and Australasia to these hubs. Laos is only accessible from within Asia.

There are international flights to Vientiane from the following countries: **Cambodia** (Phnom Penh and Siem Reap), **China** (Kunming), **Taiwan** (Taipei), **Thailand** (Bangkok) and **Vietnam** (Hanoi and Ho Chi Minh City). Most people visiting Laos from outside the region, travel via Bangkok. There are also flights from Bangkok and Chiang Mai to **Luang Prabang**. A cheaper option for getting to Laos from Bangkok is to fly to **Udon Thani**, Thailand, about 50 km south of the border at the Friendship Bridge and travel overland from there. For full details, see page 77. An alternative route is to fly from Bangkok to **Chiang Rai,** Thailand, before overlanding it to **Chiang Khong** and crossing into northern Laos at **Houei Xai**. From Houei Xai there are flights to Vientiane and boats to Luang Prabang via Pak Beng.

From Thailand   Bangkok (BKK) is the main gateway to Vientiane. If you want to visit Bangkok as well as Laos, the best way is to include the Bangkok–Vientiane sector on your long-haul ticket. This is a cheaper option than purchasing tickets separately in Bangkok. There are daily flights between Bangkok (Suvarnabhumi) and Vientiane operated by **THAI** (www.thaiairways.com) and **Lao Airlines** (www.laoairlines.com). The official fares on each airline vary slightly but both can be purchased from travel agents. It's worth checking the schedule on the Lao Airlines website as they are forever curtailing/adding/changing flights. **Bangkok Airways** (www.bangkokair.com) flies from Bangkok to Luang Prabang.

Chiang Mai (CNX) Lao Airlines (www.laoairlines.com) runs a daily service between Chiang Mai (northern Thailand) and Luang Prabang.

Udon Thani (UTH)   While most visitors to Laos fly into Vientiane, the preferred route in and out of Laos for many expats is via Udon Thani in northeast Thailand, about 50 km south of the Friendship Bridge border. This is because the single domestic airfare between Bangkok and Udon is a third of the international fare between Bangkok and Vientiane, while a domestic return costs half the price of the international ticket. Discount airline, **Air Asia** (www.airasia.com) flies this route so there are now around six flights a day between Bangkok and Udon. The service works very efficiently and is fairly hassle-free. From Udon Thani, you can catch a minibus or taxi to the Friendship Bridge or a bus directly to the Talaat Sao bus terminal in Vientiane for only ฿80. (You could also overland it from Udon Thani to Pakse in southern Laos.) All in all, taking the Udon/Friendship Bridge option between Bangkok and Vientiane will probably only add one hour to your journey, since immigration at Wattay Airport tends to be slow.

From Cambodia There are regular flights between Phnom Penh (PNH) and Vientiane with **Vietnam Airlines** (www.vietnamairlines.com) and **Lao Airlines** (www.laoairlines.com). **Lao Airlines** also runs flights between Siem Reap and Vientiane and between Siem Reap and Pakse and Siem Reap and Luang Prabang.

From China Lao Airlines (www.laoairlines.com) and **Southern Airlines** (merged with China Yunnan Air; www.cs-air.com/en/) both run flights between Kunming (KMG) and Vientiane.

From Vietnam Lao Airlines (www.laoairlines.com) operates flights between Vientiane and Hanoi four times a week. **Vietnam Airlines** (www.vietnamairlines.com) runs a daily service between Hanoi and Vientiane and regular flights between Ho Chi Minh City and Vientiane.

⁞ Official border crossings

Cambodia-Laos
Don Kralor-Voen Kham
(Lao visa required in advance),
page 264.

China-Laos
Mohan-Boten, page 145.

Myanmar (Burma)-Laos
Foreigners are currently not
permitted to enter or leave Laos
through Myanmar (Burma).

Thailand-Laos
Mittaphab (Friendship) Bridge,
Nong Khai-Vientiane, page 77.

Chiang Khong-Houei Xai, page 149.
Paksan-Beung Kan, page 189.
Nakhon Phanom-Thakhek, page 197.
Mukdahan-Savannakhet (either by
boat or the new bridge), page 213.
Chongmek-Vang Tao (near Pakse),
page 220.

Vietnam-Laos
Nong Het-Nam Khan, page 171.
Na Maew-Nam Xoi, page 176.
Cau Treo-Nam Phao, page 192.
Cha Lo-Na Phao (visas not available
at the border).
Lao Bao-Dansavanh, page 210.
Bo Y-Yalakhuntum, page 243.

Airport departure tax International departure from Laos is US$15 for international;
domestic airport tax is 5000 kip. ▸▸ *For airport information, see Ins and outs section throughout
the guide.*

By road and river

Laos is a land-locked country and hopes to establish itself as a regional transit point,
with new international highways dissecting the country at 100 km intervals. For the
moment, however, foreign visitors travelling overland between neighbouring
countries are restricted to a handful of key crossing points (see Official border
crossings, page 27). For much of its length, the Lao-Thai border is defined by the
Mekong, with bridges and ferries to link the two countries. To the east, the Annamite
mountain range forms a spine separating Laos from Vietnam, with a few cross-border
buses running from Vientiane and Savannakhet. There is only one official border
crossing between Laos and Cambodia in the south and between Laos and China in
the north. Foreigners are not permitted to cross between Laos and Myanmar (Burma).

Getting around

Air

Lao Airlines run domestic flights from Vientiane to Phonsavannh (Xieng Khouang),
Houei Xai, Oudomxai and Pakse within Laos. All flights using **Lao Airlines**, whether
domestic or international, have to be paid for in US dollars by foreigners. **Lao Airlines**
flies three types of aeroplane: French-built *ATR-72s*, and Chinese-built *Y-7s* and *Y-12s*.
The latter two are a risk. The most reliable, comfortable and newest machines – the
ATR-72s – operate on the most popular routes (Vientiane-Bangkok, Vientiane-Luang
Prabang, Vientiane-Pakse). Within Laos there is also a smaller, newer carrier – **Lao
Air**, laoair@laopdr.com, that run flights to Xam Neua and Phongsali. ▸▸ *For further
details, see Ins and outs sections throughout the guide.*

River

It is possible to take riverboats up and down the Mekong and its main tributaries. Boats
stop at Luang Prabang, Pak Beng, Houei Xai and around Don Deth, Don Khong as well

as other smaller towns and villages, such as Nong Khiaw. Aside from the main route down from Houei Xai to Luang Prabang often there are no scheduled services and departures may be limited during the dry season. Take food and drink and expect somewhat crowded conditions aboard. The most common riverboats are the *hua houa leim*, with no decks, the hold being enclosed by side panels and a flat roof (note that metal boats get very hot). Speedboats also chart some routes, but are very dangerous and never enjoyable. Prices vary according to size of boat and length of journey.

Road

Roads are not good, but they are slowly improving. Many have been repaired or upgraded in recent years, making journeys infinitely more comfortable, as well as faster. Quite a few bus, truck, tuk-tuk, *songthaew* (see below) and taxi drivers understand the rudimentaries of English, French or Thai, although some of them (especially tuk-tuk drivers) aren't above forgetting the lowest price you thought you'd successfully negotiated before hopping aboard! It is best to take this sort of thing in good humour. Even so, in order to travel to a particular destination, it is a great advantage to have the name written out in Lao. Many people will not know road names, even if it's the road right outside their front door. However, they will know where all the sights of interest are – for example wats, markets, monuments, waterfalls, etc.

Bus/truck It is now possible to travel to most areas of the country by bus, truck or *songthaew* (converted pickup truck) in the dry season, although road travel in the rainy season can be tricky if not downright impossible. VIP buses are very comfortable night buses, usually allowing a good sleep during the trip – but watch out for karaoke on board. In the south there is a sleeping bus that plies the route from Pakse to Vientiane. The mobile slumber party is loads of fun but make sure you book a double bed as you could wind up sleeping next to a stranger. Robberies have been reported on the night buses so keep your valuables somewhere secure.

On certain long-distance routes, such as Vientiane/Luang Prabang to Xam Neua, big Langjian (Chinese) trucks are sometimes used. These trucks have been colourfully converted into buses with a wooden structure on the back, divided wooden seats and glassless windows. In more remote places (Xam Neua to Vieng Xai, for instance), ancient jeeps are common.

In the south of the country, Japanese-donated buses are used although you may see the occasional shiny Volvo bus. Most roads are now sealed, although breakdowns are still fairly common. For some connections you may need to wait a day. During the rainy season (June to December) expect journey times to be longer than those quoted; indeed some roads may be closed altogether.

Car hire This costs anything from US$40-100 per day, depending on the vehicle, with first 150 km free, then US$10 every 100 km thereafter. The price includes a driver. For insurance purposes you will probably need an international driver's permit. Insurance is generally included with car hire but it's best to check the fine print. A general rule of thumb: if you are involved in a car crash, you, the foreigner, will be liable for costs as you have more money.

Motorbike and bicycle hire There are an increasing number of motorcycles available from guesthouses and other shops in major towns. 110cc bikes go for around US$4-10 per day, while 250cc Hondas are around US$20 per day. Bicycles are available in many towns and are a cheap way to see the sights. Many guesthouses have bikes for rent at US$1-2 per day.

Tuk-tuk The majority of motorized three-wheelers known as 'jumbos' or tuk-tuks are large motorbike taxis with two bench seats in the back. You'll find them in most cities and metropolitan areas; expect to pay around 10,000-15,000 kip for a short ride. They can also be hired by the hour or the day to reach destinations out of town.

In city centres make sure you have the correct money for your tuk-tuk as they are often conveniently short of change. Also opt to flag down a moving tuk-tuk rather than selecting one of the more expensive ones that shark around outside tourist destinations.

Maps

The **GT Rider** Lao map found in bookstores and other shops in Vientiane is probably the most accurate map of the country. The National Tourism Authority has also put together pretty good provincial maps of Laos, using the GT Rider Map as a base. These are available at provincial tourism offices. There are numerous glossy maps of Vientiane and Luang Prabang, including 3D maps, and a series of locally produced town maps which cover the major settlementsof Vientiane, Luang Prabang, Thakhek, Savannakhet and Pakse. The best selection in the UK is available from Stanfords, 12-14 Long Acre, London WC2E 9LP, T020-7836 1321.

Sleeping

Rooms in Laos are rarely luxurious and standards vary enormously. You can end up paying double what you would pay in Bangkok for similar facilities and service. However, the hotel industry is expanding rapidly. There is a reasonable choice of hotels of different standards and prices in Vientiane, Luang Prabang and Pakse and an expanding number of budget options in many towns on the fast-developing tourist trail. First-class hotels exist in Vientiane and Luang Prabang. The majority of guesthouses and hotels have fans and attached bathrooms, although more and more are providing air conditioning where there is a stable electricity supply, while others are installing their own generators to cater for the needs of the growing tourist trade. Smaller provincial towns, having previously had only a handful of hotels and guesthouses – some of them quaint French colonial villas – are now home to a growing number of rival concerns as tourism takes off. In rural villages, people's homes are enthusiastically transformed into bed and breakfasts on demand. While Vientiane may still have little budget accommodation, many towns in the north, such as Vang Vieng, Muang Ngoi, Muang Sing and Luang Namtha, have a large choice of very cheap, and in some cases very good accommodation, including dorm beds. In the southern provinces, upmarket and boutique accommodation has cropped up in Pakse and Don Khong. There are several excellent eco-lodges in the country, most notably the **Boat Landing** at Luang Namtha (page 152) and the **Kingfisher Ecolodge** at Ban Kiet Ngong (page 228). Many tour companies offer homestay in ethnic minority villages and camping as part of a package tour.

Sleeping price codes

LL **Over US$200 Luxury**: Only a couple of hotels – in Vientiane and Luang Prabang – fall into this category.

L **US$100-199 First class plus**: Business services, sports facilities, Asian and Western restaurants, bars and discos. Most of Laos' top hotels fall into this category.

A **US$50-99 First class**: Hotels in this category should be comfortable and offer reasonable business services, a range of recreational facilities, restaurants and bars. They may well make up in terms of personal service and friendliness what they lack in size and grandeur.

B **US$25-49 Tourist class**: All rooms will have air-conditioning, TV and an attached bathroom with hot water. Other services should include one or more restaurants, a coffee shop/room service and, occasionally, a swimming pool.

C **US$15-24 Economy**: Rooms should be air-conditioned and will have attached bathrooms with hot water and Western toilets. A restaurant and room service will probably be available.

D **US$8-14 Medium budget**: Probably air-conditioned rooms with en suite bathroom. Toilets should be Western-style. Bed linen will be provided, towels perhaps. There may be a restaurant.

E **US$4-7 Budget/guesthouse**: Usually fan-cooled rooms and often shared bathrooms with cold water only and basic facilities. Bathrooms are more likely to have squat toilets. Bed linen and towels provided. Rooms are small and facilities few.

F **Less than US$4 Dormitory/guesthouse**-type accommodation, with shared bathroom facilities, squat toilets, fan-cooled and probably cold-water showers. Cleanliness will vary.

Unless otherwise stated, the prices and codes in this guide are based on the cost of a double room for one night, not including service charges or meals.

Eating and drinking

Food

Lao food is similar to that of Thailand, although the Chinese influence is slightly less noticeable. Lao dishes are distinguished by the use of aromatic herbs and spices such as lemon grass, chillies, ginger and tamarind. The best place to try Lao food is often from roadside stalls or in the markets. The staple Lao foods are *kao niao* (glutinous rice), which is eaten with your hands and fermented fish or *pa dek* (distinguishable by its distinctive smell), often laced with liberal spoons of *nam pa*, fish sauce. Being a landlocked country, most of the fish is fresh from the Mekong. One of the delicacies that shouldn't be missed is Mok Pa steamed fish in banana leaf. Most of the dishes are variations on two themes: fish and bird. *Laap*, also meaning 'luck' in Lao, is a traditional ceremonial dish made from (traditionally) raw fish or meat crushed into a paste, marinated in lemon juice and mixed with chopped mint. It is called *laap sin* if it has a meat base and *laap paa* if it's fish based. Beware of *laap* in cheap street restaurants. It is sometimes concocted from raw offal and served cold and should be consumed with great caution. Overall though *laap* is cooked well for the *falang* palate.

Phanaeng kai is stuffed chicken with pork, peanuts and coconut milk with a dash of cinnamon. *Kai ping* is grilled chicken eaten with sticky rice. Another popular Lao dish is *tam som* – often called *som tam* – a spicy green shredded papaya salad

Restaurant price codes

₩₩₩	**Expensive**	over US$12
₩₩	**Moderate**	US$6-12
₩	**Cheap**	under US$6

Prices refer to the cost of a meal for one, without a drink.

served with chilli peppers, spices and fish sauce. This dish can be fiery hot at times, so you should stipulate how hot (*phet*) you want it! There are several different types of **soup** – include *keng no mai* (bamboo shoot), *keng khi lek* (vegetable and buffalo skin), *ken chut* (without pimentos) *keng kalami* (cabbage with fish or pork), *kenghet bot* (mushroom), *tom khaa kai* (chicken with coconut milk).

The most common **vegetables** are aubergines, tomatoes, cabbage, corn, cucumbers and lettuce, often cooked together, pureed and eaten with sticky rice. Soups usually accompany meals – they are usually a mixture of fish and meat infused with aromatic herbs.

The Lao are partial to **sweets**: sticky rice with coconut milk and black beans (which can be bought in bamboo tubes in the markets) and grilled bananas are favourites. One would have thought, in a place like Laos, that **fruit** would be on every menu. But, perhaps because familiarity breeds contempt, many restaurants will have no fruit of any kind – even at breakfast and particularly in places not geared to foreigners.

There is a well-ingrained **Vietnamese** culinary tradition and **Chinese** food is never hard to find. *Feu*, Vietnamese noodle soup, is itself an import from China but often masquerades in Laos as a Lao dish. It is usually served with a plate of raw vegetables. Most restaurants outside the main towns do not have menus but will nearly always serve *feu* and *laap* or local specialities. Indeed, their generic name is *raan khai feu* – restaurants that sell *feu*. Vietnamese spring rolls are also very popular – you can either have *yaw jeun* (deep-fried spring rolls) or *yaw dip* (fresh spring rolls) and both are usually served with fresh herbs and rice noodles.

The French left a legacy of sophisticated cuisine in Laos. **French** food is widely available, with street cafés, serving delectable fresh croissants, baguettes, *pain au chocolat* and a selection of sticky pastries, which can be washed down with a powerful cup of Lao coffee. Bread or *khao jii* is baked daily and often served with vegetables, pâté, fried eggs or an omelette. The Lao however have a habit of eating baguette sandwiches with fish sauce sprinkled on top (these are available in Vientiane, Savannakhet and Pakse). Menus in many of Vientiane's restaurants still have a distinctly French flavour to them. Vintage Bordeaux and Burgundies occasionally emerge from the cellars of restaurants too – although most of the fine vintages have now been consumed. Hotels in main towns often provide international menus and continental breakfasts. Even in small towns it is easy enough to create a continental breakfast: baguettes are widely available, wild honey can usually be tracked down, and fresh Boloven coffee is abundant.

Drink

Urban areas have access to safe water, but all water should be boiled or sterilized before drinking. Less than a third of rural areas have safe water. Bottled water is widely available, however, and produced locally, so it is cheap (about 1000 kip for a litre). Soft drinks are expensive as they are imported from Thailand; a can of coke in a stall costs about 5000 kip, a bottle 1500 kip. *Nam saa*, weak Chinese tea, is also served. There is now local fresh milk production, so milk and yoghurt are available.

The local brew is rice wine which is drunk from a clay jug with long straws. The

Essentials Eating & drinking

Nam pa

No meal would be complete without a small dish of nam pa to spoon onto almost any savoury dish. Like nam plaa in Thailand, nuoc mam in Vietnam and ngan-pyaye in Myanmar (Burma), nam pa is an essential element of Laotian gastronomic life. To make the sauce, freshwater fish is packed into containers and steeped in brine. Elsewhere, it is made mostly from small saltwater fish, but because Laos is landlocked, freshwater fish is used instead. The resulting brown liquid – essentially the by-products of slowly putrifying fish – is drained off and bottled. A variation is *pa dek*, *nam pa* with small chunks of fermented fish added, often with rice husks too. This variation tends to be used in cooking rather than as a condiment and is usually kept in an earthenware pot – often outside as the aroma is so strong!

white variety is called *lau-lao* (Lao alcohol) and is made from fermented sticky rice; *fanthong*, or red *lao-lao* is fermented with herbs. Bottled *lao-lao* is also widely available. Imported beers, wines and spirits can be found in hotels, restaurants, bars and nightclubs but are not particularly cheap. *Beer Lao* is available as a light lager (although the alcohol content is 5%) best served ice-cold or as a dark ale. In towns without electricity it is normal to add ice although most places are now on the grid. *Beer Lao* also has the advantage of being reasonably priced (about US$1 for a large bottle, depending on the restaurant or bar). Chinese beer is cheaper still and can be found in the northern provinces. French wines can be purchased (at a price) in some supermarkets and quite a few restaurants.

Eating out

Restaurant food is, on the whole, hygienically prepared, and as long as street stall snacks have been well cooked, they are usually fine and a good place to sample local specialities. Expect to pay between US$3-10 per head for a meal in main towns and less outside. By eating Lao food in local restaurants it is possible to pay US$1 or less for a meal.

Really classy restaurants are only to be found in Vientiane and Luang Prabang (especially the former). Good French cuisine is available in both cities. Salads, steaks, pizzas and more are all on offer. Expect to pay anywhere over US$5 for a reasonable meal. A better bet in terms of value for money are the Lao restaurants. Indian restaurants are starting to find their way around the country

Far more prevalent are lower-end Lao and Chinese-Lao restaurants which can be found in every town. Food in these places is usually good and excellent value for money. You'll find a cold beer and a good range of vegetarian and meat-based dishes all for between US$3 and US$5. In towns on the tourist trail these local restaurants are complemented by places geared to the vicarious demands of tourists. Here you'll find fruit smoothies, Indian food, burgers and more for anywhere between US$2 and US$5. Finally, right at the bottom end – in terms of price if not necessarily in terms of quality – are stalls that charge a US$1-2 for filled baguettes or simple single-dish meals.

Entertainment

If you are looking for evenings out at cultural events, or are keen to dance the night away, Laos is not the place for you and anywhere outside the capital is unlikely to provide much in the way of night-time revelry. Excepting perhaps the odd lock-in in a

Baci

The baci ceremony is a uniquely Lao boun (festival) and celebrates any auspicious occasion – marriage, birth, achievement or the end of an arduous journey, for instance. The ceremony dates from pre-Buddhist times and is therefore animist in origin. It is centred around the phakhouan, a designer tree made from banana leaves and flowers (or, today, some artificial concoction of plastic) and surrounded by symbolic foods. The most common symbolic foods are eggs and rice – symbolizing fertility and fecundity. The mophone hosts the ceremony and recites memorized prayers, usually in Pali, and ties cotton threads (sai sin) around the wrists of guests symbolizing good health, prosperity and happiness. For maximum effect, these strings must have three knots in them. It is unlucky to take them off until at least three days have elapsed, and custom dictates that they never be cut. Many people wear them until, frayed and worn, they fall off through sheer decreptitude. All this is accompanied by a ramvong (traditional circle dance) which in turn is accompanied by traditional instruments – flutes, clarinets, xylophones with bamboo crosspieces, drums, cymbals and the kaen, a hand-held pipe organ that is to Laos what the bagpipes are to Scotland.

Luang Prabang pub or at a bar in Vientiane, a quiet evening sipping Lao beer by the Mekong is as good as it gets. Today, even in towns, a 2200 curfew exists; sometimes bars and clubs will push it and stay open to 2300 or 2400.

The pace of life in Laos is slow; certainly nothing is super-developed – you can even count the number of cinemas on one hand, so the nearest you should expect to get to seeing the hottest new Hollywood blockbuster would generally be the nightly DVDs shown at some guesthouses. All this, of course, is part of the inherent appeal of the country and most visitors wouldn't have it any other way.

Most larger towns have bars and 'discos'. But a Lao disco is usually a place where live rather than recorded music is played. There are a growing number of bars and clubs in Vientiane, and a handful in the other major centres (mostly geared to locals rather than the foreign/expat markets).

Festivals and events

Being of festive inclination, the Lao celebrate New Year four times a year: the international New Year in January, Chinese New Year in January/February, Lao New Year (Pi Mai) in April and Hmong New Year in December. The Lao Buddhist year follows the lunar calendar, so many of the festivals are movable. The first month begins around the full moon in December. There are also many local festivals (see under individual regions). **Note** The list below is not exhaustive, but does include the most important festivals. There are many Chinese, Vietnamese and ethnic minority festivals which are celebrated in Laos and there are many regional variations.

January

New Year's Day (1 Jan) Public holiday celebrated by private *baci* throughout the country.

Pathet Lao Day (6 Jan) Public holiday, parades in main towns.
Army Day (20 Jan) Public holiday.
Boun Pha Vet (movable) To celebrate King Vessanthara's reincarnation as a Buddha.

Sermons, processions, dance, theatre. Popular time for ordination.

February

Magha Puja (movable) Celebrates the end of Buddha's time in the monastery and the prediction of his death. It is principally celebrated in Vientiane and at Wat Phou, near Champassak.

Chinese New Year (movable, Jan/Feb) Celebrated by Chinese and Vietnamese communities. Many Chinese and Vietnamese businesses shut down for 3 days.

March

Women's Day (8 Mar) Public holiday.
People's Party Day (22 Mar) Public holiday.
Boun Khoun Khao (movable) Harvest festival, local celebration centred around the wats.

April

Pi Mai (13-15 Apr) Public holiday to celebrate Lao New Year. The first month of the Lao New Year is actually Dec but festivities are delayed until Apr when days are longer than nights. By Apr it's also hotting up, so having hosepipes levelled at you and buckets of water dumped on you is more pleasurable. The festival also serves to invite the rains. Pi Mai is one of the most important annual festivals, particularly in Luang Prabang (see page 125). Statues of the Buddha (in the 'calling for rain' posture) are ceremonially doused in water, which is poured along an intricately decorated trench (*hang song nam pha*). The small stupas of sand, decorated with streamers, in wat compounds are symbolic requests for health and happiness over the next year. It is celebrated with traditional Lao folksinging (*mor lam*) and the circle dance (*ramwong*). There is usually a 3-day holiday. Similar festivals are celebrated in Thailand, Cambodia and Burma. It's good if you keep your money, cameras, etc, in plastic. 'Sok Dee Pi Mai' – good luck for the New Year – is usually said to one another during this period.

May

Labour Day (1 May) Public holiday with parades in Vientiane.

Visakha Puja (movable) To celebrate the birth, enlightenment and death of the Buddha, celebrated in local wats.

Boun Bang Fai (movable) The rocket festival, is a Buddhist rain-making festival. Large bamboo rockets are built and decorated by monks and carried in procession before being blasted skywards. The higher a rocket goes, the bigger its builder's ego gets. Designers of failed rockets are thrown in the mud. The festival lasts 2 days.

June/July

Children's Day (1 Jun) Public holiday.
Khao Phansa (movable) The start of Buddhist Lent and a time of retreat and fasting for monks. These are the most usual months for ordination and for men to enter the monkhood for short periods before they marry. The festival starts with the full moon in Jun/Jul and continues until the full moon in Oct. It all ends with the *Kathin* ceremony in Oct when monks receive gifts.

August

Lao Issara (13 Aug) Public holiday, Free Lao Day.
Liberation Day (23 Aug) Public holiday.
Ho Khao Padap Dinh (movable) A celebration of the dead.

September

Boun Ok Phansa (movable) The end of Buddhist Lent when the faithful take offerings to the temple. It is in the '9th month' in Luang Prabang and the '11th month' in Vientiane, and marks the end of the rainy season. Boat races take place on the Mekong River with crews of 50 or more men and women. On the night before the race small decorated rafts are set afloat on the river.

October

Freedom from the French Day (12 Oct) Public holiday which is only really celebrated in Vientiane.

November

Boun That Luang (movable) Celebrated in

The universal stimulant – the betel nut

Throughout the countryside in Southeast Asia, and in more remote towns, it is common to meet men and women whose teeth are stained black, and gums red, by continuous chewing of the 'betel nut'. This, though, is a misnomer. The betel 'nut' is not chewed at all: the three crucial ingredients that make up a betel 'wad' are the nut of the areca palm (Areca catechu), the leaf or catkin of the betel vine (Piper betel), and lime. When these three ingredients are combined with saliva they act as a mild stimulant. Other ingredients (people have their own recipes) are tobacco, gambier, various spices and the gum of Acacia catechu. The habit, though also common in South Asia and parts of China, seems to have evolved in Southeast Asia and it is mentioned in the very earliest chronicles. The lacquer betel boxes of Myanmar and Thailand, and the brass and silver ones of Indonesia, illustrate the importance of chewing betel in social intercourse. Galvao in his journal of 1544 noted: "They use it so continuously that they never take it from their mouths; therefore these people can be said to go around always ruminating." Among Westernized Southeast Asians the habit is frowned upon: the disfigurement and ageing that it causes, and the stained walls and floors that result from the constant spitting, are regarded as distasteful products of an earlier age. But beyond the elite it is still widely practised.

all Laos' *thats*, although most enthusiastically and colourfully in Vientiane (see page 70). As well as religious rituals, most celebrations include local fairs, processions, beauty pageants and other festivities.

December

Hmong New Year (movable).
Independence Day (2 Dec) Public holiday, military parades, dancing and music.

Shopping

Popular souvenirs from Laos include handicrafts and textiles, which are sold pretty much everywhere. The market is usually a good starting point as are some of the minority villagers. The smaller, less touristy towns will sell silk at the cheapest price (at about 40,000 kip a length). The best place to buy naturally dyed silk in Laos is in Xam Neua. This high-quality silk often makes its way to Luang Prabang and Vientiane but usually at much greater cost. Most markets offer a wide selection of patterns and embroidery though amongst the best places to go are **Talaat Sao** (Vientiane Morning Market) or, behind it, the cheaper **Talaat Kudin**, which has a textile section in the covered area. If you wish to have something made, most tailors can whip up a simple *sinh* (Lao sarong) in a day but you might want to allow longer for adjustments or other items. **OckPopTok** in Luang Prabang also has a fantastic reputation for producing top-shelf, naturally dyed silk. Vientiane and Luang Prabang offer the most sophisticated line in boutiques, where you can get all sorts of clothes from the utterly exquisite to the frankly bizarre. Those on a more frugal budget will find some tailors who can churn out a decent pair of trousers on Sisavangvong in Luang Prabang and around Nam Phou in Vientiane. If you get the right tailor, they can be much better than those found in Thailand both in terms of price and quality but you do need to be patient and allow time for multiple fittings. It is also a good idea to bring a pattern/picture of what you want.

Silverware, most of it is in the form of jewellery and small pots (though they may not be made of silver), is traditional in Laos. The finest silversmiths work out of

Living in sinh

A lovely experience is to wear the sinh, the Lao traditional banded sarong. It isn't at all necessary to wear one but the Lao love the fact that you are taking an interest in their culture and are likely to shower you with compliments. If you are attending a wedding, funeral or plan to visit a government office, it is a sign of respect to wear one. Depending on the fabric, a sinh can be whipped up in most markets in a day and can be bought for around US$10.

Vientiane and Luang Prabang. Chunky antique ethnic-minority jewellery, bangles, pendants, belts and earrings are often sold in markets in the main towns, or antique shops in Vientiane, particularly congregating around Nam Phou. Xam Neua market also offers a good range of ethnic minority-style silver jewellery. Look for traditional necklaces that consist of wide silver bands, held together with a spirit lock (a padlock to lock in your scores of souls). Craftsmen in Laos are still producing **wood carvings** for temples and coffins. Designs are usually traditional, with a religious theme. Gold jewellery is the preference of the Lao Loum (lowland Laos) and its bright yellow colour associated with Buddhist luck (often it is further dyed to enhance its orange goldness), this is best bought in Vientiane.

Essentials A-Z

Accident and emergency

Contact the relevant emergency service and your embassy. Make sure you obtain police/medical records in order to file insurance claims. If you need to report a crime visit your local police station and take a local with you who speaks English. **Ambulance** T195, **Fire** T190, **Police** T191.

Children

Lao people love children and it is not uncommon for waiters and waitresses to spend the whole evening looking after your child.

Food and drink

Stir-fried vegetables and rice or noodles are the best bet for children. Fruit can be bought cheaply: papaya and banana are excellent sources of nutrition, and can be self-peeled ensuring cleanliness. Powdered milk is available in provincial centres, although most brands have added sugar. Powdered food can also be bought in some towns – the quality may not be the same as equivalent foods bought in the West, but it is perfectly adequate for short periods. Avoid letting your child drink tap water as it may carry parasites. Bottled water and fizzy drinks are sold widely. A damp cloth and some antiseptic liquid (such as Dettol) are useful for wiping hands and tabletops and can help to minimize the chance of infection.

Disposable nappies

These can be bought in Vientiane and other larger provincial capitals, but are often expensive.

Sleeping

At the hottest time of year, a/c may be essential for a baby or young child's comfort. This rules out many of the cheaper hotels, but a/c accommodation is available in all larger towns.

Transport

Public transport may be a problem; long bus journeys are restrictive and uncomfortable. Chartering a car is undoubtedly the most convenient way to travel overland but rear seatbelts are scarce and child seats even rarer.

Customs and duty free

Duty-free allowance is 500 cigarettes, 2 bottles of wine and a bottle of liquor. Laos has a strictly enforced ban on the export of antiquities and all Buddha images.

Disabled travellers

Considering the proportion of the region's population that are seriously disabled, foreigners might expect better facilities and allowances for the immobile. But in Laos pavements are often uneven, there are potholes and missing drain covers galore, pedestrian crossings are ignored, ramps are unheard of, lifts are few and far between and escalators are seen only in magazines and high-end hotels and a sprinkling of shopping complexes.

RADAR, 12 City Forum, 250 City Rd, London, EC1V 8AF, T020-72503222.
SATH, 347 Fifth Av, Suite 610, New York City, NY 10016, T212 447-7284.

Drugs

Drug use is illegal and there are harsh penalites ranging from fines through to imprisonment or worse. Police have been known to levy heavy fines on people in Vang Vieng for eating so-called 'happy' foods, or for being caught in possession of drugs. Note that 'happy' food can make some people extremely sick. Though opium has in theory been eradicated, it is still for sale in northern areas and people have died from overdosing. *Yaa baa* is also available here and should be avoided at all costs.

Electricity

Voltage 220, 50 cycles in the main towns. 110 volts in the country; 2-pin sockets are common. Blackouts are common outside Vientiane and many smaller towns are not connected to the national grid and only have power during the evening.

Embassies and consulates

Australia, 1 Dalman Cres, O' Malley Canberra, ACT 2606, T02-864595.
Cambodia, 15-17 Mao Tse Toung Blvd, Phnom Penh, T023-982632.
France, 74 Ave Raymond-Poincaré 75116 Paris, T01-4553 0298.
Thailand, 502/1 Soi Ramkamhaeng 39, Thanon Pracha Uthit, Wangthonglang, Bangkok 10310, T02-539 6667.
Vietnam, 22 Tran Binh Trong, Hanoi, T04-2854576; 181 Hai Ba Trung, Ho Chi Minh City, T08-8297667.

Gay and lesbian

Gay and lesbian travellers should have no problems in Laos. However, it does not have a hot gay scene as such and the Lao government is intent on avoiding the mushrooming of the gay and straight sex industry. Officially it is illegal for any foreigner to have a sexual relationship with a Lao person they aren't married to. Openly gay behaviour is contrary to local culture and custom and visitors, whether straight or gay, should not flaunt their sexuality. Any overt display of passion or even affection in public is taboo. In Vientiane there aren't any gay bars per se although there are some bars and clubs where gays congregate. Luang Prabang has a few more gay-orientated options and is fast become one of South-east Asia's most gay-friendly destinations.

Health

See your doctor or travel clinic at least 6 weeks before your departure for general advice on travel risks, malaria and vaccinations. Make sure you have travel insurance, get a dental check (especially if you are going to be away for more than a month), know your own blood group and if you suffer a long-term condition such as diabetes or epilepsy make sure someone knows or that you have a Medic Alert bracelet/ necklace with this information on it (www.medicalert.co.uk).

Remember that it is risky to buy medicine, and in particular anti-malarials, in developing countries, as they may be sub-standard or part of a trade in counterfeit drugs.

The following are advised:

BCG It is not known how much protection this vaccination gives the traveller against lung tuberculosis but it is currently advised that people have it in the absence of any better alternative.

Hepatitis A Yes, as the disease can be caught easily from food/water.

Japanese encephalitis May be advised for some areas, depending on the duration of the trip and proximity to rice growing and pig-farming areas.

Polio Yes, if no booster in last 10 years.

Rabies Advised if travelling to jungle and/or remote areas

Tetanus Yes, if not vaccinated in last 10 years (but after 5 doses you've had enough for life).

Typhoid Yes, if none in last 3 years.

Yellow fever The disease does not exist in Laos. However, the authorities may wish to see a certificate if you have recently arrived from an endemic area in Africa or South America.

Health risks

Malaria is prevalent in Laos and remains a serious disease; about a third of the population contracts malaria at some stage in their lives. The choice of malaria prophylaxis will need to be something other than chloroquine for most people, since there is such a high level of resistance to it. Always check with your doctor or travel clinic for the most up-to-date advice.

Malaria can cause death within 24 hours. It can start as something just resembling an attack of flu. You may feel tired, lethargic, headachy, feverish; or more seriously, develop fits, followed by coma and then death. Have a low index of suspicion because it is very easy to write off vague symptoms, which may actually be malaria. If you have a temperature, go to a doctor as soon as you can and ask for a malaria test. On your return home if you suffer any of these symptoms, get tested as soon as possible, even if any previous test proved negative, the test could save your life.

The most serious viral disease is **dengue fever**, which is hard to protect against as the mosquitos bite throughout the day as well as at night. Bacterial diseases include

tuberculosis (TB) and some causes of the more common traveller's **diarrhoea**. Each year there is the possibilty that **avian flu** or SARS might rear their ugly heads. Check the news reports. If there is a problem in an area you are due to visit you may be advised to have an ordinary flu shot or to seek expert advice. There are high rates of **HIV** in the region, especially among sex workers. **Rabies** and **schistosomiasis** (bilharzia, a water-borne parasite) may be a problem in Laos.

Medical services

Hospitals are few and far between and medical facilities are poor in Laos. Emergency treatment is available at the **Mahosot Hospital and Clinique Setthathirath** in Vientiane. The Australian embassy also has a clinic for Commonwealth citizens with minor ailments (see page 79); US$60 per consultation. Better facilities are available in Thailand and emergency evacuation to **Nong Khai** or **Udon Thani** (Thailand) can be arranged at short notice.

Thailand

Aek Udon Hospital, Udon Thani, Thailand T+66 42-342555. A 2½-hr trip from Vientiane.

Bumrungrad Hospital, Soi 3 Sukhumvit, Bangkok, T+66 2-667 1000, www.bumrungrad.com. The best option: a world-class hospital with brilliant medical facilities.

Nong Khai Wattana General Hospital, T+66 42-465201, is a better alternative to the hospitals in Vientiane and only a 40-min trip from the capital.

Useful websites

www.cdc.cov US Government site which gives excellent advice on travel health and details of disease outbreaks.

www.who.int The WHO Blue Book lists the diseases of the world.

www.fitfortravel.scot.nhs.uk A-Z of vaccine/health advice for each country.

www.btha.org British Travel Health Association (UK). This is the official website of an organization of travel health professionals.

Insurance

Always take out travel insurance before you set off and read the small print carefully. Check that the policy covers the activities you intend or may end up doing. Also check exactly what your medical cover includes, ie ambulance, helicopter rescue or emergency flights back home. Also check the payment protocol. You may have to cough up first before the insurance company reimburses you. It is always best to dig out all the receipts for expensive personal effects like jewellery or cameras. Take photos of these items and note down all serial numbers. You are advised to shop around. **STA Travel** and other reputable student travel organisations offer good value policies. Young travellers from North America can try the **International Student Insurance Service** (ISIS), which is available through **STA Travel**, T1-800-7770112, www.sta-travel.com. Other recommended travel insurance companies in North America include: **Travel Guard**, T1-800-8261300, www.noelgroup.com; **Access America**, T1-800- 2848300; **Travel Insurance Services**, T1-800-9371387; and **Travel Assistance International**, T1-800-8212828. Older travellers should note that some companies will not cover people over 65 years old, or may charge higher premiums. The best policies for older travellers (UK) are offered by **Age Concern**, T01883-346964.

Internet

Internet cafés have been popping up all over Laos over the last few years. The connections are surprisingly good in major centres. Fast, cheap internet is available in Vientiane, Luang Prabang, Vang Vieng and Savannakhet for around 100-200 kip per min. Less reliable and more expensive internet (due to long-distance calls) can be found in Phonsavanh, Don Khone, Don Deth, Luang Namtha, Thakhek, Savannakhet and Udomxai. Many internet cafés also offer international phone services.

Language

Lao is the national language but there are many local dialects, not to mention the languages of the minority groups. Lao is closely related to Thai and, in a sense, is becoming more so as the years pass. Though there are important differences between the languages, they are mutually intelligible – just about. French is spoken, though only by government officials, hotel staff and many educated people over 40. However, most government officials and many shopkeepers have some command of English. See also Useful words and phrases, page 326, and Glossary, page 328.

Media

The *Vientiane Times* is published 5 days a week and provides quirky pieces of information and some interesting cultural and tourist-based features, as well as some more eye-catching stories translated from the local press and wire service. Television is becoming increasingly popular as more towns and villages get electricity. The national TV station broadcasts in Lao. In Vientiane **CNN**, **BBC**, **ABC** and a range of other channels are broadcast. Thailand's **Channel 5** gives English subtitles to news. The **Lao National Radio** broadcasts news in English. The **BBC World Service** can be picked up on shortwave.

Money

The kip is the official currency. At the time of going to press the exchange rate was US$1 = 9606 kip£1 = 19,682kip, €1 = 13,680 kip. The lowest commonly used note is the 500 kip and the highest, the recently introduced 50,000 kip kip tends to shadow the Thai baht but with a rather quaint one week delay. It is getting much easier to change currency and traveller's cheques. Banks are generally reluctant to give anything but kip in exchange for hard currency. US$ and Thai baht can be used as cash in most shops, restaurants and hotels and the Chinese Yuan is starting to be more widely accepted in northern parts of Laos (closer to the Chinese border). A certain amount of cash (in US$ or Thai baht) can also be useful in an emergency. Banks include the **Lao Development Bank** and **Le Banque pour Commerce Exterieur Lao** (BCEL), which change most major international currencies (cash) and traveller's cheques denominated in US$ and pounds sterling. Many of the BCEL branches offer cash advances on Visa/MasterCard.. Note that some banks charge a hefty commission of US$2 per TC. While banks will change traveller's cheques and cash denominated in most major currencies into kip, some will only change US$ into Thai baht, or into US dollars cash.

Thai baht are readily accepted in most towns but it is advisable to carry kip in rural areas (buses, for example, will usually only accept kip).

The BCEL has distributed several ATMs across the country but at the time of publication the majority of these were MasterCard only. Multi-card ATMS (only Visa and MasterCard) are only available in Vientiane but several more are planned in the future. At the time of writing, there were only a sprinkling of international multi-card ATMs in Vientiane (at the BCEL bank in Vientiane on Fa Gnum, near the Novotel and 500m from Wat Simuang temple and across from the Lao Plaza Hotel), but will only dispense a maximum of 700,000 kip at a time. On weekends, the only other options for exchange or obtaining cash are the BCEL booth along the river.

Payment by credit card is becoming easier – although beyond the larger hotels and restaurants in Vientiane and Luang Prabang do not expect to be able to get by on plastic. American Express, Visa, MasterCard/Access cards are accepted in a limited number of more upmarket establishments. Note that commission is charged by some places on credit card transactions. If they can route the payment through Thailand then a commission is not levied; but if this is not possible, then 3% is usually added.

Many BCEL banks will now advance cash on credit cards in Luang Prabang, Vientiane, Pakse, Phonsavanh, Savannakhet and Vang Vieng (not all cards are accepted at these banks, so it's better to check in advance).

Cost of travelling

The variety of available domestic flights means that the bruised bottoms, dust-soaked clothes and stiff limbs that go hand-in-hand with some of the longer bus/boat rides can be avoided by those with thicker wallets in Laos. Note that foreigners pay more than locals for flights in Laos. As the roads improve and journey times diminish in Laos though, buses have emerged above both planes and boats as the preferred (not to mention most reasonably priced) transportation option. Budget accommodation costs US$3-10, a mid-range hotel from US$20- 30. Local food is very cheap and it is possible to eat well for under US$2 a meal. Most Western restaurants will charge between US$2-5 a meal.

Opening hours

Banks Mon-Fri 0830-1600 (some close at 1500).

Offices Mon-Fri 0900-1700; those that deal with tourists open a bit later and also usually over the weekend. Government offices close at 1600.

Bars and **nightclubs** Usually close around 2200-2300 depending on how strictly the curfew is being reinforced. In smaller towns, most restaurants and bars will be closed by 2200.

Photography

Sensitivity pays when taking photographs. Be very wary in areas that have (or could have) military importance – such as airports, where all photography is prohibited. Also be careful when photographing official functions and parades without permission. Always ask permission before taking photographs in a monastery. You should always ask people's permission before you take a photograph of them.

Police and the law

If you are robbed insurers will require you to obtain a police report. The police may try to solicit a bribe for this service. Although not ideal, you will probably have to pay this fee to obtain your report. Laws aren't strictly enforced but when the authorities do prosecute people the penalties can be harsh, ranging from deportation through to prison sentences. If you are arrested seek embassy and consular support. People are routinely fined for drugs possession, having sexual relations with locals (when unmarried) and proselytizing. If you are arrested or encounter police, try to remain calm and friendly. Although drugs are available throughout the country, the police levy hefty fines and punishments if caught.

Post

The postal service is inexpensive and reliable but delays are common. As the National Tourism Authority assures: in Laos the stamps will stay on the envelope. Contents of outgoing parcels must be examined by an official before being sealed. Incoming mail should use the official title, Lao PDR. There is no mail to home addresses or guesthouses, so mail must be addresses to a PO Box. The post office in Vientiane has a 0oste restante service. EMS (Express Mail Service) is available from main post offices in larger towns. In general, post offices open 0800-1200 and 1300-1600. In provincial areas, **Lao Telecom** is usually attached to the post office. **DHL**, **Fedex** and TNT have offices in Vientiane.

Public holidays

1 Jan **New Year's Day.**
6 Jan Pathet Lao Day. Parades and holidays in some towns.
20 Jan Army Day.
8 Mar Women's Day.
22 Mar People's Party Day.
14-16 Apr Lao New Year. The first month of the Lao New Year is actually Dec but it is celebrated in Apr when days are longer than nights. Statues of the Buddha (in the 'calling for rain' posture) are ceremonially doused in water, which is poured along an intricately decorated trench (*hang song nam pha*). The small stupas of sand, decorated with streamers, in wat compounds are symbolic requests for health and happiness over the coming year. The New Year is celebrated with traditional Lao folksinging (*mor lam*) and the circle dance (*ramwong*). There is usually a 3-day holiday.
1 May Labour Day
1 Jun Children's Day
2 Dec Independence Day.

Safety

Travel advisories
The US State Department's travel advisories: Travel Warnings & Consular Information

Sheets, www.travel.state.gov /travel_ warnings.html.
The **UK Foreign and Commonwealth Office**'s travel warning section, www.fco.gov.uk/travel/

Crime rates are very low but it is advisable to take the usual precautions. Most areas of the country are now safe – a very different state of affairs from only a few years ago when foreign embassies advised tourists not to travel along certain roads and in certain areas (in particular Route 13 between Vientiane and Luang Prabang, and Route 7 between Phonsavanh and Route 13). Today these risks have effectively disappeared. However, the government will sometimes make areas provisionally off-limits if they think there is a security risk – take heed!

There has been a reported increase in motorcycle drive-by thefts in Vientiane, but these and other similar crimes are still at a low level compared with most countries. If riding on a motorbike or bicycle, don't carry your bag strap over your shoulder – as you could get pulled off the bike if someone goes to snatch your bag. In the Siphandon and Vang Vieng areas, theft seems more common. Use a hotel security box if available.

Road accidents are on the increase. The hiring of motorbikes is becoming more popular and consequently there are more tourist injuries. Wear a helmet.

Be careful around waterways, as drowning is one of the primary causes of tourist deaths. Be particularly careful during the rainy season (May-Sep) as rivers have a tendency to flood and can have extremely strong currents. Make sure if you are kayaking, tubing, canoeing, travelling by fast-boat, etc, that proper safety gear, such as life jackets, is provided. 'Fast-boat' river travel can be dangerous due to excessive speed and the risk of hitting something in the river and capsizing.

Xieng Khouang Province, the Boloven Plateau, Xam Neua and areas along the Ho Chi Minh Trail are littered with bombies (small anti-personnel mines and bomblets from cluster bomb units). There are also numerous, large, unexploded bombs; in many villages they have been left lying around. They are very unstable so DO NOT TOUCH. Only walk on clearly marked or newly trodden paths.

Student travellers

There are few specific student discounts in Laos. Anyone in full-time education is entitled to an International Student Identity Card (ISIC Association, Box 9048, 1000 Copenhagen, Denmark, T45-3393 9303). These are issued by student travel offices and travel agencies and offer special rates on all forms of transport and other concessions and services. They sometimes permit free admission to museums and sights, at other times a discount on the admission.

Telephone

International dialling code for Laos: T+856 (if ringing from Thailand, dial 007).
International operator: T170
Directory enquiries: T16 (national), T171 (international).

Public phones are available in Vientiane and other major cities. You can also go to **Lao Telecom** offices to call overseas. Phone cards are widely available in most convenient stores. Call 178 in Vientiane for town codes. Most towns in Laos have at least 1 telephone box with IDD facility. The one drawback is that you must buy a phonecard. Because these are denominated in such small units, even the highest-value card will only get you a handful of minutes talk time with Europe. Most call are charged between $0.80 and $2 a min. All post offices, telecoms offices and many shops sell phone cards.
Note If ringing Laos from Thailand, dial 007 before the country code for Laos.

Mobile telephone coverage is now quite good. Pay-as-you-go sim cards are available for 30,000 kip to 50,000 kip. Coverage is available in most provincial capitals.

Many internet cafés have set up call facilities that charge US$0.20 and under per min to make a call. In Vientiane, Pakse, Luang Prabang and Vang Vieng most internet cafés are equipped with Skype, including headphones and webcam, which costs a fraction of the price for international calls (as long as you have an account already established).

Time

Laos is 7 hrs ahead of Greenwich Mean Time.

Tipping

Tipping is rare, even in hotels. However, it is a kind gesture to tip guides and, in some more expensive restaurants, a 10% tip is appreciated if service charge is not included on the bill. If someone offers you a lift, it is a courtesy to give them some money for fuel.

Tourist information

Contact details for tourist offices and other information resources are given in the relevant Ins and Outs sections throughout the text.

The **Laos National Tourism Authority**, Lane Xang, Vientiane, T021-212248, www.tourismlaos.gov.la, provides maps and brochures. The provincial offices are usually excellent and as long as you are patient they will usually come through with the information you need. There are particularly good tourism offices in Thakhek, Vieng Xai, Savannakhet, Xam Neua and Luang Namtha. The authority has teamed up with local tour operators to provide a number of ecotourism opportunities, such as trekking and village homestays, www.ecotourismlaos.com.

Websites
Up-to-date information on Laos is not easy to come by. The best bet is to browse Lao-related or Lao-dedicated websites. The best sites, in our experience, are:
www.travelfish.org
www.visit-laos.com
www.ecotourismlaos.com
www.laohotelgroup.org
www.laopdr.com
www.asean-tourism.com
www.muonglao.com
www.mekongcenter.com
www.visit-mekong.com

Tour operators

For regional tour operators, such as **Asian Trails**, www.asiantrails.com, refer to the Activities and tours listings in the guide.

In the UK
Adventure Company, 15 Turk St, Alton, Hampshire GU34 1AG, T0870-7941009,

www.adventurecompany.co.uk.
Audley Travel, 6 Willows Gate, Stratton, Audley, Oxfordshire OX27 9AU, T01869-276219, www.audleytravel.com.
Coromandel, Andrew Brock Travel Ltd, 29A Main St, Lyddington, Oakham, Rutland LE15 9LR, T01572-821330, www.coromandelabt.com. Tailored individual travel to all 3 countries.
Guerba Adventure & Discovery Holidays, Wessex House, 40 Station Rd, Westbury, Wiltshire BA13 3JN, T01373-826611, www.guerba.co.uk.
Magic of the Orient, 14 Frederick Pl, Clifton, Bristol BS8 1AS, T0117-3116050, www.magicoftheorient.com. Tailor-made holidays to the Far East.
Regent Holidays, 15 John St, Bristol BS1 2HR, T0117-9211711, www.regent-holidays.co.uk.

Silk Steps, Deep Meadow, Edington, Bridgwater, Somerset TA7 9JH, T01278-722460, www.silksteps.co.uk.
Steppes Travel, 51 Castle St, Cirencester, Glos GL7 1QD, T01285-880980, www.steppestravel.co.uk. Specialists in tailor-made holidays and small group tours.
Symbiosis Expedition Planning, 3B Wilmot Place, London NW1 9JS, T0845-1232844, www.symbiosis-travel.com.
Trans Indus, Northumberland House, 11 The Pavement, Popes Lane, London W5 4NG, T020-8566 2729, www.transindus.co.uk.
Travel Indochina Ltd, 2nd Floor, Chester House, George St, Oxford 0X1 2AY, T01865-268950, www.travelindochina.co.uk. Small group journeys and tailor-made holidays.
Travelmood, 214 Edgware Rd, London W2 1DH, T0870-001002, www.travelmood.com.
Visit Vietnam (Tennyson Travel), 30-32 Fulham High St, London SW6 3LQ, T020-77364347, www.visitvietnam.co.uk. Also deals with Laos, www.visitasia.co.uk.

In North America
Adventure Center, 1311 63rd St, Suite 200, Emeryville, CA, T1-800 2278747, www.adventurecenter.com.
Global Spectrum, 3907 Laro Court, Fairfax, VA 22031, T1-800 4194446, www.globalspectrumtravel.com. Travel specialists to Southeast Asia.
Hidden Treasure Tours, 162 West Park Av, 2nd Floor, Long Beach, NY 11561, T1-888 8899906 (USA toll free), www.hiddentreasuretours.com.
Journeys, 107 April Drive, Suite 3, Ann Arbor MI 46103, T734-6654407, www.journeys-intl.com.
Myths & Mountains, 976 Tree Court, Incline Village, NV 89451, T001-775 832 5454 (T800-670-6984) www.mythsand mountains.com. Organizes travel to Laos.
Nine Dragons Travel & Tours, PO Box 24105, Indianapolis, IN 46224, T1-317-3290350, T1-800 9099050 (USA toll free), www.nine-dragons.com.

In Australia and New Zealand
Intrepid Travel, 360 Bourke St, Melbourne, Victoria 3000, T03-8602 0500, www.intrepidtravel.com.
Travel Indochina, Level 10, HCS House, 403 George St, Sydney, NSW 2000, T02-9244 2133, T1300-367666 (toll free), www.travelindochina.com.au. Small group journeys and tailor-made holidays.

In Southeast Asia
Discovery Indochina, 3A Cua Bac St, Hanoi, Vietnam, T(0084 4)7-164132, www.discoveryindochina.com. Private and customized tours covering Laos as well as Vietnam and Cambodia.

Visas and immigration

A 30-day tourist visa can be obtained at most (but not all) borders. Visa prices are based on reciprocity with countries and range from US$30-42. 'Overtime fees' are often charged if you enter after 1600 or at a weekend. To get a visa you need a passport photograph and the name of a hotel you plan on staying at. Visas are issued at Vientiane's Wattay Airport; Luang Prabang International Airport; and Pakse International Airport. Along the border with **Thailand**, visas are issued at the Friendship Bridge crossing near Nong Khai/Vientiane; Chiang Khong/Houei Xai; Chong Mek/Vang Tao (near Pakse); Nakhon Phanom/Thakhek; and Mukdahan/Savannakhet. With **China**, Lao visas are available at the Mohan/Boten crossing. With **Vietnam**, Lao visas are issued at the following border crossings: Lao Bao/Danasavanh crossing (Savannakhet); Nam Phao/Cau Treo (Khammouane Province); and Nam Khan/Nam Can (Xieng Khouang Province). **Note** At the time of publication, Lao visas were not available at the following borders: the Vietnam crossing Nam Xoi/Nameo; Na Phao/Cha Lo, Attapeu/Quy Nhon or the Cambodian crossing at Don Kralor. For these crossings, visas will need to be organized in advance. You will need 1 (sometimes 2) passport photos.

The Lao government also issues business visas (US$35) that are available for 30-days with the possibility of extending for months beyond. This is a more complicated process and usually requires a note from an employer or hefty fees from a visa broker. These visas are best organized from your home country and can take a long time to process.

Tourist visa extensions can be obtained from the **Lao Immigration Office** in the **Ministry of the Interior** opposite the Morning Market in Vientiane, T021-212529. They can be extended for up to 1 month at the cost of US$2 per day (although if you want to extend for a month it works out cheaper to cross the border); you will need 1 passport photo. It takes a day to process the extension and if you drop off early in the morning it will often be ready by the afternoon. Travel agencies in Vientiane and other major centres can also handle this service for you for a fee (ie an additional US$1-2 per day). Visitors who overstay are charged US$10 for each day beyond the visa's date of expiry on departure.

Women travellers

While women travelling alone can generally face more potential problems than men or couples, these are far less pronounced in Laos than in most countries and it is rare for women to be harassed. Nonetheless, women should take care to dress modestly, especially in the smaller, more provincial towns. Here in particular, skimpy tops and micro-shorts still arouse in locals the sort of embarrassed shock their urban counterparts have had to get used to. The best piece of advice for female travellers is to spend a while watching how Lao women behave and dress and appropriate where possible.

Though Laos is very safe, women should also take the usual precautions. It is illegal for a foreigner to be in a sexual relationship with a local unless married. You may often get asked if you are married; just a friendly conversation starter.

Affection in public is not looked upon highly, especially in rural areas. What may be considered in the West as friendly affection, such as putting your arm around someone, could be misconstrued as romantic love in Laos, so try not to be too tactile with the men.

Bring ample underwear and swim wear as the local synthetic underwear is uncomfortable (and very, very small) and some might find it hard trying to squeeze into the Madonna-style, conical brassieres. If you are bathing in a waterfall or river, please wear a sarong, as the locals are easily embarrassed or offended by the sight of bare flesh. Tampons and sanitary towels can be purchased in major towns but are in short supply elsewhere, so carry a backup supply.

Working in Laos

Work is not easily available in Laos and is in great demand. Laos has one of the highest retention rates of foreign workers in the region, as once they get there they don't want to leave. There is a vibrant expat community, mostly of aid workers (with NGOs or bilaterial/multilateral agencies; see www.directoryofngos.org) as well as the usual diplomatic corps. But, unlike Thailand, there is not great scope for people to teach English for a few months, for example. Jobs are advertised in the *Vientiane Times*. The *Vientiane Guide*, published by the **Women's International Group** and available from bookshops in Vientiane is a useful tool for those proposing to live in the country. It's a bit out of date these days but has handy tips on how to rent a house and so on. Courses available to foreigners tend to be more fun-orientated than career-focused. Details of cooking, weaving, language and meditation courses are given in the listings of the relevant areas.

Voluntary work

Volunteer opportunities exist all over the world, for people of all ages, nationalities, cultures and skills. This can take the shape of long-term professional posts for humanitarian specialists and aid workers or short-, medium- and long-term positions of 2 weeks up to 9 months for those taking sabbaticals and gap years, or young people looking for 'hands-on' practical field experience or the chance to join an expeditional conservation project. Volunteering abroad and working with local grassroots NGOs brings benefits to everyone involved. Volunteers can spend time working with local populations, exchanging cultures and gaining experience in the field in the non-profit sector, and local grassroots NGOs in turn can receive support and funding from volunteers. All of this can be done on a grassroots level without the involvement of governments and politicians. For this reason many local organizations are developing more and more volunteer programmes. As a general rule, social work and the environment are the main sectors within the programmes of local NGOs.

There are several umbrella groups offering useful information and links to vetted organizations. **Working Abroad** (www.workingabroad.com) offers information on local grassroots volunteer and professional work opportunities in over 150 countries worldwide. These include social and community development, environment and conservation, wildlife expeditions, teaching English, organic agricultural projects, human rights observing, working with children and orphans, providing medical care, nursing and lots more. A good one-stop shop is

www.yearoutgroup.org, a not-for-profit group representing, among others, SWP, i-to-i, Outreach International, Bunac, Greenforce and Raleigh International. Also worth checking out is **World Wide Volunteering** (www.wwv.org.uk), which has projects with more than 1000 organizations in over 200 countries. This service costs £10 for 3 searches in a year, or is free if used in public libraries, universities and schools in the UK.

Other worthwhile organizations include VSO (www.vso.org.uk) in the UK; the **Youth Ambassador Program** (www.ausaid.gov.au/youtham) in Australia; CUSO, (www.cuso.org) in Canada, and the **United Nations Volunteers** website, www.unv.org.

Vientiane Region

Footprint features

Introduction

In 1563, King Setthathirat made the riverine city of Vientiane the capital of Laos. Or, to be more historically accurate, Wiang Chan, the 'City of the Moon', became the capital of Lane Xang. In those days it was a small fortified city on the banks of the Mekong with a palace and two wats, That Luang and Wat Phra Kaeo (built to house the Emerald Buddha). The city had grown prosperous from the surrounding fertile plains and taxes levied from trade going upriver.

Today Vientiane is, perhaps, the most charming of all Southeast Asia's capital cities. Cut off from the outside world and foreign investment for much of the modern period, its colonial heritage remains largely intact. While the last few years have brought greater bustle and activity, it is still a quiet city of tree-lined boulevards, where the image of the past is reflected in the present.

Snuggled in a curve of the Mekong, Vientiane is also the region's most modest capital. It is much more than a town, but it doesn't quite cut it as a conventional city. Here, colourless concrete Communist edifices sit alongside chicken farmers; outdoor aerobics fanatics are juxtaposed against locals making merit at the city's wats; and a couple of traffic lights command a dribble of chaotic cars, bikes, tuk-tuks and buses on the city's streets.

Around Vientiane are a number of places of interest, some of which, including Ban Pako and Nam Ngum, make for worthwhile stopovers or weekend retreats. Vang Vieng and Kasi are on the road north to Luang Prabang and the former, particularly, merits more than just a brief visit.

★ Don't miss ...

1 That Luang Visit Laos' most revered Buddhist monument for its annual festival, when monks flock to the city, pages 53 and 70.

2 National museums Check out Wat Phra Kaeo and the Lao National Museum for a highly subjective history lesson, pages 57 and 60.

3 Floating restaurants Enjoy a sunset dinner as you cruise along the Mekong, page 68.

4 Phou Khao Khouay Protected Area Explore the mountains, rivers and waterfalls of this protected area, easily accessible from the capital, page 83.

5 Tubing on the Nam Song Vang Vieng is the adventure capital of Laos, with caving, climbing and river sports, page 93.

Vientiane

Vientiane's appeal lies in its largely preserved fusion of Southeast Asian and French colonial culture. Baguettes, plunged coffee and Bordeaux wines coexist with spring rolls, pho soup and papaya salad. Colourful tuk-tuks scuttle along tree-lined boulevards, past old Buddhist temples and cosmopolitan cafés. Hammer-and-sickle flags hang at ten-pin bowling discos, locals carry sacks of devalued currency and green and pink chickens wander the streets. But, as in the rest of Laos, the best thing about Vientiane, is its people. Take the opportunity to stroll around some of the outlying bans (villages) and meet the wonderful characters who make this city what it is. ⟫ *For Sleeping, Eating and other listings, see pages 62-80.*

Ins and outs → *Phone code: 021. Colour map 2, B2.*

Getting there

Air Most visitors arrive in Vientiane by air, the great bulk on one of the daily connections from Bangkok, with **Thai Air** (www.thaiair.com) or **Lao Airlines** (www.laoairlines.com), which also run international flights to/from Kunming, Phnom Penh and Siem Reap. **Vietnam Airlines** (www.vietnamair.com) runs flights between Hanoi and Ho Chin Minh City. **Wattay International Airport** lies 6 km west of the town centre (To21-212066). Vientiane is the hub of Laos' domestic airline system and to travel from the north to the south or vice versa it is necessary to change planes here. The international terminal is the bigger building on the west side. Both terminals have restaurants, telephone box, taxi service and information booth. The desk near the exit handles all outgoing taxis, according to posted rates depending on where you're going in Vientiane. Only taxis are allowed to pick up passengers at the airport (US$5 to the centre of town, 20 minutes), although tuk-tuks can drop off here. But tuk-tuks can be taken from the main road and sometimes lurk at the far side of the airport parking area, near the exit (40,000 kip to the centre). The dual carriageway into town is one of only a handful of such stretches of road in the country.

A cheaper alternative from Thailand is to fly from Bangkok to **Udon Thani** on the budget airline **Air Asia** (www.airasia.com). There are several flights a day to and from Bangkok, usually costing between ฿700 and ฿1500. Continue by road to Vientiane via the Friendship Bridge (see Border essentials, page 77), which lies just 25 km downstream from the capital (allow three hours). Shuttle buses from Udon Thani airport, ฿150, usually run to the border after every flight. ⟫ *For further details, see Essentials, page 26.*

Bus There are three public bus terminals in Vientiane. The **Southern bus station** is 9 km south of the city centre on Route 13. Most international buses bound for Vietnam depart from here as well as buses to southern and eastern Laos. The station has a VIP room, restaurants, a few shops, mini-mart and there's a guesthouse nearby.

The **Northern bus station** is on Route T2, about 3 km northwest of the centre before the airport, To21-260255, and serves destinations in northern Laos. Most tuk-tuks will take you there from the city for 20,000 kip; ask for *Bai Thay Song*. There are English-speaking staff at the help desk.

A third **bus station** is across the road from the Morning Market, in front of Talaat Kudin, on the eastern edge of the city centre. This station serves destinations within Vientiane Province, buses to and from the Thai border and international buses to Nong Khai and Udon Thani in Thailand. It is also a good place to pick up a tuk-tuk. Lak Sao, on the border with Vietnam, can be reached by a single 350-km public bus

24 hours in the city

The charm of Laos lies precisely in the fact that you can't find an espresso at three in the morning or a nightclub meeting your strange desire for techno. There's little point reaching for your Palm organizer and mapping out a day minutely planned to the last moment. But, for what it's worth… Get up at **dawn** and wander out on to the streets to watch the city's monks collecting alms from crouching women and girls (rarely men). After the final victory of the Pathet Lao in 1975 monks were encouraged – none too gently – to work for their living. Depending on your budget either buy a baguette from one of the roadside carts or get a Lao coffee and croissant or baguette from one of the cafés around the Nam Phou Fountain. If it's the dry season and it is still not too late in the day, **hire a bicycle** from one of the shops near here or from your guesthouse. Ride north on Lane Xang Avenue and That Luang Road to **That Luang**, the symbol of Lao nationhood and one of the holiest sites in the country. The ride back into town is slightly downhill, all the better if the day is hotting up. Near the bottom of Lane Xang Avenue are Vientiane's two finest monasteries as well as the **Morning Market**, which is being developed into a shopping mall. Among the cornucopia of tack from Thailand and China are textiles and silver from Laos. Recharged, head to **Wat Sisaket** and **Wat Phra Kaeo**. If your time (or your interest in Buddhist architecture) is limited,

head for the first of these: much more satisfying with its shaded cloisters and elegant, perfectly proportioned *sim*. By now it is time for lunch. Save the big spend for the evening and tuck into some roadside barbecued chicken – and make sure you choose a thin and scrawny Lao bird and not one of the plump, hormone-filled creatures from Thailand. The stalls around the Morning Market are usually a good bet for a meal.

Doing nothing much at all may seem the most enticing prospect during the hot season. But if it's reasonably cool, or you are full of energy, a nice outing is to cycle downstream along the **Mekong**. A track (no cars) follows the river beginning at around Km 5 off the main road. Turn onto one of the many paths and ride for as long as you like. The path, shaded by trees, passes monasteries and attractive riverside houses. There are shops for cold drinks and snacks along the way.

Make sure you get your bike back before the sun has set and make your way to **Quai Fa Ngum** and the Mekong. There are numerous tables right on the banks of the river, where beers and snacks are served to visitors and locals. Have a cold Beer Lao on ice and watch some of the aerobics (1800-1900 daily) in the pavilion before getting stuck intothe evening's revelries. Use those tens of thousands of kip you saved at lunch and have dinner at **Le Nadao** or **Le Silapa**. To round off the day, **Sticky Fingers** is good for cocktails and coffee.

Although Vientiane is the capital of Laos, it is no Bangkok. It is small and manageable and is one of the most laid-back capital cities in the world. The local catchphrase '*bopenyang*' (no worries) has permeated through every sector of the city, so much so that even the mangy street dogs look completely chilled out, often found asleep in the middle of major intersections. The core of the city is negotiable on foot and even outlying hotels and places of interest are accessible by bicycle. Although traffic has increased substantially over the last five years or so, cycling remains the best and most flexible way to tour the city. It can be debilitatingly hot at certain times of the year but there are no great hills to struggle up. If bicycling doesn't appeal, a combination of foot and tuk-tuk or small 110-125cc scooters take the effort out of sightseeing. There is a limited city bus service but it really serves outlying destinations on the Vientiane Plain rather than the city. Larger motorbikes, cars and taxis can also be hired, although these are mainly used for longer journeys and day trips.

Orientation The capital is divided into *bans* or villages, mainly centred around their local wats, and larger *muang* or districts: **Muang Sikhottabong** lies to the west, **Muang Chanthabouli** to the north, **Muang Xaisettha** to the east and **Muang Sisattanak** to the south. Vientiane can be rather confusing for the first-time visitor as there are few street signs and most streets have two names, pre- and post-revolutionary, but, because the city is so small and compact, it doesn't take long to get to grips with the layout. The names of major streets or *thanon* usually correspond to the nearest wat, while traffic lights, wats, monuments and large hotels serve as directional landmarks. When giving directions to a tuk-tuk it is better to use these landmarks as street names leave locals a little bewildered.

Maps Government-produced tourist/town maps are available from **Venus**, Samsenthai (opposite the **Asian Pavilion Hotel**). The best tourist map is the one produced by **Golden Triangle Rider**. Although it's geared towards bike riders and will cost you around US$5, it's a great all-round map for Vientiane. You can pick one up at **Phimphone Market**. The most common map of Vientiane in wide circulation is a well-produced 3-D map available free at the airport and around town. Rather large, and not particularly useful from a tourist viewpoint, it makes a nice souvenir. (It is also sold in some places with the 'free' cunningly blanked out.) The **National Geographic Office** ① *west of the Victory Monument, Mon-Fri 0900-1200 and 1300-1600,* provides plenty of maps at reasonable prices, although they may not be up to date. ▸▸ *For alternatives, see Shopping, page 70.*

Tourist information

Lao National Tourism Authority ① *Lane Xang (towards Patuxai), T021-212251, www.tourismlaos.gov.au,* can provide information regarding ecotourism operators and brilliant trekking opportunities offered in provincial areas. This is a good starting point if you want to organize a trip to Phou Khao Khouay. The **Tourist Police** ① *0830-1200, 1300-1600,* are upstairs.

History

Vientiane is an ancient city. There was probably a settlement here, on a bend on the left bank of the Mekong, in the 10th century but knowledge of the city before the 16th century is thin and dubious. Scholars do know, from the chronicles, that King Setthathirat decided to relocate his capital here in the early 1560s. It seems that it took him four years to build the city, constructing a defensive wall (hence 'Wiang', meaning a walled or fortified city), along with Wat Phra Kaeo and a much-enlarged That Luang.

Vieng Chan, as it was called, remained intact until 1827 when it was ransacked by the Siamese; this is why many of its wats are of recent construction. Francis Garnier in 1860 wrote of "a heap of ruins" and having surveyed the "relics of antiquity" decided that the "absolute silence reigning within the precincts of a city formerly so rich and populous, was ... much more impressive than any of its monuments". A few years later, Louis de Carné wrote of the vegetation that it was like "a veil drawn by nature over the weakness of man and the vanity of his works".

The city was abandoned for decades and erased from the maps of the region. It was only conjured back into existence by the French, who commenced reconstruction at the end of the 19th century. They built rambling colonial villas and wide tree-lined boulevards, befitting their new administrative capital, Vientiane. At the height of American influence in the 1960s, it was renowned for its opium dens and sex shows.

Vientiane today

Today Vientiane is a quiet capital with an urban population of perhaps 386,600 (up from 70,000 in 1960). There are around 695,500 inhabitants (about 10% of the population of Laos) in the Vientiane municipality but this extends far beyond the physical limits of the city. Before 1970 there was only one set of traffic lights in the whole city and, even with the arrival of cars and motorbikes from Thailand in recent years, the streets are a far cry from the congestion of Bangkok. Unlike Phnom Penh and Ho Chi Minh City, there are only scattered traces of French town planning; architecture is a mixture of east and west, with French colonial villas and traditional wooden Lao buildings intermingled with Chinese shophouses and more contemporary buildings. Some locals worry that foreign investment and redevelopment will ruin the city – already some remarkably grotesque buildings are going up – but officials seem to be aware that there is little to be gained from creating Bangkok in microcosm.

For the moment, the city retains its unique innocence: DJs are officially outlawed (although this is not enforced); there is a 2330 curfew; a certain percentage of music played at restaurants and bars every day is supposed to be Lao (overcome by banging out the Lao tune quota at 0800 in the morning) and women are urged to wear the national dress, the *sinh*. However, to describe the Lao government as autocratic is unfairly negative. Vientiane's citizens are proud of their cultural heritage and are usually very supportive of the government's attempts to promote it. The government has tried, by and large, to maintain the national identity and protect its citizens from harmful outside influences. This is already starting to change, as, with the government reshuffle in 2006, came a gradual loosening of the culturual stranglehold.

Sights

Most of the interesting buildings in Vientiane are of religious significance. All tour companies and many hotels and guesthouses will arrange city tours and excursions to surrounding sights but it is just as easy to arrange a tour independently with a local tuk-tuk driver; the best English speakers (and thus the most expensive tuk-tuks) can be found in the parking lot beside Nam Phou. Those at the Morning Market (Talaat Sao) are cheaper. Most tuk-tuk drivers pretend not to carry small change, so make sure you have the exact fare with you before taking a ride.

If you are out after curfew, a concerned policeman is likely to ask you if you are alright.

That Luang
ⓘ *That Luang Rd, 3.5 km northeast of the city centre; daily 0800-1200 and 1300-1600 (except 'special' holidays); admission 2000 kip. A booklet about the wat is on sale at the entrance.*

That Luang is considered Vientiane's most important site and the holiest Buddhist monument in the country. The golden spire looks impressive at the top of the hill, northeast of the city.

According to legend, a stupa was first built here in the third century AD by emissaries of the Moghul Emperor Asoka; it is supposed to have contained the breast bone of the Buddha. Excavations on the site, however, have only located the remains of an 11th- to 13th-century Khmer temple, making the earlier provenance doubtful in the extreme. The present monument, encompassing the previous buildings, was built in 1566 by King Setthathirat, whose statue stands outside. Plundered by the Thais and the Chinese Haw in the 18th century, it was restored by King (Chao) Anou at the beginning of the 19th century. He added the cloister and the Burmese-style pavilion containing the That Sithamma Hay Sok. The stupa was carefully restored again by l'École Française d'Extrême-Orient (whose conservators were also responsible for the

Vientiane

Sleeping
Beau Rivage Mekong **1**
Don Chan Palace **2**
Le Parasol Blanc **3**
Novotel Vientiane **4**

Parkview Executive
  Suites **5**
Royal Dokmaideng **6**
Sennesouk Guesthouse **7**
Thien Thong **10**

Thongbay Guesthouse **11**
Vieng Champa **12**
Vieng Thong
  Guesthouse **13**
Villa Sisavad **14**

restoration of parts of Angkor Wat at the beginning of the 20th century) but was rebuilt in 1930 because many Lao disapproved of the French restoration.

The reliquary is surrounded by a square cloister, with an entrance on each side, the most famous on the east. There is a small collection of statues in the cloisters, including one of the Khmer king Jayavarman VII. The cloisters are used as lodgings by monks who travel to Vientiane for religious reasons and especially for the annual **That Luang festival** (see page 70). The base of the stupa is a mixture of styles, Khmer, Indian and Lao – and each side has a *hor vay* or small offering temple. This lowest level represents the material world, while the second tier is surrounded by a lotus wall and 30 smaller stupas, representing the 30 Buddhist perfections. Each of these originally contained smaller golden stupas but they were stolen by Chinese raiders in the 19th century. The 30-m-high spire dominates the skyline and resembles an elongated lotus bud, crowned by a stylized banana flower and parasol. It was

Related maps
A Vientiane centre,
page 58

Villa That Luang **15**	**Eating** 🍴	Nong Vong Re **5**	**Bars & clubs** 🍸
Wonderland	Koto **1**	Sakura **6**	Abstract **10**
Guesthouse **16**	Le Nadao **2**	Tamnak Lao **8**	Spirit House **7**
	Le Ranch **3**		Wind West **11**
	Le Silapa **4**		

Vientiane Region Vientiane

designed so that pilgrims could climb up to the stupa via the walkways around each level. It is believed that originally over 450 kg of gold leaf was used on the spire.

There used to be a wat on each side of the stupa but only two remain: **Wat Luang Nua** to the north and **Wat Luang Tai** to the south. The large new wat-like structure is the headquarters of a Buddhist organization. The monument's outer walls often feature art exhibitions.

Although That Luang is the most important historical site in Vientiane, most visitors will feel that it is not the most interesting, impressive or beautiful, largely because it seems to have been constructed out of concrete. Both Wat Sisaket and Wat Phra Kaeo (see below and page 57) are more memorable. Nonetheless, it is important to appreciate the reverence in which That Luang is held by most Lao, including the many millions who live in neighbouring Thailand. The *that* is the prototype for the distinctive Lao-style angular *chedi*, which can be seen in northeast Thailand, as well as across Laos.

Revolutionary Monument

Also known as the **Unknown Soldier's Memorial**, this hilltop landmark is located just off Phon Kheng Road and is visible from the parade ground (which resembles a disused parking lot) in front of That Luang. Echoing a *that* in design, it is a spectacularly dull monument, built in memory of those who died during the revolution in 1975. The **Pathet Lao Museum**, to the northwest of That Luang, is only open to VIPs and never to the public but there are a few tanks, trucks, guns and aircraft used in the war lying in the grounds, which can be seen from the other side of the fence.

Patuxai (Victory Monument)

ⓘ *Junction of That Luang Rd and Lane Xang Av; Mon-Fri 0800-1100 and 1400-1630, (officially, but these hours seem to be posted only for fun); admission 3000 kip.*

At the end of That Luang is the Oriental answer to Paris's Arc de Triomphe and Vientiane's best-known landmark, the monstrous Victory Monument or Patuxai. It was originally called Anou Savali, officially renamed the Patuxai or Victory Monument, but is affectionately known by locals as 'the vertical runway'. It was built by the former regime in memory of those who died in the wars before the Communist takeover, but the cement ran out before its completion. Refusing to be beaten, the regime diverted hundreds of tonnes of cement, part of a US aid package to help with the construction of runways at Wattay Airport, to finish off the monument in 1969. In 2004 the Chinese funded a big concrete park area surrounding the site, including a musical fountain; it's a pity they didn't stretch the budget to finance the beautification of the park's centrepiece.

A small introductory sign explains that, although Patuxai might look grand from a distance, on closer inspection "it appears like a monster of concrete". The top affords a bird's eye view of the leafy capital, including the distant glittering, golden dome of the old Russian circus, now the rarely used National Circus. The interior of the monument is reminiscent of a multi-storey car park (presumably as a counterpoint to the parade ground next to the Revolutionary Monument), with graffiti sporadically daubed on top of unfinished Buddhist bas-reliefs in reinforced concrete. The frescoes under the arches at the bottom represent mythological stories from the Lao version of the *Ramayana*, the *Phra Lak Pralam*. Until 1990 there was a bar on the bottom floor; today Vientiane's youth hang out on the parapet.

Wat Sisaket

ⓘ *Junction of Lane Xang Av and Setthathirat Rd; daily 0800-1200 and 1400-1600; admission 5000 kip. No photographs in the sim.*

Further down Lane Xang is the **Morning Market** or **Talaat Sao** (see page 73). A major waterpark is being constructed in the park just behind Talaat Sao. Beyond the market, where Setthathirat meets Lane Xang, is one of Vientiane's two national museums, Wat Sisaket. Home of the head of the Buddhist community in Laos, **Phra Sangka Nagnok**, it is one of the most important buildings in the capital and houses over 7000 Buddha images. Wat Sisaket was built in 1818 during the reign of King Anou. A traditional Lao monastery, it was the only temple that survived the Thai sacking of the town in 1827-1828 (perhaps out of deference to its having been completed only 10 years before the invasion), making it the oldest building in Vientiane. Sadly, it is badly in need of restoration.

The main sanctuary, or **sim**, with its sweeping roof shares many stylistic similarities with Wat Phra Kaeo (see below): window surrounds, lotus-shaped pillars and carvings of deities held up by giants on the rear door. The *sim* contains 2052 Buddha statues (mainly terracotta, bronze and wood) in small niches in the top half of the wall. There is little left of the Thai-style *jataka* murals on the lower walls but the depth and colour of the originals can be seen from the few remaining pieces. The ceiling was copied from temples King Anou had seen on a visit to Bangkok. The standing image to the left of the altar is believed to have been cast in the same proportions as King Anou. Around the *sim*, set into the ground, are small *bai sema* or boundary stones. The *sim* is surrounded by a large courtyard, which originally had four entrance gates (three are now blocked). Behind the *sim* is a large trough, in the shape of a *naga*, used for washing the Buddha images during the water festival (see page 70).

The **cloisters** were built during the 1800s and were the first of their kind in Vientiane. They shelter 120 large Buddhas in the attitude of subduing Mara (see page 316), plus a number of other images in assorted *mudras*, and thousands of small figures in niches, although many of the most interesting Buddha figures are now in Wat Phra Kaeo. Most of the statues date from the 16th to 19th centuries but there are some earlier images. Quite a number were taken from local monasteries during the French period and have ended up here.

The whole ensemble of *sim* plus cloisters is washed in a rather attractive shade of caramel and, combined with the terracotta floor tiles and weathered roof, presents a most satisfying sight. An attractive Burmese-style library, or *hau tai*, stands on Lane Xang outside the courtyard. The large casket inside used to contain important Buddhist manuscripts but they have now been moved to protect them against vermin.

Just behind Wat Sisaket is an entire complex of colonial houses in a well-maintained garden.

Wat Phra Kaeo

① *Setthathirat Rd; daily 0800-1200 and 1300-1600 (closed public holidays); admission 5000 kip. No photographs in the sim.*

Almost opposite Wat Sisaket is the other national museum, **Wat Phra Kaeo**, also known as **Hor Phra Kaeo**. It was originally built by King Setthathirat in 1565 to house the Emerald Buddha (or Phra Kaeo), now in Bangkok, which he had brought from his royal residence in Chiang Mai. It was never a monastery but was kept instead for royal worship. The Emerald Buddha was removed by the Thais in 1779 and Wat Phra Kaeo was destroyed by them in the sacking of Vientiane in 1827. (The Thai's now claim the Emerald Buddha as their most important icon in the country.) The whole building was in a bad state of repair after the sackings, the only thing remaining fully intact was the floor. Francis Garnier, the French explorer who wandered through the ruins of Vieng Chan in 1860,

⁑ *Adjacent to the museum is the old royal palace, where the King from Luang Prabang resided. Today it is the presidential palace and closed to the public.*

describes Wat Phra Kaeo "shin[ing] forth in the midst of the forest, gracefully framed with blooming lianas, and profusely garlanded with foliage". Louis de Carné in his journal, *Travels in Indochina and the Chinese Empire* (1872), was also enchanted, writing when he came upon the vegetation-choked ruin that it "made one feel something of that awe which filled men of old at the threshold of a sacred wood".

The building was expertly reconstructed in the 1940s and 1950s and is now surrounded by a garden. During renovations, the interior walls of the wat were restored using a plaster made of sugar, sand, buffalo skin and tree oil.

The **sim** stands on three tiers of galleries, the top one surrounded by majestic, lotus-shaped columns. The tiers are joined by several flights of steps and guarded by *nagas*. The main, central (southern) door is an exquisite example of Lao wood sculpture with carved angels surrounded by flowers and birds; it is the only notable remnant of the original wat. (The central door at the northern end, with the larger carved angels supported by ogres, is new.) The *sim* now houses a superb assortment of Lao and Khmer art and some pieces of Burmese and Khmer influence, mostly collected from other wats in Vientiane. Although people regularly come and pray here, the wat's main purpose is as a quasi-museum.

‼ *The garden has a small jar from the Plain of Jars (page 166), which was transported to Vientiane by helicopter.*

Vientiane centre

200 metres
200 yards

Sleeping
Anou 1 *A2*
Asian Pavilion 2 *B4*
Chaleunxay 3 *B5*
Chanta Guesthouse 7 *B2*
Chanthapanya 40 *B2*
Day Inn 4 *B4*

Douang Deuane 5 *C2*
Dragon Lodge 39 *B2*
Ekkalath Metropole 6 *B4*
Green Park 38 *C6*
Intercity 8 *C1*
Joe Guesthouse 10 *C1*
KPP Guesthouse 11 *B1*
Lane Xang 22 *C3*
Lani I 9 *B2*
Lao 12 *B2*
Lao Paris 41 *B4*
Lao Plaza 25 *B3*
Laosakonh Guesthouse
 13 *B2*

Mali Namphu Guesthouse
 29 *B3*
Mimi Guesthouse 14 *B2*
Mixok Guesthouse 30 *B2*
Orchid 37 *B1*
Orchid Guesthouse 15 *C2*
Pangkham Guesthouse
 31 *B3*
Phet Phim Guesthouse
 18 *C1*
Phonepaseuth Guesthouse
 32 *B3*
Phornthip Guesthouse
 16 *B1*

Praseuth Guesthouse 17 *B3*
Sabaidee
 Guesthouse 33 *B2*
Samsenthai
 Guesthouse 19 *C2*
Santisouk Guesthouse
 & Restaurant 20 *B3*
Saysana Guesthouse 21 *B1*
Saysouly Guesthouse 34 *C2*
Settha Palace 23 *A4*
Soukchaleun
 Guesthouse 24 *B2*
Syri II Guesthouse 36 *B1*
Tai-Pan 26 *C2*

Notable exhibits in Wat Phra Kaeo A short description of each exhibit is given in French and Lao.

Nos 3, 4 and 17: Bronze Buddhas in typical Lao style.

Nos 294 and 295: Buddhas influenced by Sukhothai style (Thailand), where the attitude of the walking Buddha was first created (see page 316).

No 354: Buddha meditating made of lacquered wood, shows Burmese influence, dates from the 18th century.

No 372: Wooden, Indian-style door with erotic sculpture, dating back to the 16th century, originally from the Savannakhet region.

No 388: Copy of the Pra Bang, the revered statue associated with the origins of Buddhism in Laos (see pages 100 and 103).

Nos 412, 414 and 450: Khmer pieces.

No 415: A hybrid of Vishnu and Buddha.

Vannasinh Guesthouse 27 A2

Vayakorn Guesthouse 28 B2

Eating
Alexia 1 C2
Café Indochine 23 B2
Chinese Liao-ning Dumplings 2 A2
Côte d'Azur 3 C2
Dao Fa 9 C3
Delight House of Fruit Shakes 4 B4
Fathima 10 C2
Fuji Wara 5 B1
Full Moon Café 6 C2
Happy Garden 8 B2
Joma 11 C3
Just for Fun 15 C3
Khop Chai Deu 26 C3
Kua Lao 7 C4
La Cave du Château 27 C3
Le Provençal 30 B3
La Terrasse 28 B2
Le Croissant d'Or 12 B2
Le Vendôme 13 B1
Liang Xiang Bakery 20 B1
L'Opera 29 C3
Maison du Café 31 B3
Makphet 39 B1
Nam Nuang 14 A2
Nam Phou 32 C3
Nazim 16 C2
PVO Vietnamese Food 33 C3
Sabaidee 34 B3
Scandinavian Bakery 35 B3
Soukvimarn 36 B3
Sticky Fingers 19 C2
Sweet Home 20 B1
Tamnak Lao 40 A6
Thongphet Cakeshop 17 B2
Tokyo Kitchen 18 B2
Xayoh 21 B3

Bars & clubs
Déjà Vu 37 C3
Jazzy Brick 38 C3
Marina 22 A1
Mekong Deck 41 C3
Samlor Pub 24 B2
Spirit House 42 B1
That Dam Wine House 25 B4

No 416: A Khmer deity with four arms.

Nos 430 and 431: 18th-century copies of the famous Khmer apsaras, the celestial nymphs of Angkor in Cambodia.

No 698: This stone Buddha is the oldest piece of Buddhist art in Laos, dating from the sixth to ninth century.

Also look out for a collection of **stelae**, inscribed in Lao and Thai script, including one with a treaty delineating a 16th-century agreement between Siam and Lane Xang. There is also an 'Atom-struck Tile', found on the site of Sairenji Temple, Hiroshima.

That Dam

Travelling north on Chanta Koummane, the distinctive brick That Dam, or **Black Stupa**, can be seen. It is renowned for the legend of the seven-headed *naga*, which is supposed to have helped protect the city from Thai invaders (conveniently forgetting that the city was comprehensively sacked by the Thais in 1827). The *naga* now lies dormant inside, waiting for another chance. The stupa was renovated in 1995 but still has a neglected feel.

Lao National Museum

ⓘ *Samsenthai Rd, opposite the National Culture Hall; daily 0800-1200, 1300-1600, 5000 kip.*

This place was formerly called the Revolutionary Museum but in these post-revolutionary days it has been redesignated the National Museum. The museum's collection has grown over the last few years and now includes a selection of historical artefacts from dinosaur bones and pre-Angkorian sculptures to a comprehensive photographic collection on Laos' modern history. The rhetoric of these modern collections has been toned down from the old days, when photographic descriptions would refer to the 'running dog imperialists' (Americans). The museum features a dazzling array of personal effects from the revolutionary leader Kaysone including his exercise machine, a spoon he used and the coconut he once had a sip from. Downstairs there are ancient artefacts, including stone tools and quite poignant burial jars. Upstairs the museum features a range of artefacts and busts as well a small exhibition on various ethnic minorities. The final section of the museum comprises mostly photographs which trace, chronologically, the country's struggle against the 'brutal' French colonialists and American 'imperialists'.

Lao National Culture Hall

Facing the National Museum on the other side of the road is the Lao National Culture Hall. The hideous wedding cake-style building was a gift in kind by the Chinese and sticks out like a sore thumb. It is built in such monumental proportions that you can imagine tumbleweed blowing through the corridors at some of the ill-promoted events. ▸▸ For further details, see Entertainment, page 69.

Wat Ong Teu

Wat Ong Teu (identified by its bright orange monks' quarters) is located on Setthathirat, which runs parallel to Samsenthai. It was constructed by King Setthathirat in the 16th century, was ransacked by the Siamese in 1827 and then rebuilt during the late 19th and 20th centuries. The wat houses one of the biggest Buddhas in Vientiane, weighing several tonnes, which sits at the back of the *sim* and gives the monastery its name: Temple of the Heavy Buddha. The wat is also noted for its magnificent sofa and its ornately carved wooden doors and windows, with motifs from the *Phra Lak Pralam* (the *Ramayana*, see page 312). The monastery runs one of the larger Buddhist schools in Laos and is home to the Deputy Patriarch of the Lao monastic order, Hawng Sangkharat. The wat comes alive every year for the That Luang festival (see page 70).

The story of Quan Am

Quan Am was turned onto the streets by her husband for some unspecified wrong doing and, dressed as a monk, took refuge in a monastery. There, a woman accused her of fathering, and then abandoning, her child. Accepting the blame (why, no one knows), she was again turned out onto the streets, only to return to the monastery much later when she was on the point of death – to confess her true identity. When the Emperor of China heard the tale, he made Quan Am the Guardian Spirit of Mother and Child, and couples without a son now pray to her. Quan Am's husband is sometimes depicted as a parakeet, with the goddess usually holding her adopted son in one arm and standing on a lotus leaf, the symbol of purity.

Wat Chan

A short walk away, on the banks of the Mekong (junction of Chao Anou and Fa Ngum), is Wat Chan, or **Wat Chanthabuli**. It was wrecked by the marauding Thais in 1827 and now only the base of a single stupa remains in front of the *sim*. The stupa originally had Buddha images in the 'Calling for Rain' attitude on each side (see page 316) but only one remains. Inside the reconstructed *sim* is a remarkable bronze Buddha from the original temple on this site. The wat is also renowned for its panels of sculpted wood on the doors and windows.

Chua Bang-Long

For those who have had their fill of Theravada Buddhist wats, there is a fine Mahayana Buddhist *chua* (pagoda) tucked away down a narrow lane off Khoun Boulom, near Chao Anou. The Chua Bang-Long was established by Vientiane's large and active Vietnamese population, who are said to have outnumbered Lao in the city before the outbreak of the Second World War. A statue of the Chinese goddess Quan Am (see box, above) stands in front of a Lao-style *that* which, in turn, fronts a large pagoda, almost Cao Dai in style. The pagoda has been extensively renovated and embellished over the last few years. Not far away, at the intersection of Samsenthai and Khoun Boulom is another, much smaller and more intimate pagoda.

Wat Simuang

① *Setthathirat Rd, east of town; daily 0600-2000; during celebrations the temple stays open until 2200.*

Wat Simuang contains the town foundation pillar (*lak muang*), which was erected in 1566 when King Setthathirat established Vientiane as the capital of the kingdom of Lane Xang. It is believed to be an ancient Khmer boundary stone, which marked the edge of the old Lao capital. Although the temple means 'Holy City Monastery' many locals vouch that it's named after pregnant Madame Simuang, who sacrificed herself, her baby and her horse by jumping in the hole dug for the foundation pillar before the consecrated stone was erected. The *sim* was reconstructed in 1915 around the foundation pillar, which forms the centre of the altar. In front of the altar is a stone Buddha, which is thought to have magical powers and is often consulted by worshippers because it survived the temple's razing. It is believed that if you lift the Buddha off the pillow three times and make a wish then you are indebted to return an offering of fruit and flowers. Wat Simuang may not be charming, refined or architecturally significant but for many locals it is the most important monastery in the capital and is certainly considered the luckiest. Hawkers selling offerings of fruit, flowers, candles and incense line the surrounding streets, supplying the scores of people who come here hoping for good fortune. In the grounds of the wat are the ruins of what appears to be a Khmer laterite *chedi*.

Statue of King Setthathirat

Just beyond Wat Simaung, where Setthathirat and Samsenthai meet, is the statue of King Setthathirat, the founder of Vientiane. The original statue, carved by a Lao sculptor, apparently made the king look like a dwarf so it was destroyed. The present statue (there's a copy of it in Luang Prabang) was, peculiarly, donated by the Russians and, just as strangely, it survived the revolution.

● Sleeping

Vientiane *p50, maps p54 and p58*
There is very little quality accommodation in Vientiane under US$10 a night. There is a big difference in the quality of rooms between the US$10 and US$20-30 rooms and the extra US$10 is a worthwhile investment. Cheaper guesthouses will offer discounts in the wet season. Higher-end hotels offer better rates on the internet than the rack rate given if you walk in off the street. All of the guesthouses and boutique hotels, except for the most expensive, tend to get booked up so reserve in advance. As a rule of thumb, hotels priced over US$50 (ie our **A** category and above) accept major credit cards.
LL Green Park Hotel, www.greenpark vientiane.com, Kuvieng Rd, T021-264297. Designed in a modern East meets West style, this hotel is set alongside Vientiane's primary park. Beautiful rooms with all the mod-cons, Wi-Fi and super-duper bathtubs. Beautiful garden and excellent swimming pool. The only drawback is it is set a little further out from the city centre and river but is still within walking distance and makes a fantastic luxury option. Recommended.
LL-L Don Chan Palace, Piawat Village (off Fa Gnum Quay) T021-244288, www.donchanpalace.com. This 14-storey hotel is the largest in Vientiane and probably the ugliest. It was built for the ASEAN summit and is so close to the river that locals joke that it may sink in. Once you can get past the ugly exterior the 230 rooms and facilities are outstanding and afford the best views of both the river and the city in town. There's a restaurant, private karaoke rooms, bar, poolside massage and gym.
LL-L Settha Palace Hotel, 6 Pang Kham Rd, T021-217581/2, www.setthapalace.com. The stunning **Settha Palace** was built in 1936 and opened as a hotel in 1999. Its French architecture, stunning colonial decor, period furniture and beautiful tropical gardens and pool sit more easily with the fundamental essence of Vientiane that the other top-level hotels. Often considered the best hotel in town. Recommended.
L Lao Plaza Hotel, 63 Samsenthai Rd, T021-218800/1, www.laoplazahotel.com. Centrally located, this Thai-managed, 140-room hotel is no doubt useful for business visitors but seems rather incongruous in Vientiane. Non-guests may use the hotel's extensive facilities for a set fee. These include 2 restaurants, a fitness centre, pool, conference centre, satellite TV, IDD telephones, karaoke bar and shopping arcade. Most major credit cards accepted.
L Novotel Vientiane, Samsenthai Rd, near the junction with Luang Prabang, T021-213570/1, www.novotel.com. Large international-style hotel (332 rooms), with a good range of facilities including restaurant, pool, gym, tennis court, sauna, Lao massage, nightclub, business centre and games room. A/c throughout. The hotel often holds art exhibitions and concerts but the building itself is completely characterless and suffers from a poor location on the edge of town towards Wattay Airport (free airport transfer). Room rates include breakfast, but tax is extra; most major credit cards accepted.
A Tai-Pan, 2-12 François Ngin Rd (off Fa Ngum Rd, near Wat Mixay), T021-216906, www.travelao.com. The service here is hard to fault and facilities are good: restaurant, bar, basic gym, small pool and free airport pickup. The lobby is rather more impressive than the 36 rooms, but they are reasonably well equipped with a/c, IDD telephones, satellite TV and flowers and fruit on arrival. Room rates include a good breakfast. Most major credit cards accepted.

A-B Beau Rivage Mekong, Fa Ngum Rd, T021-243350, www.hbrm.com. One of the first Western-style boutique hotels in Vientiane is beautifully furnished with quirky decoration and fantastic baths. The pink exterior does not sit well with its surroundings but nonetheless this is a great boutique hotel with superb Mekong River views. Its location, just out of the centre of town on the river, ensures peace and quiet but it's still only a 5-min walk to the hustle and bustle. Includes breakfast. Recommended.

A-B Lane Xang Hotel, Fa Ngum Rd, T021-214100/7, www.lanexanghotel.com. This was the original 'luxury' hotel in Vientiane, built by the French in the 1960s. It has an undefinable charm, despite the fact that some of its retro-hip Soviet fittings and furniture have been ripped out to make way for a more contemporary look. The a/c rooms are now well equipped, with excellent bathrooms, making the hotel the best value in town, with a great central position on the river. Go for a deluxe room, with its own bar and velour bed fittings and indulge in a 1970s, porn-flick nostalgia trip. The service here is unmatched. The international restaurant has traditional Lao dancing shows every night and a cabaret on Wed, with a bird impressionist and contortionist. Other facilities include a dilapidated pool, nightclub and bar. Major credit cards accepted. Recommended.

A-B Orchid Hotel, Chao Anou, T021-264138, www.laoorchid.com. Beautiful spacious rooms with stunning modern furnishings, polished floorboards and large showers. Outstanding value for the price and very popular with business travellers. 4½-star accommodation for a 3-star price. Very busy so advanced bookings imperative. Includes breakfast and Wi-Fi. Café and zen fish pond. Visa and MasterCard accepted. Recommended.

A-C Hotel Day Inn, Pang Kham Rd, T021-222985, dayinn@laopdr.com. Run by a friendly Cambodian, this renovated villa is in a good position in a quiet part of town, just to the north of the main concentration of bars and restaurants. Attractive, airy, clean, large rooms, with a/c and excellent bathrooms. Also bike hire. Good value. Recommended.

A-C Intercity Hotel, 24-25 Fa Ngum Rd/Chou Anou (next to Wat Chan),

T021-242842, www.laointerhotel.com. This hotel is one of the oldest in Vientiane, now operating for over 30 years. Recent renovations have made it sparkle: mosaics, relief sculptures and murals adorn the walls, and traditional shutters, silk hangings and furniture feature in every room. The a/c rooms are light and spacious, with slick bathrooms and fantastic balconies overlooking the Mekong. Lovely atrium and excellent gift shop with beautiful antique costumes. Recommended.

B Chanthapanya, Nokeo Khoummane Rd, T021-244284, www.chanthapanyahotel.com. Fantastic modern Asian building. The rooms are spanking new and very comfortable. Beautifully furnished with modern Lao wooden furniture, comfy beds, fridge, TV, hot water, phone, a/c. Includes breakfast.

B-C Asian Pavilion, 379 Samsenthai Rd, T021-213430/1, asianlao@loxinfo.co.th. Currently being renovated so this historic hotel should soon be launching a new and improved version. It used to be the **Hotel Constellation** made famous by John Le Carré in *The Honourable Schoolboy*.

B-C Hotel Lao, 53/9 Heng Boun Rd, T021-219281, hotellao@laotel.com. Opened in early 1999, this hotel has 30 enormous a/c rooms, with satellite TV, telephone, minibar, even a hairdryer in the en suite bathrooms.

B-C Lao Paris, 100 Samsenthai Rd, opposite **Lao Plaza Hotel**, T021-213440, F021-216382. Clean but uninspired. Central location. Rooms with a/c and private bathrooms with hot water, some have TV. Cheaper rooms on top floor are drab.

B-C Le Parasol Blanc, behind National Assembly, close to Victory Monument (not very well marked), T021-216091, F021-215444. This is a very attractive leafy haven. Spacious a/c rooms, with wooden floors and sizeable bathrooms. Some look onto the garden, with sitting area in front, the most expensive are alongside the good-sized pool. Charming place, well run, mostly patronized by French visitors.

B-C Mali Namphu Guesthouse, 114 Pang Kham Rd (next door to Phonepaseuth Guesthouse), T021-215093, malinamp@laotel.com. Difficult to spot as it looks like a small shopfront but the façade is deceiving, as the foyer opens onto a beautifully manicured courtyard surrounded by quaint, terraced rooms. Clean, bright rooms are traditionally decorated with a modern twist and come with a/c, hot water, cable TV and a fantastic breakfast. The twin rooms are much nicer than the doubles. Friendly staff. Highly recommended.

B-C Vayakorn, 91 Nokeo Khoummane Rd, T021-241911. Centrally located and clean, with friendly staff. Wonderful comfortable, airy rooms, tastefully decorated with modern furniture. Polished floors, with hot water, a/c and TV. Sadly breakfast is no longer included with rooms but it is still excellent value. Recommended.

B-C Vieng Thong Guesthouse, Ban Phiawat, opposite Wat Phiavat in a side street, T/F021-212095. Family-style house in a nice garden with a café and big aviary. Large rooms with thick comforting duvets, rattan furniture, TV, china tea-sets and hot water showers. Pleasant but perhaps a little expensive.

C Douang Deuane, Nokeo Khoummane Rd, T021-222301/3, www.bookings-asia.com/la/hotels/douangdeane. From the exterior, this dilapidated building looks like a classic Communist edifice, but the a/c rooms have charm and character: parquet wood floors, art deco furniture, excellent bathrooms, satellite TV and a decent size. Try and get a balcony room for lovely patchwork views of the roofs of the city. Although the room rates are no longer competitive it is a good centrally located option-B if the others within this price-range are fully booked. Good-value motorbike rentals, 40,000 kip per day.

C-D Chaleunxay Hotel, Khou Vieng Rd, T021-223407, F021-223529. The laid-back, ramshackle, slightly untidy air persists, despite the brace of cleaners whose jobs never seem to be quite done. Temperamental hot water supply. Very friendly staff, and convenient location very close to the Morning Market and bus station. Endearing.

C-D Dragon Lodge, Samsenthai Rd, T021-250112, dragonlodge2002@yahoo.com. Somewhere between a guesthouse and a hotel. Fun, colourful downstairs restaurant area – good for a party; if you're looking for quiet this probably isn't the best choice. Nice, simply decorated comfortable rooms with hot water, TV and a/c. 5-star service. Visa accepted.

D Chanta Guesthouse, Setthathirat Rd (opposite Mixay Temple), T021-243204. The shabby foyer doesn't do this place justice. Rooms are homely, with polished floorboards, TV, good bathrooms, wooden furniture and great cotton bedclothes. Cheaper rooms have shared facilities.

D Orchid Guesthouse, 33 Fa Ngum Rd, T021-252825, F021-216588. Friendly staff, and jolly nice, spotlessly clean rooms with fan or a/c and breakfast included. Take a table and chairs onto the tiled roof for a lovely view of sunset on the river. Slap bang on the noisy Fa Ngum Rd, so only recommended for deep sleepers.

D Phonepaseuth Guesthouse, 97 Pang Kham Rd, T021-212263, www.phonepaseuth-gh.com. Popular, clean guesthouse with cable TV, hot water and good bathroom. Roof top garden. Good location.

D Phornthip Guesthouse, 72 Inpeng Rd (behind Wat Inpeng), T021-217239. A quiet, family-run and very friendly guesthouse, perhaps a trifle overpriced. Large rooms, with en suite bathrooms, some have a/c. Courtyard at the back, but no garden. Bicycle hire.

D Thongbay Guesthouse, off Luang Prabang Rd, turn right before the **Novotel**, Ban Non Douang, T021-242292, www.thongbay-guesthouses.com. Lovely traditional Lao house set in a lush tropical garden. Rooms have traditional-style fittings, mosquito nets and fan or a/c. The guesthouse also runs cooking classes on request (US$10), including purchasing ingredients at the local market. The only drawback of this place is its distance from the city centre. Perfect if you wish to relax.

D-E Joe Guesthouse, 112 Fa Ngum Rd, T021-241936, joe_guesthouse @yahoo.com. Wonderful family-run guesthouse on the riverfront. Light, clean, airy. Good coffee shop downstairs. Fantastic service.

D-E Praseuth Guesthouse, 312 Samsenthai Rd, T021-217932. This nondescript building contains 10 small a/c rooms, many without windows. Walls and floor are wooden, which enhances the gloomy feel, but facilities are clean. Some rooms have en suite bathrooms. Bikes for hire. Central location, with the popular **Xayoh Café** next door.

D-E Saysouly, 23 Manthaturath Rd, T021-218384, saysouly@hotmail.com. A variety of rooms, a bit on the musty side.

Parquet floors, cheap US$5 single fan rooms with shared bathroom. On the upside the shared bathrooms are excellent with powerful showers. Extra for a/c. The more expensive US$10 rooms are quite good value.

D-E Soukchaleun Guesthouse, 121 Setthathirat Rd (opposite Mixay temple), T021-218723, soukchaleun_gh@yahoo.com. Quaint guesthouse with a variety of rooms ranging from US$5 with shared bathroom through to US$13 with a/c. Comfy and homely. Super clean, friendy and relatively good value.

D-E Syri II Guesthouse, Setthathirat Rd, T021-241345. This is probably one of the best options within the cheaper price range. 3-storey guesthouse with a variety of rooms including fan rooms with shared bathroom US$6 and those with bathroom inside US$8. Clean and decorated simply with wooden furniture. The place is decorated with quirky curious from around Asia and is spotted with lounges and shared common areas. Helpful staff. Recommended.

E Sabaidee Guesthouse, Setthathirat Rd, sabaidy_gh@hotmail.com. The cheap price reflects the facilities. Turquoise, swimming pool-esque rooms with fans. Proprietor speaks reasonable English if cajoled out of his habitual grump. Communal washrooms, and always a queue.

E-F Mixok Guesthouse, 188 Setthathirat Rd (opposite Mixay Temple), T021-215606, bucnong@hotmail.com. This ain't the Ritz but you get what you pay for as the rooms are amongst the cheapest in town. Very basic, pokey rooms not for the claustrophobic, but they cost the same as a hamburger and beer. Shared hot-water bath. 11 rooms which are frequently booked out. Excellent location.

Serviced apartments

LL Parkview Executive Suites, Luang Prabang Rd (near the Novotel), T021-250888, Parkview@laotel.com. Serviced residence complex of 116 units, catering for both long- and short-term stays. Fitness centre, pool, sauna, jacuzzi, tennis court, office space and secretarial support. A bit off the beaten track.

🍴 Eating

Vientiane p50, maps p54 and p58
The absolutely best place to get **Lao food** is from the open-air stalls that line the banks of the Mekong along **Fa Ngum**. The restaurants are ridiculously low on price and high on atmosphere, particularly at night with their flickering candles. From time to time the government kicks all the eateries off the patch but they usually return with a vengeance. The **Dong Palane Night Market**, on Dong Palane, and the night markets near the corner of **Chao Anou** and **Khoun Boulom Rd** are also good places to go for Lao stall food. There are various other congregations of stalls and vendors around town, most of which set up shop around 1730 and close down by 2100. Be sure to sample Lao ice cream with coconut sticky rice.

The **Chinese quarter** is around Chao Anou, Heng Boun and **Khoun Boulom** and is a lively spot in the evenings. There are a number of noodle shops here, all of which serve a palatable array of vermicelli, *muu daeng* (red pork), duck and chicken.

The **Korean-style barbeque**, *sindat*, is extremely popular, especially among the younger Lao, as it is a social event and very cheap. It involves cooking finely sliced meat on a hot plate in the middle of the table, whilst forming a broth with vegetables around the sides of the tray; reminiscent of a 1970s fondue evening. **Seendat** (see below) is a favourite amongst the older Lao.

For cheap **Vietnamese** food, there's a good selection of stalls on Sisangvong Rd (Ban Sisanvong) and around Heng Boun St in **China Town**, where there is a dazzling array of fresh spring rolls and *feu* shops.

Restaurants that do good **vegetarian** dishes include Just for Fun, the **Full Moon Café** and **Nazim** (see below).

₹₹₹-₹₹ Le Nadao, Ban Donmieng (on the right-hand side of the Patuxai roundabout). Daily 1100-1400, 1700-2230. This place is difficult to find but definitely worth every second spent searching the back streets of Vientiane in the dark. Sayavouth, who trained in Paris and New York, produces delectable French cuisine: soups, venison, lamb, puddings. Fantastic. The US$5 set menu is one of the best lunches you will get in town.

₹₹₹-₹₹ Le Silapa, Sihom Rd , T021-219689. Mon-Sat 1130-1400, 1800-2200 (closed in Jul). Anthony and Fred provide a fantastic French-inspired menu and intimate atmosphere for fine dining without blowing the budget. Innovative modern meals that would be as at home in the fine dining establishments of New York and London as they are here. Great set lunch menu. Part of the profits are donated to disadvantaged families, usually for expensive but life-saving surgical procedures.

¶¶¶-¶¶ Côte d'Azur, 63/64 Fa Ngum Rd, T021-217252, jmdazur@laotel.com. Daily 1130-2230. Fine selection of dishes from the south of France, plus excellent wood-fired pizzas and delicious seafood dishes. Recommended.

¶¶¶-¶¶ Kua Lao, 111 Samsenthai Rd, T021-215777. Daily 1000-1400, 1700-2230. A tastefully refurbished colonial house-turned-restaurant provides a sophisticated atmosphere for quality Lao and Thai food. Avoid the set menu. Good Lao music and traditional dancing. Some locals believe that the restaurant has sold its Lao culinary credentials to the tourist dollar but most visitors to Laos will enjoy their meal here. Pricey for Laos.

¶¶¶-¶¶ La Cave du Château, Nam Phou Circle, T021-212192. Daily 1100-1400, 1800-2200. This restaurant around the Nam Phou Fountain is supposed to look like a grotto but is just a little odd. Pretty good set menu, with delicious grilled squid and steaks. Dine on the upstairs balcony.

¶¶¶-¶¶ Le Provençal, Nam Phou Circle, T021-216248. Daily 1100-1400, 1800-2200. Long-standing quaint Italian restaurant that generally gets dwarfed by its partners on the other side of the fountain. Serves a good plate of pasta.

¶¶¶-¶¶ L'Opera, Nam Phou Circle, T021-215099. Daily 1130-1400, 1830-2200. A/c Italian restaurant, pompous, cold and overpriced but with delicious ice cream and a wide range of pizza and pasta dishes, also barbecue steaks.

¶¶¶-¶ Sakura, Luang Prabang Rd, Km 2/ Soi 3 (the *soi* runs along the side of the Novotel), T021-212274. Mon 1730-2200, Tue-Sun 1030-1400 and 1730-2200. Regarded as the best Japanese food in town. Expensive for Vientiane but good value by international standards. The restaurant is in a converted private house.

¶¶ Tamnak Lao Restaurant, That Luang Rd, T021-413562. 1200-2200. It's well worth

deviating from the main Nam Phou area for a bite to eat here. This restaurant and its sister branch in Luang Prabang have a reputation for delivering outstanding Lao and Thai food, usually prepared with a modern twist.

¶¶-¶ Airport Buffet, Wattay International Airport. The buffet is a favourite with senior-ranking Lao government officials and local VIPs who make the long hike out during their lunch hour. It represents unparalleled value: 50,000 kip for as much Lao food (curries, fried dishes, etc), Japanese food (sushi), dessert, coffee and tea as you can stomach. Open for lunch and dinner. Highly recommended.

¶¶-¶ Alexia, 7 Fa Ngum Rd, T021-241349. Daily 1100-2300. Popular with tourists, **Alexia** specializes in Mexican cuisine. The food is a bit overpriced and can be pretty standard. On the up side there is live music after 2000.

¶¶-¶ Café Indochine,199 Setthathirat Rd, T021-216758. Daily 1030-2230. Intimate restaurant with delectable cuisine, including zucchini flower salad and grilled chicken.

¶¶-¶ Chinese Liao-ning Dumpling Restaurant, Chao Anou Rd, T021-240811. Daily 1100-2230. This restaurant is a firm favourite with the expats and it isn't hard to see why: fabulous steamed or fried dumplings and a wide range of vegetarian dishes. The place is spotlessly clean but the birds in the cages outside are a bit off-putting. No one is ever disappointed with the meals here. Highly recommended.

¶¶-¶ Dao Fa, Setthathirat Rd (across from Kop Chai Deu), T021-215657, www.daofa-bistro.com. Daily 0800-2200. Modern European restaurant offering home-made pasta, crêpes and wood-fired pizza. Great atmosphere with a miscellany of pop-art paintings adorning the white walls.

¶¶-¶ La Terrasse, 55/4 Nokeo Khoummane Rd, T021-218550. Mon-Sat 1100-1400, 1800-2200. This is the best European restaurant in terms of variety and price. Large fail-safe menu offering French, European, Lao and Mexican food. Good desserts, especially the rich chocolate mousse, and a good selection of French wine. Fantastic service. Reasonable prices with an excellent 'plat du jour' each day. Great 1970s-style comfort food. Recommended.

¶¶-¶ Nazim, 39 Fa Ngum Rd, T021-223480.

Daily 1000-2230. Authentic Indian (north and south) and Halal food, very popular with backpackers. Indoor and outdoor seating. They have another restaurant in Vang Vieng as well as a branch in Luang Prabang.

¶-¶ Seendat, Sihom Rd, T021-213855. Daily 1730-2200. This restaurant has been in existence for well over 20 years and is a favourite amongst the older Lao for its clean food (*sindat*) and good atmosphere. About US$1 per person more expensive than most other places but this is reflected in the quality. Recommended.

¶-¶ Seendat Somphouthong, Luang Prabang Rd, T021-250540. Daily 1030-2200. Distinguishes itself from many other barbecue (*sindat*) restaurants by using a delicious prawn sauce instead of the standard peanut. A bit far from the centre of town but worth the trip.

¶-¶ Xayoh, Nokeo Khoummane Rd, T021-262111, www.xayoh.com. Daily 0800-2330. Attractive bar and restaurant next to the hideous Lao National Cultural Hall. Salads, pizzas, burgers plus Lao/Thai food. The restaurant's speciality is a Sunday roast of beef and Yorkshire pud, etc, for homesick Brits. Double-check your order as the staff have a tendency to serve the wrong thing. Deliveries available.

¶ Full Moon Café, François Ngin Rd, T021-243373. Daily 1000-2200. Delectable Asian fusion cuisine and Western favourites. Huge pillows, good lighting and great music make this place very relaxing. Fantastic chicken wrap and some pretty good Asian tapas. The Ladybug shake is a winner. Also a book exchange and music And movie shop for ipods.

¶ Just for Fun, 57/2 Pang Kham Rd, opposite Lao Airlines. Good Lao food with vegetarian dishes, coffees, soft drinks and the largest selection of teas in Laos, if not Southeast Asia. The atmosphere is relaxed with a/c, newspapers and comfy chairs (also sells textiles and other handicrafts).

¶ Khop Chai Deu, Setthathirat Rd, on the corner of Nam Phou Rd. Daily 0800-2330. This lively place housed in a colonial building is one of the city's most popular venues. Garden seating, good atmosphere at night with soft lantern lighting, and an eclectic menu of Indian, Italian, Korean and international dishes (many of which come from nearby restaurants). While the food is

OK most come for the bustling atmosphere. The best value are the local Lao dishes, though, which are made on site and toned down for the *falang* palate. Also serves draft or bottled beer at a pleasant a/c bar. Excellent lunch buffet. Live performances.

¶ Makphet, Setthathirat near Wat Inpeng, T021-260587, www.friends-international.org. Fantastic Lao non-profit restaurant that helps raise money for street kids. Run by former street kids in training. Modern Lao cuisine with a twist. Selection of delectable drinks such as the iced hibiscus with lime juice. Beautifully decorated with modern furniture and painting by the kids. Also sells handicrafts and toys produced by the parents from vulnerable communities.

¶ Nong Vong Restaurant, on the street between Sisavong Rd and That Luang, T021-415818. This little, tucked away eatery is an all-time favourite with long-term expats who endearingly refer to it as 'Vongs'. Impeccable service and a huge selection of superb Lao, Thai and Vietnamese-inspired dishes. You can take 4 people to dinner and still come back with change from US$10. Open for dinner, but lunch really seems to be their forte. Highly recommended.

¶ PVO Vietnamese Food, off Fa Gnum Quay. A firm favourite. Full menu of freshly prepared Vietnamese food but best known for baguettes stuffed with your choice of pâté, salad, cheese, coleslaw, vegetables and ham. Bikes and motorbikes for rent too. Keep an eye out for the miniature dog wearing the Hannibal Lector-style dog-mask – a very popular doggy accessory with those Vientiane citizens paranoid about rabies. Brilliant cheap food makes this a fantastic choice.

¶ Soukvimarn, T021-214441. 1100-1400, 1800-2100. Heavily influenced by traditional southern Lao flavours. Well worth the experience as it offers the opportunity to tempt the tastebuds with a wider variety of Lao cuisine than most other eateries offer.

¶ Sticky Fingers, François Ngin Rd, T021-215972. Tue-Sun 1000-2300. Very popular small restaurant and bar serving Lao and international dishes including fantastic salads, pasta, burgers and such like. Everything from Middle Eastern through to modern Asian on offer. Fantastic comfort food and the best breakfast in town. Great cocktails, lively atmosphere, nice setting.

Deliveries available. **Stickies** should be the first pit-stop for every visitor needing to get grounded quickly as, food aside, the expats who frequent the joint are full to the brim with local knowledge.

Fathima, Th Fa Gnum, T021-219097. Without a doubt the best-value Indian in town. Ultra-friendly service and a large menu with a range of excellent curries.

Floating restaurants

A couple of floating restaurants are docked on the Mekong, off Fa Ngum Rd (just past the **Intercity Hotel**). They cruise down the river for an hour or so in the evening. It's a good idea to get there early so you can watch the sunset, as much of the cruise takes place in the dark. The food is as cheap as chips, so the cruises are exceptionally good value. Recommended.

Champadeng, a bit further along from Lane Xang Av, T020-5526911. Daily 1000-2200, cruise at 1930. This is probably the most popular of the two. Quite a good selection of Lao dishes and some hilarious English translations. The food here is as good as you will find anywhere else and, when you get bored, you can pop down to the lower level and belt out a few tunes on the karaoke – the Lao diners will love it.

Lane Xang, T021-243397. Daily 1000-2230, cruise at 1900. Most meals are around US$2.50.

Cafés, cakeshops and juice bars

Pavement cafés are ten a penny in Vientiane. You need not walk more than half a block for some hot coffee or a cold fruit shake. On Chao Anou you'll find **Liang Xiang Bakery**, **Sweet Home** and **Nai Xiang Chai** (good juices and shakes).

Delight House of Fruit Shakes, Samsenthai Rd, opposite the **Asian Pavilion Hotel**, T021-212200. Daily 0700-2200. A wonderful selection of fresh shakes and fruit salads for next to nothing.

Joma (aka **Healthy and Fresh Bakery**), Setthathirat Rd, T021-215265, bakers@laopdr.com. Mon-Sat 0700-2100. Hugely popular. A very modern, chic bakery with efficient service and a good selection of

tasty pastries, bagels, sandwiches, pastas, salads, pizzas, yoghurts and coffee. Wi-Fi and arctic-style a/c. However, it is starting to get a bit pricey.

Le Croissant d'Or, top of Nokeo Khoummane Rd, T021-223740. Daily 0700-1800. French bakery, small selection but good cheap croissants.

Scandinavian Bakery, 71/1 Pang Kham Rd, Nam Phou Circle, T021-215199, scandinavian@laonet.net. Daily 0700-2000. Delicious pastries, bread, sandwiches and cakes. Friendly *falang* chef/baker, who made the President of Tanzania's daughter's wedding cake – and has the photo to prove it. Great place for a leisurely coffee and pastries. Pricey for Laos but a necessary European fix for many expats. Recommended.

⊙ Bars and clubs

Vientiane *p50, maps p54 and p58*
Bars
There are a number of bar stalls, which set up in the evening along **Quai Fa Ngum** (the river road); a good place for a cold beer as the sun sets. Most bars will close at 2300 in accordance with the local curfew laws; some places seem to be able to stay open past this time although that varies on a day-to-day basis. Government officials go through phases of shutting down clubs and bars and restricting curfews.

Déjà Vu, Nam Phou Circle. Very upmarket, intimate cocktail bar, with a plethora of drinks available. Set in a small, white minimalist room, it is a bit out of place in Vientiane. The proprietor takes his cocktails very seriously. Recommended.

Jazzy Brick, Setthathirat Rd, near Phimphone Market (brown building on the corner of the lane that leads to Wat Xieng Khoune). Very sophisticated, modern den, where delectable cocktails are served with jazz cooing in the background. Garish shirts banned. Decorated with an eclectic range of quirky and kitsch artefacts. Very upmarket but a bit pretentious. Has become the place for well-heeled Lao. Head here towards the end of the night.

Khop Chai Deu, Setthathirat Rd (near the corner with Nam Phou). Probably the most

● *For an explanation of the eating and sleeping price codes used in this guide, see inside the*
● *front cover. Other relevant information is found in Essentials, see pages 29-32.*

popular bar for tourists in Vientiane. Casual setting and nightly band. Also serves food (see Eating, above).

Mekong Deck, Fa Gnum, Fantastic location on the river. Huge modern, open-air wooden deck. Limited drinks menu with beer, spirits and shakes but set to expand.

Samlor Pub, Setthathirat Rd. Snooker, darts, pizza and the only place in town where you can play table-football. Sometimes the clientele can be a bit so-so.

Spirit House, follow Fa Ngum Rd until it turns into a dirt track, past the Mekong River Commission, T021-243795. Beautiful wooden bar in perfect river location. Range of snacks and decent sushi. Good for those wanting to catch the sunset in style. Wi-Fi.

Sticky Fingers, François Ngin Rd, opposite the **Tai Pan Hotel**. The main drinking hole for expats. Small and intimate bar and restaurant run by two Australian women. Brilliant cocktails, especially the renowned Tom Yum. Very atmospheric and a lot of fun. Also serves food (see Eating, above). Highly recommended.

Sunset Bar, end of Fa Ngum Rd. Although this run-down wooden construction isn't much to look at, it is a firm favourite with locals and tourists hoping to have a quiet ale and take in the magnificent sunset overlooking the Mekong. Recommended.

Wind West, by traffic lights, Luang Prabang Rd. Usually stays open after 2300. Seedier than others; many wild nights happen here.

Clubs

Many of the discos in town, both those in hotels and independent set-ups, sometimes feature live bands usually playing a mixture of Lao and Thai music and cover versions of Western rock classics. Vientiane lacks good places to dance, since the most popular Western-style clubs were closed down in late 2004. Some Lao places are still running but you are advised to take earplugs as they like to play the music extremely loud.

Don Chan Palace (see Sleeping). For late night owls looking for a party, entrance fee, terrible music but the best bet for boogie late at night.

D'Tech, at the **Novotel** (see Sleeping). T021-213570. Quite happening. DJs and hip-hop acts from around Asia. Popular with the locals.

Marina, Luang Prabang Rd, behind the Marina Bowling Centre. Popular with wealthy young Lao. Drinks of choice are either Beer Lao or Johnny Walker Black. Bring earplugs.

⊕ Entertainment

Vientiane *p50, maps p54 and p58*
Cinema
Blue Sky Café, on the corner of Setthathirat and Chao Anou rds. DVD movies are generally shown daily at 1200 and 1900 on the 2nd floor.

French Cultural Centre, Lang Xang Rd, T021-215764. Tue and Thu 1930, Sat 1530, US$1. Screens the occasional French film and also hosts the Southeast Asian film festival. Check the *Vientiane Times* for up-to-date details.

Lao International Trade Exhibition Centre (**ITEC**), T4 Rd – Ban Phonethane Neua, T021-416374. Shows a range of international films.

Circus
The National Circus, known as **Hong Kanyasin**, holds infrequent performances in an old Russian tent, usually in conjunction with the French Cultural Centre. The performances usually include acrobatics and clowns and are worthwhile if you're in town at the right time.

Exhibitions
Keep an eye in the *Vientiane Times* for international performances at the **Lao Cultural Centre** (the building that looks like a big cake opposite the museum).

COPE Visitors' Centre, National Rehabilitation Centre compound on Kuvieng Rd (sign-posted), www.copelaos.org. At the time of publication COPE (Cooperative Orthotic and Prosthetic Enterprise) was setting up an exhibition on UXO (unexploded ordnance) and its effects on the people of Laos. The exhibition is very interesting and includes a small movie room, photography, UXO and a range of prosthetic limbs (some, which are actually crafted out of UXO). The exhibition helps raise money for the work of COPE, which includes the production of prosthetic limbs and rehabilitation of patients. Open 0900-1600, 20,000 kip.

T-Shop Lai, T021-223178, Th Inpeng (behind Wat Inpeng) has an exhibition upstairs devoted to Asian elephants.

Fairs and amusements
There's often a ferris wheel and bouncy castle at **That Luang** in the evenings, particularly if it is a public holiday or celebration. A more reliable option is to make the haul out to the **ITEC Centre**, where there is a collection of rides, including a ferris wheel, merry-go-rounds and dodgem cars. Popular at weekends.

Karaoke
This could almost be the Lao national sport and there's nothing like bonding with the locals over a heavy-duty karaoke session. Karaoke places are everywhere – just keep your ears out for the off-key bellowing. Good spots include the **Blue Note** in the Lao Plaza Hotel or the more expensive, upmarket **Don Chan Palace** (for both, see Sleeping). **Champadeng Cruise** also has a good karaoke room below deck (see Eating: Floating restaurants). And no one can hear your howling when you're out on the river. Recommended.

Live music
Bands will perform almost every night at **Khop Chai Deu** and **Alexia** (see Eating, above) and at the **Music House**, on Fa Ngum. The **French Cultural Centre**, on Lang Xang, hosts a variety of musical performances, from local bands through to hip-hop ensembles.

Occasionally, music concerts and beauty pageants are held at the **Lao National Culture Hall**, opposite the National Museum. No official notice is given of forthcoming events but announcements sometimes appear in the *Vientiane Times* and large banners will flank the building.

Traditional dance
Lao National Theatre, Manthathurath Rd, T021-242978. Daily shows of traditional Lao dancing, from 2030. Tickets, US$7, available at the theatre. Performances are less regular in the low season.

⊛ Festivals and events

Vientiane *p50, maps p54 and p58*
1st weekend in Apr Pi Mai (Lao New Year) is celebrated with a 3-day festival and a huge water fight. It is advisable to put your wallet into a plastic bag and invest in a turbo water pistol. There are numerous *bacis* (good luck celebrations) and the traditional greeting at this time of year is '*Sok Dee Pi Mai*' (good luck for the New Year).
Sep/Oct Boun Ok Phansa is a beautiful event on the night of the full moon at the end of Buddhist Lent. Candles are lit in all the homes and a candle-lit processions take place around the city's wats and through the streets. Then, thousands of banana-leaf boats holding flowers, tapers and candles are floated out onto the river. The boats signify your bad luck floating away.
Sep/Oct Boun Souang Heua, the boat-racing festival, is held towards the end of the rainy season. Boat races (*souang heua*) take place with 50 or so men in each boat; they power up the river in perfect unison. An exuberant event, with plenty of merrymaking.
12 Oct Freedom of the French Day is a public holiday.
Nov (date varies each year) Boun That Luang is celebrated in all of Vientiane's *thats* but most notably at That Luang (the national shrine). Originally a ceremony in which nobles swore allegiance to the king and constitution, it amazingly survived the Communist era. On the festival's most important day, **Thak Baat**, thousands of Lao people pour into the temple at 0600 and again at 1700 to pay homage. Monks travel from across the country to collect offerings and alms from the pilgrims. It is a really beautiful ceremony, with monks chanting and thousands of people praying. Women who attend should invest in a traditional *sinh*. A week-long carnival surrounds the festival with fireworks, music and dancing. Recommended.

⏿ Shopping

Vientiane *p50, maps p54 and p58*
Books
A selection of maps and books on Laos can be found in **Phimphone Market**. The **Full Moon Café** has a book exchange.
Kosila Books, Nokeo Khoummane Rd,

The art of ikat

In the handicraft shops and at the Morning Market in Vientiane, it is possible to buy distinctively patterned cotton and silk ikat. Ikat is a technique of patterning cloth characteristic of Southeast Asia and is produced from the hills of Burma to the islands of Eastern Indonesia. The word comes from the Malay word 'mengikat' which means to bind or tie. Very simply, bundles of warp or weft fibres (or, in one Balinese case, both) are tied with material or fibre (or more often plastic string these days), so that they resist the action of the dye. Hence the technique's name – resist dyeing. By dyeing, retying and dyeing again through a number of cycles it is possible to build up complex patterns. This initial pre-weaving process can take anything from two to 10 days, depending on the complexity of the design. Ikat is distinguishable by the bleeding of the dye which inevitably occurs no matter how carefully the threads are tied; this gives the finished cloth a blurred finish.

The earliest ikats date from the 14th-15th centuries.

To prepare the cloth for dyeing, the warp or weft is strung tight on a frame. Individual threads, or groups of threads, are then tied together with fibre and leaves. In some areas wax is then smeared on top to help in the resist process. The main colour is usually dyed first, secondary colours later.

With complex patterns (which are done from memory; plans are only required for new designs) and using natural dyes, it may take up to six months to produce a piece of cloth. Today, the pressures of the market place mean that it is more likely that cloth is produced using chemical dyes (which need only one short soaking, not multiple long ones – six hours or so – as with some natural dyes), and design motifs have generally become larger and less complex. Traditionally, warp ikat used cotton while weft ikat used silk. Silk in many areas has given way to cotton, and cotton sometimes to synthetic yarns.

T021-241352. A good selection of English, Lao, German and French books, maps and guides and a small selection of second-hand books. **Kosila** has also opened another shop near That Dam.

Monument Books, T021-243708. The largest selection of new books in Vientiane, **Monument** stock a range of Southeast Asian speciality books as well as coffee-table books. Good place to pick up Lao-language children's books to distribute to villages on your travels.

Vientiane Book Centre (previously **Raintree Books**), 54/1 Pang Kham Rd, T/F021-212031. This was the first English-language bookshop in Laos and still has the best selection in town. Coffee-table books, glossy magazines and maps as well as specialist Lao PDR publications. Book exchange and a limited but interesting selection of used books in a multitude of languages.

Clothing, fashion and textiles
Every hue and design is available in the **Morning Market**. For cheaper (but still very good-quality) fabric just pop across the road to **Talaat Kudin**; the fabric section is at the back of the market, in the covered area. A *sinh*, the traditional Lao skirt, can be made within the day for US$1-2 extra; just pick the length of fabric and the patterned band for the bottom of the skirt. See also Tailors.

Cama Craft, Mixay Rd, T021-501271. Handmade clothes in Hmong styles.

Couleur d'Asie, Nam Phou Circle. Modern-style Asian clothing, very well known and a favourite of locals and expats. Pricey but high-quality fusion fashion.

Lao Cotton, Luang Prabang Rd, out towards Wattay Airport, approximately 400 m on right from **Novotel**, T021-215840. Good range of material, shirts and handbags, ask to see the looms. Another branch on Samsenthai.

Lao Textiles by Carol Cassidy, Nokeo Khoummane Rd, T021-212123, F021-216205. Mon-Fri 0800-1200, 1400-1700, Sat 0800-1200. Exquisite silk fabrics, including *ikat* and traditional Lao designs, made by an American in a beautifully renovated colonial property. Dyeing, spinning, designing and weaving all done on site (and can be viewed). It's pricey, but many of the weavings are real works of art; custom-made pieces available on request.

Mixay Boutique, Nokeo Khoummane, T021-214534, contact@mixay.com. Exquisite Lao silk in rich colours, clothing as well as fantastic photographs and artefacts.

True Colour, Setthathirat, T021-214410. Ready-made clothes from the Hoay Women's Centre. Also outstanding tailoring, though they will need a couple of weeks to finish.

Tailors There are many Vietnamese tailors along Samsenthai and Pang Kham roads (north of Nam Phou fountain). **Queen's Beauty Tailor**, by the fountain, is quite good for women's clothes, but allow at least a week. Also try **Adam Tailleurs**, 72 Pang Kham Rd, and **TV Chuong**, 395 Samsenthai Rd. There are also a few tailors in the **Morning Market**.

Department stores

Satri Laos, Setthathirat, T021-244387. If Vientiane had a Harrods this would be it. Upmarket boutique retailing everything from jewellery, shoes, clothes, furnishings and homewares. Beautiful stuff, although most of it is from China, Vietnam and Thailand.

Food

Phimphone Market, Setthathirat Rd, opposite Khop Chai Deu Restaurant. This supermarket has everything a foreigner could ask for in terms of imported food, drink, magazines, translated books, personal hygiene products, household items and much more (and the price to go with it).

Simuang Minimarket, Samsenthai Rd, opposite Wat Simuang. Supermarket with a very good selection of produce, including a great array of Western products. Great place to pick up wine but double-check it's not past its use-by date.

Udom Pathana, Dong Palane Rd,

T021-214256. Has a reasonable range of cheap food imports.

Vinotheque La Cave, 354 Samsenthai Rd, with the big wine barrel out front, T021-217700. French wine shop with a large range of wine, run by Claude Monnier, who serves aperitifs with cheese.

Galleries

T'Shop Lai Gallery, Wat Inpeng Soi. Funky studio exhibiting local sculptures and art. Artists can be seen at work Mon-Sat. Media include coconut shells, wood and metal. Proceeds from sales are donated to Lao Youth projects. Upstairs there is an exhibition on Asian elephants.

Hair and beauty

There are several hairdressers dotted around the city. Men should be careful not to wind up with a bowl cut.

Barber Jam, just off Khou Vieng Rd. Cute Lao barbershop (and youth centre) where you can get a haircut for under US$1 while someone plays the guitar to you. Don't ask for anything too complex. Also have a 'ear coning' service.

Elly Boutique, Setthathirat Rd near the Kodak shop, T021-243675. Women's and men's fashion cuts, dyeing, facials and waxing, plus reportedly the best manicure and pedicure in Vientiane.

New Wave Hair Studio, 73/4 Pang Kham Rd, T021-216542. Soukanh Chantarath, the proprietor, trained at *Vidal Sassoon* and *Toni and Guy* in London. Great place to get a reasonably cheap hairdo from an internationally acclaimed hairdresser. Cutting, colouring, straightening, manicures, pedicures, waxing and eyelash tinting.

Handicrafts and antiques

The main shops are along Setthathirat, Samsenthai and Pang Kham. The **Talaat Sao** (Morning Market) is also worth a browse, with artefacts, such as appliquéd panels, decorated hats and sashes, basketwork both old and new, small and large wooden tobacco boxes, sticky-rice lidded baskets, axe pillows, embroidered cushions and a wide range of silver work. The likelihood of finding authentic antiques is pretty low. **Talaat Kudin** offers cheaper artefacts and silks but not as great a selection as Talaat Sao. Across the road from

Talaat Sao is a small ethnic handicraft market, which offers a range of cane baskets, trinkets, weaving and silk.

Camacraft , Nokeo Khoummane, T020-561660. NGO which retails handicrafts produced by the Hmong people. Beautiful embroidery, mulberry tea, Lao silk.

Ekhor Boutique, Pang Kham Rd. Textiles, clothes and handicrafts.

Indochine Handicrafts, Samsenthai Rd next to the big wine barrel, T021-263619, maiphone@hotmail.com. Larger size collectibles, not really suitable for the suitcase shopper.

MaiChan Fine Arts & Handicrafts, Samsenthai Rd, T021-263619, maiphone@ hotmail.com. Neat little shop with lots of treasures.

Mixay Boutique, Setthathirat Rd, Ban Mixay. Wooden and textile products.

Namsin Handicrafts, Setthathirat Rd. Wooden objects.

Jewellery and silverware

Many of the stones sold in Vientiane are of dubious quality, but silver and gold are more reliable. Gold is always 24 carat and is good value. Silver is cheap but not necessarily pure silver; nevertheless, the selection is interesting, with amusing animals, decorated boxes, old coins, earrings and silver belts. There's a particularly wide selection in the Morning Market (**Talaat Sao**). Silver, gold and gem shops on Samsenthai are concentrated along the stretch opposite the Asian Pavilion Hotel; there are also some gold shops further west towards the Chinese quarter.

Doris Jewelry, 2 shops in Lao Plaza Shopping Centre. Silverware, gems and antiques.

Tamarind, T020-5517031, Manthathurath. Great innovative jewellery designs, nice pieces. Also stocks a range of beautiful clothes made in stunning silk and organza.

Markets

Vientiane has several excellent markets.

Talaat Sao (**Morning Market**), off Lane Xang Av, is busiest in the mornings (from around 1000), but operates all day. There are money exchanges here (quite a good rate), and a good selection of food stalls selling Western food, soft drinks and ice cream sundaes. It sells imported Thai goods, electrical appliances, watches, DVDs and CDs, stationery, cosmetics, a selection of handicrafts (see above), an enormous choice of Lao fabrics, and upstairs there is a large clothing section, silverware, some gems and gold and a few handicraft stalls. There is also the newer addition to the Morning Market – a modern shopping centre-style market. This is not so popular as it is much pricier and stocked with mostly Thai products sold in baht. On the second floor there is a reasonable food court.

Talaat Khua-Din, on the other side of the bus stop, is a ramshackle market with an interesting produce section. It offers many of the same handicrafts and silks as the Morning Market but is a lot cheaper.

Talaat Thong Khoun Khum, on the corner of Khoun Khum and Dong Miang roads, is the largest produce market. It is sometimes known as the **Evening Market** but it's busiest in the mornings.

Other markets include **Talaat That Luang**, south of the parade ground, **Talaat Dong Palane**, Dong Palane Rd (there's a sign near the temple pointing down a lane as the bulk of the market has been moved just away from the main road), and **Talaat Chin**, which is good for electrical goods, CDs and DVDs, kids' toys, kitsch decorations, clothes, furniture and cheap imported tat.

Music and film

Cheap DVDs and VCDs can be bought from the **Morning Market**. **Walkman Village**, Fa Ngum Rd, T021-213609, also stocks a selection of good-quality DVDs and CDs, along with goods geared towards foreigners, from handbags to binoculars.

Photo processing

Konica Plaza, 110/5 Samsenthai Rd, is the best film developer in Vientiane and also offers cheap CD-burning and photocopying services. Next door are **Kodak Express** and **Venus Colorlab** (also on Heng Boun Rd). Many more are dotted around the town and in the **Morning Market**.

▲▲ Activities and tours

Vientiane p50, maps p54 and p58
Aerobics
Open-air aerobics sessions are held at the

amphitheatre on the riverfront (Fa Ngum) every evening 1700-1730. Locals love it when foreigners join in. Less public aerobics at **Sengdara Gym** (see below).

Cooking

Thongbay Guesthouse (see Sleeping), T021-242292. Cooking classes, covering all aspects of meal preparation, from purchasing the ingredients to eating the meal. Must be arranged in advance.

Cruises

Along Fa Ngum Rd, past the **Intercity Hotel**, there are a couple of floating restaurants docked. At 1900 the restaurants cruise down the Mekong for sunset. The cruise is complimentary when you eat there. You wouldn't even be able to go out in a small boat for the price of the meals, so the cruises are exceptionally good value. See Floating restaurants, page 68.

Cycling

Bicycles are available for hire from several places in town, see Transport, page 76. A good outing is to cycle downstream along the banks of the Mekong. Cycle south on Tha Deua Rd until Km 5 (watch the traffic) and then turn right down one of the tracks (there are a number) towards the riverbank. A path, suitable for bicycles, follows the river beginning at about Km 4.5. There are monasteries and drink sellers en route to maintain interest and energy.

Football

Football is very popular in Laos, with regular national league matches being played at the **National Stadium** in Vientiane. In fact, this is probably one of the few places in the world where you can see World Cup qualifying matches for under US$1.

Go-karting

ITECC Go Karts, in the car park underneath ITECC. Daily 1200-2200. Only 4 karts but they are very good quality on a smooth track. Helmets and racing gloves provided. You can try to solve logic puzzles to win extra laps – not as easy as it sounds. 45,000 kip for 5 mins, 70,000 kip for 10 mins or pay by the lap.

Golf

Santisuk Lane Xang Golf Club, Km 14, Tha Deua Rd, T021-812022. Daily 0700-1800. 9-hole course, open to the public, with modest green fees and caddies available. To get there, catch Bus No 14 from the Morning Market (40,000 kip).

Vientiane Golf Club, Km 6, Route 13 South, T021-515820. Daily 0630-sunset. Short 9-hole course that's a favourite for its friendly atmosphere and swimming pool. Cheap green fees include the caddy; clubs available for rent. It's customary to tip your caddy about US$1 per 9 holes. To get there, turn right at the Peugeot showroom (6 km south of town), left after bridge, right at the fork and right at the top of the hill.

Kickboxing

Held intermittently at the **Soxai Boxing Stadium** and usually on the last Fri of every month at 1700, about 200 m past the old circus in Baan Dong Paleb, 20,000 kip.

Language courses

Vientiane College, That Luang Rd, T021-414873. The best Lao courses. Ask for Seng.

Massage, saunas and spas

The best massage in town is given by the blind masseuses in a little street off Samsenthai Rd, 2 blocks down from Simuang Minimart (across from Wat Simuang). There are 2 blind masseuse businesses side-by-side and either one is fantastic: **Traditional Clinic**, T020-5659177 and **Porm Clinic**, T020-627633 (no English spoken). They are marked by blue signs off both Khou Vieng and Samsenthai roads. Recommended.

Mandarina, Pang Kham just off Nam Phou, T021-218703. A range of upmarket treatments between US$5-30. Massage, facials, body scrubs, mini-saunas, oils, jacuzzi.

Mixay Massage, Fa Ngum. Daily 1700-2100. Lao massage (US$5 per hr), facials, manicure, pedicure and sauna.

Oasis Massage and Beauty, 7 Mixay Rd, T021-243579. Very good, strong massages (*keng* – means strong in Lao).

Papaya Spa, opposite Wat Xieng Veh, T021-216550. Daily 0900-2000. A favourite among locals looking to spoil themselves. Surrounded by beautiful gardens, you feel more relaxed the minute you walk through the gates. Massage, sauna, facials. Lovely surroundings. Recommended. They also have a new branch that is more accessible on Lane Xang Av just up from the Morning Market.

Wat Sok Paluang, Sok Paluang. Peaceful leafy setting in the compound of Wat Sok Paluang. Herbal sauna, followed by herb tea (2000 kip) and massage by 2 young male masseurs (4000 kip); very relaxing but women should watch out for groping. Vipassana meditation is held every Sat 1600-1730, free, T021-216214. To get there, walk through the small stupas to the left of the Wat; the sauna is a rickety building on stilts on the right-hand side, recognizable by the blackened store underneath.

Shooting
There is a shooting range in the Southern corner of the national stadium US$1-2 for a few rounds.

Sports clubs and fitness centres
Several hotels in town permit non-residents to use their fitness facilities for a small fee, including the **Tai Pan** (rather basic), **Lao Plaza**, **Lane Xang**, **Don Chan** and **Novotel** (for all, see Sleeping).

Australia Club Recreation Centre, Km 3, Tha Deua Rd, T021-314921. A beautiful setting, with one of the nicest pools in Vientiane. It's a lovely place for a swim followed by a glass of wine as the sun sets. Also a small restaurant and a squash court. Short-term membership for US$10 per day or US$20 for a family. It is cheaper if you get a member to sign you in; loiter around some of the expat drinking holes and you might find someone willing. A tuk-tuk from the centre costs 20,000-30,000 kip.

Sengdara, 5/77 Phonthan Rd, T021-414061, sengdara_fitness@yahoo.com. Daily 0500-2200. Modern, well-equipped fitness centre with gym, pool and sauna. US$5 for use of all the facilities for a day, massage extra.

Swimming
The **Australia Club Recreation Centre** (see Sports clubs, above) has a fantastic saltwater pool with superb Mekong views. At the time of publication a major **water park** was being constructed in the park on Kuvieng Rd, just behind Talaat Kudin. Several hotels in

town permit non-residents to use their fitness facilities for a small fee.

Lane Xang Hotel (see Sleeping). Visiting the pool is a massive nostalgia trip. Swimmers are required to wear caps and the pool features a very old springboard. US$3.

Lao Plaza Hotel (see Sleeping). A very clean pool on the 3rd floor, with a great view of the city, open to non-guests for US$5.

Settha Palace Hotel, 6 Pang Kham Rd (see Sleeping). Lovely pool in landscaped gardens. The most luxurious (with a hefty entrance fee to boot).

Sokpaluang Swimming Pool, Sok Paluang Rd, south of centre. Daily 0800-2000. Good-sized pool for serious swimmers, paddling pool for children, costumes for hire, restaurant and bar. 9000 kip for the day.

Tai-Pan Hotel (see Sleeping). Open to non-guests. Rather basic.

Tennis
Vientiane Parkview, Luang Prabang Rd, T021-250888. Expensive at US$5 per hr but easily the best court in town. Book in advance.

Vientiane Tennis Club, National Stadium. 3000 kip per hr, equipment for hire. Floodlit courts stay open until 2100. Bar.

Ten-pin bowling
Bowling is very popular, particularly as the bars in the bowling centres are often the only ones open after curfew. The **Lao Bowling Centre**, behind the Lao Plaza Hotel, T021-218661, is good value at US$1 per person, shoe hire is included but bring your own socks. An alternative is on the way out to the airport (Luang Prabang Rd) where you'll find **Marina Bowling** which is aimed at a younger clientele, with retro lighting and fluorescent balls and pins. Not a great selection of larger shoe sizes for hire, though, so if your feet are over a size 9 you'll be bowling barefoot.

Tour operators
For general travel information or specific recommendations or to organize any kind of ecotour, visit the **National Tourism Authority** (see page 52). Most agents will use 'eco' somewhere in their title but this doesn't necessarily mean anything.

Asian Trails, Unit 10 Baan Khounta Thong, Sikotthanbong District, T021-263936, www.asiantrails.com. Southeast Asia specialists.

Diethelm Travel, Nam Phou Circle, Setthathirat Rd, T021-213833, www.diethelm-travel.com.

Exotissimo, 6/44 Pang Kham Rd, T021-241861, www.exotissimo.com. Various tours and travel services. Excellent but pricey.

Green Discovery Laos, Setthathirat Rd, next to Kop Chai Deu, T021-251564, www.green discoverylaos.com. Specializes in ecotours and adventure travel. Recommended.

Yoga

Vientiane Yoga Studio, Sokpaluang Rd, Soi 1 (first *soi* on the right after you turn onto Sokpaluang from Kuvieng Rd). Hatha yoga classes, 1½ hrs' duration, open level from beginner to experienced, Tue-Thu 1700-1830, Fri-Sun 1000-1130, 50,000 kip.

● Transport

Vientiane *p50, maps p54 and p58*
See also Ins and outs, page 50.

Air

Prices and schedules are constantly changing, so always check in advance. **Lao Airlines** to **Bangkok** (80 mins) 3 flights daily; to **Luang Prabang** (40 mins) up to 3 flights daily; to **Pakse** (50 mins) daily. To **Oudomxay** and **Houei Xai** 4 flights a week; to **Siem Reap** 5 times a week, 3 times a week via Pakse; **Phnom Penh** (1½ hrs) twice a week via Pakse; **Kunming** 3 times a week (2½ hrs); **Chiang Mai** daily. **Hanoi** daily. **Lao Air** operates flights to **Xam Neua** twice a week (50 mins) and **Phongsaly** twice a week (60 mins). **Thai Airways** to **Bangkok** (70 mins) daily. **Vietnam Airlines**, to **Hanoi** (60 mins) daily; to **Ho Chi Minh City** (3 hrs) daily and **Phnom Penh** daily.

Airline offices **Lao Airlines**, 2 Pang Kham Rd (near Fa Ngum), T021-212054, www.laoairlines.com, also at Wattay Airport; T021-212051. **Lao Air**, Wattay Airport, T/F021-512027, laoair@laopdr.com. **Thai Airways**, Head Office, Luang Prabang Rd, not far past the Novotel, T021-222527/9, www.thaiairways.com, Mon-Fri 0830-1200, 1300-1500, Sat 0830-1200; also on Pang Kham Rd, next to the bookshop and at Wattay Airport, 1st floor, Room 106,

T021-512024, daily 0700-1200 and 1300-1600. **Vietnam Airlines**, Lao Plaza Hotel, T021-217562, www.vietnam airlines.com.vn, Mon-Fri 0800-1200, 1330-1630, Sat 0800-1200.

Bicycle and motorbike

For those energetic enough in the hot season, **bikes** are the best way to get around town. Many hotels and guesthouses have bikes available for their guests, including **Lani I, Syri, Day Inn, Lao Paris** and **Douang Deuane** (see Sleeping). Expect to pay about 10,000 kip per day. There are also many bike hire shops around town, sometimes attached to restaurants, sometimes to shops specializing in other things. Markets, post offices and government offices usually have 'bike parks' where it is advisable to leave your bike. A small minding fee is charged.

Motorbikes are available for hire from many guesthouses and shops within the city centre. Expect to pay around US$5-10 per day and leave your passport as security. Trail bikes can be hired for around US$20 per day, although the price goes down to around US$15 per day if you hire the bike for a longer period. Insurance is seldom available anywhere in Laos on motorbikes but most places will also hire out helmets, a necessity. Check your insurance policy before you venture out, as most have a clause saying they won't cover motorbike accidents. **KT bikes**, Manthathurath St, T020-5816816, offer the best range of well-serviced Suzukis (US$7 per day) and dirtbikes (US$20 per day); discounts for longer hire. **PVO**, off Fa Ngum, also has a reliable selection of bicycles and motorbikes. Often a driving licence can be used in lieu of a motorbike licence if the police pull you over.

Boat

See also Floating restaurants, page 68. Improved roads means the old boat transport system has disappeared. The only real pier offering transport out of Vientiane is at **Tha Hua Kao Liaw**, 8 km west of the Novotel in Ban Kao Liaw. Departures are intermittent and unreliable so you may need to charter your boat if you're determined to travel by river; this will need to be organized at least a day in advance. Every now and then speed boats make the trip to **Pak Lai**

✱ Border essentials: Friendship Bridge

The bridge is 20 km southeast of Vientiane; catch the Thai–Lao International bus from the Talaat Sao terminal (15,000 kip) 90 minutes every two hours 0730 to 1530 and stop at Nong Khai bus station or hire a tuk-tuk US$5-7 (see page 78) to the border and arrange transport across. The border is open daily 0600-2200. Shuttle minibuses take punters across the bridge every 20 minutes for 5000 kip, stopping at the Thai and Lao immigration posts where an overtime fee is charged after 1630 and at weekends.

There are good facilities at the Lao border, including a telephone box, a couple of duty free shops (with quite possibly the cheapest vodka in the world), some drinks and snack stalls and a post office. Allow up to 1½ hours to get to the bridge and through formalities on the Lao side. The paperwork is pretty swift, unless you are arriving in Lao and require a visa or are leaving the country and have overstayed your visa. Thirty-day visas are processed in about 15 minutes and cost US$30-42 depending on your nationality. You will require a passport-sized photograph and the name of a guesthouse or hotel you are staying at. You will need to bargain hard, but in a friendly way, for a good price on

private transport from the border. Coming into Lao the taxis can be a bit sharkish and charge up to US$15 into the centre of Vientiane; it should be no more than US$7-10.

The Thai side is über-efficient but not nearly as friendly. Tuk-tuks wait to take punters to Nong Khai (10 minutes), ฿50 per person; Udon Thani is another hour further on; taxis from the Thai side of the border charge about ฿700 to get you there; add another ฿300 if you organize the Thai taxi from the Lao side. If you get stuck in Nong Khai, **Mut Mee Guesthouse** is recommended. From Udon Thani you can get to Bangkok easily by budget airline. Discount airlines (**Air Asia, Nok Air**) fly several times daily. From Udon Thani, you can catch a minibus or taxi to the Lao border or a bus directly to the border for ฿200. Taking the Udon/Friendship Bridge option between Bangkok and Vientiane will probably only add one hour to your journey, since immigration at Wattay Airport tends to be slow. Another option is to catch the overnight train from Nong Khai to Bangkok's Hualamphong Station (11 hours, ฿800 for a sleeper). Buses also run from both Udon Thani and Nong Khai to Bangkok.

(115 km, US$20). If you have 5 or 6 people you can charter speed boats to **Luang Prabang** (8 hrs) for US$45 per person but it isn't the most comfortable journey.

Bus

There is no real city bus service but buses, trucks and pickups to destinations around Vientiane all leave from the station next to the **Talaat Sao bus station**, next to the Morning Market (see below). Many private tour operators also run buses to popular locations like Vang Vieng and will pick up/drop off around Nam Phou or pick

up passengers from their guesthouse.

Vientiane has 3 main public bus terminals: **Southern, Northern** and **Talaat Sao** (Morning Market).

VIP buses are very comfortable night buses, usually allowing a good sleep during the trip – but watch out that they don't swap the normal VIP bus for a karaoke one! They provide snacks and have waitresses. Make sure you book a double if you don't want to be stuck with a strange bed partner. Robberies have been reported on the night buses so keep your valuables secure.

Southern bus station Route 13, 9 km south of the city centre. Public buses depart daily for destinations in southern Laos. At the time of writing bus prices were expected to increase by about 10,000 kip per trip. The southern bus station has a range of stores, pharmacy and massage. To **Paksan**, 3 daily in the early morning, 143 km, 1 hr 30 mins, 20,000 kip, continuing to **Lak Sao** (for the Vietnamese border), 334 km, 8 hrs, 50,000 kip. To **Thakhek**, 4 daily, 332 km, 6 hrs, 40,000 kip. To **Savannakhet**, 7 daily (early morning), 457 km, 8 hrs, 55,000 kip. To **Pakse**, 9 daily, 659 km, 15 hrs, 85,000 kip; there are also overnight express buses to Pakse, 11 hrs, 110,000 kip. **Thongli**, T021-242657, operate an overnight VIP service daily at 2030, which takes about the same time but has beds, water, snacks, etc, 130,000 kip. **KVT**, T021-213043, also run VIP buses to Pakse at 2030.

Banag Saigon, T021-720175, run buses to **Hanoi**, 1900, US$20, **Vinh**, 1900, US$16, **Thanh Hoa**, 1900, US$16, **Hué**, 1930, US$20, and **Danang**, 1930, US$20. These services run on odd days so check in advance.

Northern bus station Route 2, towards the airport 3.5 km from the centre of town, T021-260255. Northbound buses are regular and have a/c. For the more popular routes, there are also VIP buses which will usually offer snacks and service. To **Luang Prabang** (384 km), standard buses, 5 daily, 11 hrs, 90,000 kip; a/c buses, 3 daily, 10-11 hrs, 100,000 kip; VIP buses daily at 0800, 9 hrs, 120,000 kip. To **Udomxai** (578 km), standard buses twice daily, 14-15 hrs, 110,000 kip; a/c buses at 1630 daily, 120,000 kip. To **Luang Namtha**, 0830 daily, 676 km, 19 hrs, 140,000 kip. To **Phongsali**, 0715 daily, 811 km, 26 hrs, 150,000 kip. To **Houei Xai**, Mon, Wed and Fri 1730, 869 km, 25-30 hrs, 200,000 kip. To **Sayaboury** (485 km), standard at 1750 daily, 12-15 hrs, 90,000 kip; a/c at 0700 daily, 100,000 kip. To **Xam Neua**, 3 daily, 612 km, 14-23 hrs (depending on whether it goes via Phonsavanh), 150,000 kip. To **Phonsavanh** (374 km), standard at 4 daily, 10 hrs, 90,000 kip; a/c at 0730 daily, 110,000 kip; VIP bus at 0800 daily, 130,000 kip. A bus departs every Thu and Sun for the Chinese border at **Boten**.

Talaat Sao bus station Across the road from Talaat Sao, in front of Talaat Kudin, on the eastern edge of the city centre.

Destinations, distances and fares are listed on a board in English and Lao. Most departures are in the morning and can leave as early as 0400, so many travellers on a tight schedule have regretted not checking departure times the night before. There is a useful map at the station, and bus times and fares are listed clearly in Lao and English. However, it's more than likely you will need a bit of direction at this bus station: staff at the ticket office only speak a little English so a better option is to chat to the friendly chaps in the planning office, who love a visit, T021-216506. The times listed below vary depending on the weather and the number of stops en route.

To the **Southern Bus Station**, 0600-1800 every 30 mins, 2000 kip. To the **Northern Bus Station**, catch the Nongping bus (8 daily) and ask to get off at 'Thay Song' (1500 kip). To **Wattay Airport**, every 30 mins 0640-1800, 3000 kip. To **Vang Vieng**, 5 daily, 15,000 kip, 3½ hrs.

There are numerous buses criss-crossing the province; most aren't very useful for tourists. To **Barksarp** (via Som Sa Mai for the boat to **Ban Pako**), 6 daily, 5000 kip. To **Ban Keun** (via Ban Thabok for **Phou Khao Khouay**), 9 daily, 7000 kip. To **Xieng Khuan**, bus No 14 every 10-20 mins 0530-2030, 1 hr, 3000 kip. To **Nam Ngum**, direct bus 0700 daily, 3 hrs, or catch a bus to **Ban Talaat**, every hr 0630-1630, 2½ hrs, 8000 kip, and then get a *songthaew* to the lake. To **Kasi** (via **Vang Vieng**, 20,000 kip but, unless you're dead broke, there are much better ways of getting to Vang Vieng), twice daily. To the **Friendship Bridge** (Lao side), every 30 mins 0650-1710, 5000 kip. To **Nong Khai** (Thai side of the Friendship Bridge), 4 daily, about 1 hr including immigration, 10,000 kip.

Other private bus services To Vang Vieng, **Green Discovery**, from their office on Setthathirat, daily at 0100 and 1400, 45,000 kip; also **Sabaidee Bus** for the same price and at the same time. Both services will pick you up from your guesthouse if you arrange in advance. **Sabaidee Bus** to **Luang Prabang**, Tue and Thu, 130,000 kip, with a stopover in Vang Vieng on the way.

Car
It is not essential to hire a driver but note that in the event of an accident a foreigner is likely to shoulder the responsibility and any costs.

Car hire rates vary according to state and model of vehicle and also whether out-of-town trips are planned. Expect to pay about US$50-90 per day. Many hotels and guesthouses will have cars for hire.
Asia Vehicle Rental, 354-356 Samsenthai Rd, T021-217493, www.avr.laopdr.com, Mon-Fri 0800-1900, Sat 0800-1200. Vientiane city US$55 per day with driver up to 130 km, US$15 per additional 100 km. Outside of Vientiane rates are about US$80 per day plus petrol. Discounts for longer periods of hire. Very competitive prices and a good range of vehicles.

Taxi
These are mostly found at the Morning Market (Talaat Sao) or around the main hotels. Newer vehicles have meters but there are still some ageing jalopies. Flag fall is 8000 kip. A taxi from the Morning Market to the **airport**, US$5; to **Tha Deua** (for the Friendship Bridge and Thailand), US$10, although you can usually get the trip much cheaper but the taxis are so decrepit that you may as well take a tuk-tuk, US$6 (see below). To hire a taxi for trips outside the city costs around US$20 per day. To **Nam Ngum**, US$40.
Lavi Taxi, T021-350000 is the only reliable call-up service in town but after 2000 in the evening it is a lottery whether someone will answer the telephone.

Tuk-tuks
Tuk-tuks usually congregate around tourist destinations: **Nam Phou**, **Talaat Sao** and **Talaat Kudin**. Tuk-tuks can be chartered for longer out-of-town trips (maximum 25 km, US$10-15) or for short journeys of 2-3 km within the city (10,000 kip per person). There are also shared tuk-tuks, which run on regular routes along the city's main streets. Tuk-tuks are available around the fountain area until 2330 but are quite difficult to hire after dark in other areas of town. The tuk-tuks that congregate on the city corners are generally part of a quasi cartel, it is thus much cheaper to travel on one that is passing through. To stop a vehicle, simply flag it down. A reliable driver is **Mr Souk**, T020-7712220, who speaks good English and goes beyond the call of duty. **Saamlors** are as rare as hen's teeth in Vientiane.

⊙ Directory

Vientiane *p50, maps p54 and p58*
Banks
See Money, page 39, for details on changing money in Laos. At the time of writing there were only a handful of multicard Visa and MasterCard ATMs in the city. The **Banque Pour le Commerce Exterieur (BCEL)**, corner of Fa Ngum and Pang Kham roads, takes all the usual credit cards (maximum withdrawal 700,000 kip; much less on Sun). Other multicard ATMs can be found in front of the Novotel, the Lao Plaza Hotel and beside the petrol station near Wat Simuang. Other **BCEL** ATMs such as those on Setthathirat and near the Morning Market only take MasterCard. More ATMs are planned in the next few years. **BCEL**, 1 Pang Kham Rd, traditionally offers the lowest commission (1.5%) on changing US$ TCs into US$ cash; there is no commission on changing US$ into kip; also has an international ATM. **Joint Development Bank**, 33 Lane Xang Av (opposite market), T021-213535, offers good rastes on cash advances. ATM.
A number of Thai banks have set up in Vientiane; many are situated along Lane Xang Av. They all offer efficient and competitive exchange facilities: **Thai Military Bank**, 69 Khoun Boulom Rd; **Bangkok Bank**, 28/13-15 Hat Sady Rd, cash advance available on MasterCard for 3% commission.

Embassies and consulates
Australia, Km3 Tha Deua Rd (from Apr 2008), T021- 413602. **Britain**, no embassy; served by the Australian Embassy. **Cambodia**, Tha Deua Rd, Km 3, T021-314952, F021-312584, visas daily 0730-1030. Cambodian visas US$20. **Canada**, no embassy; served by the Australian Embassy. **China**, Thanon Wat Nak Nyai T021-315105. Visas take 4-days. **France**, Setthathirat Rd, T021-215258. **Germany**, 26 Sok Paluang Rd, T021-312110/1. **Japan**, Sisavangvong Rd, T021-414400. **Malaysia**, That Luang Rd, T021-414205. **Myanmar (Burma)**, Sok Paluang Rd, T021-314910-1, daily 0800-1200, 1300-1630. **Sweden**, Sok Paluang Rd, T021-315003. **Thailand**, Phon Kheng Rd, T021-900238 (consular section on That Luang arranges visa extensions), Mon-Fri 0830-1200. If crossing by land, 30-day visas are also issued at the Friendship

Bridge, see page 77. **USA**, That Dam Rd (off Samsenthai Rd), T021-267000. **Vietnam**, That Luang Rd, T021- 413400, visas 0800-1045, 1415-1615. One-month visa costs US$50 and you must wait 3 days. An extra US$5 for the visa in 1 day.

Emergencies

Ambulance, T195 but note that you are taking a significant risk by placing your life in their hands; in cases of medical emergency see Dr Ben at the **Australian Clinic** (see Medical services, below). **Police Tourist Office**, Lang Xang Av (in the same office as the National Tourism Authority of Laos), T021-251128.

Immigration

Immigration office, Phai Nam Rd (near Morning Market), Mon-Fri 0730-1200, 1400-1700. Visa extensions can be organized for US$2 per day. For visa information, see page 44.

Internet

Internet cafés have opened up all over the city, many on Setthathirat and Samsenthai roads. Most offer drinks and newspapers and are generally open daily 0800-2200/2300. Shop around for the best rates; you shouldn't have to pay more than 100 kip per min. Internet phones are now very popular, with most cafés providing this service for under US$1 per min. Also most major internet cafés are fitted with Skype and headphones. **Apollo Internet**, Setthathirat Rd, Mon-Fri 0830-2300, Sat and Sun 0900-2300, is a good bet.

Laundry

Laundrettes can be found all over Samsenthai Rd and the streets around Nam Phou. Try **Delight House of Fruit Shakes** (see Cafés, cakeshops and juice bars, above).

Media

Two English newspapers are available in Vientiane. Most articles pertinent to foreigners appear in the English-language *Vientiane Times*, 3000 kip, which runs items of Lao news, plus some quite interesting out-on-the-street interviews and quirky snippets that have been translated from the local newspapers. Up-to-date listings and events are at the back of the paper. There is also the French-language *Le Renovateur*, 3000 kip, which takes a more serious approach and includes lots of news on events in France.

Medical services

There are 2 pretty good **pharmacies** close to the Talaat Sao Bus Station. **Australian Clinic**, Australian Embassy, Nehru Rd, T021-413603 (or T021-511462 after hours), Mon-Fri 0800-1200, 1400-1700, for Commonwealth patients only (except in emergencies), US$60 to see the doctor. **Mahasot Hospital**, Fa Gnum, T021-214021, suitable for minor ailments only. For anything major it is advisable to cross the border to Nong Khai and visit **AEK Udon International Hospital**, T0066-42342555. For other hospitals in Thailand, see page 38. In cases of emergency where a medical evacuation is required, contact **Lao West coast Helicopters**, Hangar 703, Wattay International Airport, T021-512023. A charter to Udon Thani costs US$1500-US$2000, subject to availability and government approval.

Post

Post Office, Khou Vieng Rd/Lane Xang Av (opposite market), T021-216425, offers poste restante, local and international telephone calls and fax services (see page 41 for more detailed information). Also a good packing service and a philately counter. To send packages, use **DHL**, Nong No Rd, near the airport, T021-214868, or **TNT Express**, in the Thai Airways Building, Luang Prabang Rd, T021-261918.

Telephone

Area code: 021 for landlines and 020 for mobile phones. Dial 170 for international operator. The international telephone office is on Setthathirat Rd, near Nam Phou Rd, 24 hrs daily; fax service daily 0730-2130.

Around Vientiane

There are plenty of short trips from Vientiane, ranging from the popular backpacker hotspot of Vang Vieng, through to the stunning Phou Khao Khuoay National Park. Vang Vieng has become very popular with action sports enthusiasts, with kayaking, caving and rock climbing all on offer. For years the Nam Ngum dam has been a popular weekend escape for Vientiane residents and is starting to gain appeal with the tourist set. ▸▸ *For Sleeping, Eating and other listings, see pages 89-94.*

South of the city

Bus No 14 from the Talaat Sao bus station follows Route 2 southeast towards Tha Deua, the Friendship Bridge, to Thailand and the Garden of the Buddhas. The observation area by the bridge makes a good picnic spot, or it would be possible to take lunch in Thailand for visitors with multi-entry visas. ▸▸ *For immigration formalities at the bridge, see Border essentials, page 77.*

Along Thanon Tha Deua (Route 2)

Although it isn't officially recognized as a tourist destination, the **Beer Lao factory** ① *Km 12, Thanon Tha Deua (Route 2), T021-812000,* is surprisingly interesting and worth the trip. People who visit are likely to be welcomed with open arms, given a mini tour and plied senseless with the award-winning ale. Beer Lao has inadvertently become something of a national symbol and the locals swell with pride if you share their

Around Vientiane

THAILAND

Sleeping 🛏
Nam Ngum Resort 1

20 km
20 miles

Bridging the Mekong

In April 1994, King Bhumibol of Thailand and the President of Laos, accompanied by prime ministers Chuan Leekpai of Thailand and Keating of Australia, opened the first bridge to span the lower reaches of the Mekong River, linking Nong Khai in northeast Thailand with Vientiane in Laos.

The bridge had taken a long time to materialize. It was first mooted in the 1950s but war in Indochina and hostility between Laos and Thailand scuppered plans until the late 1980s. Then, with the Cold War ending and growing rapprochement between the countries of Indochina and ASEAN,

the bridge, as they say, became an idea whose time had come.

The 1200-m-long Friendship Bridge, or Mittaphab, was financed with US$30 million of aid from Australia. It is a key link in a planned road network that will eventually stretch from Singapore to Beijing. For landlocked Laos, it offers an easier route to Thailand and through Thailand to the sea. For Thailand, it offers an entry into one of the least-developed countries in the world, rich in natural resources and potential, while, for Australia, it demonstrated the country's Asian credentials.

enthusiasm for a tipple of their amber liquid. Two kilometres further on is **555 Park (Saam Haa Yai)**. These extensive but rather uninspiring gardens encompass Chinese pavilions, a lake and a small zoo. In the 1980s, a white elephant was captured in southern Laos. Revered in this part of the world for its religious significance, it had to be painted to ensure it was not stolen on the way to the capital. It was originally kept in the Saam Haa gardens but has since been moved to the zoo, where it is paraded in front of the crowds during the That Luang festival. White elephants are not really white, but pink.

Xieng Khuan

ⓘ *Route 2 (25 km south of Vientiane); daily 0800-1700; admission 5000 kip, plus 5000 kip for cameras. Food vendors sell drinks and snacks. Getting there: 1 hr by bus No 14 from the Talaat Sao bus station, charter a tuk-tuk for approximately US$15, hire a private vehicle for up to US$15, or take a motorbike or cycle because the road follows the river and is reasonably level the whole way.*

Otherwise known as the **Garden of the Buddhas** or **Buddha Park**, Xieng Khuan is a few kilometres beyond **Tha Deua** on Route 2, close to the border with Thailand. It has been described as a Laotian Tiger Balm Gardens, with reinforced concrete Buddhist and Hindu sculptures of Vishnu, Buddha, Siva and various other assorted deities and near-deities. There's also a bulbous-style building with three levels containing smaller sculptures of the same gods.

The garden was built in the late 1950s by a priest-monk-guru-sage-artist called Luang Pu Bunleua Sulihat, who studied under a Hindu *rishi* in Vietnam and then combined the Buddhist and Hindu philosophies in his own very peculiar view of the world. He left Laos because his anti-Communist views were incompatible with the ideology of the Pathet Lao (or perhaps because he was just too weird) and settled across the Mekong near the Thai town of Nong Khai, where he proceeded to build an equally revolting and bizarre concrete theme park for religious schizophrenics, called Wat Khaek. With Luang Pu's forced departure from Laos, his religious garden came under state control and it is now a public park. Luang Pu died in 1996 at the age of 72 and remains very popular in Laos and northeastern Thailand.

East of the city 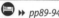 ›› *pp89-94.*

Kaysone Phomvihane Museum

ⓘ *Km 6, Route 13 south. Bus from the Morning Market or cycle.*

The Kaysone Phomvihane Museum commemorates the exploits and leadership of the Lao PDR equivalent of Vietnam's Ho Chi Minh. Kaysone was certainly the critical character in Laos' recent history: revolutionary fighter, inspired leader and statesman (see page 276). This dedicated museum is mostly visited by Lao schoolchildren.

Ban Pako → *Colour map 2, B2.*

Ban Pako lies 50 km northeast of Vientiane, on the banks of the Nam Ngum river (off Route 13). There is a quiet and secluded 'nature lodge' here, established by an Austrian couple a few years back. The owners have 50 ha of land, through which they have cut paths and planted trees. It's a lovely place to retreat to, for swimming, boating, trekking, rafting and walks to local Lao villages and, after all the physical exertion, you can unwind in the herbal sauna. To reach Ban Pako, take the Paksan bus from Vientiane's Morning Market and get off at Som Sa Mai (one hour). From Som Sa Mai, take a local boat to Lao Pako (another 25 minutes). Alternatively, the route makes a great trail bike ride; the last 20 km are on dirt and can get quite wild, especially during the wet season.

Tha Pabat Phonsanh

About 80 km down the Paksan road, is Pabat Phonsanh, built on a plug of volcanic rock in the middle of a coconut plantation. It is known for its footprint of the Buddha and has a statue of a reclining Buddha (*mudra*) rarely seen in Laos.

Phou Khao Khouay Protected Area 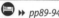 ›› *pp89-94.*

Phou Khao Khouay NPA (pronounced poo cow kway) is one of Laos' premier national protected areas. The area extends across 2000 sq km and incorporates an attractive sandstone mountain range. It is crossed by three large rivers, smaller tributaries and two stunning waterfalls at **Tad Leuk** and **Tad Sae**, which weave their way into the **Ang Nam Leuk reservoir**, a stunning man-made dam and lake that sits on the outskirts of the park. Within the protected area is a diverse array of wildlife, including wild elephants, gibbons, tigers, clouded leopards and Asiatic black bears.

Ins and outs

Getting there The park is a two-hour drive northeast from Vientiane, along Route 13 south; a good vehicle is recommended as the roads are terrible. To get to Ban Na you need to stop at Tha Pabat Phonsanh, 80 km northeast of Vientiane (see above); the village is a further 2 km from here. For Ban Hat Khai, 100 km northeast of Vientiane, continue on Route 13 to Ban Thabok, where a *songthaew* can usually take you the extra 7 km to the village. Buses to Paksan from the Talaat Sao bus station and That Luang market in Vientiane stop at Thabok.

Tourist information Although treks can be organized in Ban Na (T020-2208286) and Ban Hat Khai (T020-2240303), advance notice is required so it's advisable to go with a tour operator from Vientiane instead. Visit www.trekkingcentrallaos.com and contact the **National Tourism Authority** in Vientiane (T021-212248), or **Green Discovery Laos** (see page 76).

Tad Leuk

Accessed by dirt track (one hour) or boat from Ban Thabok (the waterfall sign is easily seen on the left), these are the most visited falls in the park and contain several large, undulating tiers. It is a good picnic spot, with swimming possible in the lake behind the waterfall although it is sometimes too rough. Tad Leuk has a visitor information centre which has toilets and washing facilities and also rents camping equipment. There's also a nice little snack stand on a platform, offering a view of the falls. Mr Khamsavay Kingmanolath, the supervisor at Tad Leuk, organizes cheap treks from Tad Leuk (about US$7-10 per group).

Tad Sae

These are the most stunning falls in the park but don't boast the facilities of Tad Leuk. The falls tumble down seven tiers, flowing for about 800 m before plummeting 40 m into a magnificent river gorge. There is a small, clear pool that's perfect for swimming. To get to the waterfall, take the road from Ban Thabok and turn right at the fork – it's signposted.

Ban Na

These days the principal draw-cards for Phou Khao Khouay are the organized treks and the elephant observation tower, both of which are based out of the small farming village of Ban Na (meaning rice field). The village's sugar cane plantations and river salt deposits attract a herd of wild elephants (around 30), which have, in the past, destroyed the villagers' homes and even killed a resident. This has limited the villagers' ability to undertake normal tasks, such as collecting bamboo, fearing that they may come across the wild elephants. To help compensate, the village, in conjunctions with some NGOs, has constructed an **elephant observation tower** 4 km from Ban Na and has started running trekking tours to see these massive creatures in their natural habitat. It possible to stay overnight at the elephant tower, to try and catch a glimpse of the giant pachyderms, who come to lap up salt from the nearby salt lick in the early evening hours. One- to three-day treks through the national park cross waterfalls, pass through pristine jungle and, with luck, offer the opportunity to hear or spot the odd wild elephant. It is too dangerous to get close to these creatures. This is an important ecotour that contributes to the livelihood of the Ban Na villagers and helps conserve of the elephant population. Advance notice is required so it's advisable to book with a tour operator in Vientiane (see page 75). If you are travelling independently you will need to organize permits, trekking and accommodation with the village directly. To do this, contact Mr Bounthanam (T020-2208286). Visit www.trekkingcentrallaos.com and contact the National Tourism Authority in Vientiane or **Green Discovery Laos** (see page 76). Visitors will need to bring drinking water and basic snacks. Do not try to feed the elephants, they are very dangerous.

Ban Hat Khai

This village is home to 90 families from the Lao Loum and Lao Soung ethnic groups and is another starting point for organized treks through amazing mountain landscapes, crossing the Nam Mang river and the Phay Xay cliffs. Most treks take in the Tad Sae falls. Homestay accommodation is available in the village.

North of the city ● » *pp89-94.*

Route 13 North

Tad Kaukhanna ① *10,000 kip per car plus 2000 kip per person*, is 11 km off the Phonhong road (Route 13), about 18 km north of Vientiane. It's a lesser known waterfall with a campsite and a restaurant. Tuk-tuks normally only head this way on public holidays, so a private car or taxi may be necessary to get here. A day trip in a *songthaew* should cost about US$15-20 return.

About 30 km from Vientiane, on the Luang Prabang road, is **Dane Soung**, an area where large fallen rocks have formed a cave. There are Buddhist sculptures inside and a footprint of the Buddha on the left of the entrance. This is a popular spot with locals at the weekend. Too steep for tuk-tuks, it tends to be only private cars and motorbikes that make it here. Turn left at the 22 km mark towards Ban Houa Khoua. Dane Soung is 6 km down the track and is only accessible in the dry season.

Vientiane Zoo
ⓘ *Route 10, near Ban Keun, 50 km north of Vientiane. Daily 0800-1630, 5000 kip.*
This zoo is really not much to get excited about: a small collection of animals and nothing of great zoological note. There's a café and picnic area. Take a public bus bound for Ban Keun and ask to be let off at the '*Suan Sat Wiang Chan*'.

Vangxang
Located 80 km north of Vientiane on Route 13, Vangxang, which means elephant drinking hole, is a lovely place to stop on the way to Vang Vieng. Worth a look are the amazing Buddha sculptures carved into a cliff face 2 km from the Vangxang Resort. The 10 Angkorian relief sculptures are believed to be over 500 years old, with two of them hovering at about 4 m. Aside from the Buddha carvings, walks through the jungle are the only diversion.

Nam Ngum dam and reservoir � ⊘ » *pp89-94.*

The Nam Ngum dam, 90 km from Vientiane, is the pride of Laos and figures prominently in picture postcards. It provides electricity for much of the country and its energy exports to Thailand are the country's second biggest foreign exchange earner. The lake is very picturesque and is dotted with hundreds of small islands.

Background
Many people believe that the dam was built with Soviet aid and assistance following the victory of the Communists in 1975. In fact construction began in the 1960s under the auspices of the Mekong Development Committee and was funded by the World Bank and Western nations. Indeed a large slice of the country's aid budget went into the construction of the dam, which was officially opened in the early 1970s. After the Communist victory, two of the lake's islands came in handy as open prisons for the most 'culturally polluted' of Vientiane's population. Two thousand drug addicts, prostitutes and other assorted hippies and 'low lifers' were rounded up and shipped out here. One island was allocated for men and the other for women. In addition to the islands, huge semi-submerged tree-trunks pose a navigational hazard, as no one had the foresight to log the area before it was flooded. The untapped underwater cache of timber has now been spotted by the Thais looking for alternative sources of timber; sub-aqua chainsaws are used to take out the 'treasure'.

❗ *No photographs are allowed at the dam wall or at the power plant.*

Exploring the lake
Access to the Nam Ngum reservoir is via Phonhong on Route 13: turn right at the strategically placed concrete post in the middle of the road, then head left to the village of **Ban Talaat** on the southwest shores of the reservoir. The market here is worth a browse (the word '*talaat*' means market), as minority groups from the surrounding area come here to sell their produce. From Ban Talaat, turn right across the narrow bridge to reach the dam, about 4 km up the road. An alternative route to the dam is via Route 10 out of Vientiane, which passes through much prettier countryside and traverses the Nam Ngum by ferry. Turn right at the end of the road for the dam. One bus leaves the

Morning Market in Vientiane daily for Nam Ngum, otherwise you will need to catch a bus to Ban Talaat and organize a *songthaew* from there. There are boats from the dam to **Ban Pao Mo** on the other side of the reservoir. The trip should take around two hours and cost about US$10 per hour but it is necessary to bargain hard with boatmen before crossing the lake. Boats can also be hired out; again, barter hard to get a good hourly rate. Vang Vieng is two hours' ride from the dam.

Vang Vieng and around ⊜⊘⊙⊕⊛⊜⊜ ▸▸ *pp89-94.*

The drive to Vang Vieng, on the much improved Route 13, follows the valley of the Nam Ngum north to Phonhong and then climbs steeply onto the plateau where Vang Vieng is located, 160 km north of Vientiane. The surrounding area is inhabited by the Hmong and Yao hill peoples and is particularly picturesque: craggy karst limestone scenery, riddled with caves, crystal-clear pools and waterfalls. In the early morning the views are reminiscent of a Chinese Sung Dynasty painting.

The town itself is nestled in a valley on the bank of the Nam Song river, amid a misty jungle. It enjoys cooler weather and offers breathtaking views of the imposing mountains of Pha Tang and Phatto Nokham. There are a number of 16th- and 17th-century **monasteries** in town of which the most notable are **Wat That** at the northern edge of the settlement and **Wat Kang**, 100 m or so to the south.

The town's laid-back feel has made it a popular haunt for the backpacker crowd, while the surrounding landscape has helped to establish Vang Vieng as Laos' premier outdoor activity destination, especially for rock climbing, caving, and kayaking. (It is also a convenient stop-off point on the gruelling journey to Luang Prabang.) Its popularity in many ways has also become its downfall: Vegas-like neon lights, pancake stands, and 'happy' this, 'happy' that now pollute this former oasis. Nevertheless, the town and surrounding area is still full of wonderful things to do and see.

Ins and outs

Getting there and around Vang Vieng is on Route 13 between Vientiane and Luang Prabang so a bus between Vientiane and anywhere up north (or vice versa) will pass Vang Vieng even if it is not on the itinerary. The journey to/from the capital takes about three to four hours and buses come and go from a inconspicuous spot on the side of the road along the old airstrip near the centre of town. You generally don't have to wait too long for a bus that's heading in your direction.

Safety Laos is a very safe country for tourists but a disproportionate number of accidents and crimes seem to happen in Vang Vieng. **Theft** is routinely reported, ranging from robberies by packs of kids targeting tubers on the river to the opportunist theft of items from guests' rooms. It is usually advisable to hand in any valuables to the management of your guesthouse or to padlock your bag and leave cash stashed in a very good hiding spot. Another major problem is the sale of illegal **drugs**. Police often go on sting operations and charge fines of up to US$600. There have even been unsubstantiated reports of the police planting drugs on tourists. Legal issues aside, numerous travellers have become seriously ill from indulging in the 'happy' supplements supplied by the restaurants. ▸▸ *For details of the significant safety risks involved in adventure activities, see Tour operators, page 92.*

Nam Song River

Vang Vieng has become synonymous with tubing down the Nam Song. Tubes can be picked up from the Old Market area where the tubing company has formed a cartel. Without stops the 3-km tubing from the **Organic Mulberry Farm** back to town can take one to two hours if done quickly, but most people do it in three to four hours, choosing

to stop along the way to drink, play volleyball or use the flying fox swings at the many
bars dotted along the river on the way into town. ▸▸ *See also Tubing, page 93.*

Many tour operators offer kayaking trips as well. Popular routes include kayaking down the Nam Song to incorporate the caves (especially Tham Nam – water cave), or the trip back to Vientiane via the drop-off point at Nam Lik. If you want to break the journey there are several nice guesthouses at Nam Lik. ▸▸ *See also Kayaking and rafting, page 92.*

Caves

Vang Vieng is best known for its limestone caves, sheltered in the mountains flanking the town. Pretty much every guesthouse and tour operator offers tours to the caves (the best of these is **Green Discovery**) and, although some caves can be accessed independently, it is advisable to take a guide to a few as they are dark and difficult to navigate. Often children from surrounding villages will take tourists through the caves for a small fee. Don't forget to bring a torch, or even better a head-lamp, which can be picked up cheaply at the market both in Vang Vieng and Vientiane. Each cave has an entrance fee of 3000-10,000 kip and many have stalls where you can buy drinks and snacks. You can buy hand-drawn maps from the town but all the caves are clearly signposted in English from the main road so these are not really necessary.
▸▸ *For further details, see Activities and tours, page 92.*

Of Vang Vieng's myriad caves, **Tham Chang** ① *access via the* Vang Vieng Resort *(see Sleeping), 2000 kip*, is the most renowned of all. Tham Chang penetrates right under a mountain and is fed by a natural spring perfect for an early-morning dip. From the spring it is possible to swim into the cave for quite a distance (bring a waterproof torch, if possible). The cave is said to have been used as a refuge during the 19th century from Chinese Haw bandits and this explains its name: *chang* meaning 'loyal' or 'steadfast'. Entrance is via Vang Vieng resort south of town. For your US$1 or 10,000 kip entrance fee you not only get into the caves but the lighting system will also be turned on. Although the cave is not the most magnificent, it serves as a superb lookout point.

Another popular cavern is **Tham Poukham** ① *7 km from Vang Vieng, 5000 kip.* The cave is often referred to as the cave of the Golden Crab and is highly auspicious. It's believed that if you catch a golden crab you will have a lifetime of fortune. To get there you need to cross the foot-bridge near the **Villa Nam Song**, and then follow the road for a further 6 km until you reach the village of Ban Nathong. From the village the cave is a short climb up quite a steep hill. Mossy rocks lead the way into the main cavern area where a large bronze reclining Buddha is housed. Here there is an idyllic lagoon with glassy green-blue waters, perfect for a dip.

Tham None ① *4 km north of Vang Vieng, 5000 kip*, is known locally known as the 'Sleeping Cave' because 2000 villagers took refuge there during the war. The large cave is dotted with stalagmites and stalactites, including the 'magic stone of Vang Vieng', which reflects light. There are also lots of bats residing in the grotto. This cave is very popular with tour groups and rock climbers.

Tham Xang ① *14 km north of Vang Vieng on the banks of the Nam Song, 2000 kip*, also known as the 'Elephant Cave', is named after the stalagmites and stalactites that have created an elephant formation (you may need to squint to see it). The cave also contains some Buddha images, including the footprint of Buddha. Although the cave itself is relatively nondescript the bell used by monks is made of a former bomb. From this cave there is a signposted path that leads to **Tham Nam** (water cave) ① *15 km from town, 5000 kip*, a long spindly cave that is believed to stretch for at least 7 km. It takes about two hours to explore the cavern and at the entrance there is a crystal-clear pool, perfect for a dip. This is one of Vang Vieng's most interesting caves and in the wet season needs to be explored with an inner tube or by wading, while pulling yourself along a rope. It's not an easy task and should not be attempted alone. At times the cavern is an extremely tight fit and commando-type crawling is required; a hard helmet with lamp attached is necessary. However, it is an incredible caving experience. To get to these two caves follow Route 13 north and turn left at Km 14, follow this dirt road for 1 km until you reach the river. Boats charge 10,000 kip to cross the river to see Tham Xang, from which you can walk to Tham Nam.

There are many more caves in the vicinity of town, most to the west and north. It is possible to hire a bicycle in Vang Vieng (around 10,000 kip per day), take it across the

Vang Vieng

To 11 15, New Market, New Bus Terminal & Luang Prabang

Wat That

Route 13

Lao Development

Wat Kang

BKC Bookshop
Riverside Tour
Green Discovery
Tubing Pickup

Nam Song

Disused Airstrip

Motorbike Rental

Agricultural Promotion

Motorbike Rental

To Tham Poukham (6 km)

Footbridge

Wat Si Souman

Wat Mixay Yaram

To Vientiane

12 & Tham Chang

N
100 metres
100 yards

Sleeping
Ban Sabai Bungalows **17**
Bountang **2**
Chanthala **3**
Dokkhoun **4**
Elephant Crossing **1**
Grandview **6**
Le Jardine Bungalows **18**
Malany Guesthouse **5**
Maylyn Guesthouse **7**
Organic Mulberry Farm **11**
Phou Bane **10**
Saysong Guesthouse **14**
Thausouk **21**
Thavonsouk Resort **16**

Thavisouk **19**
Vang Vieng Eco-Lodge **15**
Vang Vieng Orchid **20**
Vang Vieng Resort **12**
Vansana **22**
Villa Nam Song **8**

Eating
Luang Prabang Bakery **11**
Nangbot **3**
Nazim's **4**

Nisha **5**
Organic Farm Café **6**
Rising Sun **13**
Vieng Champa **15**
Xayoh **16**

Bars & clubs
Oh La La **1**
Sakura **12**

are between 2 km and 15 km from Vang Vieng. Alternatively you can catch a Lao-style tractor on the far side of the river (5000-8000 kip depending on distance; bargain hard).

Kasi → Colour map 2, A2.

This is one of those towns that seem to exist for no better reason than that people need to rest and have a bite to eat. It is a trucking stop on Route 13 and, as it is only 60 km north of the much more attractive town of Vang Vieng, it entices few people to tarry here for longer than necessary. According to some of the locals, the countryside around Kasi boasts what is reputedly the second largest cave in the world, Khoun Lang. To date, this has remained a well-kept secret; the cave hasn't popped up on the tourism radar yet and no official tours have been established. Delightfully, the introduction of tourists to the area looks set to be done in a traditional Lao style, with trips incorporating local food and living, including showers in the river and such like. There is plenty of interest to be had by walking around local ethnic villages. The children learn English at school and welcome the opportunity to talk to strangers.

The 45-km stretch of hilly road north of Kasi, up towards **Muang Phou Khoun**, is notorious for Hmong rebel attacks, although it has calmed down in the last few years. **Muang Phou Khoun** is an old colonial garrison at the junction of Route 13 and Route 7. Its strategic position was heavily fought over during the second Indochina war.

● Sleeping

Ban Pako p83, map p81
B Ban Pako Resort, T021-451841, F021-451844. Accommodation is in a Lao-style longhouse or in single bungalows overlooking the river. You can also sleep under the stars on the veranda. Can be crowded at weekends. The restaurant (🍴) serves excellent Lao and European food.

Phou Khao Khouay Protected Area p83
The visitor centre at Tad Leuk rents out tents, mattresses, mosquito nets and sleeping bags. It costs 40,000 kip per night to rent a tent and 15,000 kip a night to hire a sleeping bag. Toilets and washing facilities on site. It is also possible to organize a homestay in one of the surrounding villages. It is also possible to stay overnight in the Elephant Observation Tower near Ban Na.

Vangxang p85
E Vangxang Resort, 13 Neau Rd, Ban Phonegnern, T021-211526. The resort has cute little cottage-style bungalows, with hot water. Great Lao restaurant and scenic man-made lake. US$6 a night.

Nam Ngum dam and reservoir p85, map p81
A-B Nam Ngum Resort, southern end of Nam Ngum, T021-217592,

www.dansavanh.com. Perplexingly advertised as an ecotourist option, this is a Malaysian and Lao government joint-venture hotel with 209 rooms, Chinese and Thai restaurant, health centre, video games. Future plans include marine sports facilities, funfair and golfing links. Rates include breakfast and a shuttle bus from Vientiane.
B-C Nam Lik Eco Resort, Ban Vang Mong, about 8 km from Ang Nam Ngum, turn off Route 13 at Km 75, T020-5508719. Lovely bungalow rooms affording brilliant views. Lots of adventure sports, from kayaking to rock climbing.

Vang Vieng and around p86, map p88
The town's popularity has ensured a uniformity among almost all places catering to budget tourists: most restaurants feature the same menu and there isn't much individuality in the cheaper guesthouses either. The majority are geared to the needs of travellers and offer a laundry service, guides and bicycles. However, in the last 2 years a couple of higher-end hotels have cropped up, providing more attractive options. Although the accommodation in the centre of town is usually cheaper, try and get a room with a view of the river as it is simply stunning.

A-B Vansana, by the river, T023-511598, vansana@laotel.com. Despite the soulless exterior this hotel has the best rooms and facilities in town. Large bedrooms fitted with all the mod cons and stunning mountain and river views. Modern wooden furniture, minibar and local handicrafts decorate the room. Beautiful pool and bar by the river, with deckchairs. Ask for a room with a view. Recommended.

A-C Thavonsouk Resort, on the river, T021-511096, www.thavonsouk.com. This lovely place offers 5 different styles of accommodation across their sprawling riverfront premises. Bungalows range from US$18 to US$75. The US$35 bungalows are great value with massive balcony fitted with sunbeds. There is a traditional Lao house, decorated with Lao furnishings, suitable for a family or big group, plus suites (TV, fridge, bath, a/c) and standard accommodation. Fantastic restaurant. Keep your eye out for local home-grown pop star, Aluna and her father Alom who run this family business.

B Elephant Crossing, on the Nam Song River, T023-511232, www.theelephant crossinghotel.com. A great mid-range option. Australian-owned riverfront hotel classically decorated with modern wooden furnishings. The big bathtub and sliding window between the bedroom and bath-room will be a big hit with romantics. All rooms have view, fridge and a/c. Breakfast included.

B Villa Nam Song, reservation@villa namsong.com, milestone at the gate. Quaint terracotta villas set in manicured gardens overlooking the Nam Song. Parquet floors, hot water. Restaurant attached. Although this is a beautiful hotel there is better value for money in town.

B-C Ban Sabai Bungalows, on the banks of the river, T021-511088, F021-511403. A stunning complex of bungalows in a spectacular location, with all the modern fittings. Hot water, a/c, breakfast included.

B-C Vang Vieng Resort, close to Tham Chang, T021-219380. A Chinese-owned resort, with bar and noodle restaurant. Some chalets have bathrooms but there's no a/c and the rooms smell musty.

C-D Grandview, on the river, T023-511474, grandviewguesthouse@gmail.com. This newcomer offers spotless rooms with attached hot water bathroom. Beautiful balcony views, cheaper rooms without view. Option of paying US$4 extra for a/c. Excellent value. Highly recommended.

D-E Thavisouk, in the centre of town, T023-511340. If you are looking for a budget option in town this is perfect. No frills but very clean. Rooms with hot water bath attached US$3-4. Bit of an ant problem. While the accommodation is good value their tours, tickets and other services aren't.

D-E Vang Vieng Orchid, on the river road, T023-5111172. Comfortable fan or a/c rooms. Hot water in the bathrooms, clean tiled floors, very comfortable rooms. Friendly owners. The rooms with the private balconies are well worth the few extra dollars because you will have your own personal piece of the phenomenal view.

E Malany Guesthouse, on the main road, T021-511083. Smack bang in the centre of town. Big concrete building, not the most forthcoming in friendliness. The rooms are very clean and surprisingly nice, with en suite bathrooms, hot water and fan. Hardish beds, though.

E Maylyn Guesthouse, T020-5604095. Very atmospheric setting on the opposite side of the river to town. Basic rattan-style bungalows, with shared facilities. In summer a footbridge leads to the bungalows, some with shared facilities others with ensuite; in the wet season small boats make the short trip for around 2000-5000 kip. Trail bike and bike hire.

E-F Dokkhoun, T021-511032. Villa with 2 storeys and balcony area, clean rooms with hot water en suite bathrooms and hot water. A/c rooms for a few dollars extra.

E-F Le Jardine Bungalows, on the river, about 900 m from the centre of town, T020-5474643. There are 3 sets of bunalows here: the best are superb; the worst are falling down, soulless, concrete blocks. It is far enough from town for the surrounding beauty to remain undisturbed but close enough for convenience. The views are remarkable and the restaurant is quite good too. The owners are lovely and don't suffer from Vang Vieng jadedness quite often found in these cheaper bungalows.

E-F Saysong Guesthouse, by the river behind the post office, T021-511130.

The cheaper rooms (US$3) have en suite bathrooms and are a bit mouldy. The doubles are substantially better, cleaner and bigger. There's a small coffee shop downstairs and a fantastic communal balcony overlooking the river.

F Bountang, near Wat Kang. Large 3-storey white villa with weaving loom and handicrafts in the garden. Choice of cold and hot showers.

F Chanthala, next to Wat Kang. One of the older cheap guesthouses in Vang Vieng, with shared toilet facilities, clean.

F Phou Bane, close to the market and the bus station. One of the original guesthouses in Vang Vieng which may lend the place atmosphere, but the rooms are not as clean or well-equipped as others; shared shower and toilet downstairs. Good restaurant and nice garden to lounge in. A friendly place.

F Viengvilay, T021-511177. Bit of a mixed bag, this one: all rooms are reasonably clean and have en suite bathrooms, some on the 2nd floor offer spectacular views of the mountains.

Out of town

The places out of town are great for those who wish to escape into a more natural landscape. The lack of facilities and transport in the area ensures tranquillity but also makes it quite difficult to get to town.

B-C Vang Vieng Eco-Lodge, 7 km north of town, T020-2247323, tatluang@laotel.com. Although this isn't an eco-lodge it is still an exceptionally beautiful place to stay. Set on the banks of the river with stunning gardens and beautiful rock formations, it is a perfect place to get away from it all. The 10 chalet-style bungalows have been nicely decorated, with beautiful balconies, comfortable furnishings and a big hot-water bathtub. Management assures a tuk-tuk is just a phone call away. Good Lao restaurant. Also arranges activities. Low-season discount.

E-F Organic Mulberry Farm, 3 km north of town, T021-511220, www.laofarm.org. This mulberry farm has basic rooms with mosquito net, dorm accommodation and full board. Cheaper rates in the low season. Hugely popular restaurant, serving great starfruit wine and famous mulberry pancakes. It is a very popular drop-off spot for tubers.

Kasi *p89*

Rooms are available at several guesthouses.

E Somchith, Route 13 Main Rd. The most popular place is this small guesthouse above a restaurant in the centre of town.

---

❷ Eating

Nam Ngum dam and reservoir *p85, map p81*

¶¶-¶ Lao Food Rafts, there are several floating restaurants lining the shore.

Vang Vieng and around *p86, map p88*

There is a string of eating places on the main road through town, with the same menu duplicated in almost every establishment. Generally available are hamburgers, pasta, sandwiches and basic Asian. Most of the restaurants offer 'happy' upgrades – marijuana or mushrooms in your pizza, cake or lassi, or opium tea. Although many people choose the 'happy' offerings, some of these wind up very ill. The police have also been known to go on drug-busting sprees.

¶ Luang Prabang Bakery Restaurant, just off the main road. Excellent pastries, cakes and shakes and pretty delicious breakfasts. Make sure you ask for the freshest batch as they have a tendency to leave cakes on the shelf well past their use-by date. Recommended.

¶ Nangbot, on the main road, T021-511018. This proper sit-down restaurant is one of the oldest tourist diners in town and serves a few traditional dishes, such as bamboo shoot soup and *laap* with sticky rice, alongside the usual Western fare.

¶ Nazim's, on the main road, T021-511214. Largest and most popular Indian joint in town. Good range of South Indian and *biriyani* specialities, plus selection of vegetarian meals.

¶ Nisha Restaurant, on the main road, T020-5685538. Pretty good-value Indian food and Lao dishes.

¶ Organic Farm Cafe, further down the main road. Small café offering over 15 tropical fruit shakes and a fantastic variety of food. Mulberry shakes and pancakes are a must and the harvest curry stew is absolutely delicious. Try the fresh spring rolls, with pineapple dipping sauce as a starter. The food is highly recommended, the service could do with a little work. The sister branch is at the **Organic Mulberry Farm** (see Sleeping). You can while away the afternoon sipping star-fruit wine and watching the world go by on the river. Highly recommended.

¶ **Rising Sun**, just off the main road. They have tried to cultivate a different atmosphere here to other restaurants in town. The decor is brightly coloured and the menu features good comfort food, such as cottage pie.

¶ **Vieng Champa Restaurant**, on the main road, T021-511037. Refreshingly, this family-run restaurant seems to have a greater selection of Lao food than most other places on the street. The only drawback is the highly unflattering green fluorescent lighting.

¶ **Xayoh**, on the main Luang Prabang Rd, T023-511088. Restaurant with branches in Vientiane and Luang Prabang offering good Western food in a comfy environment. Pizza, soups and roast dinners.

◯ Bars and clubs

Vang Vieng and around *p86, map p88*
The latest hotspot in Vang Vieng changes week to week.
Oh La La Bar, off the main street.
Very popular, open bar with pool table.
Sakura Bar, between the main road and the river. Big open bar with loud, blaring and often live music.

◯ Shopping

Vang Vieng and around *p86, map p88*
BKC Bookshop, next door to Fathima restaurant, T021-511303. A reasonable but limited bookshop and exchange.
New Market, 2 km north of town, has the greatest selection of goods.

▲ Activities and tours

Vang Vieng and around *p86, map p88*
Kayaking and rafting
See also Tour operators, below. Kayaking is a very popular activity around Vang Vieng and competition between operators is fierce. There is a wide variety of trips available, ranging from day trips (with a visit to the caves and surrounding villages), to kayaking all the way to Vientiane via the stop-off point

at Nam Lik, US$15-25, about 6 hrs, including a 40-min drive at the start and finish. All valuables are kept in a car which meets kayakers at the end of their paddle. A few companies also offer 2-day rafting trips down the Nam Ngum river, one of the only ways to see the seldomly visited and formerly off-limits Saysamboun Special Zone. The trip includes several grade 4 and 5 rapids and usually an overnight camp on an island on Nam Ngum Lake. US$100 per person or less for groups of more than 3. The trips can be tailormade to include other attractions.

Be wary of intensive rafting or kayaking trips through risky areas during the wet season as it can be very dangerous. Check equipment thoroughly before committing.

Rock climbing
Vang Vieng is the only really established rock-climbing area in the country, with over 50 sites in the locality, ranging from grade 5 to 8A+. Almost all of these climbs have been 'bolted'. There are climbing sites suitable for beginners through to more experienced climbers. **Green Discovery** (see Tour operators, below) runs climbing courses almost every day in high season (US$20-45 per day, including equipment rental). The best climbing sites include:
Sleeping Cave (**Tham None**, see page 87). A popular destination, accessed by dug-out canoe across the Nam Song river. The cave offers 14 separate routes, after which you can jump into the water on one of the rope swings to cool off.
Sleeping Wall, near Sleeping Cave. A tough 20-m crag, which features 19 separate climbs, including a few ascents requiring some tricky manoeuvring and steep overhangs. Boatmen offer climbers a lift along the Nam Song river (5000 kip) to get to the wall. There are refreshment stalls at both Sleeping Wall and Sleeping Cave.
Tham Nam Them, 7 km from town. Fantastic clambers around the entrance of the cave. There are 19 bolted tracks here, both inside and outside the cave.

Tour operators
Tour guides are available for hiking, rafting, visiting the caves and minority villages from most travel agents and guesthouses. Safety issues need to be considered when taking

part in any adventure activity. There have been fatalities in Vang Vieng from boating, trekking and caving accidents. The Nam Xong river can flow very, quickly during the wet season (Jul and Aug) and tourists have drowned here. Make sure you wear a life-jacket during all water-borne activities and time your trip so you aren't travelling on the river after dark. A price war between tour operators has led to cost cutting, resulting in equipment that is not well maintained or does not exist at all. With all tour operators it is imperative that you are given safety gear and that canoes, ropes, torches and other equipment is in a good state of repair. The more expensive, reputable companies are often the best option (see also Vientiane Tour operators, page 75).

Green Discovery, attached to Xayoh Café, T023-511440, www.greendiscoverylaos.com. By far the best operator in town. Caving, kayaking, hiking and rock climbing. Very professional and helpful. Recommended.

Riverside Tour, T020-2254137, www.riversidetourlaos.com. Kayaking and adventure tours.

Trekking

Almost all guesthouses and agents in town offer hiking trips, usually incorporating a visit to caves and minority villages and, possibly, some kayaking or tubing. The best treks are offered through the major tour operators who will provide an English-speaking guide, all transport and lunch for US$10-15 per day.

Tubing

No trip to Vang Vieng is complete without tubing down the Nam Song. Floating slowly along the Nam Song is an ideal way to take in the stunning surroundings of misty limestone karsts, jungle and rice paddies. The drop-off point is 3 km from town near the **Organic Mulberry Farm**, where several bars and restaurants have been set up along the river. Start early in the day as it's dangerous to tube after dark and the temperature of the water drops sharply. Please take a sarong with you and do not walk through town in a bikini as it is culturally unacceptable and highly offensive to the locals.

Tour operators and guesthouses offer tube rental, life jackets and drop-off for US$4. A US$7 fine is charged for lost tubes (people may offer to return the tubes for you; it is best to decline this offer). Dry bags can be rented for 10,000 kip. It is essential that you wear a life jacket as people have drowned on the river, particularly in the wet season (Jul and Aug) when the river swells and flows very, very quickly. Without stopping expect the journey to take 1-2 hrs. Most people stop along the way and make a day of it.

⊖ Transport

See also Vientiane Transport, page 76.

Vang Vieng and around *p86, map p88*
Bicycle and motorbike hire
There are many bicycles for rent along the road east up from the market (10,000 kip per day). There are also a few motorbike rental places (US$5 per day); the best of these is opposite the **Organic Farm Café** in town.

Bus

Buses leave from the make-shift bus terminal on the east side of the airstrip, T021-511341. There are plans to relocate all buses to the terminal at the New Market, 2 km north of town. Check before going to either station. This station has been built for 2 years now and the buses still haven't relocated. Minibuses leave from most guesthouses to both Vientiane and Luang Prabang – this service is notoriously unreliable with passengers packed in like sardines and minivans often breaking down. Best to opt for the local bus. You can catch northbound buses headed from **Vientiane** to **Luang Prabang** hourly between 1200 and 2000 (70,000 kip, 8-10 hrs). The bus en route from Vientiane to **Phonsovan** passes through town at 0900, 85,000 kip. Public buses leave for **Vientiane** at 5 times daily, (3½-4 hrs) 25,000 kip; *songthaews* depart every hour. Public buses leave for **Vientiane** 6 times daily, 20,000 kip; *songthaew* depart every hour or so.

Private transport and VIP buses
Tickets are usually sold by guesthouses and will include a tuk-tuk pickup at your hotel to the bus. VIP buses leave to **Luang Prabang** at 1000, US$10, 6 hrs. The minivans leave at 0900. VIP bus to **Vientiane** 1000 and 1300 (3 hrs) 55,000 kip (you are actually better off on the local bus for short stints like this). Mini-

van to **Vientiane** 0900, 70,000 kip, 3½ hrs
(not recommended). Minibus to **Luang
Prabang** 0900, 105,000 kip (5 hrs). Every
guesthouse and travel agent can book the
VIP/minivans and they will pick up from
your guesthouse. Seats get booked up really
quickly.

Tour companies sell tickets from Vang
Vieng to **Bangkok** for ฿825 but there are
better, more efficient and cost-effective
ways to get back to the Thai capital.

Tuk-tuk
A day trip to the caves should cost US$10
but there have been reports of some drivers
offering trips to the caves for 10,000 kip per
person and then demanding an outrageous
fee for the return leg. Make sure all prices are
set in stone before leaving town.

Kasi *p89*
Bus/truck
There are connections south to **Vang Vieng**
(2 hrs) and north to **Luang Prabang** (4 hrs).

● Directory

Vang Vieng and around *p86, map p88*
Banks Agricultural Promotion Bank and the
Lao Development Bank, on the main road,
both exchange cash, 0830-1530 daily. BCEL,
T021-511480, exchanges cash and TCs and
will also do cash advances on Visa and
MasterCard, daily 0830-1530. MasterCard
ATM. **Internet** There are a number of
internet cafés along the main drag, all 300 kip
per min (but prices are expected to go
down); most offer international net calls
from 3000 kip per min. **Magnet** is the best of
the internet cafés; as well as internet it offers
music/movie transfer to iPod and cash
advances from the EFTPOS facility for 3%
commission. **Medical services** Vang
Vieng Hospital is located on the road that
runs parallel to the river; it's terribly
under-equipped. The hospital is proof
positive of the need for travel insurance. In
most cases it is better to go to Vientiane or
even into Thailand, see pages 38 and 80.
Post The post office is next to the old
market, daily 0830-1600.

✱ Footprint features

Introduction

Much of Laos' northern region is rugged and mountainous, a remote borderland with a significant minority population of hill peoples. Until recently, in some areas at least, the only way to travel was by boat, along one of the rivers – many fast-flowing – which have cut their way through this impressive landscape. Today road travel is much improved, although still not easy. The key centre of the north is the old royal capital of Luang Prabang, one of the world's most beautiful cities. To the east is the Plain of Jars and Vieng Xai, a former stronghold of the Pathet Lao, while to the north is a string of small towns that are becoming increasingly popular places to visit. Eco-resorts in peaceful forest settings, treks to upland villages, dips in icy mountain streams and rafting trips down innumerable rivers are among the highlights of this region. And, as tourist numbers rise, local people are learning to cater for the peculiar demands of foreigner visitors.

★ Don't miss ...

1 **Luang Prabang** Saunter through the old royal capital, taking time to visit the incomparable Wat Xieng Thong and to climb Mount Phousi, see page 98.

2 **Pak Ou caves** Catch a boat upstream to cliff-side caves, stuffed with 4000 images of the Buddha, see page 117.

3 **Tad Kwang Si** Take a dip in these cascades, south of Luang Prabang, page 118.

4 **Cruising on the Mekong** Take a slow boat along the river between Luang Prabang and Houei Xai on the border with Thailand, pages 129, 148 and 160.

5 **Trekking around Phongsali** Head north to this upland town for hiking amid stunning scenery, page 135.

6 **Muang Sing** Use the attractive hill town as a base for exploring the hill villages and minority peoples of the area, page 146.

7 **Boat Landing Guesthouse** Stay at the country's premier ecotourism resort on the river in Luang Namtha and enjoy great food too, page 152.

8 **Plain of Jars** Construct your own hypothesis for the creation of Xieng Khouang's giant stone jars, page 166.

9 **Vieng Xai** Explore the caves that served as the stronghold of the Pathet Lao, page 179.

Northern Laos

Luang Prabang and around

In terms of size, Luang Prabang hardly deserves the title 'city' – the district capital has a population of around 26,000. But in terms of grandeur the appellation is more than deserved. Luang Prabang is the town that visitors often remember with the greatest affection. Its rich history, incomparable architecture, relaxed atmosphere, good food, friendly population and stunning position, surrounded by a crown of mountains, mark Luang Prabang out as exceptional.

Anchored at the junction of the Mekong and Nam Khan rivers, the former royal capital is home to a spellbinding array of gilded temples, weathered French colonial shopfronts and art deco shophouses. Luang Prabang was founded on Mount Phousi – a small rocky hill with leafy slopes – and has been a mountain kingdom for over 1000 years. Despite a few welcome concessions to modern life, including great food, internet cafés, electricity and the occasional car, Luang Prabang still oozes the magic of bygone days. In the 18th century there were more than 65 wats in the city; many have been destroyed over the years but over 30 remain intact, including the former royal Wat Xieng Thong; Wat Visoun, built in 1513 (the oldest operational temple in Luang Prabang); That Pathum (Lotus Stupa), noted for its odd watermelon-like shape, and Wat Aham, formerly the seat of the Lao Supreme Patriarch. The continuing splendour and historical significance of the town led UNESCO to designate Luang Prabang a World Heritage Site at the end of 1995 and declare it the best-preserved traditional city in Southeast Asia.

Yet for all its magnificent temples, this royal 'city' feels more like an easy-going provincial town: in the early evening children play in the streets, while women cook, old men lounge in wicker chairs and young boys play takro. The town's timelessness can be observed by simply walking the ancient cobbled paths. ▶▶ *For Sleeping, Eating and other listings, see pages 119-131.*

Ins and outs → *Phone code: 071. Colour map 2, A2.*

Getting there Visitors to Luang Prabang used to be advised by Vientiane's foreign consular staff to fly rather than risk the road journey. This was because vehicles on the stretch of Route 13 between Vientiane and Luang Prabang, particularly north of Kasi, were periodically attacked by Hmong bandits. Although there have been no attacks on this stretch for several years now, flying is still the easiest option, with daily connections from Vientiane, plus flights from Bangkok and Chiang Mai to **Luang Prabang International Airport** (LPQ) ① *4 km northeast of town, T071-212172/3*. Don't expect anything too jazzy but the airport does have a phone box, a couple of restaurants and handicraft shops. There is a standard US$5 charge for a tuk-tuk ride from the airport into the centre; on the way back you can probably negotiate a cheaper price.

Route 13 is now safe, with no recent attacks reported, and the road has been upgraded, shortening the journey from Vientiane to a relatively painless eight or nine hours. There are also overland connections with other destinations in northern Laos including Sayaboury, Nong Khiaw, Xieng Khouang (Phonsavanh), Xam Neua, Luang Namtha, Udomxai, Muang Ngoi and Pak Mong. Luang Prabang has two main bus stations: **Kiew Lot Sai Nuan** (northern bus station), located on the northeast side of Sisavangvong Bridge, for traffic to and from the north; and **Naluang** (southern bus

● Luang Prabang's famously laid-back atmosphere even extends to its prison. Inmates at the
● Nam Pha 'free-range' jail were reportedly reluctant to be released. It is also reported that
  relatives can 'stand-in' for prisoners over a weekend if they want to see the outside world.

station) for traffic to and from the south. Occasionally buses will pass through the opposite station to what you would expect, so be sure to double-check. The standard tuk-tuk fare to/from either bus station is about 15,000 kip. If there are only a few passengers, it's late at night or you are travelling to/from an out-of-town hotel, expect to pay 20,000 kip. These prices tend to fluctuate with the international cost of petroleum. There is a third, smaller station, south of town, on the road to the falls, which operates as a terminal for buses to Sayaboury.

A third option is to travel by river: a firm favourite is the two-day trip between Houei Xai (close to the Thai border) and Luang Prabang, via Pak Beng. Less frequent are the boats between Luang Prabang and Vientiane, via Pak Lai, and to Muang Ngoi and Nong Khiaw, via Muang Khua. ▸▸ *For further details, see Transport, page 129.*

Getting around Luang Prabang is a small town and the best way to explore is either on foot or by bicycle. Bicycles can be hired from most guesthouses for US$1 per day. Strolling about this beautiful town is a real pleasure but there are also tuk-tuks and saamlors available for hire. Motorbikes can't be hired or ridden around town. Note that road names are not widely used and there seems to be some confusion over precisely what some of the roads are called. Buses provide links with out-of-town destinations (although the service is limited and intermittent), and there are also boats and minibuses for charter.

Best time to visit Luang Prabang lies 300 m above sea-level on the upper Mekong, at its confluence with the Nam Khan. The most popular time to visit the town is during the comparatively cool months of November and December but the best time to visit is from December to February. After this the weather is warming up and the views are often shrouded in a haze, produced by shifting cultivators using fire to clear the forest for agriculture. This does not really clear until May or even June. During the months of March and April, when visibility is at its worst, the smoke can cause soreness of the eyes, as well as preventing planes from landing.

Tourist information Luang Prabang Tourist Information Centre ⓘ *Sisavangvong Rd, T071-212487.* Aside from provincial information, it offers a couple of good ecotourism treks (which support local communities), including one to Tad Kwang Si and one in Chompet district. The Chompet trek receives quite good reviews and includes visits to hot springs, villages and the chance to watch a traditional performance from Hmong performers.

Probably the best city map is the one compiled by the **Lao National Tourism Authority,** with support from the Asian Development Bank and GT Rider; the tourist office should have free copies. Other maps are increasingly available, including a detailed one by Hobo maps.

History

According to legend, the site of Luang Prabang was chosen by two resident hermits. Buddha was believed to have glanced in Luang Prabang's direction, saying a great city would be built there. The discovery of large, stone container-like artefacts nearby allude to an ancient history yet to be unravelled by archaeologists. Some believe the artefacts are linked with the Vietnamese Dong Son period (500 BC-AD 100), while others suggest a prehistoric connection to the Plain of Jars. Details are sketchy regarding the earliest inhabitants of Luang Prabang but historians imply the ethnic Khmu and Lao Theung groups were the initial settlers. They named Luang Prabang, 'Muang Sawa', which literally translates as Java, hinting at some kind of cross-border support. By the end of the 13th century, Muang Sawa had developed into a regional hub.

A major turning point in the city's history came about in 1353, when the mighty Fa Ngum barrelled down the Nam Ou river, backed by a feisty Khmer army, and captured Muang Sawa. Here, the warrior king founded Lane Xang Hom Khao, the Kingdom of a Million Elephants, White Parasol and established a new Lao royal lineage, which was to last another 600 years. The name of the city refers to the holy Pra Bang, Laos' most sacred image of the Buddha which was given to Fa Ngum by his father-in-law the King of Cambodia.

Fa Ngum imported Khmer traditions including Theravada Buddhism and great architecture, but his constituents and army, wary of his warmongering ways, exiled him in 1373, and his son, Oun Heuan, then assumed the throne. Oun Heuan was known as 'Samsenthai', a name that indicated the size of his army – a man-force of 300,000 – and, during his reign, the city was renamed Muang Xieng Thong, the City of Gold.

In 1478 the city was invaded by Vietnamese. After several years occupying and ransacking the place, they were finally driven out and the Kingdom embarked upon a massive reconstruction campaign. During this period some of Luang Prabang's finest monuments were built, including Wat Xieng Thong. The city had been significantly built up by the time King Visunarat came to power in 1512 and remained the capital until King Setthathirat, fearing a Burmese invasion, moved the capital to Vieng Chan (Vientiane) in 1563.

Luang Prabang was a religious as well as a trading centre. To begin with, it seems that Theravada Buddhism was creatively combined with ritualistic elements from the Hinduist and animist past. Mendez Pinto, in his account of 1578, describes Luang Prabang (or what historians take to be Luang Prabang) as having 24 religious sects and writes that there is "so great a variety and confusion of diabolical errors and precepts, principally in the blood sacrifices they employ, that it is frightful to hear them". The royal chronicles of the 16th century describe successive attempts to erase these sects from the kingdom.

Luang Prabang's importance diminished in the 18th century, following the death of King Souligna Vongsa and the break-up of Lane Xang, but it remained a royal centre until the Communist takeover in 1975. During the low point of Laos' fortunes in the mid-19th century, when virtually the whole country had become tributary to Bangkok (Siam), only Luang Prabang retained a semblance of independence. The tiny kingdom, shorn of most of its hinterland, paid tribute to Siam, Hué and Peking, hoping to play one off against the other. (The country's approach to foreign affairs since 1975 neatly mirrors this strategy.) What the king in Luang Prabang did not envisage, however, was the arrival of a power stronger than all three of these: the French.

The French and the British competed diligently for control of mainland Southeast Asia. France's piece of the cake became French Indochina and their attempt to wrest control of Laos from Siamese suzerainty was linked to the energy, perseverance and force of will of one man: Auguste Pavie. Contemporary accounts describe Pavie as "thin and weak-looking" but this physical demeanour disguised a man of extraordinary abilities. He was appointed French vice-consul in Luang Prabang in May 1886, after accumulating 17 years' experience in Cambodia and Cochin China (south Vietnam). According to Martin Stuart-Fox in *A History of Laos* (1997), Pavie had not only acquired a comprehensive knowledge of the people, cultures and languages of the area, but also developed a deep dislike of the Siamese. His part in securing Laos for France was achieved when he rescued King Unkham from marauding Haw and Tai bandits in 1887. The protecting Siamese and their Lao soldiers had departed from Luang Prabang, leaving Pavie with the opportunity to save the day. He plucked the aged king from a burning palace, escaped downstream and was rewarded when the king requested France's protection. The events marked the dispossession of the Siamese by the French. The city had been ransacked and set ablaze by the bandits but the French helped to rebuild the city, using indentured labour from Vietnam and giving Luang Prabang much of the look it has today.

⁑ Mekong monsters, real and imagined

It is said that the pla buk, the giant catfish of the Mekong, was only described by Western science in 1930. That may be so, but the English explorer and surveyor, James McCarthy, goes into considerable detail about the fish in his book Surveying and exploring in Siam, which was first published in 1900 and draws upon his travels in Siam and Laos between 1881 and 1893.

He writes: "The month of June in Luang Prabang is a very busy one for fishermen. Nearly all the boats are employed on fishing, each paying a large fish for the privilege. Two kinds of large fish, pla buk and pla rerm, are principally sought after... A pla buk that I helped to take weighed 130 lbs; it was 7 ft long and 4 ft 2 in round the body; the tail measured 1 ft 9 in. The fish had neither scales nor teeth, and was sold for 10 rupees. The roe of this fish is considered a great delicacy. The fish is taken in ... June, July and August, when on its upward journey. Returning in November, it keeps low in the river, and a few stray ones only are caught."

McCarthy also recounts the story of a mythical river serpent of the Mekong: "It lives only at the rapids, and my informant said he had seen it. It is 53 ft long and 20 ft thick. When a man is drowned it snaps off the tuft of hair on the head [men wore their hair in this manner], extracts the teeth, and sucks the blood; and when a body is found thus disfigured, it is known that the man has fallen victim to the nguak, or river serpent, at Luang Prabang."

James McCarthy, an otherwise rather plodding recorder of events and sights, wrote of Luang Prabang at the end of the 19th century: "In a clear afternoon, Luang Prabang stood out distinctly. At evening the pagoda spires and the gilded mouldings of the wats, glancing in the light of the setting sun, added their effect to that of the natural features of the landscape – and caused in me a feeling of irresistible melancholy. Since my visit in February 1887, Luang Prabang had passed through much suffering. It had been ravaged by the Haw; its people had been pillaged and murdered or driven from their homes, and the old chief had only been rescued by his sons forcing him to a place of safety. The town seemed doomed to suffer, for within two months past it had again been burned, and, more recently still, about 500 of its inhabitants had died of an epidemic sickness." Yet, by 1926 American Harry Franck could find paradise in Luang Prabang, as recorded in his book, *East of Siam*: "It is not a city at all, in the crowded, noisy, Western sense, but a leisurely congregation of dwellings of simple lines, each ... with sufficient ground so that its opinions or doings need not interfere with its neighbours. In short, Luang Prabang town is in many ways what idealists picture the cities of Utopia to be".

Luang Prabang didn't suffer as greatly as other provincial capitals during the Indochina wars, narrowly escaping a Viet Minh capture in 1953. Rumour has it that as the Vietnamese troops approached Luang Prabang, the citizens remained calm because a blind monk had prophesized that the city wouldn't be taken. During the Second Indochina War, however, the Pathet Lao cut short the royal lineage, forcing King Sisavang Vatthana to abdicate and sending him to a re-education camp in northeastern Laos where he, his wife and his son died from starvation.

Despite the demise of the monarchy and years of revolutionary rhetoric on the city's tannoy system, Luang Prabang's dreamy streets have somehow retained the aura of old Lane Xang. In the early 1990s it was suggested that a highway be constructed through Luang Prabang, to the Chinese border. Fortunately, with UNESCO's designation of Luang Prabang as a World Heritage Site, the scope for redevelopment was substantially restricted. The old town – essentially the promontory – is fully protected while elsewhere only limited redevelopment and expansion is permitted (no building, for example, can be higher than three storeys). The road building went ahead but the local authorities constructed a bypass to ensure that the fragile town wasn't disrupted.

Sights

The sights are conveniently close together in Luang Prabang. Most are dotted along the main Sakkaline, Sisavangvong and Souvanna Khampong roads. Most are walkable – the important ones can be covered within two leisurely days – but a bike is the best way to get around. To begin with it may be worth climbing Phousi or taking a stroll along the Mekong and Nam Khan river roads to get a better idea of the layout of the town. Most of Luang Prabang's important wats are dotted along the main road, Phothisarath. When visiting the wats it is helpful to take a guide to obtain entry to all the buildings, which are often locked for security reasons. Without a guide, your best chance of finding them open is early in the morning. ▶▶ *For a walking tour of the town, see page 111.*

▶ At daybreak, scores of saffron-robed monks silently amble out of the monasteries bearing gold-topped alms boxes in which to collect offerings from the town's residents.

▶▶ *For a walking tour of the town, see page 111.*

Northern Laos Luang Prabang & around

Luang Prabang

| 100 metres |
| 100 yards |

Sleeping 🛏

Ancient Luang
  Prabang **12** *B3*
Ban Lao **1** *C2*
Boun Gning
  Guesthouse **2** *B2*

Jaliya **3** *C3*
Kounsavan **19** *B3*
Lane Xang &
  Lane Xang Travel **5** *C4*
La Résidence Phou Vao **15** *D2*
Le Parasol Blanc **6** *B1*

Maison Souvannaphoum **18**
Mano Guesthouse **7** *C3*
Manoluck **9** *D1*
Mouang Luang **10** *C2*
Muang Swa **11** *C1*
New Luang Prabang **13** *B3*

Royal Palace

ⓘ *Sisavangvong Rd, daily 0800-1100 and 1330-1600, admission 20,000 kip. Shorts, short-sleeved shirts and strappy dresses are prohibited; shoes should be removed and bags must be put in lockers. No photography.*

Also called the **National Museum**, the Royal Palace is right in the centre of the city on the main road, Sisavangvong, which runs along the promontory and allowed royal guests ready access from the Mekong. Unlike its former occupants, the palace survived the 1975 revolution and was converted into a museum the following year. It replaced a smaller wooden palace on the same site.

Construction of the palace started in 1904, during the reign of Sisavang Vong, and took 20 years. It was built by the French for the Lao king, in an attempt to bind him and his family more tightly to the colonial system of government. Although most of the construction was completed by 1909, the two front wings were extended in the 1920s and a new, more Lao-style roof was added. These later changes were accompanied by the planting of the avenue of palms and the filling in of one of two fish ponds. Local residents regarded the ponds as the 'eyes' of the capital, so the blinding of one eye was taken as inviting bad fortune by leaving the city unprotected. The subsequent civil war seemed to vindicate these fears. The palace is Khmer in style, cruciform in plan and mounted on a small platform of four tiers. The only indication of French involvement can be seen in the two French lilies represented in stucco on the entrance, beneath the symbols of Lao royalty. There are a few Lao motifs but, in many respects, the palace is more foreign than Lao: it was designed by a French architect, with steps made from Italian marble; built by masons from Vietnam; embellished by carpenters from Bangkok; and funded by the largesse of the colonial authorities. While the palace itself is modest, its contents are spectacular.

The museum now contains a collection of 15th- to 17th-century Buddha statues and artefacts from many of the wats in Luang Prabang such as the Khmer bronze drums from Wat Visoun. Notable pieces include an ancient Buddha head, an offering from Indian dignitaries; and a reclining Buddha with the unusual addition of mourners. The most important piece, however, is the Pra Bang, or **Golden Buddha**, from which the city derives its name. The Buddha is in the attitude of Abhayamudra or 'dispelling fear' (see page 316). Some believe that the original image is kept in a bank vault, although most dispel this as rumour. It is 90% solid gold, stands 83 cm high and weighs around 53 kg. Reputed to have originally come from Ceylon, and said to date from any time between the first and ninth centuries, the statue was brought to Cambodia in the 11th century, given to King Phaya Sirichanta, and was then taken to Lane

Related maps
A Luang Prabang detail, p106

Map labels: Mekong River; Tourist Boats to Pak Ou; Souvanna Khampong; Sakkaline; Nam Khan; To Pak Ou & Xang Hai; To Airport, Northern Bus Terminal & Ban Hat Hien; Wat Tao Hai

Margin: **Northern Laos** Luang Prabang & around

Xang by King Fa Ngum, who had spent some time in the courts of Angkor and married into Khmer royalty. An alternative story has the Pra Bang following Fa Ngum to the city. It is said that he asked his father-in-law, the King of Angkor, to send a delegation of holy men to assist him in spreading the Theravada Buddhist faith in Lane Xang. The delegation arrived bringing with them the Pra Bang as a gift from the Cambodian King. The Pra Bang's arrival heralded the capital's change of name, from Xieng Thong to Nakhon Luang Prabang – 'The great city of the big Buddha'. In 1563 King Setthathirat took the statue to Lane Xang's new capital at Vientiane. Two centuries later in 1779 the Thais captured it but it was returned to Laos in 1839 and rediscovered in the palace chapel in 1975. The Pra Bang is revered in Laos as its arrival marked the beginnings of Buddhism in Lane Xang. The Pra Bang is currently kept in a small enclosure to the right of the entrance but is expected to be moved to the Wat Ho Prabang some time in the future.

Entrance Hall The main entrance hall of the palace was used for royal religious ceremonies, when the Supreme Patriarch of Lao Buddhism would oversee proceedings from his gold-painted lotus throne.

King's Reception Room The room to the immediate right of the entrance was the King's Reception Room, also called the **Ambassadors' Room**. It contains French-made busts of the last three Lao monarchs, a model of the royal hearse (which is kept in Wat Xieng Thong) and a mural by French artist Alex de Fontereau, depicting a day in the life of Luang Prabang in the 1930s.

Coronation Room (Throne Room) To the rear of the entrance hall, the Coronation Room was decorated between 1960 and 1970 for Sisavang Vatthana's coronation, an event which was interrupted because of the war. The walls are a brilliant red with Japanese glass mosaics embedded in a red lacquer base with gilded woodwork. They depict scenes from Lao festivals, such as boat racing. The carved throne has a gold three-headed elephant insignia; on one side is a tall pot to hold the crown. To the right of the throne, as you face it, are the ceremonial coronation swords and a glass case containing 15th- and 16th-century crystal and gold Buddhas, many from inside the 'melon stupa' of Wat Visoun. Because Luang Prabang was constantly raided, many of these religious artefacts were presented to the king for safekeeping long before the palace became a national museum. At the back of the room to the right of the entrance is the royal *howdah*, a portable throne that was used during battle. The throne is covered with shields to protect it.

Private Apartments In comparison to the state rooms, the royal family's private apartments are modestly decorated. They have been left virtually untouched since Sisavang Vatthana and family left for exile in Xam Neua Province. The **King's Library** backs onto the Coronation Room: Sisavang Vatthana was a well-read monarch, having studied at the École de Science Politique in Paris. Behind the library, built around a small inner courtyard are the queen's modest bedroom, the king's bedchamber and the royal yellow bathroom, with its two regal porcelain thrones standing side by side. These rooms are cordoned off but you can still see them. The king's bed is a marvellous construction with a three-headed elephant insignia. The remaining rooms include a small portrait gallery, dining room and the former children's bedroom, which is decorated with musical instruments and headdresses for *Ramayana* actors. In the hallway linking the rooms is a miscellany of interesting objects, including a an intricately patterned *sinh*, worn by the queen, and a royal palanquin (the king's tuk-tuk), which would have been tied to an elephant. Domestic rooms, offices and library are located on the ground floor beneath the state apartments.

Other reception rooms To the left of the entrance hall is the reception room of the **King's Secretary**, and beyond it, the **Queen's Reception Room**, which together house an eccentric miscellany of state gifts from just about every country except the UK. Of particular note is the moon rock presented to Laos by the USA following the Apollo 11 and 17 lunar missions. Also in this room are portraits of the last King Sisavang Vatthana, Queen Kham Phouy and Crown Prince Vongsavang, painted by a Soviet artist in 1967.

King's Chapel On the right wing of the palace, next to the King's Reception Room, is the king's private chapel, which housed the Pra Bang until 2005. It also contains four Khmer Buddhas, ivories mounted in gold, bronze drums used in religious ceremonies and about 30 smaller Buddha images from temples all over the city.

Wat Ho Prabang This small ornate pavilion is located in the northeast corner of the palace compound, to the right of the entrance to the Royal Palace. It was designed by the Royal Secretary of the time to house the Pra Bang and was paid for by small donations sent in from across the country. The Pra Bang should move here some time in the future.

Other buildings In the left-hand corner (south) of the compound, is the **Luang Prabang Conference Hall**, built for the official coronation of Savang Vatthana, which was terminally interrupted by the 1975 revolution. The southwestern corner of the compound is now used as the **Royal Theatre**, where traditional performances are held.

Wat Mai

ⓘ *Sisavangvong Rd, daily 0800-1700, admission 5000 kip.*

Next to the Royal Palace is Wat Mai. This royal temple, inaugurated in 1788, has a five-tiered roof and is one of the jewels of Luang Prabang. It took more than 70 years to complete. It was officially called Wat Souvanna Phommaram and was the home of the Buddhist leader in Laos, Phra Sangkharath, until he moved to That Luang in Vientiane. Auguste Pavie and his crew took up residence here while trying to win Luang Prabang over from the Siamese who controlled the Lao court at the time. The Siamese thought that detaining Pavie in the compound would keep him out of their way but the Frenchman struck up a friendship with a local abbot, who acted as a runner between the king and Pavie. The temple housed the Pra Bang from 1894 until 1947 and, during Pi Mai (New Year), the Pra Bang is taken from the Royal Palace and installed at Wat Mai for its annual ritual cleansing, before being returned to the palace on the third day.

Today, Wat Mai is probably the most popular temple after Wat Xieng Thong. The façade is particularly interesting: a large golden bas-relief tells the story of Phravet (one of the last reincarnations of the Gautama or historic Buddha), with several village scenes, including depictions of wild animals, women pounding rice and people at play. The interior is an exquisite amalgam of red and gold, with supporting pillars similar to those in Wat Xieng Thong and Wat Visoun. The temple is indicative of Luang Prabang architecture aside from the standout roofed veranda, whose gables face the sides rather than the front. The central beam at Wat Mai is carved with figures from the Hindu story of the birth of Ravanna and Hanuman. Behind the temple is an open construction where two classical racing boats are kept, ready to be brought out for Pi Mai (Lao New Year) and the August boat racing festival. ⏵ *For details, see Festivals and events, page 125.*

Mount Phousi

ⓘ *The western steps lead up from Sisavangvong Rd, daily 0800-1800, admission at western steps 10,000 kip. If you want to watch the sun go down, get there early and jostle for position – don't expect to be the only person there.*

Directly opposite the Royal Palace is the start of the steep climb up Mount Phousi, the spiritual and geographical heart of the city and a popular place to come to watch the sunset over the Mekong, illuminating the hills to the east. Luang Prabang was probably sited at this point on the Mekong, in part at least, because of the presence of Phousi. Many capitals in the region are founded near sacred hills or mountains, which could become local symbols of the Hindu Mount Mahameru or Mount Meru, the abode of the gods and also the abode of local tutelary spirits.

As you start the ascent, to the right is **Wat Pa Huak**, a disused wat suffering from years of neglect. It is usually locked but, occasionally, monks will open the building up for a small donation. It is worth the trouble because the monastery has some fine 19th-century murals, depicting classic scenes along the Mekong. There are a few Buddha images here that date from the same period and a fine carved wooden mosaic on the temple's exterior, depicting Buddha riding Airavata, the three-headed elephant from Hindu mythology.

From Wat Pa Huak, 328 steps wind up Phousi, a gigantic rock with sheer forested sides, surmounted by a 25-m-tall *chedi*, **That Chomsi**. The *chedi* was constructed in 1804, restored in 1914 and is the designated starting point for the colourful Pi Mai (New Year) celebrations in April (see Festivals and events, page 125). Its shimmering gold-spired stupa rests on a rectangular base, ornamented by small metal Boddhi trees. Next to the stupa is a little sanctuary, from which the candlelit procession descends at New Year, accompanied by effigies of Nang Sang Kham, the guardian of the New Year, and naga, protector of the city. The drum, kept in the small *hor kong* on the east side of the hill, is used only on ceremonial occasions. The summit of Phousi affords a splendid panoramic view of Luang Prabang and the surrounding mountains. The Mekong lies to the north and west, with the city laid out to the southeast.

A path next to the *ack-ack* cannon leads down to **Wat Tham Phousi**, which is more like a car port than a temple, but which is home to a rotund Buddha, Kaccayana (also called Phra Ka Tiay). At the top of the steps leading out of the wat are two tall cacti, planted defiantly in the empty shell casings of two large US bombs – the local monks' answer to decades of war.

Luang Prabang detail

Mekong

Nam Khan

100 metres
100 yards

Sleeping
Ammata Guesthouse 20 *A3*
Apsara 1 *B4*
Bougnasouk Guesthouse 2 *A2*
Bounthieng Guesthouse 3 *A3*
Chantanome Guesthouse 4 *A2*
Kongsavath 18 *A3*
Le Calao Inn 5 *A4*
Merry Lao Swiss 6 *B1*
Oui Guesthouse 21 *B5*

Pack Luck 7 *A3*
Pa Phai 8 *A2*
Sala Luang Prabang 9 *A1*
Say Nam Khan 10 *B2*
Sayo Guesthouse 11 *A1*
Silichit Guesthouse 12 *A2*
Sok Dee Guesthouse 13 *A2*
Three Nagas 14 *B3*
Tum Tum Cheng 15 *A4*
Villa Santi 16 *B3*

Villa Santi Annexe 22 *B3*
Villa Savanh 17 *B3*

Eating
Blue Lagoon 21 *A1*
Café Ban Vat Sene 1 *B3*
Café des Arts 2 *B3*
Couleur Café 6 *A2*
Dao Fa 3 *B2*
Khemkhan Food Garden 5

Wat Siphouttabath (Wat Pha Phoutthabat)

Located down a path to the north of Wat Tham Phousi, just off the central road running along the promontory, is a compound containing three monasteries. Of them, **Wat Pa Khe** is most notable, predominantly for its carvings of 17th-century Dutch and Italian traders. Why these traders are depicted in a Buddhist temple in Luang Prabang remains a mystery, although many suspect it may have been influenced by trading merchants from the East India Company, who travelled through the area in the late 16th century. Behind the *sim* is a shrine housing a 3-m-long footprint of the Buddha. The shrine is normally only open during festive occasions, so you will need to ask someone on the premises for a key. Flanking the shrine is a small pavilion where Cambodia's former King Sihanouk entertained the press (in his usual publicity-centric fashion) during King Sisavang Vong's cremation ceremony.

Wat Xieng Muang and Wat Pha Phai

A block back from Sisavangvong Road is the old monastery site of **Wat Xieng Muang**. The *sim* here was constructed in 1879, although initial construction is believed to have started decades earlier. The temple features a few impressive sculptures and an imposing fresco of *nagas* on the ceiling. UNESCO has funded an artistic training centre for monks here to ensure that adequate skills are available to continue restoration work in the future. The novices are being taught the crafts of wood-carving, painting and Buddha-making. Also in the same block is **Wat Pha Phai**, called the Bamboo Monastery, although there isn't an overwhelming amount of bamboo in evidence. The *sim*, however, is decorated with colourful serpents and peacocks.

Wat Sene (Wat Saen)

Further up the promontory, Wat Sene was built in 1718 and was the first *sim* in Luang Prabang to be constructed in Thai style, with a yellow and red roof. The exterior may lack subtlety, but the interior is delicate and rather refined, painted red, with gold patterning on every conceivable surface. *Sen* means 100,000 and the wat was built with a local donation of 100,000 kip from someone who discovered 'treasure' in the Nam Khan river. At the far end of the wat compound is a building containing a large, gold, albeit rather crudely modelled, image of the Buddha in the 'calling for rain' *mudra* (standing, arms held stiffly down). Note the torments of hell depicted on the façade of the building (top, left). The temple was restored in 1932, with further renovations in 1957. One of Laos' most sacrosanct abbots, Ajahn Khamjan, was ordained at the temple in 1940.

Wat Xieng Thong

① *Xiengthong Rd, daily 0800-1700, admission 10,000 kip.*

Wat Xieng Thong Ratsavoraviharn, usually known as just Wat Xieng Thong, is set back from the road, at the top of a flight of steps leading down to the Mekong. It is arguably the finest example of a Lao monastery, with graceful, low-sweeping eaves, beautiful stone mosaics and intricate carvings. The wat

Northern Laos Luang Prabang & around

has several striking chapels, including one that houses a rare bronze reclining Buddha and another sheltering a gilded wooden funeral chariot. The back of the temple is encrusted with a stunning glass mosaic depicting a boddhi tree, while inside, resplendent gold-stencilled pillars support a ceiling with *dharma* wheels. The temple's tranquillity is further enhanced by beautiful gardens of bougainvillea, frangipani and hibiscus, shaded by banyan and palm trees.

This monastery was a key element in Luang Prabang's successful submission to UNESCO for recognition as a World Heritage Site. The striking buildings in the tranquil compound are decorated in gold and post-box red, with imposing tiled roofs, intricate carvings, paintings and mosaics, making this the most important and finest royal wat in Luang Prabang. It was built by King Setthathirat in 1559, and is one of the few buildings to have survived the successive Chinese raids that marked the end of the 19th century. It retained its royal patronage until 1975 and has been embellished and well cared for over the years: even the crown princess of Thailand, Mahachakri Sirindhorn, has donated funds for its upkeep.

The sim The *sim* is a perfect example of the Luang Prabang style, with its low, sweeping roof in complex overlapping sections. The roof is one of the temple's most outstanding features and is best viewed at a distance. Locals believe that the roof has been styled to resemble a bird, with wings stretched out to protect her young. The eight central wooden pillars have stencilled motifs in gold and the façade is finely decorated. The beautiful gold-leaf inlay is predominantly floral in design but a few images illustrate Ramayana-type themes and the interior stencils depict *dharma* wheels and the enigmatic King Chantaphanit.

In an ancient form of the modern-day Mousetrap game, a serpent-like aqueduct sits above the right-hand side of the main entrance. During Lao New Year water is poured into the serpent's tail, causing it to gush along to its mouth and tip onto the Buddha image below. The water then filters down a drain, flowing under the floor and eventually spouting out of the mouth of the mirrored elephant on the exterior wall.

At the rear of the *sim* is a mosaic representation of the thong copper 'Tree of Life' in glass inlay. This traditional technique can also be seen on the 17th-century doors of That Ingheng, near Savannakhet in central Laos (see page 207).

Side chapels Behind the *sim* are two red *hor song phra* (side chapels): the one on the left is referred to as **La Chapelle Rouge** (the Red Chapel) and houses a rare Lao reclining Buddha in bronze, dating from the 16th century, which was shown at the 1931 Paris Exhibition. The image was kept in Vientiane and only returned to Luang Prabang in 1964. Several other Buddha images, of varying styles, dates, and materials, surround the altar. The exterior mosaics on the *hor song phra*, which relate local tales, were added in 1957 to honour the 2500th anniversary of the Buddha's birth, death and enlightenment. Somewhat unusually, the fresco features a heroic character from local Lao folklore, Siaw Sawat. The other *hor song phra*, to the right of the *sim*, houses a standing image of the Buddha which is paraded through the streets of the city each New Year and doused in water. A small stone chapel with an ornate roof stands to the left of the *sim*.

Chapel of the Funeral Chariot The **hor latsalot** (chapel of the funeral chariot) is diagonally across from the *sim* and was built in 1962. The centrepiece is the grand 12-m-high gilded wooden hearse, with its seven-headed serpent, which was built for King Sisavang Vong, father of the last sovereign, and used to carry his urn to the stadium next to Wat That Luang (see below) where he was cremated in 1959. It was built on the chassis of a six-wheel truck by the sculptor Thid Tan. On top of the carriage sit several sandalwood urns, none of which contain royal ashes. Originally the urns would have held the bodies of the deceased in a foetal position until cremation. The mosaics inside the chapel were never finished but the exterior is decorated with some almost erotic scenes from the *Ramakien* (or local *Ramayana*), sculpted in enormous panels of teak wood and covered with gold leaf. Glass cabinets feature several puppets that were once used in royal performances.

Other structures The **Tripitaka Library**, near the boat shelter, was added in 1828. The **hor kong** at the back of the garden was constructed in the 1960s and near it is the site of the copper tree, from which Wat Xieng Thong took its name.

Wat Pak Khan

At the far northeast end of Phothisarath Road is Wat Pak Khan, which is not particularly noteworthy other than for its scenic location overlooking the confluence of the two rivers. It is sometimes called the Dutch Pagoda, as the sculptures on the south door are of figures dressed in 18th- and 19th-century Dutch costume.

The Pra Bang was housed here from 1507 to 1715 and again from 1867 to 1894.

Wat Visunnarat (Wat Wisunarat)

ⓘ *Daily 0800-1700, admission 10,000 kip.*

This is better known as Wat Visoun and is on the south side of Mount Phousi. It is a replica of the original wooden building, constructed in 1513, which had been the oldest building in Luang Prabang, until it was destroyed by marauding Chinese tribes. Louis Delaporte's sketches from the 1860s show the original temple as boat- or coffin-shaped. The wat was rebuilt in 1898 and, in keeping with the original style, renovators tried to ensure that the brick and stucco construction resembled the original medieval shapes of the lathed wood. The arch on the northwest side of the *sim* is original and the only remaining piece of the 16th-century building.

The *sim* is virtually a museum of religious art, with numerous 'Calling to the Rain' Buddha statues: most are more than 400 years old and have been donated by locals. One of the biggest philanthropists was Prince Phetsarat who donated them in order to redeem the temple after the Haw invasion. Wat Visoun also contains the largest Buddha in the city and old stelae engraved with Pali scriptures (called *hiu chaluk*).

The big stupa, commonly known as **That Makmo** ('melon stupa'), was built by Queen Visunarat in 1504. It is of Sinhalese influence with a smaller stupa at each corner, representing the four elements. The stupa originally contained hundreds of small Buddha images, many of which were pilfered by the Haw. The remaining images were relocated to the Royal Museum for safe-keeping.

Wat Aham

ⓘ *Next door to Wat Visoun, daily 0800-1700, admission 10,000 kip.*

Wat Aham was built by a relative of the king in 1823 and, before Wat Mai took over, Wat Aham was the residence of the Supreme Patriach of Lao Buddhism, Sangkharat. The interior has rather beautiful pillars and roof and overbearing modern murals of the torments of hell, as well as a panoramic view of Luang Prabang. The two huge banyan trees outside are important spirit shrines.

Wat Phra Maha That

Close to the **Hotel Phousi** on Phothisarath Road, this is a typical Luang Prabang wat, built in the 1500s and restored at the beginning of this century. The ornamentation of the doors and windows of the *sim* merit attention, with their graceful, golden figures from the *Phra lak phra lam* (the *Ramayana*). The pillars, ornamented with massive *nagas*, are also in traditional Luang Prabang style and reminiscent of certain styles adopted in Thailand. The front of the *sim* was renovated in 1991. The monastery contains a stupa, holding the ashes of Prince Phetsarat and his younger brother Prince Souvanna Phouma.

Wat Phra Bath

Behind the market at the far northwest end of Phothisarath Road is Wat Phra Bath (or Phraphoutthabat Tha Phralak). The original wooden temple on this site dated back to the 17th century but most of the present structure was built in 1959 by the local Chinese and Vietnamese community. It certainly doesn't evoke the grandeur of other temples in town but is worth a visit for its picturesque position above the Mekong. It is renowned for its huge Buddha footprint – 'bath' is the Pali word for footprint.

Wat That Luang

Close by, behind the stadium, on Phou Vao Rd, is Wat That Luang. Rumour suggests that the original structure was built by Indian missionaries, although this is probably no more than hearsay as all evidence suggests that the royal wat was built in 1818 by King Manthaturat. Note the bars on the windows of the *sim* in wood and gold leaf, typical of Luang Prabang. The gold stupa, at one end of the compound, was built in 1910 and contains the ashes of King Sisavang Vong and his brother. King Sisavang Vong is remembered fondly in the city and many offerings are left here. The stone stupa contains relics of the Buddha and is the site of the Vien Thiene (candlelit) festival in May (see Festivals and events, page 125). There are also some traditional style *kuti*, or monks' quarters, with carved windows and low roofs.

When James McCarthy visited Wat Luang at the end of the 19th century, he was told of the ceremonies that were performed here on the accession of a new 'chief'. In his book *Surveying and exploring in Siam* (1900) he writes that the "Kamus assembled and took the oath of allegiance, swearing to die before their chief; shot arrows over the throne to show how they would fight any of its enemies, and holding a lighted candle, prayed that their bodies might be run through with hot iron and that the sky might fall and crush them if they proved unfaithful to their oaths".

Wat Manolom

South of Wat That Luang (between Phou Vao and Kisarath Settathirat), Wat Manolom was built by the nobles of Luang Prabang to entomb the ashes of King Samsenthai (1373-1416) and is notable for its large armless bronze Buddha statue, one of the oldest Lao images of the Buddha, which dates back to 1372 and weighs two tonnes. Locals maintain that the arm was removed during a skirmish between Siamese and French forces during the latter part of the 19th century. The Lao have unsuccessfully replaced the missing appendage with a concrete prosthetic. The monastery has an attractive weathered look and the usual carved doors and painted ceilings. While it is not artistically significant, the temple – or at least the site – is thought to be the oldest in the city, dating back, so it is said, to 1375 and the reign of Fa Ngum. Close by are the ruins of an even older temple, **Wat Xieng Kang**, which dates back to 1363.

Wat Pa Phon Phao and Wat Phra That Chedi

ⓘ *3 km out of town to the northeast, near Ban Phanom, daily 0800-1000 and 1300-1630, donation expected.*

Outside town, **Wat Pa Phon Phao** is a forest meditation centre renowned for the teachings of its famous abbot, Ajahm Saisamut, one of the most popular monks in Lao history. Better known to tourists, though, is **Wat Phra That Chedi**, known as the Peace Pagoda. It looks as though it is made of pure gold from a distance and it occupies a fantastic position. The wat's construction, funded by donations from Lao living abroad and from overseas Buddhist federations, was started in 1959 but was only completed in 1988; the names of donors are inscribed on pillars inside. It is modelled on the octagonal Shwedagon Pagoda in Yangon (Rangoon) and its inner walls are festooned with gaily painted frescoes of macabre allegories. The lurid illustrations depict the fate awaiting murderers, adulterers, thieves, drunks and liars who break the five golden

❧ *The small huts to the right of the entrance are meditation cells or 'kutis'.*

document the life of the Buddha. On the second level, it is possible to duck through a
tiny opening to admire the Blue Indra statues and the view of Luang Prabang.

Traditional Arts and Ethnology Centre

ⓘ *Ban Khamyong, T071-253364, www.taeclaos.org, Tue-Sun 0900-1800, 20,000 kip.*
This fantastic museum is dedicated to the various ethnic groups in Laos. It is a
non-profit centre with a permanent exhibition featuring photographs, religious
artefacts, clothing, household objects and handicrafts. Within the exhibition there is
a focus on the Hmong and their New Year celebrations; the Khmu and their baskets
and art of backstrap looms; the Mien Yao embroidery and Lanten Taoist religious
ceremonies; the Tai Dam bedding and Tai Lue culture. This museum really is worth a
visit – particularly for anyone who is venturing further north to go trekking. Attached to
the centre is a handicraft shop that directly supports ethnic artisan communities.
There's also a café and a small library.

...ectural tour of Luang Prabang

→ *Numbers in the text are marked on the map below.*

In a town as small as Luang Prabang, it is easy enough just to set out and find your
own route. However, we have provided a walking tour that takes in Luang Prabang's
architectural highlights (secular as well as religious). It concentrates on the peninsula
and the streets that form the original core of the city. The route and the most
interesting buildings are shown on the map below. ⟫ *For a guide to the secular architectural*
styles described in this tour, see page 112.

The start of the tour is on Thanon Phothisarath in front of the **Royal Palace (1**; see
page 103). Historically, the area to the west of the palace was considered the noble
quarter of town, the east was inhabited by the middle classes, while the working class
lived around the foot of Phousi. Walking from the Royal Palace along Phothisarath
Road southwest towards the post office, look out for the **traditional Lao house (2)** in

Luang Prabang walking tour

Royal Palace **1**	Wat Xieng Muang **8**	Calao Inn **16**
Traditional Lao house **2**	Traditional Lao house **9**	Lao houses with French
Gendarmerie **3**	Compartment buildings **10**	colonial influence **17**
Lao Bank **4**	French colonial	School of Fine Arts **18**
Lao-French colonial	school **11**	French colonial
house **5**	Villa Santi Hotel **12**	hospital **19**
Lao-French colonial	Villa Savanh **13**	Lao-French colonial
house **6**	Wat Xieng Thong **14**	buildings **20**
Royal Taxes office **7**	Bamboo house **15**	Maison Souvannaphoum **21**

100 metres
100 yards

A guide to Luang Prabang's secular buildings

Traditional Lao The traditional Lao house is rectangular, supported on timber stilts, with a two-sided steep roof and built of bamboo, wood or daub. The stilts help to protect the occupants against wild animals at night and also help to keep the living area dry, especially during the rainy season. The underside also provides a shaded spot for working during the day, as well as area for storage. Living above ground is said to be a characteristic of the Lao and a 16th-century Lao text, the Nithan Khun Borom, records that the Lao and Vietnamese Kingdoms of Lane Xang and Dai Viet agreed to demarcate their respective zones of influence according to house style: people living in houses raised on stilts would owe allegiance to Lane Xang, those living on the ground, to Dai Viet.

The traditional Lao house is divided into three principal sections, recognizable from the exterior: the sleeping room, the veranda, and the kitchen. Under the main roof is the sleeping area and the very characteristic veranda is contiguous to it. The kitchen is linked to the main building by an open deck commonly used for bathing and washing. Roof, gables, rafters and balustrade are ornamented with lots of savoir-faire. The building process of traditional Lao houses was governed by strict rules: its orientation, the date when building could commence, the setting of the wooden piles, and so on, had to conform to spiritual guidelines.

French colonial The French introduced new technologies and materials into house construction, in particular the fired brick and the ceramic roof tile. Traditionally, these materials were reserved for wat construction – explaining why almost all buildings of pre-colonial vintage in Laos today are religious. The main characteristics of French colonial architecture are: extensive roof area to protect against sun and rain; large window openings, paned and shuttered; verandas; arcades; a monumental entrance; a fireplace and chimney breast; brick and wooden decorative details expressing different construction systems (for instance, columns, capitals, rafters and lintels) and ceramic roof tiles.

front of Wat Mai. This is a construction on stilts with a closed veranda. Continuing along Phothisarath Road, the former French colonial **Gendarmerie** (**3**) – now the information and culture department – is on your left, with gables on the façade. There's another example of a French colonial building, the **Lao Bank** (**4**), on your right.

Turn right onto Kittsarath Setthathirat Road and walk down towards the Mekong. Past the post office, on the right, is a **Lao house showing French colonial influences** (**5**). Take the first road on your right to see more examples of traditional Lao houses. In some cases the formerly open ground level area has been enclosed to increase the habitable space, using a variety of different materials: bricks, wood and bamboo, for example. (This is also very common in Thailand. Traditionally the under-house area was used for weaving and lounging during the hottest hours of the day. At night, animals were corralled under the house to keep them safe. Fires were also lit here at night at the coldest times of year.)

At the very end of this street, just beside the Royal Palace, are two opulent **Lao-French colonial-style houses** (**6**). Turn left to reach the Mekong River road and then right to walk along the riverbank. The **Royal Taxes office** (**7**), now operating as a tourism company, lies behind the Royal Palace. It is decorated with the classic three-headed elephant insignia. To see some truly beautiful examples of traditional

Lao-French colonial As French influence grew, so Lao builders began to incorporate some aspects of French design into their constructions. For example, some houses which in all other respects conform to the traditional Lao house style, have French openings and a grandiose doorway leading to a flight of impressive stairs.

French colonial-Lao In the same way as Lao builders adopted some French elements, so French architects and builders embraced Lao stylistic features. This is most evident in the use of temple-style ornamentation, on the roof for example.

International-modern Many houses are now built of concrete and the bungalow has become common. In many cases, traditional Lao architectural motifs and designs are merely made from concrete rather than the traditional wood. But concrete has also allowed some innovations in design: cantilevers, flat roofing, pre-fabricated elements and geometric ornamentation are all linked in part to the change in building medium from wood and bamboo, to concrete. 'International modern' includes both domestic buildings and compartments (shophouses).

Lao contemporary

Lao contemporary houses tend to fall into two categories. Either they are respectful of traditional Lao style; or they embrace modern design and construction materials wholesale. Houses in the first category can be seen to be part of an evolution of the traditional Lao house: the main entrance has shifted to the gable side, the veranda is smaller, while the open area between the piles below the main house is enclosed with brick or concrete walls and has physically become part of the house. Wood is still used for exterior facing for the first floor, but the walls of the ground level floor are made from stone and bricks. This is the most common form of house built today.

The second category of Lao contemporary house is built entirely of brick and concrete and most Lao consider it to be more luxurious.

architecture, enter **Wat Xieng Muang** (**8**; see page 107) and take the exit into the alley behind the temple. Opposite the wat is a **traditional Lao house** (**9**).

Continue up to Phothisarath Road, turn left and take a look at the **compartment buildings** (**10**) on both sides of the street. These skillfully combine commercial and residential functions under the same roof, much like the Chinese 'shophouse' found throughout Southeast Asia, in which the ground floor serves as a business, shop or workshop. The Lao traditionally never lived and worked in the same building; they always ran their businesses from some other location, even if it was a street-side stall just a few yards away from their home. It is therefore safe to assume that these 'compartments' were used by Chinese and Vietnamese immigrants. They are built in a variety of styles, mainly French colonial and Lao-French colonial.

Walking on towards the tip of the peninsula, there are several other notable buildings, including the **French colonial school** (**11**) and the **Villa Santi Hotel** (**12**), on the left-hand side of the road, and **Villa Savanh** (**13**), a traditional Lao compartment building on the right. At **Wat Xieng Thong** (**14**; see page 107) take the exit from the monastery on the east side to look at the modest **bamboo house** (**15**) down the alley.

At the tip of the peninsula, turn back along the Mekong River road. On the left is the **Calao Inn** (**16**), an example of a renovated colonial building and the only Portuguese building on the peninsula. Immediately after the inn, take the first road on your left and then turn right. Along this road, at the first intersection, are two very fine **Lao houses** showing **French colonial influences (17)**. Past the intersection further along the same street, the **School of Fine Arts (18)** is one of few Lao traditional-style buildings in Luang Prabang, with two adjoining roofs. Return to the Mekong River road along which are a number of buildings showing various degrees of international influence.

Cross the peninsula to the Nam Khan river road and then follow the road south around Phousi. Along the road are a number of examples of Lao traditional and Lao-French colonial buildings. On Rathsavong Street is the **French colonial hospital (19)**. Further along, turn right towards Nam Phou. This street has a number of **Lao-French colonial buildings (20)**, showing French influences on Lao architecture. Follow the road until it reaches the **Maison Souvannaphoum (21)** on the left. Take a minute to have a look at the main building (not the new annexes), which was built in 1962 in a modern French-colonial style. The tour ends north of here at the post office.

West bank of the Mekong 🛏 ›› *pp119-131.*

The monasteries and villages on the right bank of the Mekong are accessible by boat from Luang Prabang. For anyone who does not fancy spending three hours on a boat travelling to and from the Pak Ou caves, this makes for an enchanting alternative excursion. Also on the right bank are two hills, **Phou Thao** and **Phou Nang**, named after Luang Prabang's very own Romeo and Juliet. Thao Phouthasene and Nang Kang Hi were two lovers who died in tragic but romantic circumstances only to find themselves transformed into rock and incorporated in the local landscape. The hills are said to look like a man and woman sleeping next to each other.

Ins and outs

It is simpler to explore sights outside the city with a tour operator, as roads are unmarked and rural communities are less used to tourists. Many hotels organize trips. Boats run from the boat pier downstream from the Royal Palace to the other side of the river, near Wat Long Khoun or Ban Xiang Men, 35,000 kip return. If you can't find a boat here, try the pier behind the Royal Palace. Remember to fix a return time with the ferryman. Ferries also run irregularly across the river for 2500 kip. ›› *For further details, see Tour operators, page 127, and Transport, page 129.*

Wat Long Khoun
ⓘ *Daily 0800-1700, admission 5000 kip for foreigners.*
The first stop is usually Wat Long Khoun at the top of a flight of steps leading up from the riverbank, almost opposite Wat Xieng Thong. This wat was built in two stages and

Excursions from Luang Prabang

was renovated by the École Française de l'Extrême-Orient in January 1994 at a cost of FF400,000. The oldest section is at the back and dates from the 18th century. The beautifully sculpted door was made in 1937. The *sim* on the river side of the compound is a delightful building, small, well-proportioned and intimate. It has some vibrant but fading Jataka murals. On the exterior, either side of the main doorway, are two bearded warriors, with swords slung over their backs, that seem to be representations of Chinese Haw soldiers. The kings of Lane Xang are said to have come on three-day retreats to this spot, to prepare for their coronation.

Wat Tham

ⓘ *100 m upstream from Wat Long Khoun, daily 0800-1700, admission 5000 kip.*
A well-trodden path leads upstream to Wat Tham, literally 'cave monastery', nestled in Sakkarin Savannakuha cave, above a dilapidated sala. The wat is a limestone cave temple with stairs and balustrades cut out of the stone. The interior is very dark but is worth exploring, as it is stacked with ancient, rotting Buddha images. During Pi Mai celebrations the temple comes alive with pilgrims, candles and those coming to worship the images in the masses. A resident monk, with the aid of dim torches, will lead visitors down into the airless cavern pointing out rock formations and Buddha images. Fearful that the torches may not be powered by long life batteries, visitors may emerge into the light with a degree of relief. Not for the claustrophobic. If the cave is locked ask someone at Wat Long Khoun to let you in.

Wat Chom Phet and Wat Xiang Men

Leading from Wat Long Khoun downstream is another well-trodden track. Before reaching the small community of Ban Xiang Men, a stairway leads up to **Wat Chom Phet** ⓘ *entry 5000 kip*, a hilltop *sim* offering fine views over the Mekong and Luang Prabang. The site has been apparently abandoned as a religious site, although the mouldering *sim*, kiltering *chedis* and profusion of apricot-coloured lilies give the place a rather attractive 'lost wat in the forest' feel. It also enjoys a perfect view at sunset.

Continuing downstream, the track passes through **Ban Xiang Men**, a peaceful village where households cultivate the exposed riverbanks during the dry season, taking advantage of the annual deposition of silt. **Wat Xiang Men** was originally built in 1592 by Chau Naw Kaewkumman, son of Setthathirat, and has undergone extensive renovations since. The doors date from the original construction, as do several artefacts within the wat. This temple is particularly sacred to local residents because the Pra Bang was located here for a week when it first returned to Luang Prabang from Vientiane in 1867. About 1 km downstream, in a clearing in the middle of the forest, is the **royal cemetery**. There are sculptures depicting those members of the royal family who could not be cremated for religious reasons, such as children who died as infants and victims of contagious diseases. It is hard to find a local guide willing to take you there as most are terrified of ghosts.

Ban Chan

Ban Chan is on the northern bank of the Mekong, 5 km downstream from Luang Prabang (about 15 minutes by boat; US$6) or 4 km on the road beyond the evening market to Ban Sangkhalok and a short crossing by boat (villagers will paddle you across). The village is known for its local pottery industry and mostly produces thongs (large water storage jars) and salt pots. Boats regularly cross the river – although the fare varies depending on the number of passengers. You can charter a boat from the main pier on the Mekong for a couple of hours (about 70,000 kip). It is possible to cross over to Wat Long Khoun, walk downstream and catch another boat back to the Luang Prabang bank of the river either at Ban Xiang Men or Ban Chan. Or the circuit can be completed in the reverse direction. There are a couple of food stalls in Ban Xiang Men.

Tad Hoykhua

Hoykhua Waterfall is 14 km west of Luang Prabang in Ban Pakleung. The beautiful two-tiered cascades plummet 50 m, with a deep pool at the bottom. There are several Hmong and Khmu villages in the vicinity. To get to the falls cross the Mekong by boat at Tha Heua (boat station) in Luang Prabang to Xiang Men Village and then travel the rest by road. There are three bungalows here at **Tad Hoykhua Guesthouse** (T020-5570825).

East of the city ⓐ ➤ *pp119-131.*

Ban Phanom and around

Ban Phanom, or Tit Cliff Village, is 6 km east of Luang Prabang. This is a 300-year-old weaving village, where shawls (*pha biang*) and sarongs (*pha sin*) are made from silk

> ❦ *A trip to this village can be combined with a visit to Phra That Kong Chedi and Henri Mouhot's tomb. A tuk-tuk to all three will cost US$8-9 return.*

and cotton. Although best known for its weaving, the village's main economic activity is rice cultivation. The 100 or so families in Ban Phanom are members of the Lue minority, who originated from Yunnan in southern China. They were traditionally the king's weavers, soldiers and palace servants. King Sisavang Vong's dancers were traditionally hand-picked from this village at the age of six or seven and were required to undergo intensive training aimed at increasing their flexibility.

A few years ago cloth was sold from a street market in the middle of the village. However, some of the larger producers have turned their houses into small shops and it is now possible to buy lengths of cloth at any time. Tourists are more than welcome to wander around and look at the process of silk manufacture, from the silk worm's inception to finish, with the weavers clacking away at their looms. The village has turned into somewhat of a tourist trap and those looking for a bargain might be disappointed to find that the silk is almost the same price as in town.

The French explorer Henri Mouhot stumbled across Angkor Wat in 1860 but succumbed to a malarial attack in Luang Prabang on 10 November the following year: his last journal entry read, "Have pity on me, O my God". Resident foreign aid workers spent months searching for his grave before rediscovering it in 1990, 2 km beyond Ban Phanom, at the top of a bank looking down into the Nam Khan, a tributary of the Mekong. **Henri Mouhot's tomb**, 3 km from Ban Phanom, was constructed six years after his death, in 1867, and was designed by another French explorer, Doudart de Lagrée. The town of Mouhot's birth, Montbéliard, donated a plaque inscribed simply, 'Proud of Our Son', and the French government has granted an allowance for the tomb's upkeep. When going to the tomb on foot, bicycle or motorbike, follow the road along the river until you see the sign and turn left; follow this path for a further 300 m. It is also possible to get a boatman to take you the extra kilometres for a couple of dollars. If you are unsure ask villagers in Ban Phanom for directions; children will sometimes show visitors the way.

Ban Hat Hien

This village is on the airport road; fork right before the terminal and at the end of the road is Luang Prabang's knife-making village. Residents beat scrap metal over hot stoves to make blades and tools. The flames are fanned by bellows, originally made from teak tubes and operated with plungers; several craftsmen use old 155-mm Howitzer propellants and say their "little presents from the US come in very handy". One shed is stacked with hundreds of old car batteries from which the lead is extracted and poured into moulds for ball bearings and gunshot. The results of their labours can be seen in the markets in town. From the nearby Nam Khan, villagers harvest 'seaweed', which is dried, fried and eaten with sesame in a dish known as *khai pehn*; it is sold all over the country.

Pak Ou caves

The Pak Ou caves are perhaps the most popular excursion from Luang Prabang and are located 25 km upstream from the city, set in a limestone cliff opposite the mouth of the Nam Ou tributary (Pak Ou means 'Mouth of the Ou'). The two caves are studded with thousands of wood and gold Buddha images – 2500 in the lower cave and 1500 in the upper – and are one of the main venues for Pi Mai in April, when hundreds make the pilgrimage upriver from Luang Prabang. During the dry season the river shrinks, exposing huge sandbanks, which are improbable gold fields. Families camp out on the banks of the Mekong and pan for gold, most of which is sold to Thailand.

Ins and outs

Many restaurants, hotels, guesthouses and tour companies in Luang Prabang will arrange this boat trip, which is the best way to reach the caves. Otherwise, boats can be chartered from Tha Heua Me or from one of the stairways leading down to the river along Manthatourath, where boatmen wait for business. The going rate for the journey – about two hours upstream and one hour down with stops en route – is US$10-15. Boats vary in size but the larger ones can take up to eight people. Long-tailed boats also depart from the pier in Luang Prabang and charge US$25 for up to five people. Boats will often stop at Xang Hai (see below) and Ban Pak Ou, across the water from the caves, where enterprising villages have set up thatched stalls serving sticky rice, barbecued Mekong fish and *somtam*, plus cold drinks and snacks. Although rest houses, tables and a basic toilet have been built below the upper cave, there is no restaurant and no drinks stall at the caves themselves.

Background

The two sacred caves were supposedly discovered by King Setthathirat in the 16th century but it is likely that the caverns were associated with spirit (*phi*) worship before the arrival of Buddhism in Laos. For years the caves, which locals still believe to be the home of guardian spirits, were inhabited by monks. The king visited them every New Year, staying at Ban Pak Ou on the opposite bank of the Mekong, where there is a royal wat with beautiful old murals on the front gable. The famous French traveller, Francis Garnier, also visited the caves on his travels in the 1860s.

Some of the Buddha images in the caves are thought to be more than 300 years old, although most date from the 18th and 19th centuries. In the past, gold and silver images were in abundance but these have all been stolen; now the Buddha images are crafted from wood, copper or stone. Both the caves and the many Buddhas they contain were restored with Australian funds but since the Australian government completed its conservation project in 1998, theft has been a chronic problem, particularly between 2001 and 2002, when hundreds of statues were stolen and sold to Thai antique dealers and tourists in Luang Prabang.

Exploring the caves

① *Admission US$1, free for children*. Torches are available but candles make it possible to see reasonably well after your eyes have become accustomed to the dark. The lower cave, really a deep overhang, is named **Tham Thing**, while the upper, an enervating climb up 100 or so slippery steps, is called **Tham Phum**. A carved wooden frieze, supporting two massive wooden doors flanks the entrance. Aside from the numerous Buddha images, the cave features a statue of one of Buddha's disciples and a carved wooden water channel for the ceremonial washing of the sculptures. The cave is around 54 m long and the sculptures range from 10 cm to 1.5 m in height. Many of the images are in the distinctive attitude of the Buddha calling for rain (with arms held by the side, palms turned inwards).

Xang Hai is 20 km upstream from Luang Prabang, on the way to Pak Ou caves and a popular stop-off. The name of this village translates as 'making wine pots'. In the rainy season the villages grow glutinous or 'sticky' rice and in the dry season they

> **❗** *Lao for 'cheers' is seung dium!*

ferment it in water and yeast to brew *lao-lao*, a moonshine whisky, which is sold illegally in Luang Prabang. The village has now become rather touristy, with scores of stalls selling textiles, ceramics, souvenirs from Thailand, opium pipes and weights, ethnic clothes, and some *lao-lao* too. Villagers are delighted to give visitors a tasting session.

South of the city ⊖ ⤞ *pp119-131.*

Tad Sae

Seventeen kilometres (one hour) south of Luang Prabang are the beautiful multi-tiered, limestone cascades of Tad Sae, which make for a great half-day trip during the rainy season. (In the dry season, the waterfall is reduced to a mere trickle.) The falls sit at the confluence of the Huay Say and Nam Khan rivers and feature a multitude of crystal-clear swimming holes, similar to Kwang Si but on a smaller scale. They are not as touristy as Kwang Si and offer greater privacy. To get there, head south along Route 13 for 17 km and turn off for Ban En (signposted); follow this track for 2 km. From the village you can hire a boat for around US$1 to take you to the falls. Food stalls and facilities are also available. A tuk-tuk from Luang Prabang will cost about US$8-9.

Tad Kwang Si

ⓘ *30 km south Luang Prabang; admission 20,000 kip, parking 2500 kip.*

These waterfalls are 30 km south of Luang Prabang on a tributary of the Mekong. The trip to the falls is almost as scenic as the cascades themselves, passing through small Hmong and Khmu villages and vivid green, terraced rice paddies. Travel agents run tours to the falls or you can charter a tuk-tuk for about US$15 return (make sure you agree how long you want to spend at the falls). Slow boats take one hour down and two hours back up river, via **Ban Muang Khai** (a pretty little village), where it is necessary to take a tuk-tuk the last 6 km or so to the falls. A third possibility is to take a speedboat from either Tha Leua Sing Kaeo (about 3 km downstream from Luang Prabang) or Ban Don, a few kilometres upstream.

The falls are stunning beautiful, misty cascades flowing over limestone formations, which eventually collect in several tiered, turquoise pools. In 2003 a large section of the limestone cliff collapsed, so the falls are a little shorter these days but just as scenic. Originally the waterfall's surroundings were inhabited by numerous animals, including the deer that give the falls their name, Kwang Si. However, the only wildlife you're likely to see today is Phet the tiger and some Asiatic black bears, rescued from poachers, in enclosures halfway between the entrance and the falls. The United Nations Development Programme (UNDP) has cleared a path to the falls which winds right up to the top. The bottom level of the falls has been turned into a park and viewing area, with a small platform that affords good photo opportunities. The local village's economy seems increasingly to depend on the tourist business, so you'll find a large number of vendors selling snacks and drinks and some souvenirs. The site also has public toilets and changing rooms.

Although the waterfall is impressive year round, in the summer, the water cascades so gently over the various tiers of the falls that it's possible to scramble behind the curtains of water without getting wet. In the rainy season, the gallons of water roaring down the mountain catch the imagination and could form the backdrop for any Indiana Jones or James Bond adventure. Best of all, and despite appearances, it's still possible to take the left-hand path halfway up the falls and strike out through the pouring torrents and dripping caves to the heart of the waterfall. Exhilarating and highly recommended. The pools above the falls are sheltered and comparatively private and make a wonderful spot for a swim; the second tier is best for a dip. If you follow the water either upstream or downstream there are plenty of other shady swimming spots. Note that swimming is only permitted in designated pools and, as the Lao swim fully clothed, you should wear modest swimwear and bring a sarong.

Hmong villages

There are numerous Hmong villages within a shortish distance of Luang Prabang and on the way to Kwang Si falls. Hmong children will usually come out on the road and stop your vehicle to sell you wristbands or embroidery. It is better to buy something from them than to give them cash or lollies. ▸▸ *For more information about the Hmong, see page 304.*

Ban Longlan is east of town. To get there, take the main road upstream. At Ban Pak Xuang, just before the bridge over the river Xuang, turn right to follow this tributary of the Mekong. Just before reaching Ban Kokvan turn right onto a track to Ban Natan. From here an even smaller track leads off to the left. It follows the Houei Hia, a small stream, between two mountains and works its way upwards to the mountain village of Ban Longlan. Allow two hours to get there. Few tourists visit this village so dress modestly and be especially sensitive to local sensibilities. In the rainy season you will need a trail bike or 4WD to get there.

Another Hmong village downstream from Luang Prabang is **Ban Long Lao** (one hour by tuk-tuk, US$15). Take the road southwest from town and after about 8 km turn left (after Ban Lekpet and before Ban Naxao). At the radio transmitter, continue straight ahead (rather than turning right to a waterfall). The road climbs steeply, passing a small dam and ends at the village of Long Lao. Again this is a village rarely visited by tourists. ▸▸ *For more details of how to get to the villages, see Transport, page 129.*

● Sleeping

Luang Prabang *p98, maps p102 and p106*
Accommodation in Luang Prabang continues to expand at the rate of knots. There were a few new places in development at the time of publication worth keeping an eye out for, in particular a new hotel from the **Aman** chain (www.amanresorts.com) which will be in the old hospital and will probably be completed in 2008.

The restored colonial villas on the peninsula and along Phou Vao tend to get booked up, particularly during national holidays, so, if you are thinking of plumping for an upper-range hotel, it is advisable to arrange accommodation in advance. Around Lao New Year, hotels and guesthouses can almost charge what they like but in the wet season, prices tend to be a lot lower, with most smaller establishments quoting approximately half the price given here and more expensive hotels generally knocking

off about 20%. For the more upmarket hotels, check their websites, as internet rates are usually cheaper than rack rates. Also contact **Lao Airlines** as they usually have deals with some of the top-notch hotels. Advance bookings are recommended at all times except the wet season.

There are plenty of hurriedly constructed budget guesthouses springing up all the time, particularly in the narrow streets between the post office and the river and now also inland from Phothisarath Rd. However, many of them are distinctly mediocre and the older ones tend to get run down pretty quickly. New establishments can be found on the tip of the peninsula heading towards Wat Xieng Thong and in the quiet streets around Phou Vao.

LL La Résidence Phou Vao, on a hill slightly out of town, T071-2125303, www.residence phouvao.com. Best hotel in town by a mile. Every little detail in this plush hotel is perfect, from the fragrance of frangipani that wafts through the foyer, to the beautiful, carefully lit infinity pool with lines of lamps. Massive, beautiful rooms with lounge area, fresh fruit and a simply divine bathroom. A luxury hotel through and through. In the low season they drop their rates by about US$100.

L Three Nagas Boutique Hotel (Auberge les 3 Nagas) Sakkaline Rd, T071-253888, www.3nagas.com. Housed in a beautifully restored building, with an annex across the road, this boutique hotel is a running contender for best room in town. Attention to detail is what sets it apart: from the 4-poster bed covered with local fabrics to the large deep-set bathtub with natural handmade beauty products. Private balconies or rooms lead onto a stunning courtyard. There's a lovely sitting area in each room, plus traditional *torchis* walls and teak floors. Breakfast (included) is served in the fantastic café downstairs. Internet facilities for those travelling with laptop.

A Ancient Luang Prabang, Sisavangvong Rd, T071-212264, www.ancientluang prabang.com. 12 fantastically designed open-plan rooms featuring a big modern tub (separate toilet). The perfect romantic retreat for couples but not the place to bunk down with your mother. At US$65 these rooms represent good value. Lovely wooden furninshings. Café downstairs with Wi-Fi and a good range of coffees including frappés.

A Le Calao Inn, river road, T071-212100, www.calaoinn.laopdr.com. Enclosed by yellow walls, this Portuguese/French colonial (1902) building boasts beautiful rooms in an incomparable position overlooking the Mekong. The balcony view is a real plus, so ensure you ask for a room with water views.

A Maison Souvannaphoum, Phothisarath, T071-212200, www.coloursofangsana. com/souvannaphoum. Formerly Prince Souvanna's residence, this place really is fit for royalty. There are 4 spacious suites and 18 rooms, with a/c, aromatherapy burners and special treats left in the rooms. The service is top-notch.

A Pack Luck, opposite L'Éléphant, T071-253373, packluck@hotmail.com. This boutique hotel has 5 rooms that you couldn't swing a cat in but are tastefully decorated with beautiful fabrics and the bathrooms have deep slate bathtubs.

A Villa Maydou, set very close to the grounds of Wat Meuna, T071-254601, www.villamaydou.com. Slightly on the expensive side but beautiful nonetheless. The hotel has a very evocative Buddhist feel due to its location right on the doorstep of Wat Meuna. The French-owned hotel is set in restored government buildings, originally built in 1925. Spacious airy a/c rooms simply decorated in a modern style with modern bathtub, minibar.

A Villa Santi Hotel, Sisavangvong Rd, T071-252157, www.villasantihotel.com. Almost an institution in Luang Prabang, this is a restored house from the early 20th century that served as the private residence of the first King Sisavong's wife and then Princess Manilai. It's a charming place, full of character and efficiently run but it is starting to look a bit run down. There are 11 traditional rooms in the old building, each of a different size, and 14 newer rooms, with baths and showers, in a stylishly built annexe. The daughter of the official royal cook rustles up mouthwatering French cuisine in the **Princess Restaurant** and there are attractive seating areas in the garden, lobby or on the balcony.

A-B Le Parasol Blanc, Phou Vao Rd, T071-252194. A modern construction with teak finish houses 30 nicely decorated rooms, with minibar, surrounded by secluded, beautiful gardens.

A-B Manoluck (sometimes **Manoruck**), 14/3 Phou Vao Rd, T071-212250, Manoluck@laotel.com. Quasi-classical hotel. Rooms have good facilities (a/c, cable TV, minibar, polished wooden floors) but there's a surfeit of ostentatious furnishings in the lobby. Western/Asian restaurant. Credit cards accepted.

A-B Mouang Luang, Boun Khong Rd, T/F071-212790. Rather grandiose and lavish 2-storey reinterpretation of traditional Lao architecture. There are 35 beautifully decorated a/c rooms, with polished wooden floors, marble bathrooms and enthusiastic staff but it's starting to look a bit run down. Lao and European food in the

● *For an explanation of the eating and sleeping price codes used in this guide, see inside the*
● *front cover. Other relevant information is found in Essentials, see pages 29-32.*

restaurant, small kidney-shaped pool. Credit cards accepted.

A-B Sala Luang Prabang, 102/6 Ounkham Rd, T071-252460, www.salaprabang.salalao.com. Very chic, renovated 100-year-old building overlooking the Mekong. Nice use of exposed beams and stone inlay in communal areas. Rooms can be quite small, but have a minimalist, up-to-date edge with a/c and modern bathrooms and doors either opening onto a small courtyard or river balcony (more expensive). Bus, car, bicycle hire available.

A-B Tum Tum Cheng, off Sisavangvong Rd, T071-253262, tumtumcheng@yahoo.com. Large white building with murals lining the walls. Big rooms have local artefacts, a/c and hot water. A very tranquil atmosphere but perhaps a bit pricey at US$30 for a double.

A-C The Apsara, Kingkitsarath, T071-212420, www.theapsara.com. Ivan Scholte, wine connoisseur and antique collector, has done a perfect job on this establishment. It oozes style. The stunningly beautiful rooms are themed by colour, with 4-poster beds, changing screen, big bathtub and lovely balcony. Very romantic with a modern twist. The rooms in the second building are also magnificent with terrazzo showers you could fit an elephant in. The foyer and lovely restaurant (see Eating) are decorated with Vietnamese lanterns, Burmese offering boxes and modern art. Room rate includes breakfast. Ivan has some very exciting plans in the pipeline so watch this space. Get in early as it is popular and gets booked up in advance. Recommended.

A-C Merry Lao Swiss, Kingkitsarath Rd, T071-260211, samoraphouma@hotmail.com. Clean rooms with traditional-style furniture. Funky chequered floor. All have a/c, TV. Prices vary between US$20 and US$80 and include breakfast.

A-C Say Nam Khan, overlooking the river, T071-212976, saynamkhan_lp@hotmail.com. Attractive renovated building with a homely feel created by its friendly owners. White paint and wooden furnishings, clean a/c rooms, although the inner ones are quite dark. Private bathrooms and hot water. Sitting on the terrace overlooking the Nam Kham emphasizes the lovely setting. Very friendly and helpful. Often booked up.

A-C Sayo Guesthouse, Sotikoumman Rd, T071-252614, sayo@laotel.com. A lovely

hotel set in a colonial mansion. The front rooms are beautifully and tastefully decorated with local fabrics and woodwork, polished wooden floors and furniture, and they have a fantastic view over Wat Xieng Muang – you can watch the monks painting and woodworking. The back rooms aren't as good value but are still recommended.

B Ammata Guesthouse, T071-212175, phetmanyp@yahoo.com.au. Very popular guesthouse with largish rooms decorated simply and stylishly with wooden furniture and polished floorboards, hot water and en suite bathroom.

B Oui Guesthouse, at the end of the peninsula in Ban Khille on Sukkaserm, ouisguesthouse@gmail.com, T071-252374. Charming little guesthouse with sparkling new rooms and polished floorboards, hot water, TV and fridge. Nicely decorated with local artefacts. Fantastic wine bar next door.

B-C Muang Swa, Phou Vao Rd, T071-212192. A/c, restaurant, noisy disco. 17 reasonable rooms, with en suite bathrooms.

B-C New Luang Prabang Hotel, Sisavang-vong Rd, T071-212264, F071-212804. Rather an ugly building with 15 rooms over 4 floors, decorated with the odd piece of local tapestry. Rooms are liveable but a bit pricey. Free pickup to and from the airport.

B-D Ban Lao, Souvannaphoum Rd, T071-252078. An impressive white mansion with polished wooden floors. Large double rooms have en suite bathrooms and a/c; others have shared facilities. New annexe has reasonable, clean rooms with showers, hot water and satellite TV. Good value for money.

B-D Kongsavath Hotel, Ounkham Rd, T071-212994, khongsavath@hotmail.com. Nice clean guesthouse overlooking the Mekong, with comfy beds, a/c, hot water and lovely views from the window. Teak doors throughout this wonderful, restored building. Restaurant attached with good breakfast selection, stir-fry and drinks (US$2-3).

B-D Lane Xang, Visunnarat Rd, T071-212749. This attractive chalet-style hotel is run by **Lane Xang Travel Co**. Clean doubles with en suite bathroom and fridge. Good views of Wat Visunnarat.

B-D Silichit Guesthouse, just off Ounkham Rd, T071-212758. Despite the dubious sounding name, this clean guesthouse is excellent value and well located. The rooms are comfortable with fan, en suite bathroom and hot water. Very friendly owners can speak English and French, and often invite guests to sit down for a family dinner or have a Beer Lao. As with most budget places, its prices drop dramatically in the low season.

B-D Tam Tam, Sisavangvong Rd, T071-253300, chantavong@hotmail.com. You're paying for the great location here. The big rooms are reasonably good, with bathroom, hot water and a/c. Pay US$25 for a TV and fridge. Large restaurant attached with outdoor seating, serving a wide selection of drinks, big breakfast menu (around US$2-3), burgers, salads, spaghetti and some Lao food.

D Bougnasouk Guesthouse, Ounkham Rd, T071-212749. This riverfront guesthouse has rather cramped, fan-cooled rooms and en suite bathrooms with hot water. Lao restaurant serves exceptionally cheap Asian breakfast. A pungent odour of old pipe tobacco wafts through the place.

D Bounthieng Guesthouse, Khem Kong Rd, T071-252488, bounthiengsolo@yahoo.com. Riverside guesthouse with great communal balcony overlooking the river. Rooms are comfortable enough with fan and en suite bathrooms with hot water. Cheaper rooms have shared facilities. Pretty good value. Recommended.

D Chantanome Guesthouse, off Ounkham Rd, T020-770060. Neat rooms with fan and hot water. Very snazzy stone-inlay bathrooms.

D-E Boun Gning Guesthouse, 109/4 Ban That Luang, T071-212274. Attractive balcony, triples available, rooms are quite bare. Friendly and helpful English-speaking management.

E Mano Guesthouse, Phamahapasaman Rd, T071-253112. Clean, with a tiled ground floor and wooden upstairs, this place is a relaxed and charming, family-run option, offering some a/c. Ideal for chess enthusiasts, as a large chess set is carved into one of the stone tables outside. Owners speak good English and some French.

E Sok Dee Guesthouse, just off Ounkham Rd, T071-252555. Down a quiet, pleasant side street. Clean rooms with TV, fan and hot water baths. Small restaurant attached that offers a limited breakfast menu. Bicycle rental. Pretty good value. Recommended.

E Vanvisa Villa, T071-212925, vandara1@hotmail.com. Brightly coloured guesthouse down a quaint street. This is a little gem, with teak floors, large, characterful and immaculate rooms and friendly owners. The downstairs has beautiful handicrafts and antiques. It's a bit run down but has a homely feel.

E-F Jaliya, Phamahapasaman Rd, , T071-252154. The ever-popular **Jaliya** has a range of bungalow-type rooms on offer, with varied facilities, from shared bathrooms and fan through to a/c and TV, so take a look around. Relaxing garden area with friendly pet deer. Bicycle and motorbike rental.

E-F Kounsavan, Chaotonkham Rd, T071-212297. This beautifully situated guesthouse is easy to miss because it's halfway down a sleepy-looking street but it's definitely worth tumbling upon as it's an oasis of tranquillity. Green grass, flowers, balconies, showers with hot water. Some rooms have en suites, others share facilities. This place is extremely friendly, and within easy striking distance of the town centre. Recommended.

F Pa Phai, opposite Wat Pha Phai. This guesthouse is run by an elderly lady who speaks good English and French. It is a bit run down but classic Laos: an attractive little wooden place with a shady garden and a veranda on the first floor. 10 clean rooms (separated only by rattan walls – which don't leave much to the imagination), very clean bathrooms, bikes for rent and same day laundry service. Recommended.

F Saylom Khem Khong, T071-212304, wonmany2001@yahoo.com. Basic rooms on the river with fan and shared facilities. A bit cramped. Not much English spoken.

F Sunkeo II, just behind the post office, T071-252804. Basic rooms, shared hot water bathrooms. Friendly, clean.

Self-catering

Villa Savanh, Sisavangvong Rd, T071-212420, info@theapsara.com. A traditional wooden but fully restored, self-contained house, with 3 double bedrooms and bathrooms. Good use of Lao fabrics and furniture. Set in beautiful gardens. Steep stairs could pose a difficulty for some. Same management as the **Apsara** (see above). Short-term stays US$250 per night, discount for longer rental.

West bank of the Mekong p114
L-A Grand Luang Prabang Hotel & Resort, Ban Xiengkeo, 4 km from town, T071-253851/7, www.grandluangprabang.com.

Very beautiful restored hotel in the former Prince Phetsarath's residence. Simple, classically decorated rooms set in lovely gardens. Try to get a room with the stunning Mekong River view. The 80 rooms have all the mod cons including IDD telephone, minibar, TV and marble bathroom. The drawback is that it is a bit of a hike from town.

East of the city p116
A **Lao Spirit Resort**, 15 km east of Luang Prabang, T071-252655, www.tigertrail-laos.com. Eco-friendly accommodation in bungalows with open-air bathrooms. The **Tiger Trail Elephant Camp** is located on the opposite side of the river and elephant treks can be organized. The beautifully decorated glass-fronted bungalows are usually booked in conjunction with one of the Tiger Trail tours but can be booked independently. Restaurant with Asian and European food. US$70 including breakfast and transfer. Discounts in low season. Gets rave reviews. Recommended.
C **Thongbay Guesthouse**, Ban Vieng May, 3 km southeast of the centre of Luang Prabang, T071-253234, www.thongbay-guesthouses.com. Absolutely stunning set-up of modern bungalows overlooking the Nam Khan. 12 bungalows including 2 extra large family-sized ones. Beautiful tropical garden with a small pond as a centre piece. The rooms overlooking the river are the best, affording fantastic views of the laid-back rural life. Bungalows have a fridge, 4-poster bed and hot water. Popular with tour groups so advanced booking is necessary. Recommended.

South of the city p118
A **Villa Santi Resort**, Ban Na Dui, T071-252157, www.villasanti hotel.com. This new 55-room resort, under the same management as **Villa Santi Hotel**, could hardly be more dreamy. It's set in 10 ha of beautiful countryside 6 km from town on the road to Kwang Si falls and backs onto a local village and fields of rice paddies. The foyer is decorated with beautiful art deco-style furniture and the rooms are very comfortable. There is a pool but it is often empty of water. If you can get on one of the **Laos Airlines** deals, this hotel is very good value. Shuttle buses into town are scheduled to leave every 30 mins throughout the day. Recommended.

🍴 Eating

Luang Prabang *p98, maps p102 and p106* Note that Luang Prabang has a curfew; most places won't stay open past 2200.

Luang Prabang produces a number of culinary specialities that make interesting souvenirs. The local market is a good starting point, although most restaurants have now clicked onto the popularity of the local delicacies. The most famous is *khai pehn*, dried river weed, mainly from the Nam Khan, which is mixed with sesame and eaten nationwide. It is particularly good fried as a sandwich between garlic and sesame. *Chao bong*, a mildly hot pimento purée, is also popular throughout the country. Other delicacies include: *phak nam*, a watercress that grows around waterfalls and is commonly used in soups and salads; *mak kham kuan*, tamarind jam, and *mak nat kuan*, pineapple jam.

One of the best local culinary experiences is to grab some Lao takeaway food from the night market that runs off **Sisavangvong Rd**, 1600-2200. Here you can pick up fresh spring rolls (*nem nip*) papaya salad (*tom som*), sticky rice (*cow niao*), the local delicacy Luang Prabang sausage (*Sai Hua*), BBQ chicken on a stick (*gai*) or fish (*pa*), dried buffalo (*sin savanh*) and dried seaweed. There are also a number of cheap buffets where you can get a selection of local curries and dishes. If you don't want your food too hot ask for '*bo pet*'.
🍴🍴-🍴 **L'Éléphant**, Ban Vat Nong, T071-252482, contact@elephant-restau.com. About as fine as dining gets in Luang Prabang. Very upmarket and utterly delectable cuisine. Pan-fried fillet of snapper, with capers and basil-flavoured mash is delicious, as are the simmered scallops. Also a number of Lao dishes. There are 3 set menus and an extensive wine list. Good place to treat yourself. Highly recommended.
🍴🍴 **Café des Arts**, Sisavangvong Rd, T071-252162. Pleasant and reasonably priced French restaurant with artwork for sale on the walls but a bit lacking in atmosphere. Good salads, disappointing pizzas, scrumptious crème caramel. Some of the steak dishes are a bit expensive, US$6-7, but the chicken dishes are delicious.
🍴🍴-🍴 **The Apsara**, see Sleeping. Lao/Thai restaurant offering dishes such as braised

pork belly and pumpkin, great fish cakes. Try their delicious red curry cream soup with lentils and smoked duck or braised beef shin Chinese style. Good value.

♥♥-♥ Blue Lagoon, beside the Royal Palace, www.blue-lagoon-cafe.com, T071-253698. This restaurant offers a great selection of delicious hearty European meals – especially Swiss-inspired meals such as the fondue chinoise. Great steaks and pasta and ice creams to die-for. Indoor and outdoor seating in comfortable candlelit garden setting.

♥♥-♥ Café Ban Vat Sene, Sakkaline Rd, opposite Wat Sene. A very pleasant option, with a breezy, colonial air. White walls and polished dark wooden floors, tables and chairs. Great for breakfast. The food (French) is a treat. Good place for coffee or tea.

♥♥-♥ Couleur Café/Restaurant, Ban Vat Nong, T020-5621064. The French expats in town have nothing but praise for this place with its French and Lao meals and ambient setting. Good wine. This is the place for carnivores as it has become renowned for its steaks.

♥♥-♥ Luang Prabang Pizza, Sisavangvong Rd. No surprises for guessing what their signature dish is. Pizzas and pasta are cheap and passable but the real highlight here is the fantastic Lao staff.

♥♥-♥ Nazim's Indian Restaurant, Sisavangvong Rd. Luang Prabang's first Indian restaurant appears to be a roaring success. The menu offers a huge selection of authentic Indian food from both north and south of the country, plus halal dishes. The management and the chefs are all Indian which ensures that the food is traditionally prepared. The servings are huge, and the service is efficient; the interior remains bare.

♥♥-♥ Nisha's, Sisavangvong Rd, Mt Phousi. Whoever goes into **Nisha's** emerges singing its praises. The varied Indian dishes are delicious as well as reasonably priced.

♥♥-♥ Tamnak Lao, Sisavangvong Rd, opposite **Villa Santi**, T071-252525. Brilliant restaurant, serving modern Lao cuisine, with a strong Thai influence. Very popular with tour groups. The freshest ingredients are used: try fish and coconut wrapped in banana leaf or pork-stuffed celery soup. Atmospheric surroundings, particularly upstairs, and exceptional service. Best for dinner. Unmissable.

♥♥-♥ Tum Tum Cheng, Sakkaline Rd, T071-252019. Lao food prepared by a Hungarian returnee. Tasty fusion-style meals. Very comfy outdoor seating. Also offers classes in Lao cooking and classical Lao dancing.

♥ Dao Fa, Sisavangvong Rd, T071-215651, www.daofa-bistro.com. Great selection of teas and coffees, fab ice creams and tasty homemade pasta. The latter is the real draw and is recommended. Brightly decorated space with pavement seating.

♥ Khemkhan Food Garden, Nam Khan Rd, T071-212447. A reasonable line in spicy foods but it's better for a beer than a feed. Very pleasant terrace setting overlooking the Nam Khan.

♥ Morning Glory , Sakkaline Rd. 0800-1600. Small but cosy Thai restaurant decorated with the proprietor's photographs and paintings. Intimate open-style kitchen serving up fantastic home-style meals – great juices, breakfasts and curries. Try the *Tom Kha Gai* and zesty juice.

♥ Tamarind, facing Wat Nong, T020-7770484, www.tamarindlaos.com. Mon-Sat 1100-1800. Brilliant restaurant offering modern Lao cuisine; an utterly exceptional dining experience. Try the five-bites (the Lao equivalent to tapas), the pumpkin soup is to die for and the tamarind juice is exceptional. Even better than their à la carte menu are the 'dining experiences' such as traditional Lao Celebration meal 'Pun Pa', which includes succulent marinated fish and a purple sticky rice dessert, or the Adventurous Lao Gourmet degustation menu, which comes with clear explanations of what each dish is. They also do **market tours** with in-depth explanations of Lao delicacies (advance booking is essential) and can organize picnics. The owners Joy and Caroline have been receiving accolades from around the region.

♥ View Khaem Khong, Ounkham Rd, T071-212726. The most popular of the dining establishments along the river. Good for a beer at sunset. The locals call the manager the 'King' because he seems to survey his mini outdoor kingdom from a throne. Service is a bit swifter during the day. Tasty Luang Prabang sausage and *laap*. Recommended.

Foodstalls

A tempting choice of early evening stalls is to be found on Kittsarath Setthathirat, towards the river, and on the sidestreet down towards the river near the night market on Sisavangvong Rd. Roast chicken and sticky rice, a Lao favourite, are among the foods on offer. Very cheap and usually pretty good food. Baguettes can be bought at many roadside stalls.

Cafés and bakeries

Joma, Sisavangvong Rd near Nam Phou fountain, T071-252292. Utterly delicious array of comfort foods: shakes, coffee, sandwiches, lasagne, quiche and more. Nice and cool a/c interior. **Mulberry Handicrafts** is upstairs.

L'Étranger, Kingkitsarath Rd, near **Hive Bar**, T020-5471736. Great little bookshop-cum-café. The upstairs is exceptionally comfortable with cushions and low tables. This is the perfect place to wind down, grab a book and have a cuppa. Outstanding breakfasts. Books are rented here for 5000 kip per day. A movie is shown daily at 1900.

Luang Prabang Bakery, Sisavangvong Rd, T071-252499. Croissants, lemon bars, raisin slices, brownies, muffins, coffee, rolls, all to eat on premises or take away. Also sells muesli, making it a good place for breakfast. One of the best selections of chocolate cakes in the country.

See also **Café Ban Vat Sene**, page 124.

🍸 Bars and clubs

Luang Prabang *p98, maps p102 and p106*
L'Éléphant, **La Résidence Phou Vao** and **Apsara** provide attractive settings for a drink. A sunset beer at one of the restaurants overlooking the river is divine. After everything closes between 2200 and 2300 most locals head to either the bowling alley for a beer (open until 0300) or to have a bowl of soup and a cold beverage on Phou Vao Rd at one of the many *pho* noodle shops.

Dao Fa nightclub, on the way to the South Bus Station. Extremely popular with locals and plays Asian dance music.

Hive Bar, Kingkitsarath Rd, next to **L'Étranger**. Luang Prabang's most happening bar-club is good for a dance, though it has become quieter now that the competition around it has started to grow.

Khily Wine Bar, tucked away next door to **Oui Guesthouse** at the end of the peninsula. The secret hotspot for locals. This intimate

bar has high chairs with a long bar stocked with an extensive selection of Lao wines. Great for a quiet drink.

Khob Jai, Kingkitsarath Rd, opposite **Hive Bar** (sometimes known as **LPQ**). A dedicated gay-friendly bar but open to all and sundry.

Lao Lao Garden, Kingkitsarath Rd. A tiered landscaped terrace, with low lighting, that's become a favourite backpacker haunt with cheap, delicious cocktails.

Pack Luck, Sisavangvong Rd. For a more upmarket drink, this cosy wine bar has a great selection of tipples and well-selected wines. This modern establishment is high on atmosphere with comfy beanbags, modern art adorning its walls and candlelit tables.

🎭 Entertainment

Luang Prabang *p98, maps p102 and p106*
Cinema
There isn't a cinema in Luang Prabang anymore. **L'Étranger** (see Cafés and bakeries, above) shows arthouse and other well-reviewed movies every evening.

Theatre and dance

Traditional dance performances, influenced by the *Ramayana*, are held at the **Theatre Phalak Phalam** in the Royal Palace compound, T071-253705, Mon, Wed and Sat at 1800, US$6-15. The traditional dance of Luang Prabang, which is incorporated into most shows, is over 600 years old.

🎉 Festivals and events

Luang Prabang *p98, maps p102 and p106*
April
Pi Mai (Lao New Year; movable) is the time when the tutelary spirits of the old year are replaced by those of the new. It has special significance in Luang Prabang, with certain traditions celebrated in the city that are no longer observed in Vientiane. In the past the King and Queen would symbolically clean the principal Buddha images in the city's main wats, while masked dancers pranced through the streets re-enacting the founding of the city by 2 mythical beasts. Today, people from all over the province, and even further afield, still descend on the city. The newly crowned Miss New Year (Nang Sang Khan) is paraded through town, riding on

the back of the auspicious animal of the year.

Day 1 Bazaar is held in the streets around the post office; sprinkling of Buddha statues with water; release of small fish into Mekong from pier behind Royal Palace – a symbolic gesture, hoping for good luck in the New Year; construction of sand stupas on western bank of Mekong, next to Wat Xiang Men; fireworks in the evening.

Day 2 1st procession from Wat That to Wat Xieng Thong; dance of the masks of Pou Nheu Nha Nheu and Sing Kaeo Sing Kham; fireworks and festivities in the evening.

Day 3 2nd procession from Wat Xieng Thong to Wat That; procession of monks; *baci* celebrations; fireworks in evening.

Day 4 Pra Bang is moved from the Royal Palace to Wat Mai.

Day 5/6 All-day traditional washing of Pra Bang at Wat Mai.

Day 7 Pra Bang Buddha is returned to Royal Palace.

Days 9-11 Wat Xieng Thong Phraman image brought outside for ritual washing.

May
Vien Thiene (movable), the candlelit festival.

September
Boat races (movable). Boats are raced by the people living in the vicinity of each wat.

O Shopping

Luang Prabang *p98, maps p102 and p106*
Antiques
Authentic antiques are almost impossible to find as the Thai dealers have whole-heartedly scavenged through the place. Real antiques are considered immensely valuable and will usually be priced accordingly.
Patthana Boupha Antique Gallery, Ban Visoun, T071-212262. This little gem can be found in a partitioned-off area in a fantastic colonial building. Antique silverware and jewellery, Buddhas, old photos and fine textiles. Less common are furniture and household items. Reasonable prices. Often closed, so ring beforehand.

Baskets
The best collection can be found in several shops along Sisavangvong Rd, near to Villa Santi.

Books
A small selection of second-hand books is available at **Luang Prabang Bakery Restaurant**, Sisavangvong Rd (not to be confused with the Luang Prabang Bakery Restaurant that sells all the chocolate cakes, see Cafés). A wider selection of books can be purchased or rented from **L'Étranger** (see Cafés), the best bookshop in the country.

Fashion and textiles
Mulberries, above **Joma Café** (see Eating), sells a range of silk homewares and clothes, as well as local teas.
OckPopTok, near **L'Éléphant** restaurant, T071-253219. **OckPopTok**, which literally translates as 'East meets West', truly incorporates the best of both worlds in beautiful designs and fabrics. It specializes in naturally dyed silk, which is of a much better quality than synthetically dyed silk as it doesn't run. Clothes, household items, hangings and custom-made orders are also available (if ordered well in advance). Check out the **Fibre2Fabric** gallery next door (see Galleries, below). Recommended.
Satri Lao Silk, Sisavangvong Rd, T071-219295. Truly beautiful silks and handicrafts for sale. Sometimes a bit overpriced, but definitely worth a look.

Galleries
Quite a few little operations are popping up now, since the German owner of **Ban Khilly Paper Gallery**, Sakkaline Rd, T071-212611, opened his place, trained up all his staff, and then had to watch as most of them went off with their newly learnt skills to set up on their own. This is a *sa* crafts centre (*sa* is a rough, leaf-effect paper) selling scrolls, temple stencils, paper lanterns, cards and beautifully decorated and painted paper.
Fibre2Fabric, 71 Ban Vat Nong (next door to **Ock Pop Tok**), T071-254761, www.fibre 2fabric.org. A fantastic gallery exhibiting textiles and a display on the culture surrounding the textiles of different ethnic groups. Exhibition with photography, weaving and explanations of local ethnic customs and cultures associated with textile production. Local weavers are often on hand to explain the processes.
Kop Noi, Ban Aphay, www.kopnoi.com. This little shop has a rotating exhibition on

the second storey of their shop. They also exhibit a selection of photographs from renowned Lao photographer Sam Sisombat. **Kinnaly Gallery**, Sakkaline Rd, T020-5557737. Gallery featuring photographic work and local art.

Handicrafts

There is a handicraft market, geared to tourists, close to the intersection of Phou Vao Rd and the river road. A row of shops lines Phothisarath Rd.

Jewellery

Naga Creations, Sisavangvong Rd, T071-212775. A large collection of jewellery and trinkets, combining Lao silver with quality semi-precious stones. Both contemporary and classic pieces. Some truly innovative work by the jeweller **Fabrice**, including beautiful use of beetle wings (the same style that was once used to adorn royal clothing).

Markets

The **night market** sprawls down several blocks of Sisavangvong Rd (this market has been moving around the last few years but is expected to return to Sisavangvong Rd). Daily 1700-2230. Hundreds of villagers flock to the market to sell their handicrafts, ranging from silk scarves through to embroidered quilt covers and paper albums. The market shouldn't be missed and most visitors won't leave without a great souvenir or two.

Phousi market, 1.5 km from the centre of town. The latter is a fantastic place to pick up quality silk garments. Pre-made silk clothes are sold here for a fraction of the price of the shops in town. The clothes just need the odd button sewn on here or the hem taken up there. Make sure that you are very detailed with instructions though and ensure the same colour thread is used in any alterations.

Talat Dala, housed in market building in the middle of town on the corner of Setthathirat and Chao Sisophon roads, at the time of publication the market was being gloriously revamped to become a major market for artisans and jewellers to sell their wares.

Silver

One of Luang Prabang's traditional crafts is

silversmithing. During the Communist era between 1975 and 1989 many silversmiths turned to other occupations, such was the lack of demand. However, with the rise in tourism and the economic reforms, demand has increased and many silversmiths have returned to their craft.

Most tourists buy their silver – and other crafts – from the main market in Luang Prabang (see above). However, almost none of the pieces on sale here are from the Luang Prabang area – despite what the marketeers might say. Most are made in Vientiane and trucked to the royal capital. Expert silversmiths like Thithpeng Maniphone maintain that these Vientiane-made pieces are inferior, and certainly the engraving and silverwork does appear cruder.

The silversmith along the river, near the rear of the Royal Palace, produces good workmanship; his father made one of the King's crowns. There are also several other Lao silversmiths around the Nam Phou area (fountain), where you can watch the artisans ply their trade. **Thit Peng**, signposted almost opposite Wat That, is a workshop and small shop with jewellery and pots.

Woodcarving

Caruso Gallery, Sisavangvong Rd (towards the Three Nagas Hotel) has some stunning but expensive wooden furniture and artefacts.

▲▲ Activities and tours

Luang Prabang *p98, maps p102 and p106*
Cookery classes
There are a number of classes offered in Luang Prabang. The cooking classes are ordered in preference.
Tamarind, www.tamarindlaos.com, facing Wat Nong, T020-777 0484. This successful restaurant has been running specialized custom-made classes for 1 or 2 people at a time. However, due to their immense popularity they will expand these courses to larger groups. Recommended.
Tamnak Lao, T071-252525, www.laocookingcourse.com, US$25 per person for 1-day cooking class, including shopping at the markets.
Tum Tum Cheng, Sakkaline Rd, T071-253388, www.tumtumcheng.com. Mon-Sat. Popular cooking classes operating

since 2001. 1 day, US$25; 2 day, US$45; 3 day US$60. Advance bookings are required.

Elephant tours and activities

Elephant Park Project, 25 km from Luang Prabang (visits and activities can be organized through Tiger Trails office on Sisavangvong Rd, www.laos-adventures.com, T071-252655).This has been established in conjunction with Tiger Trails in Luang Prabang. They have bought up old elephants that were chained up in Hongsa as they were no longer useful for hauling timber. In order to keep the old elephants active the operators run a number of activities. Tourists can participate in up to 25 activities at the elephant park, including experiencing life as a *mahout* (elephant keeper) and washing the elephants or trekking with them. There are a few other similar elephant park projects but these are pale imitations which have compromised on quality.

Sauna and massage

Aroma Spa, Sisavangvong Rd, T020-7611255. Another mid-priced spa offering aroma-therapy, facials, body scrubs, etc.

Khmu Spa, Sisavangvong Rd, T071-212092. A range of cheaply priced massages including the Khmu massage (gentler, lighter strokes) Lao massage (stretching, cracking and pressure points) and foot massage. Also has herbal sauna. Open until 2200.

Maison Souvannaphoum (see Sleeping). A spa with a range of luxurious and expensive treatments. For sheer indulgence.

Red Cross Sauna, opposite Wat Visunnarat, reservations T071-212303. Daily 0900-2100 (1700-2100 for sauna). Massage 30,000 kip per hr, traditional Lao herbal sauna 10,000 kip. Bring your own towel/sarong. Profits go to the Lao Red Cross.

The Spa at La Résidence Phou Vao (see Sleeping) offers very expensive 3-hr massage courses, US$190 for 2 people. This includes a 1-hr massage for each person, the class, a handbook and oils. www.residence phouvao.com, T071-212530.

Spa Garden, Ban Phonheauang, T071-212325, spagardenlpb@hotmail.com. More upmarket. Offers a wide selection of massage and beauty treatments including aromatherapy massage US$12 per hr, sports

body massage, facial treatments, skin detox US$25 per hr. The best value for money in luxury massages, pedicure or manicure all set in a relaxing building with oil burners, wind chimes and dolphin-esque sounds playing in the background. Packages between US$5 and US$38.

Steam Bath Massage, near Wat Xieng Thong on Souvanna Khampong Rd. Daily 1600-2030. A low-key affair where one entrepreneurial family have set up a sauna and massage in their home. Very friendly. Bring a towel and shower first.

Tour operators

All Laos Service, Sisavangvong Rd. Large successful travel agency organizing ticketing and travel services.

Asian Trails, Unit 06, Baan Vat That, Khaem Khong Rd, PO Box 779, T071-252764, www.asiantrails.com.

Green Discovery, T071-212093, www.greendiscoverylaos.com. A range of rafting and kayaking trips that pass through grade 1 and 2 rapids. Cycling trips around Luang Prabang and surrounding countryside. Homestays, rafting, kayaking, trips to Pak Ou caves, etc.

Tiger Trail, Sisavangvong Rd, T071-252655, www.tigertrail-laos.com. Adventure specialists: elephant treks, trekking, mountain biking tours, rafting, rock climbing, etc. Their resort gets rave reviews, see Sleeping.

Treasure Travel Laos, Sisavangvong Rd, T071-254403. Almost every travel service possible, from tours to Phonsavanh, through to ticketing and transport. Good local operator. Recommended.

Weaving classes

Weaving Centre, 2 km out of town on the river (bookings at **Ban Vat Nong Gallery**, T071-253219. info@ockpoptok.com). The team behind the fabulous creations at **Ock Pop Tok** have opened a weaving centre. Half-day dyeing classes introduce students to the world of silk dyes (US$35). A variety of 1- to 3-day weaving classes are offered at US$35 per day. Tailor-made courses are also available. Classes are run by professional weavers and their English-speaking assistants. At the time of publication a small café was going to be opened on site.

⊝ Transport

Luang Prabang *p98, maps p102 and p106*
See also Ins and outs, page 98.

Air

Luang Prabang International Airport (LPQ) about 4 km from town, T071-212172/3. **Lao Airlines**, Phamahapasaman Rd, T071-212172, has 3 daily connections with **Vientiane**, 40 mins, and a service to **Chiang Mai**, **Pakse** and **Phonsavanh**. It also runs 3 flights a week between **Bangkok** and Luang Prabang. These flights are notoriously prone to change so check schedule well in advance. **Bangkok Airways** runs daily flights to **Bangkok**. In the high season **Siem Reap Airways** runs flights to **Siem Reap** via Pakse.

Early morning departures are often delayed during the rainy season, as dense cloud can sometimes make Luang Prabang airport inoperable until about 1100. Airline tickets are more often than not substantially cheaper from travel agents (see Tour operators, above) than from the actual airline. Confirm bookings a day in advance and arrive at the airport early as flights have been known to depart as soon as they're full.

Bicycle hire

There is no doubt that the best way to explore Luang Prabang is by bicycle. Bikes can be rented for US$1 per day from most guesthouses.

Boat

Luang Prabang was established at the confluence of the Mekong and Nam Khan rivers because of the transport and communication opportunities that such a position affords in an otherwise mountainous and inaccessible area. However, with the development of overland links and the upgrading of the Vientiane–Luang Prabang road, river transport has languished. Nonetheless, while few passengers take the boat option south to Vientiane via Pak Lai, the route upstream to Houei Xai via Pak Beng, on the border with Thailand, remains very popular. There are 3 departure areas, with most boats leaving from the 2 docks behind the Royal Palace. **Tha Heua Me Pier** is the most popular departure point and has a blackboard listing all the destinations and prices available (daily 0730-1130 , 1300-1600). Prices are largely dependent on the cost of gasoline. There is also a dock at **Ban Don** (15 mins north of town by tuk-tuk, US$1-2).

To Houei Xai/Pak Beng The 2-day boat trip down the Mekong between Houei Xai and Pak Beng has become a rite of passage for travellers in Southeast Asia. There are a range of boat options to suit everyone from the flashpacker to the backpacker.

The **slow boat** to Houei Xai leaves from the boat pier on Khem Khong Rd called the Tha Heua Mea pier, 2 days, with a break in Pak Beng after 6-7 hrs on the 1st day. It costs US$11 for each leg of the trip and almost all travel agents sell tickets. It's often packed to the brim so wear something comfortable and bring some padding to sit on. Seats are usually basic wooden benches though you may luck it with one that has bus seats. The trip from Luang Prabang to Houei Xai (via Pak Beng overnight) is usually less busy than in the other direction. (If the boat to Pak Beng is full, you can charter your own for about US$200-300.) Tickets for the onward trip to Houei Xai, can be purchased in Pak Beng. Take a good book and a grab some goodies from one of the bakeries to take on board. Most boats will have a vendor selling basic drinks. The boat usually leaves between 0800 and 0900 (changeable so check) but it is necessary to get there early to secure yourself a good seat.

A mid-range option is the **Nagi**, a more comfortable, quicker boat than the regular slow boat. From Houei Xai the *Nagi* makes the trip to Luang Prabang in 1 day. The boat departs at 0830 and arrives at approximately 1730. Going upstream from Luang Prabang to Houei Xai the journey takes 2 days. Hot food and cold drinks are served on board. Email bookings. From Houei Xai to Luang Prabang – 1 day US$80; From Luang Prabang to Houei Xai (via Pak Beng) US$70 (not including accommodation in Pak Beng where you have to stay overnight).

The most luxurious way to make the trip is on the **Luangsay Cruise**, office on Sisavangvong Rd, T071-252 553, www.asian-oasis.com, which makes the trip in 2 days and 1 night, stopping over at Pak Ou Caves en route and staying overnight at their luxurious lodge in Pak Beng (page 154).

The boat is extra comfortable and has lounges, a stocked bar and lots of board games. Very popular in high season and will need to be booked 6 months in advance. In low season the boat runs from Houei Xai to Luang Prabang on Mon and Fri and in the opposite direction on Wed and Sat (US$243 twin/ US$300 single). In the high season the boat runs from Houei Xai to Luang Prabang on Mon, Thu and Fri, and in the opposite direction Luang Prabang–Houei Xai on Tue, Wed and Sat (US$358 twin/US$422 single). In the low season it may be possible to get a standby rate if there is availability.

Speedboats (which are not recommended) depart from Ban Don to **Houei Xai** (on the Thai border; see page 149), US$30, around 6 hrs, with a short break in **Pak Beng**. Tickets are available from most travel agents. The boats are horribly noisy and dangerous (numerous fatalities have been reported from boats jack-knifing when hitting waves). Ear plugs are recommended and ensure boatmen provide a helmet and life jacket.

To Vientiane via Pak Lai The passenger service between Vientiane and Luang Prabang has ceased but you may be able to squeeze yourself on to one of the rare southbound cargo boats. This is difficult and unreliable. Larger boats only travel in the rainy season and you may have to hang around for several days, while the freight is loaded. It may be helpful to use a translator in order to negotiate the price. The stretch of river from Luang Prabang to Pak Lai is quite hazardous, with a fair number of rapids, so a more practical alternative may be to take the bus to **Sayaboury** (see Bus, below) and on to **Pak Lai**, where there is a basic guesthouse, then catch the boat to Vientiane from there. Slow boats depart Pak Lai for Vientiane at 0730 and take all day (US$10). Or you can hire a speed boat, 5-6 hrs, US$150 for up to 6 people. It is possible to see working elephants on the journey between Pak Lai and Sanakham (Xana Kham), the next significant settlement downstream. Sanakham has 3 wats, one with a ruined stupa and another with an unusual Buddha image. There is a river border crossing here to Chiang Khan in Thailand, but foreigners are not permitted to cross (although frequent boats ply the Mekong and it is said

that no-one asks for your passport). Boats from Sanakham to Vientiane are intermittent, and take about 8 hrs, arriving at the northern jetty.

To Nong Khiaw and Muang Khua
A few boats travel up the Nam Ou to Nong Khiaw and Muang Ngoi. However, these are infrequent, especially when the river is low. The journey usually takes 6 hrs to Nong Khiaw, 120,000 kip, and a further 1 hr to Muang Ngoi. The Nam Ou joins the Mekong near the Pak Ou caves, so it is possible to combine a journey with a visit to the caves en route. The irregular travel dates to Nong Khiaw are posted on a board outside the boat pier or you can ask one of the travel agents on Sisavangvong Rd when the next departure is. It is possible to charter a boat for 1-6 people for US$150. Speedboats to Nong Khiaw sometimes leave from Ban Don (5 km from Luang Prabang), expect to pay 160,000 kip. The speedboats are hazardous, uncomfortable and not environmentally friendly.

Bus/truck
The northern bus terminal is for northbound traffic and the southern for traffic to/from the south. Always double-check which terminal your bus is using, as unscheduled changes are possible. There's a third, smaller station, south of town on the road to the falls, for buses to Sayaboury.

From the northern terminal To **Luang Namtha**, daily 0900 and 1730, 10 hrs, usually via Udomxai, 70,000 kip. The roads are reasonable and paved but quite hilly. The 1730 bus has usually come from Vientiane and is often full. An alternative is to break the journey by catching the bus to **Udomxai**, 0900 and 1130 daily, 5 hrs, 45,000 kip, and then continuing on to Luang Namtha in the afternoon. There are also daily departures (usually in the morning) to **Houei Xai** on the Thai/Lao border, 100,000 kip, 11-12 hrs. A VIP bus to Houei Xai passes through on Mon, Wed, Fri and Sun, 1000, 10 hrs, 160,000 kip. There is a very long bus journey to **Xam Neua**, 1630, they say it takes 14 hrs but it can be up to 20 hrs, 100,000 kip. **Phongsali**, 1600, 13-15 hrs 100,000 kip. To Nong Khiaw, by *songthaew*, regular departures usually in the morning 32,000 kip.

From the southern terminal There

are up to 8 daily buses to **Vientiane**, although scheduled departures tend to decline in the low season, 10-11 hrs, 90,000 kip; most of these services stop in **Vang Vieng**, 6 hrs, 75,000 kip. VIP buses to Vientiane depart 0800 and 0900, 9 hrs, 115,000 kip; both these services stop in Vang Vieng, 100,000 kip.

To **Phonsavanh**, daily 0830, 8-9 hrs, 85,000 kip. It should cost 10,000-15,000 kip to get to the centre of town from the station.

From the Sayaboury terminal
Songthaew for **Pak Khon**, on the Mekong, depart several times a day, when full, 3 hrs. From Pak Khon there is a Mekong ferry to **Tha Deua**, from where buses continue to **Sayaboury**, 1 hr. This is the route you need to take if you want to catch a boat from Pak Lai to Vientiane (see above).

Minibus

Minibuses with driver are available from several hotels and the tour companies, US$50 per day around Luang Prabang, US$60 per day if travelling further afield. Check out the notice boards for services to **Vang Vieng**, 5 hrs, and **Vientiane**, 7 hrs; quicker than the bus, but more expensive. If you have a big group you can organize independent minivan rental.

Saamlor and tuk-tuk

Lots around town, which can be hired to see the sights or to go to nearby villages. A short stint across town should cost about 10,000 kip per person, but expect to pay 20,000 kip for anything more than 1 km. Most of the nearby excursions will cost US$10-15.

● Directory

Luang Prabang *p98, maps p102 and p106*
Banks Lao Development Bank, 65 Sisavangvong Rd, Mon-Sat 0830-1200

and 1330-1530, will change US$/Thai ฿/ TCs into US$ or kip, but doesn't accept credit cards; there's another branch on Sisavangvong Rd, near Nisha Restaurant.
Banque pour le Commerce Exterieur Lao (BCEL), Sisavangvong Rd, Mon-Sat 0830-1200 and 1330-1530; all transactions in kip, will exchange Thai ฿, US$, AU$, UK£, € and TCs, also cash advances on Visa cards; they also have an ATM but at the time of publication this was only for MasterCard. Many of the jewellery stalls in the old market, plus restaurant and tourist shop owners, will change US$ and Thai ฿. Many of the travel agencies will give credit card advances if you get stuck after hours without money but charge a whopping 6-8% commission.
Internet Plenty of internet cafés have cropped up around town, with a concentration on Sisavangvong Rd. **Luang Prabang Internet**, opposite Silichit Guesthouse, is probably the best value deal in town, with the friendliest service.
Medical services Facilities in Luang Prabang are limited. The **main hospital**, on Settathirat, T071-252049, is only useful for minor ailments. For anything major you're better off getting a flight to Bangkok. There are a few quite well-equipped pharmacies towards Villa Santi on Sisavangvong Rd.
Post, telephone and internet Post and telephone office on the corner of Chau Fa Ngum and Setthathirat streets, Mon-Fri 0830-1730, Sat 0830-1200, express mail service, fax and international telephone facilities, philately section. There are IDD call boxes around the post office and on Sisavangvong Rd. Hotels and some guesthouses also allow international calls from their reception phones (about US$5 a min). You are better off making international calls from one of the many internet cafés, which are dramatically cheaper and have usually installed Skype.

North of Luang Prabang

In recent years the settlements of Nong Khiaw and Muang Ngoi Neua in the north of Luang Prabang Province have become firm favourites with the backpacker set. In fact, idyllic Muang Ngoi Neua is often heralded as the new Vang Vieng, surrounded by stunning scenery and the fantastic ebb of life on the river. It is far more pleasant to travel between Luang Prabang and Nong Khiaw/Ban Saphoun by long boat, than by bus. The Nam Ou passes mountains, teak plantations, dry rice fields and a movable water wheel mounted on a boat, which moves from village to village and is used for milling. But with the improvements that have been made to Route 13, road travel has now become the preferred option for many – partly because it is cheaper, and partly because it is quicker. Route 13 north runs parallel with the river for most of the journey to Nam Bak. There is trekking around Muang Khua further north upriver. ▸▸ For Sleeping, Eating and other listings, see pages 136-141.

Nam Bak → *Colour map 1, B3.*

The town of Nam Bak lies on the banks of the Nam Bak. It is a rather beautiful place and is worth an overnight stop. The market is interesting in the very early morning, when hill people including Blue Hmong converge to sell a miscellany of pickings from the forest. There is a small wat on the right, at the end of town as you come from Luang Prabang, called **Wat Tiom Tian**. From here there are good views of the surrounding countryside. There is a small children's graveyard behind the wat.

> ❢ *The road west from Nam Bak to Udomxai is beautiful, passing Blue Hmong villages.*

Nong Khiaw and Ban Saphoun ●❶❷❸●

▸▸ *pp136-141. Colour map 1, B4.*

Nong Khiaw lies 22 km to the northeast of Nam Bak and is a delightful little village on the banks of the Nam Ou, surrounded by limestone peaks and flanked by misty mountains, the largest aptly named Princess Mountain. The remote little town is one of Laos' prettiest destinations. There are, in fact, two settlements here: Ban Saphoun on the east bank of the Nam Ou and Nong Khiaw on the west. Of the two, Ban Saphoun offers the best views and has the best riverside accommodation. Confusingly, the combined village is sometimes called one name, sometimes the other and sometimes **Muang Ngoi**, which is actually another town to the north (see opposite) and also the name of the district.

One reason why Nong Khiaw/Ban Saphoun has become such a popular stopping place for travellers is because of its pivotal position on the Nam Ou,

Nong Khiaw & Ban Saphoun

To Muang Ngoi Neua & Muang Khua

NONG KHIAW — Truck Stop — Wat Saphoun

Boats North & South

Nam Ou

BAN SAPHOUN

Kaysone Monument — School

To Tham Pha Thok Cave, Vieng Thang & Nam Nouan

To Tham Pha Kwong Caves, Nam Bak, Udom Xai & Luang Prabang

To Luang Prabang

N

Not to scale

Sleeping ●
Manipoon Guesthouse 1
Mexay Guesthouse & Restaurant 2

Phanoy Guesthouse, Bakery & Bookshop 4
Phosoi Guesthouse 5
Sanhty Guesthouse & Restaurant 7
Sendoro Guesthouse 6
Somgnot Guesthouse & Restaurant 8
Sunset Guesthouse & Restaurant 9

Northern Laos North of Luang Prabang

alternate route to Xam Neua/Udomxai. The road trip between Udomxai and Xam Neau
that Nong Khiaw sits upon is one of the most spectacular in Laos, moving through
remote villages. Despite its convenience as a staging post this town is a destination in
its own right. It is a beautiful spot, the sort of place where time stands still, journals
are written, books read and stress is a deeply foreign concept.

It is possible to swim in the river (women should wear sarongs) or walk around
the town or up the cliffs. The bridge across the Nam Ou offers fine views and photo
opportunities.

Around Nong Khiaw

The most obvious attractions in the area are the caves that were used by locals when
the US bombed the area. **Tham Pha Thok** ① *2.5 km southeast of the bridge, entry
5000 kip*, was a Pathet Lao regional base during the civil war. It was divided into
sections – a hospital section, a police section and a military section. Old remnants
exist like campfires and ruined beds but other than that there is little evidence of it
being the PT headquarters until you see the bomb crater at the front. To get there you
walk through beautiful rice paddies. There is a second cave, **Tham Pha Kwong**, about
300 m further down on the left, which was the Pathet Lao's former banking cave. The
cave is a tight squeeze and is easier to access with the help from a local guide. It splits
into two caves, one of which is the financial office and the accountants office.

To walk to the caves, turn left out of the village heading towards Nam Bak and the
Tham Pha Kwong caves are about 30 minutes' walk, up on the right. There is a shrine to
the Buddha, various relics, and a pile of old ammunition and bombshells inside. Take a
strong torch to explore the tunnel at the back. It's a 30-minute trek to Tham Pha Thok:
go over the bridge and follow the main road. The caves are signposted.

A further 2 km along the road, at Ban Nokien, is the **Than Mok** waterfall. To get
there, you can either walk for about 3 km or charter a boat (around 20,000 kip per
person for the return trip); remember to agree a return time. There's a 2000 kip fee to
see the waterfall, and some cheeky little child will likely charge you a further
10,000 kip to guide you there (40 minutes each way). It's difficult to find on your own.
It's best to go in the morning, so as not to have to rush the climb up to the falls or cut
short your time there before dark.

If you go to the boat landing it is also possible to organize a fishing trip with one of
the local fishermen for very little money. You might need someone to translate for you.

Muang Ngoi Neua ⊜❼▲⊜❽ ⇥ *pp136-141. Colour map 1, B4.*

The town of Muang Ngoi Neua lies 40 km (one hour) north of Nong Khiaw, along the
Nam Ou. This small town surrounded by ethnic villages has become very popular with
the backpacker set over the last few years, with many calling it the new Vang Vieng.
The town is a small slice of utopia, set on a peninsula at the foot of Mount Phaboom,
shaded by coconut trees, with the languid river breeze wafting through the town's
small paths. Most commonly known as **Muang Ngoi**, the settlement has had to
embellish its name to distinguish it from Nong Khiaw, which is also often referred to
as Muang Ngoi (see above). It's the perfect place to go for a trek to surrounding
villages, or bask the day away swinging in your hammock. A market is held every
10 days to which the villagers come to sell their produce and handicrafts.

Around Muang Ngoi Neua

Tham Kang cave, a large limestone cave, with a glassy river running through it, is a
pleasant 30-minute walk south of town. Follow the road out of town, turn left near
Kaikaew Restaurant and head through the school grounds and along a narrow path
through vegetation. Follow the path on the left to avoid wading through very deep and

very cold water. Just past the school, villagers will collect the entrance fee of 2000 kip. The cave is over 30 m high and exceptionally dark inside, so bring a torch. There's a swimming hole at ground level. **Tham Pa Kaew** is a further five minutes' walk along the trail. Inside the cave is a small Buddha image and there's also a crystal-clear pool that's great for a dip. On the other side of the path are sticky rice paddies, where you can catch a glimpse of locals planting or harvesting the rice by hand. Another 30 minutes' walk along the same path leads to some friendly Khmu and Lao villages; the people of **Ban Ha** are exceptionally friendly. Another 30 minutes' walk leads to **Ban Huay Baw**, from where you can reach the **Than Mok** waterfall by boat (see page 133). It is a 20-minute trip downstream to **Ban Sopkhong** (60,000 kip per boat), where you disembark for a one-hour walk to the waterfall. Villagers are more than obliging to assist in directions.

> ✦ Word on the ground is that the caves are connected via an underground tunnel; but don't even think of exploring, it's far too dangerous!

Muang Khua ⬤⬤⬤▲⬤ ‣‣ pp136-141. Colour map 1, B3.

→ Phone code: 081.

Muang Khua is nestled into the banks of the Nam Ou, close to the mouth of the Nam Phak, in the south of Phongsali Province. Hardly a destination in itself, it's usually just a stopover between Nong Khiaw and Phongsali. But Muang Khua is a great place to kick back for a few days, if you want to take a break from the well-worn travellers' path.

Located at the junction of two rivers and on Route 4 to Vietnam, the town has long been a crossroads between Vietnam and Laos. A French garrison was based in Muang Khua until 1954, when it was ousted by Vietnamese troops in the aftermath of the battle at Dien Bien Phu. For a brief period from 1958, Polish and Canadian officials of the Comité International de Contrôle were quartered in the town to monitor the ceasefire between the Pathet Lao and the Royal Lao government. Nowadays, Muang Khua is home to a burgeoning market in Vietnamese goods, trucked in from Dien Bien Phu. There is speculation that the border with Vietnam will soon open to tourists, which will certainly change the character of the town, for better or worse.

Muang Khua is an attractive town to walk about, but be prepared for a group of children to join you on your saunter. There is a small new wat and a 30-m-long wood and iron pedestrian bridge across the Nam Phak to a small village on the other side. The bridge offers excellent views up and down the river but, as it tends to wobble, it is not for vertigo-sufferers. The morning market, which sometimes attracts Akha women, sells fresh vegetables and meat, while the goldsmith, just off the main square, is usually surrounded by a small group watching his very delicate work.

Around Muang Khua

The Akha, Khmu and Tai Dam are the main hilltribes in the area. The nearest villages are 20 km out of town and you will need a guide if you want to visit them. Trekking around Muang Khua is fantastic and still a very authentic experience, as this region remains largely unexplored by backpackers. The friendly villagers are very welcoming to foreigners, as they don't see as many here as in somewhere like Muang Sing. For these very reasons, it is important to tread lightly and adopt the most culturally sensitive principles: don't hand out sweets and always ask before taking a photograph. Treks usually run for one to three days and involve a homestay at a villager's house (usually the Village Chief). ‣‣ For further details, see Activities and tours, page 139.

Towards Phongsali

You can travel from Muang Khua to Phongsali either by truck, bus or boat. Trucks, on their way from Udomxai, depart from the nearby village of **Pak Nam Noi**; buy lunch from the market there before departure. The ride is a long one, made more difficult when the pickup is full. However, it's a great experience and the hilltribes you come across along the way are very interesting and the scenery toward the Phongsali end of the trip is utterly breathtaking. Alternatively, catch a boat direct from Muang Khua. It's also a beautiful trip, especially for birdwatching, with kingfishers everywhere. The river is quite shallow in places and there is a fair amount of white water, so take a blanket. Boats stop at **Hat Xa**, 20 km or so to the northeast of Phongsali, where you may find yourselves stuck, as there are no buses to Phongsali after mid-afternoon. Note there is no electricity in Hat Xa. ›› *For further details, see Transport, page 140.*

Phongsali ●●▲●● ›› *pp136-141. Colour map 1, A3.*

→ *Phone code: 088.*

High up in the mountains at an altitude of about 1628 m, this northern provincial capital provides beautiful views and an invigorating climate. It is especially stunning from January to March, when wildflowers bloom in the surrounding hills. The town can be cold at any time of the year, so take some warm clothes. Mornings tend to be foggy and it can also be very wet. There is an end-of-the-earth feel in the areas surrounding the main centre, with dense pristine jungle surrounded by misty mountains.

Phongsali was one of the first areas to be liberated by the Pathet Lao in the late 1940s. The old post office (just in front of the new one) is the sole physical reminder of French rule. The town's architecture is a strange mix of Chinese post-revolutionary concrete blocks, Lao wood-and-brick houses with tin roofs, and bamboo or mud huts with straw roofs. The town itself is home to about 20,000 people, mostly Lao, Phou Noi and Chinese, while the wider district is a pot pourri of ethnicities, with around 28 minorities inhabiting the area.

The **Provincial Tourism Office** ① *on the way to Phou Fa Hotel (now simply a restaurant), To88-210098, Mon-Fri 0730-1130, 1330-1630*, can arrange guided eco-treks, including village homestays, for up to five nights.

Around Phongsali

Many paths lead out of town over the hills; the walking is easy and the views are spectacular. It is not possible to hire bikes, tuk-tuks or even ponies here so walking is the only way to explore the fantastic landscapes of this region. Climb the 413 steps to the top of **Mount Phoufa** for humbling views of the surrounding hills. Some people trek north from Phongsali to **Muang Uthai**, staying in Akha villages en route. Muang

Northern Laos North of Luang Prabang

Phongsali

Kaysone Monument
Lao Development
Museum of Tribes 🏛
Lao Airlines
Bus Station to Hat Xa
To Mount Phou Fa
To Hat Xa (1 km)
To Bus Station (3 km) & Muang Xai
Wat Kaew Fa

N
Not to scale

Sleeping ●
Phongsaly 1
Sengsaly Guesthouse 2
Viphahone 4
Yu Houa Guesthouse 3

Uthai is probably as remote and unspoilt as it gets. During the rainy season, it may be possible to take a boat back downriver from Uthai to Luang Prabang. ▸▸ *For further details, see Activities and tours, page 139.*

Towards Udomxai

The road from Phongsali to Udomxai has been upgraded relatively recently and, although it remains only partially sealed, is in good condition. The surroundings and scenery are incredible. It is possible to break the journey at **Pak Nam Noi,** which lies at the intersection of the two roads going either to Muang Khua or Udomxai. There's an elephant farm near Km 14 and elephants can sometimes be seen from the road.

● Sleeping

Nam Bak *p132*

F **Bounthiem,** canary yellow building opposite the wat at the opposite end of town to the market, T071-253640. Friendly place with 5 double or twin rooms, clean, comfy mattresses, fans and mosquito nets. Balcony area, Western-style toilet downstairs and shower with hot water. Recommended.

F **Khounvilay Guesthouse,** next door to Bounthiem, T071-253647. Basic doubles, triples and twins. Quite scruffy with a squat toilet and shower out the back. Mosquito nets, cold drinks available. The wonderfully friendly family owners are likely to invite you to share their evening meal – an extravaganza of spices that is liable to blow your mouth away! Mr Somchith is a good source of travel information.

F **Viengthong Guesthouse,** 100 m past the bridge on the right. 9 very clean and comfortable rooms, singles, twins and doubles, with fan and mosquito nets. Separate Western-style toilet and scoop showers downstairs. Free bottle of water on check-in.

Nong Khiaw and Ban Saphoun *p132, map p132*

B-C **Riverside,** turn off right beside the bridge in Ban Saphoun, T071-254770. www.nongkhiau.com. Stunning modern bungalows and restaurant. Beautifully decorated upscale rooms with 4-poster bed, mosquito net and tiled hot-water bathrooms. Stunningly decorated in modern Asian East-meets-West style. For those looking for something upmarket this exquisite place fits the bill perfectly. The restaurant has a great selection of wines and internet. Book in advance as it is a favourite of the tour groups. Recommended.

F **Manipoon Guesthouse,** near the post office, Nong Khiaw, T071-253908. Slightly grander rooms than the other guesthouses, separated by wooden walls rather than just bamboo. Verandas offer unspectacular views of nearby rooftops. Bathroom downstairs.

F **Mexay Guesthouse,** on the Ban Saphoun side of the bridge. 6 dirt-cheap but clean and comfortable doubles and twins. Separate squat bathroom downstairs. The food is not as inviting as that of its more successful neighbour, **Sunset** (see below).

F **Phanoy Guesthouse, Bakery and Bookshop,** 50 m past the bridge, Ban Saphoun, T071-253919. Guesthouse has 7 basic but clean and comfortable thatched bungalows with mosquito nets and squat toilets. Inside bathroom. Fantastic verandas overlooking the river. Some bungalows (50,000 kip) have hot water. If you are extra lucky the owner will show you his display of butterflies and beetles; he can explain the history of each one. Very nice family-owned business with a great atmosphere. The best of the cheaper options.

F **Phosoi Guesthouse,** south of the boat landing and opposite the school. A small, rickety 2-floored structure with 5 small doubles and twins. Balcony upstairs, café downstairs, with small Lao menu. Squat toilet and scoop shower in garden. Recently renovated. Friendly owners can speak a little English.

F **Sanhty Guesthouse,** a few doors down from the post office facing the river, Nong Khiaw. 6 tiny twin and double rooms, squat toilet and shower at the back.

F **Sendoro Guesthouse,** on the left just before crossing the bridge, Nong Khiaw. 5 double and twin bungalows with balconies looking out across the river, and 5 more set a little more inland, separate squat toilet and scoop showers, with a washing machine. Also a large restaurant with a good selection.

F Somgnot Guesthouse, a few doors down from the **Sanhty Guesthouse**, close to where the boats leave, Nong Khiaw. 5 'spaces' – it's difficult to call them rooms – separated by bamboo screens, Oriental feel, with Indian paintings. Run by a friendly old man with a little English. Tasty cheap Lao food served downstairs.

F Sunset Guesthouse, down a lane about 100 m past the bridge, Ban Saphoun, T071-253933. Slap bang on the bank of the river – you couldn't ask for a more picturesque setting from which to watch the sunset. The charming, sprawling bamboo structure looks out onto tables and sun umbrellas liberally arranged over the various levels of decking that serve as a popular restaurant in the evenings. Western toilet and hot water shower outside. 8 rooms with hard mattresses. A bit dirty. Slow internet.

Muang Ngoi Neua *p133*

All the accommodation in town is dirt cheap and of the same standard: bungalows with extremely welcoming hammocks on their balconies. Most offer a laundry service for around 10,000 kip per kilo and all have electricity 1800-2200 only. Rats are a problem here but, luckily, mosquito nets tend to keep them at bay.

F Lattanavongsa. Concrete building housing relatively comfortable rooms with attached bathroom.

F Ning Ning Guesthouse, beside the boat landing. Double and twin bungalows, overlooking the river, with separate Western toilet and shower. The food in the adjoining restaurant is great and the owner speaks good English. Popular spot.

F Phet Davanh Guesthouse, on the main road, near the boat landing. Concrete guesthouse, with 10 double and twin rooms. Much cleaner than the other alternatives. Comfy mattresses on the floor, Western toilet and shower, restaurant with Lao menu. Good for those who don't want to stay in a bungalow.

F Sainamngoi Bungalows, at the south end of the main road (on the left-hand side). 5 run-down bungalows with double beds

overlooking the stream to Mount Phaboom. Squat toilet and shower outside. Very tranquil; you won't be disturbed.

F Tali Guesthouse, just beyond the south end of the main road, by the Nam Ou. Set in a shady area amid trees. Basic rooms, separate Western toilet and scoop shower. Restaurant with a few Lao dishes.

Muang Khua *p134*

D Sernnali Hotel, in the middle of town, near the top of the hill, T081-212445. By far the most luxurious lodging in town. 18 rooms with large double and twin beds, hot water scoop showers and western-style toilets, immaculately clean. Balconies overlook the Nam Ou. Chinese, Vietnamese and Lao food served in the restaurant.

E-F Nam Ou Guesthouse & Restaurant, follow the signs at the top of the hill, T081-210844. Looking out across the river where the boats land, this guesthouse is the pick of the ultra-budget bunch in Muang Khua. Singles, twins and doubles, some with hot water en suites, and 3 newer rooms with river views. Great food (see Eating, below). A popular spot. Go for an upstairs room.

F Keophila Guesthouse, almost at the top of the hill, T081-210907. A reasonably new building with 7 clean, completely tiled double and twin rooms, with hard beds, hot water showers and squat toilets, interesting decor in the bathrooms.

F Ketsana Guesthouse, down a lane at the bus station, T081-210821. Basic rooms with mosquito nets and fan, some have squat toilet and shower. A balcony out front for relaxation. The cheery family that own it don't speak any English.

F Singsavanh Guesthouse, on the top of the hill next to the market, T088-210812. Clean concrete structure. Basic twins and doubles, with mosquito net, some have toilet and shower attached. Very friendly staff. The budget rooms in the basement have an eclectic collection of buffalo and deer heads – an experience.

Towards Phongsali *p134*

F Hat Xa now has a guesthouse, run by the chief, 15,000 kip for a space in a bamboo shelter with a pillow and mattress. The Nam Ou serves as the toilet and shower!

D **Viphahone Hotel**, next to the post office, T088-210111. This 3-storey building has 24 very clean, large and airy twin and double rooms, with excellent hot water bathrooms, some with Western flush toilets, some with squats. There is a coffee table with chairs in most rooms as well as Laos tea. Good value. Restaurant on the ground flor.

E **Sengsaly Guesthouse**, up the hill and around the bend from the market, T088-210165. Worn but comfortable rooms in a concrete building, with squat toilets and scoop showers. The friendly owners will bring you hot water in the evening for the Lao tea provided in your room or, if you prefer, to shower with.

F **Phongsaly Hotel**, opposite Kaysone Monument. This Chinese 4-storey monstrosity is the tallest building in town. There are 2 floors of large and airy triple rooms, some with hot-water bathrooms. Excellent views from the roof and a good restaurant. The Chinese owner is rumoured to have come by his money by poaching elephants. Price negotiable for longer stays.

F **Yu Houa Guesthouse**, across the road from the market, T088-210186. A 3-storey building with 6 clean fresh twin and double rooms. The more expensive rooms have a bathroom with Western toilet. Shared shower on the 2nd floor with squat toilet for the other rooms. Sweeping views of the valley from the rooms at the back. Restaurant downstairs.

Towards Udomxai *p136*
F **Sinsay Guesthouse**, Pak Nam Noi. Simple rooms for 20,000 kip.

❷ Eating

Nam Bak *p132*
❡ **Han Nang Nit**, opposite the market. The best of 2 or 3 noodle shops. No English but very friendly service – good place to wait for onward transport as the trucks stop outside.

Nong Khiaw and Ban Saphoun *p132, map p132*
Most of the guesthouses have cafés attached. For some fine dining the restaurant at the Riverside is absolutely fantastic, with an extensive wine menu to boot. For those

on a budget the **Phanoy Guesthouse** and **Bakery Bookshop** does reasonably good food. Ask for dishes to be served with *jeow* (chilli jam) delicious. Good selection of cakes.

Muang Ngoi Neua *p133*
Aside from the guesthouse restaurants, which serve quality Lao food, there are also a number of places to eat along the main road. Most have exactly the same food; in fact, many of them just copy their competitors' menus. The fruit shake stands in the centre of town are good value.

❡❡-❡ **Sainamgoi Restaurant & Bar**, in the centre of town. Tasty Lao food in a pleasant atmosphere, with good background music. The bar, the only one in town, is in the next room.

❡ **Nang Phone Keo Restaurant**, next to **Banana Guesthouse**. All the usual Lao food plus some extras: try the 'Falang Roll' for breakfast (a combination of peanut butter, sticky rice and vegetables).

❡ **Sengdala Restaurant & Bakery**, along the main road, with a bomb casing out front. Very good, cheap Lao food, terrific pancakes and freshly baked baguettes.

❡ **Sky Restaurant** is ambient in the evening although the food is not great.

Muang Khua *p134*
This is a small town with very few eateries, although what it lacks in restaurants, it makes up for in pool tables; very small children show a frightening aptitude and you should be prepared to have an instant audience if you try your hand; there is usually a box in which you are expected to make a donation.

Noodles and baguettes are available in the market.

❡❡-❡ **Nam Ou Guesthouse & Restaurant** (see Sleeping), up the mud slope from the beach. An incomparable location for a morning coffee overlooking the river; it has an English menu and friendly staff.

❡❡-❡ **Restaurant** opposite the **Singsavanh Guesthouse** has tasty fried noodles and rice dishes and an English menu.

❡ **Restaurant** next door to Keophila Guesthouse serves nice and cheap Vietnamese-style *feu*.

Towards Phongsali *p134*
❡ **Hat Xa**. The chief runs a very pricey and

basic restaurant, and has the only shop with a fridge. There is a small noodle shop on the hill towards Phongsali which serves much better and cheaper fare.

Phongsali *p135, map p135*
The rice here is steamed rather than sticky. There are *feu* stalls opposite the market.
♀ **Phongsaly Hotel** (see Sleeping). A good bet, with a variety of dishes including Thai, Chinese and Lao.
♀ **Yu Houa Guesthouse** (see Sleeping). A short Lao and Chinese section on an English menu. Cheap and good.

▲ Activities and tours

Muang Ngoi Neua *p133*
Trekking, hiking, fishing and kayaking, trips to the waterfalls and boat trips can be organized through most of the guesthouses for US$10 per day. Tubing can be arranged for US$2 per day.
Lao Youth Travel, www.laoyouthtravel.com. Daily 0730-1800. Half-day, day, overnight or 2-night treks, starting from US$10 per person. Also kayaking trips.

Phongsali *p135, map p135*
Trekking
A few independent local guides lead treks in the region. The **tourism office**, on the way to Phou Fa Hotel, T088-210098, Mon-Fri 0730-1130 and 1330-1630, can also arrange guided treks for up to 7 nights for around US$25 per day (1 person) or US$35 (2 people). **Chantha Sone**, T020-5688315, offers 1- or 2-day treks over the weekend for US$17 per person per day (1 person) or US$12 (2 people), including food and accommodation; he has a number of different routes, visiting some of the 35 ethnic villages in the area. **Mr Phonsai**, T020-5688357, is another local guide who comes recommended. Agencies in Luang Prabang and Luang Namtha also organize group treks around Phongsali.

☉ Transport

Nam Bak *p132*
There are regular trucks/buses to **Luang Prabang**. To **Nong Khiaw**, 1 hr by truck on a good road. In theory, the trucks wait for

the boats to arrive from Luang Prabang and Muang Khua. To **Muang Ngoi Neua**, 0700 and throughout the day as soon as they're full, 7000 kip; be prepared to wait around for a few hours, tuk-tuks are more frequent for the same price. To **Udomxai** (94 km), you need to take a *songthaew* to **Pak Mong**, 10 km west of Nam Bak, 8000 kip, and change there for a bus to Udomxai, 3 hrs, 15,000 kip. Don't be surprised if you have to wait in Pak Mong. To **Nam Nouan**, flag down one of the vehicles from Vientiane travelling east along Route 1, which usually pass the market at around 2000, 60,000 kip.

Nong Khiaw and Ban Saphoun *p132, map p132*
Boat
Boat services have become irregular following road improvements, although you may find a service to **Muang Ngoi Neua**, 1 hr, 20,000 kip, from the boat landing. However, these boats won't run unless there are enough passengers. Likewise, boats to Luang Prabang only run if enough people want to make the trip, so you might find yourself waiting a couple of days. Some vessels also head upriver to **Muang Khua**, 5 hrs, 100,000 kip. The river trips from Nong Khiaw are absolutely spectacular. It is possible to charter boats to both of these destinations.

Bus/truck
Buses en route from surrounding destina-tions stop in Nong Khiaw briefly. Basic time-tables are offered but buses can be hours early or late, so check details on the day. It is often a matter of waiting at the bus station for hours and hoping to catch the bus on its way through. Plonking yourself in a restaurant on the main road usually suffices but you will need to flag down the bus as it passes through town. Regular connections to **Luang Prabang**, 3-4 hrs, 0830 and 1100, 32,000 kip. Also several departures daily to **Nam Bak**, 30 mins, 10,000 kip and on to **Udomxai**, 1130, 4 hrs, 31,000 kip.
Alternatively, take one of the more regular *songthaew* to **Pak Mong**, 1 hr, 20,000 kip, where there is a small noodle shop-cum-bus station on the west side of the bridge, and then catch a vehicle on to Udomxai/ Vientiane (see Nam Bak Transport, above).

Travelling east on Route 1, there are buses to **Vieng Kham**, 2 hrs, 25,000 kip, and a village 10 km from **Nam Nouan**, where you can change and head south on Route 6 to **Phonsavanh** and the **Plain of Jars**. There are direct buses north to **Xam Neua** and the village near Nam Nouan, which can be caught from the toll gate on the Ban Saphoun side of the river when it comes through from Vientiane at around 2000-2200, 100,000 kip; it's usually quite crowded. If you miss a bus to or from Nong Khiaw you can always head to **Pak Mong** which is a junction town sitting at the cross-roads to Luang Prabang, Nong Khiaw and Udomxai. Aim to get here earlier in the day to catch through traffic otherwise you may have to stay overnight. (If you do, try the **Pak Mong Guesthouse Restaurant**, T020-5795860, or any of the other 6 places in town.

Muang Ngoi Neua p133
Boat

From the landing at the northern end of town, slow boats travel north along the beautiful Nam Ou surrounded by mountainous scenery to **Muang Khua**, 5 hrs, US$10, or charter your own for US$50 per boat. Slow boats also go south (irregularly) to **Nong Khiaw**, 1 hr, 20,000 kip, and **Luang Prabang**, 8 hrs, US$100 per boat. Departure times vary and whether they depart at all depends on there being sufficient passengers. For more information and tickets, consult the booth at the landing.

Muang Khua p134
Boat

Road travel is now more popular but irregular boats still travel south on the Nam Ou to **Muang Ngoi Neua/Nong Khiaw**, 4-5 hrs, 100,000 kip, if there is enough demand. Also north to **Phonsali** via **Hat Xa**, 6 hrs, 100,000 kip. Boats can be charted to Phonsali for around US$110. A jeep or truck transports travellers on from Hat Xa to Phonsali, 20 km, 2 hrs along a very bad road, 50,000 kip. Alternatively, charter a jeep, US$15.

Songthaew/truck

To get to **Phonsali**, take a *songthaew* to nearby village **Pak Nam Noi**, daily 0800, 1hr, 30,000 kip, then take the *songthaew* or bus

that passes through from Udomxai at around 1000, 9 hrs, 50,000 kip.

To **Udomxai**, pickups and buses leave daily 0700-0800 from the bus station alongside the market, 4 hrs, US$5, and to Luang Prabang, 8 hrs, US$7.

Phongsali p135, map p135
Air

Lao Airlines, T088-210794, fly to/from **Vientiane** twice a week, although flights can be cancelled at short notice. Lao Airlines on-and-off flights are a bit of a gamble and are often cancelled. At the time of publication we were told they had been discontinued. Another, newer option, is to fly with Lao Air, T021-512027, laoair@laopdr.com, which has 2 scheduled flights a week US$75 each way.

Bus/truck and boat

You can travel from **Muang Khua** to Phongsali either by truck or by boat. Trucks also depart from **Pak Nam Noi** (near Muang Khua); buy lunch from the market there before departure. The ride is long and difficult when the pickup is full, but it's a great experience: the hilltribes along the way are very interesting and the scenery towards the Phongsali end of the trip is utterly breathtaking. Alternatively, catch a boat from Muang Khua to **Hat Xa**, 20 km or so to the northeast of Phongsali, 5-6 hrs, 100,000 kip. In the low season, there may not be any scheduled boats so it may be necessary to gather a few extra tourists and charter a boat US$80-100. It's a beautiful trip, especially for birdwatching. Depending on the season, the river is quite shallow in places, with a fair amount of whitewater. It can be cold and wet so wear waterproofs and take a blanket. Note that you may find yourselves stuck in Hat Xa, as there are no onward buses to Phongsali after mid-afternoon.

❶ Directory

Nam Bak p132
Bank There's an exchange by the market.
Post The post office is 100 m west of the market.

Nong Khiaw and Ban Saphoun p132, map p132
Internet Sunset and Riverside guesthouses

(see Sleeping) have access. **Post** The post office is at the bridge, on the Nong Khiaw side.

Muang Ngoi Neua *p133*
Bank Lattanavongsa Money Exchange is on the main road at the northern end of town.

Muang Khua *p134*
Bank Lao Development Bank, near the truck stop, Mon-Fri 0800-1130 and 1300-1630, can change US$, Thai ฿ and Chinese ¥ for kip at quite bad rates. They won't change TCs or do cash advances on credit cards, so make sure you have plenty of cash before you come here. **Electricity** Daily 1830-2200. **Post** The post office is

opposite the wat; turn right at the top of the hill. **Telephone** International calls can be made from the Telecom office, a small unmarked hut with a huge satellite, halfway up the winding road, behind the bank, daily 0700-1130, 1300-1630.

Phongsali *p135, map p135*
Banks There is a branch of the Lao Development Bank, 20 m along from Phonsaly Hotel. It will only change US$, Thai ฿ and Chinese ¥. **Post** The post office is just down the road from the Viphahone. **Telephone** Calls can be made from Lao Telecom Office, next door to the post office or else there is an IDD call box on the opposite side of the road.

Northwest Laos

Northwestern Laos is comprised of dramatic, misty mountainous scenery, clad with thick forests and peppered with small villages. This area is home to a large variety of ethnic minority groups including the Akha, Hmong, Khmu and Yao and has become a firm favourite with trekkers. The mighty Mekong forges its way through picturesque towns, such as Pak Beng and Houei Xai, affording visitors a wonderful glimpse of riverine life. ▸▸ *For Sleeping, Eating and other listings, see pages 151-162.*

Udomxai (Oudom Xai) and around ●❷▲❸❶

▸▸ *pp151-162. Colour map 1, B3.*

→ *Phone code: 081.*

Udomxai, the capital of Udomxai Province, is a hot and dusty town. It was razed during the war and the inhabitants fled to live in the surrounding hills; what is here now has been built since 1975, which explains why it is such an ugly settlement. Since the early 1990s, the town has been experiencing an economic boom – as a result of its position at the intersection of roads linking China, Vietnam, Luang Prabang and Pak Beng – and commerce and construction are thriving. It also means that Udomxai has a large Chinese and Vietnamese population, a fact that appears to rile the locals.

The town's truck-stop atmosphere doesn't enamour it to tourists and, unfortunately, the other bad elements which come with major transport thoroughfares seem to be raising their heads here too, such as prostitution and increased HIV/AIDS. However, the town does make a decent stop-off point at a convenient junction; it's one of the biggest settlements in northern Laos and has excellent facilities. The **Provincial Tourism Office** ① *near the river on the main road in the centre of town, T081-211797, Mon-Fri 0800-1630*, can offer helpful advice.

Around Udomxai

Udomxai Province is populated by 23 different ethnic minority groups, with strong contingents of Hmong, Akha and Khmu. The village of **Ban Ting**, behind Udomxai is interesting to wander through. Its wat, just the other side of the stream, has a ruined monastery and a bizarre life-size tree made of concrete, with tin leaves, concrete animals in the foliage and two reclining Buddhas on the topmost branches. The wat

⁑ Visiting an Akha village

Many people have complained that visiting tribal villages is similar to visiting a human zoo. Here are some tips on how to avoid this experience:

→ Always visit with an Akha or locally endorsed guide rather than on your own.
→ Do not touch the spirit symbol, spirit gate, spirit house or swing and do not walk through the Akha entrance gate. Touching any of these things is believed to bring incredibly bad luck to the village.
→ If you wish to give gifts, such as money, these should be offered only to the Village Chief.
→ Accept food and drink if it is offered. The Akha may also offer you a massage; it's OK to accept.
→ Rather than watching people go about their work, ask if you can help them.

also includes a Buddhist high school for monks and offers a good view of the town and surrounding mountains.

Ban Mok Kho is a Hmong village 16 km along Route 1 to Nam Bak, where the inhabitants wear traditional dress and live in longhouses. To get there, catch a ride on a pickup going to Nam Bak, or negotiate a price with a taxi or tuk-tuk.

The local tourism authorities have teamed up with **Udomxai Travel** to offer treks in the **Houay Nam Kat Nature Reserve** and to the **Nam Kat** waterfall. A few tourists who have gone on the trip have reported only a trickle of water from the falls. ▶▶ *For further details, see Activities and tours, page 157.*

Muang La

Muang La is located 28 km north of Udomxai, off Route 4 to Phongsali and makes a lovely stop en route. **Wat Ban Pakkla** is considered one of the most sacred temples in the area, due to the presence of a 400-year-old, gold-plated Buddha image, known as the Pra Xaek Kham. Steeped in superstition and highly auspicious, the temple is the place to go if you want to make your dreams come true.

Muang La has gained popularity with travellers for its **hot springs**. Set in beautiful surroundings, the springs are a favourite afternoon bathing spot for the locals who come for a dip in the very hot waters. If you bathe here, wear a sarong or something discreet. The springs haven't really been developed and, at the time of publication, were full of algae but the authorities are trying to improve the site, so it is worth enquiring in Udomxai before you make the trip.

Muang Houn → *Colour map 1, B2.*

This is a new town (although it looks as old as any other), built in 1986 by the government to entice people down from the hills, in an attempt to stop them growing opium. There are quite a number of Blue Hmong in town.

Luang Namtha and around ⬤⬤⬤⬤⬤⬤ ▶▶ *pp151-162.*

Colour map 1, B2.
→ *Phone code: 086.*
The provincial capital was obliterated during the war and the concrete structures erected since 1975 have little charm. Like other towns in the north, the improvement in transport links with China and Thailand has led to burgeoning trade. The main attraction is the food market, where members of the many minorities who inhabit the

area can be found selling exotic species. Despite this dubious trade, the area has firmly established itself as a major player in Laos' ecotourism industry, primarily due to the Nam Ha National Protected Area (see page 144) and the environmentally friendly **Boat Landing Guesthouse** (see page 152).

Sights

The **Luang Namtha Museum** ⓘ *near the Kaysone Monument, daily 0830-1130, 1330-1530, 5000 kip*, is also worth a visit (although it was undergoing renovations at the time of publication). The museum houses a collection of indigenous clothing and artefacts, agricultural tools, weapons, textiles and a collection of Buddha images, drums and gongs.

In the centre of town is the fledgling **night market** with a range of food stalls. Only in its infancy, the local authorities have aspirations to expand the market to include ethnic handicrafts like the one in Luang Prabang.

That Poum Pouk sits in a ruinous state on a hill, 3 km west of the airfield. Local sources suggest that the stupa was built as part of a competition between the Lanna Kingdom (in northern Thailand) and the Lane Xang Kingdom to prove who had the most merit. Severe damage due to bombing in 1964 led local villagers and monks to reconstruct the stupa but this proved a somewhat fruitless exercise as further bombing in 1966 dislodged the stupa, parts of which still remain on the ground. Incredibly, much of the original stucco and an incripted stelae survived. The trip to the stupa is most pleasant in the afternoon; tuk-tuks will do the return trip from the market for US$5.

Villages around Luang Namtha

Luang Namtha Province has witnessed the rise and decline of various Tai Kingdoms and now over 30 ethnic groups reside in the province, making it the most ethnically diverse in the country. Principal minorities include Tai Lu, Tai Dam, Lanten, Hmong and Khamu. There are a number of friendly villages around the area. As with all other minority areas, you should only visit the villages with a local guide or endorsed tourism organization.

Ban Nam Chang is a Lanten village 3 km walk along a footpath outside Luang Namtha; ask the way. Lanten women are easily recognized: they wear their hair back and pluck their eyebrows from the age of 15. Their clothes are black, with coloured borders, and they wear a lot of delicate silver jewellery.

Ban Lak Khamay is quite a large Akha village 27 km from Luang Namtha on the road to Muang Sing. It was resettled from a nearby location higher in the hills in 1994 as part of a government policy to protect upland forests. The community now grows teak and rubber trees. The village chief speaks Lao. The settlement features a traditional Akha entrance; if you pass through this entrance you must visit a house in the village, or you are considered an enemy. Otherwise you can simply pass to one side of the gate but don't touch it. Other features of interest in Akha villages are the swing, located at the highest point in the village and used in the annual swing

Luang Namtha

To Muang Sing & Udomxai
Luang Namtha Museum
Kaysone Monument
Lao Telecom
BCEL
Luang Namtha Guide Service
Bike Rental
Night Market
Green Discovery
KNT
To Boat Landing, Airport, Lao Airlines & Houei Xai

N
100 metres
100 yards

Sleeping 😊
Boat Landing Guesthouse & Restaurant **12**
Luang Namtha Guesthouse **7**
Manychan Guesthouse **4**
Palanh Guesthouse **2**
Vila Guesthouse **10**
Zuela Guesthouse **5**

Eating 🍴
Bakery **1**
Banana **3**
Coffee House **6**
Panda **2**
Yamuna **4**

festival (you must not touch the swing), and the meeting house, where unmarried couples go to court and where newly married couples live until they have their own house. There is another, smaller Akha village a few kilometres on towards Muang Sing. ▶▶ *For further information, see Visiting an Akha village, page 142.*

Ban Nam Dee is a small bamboo papermaking Lanten village about 6 km northeast of Luang Namtha. The name of the village means 'good water' and not surprisingly, if you continue on from Ban Nam Dee 1 km there's a waterfall. The trip to the village is stunning, passing through verdant green rice paddies dotted with huts. A motorbike rather than a bicycle will be necessary to navigate these villages and sights as the road can be very rocky. Villagers usually charge 3000 kip for access to the waterfall.

The small Tai Lue village of **Ban Khone Kam** is also worth a visit. The settlement is based on the banks of the Nam Tha, halfway between Luang Namtha and Houei Xai, and is only accessible by boat or by foot. The friendly villagers offer **homestays** here (30,000 kip per night, includes meals), for one or two nights, providing an interesting cultural insight into the daily lives of the region's boatmen and rice farmers. For trips between Luang Namtha and Houei Xai contact the **Luang Namtha Boat Station** ① *T086-211305*, or the environmentally friendly **Boat Landing Guesthouse** in Luang Namtha.

Ban Vieng Nua, 3 km from the centre of town, is a Tai kolom village famous for its traditional house where groups can experience local dancing and a good luck baci ceremony (US$30 for the group). Contact the tourist information office (see page 141) to make bookings. Dinner can also be organized here at a cost of US$6 per head.

Vieng Phouka and around

Before the roads were upgraded, Vieng Phouka was the place to stay overnight when travelling between Luang Namtha or Muang Sing and the Mekong. Located south of Luang Namtha (and 125 km north of Houei Xai), the town is surrounded by minority villages, Akha, Hmong, Lahu and Khmu, with the Khmu comprising about 90% of the population. The local tourism authority runs treks around the area. ▶▶ *For further details, see Activities and tours, page 157.*

The 5-km-long **Nam Aeng cave**, 12 km north of Vieng Phouka, is famous locally for an annual ceremony on 13 January, when elders call up the large fish in the cave. The **Nom cave**, a four-hour walk from the town, was once home to a famous sacred Buddha, which has now been pilfered. During the revolution it served as a hideout. Around the area are a few scattered remains of the wall from the ancient city of Kuvieng, much of which has been dismantled by local villagers at the government's insistence.

Both Luang Namtha and Vieng Phouka make great bases from which to venture into the **Nam Ha National Protected Area** (NPA), one of a few remaining places on earth where the rare black-cheeked gibbon can be found. If you're lucky you can hear the wonderful singing of the gibbons in the morning.

Nam Ha National Protected Area

This area has firmly established itself as a major player in Laos' ecotourism industry, primarily due to the **Nam Ha Ecotourism Project**, which was established in 1993 by NTA Lao and UNESCO to help preserve Luang Namtha's cultural and environmental heritage in the Nam Ha National Protected Area. The Nam Ha NPA is one of the largest protected areas in Laos and consists of mountainous areas dissected by several rivers. It is home to at least 38 species of large mammal, including the black-cheeked crested gibbon, tiger and clouded leopard, and over 300 bird species, including the stunning Blythe's kingfisher. The Nam Ha project has won a UN development award for its outstanding achievements in the area.

The organization currently leads two- and three-day treks in the area for small

● *The residents of Ban Boolahn Village, about 14 km north of Vieng Phouka, are renowned*
● *locally as bat hunters; the creatures are used for cooking.*

⠿ Border essentials: Boten-Mohan (China)

The border between Boten (Laos) and Mohan (China) is open to international traffic daily 0800-1600. There have been reports of some citizens getting Chinese visas here but it depends on nationality so you'll need to check in advance. (The nearest Chinese embassy is in Vientiane.) Travelling from Luang Namtha or Udomxai to China, the earliest you can arrive in Boten is 1100. This means that when you cross into China you have to stay in Mengla (2 hours away). Mengla is a nasty introduction to China, reverberating with the tiresome sounds of karaoke and prostitutes until the early hours. It is better to stay in Boten overnight and then make an early start to reach the much nicer town of Jinghong (5-6 hours from Mengla).

Coming into Laos, you can pick up a 30-day Lao visa at the border or in advance from the Lao consulate in Kunming, which is inside the Camelia Hotel (T0871-3176624); the latter takes three working days to process or 24 hours on payment of a surcharge.

You can change remaining yuan into Lao kip at the border. The bus station is a walk down the hill. There is limited accommodation in Boten so if you want to make it to the bigger settlement of Luang Namtha, you should aim to cross in the morning when transportation is ubiquitous, rather than in the afternoon when you could find yourself stranded. If there isn't a direct bus, take the bus to Udomxai and change at Natuei. If you want to go to Vientiane and there isn't a direct bus, your best bet is to catch a bus to Udomxai and transfer there to Vientiane/Luang Prabang.

groups of four to eight culturally sensitive travellers. The treks offer the chance to visit traditional villages, explore various forest habitats, take river trips and support local conservation efforts. A relatively new trek to **Phu Sam Yord**, Three Peak Mountain, has recently been unveiled. The trek is a fantastic way to witness a variety of cultures, partake in local village activities and see stunning landscapes. New, longer routes to other villages are also being explored. Treks leave three to four times a week; check with the **Luang Namtha Guide Service Unit** or **Green Discovery** (see Tour operators, page 157) for departure days; an information session about the trek is given at the Guide's Office. The price will cover the cost of food, water, transportation, guides, lodging and the trekking permit. All the treks utilize local guides who have been trained to help generate income for their villages. Income for conservation purposes is also garnered from the fees for trekking permits into the area. Several vendors on the main road offer inflated inner tubes for tubing on the Nam Ha River, though this is organized without the expertise in tubing and river awareness of other places in the country and is not always safe, particularly when the waters are high. ▶▶ *For further details, see Activities and tours, page 157.*

Nateui → *Colour map 1, B2.*

Nateui is a small roadside settlement northeast of Luang Namtha at the junction of Route 3 and Route 1. Route 3 runs southeast from here to Udomxai, while Route 1 runs north 18 km to the border settlement of Boten and then into China. This stretch of road is currently being rebuilt as part of the Chinese highway through to Myanmar; as a result it's quite painful and dusty at the the moment but in the near future will be one of the more enjoyable bits of travelling in Laos. Nateui has become a stopover town for trucks driving from Luang Prabang, through Boten, to Mengla in China.

Boten lies on the border with China and, until recently, was nothing more than a trucking stop for drivers, with a couple guesthouses here and a handful of noodle shops. However, the town is set for dramatic change, with the construction of the massive Chinese-funded 'Golden Boten City' project. The 10-year project aims to build warehouses, several marketplaces, 2000 hotel rooms and 500 guesthouses, entertainment venues and a golf course. The first foundation stone was laid in 2005 but whether these grandiose plans actually come to fruition remains to be seen. The city project is hoping to capitalize on the upgrading of Highway R3, which will eventually run from Kunming, China, through Luang Namtha and Bokeo provinces to Bangkok, Thailand.

> ❗ *A road leads from Muang Sing to the Chinese border but the crossing is not open to foreigners – at least officially. Boten is still the only point where foreign nationals can cross to or from China.*

Muang Sing ▨▨▨▲▨▮

▶▶ *pp151-162. Colour map 1, B2.*

Many visitors consider this peaceful valley to be one of the highlights of the north. Lying at the terminus of the highway in the far northwest corner of Laos, it is a natural point to stop and spend a few days recovering from the rigours of the road, before either heading south or moving on to China. This area is a border region that has been contested by the Chinese, Lao and Thai at various points in the last few centuries. While it is now firmly Lao territory, there is a gnawing sense that the Chinese have again invaded by stealth; their economic presence is all too evident. There are also several NGOs, as well as bilateral and multilateral development operations, in the area. The only way to get to Muang Sing is by truck or pickup from Luang Namtha. The road is asphalt but is sometimes broken and the terrain on this route is mountainous with dense forest.

Sights

Muang Sing itself is little more than a supremely picturesque village, situated on an upland plateau, where golden rattan huts glow among misty, blue-green peaks. The town features some interesting old wooden and brick buildings and, unlike nearby Luang Namtha and several other towns in the north, it wasn't bombed close to oblivion during the struggle for Laos. The **old French fort**, built in the 1920s, is off limits to visitors, as it is occupied by

Muang Sing

To ① & Chinese Border
School ▨

Bikes for hire

Nam Sing

To Morning Market

Muang Sing Exhibition ▨
Wat Sing Jai ▨
Tour Guide ▨
Library ▨ ③
⑫
⑤
②
⑬
⑩
ℹ

To Museum

Lao Development ▨ ⓢ ▨ ▨
Kaysone Monument ▨

⑦

To ⑧, Xieng Kok, Luang Namtha & Burmese Border

N
Not to scale

Sleeping ▨
Adima Guesthouse & Restaurant 1
Daenneua Guesthouse 3
Muang Sing Guesthouse 5
Phoulou 2 7
Phoutat Guesthouse/ Black Stupa 8

Sengdeuane Guesthouse & Restaurant 9
Sengkhatiyavang Guesthouse 10
Taileu Guesthouse & Restaurant 12
Viengxai Guesthouse & Restaurant 13

Eating ❼
Viengphone 2

Opium

Most ethnic groups in Muang Sing still live traditionally and practise slash-and-burn agriculture, growing rice, corn and even some cotton. Many of the local Akha villages were originally built on slopes as high as 600-1500 m but the government relocated villages down to 400-600 m in an attempt to eradicate opium farming in the hills. For a long time Muang Sing was highly reliant on the opium trade, with the drug used for medicinal purposes for over a hundred years. The government crackdown (in the face of international pressure) has impoverished many farmers but, despite the government's best efforts, opium is still readily available to buy in the town. Needless to say, don't buy it under any circumstances.

One tourist who had taken too much opium ran naked into an ethnic minority village in the middle of the night, only to be beaten up by local villagers who thought an evil ghost (*pii*) had come to attack their village. There are two morals to this story: never take opium and always dress modestly in Laos.

the Lao army, but the **market** is certainly worth a look if you're up very early in the morning; it starts about 0545 and begins to wind down after 0730. Along with the usual array of plastic objects, clothes and pieces of hardware, local silk and cotton textiles can be purchased. Numerous hill peoples come to the market to trade, including Akha and Hmong tribespeople, along with Yunnanese, Tai Dam and Tai Lu.

The **Muang Sing Ethnic Museum** ① *in the centre of town, Mon-Fri 0900-1200, 1300-1600, 5000 kip*, is a beautiful building housing a range of traditional tools, ethnic clothes, jewellery, instruments, religious artefacts and household items, like the loom. The building was once the royal residence of the Jao Fa (Prince), Phanya Sekong. There is another, enigmatic museum, near the central market, although it is not officially open. If you knock on the building next door the occupants might be able to point you in the direction of the gate-keeper, who holds the key. Most Buddhist monasteries in the vicinity are Tai Lue in style. The most accessible is **Wat Sing Chai**, on the main road.

‡ *The tourist office has loads of information, from transport details through to local history.*

Around Muang Sing

The area around Muang Sing is home to many minorities who have been resettled, either from refugee camps in Thailand or from highland areas of Laos. The town is predominantly Tai Lue but the district is 50% Akha, with a further 10% Tai Neua. The population of the district is said to have trebled between 1992 and 1996 and, as a result, it is one of the few places in northern Laos where hilltribe villages are readily accessible. The main activity for visitors is to hire bicycles and visit the villages that surround the town in all directions; several guesthouses have maps of the surrounding area and trekking is becoming increasingly popular. However, please do not undertake treks independently as it undermines the government's attempts to make tourism sustainable and minimize the impact on the culture of local villages.

From Muang Sing, trek uphill past **Phoutat Guesthouse** for 7 km to reach **That Xieng Tung**, the most sacred site in the area. The stupa was built in 1256 and is believed to contain the Buddha's adam's apple. It attracts lots of pilgrims in November for the annual full moon festival. Originally a city was built around the

● *Local folklore suggests that Muang Sing was founded hundreds of years ago, when two lions (sing) came down from the Himalayas and settled here.*

stupa but everyone migrated down to lower lands. There is a small pond near the stupa, which is also believed to be very auspicious: if it dries up it is considered very bad luck for Muang Sing. It is said that the pond once dried up and the whole village had no rice and starved. Most tourism operators will run treks up to the stupa and will also stop at **Nam Keo** waterfall, a large cascade with a 10-m drop that trickles down into a little brook. It's a nice place for a picnic lunch. The local tourism authority runs treks to the falls for upwards of US$10. Bring good shoes. ▶▶ *For further details, see Activities and tours, page 157.*

Along the Mekong 🏠🏊▲🚌🎫 ▶ *pp151-162.*

Houei Xai (Houay Xai) and around → *Phone code: 084. Colour map 1, B1.*

This town is in the heart of the Golden Triangle and used to derive its wealth from the narcotics trade on the heroin route to Chiang Mai in Thailand. Today trade still brings

‼ *Houei Xai is a good place to shop for Lao weaving and gems, as it is cheaper than Vientiane.*

the town considerable affluence, although it is rather less illicit: timber is ferried across the Mekong from Laos to the Thai town of Chiang Khong and, in exchange, consumer goods are shipped back. Sapphires are mined in the area and, doubtless, there is also still some undercover heroin smuggling.

Houei Xai is a popular crossing point for tourists travelling to and from Thailand and a considerable amount of money flows in from the numerous guesthouses and restaurants that have been built here. However, few people spend more than one night in the town. Most passengers arrive close to the centre at the passenger ferry pier. The vehicle ferry pier is 750 m further north (upstream), while the post office is about 500 m south, at the edge of town.

Although the petite, picturesque town is growing rapidly as links with Thailand intensify, it is still small and easy enough to get around on foot.

Wat Chom Kha Out Manirath, in the centre of town, is worth a visit for its views. The monastery was built at the end of the 19th century but, because it is comparatively well endowed, there has been a fair amount of re-building and renovation since then. There is also a large former French fort here called **Fort Carnot** now used by the Lao army (and consequently out of bounds).

The **Morning Market** can be entertaining, particularly for first-time visitors who have entered from Thailand, as this will be their first experience of a Lao market. There is little of note about the products on display but local tribespeople come from their villages to sell things here. To get there, take a tuk-tuk (3000 kip). There is a **sapphire mine** south of the town, near the fast boat terminal. The miners pan in the morning and clean the stones in the afternoon, so the afternoon is the best time to visit.

Most visitors who stick around Houei

Houei Xai

To Nam Khong Hills

Vehicle Ferry Pier

Red Cross ✚

Mekong

Sebong

Gibbon Experience ▣

Passenger Ferry Pier, Immigration & Customs

▲ Wat Chom Kha Out Manirath

Bokeo Travel Agency ▣

✉ Morning 🚌

To Tin That Pier (2km), That Nevsouvanna (3km) & Airport (9km)

N

Not to scale

Sleeping 🛏
Arimid Guesthouse 1
BAP Guesthouse 2
Houay Xai 3

Sabaydee 5
Thanormsub Guesthouse 6
Taveensinh Guesthouse 7

Eating 🍴
Khemkhong 1
Nutpop 3
Riverside 4

Border essentials: Houei Xai-Chiang Khong (Thailand)

Small boats ferry passengers across the Mekong between Houei Xai (Laos) and Chiang Khong (Thailand) every 10-20 minutes throughout the day, 10,000 kip, five minutes. Thai immigration is open daily 0800-1800. A one-month Thai visa is available at the border. Buses and taxis travel from Chiang Kong to Chiang Rai Airport where there are connections

to Bangkok. From Chaing Khong there are regular buses to Chiang Rai, 0600-1700, and Chiang Mai, 1100.
 Crossing into Laos, immigration is open daily 0800-1700, but expect to pay a US$1 overtime fee at the weekend or after 1600. Tourist visas (30 days) are available at the border for US$30-42. There is also a bank at the Lao border (daily 0830-1600).

Xai do so to visit the **Gibbon Experience** ① T084-212021, www.gibbonx.org, a three-day trip into **Bokeo Nature Reserve** where a number of tree houses have been built high up in the jungle canopy and linked with a course of interconnected zip-lines. The experience of staying in one of these tree houses and being awoken by singing soprano gibbons is truly awe-inspiring, as is zip-lining through the mist above the jungle canopy. In the morning well-trained guides take visitors for hikes to see if they can spot the elusive gibbons and other plant and animal species. Such species include the giant squirrel, one of the largest rodents in the world, and the Asiatic black bear, whose numbers are in decline due to hunting for their bile and gall bladders. First and foremost this is a very well-run conservation project. The **Gibbon Experience** was started to help reduce poaching, logging, slash-and-burn farming and the destruction of primary forest by working with villagers to transform the local economy by making a non-destructive living from their unique environment. Already the project has started to pay dividends: the forest conservation and canopy visits can generate as much income year on year as local logging company could do only once. The cost is US$150 for three days and includes tree house accommodation, transport, food, access to Bokeo Nature Reserve and well-trained guides who can explain the surrounding environment.

Ban Nam Chan is a pleasant Chinese-speaking village, about 17 km from Houei Xai. The Lanten tribespeople who live here are famous for their textiles: the women wear black, kaftan-style dresses and shave their eyebrows and wear a headpiece once they are married; the men wear black shirts and blue trousers. Along the way, the road passes Hmong villages (15 km in). **Ban Nam Keun**, a small traditional village on the high plateau not far from the main town, is worth a visit for its natural beauty.

Pak Beng → Colour map 1, C2.
This long thin strip of a village is perched halfway up a hill, with fine views over the Mekong. Its importance lies in its location at the confluence of the Mekong and the Nam Beng. There is not much to do here but it's a good place to stop on the slow boat between Houei Xai and Luang Prabang (or vice versa). The village is worth a visit for its traditional atmosphere and the friendliness of the locals, including various minorities. Just downstream from the port is a good spot for swimming in the dry season, but be careful as the current is strong. There are also a couple of monasteries in town. The locals are now organizing guided treks to nearby villages; check with **Bounmy Guesthouse** (see Sleeping).

Hongsa and around
From Pak Beng you can take a boat downriver to the small town of **Tha Suang** and then catch a songthaew, through beautiful jungled hills, to the valley of Hongsa. Hongsa

district is renowned for its 70 working elephants, which are used as all-purpose heavy 'machinery' for the timber trade and other agricultural purposes. Hongsa town is usually just a jump-off point for excursions to nearby **Vieng Ghiaw**, whose men have a long tradition as *mahouts* (elephant handlers), training elephants specifically for use in the local timber trade. ►► *For details of elephant treks, see Activities and tours, page 157.*

❗ *Hongsa is under 50 km from the Thai border. At the time of publication the crossing at Muang Ngeun wasn't open to foreigners, though it is said to be opening up soon.*

Vieng Ghiaw is surrounded by overgrown, ruined city walls, believed to be hundreds of years old, and an extensive moat system that spans several kilometres. The predominatly Tai Lue village features traditional stilt houses, made of solid Mai Du (an Asian rosewood) and designed to house both elephants and humans, with a large spacious area underneath so that the mahout can step straight off his veranda onto the elephant's back. Locals are actively involved in the preservation of these unique houses and are hoping, through sponsorship, to keep their village homes rather than replacing them with ugly, concrete equivalents. Displayed beneath the veranda are miscellaneous items, usually weaving looms or elephant saddles, which symbolize the family's social status. The Tai Lue use a variety of saddles, separate ones for training, hunting, weddings or religious celebrations. The village is also well known for its textiles, woven by the Tai Lue women.

Sayaboury (Xayaboury) 🚌🚻🚐🌑 ►► *pages 151-162.*

Colour map 1, C2.
→ *Phone code: 074.*

Sayaboury is not on many visitors' agendas. This is partly because it is a difficult place to get to and partly because there doesn't seem any obvious reason to make the effort. There is no direct road between Vientiane and Sayaboury so the only way to get here from the capital is to take a boat upriver to Pak Lai and then to catch a bus – if the road isn't washed away. Rather easier is to catch a bus from Luang Prabang through Muang Nan, cross the Mekong by ferry, and then take a bus to Sayaboury – a comparatively painless four- to seven-hour journey. Having reached Sayaboury and sampled its limited enticements, it is then necessary to retrace your steps or set out for Pak Lai and hope for a downstream boat to Vientiane – wishful thinking for the most part.

These transport difficulties have given Sayaboury a rather charming forgotten atmosphere. It may be the capital of a province covering over 16,000 sq km – equivalent to the area of Hawaii or Northern Ireland – and with 300,000 inhabitants, but it doesn't feel like it. The town is located in an attractive setting on the Nam Houn – a tributary of the Mekong – and has a number of monasteries; those of note, according to local historians, are **Wat Thin**, **Wat Pha Phoun**, **Wat Natonoy** and **Wat Sisavang Vong**, named after the king who reigned during the de facto Japanese occupation of French Indochina. The province is mountainous with Phu Khao Mieng, Laos' ninth highest peak, just exceeding 2000 m.

Gluttons for punishment or very adventurous souls, depending on which way you look at it, may care to take the seven- to 10-hour *songthaew* trip from Sayaboury to Hongsa (see page 149). The trip covers some stunning territory and you may see some working elephants en route but it is a bone-jarringly bumpy trip on unsealed roads and, in the rainy season, they are often flooded.

Pak Lai → *Colour map 2, B1.*

Pak Lai is not very much more than a convenient place to stop on the long river

⬤ *Sayaboury has more alternative spellings than most – and this in a country which is replete with imaginative transliterations: you'll come across Sainyabuli, Sayabouri, Sayaboury, Sayaburi, Xaignabouli, Xaignabouri, Xayabury and others.*

journey between Vientiane and Luang Prabang and it grew up as a boating equivalent to a truck stop. There are a sprinkling of colonial shopfronts and old wooden Lao houses, a couple of guesthouses, a few restaurants and shops, and a desultory branch of the Lao Development Bank.

Pak Lai does, however, enjoy a footnote in Laos' colonial history which is worth recounting. In 1887 Luang Prabang was attacked by a band of Chinese Haw and northern Tai bandits. Auguste Pavie, the newly appointed French vice consul, rescued King Unkham from his burning palace and escaped downstream to Pak Lai. Here they remained while the old and frail king recovered from the journey and Pavie researched the early history of Lane Xang. This piece of quick-thinking indebted the king to Pavie and therefore also to the French. Within five years of this heroic rescue Laos was French and the Siamese had lost control of the country.

● Sleeping

Udomxai *p141, map p151*

D Fu Shan, 2 doors down from the Sing Tong (and a step up in the friendliness stakes), T081-312198. A Chinese establishment, offering bare doubles with en suite hot shower and Western toilet, TV and fan. Restaurant downstairs.

D Surinphone, T081-212789, srphone@laotel.com. Very comfortable, clean and modern a/c rooms with TV and comfortable beds, hot-water bathrooms with bathtub. All in all a good choice. Very friendly.

D-E Litthavixay Guesthouse, about 100 m before the turning onto the airport road, T081-212175. This place has the best rooms in town, large single, double and triple rooms and all very clean. Rooms with lots of facilities. Hot water shower attached. Best-value internet in town. The restaurant has a small but good selection of foreign breakfast dishes.

E Saylomyen Guesthouse, about 200 m from the airport, T081-211377. Very clean, comfortable rooms, some with adjoining bathrooms and hot water. Also an 'open-air' room for use in the warmer months.

F Dokbouadeng, T081-312142. Rooms with en suite shower and Western toilet, small restaurant downstairs.

F Linda Guesthouse, downhill from the market and across the bridge, T081-312147. Reasonably new 3-storey white building, with gold frescoes and lobby with comfortable sofa. Clean, furnished rooms, some with bathroom en suite, Western toilet and hot water. Rooms have fan and balcony.

F Linda No2 Guesthouse, on the street behind the Kaysone Monument, T020-5681188. Clean rooms with hot water, bath and TV. Although their English is not great, the staff here are friendly. Restaurant downstairs. Good value.

Udomxai map — Sleeping: Dokbouadeng 1, Fu Shan 2, Linda 4, Linda No 2 Guesthouse 5, Litthavixay Guesthouse 6, Phuxay 8, Saylomyen Guesthouse 10, Somphou Guesthouse 12, Yang Lu 13, Thanousin 3. Eating: Sinphet Guesthouse & Restaurant 1. Not to scale.

F Phuxay, downhill on the main street from the market and across the bridge, turn right after the petrol station (there is a sign at the petrol station), up the road from the police counter-narcotics unit, T081-312140. Newly revived, clean rooms with en suite hot shower and toilet, TV and minibar. The double beds are massive. Nice garden with sitting area.

F Somphou Guesthouse, next to Linda Guesthouse. Not-so-clean doubles with en suite hot-water baths and Western toilets. Comfy lounge with a TV. Also dorm beds for 10,000 kip each, with shared toilet and shower. Restaurant downstairs.

F Yang Lu Guesthouse, a few doors up from the Sai Xi, T081-312067. Large rooms with TV, en suite shower, hot water and toilet; a bit gloomy but the staff are friendly.

Around Udomxai *p141*

A-B Kamu Lodge, Ban Nyong Hay, Udomxai Province, T071-241861. On the banks of the Mekong, 3 hrs upstream from Luang Prabang. Visitors usually stay here en route from Houei Xai, when booking an ecotour with **Exotissimo** (see Tour operators, page 111), but you can also stay here independently. Good if you're after a few days' isolation. Management plans to turn this into a major eco-resort but for now accommodation is in modern canvas tents, decorated with local furnishings. The Lao restaurant serves excellent fish. Also runs some treks and activities, such as gold panning. **Exotissimo** will arrange transport too (extra).

Muang La *p142*

F Hot Springs Resort. If you wish to stay, this is your only option, with US$3 accommodation in basic wood and bamboo constructions, with fan and river-water showers. The resort also has a very basic restaurant.

Muang Houn *p142*

F Bounnam Guesthouse, T081-212289. Basic no-frills guesthouse, with reasonable facilities for a short stay.

F Miss Manyvane. A 2-storey concrete house, with a little balcony upstairs. Basic facilities, 4 rather mouldy twin rooms, with tattered mosquito nets, shared toilet and scoop shower. The family lives downstairs.

Luang Namtha *p142, map p143*

There has been a sudden rush of guesthouses popping up here over the last few years yet, despite this, Luang Namtha has very little in the way of decent accommodation aside from the **Boat Landing**, the best ecotourism venture in the country and the stand-out choice in the area.

B Boat Landing Guesthouse & Restaurant, T086-312398. Further out of town than most other guesthouses, this place is located right on the river. Time stands still here. It's an eco-resort that has got everything just right: pristine surroundings, environmentally friendly rooms, helpful service and a brilliant restaurant serving traditional northern Lao cuisine. The rooms are very homely, combining modern design with traditional materials and decoration. The gardens are beautiful and brimming with butterflies and birds. Great restaurant attached serving local indigenous dishes. Recommended.

C Vila Guesthouse, on the southern side of town, T086-312425. A 2-storey building with 11 of the cleanest rooms in town, lounge and sparkling en suite bathrooms, with hot water.

E Manychan Guesthouse, on the main road in the centre of town, T086-312209. One of the most popular places in town, probably due to the location and its good restaurant. Decent, clean rooms with fan and hot water bathrooms. Bikes can be hired next door for 15,000 kip per day. Very friendly staff.

E Palanh Guesthouse, T086-312439. Relatively clean rooms, with fan. Big ones are airy and spacious with en suite bathrooms; smaller (and cheaper) rooms have no attached bathrooms but, rather delightfully, you walk along the veranda to get to the communal facilities. Rustic.

E Zuela Guesthouse, T086-312183. Fantastic value guesthouse in a beautiful modern wooden building with extremely comfortable beds and linen. Immaculate rooms with fan and attached hot water bathrooms. This family-run guesthouse is truly a league apart from other budget options in town. Restaurant attached. Highly recommended.

F Luang Namtha Guesthouse, 2 blocks

For an explanation of the eating and sleeping price codes used in this guide, see inside the front cover. Other relevant information is found in Essentials, see pages 29-32.

west of the main centre, T086-312087. Run by 2 friendly Hmong brothers, one of whom speaks English. The house is an impressive building for Luang Namtha, with a grand staircase. All rooms are beautifully clean and furnished, with en suite hot-water bathrooms and balconies. Satellite TV in the more pricey rooms.

Vieng Phouka p144
There are a few very, very basic guest-houses in town, try the **Don Vieng**, T084-212394, US$2-3, or the **Bo Kung**.

Nateui p145
E **Tali Guesthouse**, on the main road. No traffic in the evening, so it is quiet and serves reasonably good food.

Boten p146
At present there is a small, unmarked guesthouse right on the border (**E**). Basic doubles, clean enough, geared to Chinese, Vietnamese and Lao truckers. Expect a few more to crop up soon as the major construction work begins. Boten also has a couple of *feu* stalls but little else.

Muang Sing p146, map p146
D **Phoulou 2**, at the southern end of town, T086-212348. Has great double bungalows and provides towels and bottled water. The lack of scenery is its only downfall.
D **Phoutat Guesthouse/Black Stupa**, 6 km out of Muang Sing on the main road towards Luang Namtha, T020-5686555. This place changes its name about every 6 months but remains the best accommo-dation in the vicinity. 10 wooden bungalows perched on the side of a hill, looking over the small town, mountains and rice paddies. Quaint gardens, home to an abundance of butterflies, link the bungalows via a small paved path. Hot water, fan, Western toilet and fantastic balcony. Stunningly beautiful. There is also quite a decent restaurant on site, whose views extend all the way to China. Very good value. Recommended.
D-E **Adima Guesthouse**, near Ban Oudomsin, north of Muang Sing towards the Chinese border, T020-2249008. A little hard to get to but the location is scenic. Peaceful bungalows constructed in traditional Yao and Akha style, plus a lovely open-air

restaurant. A calm retreat surrounded by rice fields. Minority villages are literally on the doorstep. Footprint does not endorse DIY treks using the guesthouse map, which are having a negative effect on local villages. If you wish to trek please visit the local tourism office or contact **Exotissimo**, see page 157, to organize a bonafide eco-trek. To get there, take a tuk-tuk (20,000 kip) or hire a bike. Alternatively, the owner runs in and out of town about 3 times a day (depending on bus arrival times) and will pick you up from the bus station for a small fee.
E **Sengdeuane Guesthouse**, at the far end of town from the bus stop, T086-212376. A quiet spot. Rooms have iron doors which make the place resemble a dungeon, but there's an attractive view from the roof. Shared bathroom outside. The owners have built large clean rooms out the back, which boast adjoining bathrooms, hot water and enormous double beds.
F **Daenneua Guesthouse**, on the main road, T086-212369. Friendly staff, good restaurant, slightly better rooms than **Taileu**, now with hot water and laundry service.
F **Taileu Guesthouse**, on the main road, T030-1212375. Above the restaurant, 8 very basic rattan rooms with bamboo style, 4-poster beds (the rickety backpacker version not the romantic type), squat toilets and temperamental hot water via solar power. The owners are lovely, lovely people.
Additional guesthouses (**F**) in the centre of town include **Muang Sing**, **Viengxai** (see Eating) and **Sengkhatiyavang**. There's nothing to really distinguish between them: basic, cramped double rooms, with shared squat toilets and shower and paper-thin walls, although the **Viengxai** now has some en suite bathrooms.

Houei Xai p148, map p148
There is a cluster of hotels on Sekhong Rd, which is the main street running through the town.
D-E **Arimid Guesthouse**, northwest end of the town, T084-211040. The owners Mr and Mme Chitaly speak excellent French and a little English. Comfortable individual rattan-style bungalows, bathroom attached, hot water, nice garden area and great balconies. Some with a/c. Mme Chitaly will cook tasty food and serve it to you at your

bungalow. Close to the slow boat terminal.

D-E Taveensinh Guesthouse, northwest end of the town, T084-211502. The best value in town fan, TV hot water bathrooms. Great communal balconies overlooking the river.

E BAP Guesthouse, on the main Sekhong Rd, T084-211083. One of the oldest guesthouses in town consisting of a labyrinth of additions and add-ons as their business has grown over the years. A range of rooms, though the newer tiled ones with hot-water bathrooms are the best. The female proprietor here is hard as nails but has loads of charisma and a wily sense of humour.

E Houay Xai, in the centre of town. Rooms with en suite bathroom, including hot shower. Basic but clean hotel, friendly staff.

E Sabaydee, T020-5483233. Big, tiled rooms, with en suite hot showers and Western toilets. Recommended.

F Thanormsub Guesthouse, on the main Sekhong Rd, T084-211095. Double rooms, clean, hot water, fan and satin curtains to boot. Nice, helpful staff.

Pak Beng p149, map p154

During peak season, when the slow boat arrives from Luang Prabang, about 60 people descend on Pak Beng at the same time. As the town doesn't have an endless supply of great budget guesthouses, it is advisable to get someone you trust to mind your bags, while you make a mad dash to get the best room in town. There are a number of shack-like bamboo lodgings running up the hill.

A-B Pakbeng Lodge. A wooden and concrete construction, built in Lao style, this stunning guesthouse sits perched on a hillside above the Mekong and includes 20 rooms with fan, toilet and hot water. Good restaurant and wonderful views. Owned by the same people who own the **Elephant Lodge** in Hongsa (see page 155).

B Luangsay Lodge, about 1 km from the centre of town, T081-212296, www.mekongcruises.com. This is the most beautiful accommodation available in Pak Beng. An attractive wooden pathway curves through luscious tropical gardens to several wooden bungalows with fantastic balconies and large windows overlooking the river and misty mountains. Hot water bathrooms and romantic rooms make this a winner. Great

restaurant. Book in advance as it tends to get booked up by customers on the Luangsay Cruise. Recommended.

B Phetsoxkai Hotel, T081-212299. Large Lao-owned hotel which looks grand but doesn't live up to expectation. Nonetheless the 28 rooms are beautifully decorated, though on the smallish side. Hot water bathroom, DVD player. Restaurant with Western, Lao and Thai cuisine. Very friendly owners.

D-E Salika, T081-212306. This is an elegant structure on the steep cliff overlooking the river. Big, clean rooms with toilet and shower en suite (mostly cold), tiled floors. There is a great restaurant, serving reasonably priced meals (see Eating). Fantastic service.

E-F Donevilisack Guesthouse, T081-212315. The popular **Donevilasack** offers a pretty reasonable choice of rooms. In the older, wooden building are basic budget rooms, with fan, mosquito net and

Pak Beng

To Udom Xai

Wat Sin Jong Jaeng

Wat Khok Kho

Nam Beng

Ticket Office for Boats

To **3** | Boat Landing

To Houei Xai

To Luang Prabang

Mekong

N

Not to scale

Sleeping
Bounmy Guesthouse **1**
Donevilisack Guesthouse **2**
Luangsay Lodge **3**
Monsavan **5**
Pakbeng Lodge **6**
Salika Guesthouse & Restaurant **7**

shared hot-water showers. More expensive rooms in the newer concrete building have private cold water bathrooms.

E-F Bounmy Guesthouse. Smallish bamboo rooms, with bed, fan, mosquito net and good, clean, bathrooms with hot water (some shared facilities). Although it occupies a quiet location, the walls are paper thin, which can be a bit annoying.

F Monsavan. Comparatively clean, bamboo rooms, with fan and mosquito net. It is reportedly rat-free, which is a plus, but the shared toilets are a bit of a hike away, on the other side of the road! Guests say the owner prepares good sandwiches for the boat-trip to Luang Prabang.

Hongsa *p149*
A-B Elephant Lodge, T074-252841. An upmarket choice that must be booked in conjunction with a tour from **Lao Travel Ecotourism**, T021-213180. The tour is quite expensive. Restaurant.
F Sunflower Guesthouse. Clean 2-storey guesthouse next to a beautiful lotus pond. The nearby **Lotus Café** is the best place for a quick bite to eat, with a surprising menu which includes a few Italian dishes and a Korean BBQ plus the usual Lao fare.

Sayaboury *p150*
F Hongvilai Guesthouse, south of the centre on the banks of the Nam Houn, T074-211068. This place has a good outlook but the rooms are a bit squalid – shared cold-water bathrooms and not quite clean. Even so, it makes a nice spot to stay.
F New Sayaboury Hotel. Large, 3-storey hotel with clean, fair-sized rooms boasting fan, en suite bathroom and hot water. For a few extra dollars you can get a/c. Recommended.

Pak Lai *p150*
F Banna Guesthouse, along the river road, east of the boat landing, T074-211995. Very clean, 3-storey guesthouse, 17 rooms with fan and shared facilities.
F Lamdouan Guesthouse, to the west of the boat landing, along the river road. Very friendly, family-run guesthouse, basic rooms with shared facilities.

There is a nice little restaurant beside the boat landing that serves *feu* and *pad gow*.

🍴 Eating

Udomxai *p141, map p151*
As well as those listed below, **Litthavixay Guesthouse** (see Sleeping) can whip up some good dishes, including Western-style pancakes and breakfasts. **Somphou** and **Dokbouadeng** guesthouses (see Sleeping) also have small cafés on the ground floor. There are a number of restaurants on the 1st left turn after the bridge; all do good Laos and Chinese food. Noodle soup shops are scattered throughout town and stalls in front of the market sell beer and snacks from nightfall.

🍴 Sinphet Guesthouse & Restaurant, opposite **Linda Guesthouse**. One of the best options in town. English menu, delicious iced coffee with ovaltine, great Chinese and Lao food. Try the curry chicken, *kua-mii* or yellow noodles with chicken. Also stocks some French wines.
🍴 Thanousin, on the corner of the road to the airport. Friendly service, menu in English, good basic Lao food.

Muang Houn *p142*
There are 2 eating places facing each other next to the market. Both serve noodles, eggs and sticky rice, no menu. Fresh baguettes are available from the market in the morning.

Luang Namtha *p142, map p143*
🍴-🍴 Boat Landing Guesthouse & Restaurant, see Sleeping, T086-312398. Best place to eat in town, with a beautiful dining area and exceptionally innovative cuisine: a range of northern Lao dishes made from local produce that supports local villages. Highly recommended.
🍴-🍴 Manychan, see Sleeping. A very popular restaurant with outdoor seating and a variety of toned-down Lao dishes plus a few Western interpretations.
🍴 Banana Restaurant, on the main road, towards **KNT Internet**, T020-5718026. This restaurant is gaining flavour with locals and tourists for its good fruit shakes and Lao food. A few Western dishes, too.
🍴 Coffee House, off the main road around the corner from **Green Discovery**, T030-5257842. This fantastic little hole-in-the-wall Thai restaurant serves a range of delicious Thai meals all under 10,000 kip. The meals are served on brown rice imported from

Thailand. Massaman curry, Tom Yum soup plus a great variety of other Thai staples. Fantastic espresso coffee and cappuccinos. Mr Nithat, the owner's husband, is good for a chat. Recommended.

Panda Restaurant, T086-211304. A goodie, housed in a beautiful stilted building overlooking rice paddies. Cheap and tasty food. The curries are outstanding. The friendly owner speaks English.

Yamuna Restaurant, on the main road, T020-5405698. A delicious Indian restaurant with veg and non-veg dishes and halal cuisine. Extensive, predominantly south Indian menu.

Bakeries, cafés and street stalls
There is a bakery and cake shop near the market that sells mouthwatering treats; try the green tea cake. There are a few *feu* stalls by the main market and the morning market near the bus stop, useful when waiting for those ever-delayed *songthaew*. At night, food vendors gather along the main road, with pretty, candlelit stalls, selling meat on a stick and waffles. For those with a sweet tooth, **KNT Internet** sells home-made cakes.

Muang Sing *p146, map p146*
It is highly recommended that you eat some of the delicious ethnic food while you're in Muang Sing as there aren't many other places where you will be able to sample these meals.

Adima Guesthouse, see Sleeping. Western offerings, such as the usual backpacker pancakes or fried eggs, as well as some Lao-inspired meals.

Sengdeuane Guesthouse and Restaurant. A quiet option with an English menu, which is mostly just for show. Nice garden setting and an ancient karaoke machine. Korean BBQ only (*sindat*). It opens from 1700. Popular with the locals.

Taileu Guesthouse and Restaurant, see Sleeping, T081-212375. The most popular place to eat due to its indigenous Tai Leu menu. Well worth the trip with some unique and tasty meals including baked aubergine, with pork, soy mash and fish soup. One of the few places in the country where you can sample northern cuisine. Try their local piña colada with *lao lao*, their *sa lo* (Muang Sing's answer to a hamburger) or one of the

famous *jeow* dishes. The banana flower soup is fantastic. This id the stand-out option in town and an eating experience you won't find elsewhere in Laos. Noi, the owner, is very friendly. Highly recommended.

Viengphone, next door to the **Viengxai Restaurant**, T081-212368. This place has an English menu offering the usual fare. Excellent fried mushrooms, although the service is a bit *bopenyang*.

Viengxai Restaurant, see Sleeping. Very good food, with some of the best chips in Laos, English menu, friendly service, reasonable prices. Good selection of shakes. Clean.

Houei Xai *p148, map p148*
Riverside, just off the main road, near the **Houay Xai Guesthouse**, T084-211064. Huge waterfront restaurant on large platform. Perfect position for taking in the sunset. Great shakes. Extensive menu that's a mixture of Lao and Thai food. The curries are quite good. Usually there is live music, some of it decidedly off-key, played here.

BAP Guesthouse, see Sleeping. Without doubt the best breakfast menu in town: wide range of dishes including pancakes, croissants and eggs.

Deen Restaurant, on the main road, T020-5901871. Indian restaurant with a very extensive menu of dishes including a large selection of halal and vegetarian food. Sparkly clean with very formal table-clothes and table settings. The owner is very accommodating.

Khemkhong Restaurant, across from the immigration stand. Good option for those who want a drink after the cross-border journey. Lao and Thai food.

Nutpop, on the main road, T084-211037. The fluoro lights and garish beer signs don't give a good impression. However, this is quite a pleasant little garden restaurant, set in an atmospheric lamp-lit building. Good Lao food – fried mushrooms and good curry. The fish here is excellent.

Pak Beng *p149, map p154*
Restaurants serve breakfast (baguettes, pancakes and coffee) really early. The eco-lodges have pretty upscale restaurants.

Kopchaideu Restaurant, overlooking the Mekong. This restaurant has a wide selection of Indian dishes with a few Lao favourites thrown in. Great shakes and fantastic service. ¶ **Salika**, see Sleeping. An atmospheric restaurant downstairs has wonderful river views, fresh flowers on the table, amazing variety on the menu, including cheese omelette, but interminably slow service.

There are several restaurants lining the main road towards the river; all seem to have the same English menu, basic Lao dishes, eggs and freshly made sandwiches. The local market has an array of dishes from *feu* through to frogs!

Sayaboury *p150*
There are a number of restaurants, along with the usual noodle shops and stalls, near the market and on the streets leading off the market. None is particularly noteworthy. Simple Chinese and Lao dishes.

✪ Festivals and events

Pak Lai *p150*
Mid-Feb Elephant Festival. Check www.elefantasia.org. Recommended.

✪ Shopping

Luang Namtha *p142, map p143*
KNT internet Shop sells textiles woven by the women of Luang Namtha: silk skirts, curtains, cushions, etc. There is also a handicrafts store around the corner from Saikhonglongsack.
Panfa Art, on the main road, offers a range of beautiful handicrafts, silk and other local artefacts.

There are plans to develop the small night-market, into a more extensive handicraft market, yet at the time of publication this looked unlikely.

▲ Activities and tours

Udomxai *p141, map p151*
Traditional Lao herbal sauna and massage is offered by the **Red Cross Centre**, behind the main stupa past the **Phuxay Hotel**, daily 1500-1900, 40,000 kip per hr. Look out for the signs on the main road.
Udomxai Travel, near the bus station, T081-212020, travel_kenchan@yahoo.com, offers ecotours and travel services.

Massage and sauna
There's a herbal sauna not far from Sengchanh film processing, daily 1630-1730, 15,000 kip for a sauna; 25,000 kip for a massage, 50 mins. The towels they provide are disgusting, so bring your own.

Tour operators
Green Discovery, near Manychan Guesthouse, T086-211484, www.green discoverylaos.com. Offers 1- to 7-day kayaking/rafting, cycling and trekking excursions into the Nam Ha NPA.
Luang Namtha Guide Service Unit, T086-211534. Information on treks into the Nam Ha NPA.

Vieng Phouka *p144*
The local tourism authority runs treks around the local villages, the Nam Ha National Park and caves with food and accommodation and camping with a host family. The guides are usually Khmu and Akha locals from the surrounding villages and have excellent local knowledge. Contact the **Vieng Phouka Guide Service Unit**, T084-212400, or speak to the **National Tourism Authority** in Vientiane.

Muang Sing *p146, map p146*
Trekking
Trekking has become a delicate issue around Muang Sing as uncontrolled tourism was beginning to have a detrimental effect on some of the surrounding minority villages. Luckily some sensible procedures and protocols have been put in place to ensure low-impact tourism which still benefits the villages concerned.

Exotissimo, www.exotissimo.com, in cohoots with **GTZ**, a German aid agency, have launched more expensive but thoroughly enjoyable treks such as the **Akha Experience**, which include tasty meals prepared by local Akha people. Closed at weekends.

The **tourism office and trekking centre**, in the centre of town, T020-2393534, can also organize pretty good treks for 1, 2 or 3 days, including accommodation and food. The guides are supposedly from local villages and can speak the native tongue, Akha or Tai Lue. Most treks cost around US$25 per day and have received glowing reports from tourists, particularly the **Laosee Trek**. Trek prices are reduced with larger numbers. The tourism office, next door to **Exotissimo**, is open Mon-Fri 0800-1130, 1330-1700. Treks organized during the working week.

Houei Xai p148, map p148
Tour operators

Gibbon Experience, T084-212021, www.gibbonx.org. This unique ecotourism operation provides the rare opportunity to see or hear the soprano-singing, black-cheeked crested gibbons (once thought to be extinct) from a network of canopy huts and zip-lines. Sightings are seasonal. Accommodation is in a tree house, affording sensational views of the surrounding Bokeo Forest Reserve.
Phoudoi Travel and Tours, in the centre of town, T084-211676. Arranges tours to the mines and hilltribe villages and offers an international phone service, helpful people.

Pak Beng p149, map p154
Massage

Next door to **Bounmy Guesthouse** is an understated but fantastic massage place.

Hongsa p149
Elephant trekking

Elephant treks can also be organized independently for US$18 for 2 hrs for 2 people.

● Transport

Udomxai p141, map p151
Air

There are flights to **Vientiane**, Tue, Thu and Sat, US$72. **Lao Airlines** has an office at the airport, T081-312047.

Bus/truck/songthaew

Udomxai is the epicentre of northern travel. If arriving in Udomxai to catch a connecting bus, it's better to leave earlier in the day as transport tends to peter out in the afternoon. These prices are subject to change.

One of the nicest ways to get to Udomxai from either Luang Prabang or Houei Xai is to catch the boat to Pak Beng (see pages 129 and 160) and then take a bus from there.

The bus station is 1 km east of the town centre. Departures east to **Nong Khiaw**,

3 hrs, trucks are fairly frequent, most departing in the morning. If you get stuck on the way to Nong Khiaw it is possible to stay overnight in **Pak Mong** where there are numerous rustic guesthouses. The bus to **Nong Khiaw** leaves at 0900, 114 km. **Pak Mong**, 1400 and 1600, 2 hrs, 82 km, 22,000 kip. To **Luang Prabang**, 3 daily, 194 km, direct, 5 hrs, 48,000 kip. Direct bus to **Vientiane**, 1530 and 1800, 15 hrs, 100,000 kip. Vientiane **VIP** bus, 1600 and 1800, 121,000 kip (also runs via **Luang Prabang**). **Xam Neua**, Tue-Sat 1230, 100,000 kip. **Luang Namtha**, 3 daily, 115 km, 4 hrs, 32,000 kip. **Boten** (the Chinese border) 0800, 82 km, 28,000 kip. It is possible for some nationalities to obtain Chinese visas at the border. However, you will need to check if you are eligible in advance (at the time of publication UK citizens could but US citizens could not get a Chinese visa at the border).

There are services north on Route 4 to **Phongsali**, 0800, 232 km, 9 -12 hrs, 60,000 kip; this trip is long so bring something soft to sit on and try to get a seat with a view.

There are plenty of *songthaew* on standby waiting to make smaller trips to destinations like **Pak Mong** and **Nong Khiaw**; if you miss one of the earlier buses it is worthwhile bargaining with the drivers, as, if they can get enough money or passengers, they will make the extra trip.

At the bus station there is a range of food stalls, a Chinese restaurant and a tempera-mental internet café, 10,000 kip per hr.

Muang Houn p142

Regular buses south to **Pak Beng**, 2 hrs, 15,000 kip, and north to **Udomxai**, 4-5 hrs, 25,000 kip.

Luang Namtha p142, map p143
Air

The airport is 7 km south of town – 15,000 kip by tuk-tuk. At the time of publication there were no domestic flights to or from Luang Namtha as the airport was being upgraded to an international airport. **Lao Airlines**, T086-312180, has an office south of town on the main road. When flights do reopen it is imperative to book in advance.

Bicycle/motorbike

Bicycles for hire from next door to the **Manychan Guesthouse** for 15,000 kip a day. Motorbikes for hire for US$5 a day from **Zuela Guesthouse**.

Boat

Call T020-5686051 for information. Officially, fast boats are not allowed on the Nam Tha. Slow boats are the best and most scenic travel option but their reliability will depend on the tide and, in the dry season (Mar–May) they often won't run at all as the water level is too low. There isn't really a regular boat service from Luang Namtha, so you will have to either charter a whole boat and split the cost amongst the passengers or hitch a ride on a boat making the trip already. If you manage to organize a boat it should cost around US$150 to **Houei Xai**; it is cheaper to go from Luang Namtha to Houei Xai than vice versa. The **Boat Landing Guesthouse** is a good source of information about boats; if arrangements are made for you, a courtesy tip is appreciated.

Bus/truck/songthaew

The main bus station and its ticket office are about 100 m north of the Morning Market, T086-312164, daily 0700-1600. This bus station is set to be abolished to make way for a new Malaysian hotel. A new bus station is planned on the corner near **Panda Restaurant**, on the main road.

To **Muang Sing**, 3 daily, 1½ hrs, 20,000 kip, additional pickups may depart throughout the rest of the day, depending on demand. To **Udomxai**, 3 daily, 100 km, 4-6 hrs, 32,000 kip, additional services will leave in the early afternoon if there is demand, otherwise jump on a bus to Luang Prabang.

To **Houei Xai**, 0900 and 1330, 55,000 kip. To **Luang Prabang**, 0930 daily, 10 hrs, 70,000 kip. To **Vientiane**, 20 hrs, 140,000 kip. To get to **Nong Khiaw**, 60,000 kip, you need to go via Udomxai (leave early).

To **Boten** (Chinese border) 3 daily, 1½ hrs, 25,000 kip. Many travellers have reported obtaining a visa at this border crossing; however, it is less risky to organize a visa in advance in Vientiane. Tourist visas cost US$70-150, depending on nationality. US citizens are unable to obtain visas at this crossing. Check with the Chinese embassy beforehand.

Vieng Phouka *p144*

Buses and *songthaew* depart for **Houei Xai**, a few times daily from the market, usually in the morning, 5 hrs, US$5. It is also possible to get buses to **Luang Namtha** and **Udomxai**.

Nateui *p145*

Infrequent *songthaew* connections with **Luang Namtha**, 34,000 kip, and **Udomxai**, 80 km, 15,000 kip, and rather more frequent departures for the border at **Boten**, 18 km.

Boten *p146*

Pickups to **Luang Namtha**, 0830, 1100 and 1300 daily, 15,000 kip. To **Udomxai**, 0930, 1200 and 1400 daily, 23,000 kip. For international connections with China, see Border essentials, page 145.

Muang Sing *p146, map p146*
Bicycle

Available for rent from some of the guest-houses. There are also some bicycle hire shops on the main street. The going rate is 10,000 kip per day. The Muang Sing tourism office hires bikes for 20,000 kip per day.

Boat

It is sometimes possible to charter boats from **Xieng Kok** downstream on the Mekong to **Houei Xai**, 3-4 hrs. This is expensive – around US$150-200.

Bus/truck/songthaew

The bus station is across from the main market. To **Luang Namtha**, by bus or pickup, 5 daily, 2 hrs, 20,000 kip. To charter a *song-thaew* or tuk-tuk to Luang Namtha costs at least 200,000 kip. *Songthaew* also leave sporadically to **Xieng Kok**, 30,000 kip, 4 hrs.

There are trucks to **Muang Long**, daily 1100 and 1430, 48 km, 2 hrs, 13,000 kip, and to **Xieng Kok** (located on the Mekong at the Myanmar/Burma border), several times a week, 75 km, 2½ hrs, 25,000 kip. Foreigners are not officially permitted to cross into Myanmar (Burma) here, but there have been reports of travellers being granted a visa and entering.

Houei Xai *p148, map p148*

Lao National Tourism State Bokeo, on the main street up from immigration, T084-211555, can give advice on the sale of boat, bus, pickup and other tickets. Numerous travel agencies congregate around the immigration centre offering bus and boat ticket sales. See page 129 for extensive information on boat travel between Houei Xai and **Luang Prabang**.

Air
The airport is located 5 km south of town and has flights to **Vientiane**, Tue and Thu, US$85; book in advance as it is a small plane and tends to fill up quickly.

Boat
The BAP Guesthouse is a good place to find out about boat services. For services across the Mekong to Thailand, see Border essentials, page 149.

The 2-day trip down the Mekong to Luang Prabang has become part of the Southeast Asian rite of package. The slow boat to **Pak Beng** is raved about by many travellers. However, in peak season the boat can be packed to the rafters and the wooden chairs (or ground) are extremely uncomfortable. It is advisable to bring something soft to sit on, a good book to read and a packed lunch. The boat leaves from a jetty 1½ km north of town, 0930-1000 daily, 6-7 hrs, US$11 or US$22 for the 2-day trip (usually you buy the ongoing ticket at Pak Beng). If you can get enough people together it is possible to charter your own boat for US$600. It is worth noting that the trip, done in reverse, usually has fewer passengers.

For a luxury option there is the Luangsay Cruise, T071-252553, www.asian-oasis.com, which undertakes a 2-day/1-night cruise down the river in extreme comfort with cushioned deckchairs, a bar, wooden polished interior and games on board. Guests stay at the beautiful Luangsay Lodge in Pak Beng.

For a mid-range option, **Phoudoi Travel**, on the main road in Houei Xai, sells tickets for US$60 on a boat direct to Luang Prabang that is roomier than the standard cattle-class boat yet not as cosy as the *Luangsay*. The *Nagi*, for US$80, does the trip in one day in comfort. www.travel-thailand.com/article.php/cruise_the_mekong.

Speedboats are a noisy, nerve-wracking, dangerous alternative; they leave from the jetty south of town, to **Pak Beng**, 3 hrs,

US$15, and to **Luang Prabang**, US$29. There have been reports of unscrupulous boatmen claiming there are no slow boats in the dry season to encourage travellers to take their fast boats. This is usually untrue.

Bus/truck/songthaew
The bus station is located at the Morning Market, 7 km out of central Houei Xai; a tuk-tuk to the centre costs 20,000 kip. To **Nam Chan** by taxi, 1 hr, 80,000 kip, for the whole vehicle.

Trucks, buses and minivans run to **Vieng Phouka**, daily 0930-1030, 5 hrs, 45,000 kip; to **Luang Namtha**, daily 0930-1130, 170 km, 7 hrs, 65,000 kip; to **Udomxai**, daily 0930, 7 hrs, 120,000 kip; to **Luang Prabang**, Fri 1130, 11 hrs, 140,000 kip; to **Vientiane**, daily 1130, 20 hrs, 200,000 kip.

Pak Beng *p149, map p154*
Boat
The times and prices for boats are always changing so it's best to check beforehand. The slow boat to **Houei Xai** leaves at around 0800-0900 from the port and takes all day, US$11. The slow boat to **Luang Prabang** leaves around the same time. Get in early to get a good seat. Speedboats to Luang Prabang (2-3 hrs) and Houei Xai leave in the morning, when full. You can also take a boat downriver to **Tha Suang**, 1 hr, US$5, and then catch a *songthaew* from here to **Hongsa**, US$3.

Bus/truck/songthaew
Buses and *songthaew* leave about 2 km from town in the morning for the route north to **Udomxai**, 6-7 hrs, 40,000 kip. Direct *songthaew* to Udomxai are few, so an alternative is to take one to Muang Houn and catch a rather more frequent service from there. The road to Udomxai passes through spectacular scenery.

Sayaboury *p150*
Air
Flights to **Vientiane**, Sat and Wed, 45 mins, US$51/US$97. On each occasion the plane makes a round trip. Tickets can be purchased at the airport, about 1 km south of town.

Bus
There are 2 bus terminals, the South Bus

Station, 2 km southeast of town, and the North Bus Station, 2 km north of town.

There are no direct road links with Vientiane. The road south from Sayaboury only goes as far as Muang Ken Thao, close to the border with Thailand. This road passes through Pak Lai, on the Mekong, where it is possible to catch a boat downstream to **Vientiane**. There are buses to **Pak Lai** at daily 0730-1000, 4 hrs, US$2.50. Note that the road is in poor condition – although it is gradually being upgraded – and transport during the wet season (Jun/Jul-Oct/Nov) is difficult and sometimes impossible.

You can catch a *songthaew* north to **Tha Deua** on the Mekong, 23 km, 1 hr, from where a ferry crosses to **Pak Khon**, 3000 kip. There are regular buses from Pak Khon to **Luang Prabang**, 4 hrs, US$1.50. Speedboats also run from Tha Deua direct to Luang Prabang, 1 hr, US$20, but you may have to rent the whole boat which is costly.

Pak Lai *p150*
Boat
There are connections by slow boat (downriver) to **Vientiane**, daily 0730, 8 hrs, US$7. However, due to the upgrading of Route 13 between Vientiane and Luang Prabang, there are no longer any scheduled boats upriver to Luang Prabang; instead you need to head to Sayaboury then Tha Deua (see above).

Songthaew
Songthaew services terminate 3 km out of town; share a tuk-tuk into the centre. *Songthaew* run north to **Sayaboury**, 4 hrs, US$3, twice daily.

● Directory

Udomxai *p141, map p151*
Banks Lao Development Bank, just off the road on the way to Phongsali, changes US$, Chinese ¥ and Thai ฿. The BCEL Bank, on the main road near the Kaysone Monu-ment, T081-211260, is much more convenient and offers the same services. No credit card advances. **Electricity** Available 24 hrs. **Internet** Available at Litthavixay Guest-house, at the bus station, on the main road at **Samlaan Cycling** and around the corner from there at the English school,

100-200 kip per min. Quite often the whole town's internet is down. **Post and telephone** Post office and Lao Telecom, opposite the Sai Xi Hotel, uphill from the Chinese market; international calls available.

Luang Namtha *p142, map p143*
Banks Banks open Mon-Fri only. **Lao Development Bank**, in the centre of town, changes US$ and Thai ฿ to kip, also exchanges TCs but charges a sizeable commission. The BCEL opposite the Telecom Office, changes US$ and Thai ฿ and does cash advances on Visa. It has an ATM but it only accepts MasterCard. **Electricity** Available 24 hrs. **Internet** KNT Computers, on the main road, south of Manychan Guesthouse, 200 kip per min. **Telephone** You can make international calls from **Lao Telecom**, near Saikhonglongsack Guesthouse.

Muang Sing *p146, map p146*
Banks There is a small branch of the **Lao Development Bank** opposite the market which will exchange Thai ฿, Chinese ¥ and US$.

Houei Xai *p148, map p148*
Banks Lao Development Bank, right next to the immigration office, changes TCs, US$ cash and Thai ฿, daily 0830-1600. **Immigration** At the boat terminal and the airport, daily 0800-1800, a small overtime fee is charged Sat and Sun and after 1600 (see also Border essentials, page 149). Quite possibly the friendliest immigration post in the country. **Internet** There is a small internet shop on the main street which charges 15,000 kip per hr. **Post and telephone** Post office with telephone facilities is about 500 m south (downstream) from the centre of town.

Pak Beng *p149, map p154*
Banks There is no bank in town, but most of the guesthouses and restaurants will exchange Thai ฿ and US$ cash and charge a hefty commission. **Electricity** Sporadic and sometimes only available daily 1800-2200. **Internet** Available at the boat ferry office for a whopping 500 kip per min. High-speed internet is also available past the

Pak Beng Market 500 kip per min. **Post** The post office is up over the hill on the main road.

Sayaboury *p150*

Banks There is only one bank in town, the Lao Development Bank, just down from the Kaysone Monument, Mon-Fri 0830-1600. It does not accept TCs but will change US$ and Thai ฿. The rate of exchange is poor.
Post and telephone The post office,

Mon-Fri 0800-1100 and 1300-1700, and **Lao Telecom Office** are in the centre of town, on the other side of the road from the market. International call cards are available.

Pak Lai *p150*

Banks The Lao Development Bank, a block north of the boat landing, will change Thai ฿ and US$. **Post and telephone** There is a small telephone office and post office a block west of the bank.

Xieng Khouang Province

Apart from the historic Plain of Jars, Xieng Khouang Province is best known for the pounding it took during the war. Many of the sights are battered monuments to the plateau's violent recent history. Given the cost of the return trip and the fact that the jars themselves aren't that spectacular, some consider the destination oversold. However, for those interested in modern history, it's the most fascinating area of Laos and helps one to gain an insight into the resilient nature of the Lao people. The countryside, particularly towards the Vietnam border, is beautiful – among the country's best – and the jars, too, are interesting by dint of their very oddness: as if a band of carousing giants had been suddenly interrupted, casting the jars across the plain in their hurry to leave. ▸▸ For Sleeping, Eating and other listings, see pages 172-175.

Ins and outs

Getting there Phonsavanh Airport (aka Xieng Khouang airport) is 4 km west of Phonsavanh. **Lao Airlines** flies to and from Vientiane; check www.laoairlines.com for up-to-date information. A tuk-tuk to town costs 20,000 kip per person. The most direct route by road from Luang Prabang to Xieng Khouang Province is to take Route 13 south to Muang Phou Khoun and then Route 7 east. You might want to take travel sickness tablets as it's quite a bumpy trip. An alternative, scenic, albeit convoluted, route is via Nong Khiaw (see page 132), from where there are pick-ups to Pak Xeng and Phonsavanh via Vieng Thong on Route 1 or Nam Nouan.

The bus station is 4 km west of Phonsavanh on Route 7, although many buses still pass by the old bus station near the dry market; a tuk-tuk to/from the centre costs 10,000 kip.

Getting around Public transport is limited and sporadic. Provincial laws have occasionally banned tuk-tuks and motorbikes from ferrying customers around the area. These regulations have been relaxed recently but don't be surprised if they are brought into force again. ▸▸ *For further details, see Transport, page 174.*

Best time to visit It is cold here from November to March. Several jumpers and a thick jacket are required.

Background

Xieng Khouang Province has had a murky, blood-tinted, war-ravaged history. The area was the most bombed province in the most bombed country, per capita, in the world as it became a very important strategic zone that both the US and Vietnamese wanted to retain control of. The town of Phonsavanh has long been an important transit point between China to the north, Vietnam to the east and Thailand to the south and this status historically made the town a target for neighbouring countries. What's more, the plateau of the Plain of Jars is one of the flattest areas in northern Laos, rendering it a natural battleground for the numerous conflicts that ensued from the 19th century to 1975. As a result, the region holds immense appeal for those interested in the modern history of the country.

The earliest known settlers in this area were believed to be of the ethnic Tai origin and a Phuan kingdom was established in the region in the 14th century. The kingdom suffered numerous sackings by the Vietnamese over hundreds of years, until, in 1832, they invaded Phonsavanh, executing the Phuan king and turning the area into an Annan vassal state. The region was incorporated into the kingdom of Lane Xang by King Fa Ngum briefly in the 16th century but was more often than not ruled by the Vietnamese (who called it Tran Ninh) because of its proximity to the border. The Chinese Haw also ravaged Phonsavanh in the 19th century, an event that, along with the sacking of Luang Prabang, became a catalyst for the government's acceptance of French protection.

Under the French, Xieng Khouang supported tea plantations and many colonial settlers took to the temperate climate. Like the Boloven Plateau to the south, the French colonial administration had visions of populating the Plain of Jars with thousands of hard-working French families. Only in this way, it was reasoned, could Laos be made to pay for itself.

Once the French departed, massive conflicts were waged in 1945-1946 between the Free Lao Movement and the Viet Minh. The Pathet Lao and Viet Minh joined forces and, by 1964, had a number of bases dotted around the Plain of Jars. From then on, chaos ensued, as Xieng Khouang got caught in the middle of the war between the Royalist-American and Pathet Lao-Vietnamese (see also page 164). The extensive US bombing of this area was to ensure it did not fall under Communist control of Pathet Lao. The Vietnamese were trying to ensure that the US did not gain control of the area from which they could launch attacks on North Vietnam.

During the 'Secret War' (1964-1974) against the North Vietnamese Army and the Pathet Lao, tens of thousands of cluster bomb units (CBUs) were dumped on Xieng Khouang Province. Other bombs such as the anti-personnel plastic 'pineapple' bomblets were also used. As 30% of the original CBUs did not explode, these cluster bombs continue to kill and maim today. The Plain of Jars was also hit by B-52s returning from abortive bombing runs to Hanoi, who jettisoned their bomb loads before heading back to the US air base at Udon Thani in northeast Thailand. One bombing raid destroyed 1600 buildings in Xieng Khouang town alone. Suffice it to say that, with over 580,944 sorties flown (one-and-a-half times the number flown in Vietnam), whole towns were obliterated and the area's geography was permanently altered. Today, as the **Lao Airlines** Y-12 turbo-prop begins its descent towards the plateau, the meaning of the term 'carpet bombing' becomes clear. On the final approach to the town of Phonsavanh, the plane banks low over the cratered paddy fields, affording a T-28 fighter-bomber pilot's view of his target, which in places has been pummelled into little more than a moonscape. Some of the craters are 15 m across and 7 m deep. Testament to the Lao people's resilience, symbolically, many of these craters have been turned into tranquil fish ponds; the bombs transformed into fences and the CBU carriers serving as planter pots.

The so-called 'collateral damage' was also staggering. There is no official figure on the number of dead but, since over 80% of the population is believed to have inhabited the northern and southern provinces targeted by US bombing, some sources estimate 300,000 Lao were killed – between a ninth and a tenth of the

Both the Vietnamese and the US signed a 1962 Geneva Accord, prohibiting military involvement in Laos, yet more bombs were dropped on Laos during the 1960s and 1970s than on both Germany and Japan combined in the Second World War.

Secret War on the Plain of Jars

The plain occupies an important niche in modern Lao history as it became one of the most strategic battlegrounds of the war. For General Vang Pao's Hmong, it was the hearthstone of their mountain kingdom; for the royalist government and the Americans it was a critical piece in the Indochinese jigsaw; for Hanoi it was their back garden, which had to be secured to protect their rear flank. From the mid-1960s, neutralist forces were encamped on the Plain (dubbed 'the PDJ' during the war). They were supported by Hmong, based at the secret city of Long Tien, to the southwest. US-backed and North Vietnamese-backed forces fought a bitter war of attrition on the PDJ; each time royalist and Hmong forces were defeated on the ground, US air power was called in to pummel from above. In mid-February 1970, American Strategic Air Command, on presidential orders, directed that B-52 Stratofortress bombers should be used over the PDJ for the first time. Capable of silently dumping more than one hundred 500-lb bombs from 40,000 ft, they had a devastating effect on the towns and villages of the plain but a minimal effect on Communist morale. Even if the B-52s had managed to wipe out North Vietnamese and Pathet Lao forces, the US-backed troops were unable to reach, let alone hold, the territory. Hanoi had garrisons of reinforcements waiting in the wings.

On the plain, the B-52 proved as inappropriate and ineffective a weapon as it would later on the Ho Chi Minh Trail. As US bomber command increasingly turned its attention to the trail, the Pathet Lao quickly seized the upper hand and retook the PDJ. The Communists were beaten back onto the surrounding hills and ridges by Vang Pao's forces and American bombers but they kept swarming back and, by March 1972, the North Vietnamese Army had seven divisions in Laos supporting the Pathet Lao. The so-called 'Mountain of Courage' – the hill behind the new airport to the northwest) – was the scene of some particularly hard fighting. It was here that the royalists, encamped on Phu Kheng, were trapped on two fronts by the Communists. When the Pathet Lao retook Xieng Khouang for the last time in 1973, they consolidated their position and bided their time.

country's total population at the time. One survivor from just outside Phonsavanh recalled his experiences of the bombing campaigns: "I was just a boy, coming home and saw a bomb hit my house. It exploded and split my home right in two! My parents and my brother were killed; my sister, killed; the family, killed; my dog was killed, the buffaloes, killed. Everything gone." He remembers how "the kids would run out to the streets and pick up these things that had fallen from the sky, like parachutes, thinking they were chocolate bars or something, and their arms would catch fire and no matter how hard you tried you couldn't put it out, these screaming children on fire. It was horrific, truly horrific."

Today, hundreds of thousands of bomblets – and equally lethal impact mines, which the Lao call *bombis* – remain buried in Xieng Khouang's grassy meadows. Because the war was 'secret', there are few records of what was dropped and where and, even when the unexploded ordnance (UXO) has been uncovered, their workings are often a mystery – the Americans used Laos as a testing ground for new ordnance so blueprints are unavailable. One aid worker relates how in the mid-1980s, a specially designed, armour-plated tractor was terminally disabled by *bombis*, while attempting to clear them from the fields. The UK-based **Mines Advisory Group** (MAG) ① *on the main road in the centre of town, daily 0800-1200 and 1300-2000 (except the 12th and 18th of every month)*, is currently engaged in clearing the land of Unexploded Ordnance. They have an exhibition of bombs, photographs and information on the bombing campaign and ongoing plight of Laos with UXO. Usually there is staff on hand to explain exactly how the bombs were used. All T-shirts sold here help fund the UXO clearance of the area and are a very worthwhile souvenir.

Uncle Sam has, however, bequeathed to local people an almost unlimited supply of twisted metal. Bombshells and flare casings can frequently be seen in Xieng Khouang's villages where they are used for everything from cattle troughs and fences, to stilts for houses and water-carriers. In Phonsavanh steel runway sheets make handy walls, while plants are potted out in shell casings.

Xieng Khouang remains one of the poorest provinces in an already wretchedly poor country. The whole province has a population of only around 250,000, a mix of different ethnic groups, predominantly Hmong, Lao and a handful of Khmu. Government attempts to curtail shifting cultivation and encourage the Hmong to settle have not been very successful, largely because there are no alternative livelihoods available. Travelling through the province there is a sense not just that the American air war caused enormous suffering and destruction, but that the following decades have not provided much in the way of economic opportunities.

Phonsavanh ●❶❷❸❹▲❺❻ ↠ *pages 172-175. Colour map 1, C4.*

→ *Phone code: 061.*

Phonsavanh is the main town of the province today – old Xieng Khouang having been flattened – and its small airstrip is a crucial transport link in this mountainous region. Surrounding the town are huge mountains, among them Phu Bia, one of the country's highest. The town itself is notable mainly for its ugliness. It was established in the mid-1970s and sprawls out from a heartless centre with no sense of plan or direction. While Phonsavanh will win no beauty contests, it does have a rather attractive 'Wild

Phonsavanh

Not to scale

Sleeping 🛏
Auberge de la
 Plaine Des Jarres **1**
Dok Khoun **3**
Khou Kham
 Guesthouse **10**
Maly **6**
Orchid **15**

Nice Guesthouse **8**
Phonsavanh **9**
Vansana **14**

Eating 🍴
Craters **2**
Nisha Indian **3**
Phonexay **5**

Sangah **6**
Simmaly **7**

Bars & clubs 🍸
Maliyona Pub **8**

West' atmosphere. As journalist Malcolm Macalister Hall wrote in 1998: "I liked this ugly, rough-hewn town: for its unlikely invitations, its mad breakfasts, and the beautiful landscapes that surrounded it". What's more, it's the only base from which to explore the Plain of Jars (see below), so it has a fair number of hotels and guesthouses. The daily market is busy but rather undistinguished, with the usual assortment of cheap Chinese bric-a-brac. The food market, behind the post office, is more lively and worth a look.

> **!** *Note that travel agents and airlines tend to refer to the provincial capital, Phonsavanh, as 'Xieng Khouang', while the old town of Xieng Khouang is now usually known as 'Muang Khoune'.*

South of Phonsavanh, on two small hills, a pair of white and gold monuments can be seen. It is worth the short hike up, if only for the views they afford of the surrounding countryside. The **Vietnamese war memorial** ① *daily from dawn till dusk, 1000 kip*, on the west side, was built to commemorate the death of over one million Vietnamese troops in the war against the anti-Communists. It contains the bones of Vietnamese soldiers and is inscribed 'Lao Vietnamese Solidarity Forever'. The newer **Lao war memorial** ① *daily from dawn till dusk, 1000 kip*, to the east, is more rounded in the Lao style and was built later in memory of 4500 Pathet Lao soldiers who died, including Hmong and Khmu fighters (often only remembered as fighting for the US).

Plain of Jars 🏠🍴🚆 ➤ *pages 172-175. Colour map 1, C5.*

The undulating plateau of the Plain of Jars (also known as Plaine de Jarres, or **Thong Hai Hin**), stretches for about 50 km east to west, covering an area of 1000 sq km at an altitude of 1000 m. In total there are 136 archaeological sites in this area, containing thousands of jars, discs and deliberately placed stones. Of these only three are open to tourists. Note that the plateau can be cold from December to March.

Ins and outs
Getting there and around
Provincial laws have sporadically banned tuk-tuks and motorbikes from ferrying customers around the area. These regulations have been relaxed recently but don't be surprised if they are brought into force again. It should be possible to drive to the Plain of Jars, see Site one and return to town in two hours. Expect to pay in the region of US$30 for an English-speaking guide and vehicle for four people, or US$60 for seven people and a minivan. A tuk-tuk to Site one costs approximately US$7 per person. Alternatively, hotels, guesthouses and tour companies in Phonsavanh run set tours to the Plain of Jars, Muang Khoune (Xieng Khouang) and to Hmong villages to the northeast of Phonsavanh. If you arrive by air, the chances are you'll be inundated with official and unofficial would-be guides as soon as you step off the plane. Note that it is not possible to walk from the airport to Site one, as there is a military base in between. It is recommended that you hire a guide, for at least a day, to get an insight into the history of the area. The cost of admission to each site is 7000 kip. ➤ *For further information, see Activities and tours, page 174, and Transport, page 174.*

> **!** *The road to the Plain passes through a Hmong resettlement village. Their distinctive homes are not built on stilts and there is no separate kitchen area on the side.*

Background
Most of the jars are generally between 1 m and 2.5 m high, around 1 m in diameter and weigh about the same as three small cars. The largest are about 3 m tall. The jars have long presented an archaeological conundrum, leaving generations of theorists nonplussed by how they got there and what they were used for. Local legend relates that King Khoon Chuong and his troops from Southern China threw a stupendous party after their victory over the wicked Chao Angka and had the jars made to brew

outrageous quantities of *lao-lao*. However attractive this alcoholic thesis, it is more likely that the jars are in fact 2000-year-old stone funeral urns. The larger jars are believed to have been for the local aristocracy and the smaller jars for their minions.

Some archaeologists speculate that the cave below the main site was hewn from the rock at about the same time as the jars themselves and that the hole in the roof possibly indicates that the cave was used for cremation or that the jars were made and fired in the cave. But this is all speculation and the jars' true origins and function remain a mystery. In fact, the stone from which the jars at Site one are made doesn't seem to come from that area. Instead, using the evidence of some half-hewn jars made of the same stone found near Sites two and three, archaeologists have postulated that the jars were carved here and then transported to Site one.

Tools, bronze ornaments, ceramics and other objects have been found in the jars, indicating that a civilized society was responsible for them but no-one has a clue which one, as the artefacts bear no relation to those left behind by other ancient Indochinese civilizations. Some of the jars were once covered with round lids and there is one jar, in the group facing the entrance to the cave, which is decorated with a rough carving of a dancing figure.

Over the years, a few jars have been stolen and a number have been transported by helicopter down to Vientiane's Wat Phra Kaeo and the backyard of the National Museum (see pages 59 and 60). Local guides will claim that despite four or five B-52 bombing raids on the plain every day for five years during the Secret War (see page 164), the jars remained mysteriously unscathed. However, several bomb craters and damaged jars at the main site show this to be a fanciful myth. During heavy fighting on the plain in the early 1970s, the Pathet Lao set up a command centre in the cave next to the jars and then posed among the jars for photographs (which can be seen in the Revolutionary Museum in Vientiane). Around the entrance to the cave are

Plain of Jars

To Nam Nouan & Xam Neua

To Muang Sui & Luang Prabang

Phiu San (2218m)

Tham Phiu

○ Ban Na Meun

Nam Keua

Muang Kham

Phu Leng (1582m)

○ Ban Na Sala

To Nong Het & Vietnam border

Hot Springs

Old Airport

○ Ban Tha Jok

New Airport

○ Ban Xon

Nam Mat

○ Phonsavanh

Hmong Resettlement Village

Site 1 Cave

Plain of Jars (Thong Hai Hin)

Phu Gnouan (1825m)

N

To Muang Khoune (Xieng Khouang) & Sites 2 & 3

Not to scale

Sleeping
Auberge de la Plaine des Jarres 1

Eating
Restaurant 1

numerous bomb craters, as the US targeted the sanctuary in a futile attempt to dislodge the Communists.

A vast aviation fuel depot was built next to the jars, early in the 1990s, to supply the huge new airbase just to the west. The base, designed by Soviet technicians, is the new headquarters for the Lao Air Force, although why the government needs a large airbase here remains a mystery and something of a political minefield. On the grasslands around the jars are stumpy little flowers, known as 'baa' by the Hmong and 'dok waan' by the Lao; the stems are boiled to make a soup, while the red buds are fried. Once the flower has bloomed (turning yellow), they are no longer tasty. Along with the bomb craters that scar the landscape there are also patches of bare earth that have nothing to do with the Indochina conflict. These are sparrow free-fire zones: after the first rains, local people clear the land of grass over an area of about 10 sq m and build a small hide; they then put sticky rice down and wait for the poor creatures to alight for a leisurely lunch before being blasted.

Site one

More than 300 jars survive, mainly scattered on one slope at so-called 'Site one' or **Thong Hai Hin**, 10 km southwest of Phonsavanh. This site is closest to Phonsavanh and has the largest jar – along with a small restaurant. A path, cleared by MAG, winds through the site, with a warning not to walk away from delineated areas as UXO are still around. There are 250 jars at the site, each of which weighs about a tonne, although the biggest, called **Hai Cheaum**, is over 2 m tall and weighs over 6 tonnes. Folklore suggests that the jar is named after a Thai-Lao liberator, who overthrew Chao Angka. Further downhill is another smattering of jars, some of which feature carvings. The smallish cave in the hill to the left was used by the Pathet Lao as a hideout during the war and may have been the ancient kiln in which the jars were fired (see Background, above).

Site two

True jar lovers should visit Site two, known as **Hai Hin Phu Salatao** (literally 'Salato Hill Stone Jar Site'), and Site three (see below). Site two is 25 km south of Phonsavanh and features 90 jars spread across two hills. The jars are set in a rather beautiful location, affording scenic views.

Site three

A further 10 km south of Site two, Site three, also called **Hai Hin Laat Khai**, is the most atmospheric of all the sites, set in verdant green rolling hills, swiss-cheesed with bomb craters. To get there you have to walk through some rice paddies and cross the small bamboo bridge. There are more than 130 jars at this site, which are generally smaller and more damaged than at the other sites. There's also a very small, basic restaurant here, serving feu. Nearby is **Ban Xieng Dai**, a friendly village, home to a monastery featuring some Buddha images, which were badly damaged during the war. Villagers will lead treks to the nearby Lang waterfall for 10,000 kip.

Muang Khoune (old Xieng Khouang) ›› Colour map 1, C4.

The old town of Xieng Khouang – now rebuilt and renamed Muang Khoune – was destroyed during the war, between 1964 and 1969, and now the population is reduced to a mere 14,000. Prior to the bombing, the town was extremely picturesque, similar to Luang Prabang, with over 400 old colonial buildings and 30 wats and pagodas but today it holds nothing in the way of aesthetic charm and a sense of impermanence pervades; it consists of a row of wooden Lao houses and a market area. However, while Muang Khoune itself is spectacularly unimpressive, its position, surrounded by mountains, is noteworthy.

Background

Xieng Khouang was founded by Chao Noi Muang and was a stronghold for the Xieng Khouang royal family. In 1832 the Hmong mountain state was annexed by Vietnam and renamed Tran Ninh; the king was marched off to Vietnam and publicly executed in Hué, while the population of Xieng Khouang was forced to wear Vietnamese dress.

Many important temples were built here in the distinctive Xieng Khouang style but these were completely obliterated by the American bombing. The religious architecture of the province was one of Laos' three main architectural styles (Luang Prabang and Vientiane styles being the other two). The town was also the main centre for the French in this area during the colonial period and remnants of French colonial architecture are still in evidence.

Xieng Khouang was most heavily bombed during 1969 and 1970, when US air power was called in to reverse the success of the Communists' dry season offensive on the Plain of Jars. In his book *The Ravens*, Christopher Robins interviews several former US pilots who describe the annihilation of the town in which 1500 buildings were razed, together with another 2000 across the plain. Three towns, he says, "were wiped from the map. By the end of the year (1970) there would not be a building left standing". During this time most villagers left their homes and lived in caves or in the forest, subsisting on rice from China and Vietnam. So incessant was the bombing and strafing that peasants took to planting their rice fields at night. One brave woman recalled, "I would have to get the rice at two or three in the morning so as not to be seen. I would carry it on my back, sometimes 100 kg, it was so heavy that I was doubled over, my head almost touching the ground."

The town, which is in fact little more than a village, was rebuilt after 1975 and renamed Muang Khoune.

Sights

Those excited about the prospect of visiting a unique collection of 500-year-old wats must, for the most part, be content with piles of bricks. There is virtually nothing left of the 16th-century **Wat Phia Wat** (at the far end of town on the right-hand side by the road), except the basement and several shrapnel-pocked Buddha statues, including a large, seated Buddha which is believed to be over 600 years old. The once-picturesque wat underwent a series of renovations in 1930 only to be bombed into oblivion by the Americans. The half-hearted attempt at further renovation is barely noticeable. Walking up the hill, the remains of the French colonial Governor's house, built in the 1930s, can be seen, with some old tile floors still in place and a hospital, patched together Lao-style.

Two stupas perch on a pair of hills above the town. **That Chompet** is a stump of its former self and is relatively overgrown. A better alternative is the 16th-century **That Foun**, which is quite sizeable and similar to That Dam in Vientiane. The *that* is said to contain relics of the Indian emperor Asoka but this legend should be taken with a large pinch of *nam pa*. It may, however, explain why the heart of the stupa has been hollowed out, as thieves have searched, apparently in vain, for buried treasure, in particular old Buddha images.

Wat Si Phoum (opposite the market below the main road) was also destroyed by the war and now a new inelegant wat has been built next to the ruined *that*. There is a small monastery attached.

The market in Muang Khoune holds little interest for the tourist, with nothing on sale but the bare essentials. Head to the Black Tai village, about 500 m northwest of town, to buy local handicrafts and scarves.

West of Phonsavanh

Muang Sui

Muang Sui lies 45 km west of Phonsavanh on Route 7. The town was formerly known for its vast array of old Buddhist temples and traditional Lao architecture but its fate was sealed once it became a primary landing site for US planes. The town was later razed by

❧ When travelling between Phonsavanh and Muang Sui, stop off to look at the old Russian tank, about 20 km west of Phonsavanh.

the North Vietnamese Army. It is part of a district called Phu Kut, an area known for Hmong insurgency, so don't be surprised if you see armed personnel around. The strip of road, in particular, has experienced ongoing difficulties with Hmong insurgents and, although things are settling down now, with a large group surrendering to the government in 2005, there is still a small risk of attack. There aren't many sights in the actual town and a day trip

from Phonsavanh should be more than sufficient to take in the outlying caves and picturesque **Nong Tang Lake**, a short drive east of town. The lake is crowned by limestone karst formations and believed to be very deep.

The caves around Muang Sui make the trip worthwhile; a US$1 entrance fee is paid at **Buddha Cave** (Tham Pha), a large honeycomb network of labyrinthine passages, grottoes and caverns that is said to house over 1000 Buddha images, many dating back 1200 years. Another nearby cave, was used by the Vietnamese Army as a hospital and is still known as **Hospital Cave**. **Water Cave** is named after the water that falls though its roof but it isn't as interesting as the other caves. Nearby is the large **Stupa Cave** (Tham That), which contains the ruins of an old stupa believed to be several hundred years old. Within walking distance is **Coffin Cave**, nestled high up in a limestone cliff. It's a bit of a climb to the cave but worth it as it contains prehistoric coffins carved out of old tree trunks. The caves have been raided but there are a few human remains and remnants scattered around the floor.

East of Phonsavanh 🚐🚌 ▸ pp172-175.

Route 7 heads east from Phonsavanh towards Muang Kham and the border with Vietnam (see page 171). The journey is characterized by attractive rolling hills and grassy meadows in the wet season but becomes very barren in the dry season, especially where the bomb craters have pock-marked the landscape. The drive is an abject lesson in the potentially destructive nature of some forms of shifting cultivation. Some authorities estimate that up to 100,000 ha of forest were being destroyed in this area by slash-and-burn agriculture before the government implemented a policy to minimize the practice. The difficulty is that minority shifting cultivators – especially the Hmong – often farm land that has already been logged by commercial timber firms (for the simple reason that it is easier to cultivate) and then find themselves blamed for the destruction.

About 12 km east of Phonsavanh is the village of **Ban Xon**, which lays claim to two famous daughters, Baoua Kham and Baoua Xi, who are reported to have shot down a US B-52 with small arms fire. War historians are very sceptical about this claim but a Lao popular song was nonetheless written about them. The ballad is said to extol the beauty and courage of the women of Xieng Khouang.

Hmong villages

Route 7 winds its way down off the plateau along the Nam Keua, a fertile area where Hmong villagers grow rice and maize. About 25 km east of Phonsavanh is the Hmong market, held on Sundays from 0400 to 1000. Hundreds of people come in from surrounding villages to the colourful market to sell local produce, animals and

Border essentials: Nong Het-Nam Khan (Vietnam)

Nong Het is approximately 60 km east of Muang Kham. It is deep in Hmong country and is an important trading post with Vietnam, which is just a few kilometres down the road at Nam Khan. Not many tourists seem to use this border crossing, although trucks and *songthaew* ply between

Phonsavanh and the border daily, 4-5 hours, US$4-5. There are also buses via Nong Het from Phonsavanh's central bus station Tuesday and Friday at 0630, US$10. Lao visas (30 days) are available at the border for US$30-42; Vietnamese visas are required in advance.

handicrafts. Many of the older people wear traditional attire. Seven kilometres further east is the roadside Hmong village of **Ban Tha Jok**, where there are some old Hmong houses that use old bomb casings as stilts.

If you wish to visit a more traditional Hmong settlement, leave your vehicle at Ban Na Sala Mai on the main road and walk south for 5 km, up a very pleasant valley to **Ban Na Sala**. This is a very beautiful village, perched in the hills. During the war, the Pathet Lao occupied the hills surrounding this village, so the US army was not able to go anywhere near it. Ban Na Sala is one of the best places to see the creative architectural and household application of war debris, as here, too, the people have utilized bomb casings to construct their houses.

Muang Kham

This small trading town, 53 km east of Phonsavanh, is situated in the centre of a large open valley on the route to Vietnam. It was devastated during the war but now has a thriving economy dealing in Vietnamese and Chinese goods. The valley is an important fruit- and rice-growing area. There's a market early every morning in the centre of town and there are also a couple of groups of stone jars close by.

Tham Phiu

ⓘ *East of Muang Kham, off Route 7, just after the Km 183 post, entry to caves 5000 kip. A rough track leads down to an irrigation dam, built in 1981. To get to Tham Phiu, either go the easy way and hire a vehicle and driver US$30-40 from Phonsavanh, or go the hard way, by public transport. For the latter, take the bus to Nong Het, and request to stop at the Tham Phiu turn-off. From here walk towards the towering limestone cliff and follow the small trails for the last kilometre. It is best to do this with a guide as UXOs still litter in the area.*

Evidence of the dirty war can be seen in the area immediately surrounding Muang Kham. The intensity of the US bombing campaign under the command of the late General Curtis Le May was such that entire villages were forced to take refuge in caves. (Curtis Le May is infamously associated with bragging that he wanted to bomb the Communists "back into the Stone Age".) In Tham Phiu, a cave overlooking the valley, 365 villagers from nearby Ban Na Meun built a two-storey bomb shelter and concealed its entrance with a high stone wall. They lived there for a year, working in their rice fields at night and taking cover during the day from the relentless bombing raids. On the morning of 8 March 1968 two T-28 fighter bombers took off from Udon Thani air base in neighbouring Thailand and located the cave mouth which had been exposed on previous sorties. It is likely that the US forces suspected that the cave contained a Pathet Lao hospital complex. Indeed, experts are at odds whether this was a legitimate target or an example of collateral damage. The first rocket destroyed the wall; the second, which was fired as the planes swept across the valley, carried the full length of the chamber before exploding. There were no survivors and 11 families were completely wiped out; in total 437 people died, many reportedly women and children. Local rescuers claim they were unable to enter the cave for three days, but eventually the dead were buried in a bomb crater on the hillside next to the cave mouth. Today there is no official memorial, just the eerily black walls. The interior of the cave was completely dug up by rescue parties and relatives and today there is nothing but rubble inside. It makes for a poignant lesson in military history and locally it is considered a war memorial. Further up the cliff is another cave, **Tham Phiu Song**, which fortunately didn't suffer the same fate. Visitors are welcome to explore but you will need a torch.

Bor Yai and Bor Noi

① *Hot Springs Resort, off Route 7, daily 0900-1900, 5000 kip. Taxi from Muang Kham 50,000 kip or tour from Phonsavanh.*

Not far from Muang Kham, off the Vietnam road, are two hot springs (*bor nam lawn*) on the Nam Mat, imaginatively named Bor Yai (Big Spring) and Bor Noi (Little Spring). They are locally known for their curative properties and are said to have enormous potential for geothermal power but this is hard to believe as they do not appear to be particularly active. The murky water is distinctly uninviting but it is piped to showers and wooden tubs, where a therapeutic soak can be quite pleasant. The springs are owned and operated by the government, so to bathe you have to go to the resort, which has a number of private bathrooms that tourists can use for the day. The resort was purportedly built by Kaysone Phomvihane's wife for visiting dignitaries.

● Sleeping

Phonsavanh *p165, map p165*

None of the streets in Phonsavanh are named – or at least the names aren't used. Consult the map on page 165 to check the exact locations of hotels, guesthouses and restaurants.

A-B Auberge de la Plaine des Jarres (aka Phu Pha Daeng Hotel), 1 km from the centre of Phonsavanh, T/F061-312044. In a spectacular position on a hill overlooking town are 16 attractive stone and wood chalets, with living room, fireplace and shower-room (occasional hot water). Clean and comfortable, lovely views, roses, geraniums and petunias planted around the chalets. Restaurant serves good food. More expensive Oct-May. They sell keyrings made of bullets.

A-B Phu Chan Resort, on a hill on the outskirts of town, T061-312264. Cosy spacious wooden bungalows with all the modern fittings. Nice view of town and the cemetery.

A-B Vansana, on a hill about 1 km out of town, T061-213170. Big, modern rooms with telephone, TV, minibar, polished floorboards and tea/coffee-making facilities. Phenomenal views of the countryside. Opt for the rooms upstairs, with free-form bathtub and picturesque balcony views. Restaurant offers Lao and foreign cuisine. Excellent value, especially the VIP room for US$50. Highly recommended.

B-D Maly Hotel, down the road from local government offices, T061-312031, F061-312003. All rooms have hot water and are furnished with a hotchpotch of local artefacts, including a small (defused!) cluster bomb on the table. More expensive rooms on the upper floors have satellite TV, internet for those who have laptops, out-of-place baths, sitting area and other luxuries. Restaurant. The owner, Mr Sousath Phetrasy, runs tours in this area and to the north around Xam Neua (see Activities and tours, page 174).

C-D Orchid, just off the main road in the centre of town, T061-312403. You can't miss this big green-blue building. Guesthouse, not quite at hotel standard but close enough to be good value. Rooms with TV, hot water, comfy beds and bath. Nicely decorated. Free breakfast and airport pickup (if you ring in advance).

E Khou Kham Guesthouse, on the main road through town. A Hmong-owned hotel. Large rooms with bathroom and hot water but beds are a bit like sleeping on a rock face. Mai and Khou, the friendly owners, speak English. A large selection of ethnic hats for sale in the foyer.

E Nice Guesthouse, on the main road, T0205-616246, naibhoj@hotmail.com. Has a Chinese feel about it but owned by local Lao. Clean decent-sized rooms with hot water and comfy beds. Reasonable value.

E-F Sabaidee, a block back from the main road, T020-5067990, sabaidee2000@hotmail.com. Tiled, clean rooms with hot-water bathroom. Very low hobbit-like doors. Central location, family atmosphere.

F Dok Khoun, Route 7, T061-312189. Tiled rooms with desk. So clean that the smell of ammonia could knock you out. The bathroom is in what looks like a cupboard. Foyer decorated with UXO.

F Phonsavanh Hotel, T061-312206, T020-5561193. Mammoth building houses huge dark rooms with en suite bathrooms or shared facilities – the water supply is erratic. Also operates as a part-time brothel. Unhelpful staff.

Plain of Jars *p166*

There are no hotels or guesthouses in the town of **Muang Khoune**.

Bor Yai and Bor Noi *p172*

D Hot Springs Guesthouse, Bor Yai. 2 lovely wooden bungalows, each with 4 rooms and 1 bathroom. Recommended.

D Senebot, around the corner from **Hot Springs Guesthouse**. Rooms are on the small side.

🍴 Eating

Phonsavanh *p165, map p165*

🍴 Maly Hotel, see Sleeping. A great little restaurant serving fantastic food from a very extensive menu: everything from duck curry to beef steak.

🍴-🍴 Auberge de la Plaine de Jarres, see Sleeping. Reasonable menu of Lao dishes and some French food, somewhat overpriced given the competition.

🍴-🍴 Craters, main street, T020-7805775. Modern, Western restaurant offering burgers, pizza and sandwiches. Comfortable cane sofas, good music, attentive service. Delectable but pricey cocktails.

🍴 Nisha Indian, on the main road. 0600-2230.

Wins the prize for most unexpected find in Phonsavanh. North and south Indian food – very welcome if you need a reprieve from the same Asian dishes found throughout the north of Laos. The owner, endeavouring to exhibit some marketing prowess, has handwritten his name and phone number on every single water bottle.

🍴 Phonexay, on the main road, towards the Tourism Office. Excellent fruit shakes and good Asian dishes – fried noodles, sweet and sour. Exceptionally friendly service.

🍴 Sangah, main street. Thai, Lao and Vietnamese (good noodle soup) dishes all available, as well as some Western fare including steak and chips. Enormous portions.

🍴 Simmaly, main street, T061-211013. What this place lacks in atmosphere it makes up 10-fold with food. Fantastic *feu* soup. Great service and immensely popular. Recommended.

Plain of Jars *p166*

There are many good restaurants in **Muang Khoune**. Manivanh, for example, has good soup and fried rice/noodles dishes. There's also good *pho* opposite the market.

🍸 Bars and clubs

Phonsavanh *p165, map p165*
Maliyona Pub, on the main road. This graffiti-decorated bar on the main drag sticks out like a sore thumb. Ear-blastingly loud hip-hop and Thai music. Beer Lao and BYO spirits. Rather void of customers.

🛍 Shopping

Phonsavanh *p165, map p165*
There are a multitude of shops at the town's market. The dry market is beside the town bus station and sells local handicrafts including the famous Phonsavanh parasols, textiles and silver. Most products from shoes to biscuits can be purchased here. West of the centre of town is the Chinese Market, which stocks a good variety of ethnic clothes and jewellery as well as many cheap tacky imported products. Behind the post office is a fresh produce market with a gamut of fruit and vegetables on offer. There is a surprisingly well-equipped camera shop on

Parasol renaissance

Aside from the war paraphernalia, Phonsavanh is also the best place in Laos to pick up a traditional paper parasol. The art of making paper and wood umbrellas, also known as khan nyu, has undergone a renaissance in the last decade. The tradition is a centuries-old practice, originally bequeathed to the domain of monkhood. Novices and monks would make the parasols to give as gifts to the villages they were visiting. After 1975, the paper umbrellas were quickly usurped by plastic and metal ones from China. The frame of the umbrella is formed from bamboo and the paper made from a pulp of mulberry trees and usually dyed with colour from fruits, such as apple. The paper is stuck to the frame with glue made from persimmon resin and the outside spokes are painted with a charcoal compound. The umbrellas sell from US$5 upwards and can be found in the market and at guesthouses, such as Seng Tavanh.

the corner, adjacent to the town's bus station. Many of the guesthouses sell local handicrafts and war paraphernalia.

✸ Festivals and events

Phonsavanh p165, map p165
Dec National Day on 2 Dec is celebrated with horse-drawn drag-cart racing. Also in Dec is **Hmong New Year** (movable), which is celebrated in a big way in this area. Festivities centre around the killing of a pig and offering the head to the spirits. Boys give cloth balls, known as *makoi*, to girls they've taken a fancy to.

▲▲ Activities and tours

Phonsavanh p165, map p165
Tour operators
There are no shortage of tour operators in Phonsavanh and most guesthouses can now arrange tours and transport. A full-day tour for 4 people, travelling about 30 km into the countryside, should cost up to US$50-60, although you may have to bargain for it. The tourist office, just off the main road, is also quite helpful and runs tours to the hot springs near Muang Kham. Most of the travel agencies are located within a block of each other on the main road.
Indochina Travel, on the main road, T061-312409. Expensive but well-regarded minivan tours (cheaper if you can organize a group).

Inter-Lao Tourisme, on the main road in town. Offers a range of minivan tours to the jars and outlying villages.
Lao Youth Travel, on Route 7, T020-5761233, www.laoyouthtravel.com. Offers a wide range of tours to the jars and post conflict sites.
Sousath Phetrasy, owner of the **Maly Hotel** (see Sleeping) is the most knowledgeable tour guide, however. He spent his teenage years in a cave at Xam Neua during the war and has helped foreign researchers with projects in the region. He also claims to be able to access some of the sites other guides can't reach, such as Long Tien. He is probably the best guide you can get, in terms of local and historical knowledge, and speaks fluent English and German. His tours are slightly more expensive than others but well worth it.

◉ Transport

Phonsavanh p165, map p165
Air
As you fly into Phonsavanh, the pock-marked landscape comes into view and the war's collateral damage becomes apparent.
   Lao Airlines, T061-212027, runs flights to **Vientiane**, Fri-Mon and Wed; check www.laoairlines.com for current schedules. In peak season it is often possible to fly via **Luang Prabang**.

Bus
To **Muang Sui** in Phu Kut district, 50,000 kip.
To **Luang Prabang**, 0800 daily (both local

and VIP bus), 265 km on a sealed road, 7-8 hrs, 90,000 kip. To **Vientiane**, 3 daily, 9-10 hrs, 90,000 kip, also a VIP bus (with a/c and TV) daily at 0730, 100,000 kip. Also north to **Vang Vieng**, daily at 0720, 75,000 kip, and a VIP bus at 0730, 100,000 kip. To **Muang Kham**, 3 hrs, 30,000 kip. Also north to **Nam Nouan**, 0900, 4 hrs, 35,000 kip (change here for transport west to **Nong Khiaw**). To **Xam Neua**, daily 0800, 1600, 70,000 kip, a 10-hr haul through some of the country's most beautiful scenery and very windy roads towards the end (you may want to take travel sickness medicine).

Buses also travel to **Vinh**, Vietnam, Tue, Thu and Sat 0630, 12 hrs, US$12. If you want to cross the border here you will need to organize a visa in advance as there is no consulate in Phonsavanh or agencies that will send your passport to Vientiane.

Car with driver/songthaew
A car with driver is the easiest way of touring the area. A full car to the **Plain of Jars** will cost US$20 (US$5 each) to Site one, or US$30-40 to all 3 sites. The tour could be combined with a trip to the hot springs, west of Muang Kham, for an extra US$20-30. To **Muang Sui**, US$60-80 return. To hire a *songthaew* to go to **Tham Phiu** is US$30-40 for the day, a minivan here costs US$60.

Plain of Jars *p166*
Route 1D is surfaced between Muang Khoune and Phonsavanh (32 km). Buses to **Phonsavanh** depart daily from the Morning Market, 45 min, 15,000 kip.

Muang Kham *p170*
The only way to visit the minority villages en route to Muang Kham is by hiring a taxi. A taxi from Muang Kham to the hot springs costs 50,000 kip

❶ Directory

Phonsavanh *p165, map p165*
Banks Lao Development Bank, near Lao Airlines Office, 2 blocks back from the dry market, changes cash and TCs, Mon-Fri 0800-1200, 1330-1600, no advances on Visa. **Indochine Travel** has an exchange booth with Visa advance, the only place in town, but they charge a whopping 6.9% commission. Moneygram service.
Hairdressers Unlikely that you would want a new hairstyle here but there are several hairdressers dotted around town that will give you a good head massage and hairwash for 10,000 kip. **Internet** At the photo shop, 200 kip per min, and across from the *songthaew* station in town. Slow internet access. **Medical services** Lao-Mongolian Hospital, T061-312166, Sufficient for minor ailments. **Pharmacies** are ubiquitous in town, particularly around the market. **Post and telephone** The post office is opposite the dry market and has IDD phone boxes outside.

Hua Phan Province

Hua Phan Province has a total population of 270,000 and is one of the most isolated areas of the country. Over 20 ethnic groups, mostly mountain-dwellers, inhabit the province, whose character has been shaped over the centuries by a variety of shifting rulers: it was part of the Tai Neua Kingdom, then integrated into the Annamese state of Ai Lao and also experienced stints as a Siamese protectorate and French colonial outpost. Until recently, Hua Phan remained relatively sheltered from the free market ethos that has spilled into towns along the Thai and Chinese borders, and memories of the period when it was the base for the revolutionary struggle are still close to the surface. Traders from China and Vietnam are more common these days but Hua Phan is still known in Laos as the 'revolutionary province'.

Hua Phan is spectacularly beautiful but largely overlooked by tourists. This is a shame, as it is one of the most scenic parts of the country. It is also one of the country's poorest provinces, with over 75% of the population living below the poverty line. Local authorities hope that the area's large tourism potential will help to alleviate the plight and they have teamed up with the NGO SNV to develop infrastructure. There are plans

Border essentials: Na Maew-Nam Xoi (Vietnam)

Route 6A heads east from Xam Neua to the border crossing between Na Maew (Laos) and Nam Xoi (Vietnam), which was opened to tourists in 2004. You'll need to get your Laos/Vietnam visa in advance. The border is open 0730-1130, 1330-1700. It may be necessary to pay a processing or overtime fee.

The trip to the border is two hours from Vieng Xai. *Songthaew* leave Vieng Xai at 0640 from the main Xam Neua–Na Maew road, 1 km from the centre of Vieng Xai, 20,000 kip. It is also possible to take a *songthaew* from Xam Neua station at 0630-0715 (3-4 hours), 30,000 kip, or to charter a *songthaew* to the border from Xam Neua for about US$50.

Footprint has received several complaints about difficulties with unethical tourism operators on the Vietnamese side of this border crossing, charging a fortune for transport. A motorbike taxi to Quan Son should cost around US$10. If you get really stuck on the Vietnam side contact Mr Pham Xuan Hop in Na Maew, T(00 84) 9923 7425, who may be able to organize minivan rental (US$42-50 to Quan Son).

There are two guesthouses in Na Maew (**Phucloc Nha Tru** and **Minhchien**) offering rudimentary facilities for US$3-5 per night).

A bus runs from Na Maew to Thanh Hoa every Tuesday, Thursday and Saturday at 1130, US$8.

for new guesthouses, a new runway, a visa facility at the Vietnam border and, generally, more open access. ▸▸ *For Sleeping, Eating and other listings, see pages 183-184.*

Ins and outs

Getting there Tourists are often put off visiting Hua Phan by the long bus haul to get there but, considering the road passes through gorgeous mountain scenery, the trip is well worth the endeavour. There are three main sealed roads to Xam Neua: Route 6 from the south, linking Xam Neua with Phonsavanh; Route 1 from Vieng Thong and the west, and Road 6A from the Vietnamese border. Due to the upgrading of Route 6, it is now possible to make the journey between Phonsavanh and Xam Neua in a day without an overnight stop in Nam Nouan en route but always check on road conditions before setting off. There is an airport at Xam Neua, 3 km from the centre of town on the road to Vieng Xai and Vietnam. ▸▸ *For further details, see Transport, page 184.*

Getting around Tourists should exercise caution when travelling independently throughout the province, as some of the authorities harbour a residual suspicion of Westerners and there are very few guides that can speak English. The provincial tourism office is probably the best first port of call, and you can organize a car with driver/guide to Vieng Xai caves or Hintang Archaeological Park.

When to visit Summer is pleasant in Xam Neua but temperatures at night reach freezing in winter and you should bring a pullover, even in summer. The area is at its most picturesque in October, when the rice is almost ripe. Mosquitoes are monstrous here, so precautions against malaria are advised (see Health, page 38).

Background

Together with Phongsali Province, Hua Phan was the base for left-wing insurgency from the late 1940s until the final victory of the Pathet Lao over the royalist forces in 1975. Members of the Lao Issara, who had fled to Vietnam after French forces smashed the movement in 1946, infiltrated areas of northeast Laos in 1947-1949 under the sponsorship of the Viet Minh. The movement coalesced when Prince

Souphanouvong, who had fled to Thailand, arrived in Hanoi and organized a conference in August 1950 at which the Free Lao Front and the Lao Resistance Government were formed. Thereafter, the Pathet Lao adopted strategies developed by the Viet Minh in Vietnam, who in turn drew on the strategies of Mao Zedong and the Chinese Communists: establishment of bases in remote mountain areas; use of guerrilla tactics; exploitation of the dissatisfaction of tribal minorities, and mobilization of the entire population of liberated areas in support of the revolutionary struggle. By the time of the Geneva Agreement of 1954, following the French defeat at Dien Bien Phu, Communist forces effectively controlled Hua Phan and Phongsali provinces, a fact acknowledged in the terms of the settlement, which called for their regroupment inside these provinces pending a political settlement. The Pathet Lao used the breathing space and the succession of coalition governments in the late 1950s and early 1960s to reorganize their operations. The Lao People's Revolutionary Party was formed at Xam Neua in 1955 and the Neo Lao Hak Sat, or National Front, was established in 1956.

While Party President Prince Souphanouvong spent a good deal of time in Vientiane, participating in successive coalition governments between 1958 and 1964, Secretary-General Kaysone Phomvihane remained in Hua Phan overseeing the political and military organization of the liberated zone. The beginning of the American bombing campaign in 1964 forced the Pathet Lao leadership to find a safe haven from which to direct the war. Vieng Xai was chosen because its numerous limestone karsts contained many natural caves which could be used for quarters, while their proximity to each other inhibited attack from the air. American planes tried to dislodge the Communists from their mountain hideout but, protected in their caves, they survived the onslaught. Nevertheless, phosphorous rockets and napalm caused many casualties in the less-fortified caves. After the war, senior members of the Royal Lao Government were sent to re-education camps in the province.

Xam Neua (Sam Neua) ⊖🚲🚗🍴 ›› pp183-184. Colour map 1, B5.

→ *Phone code: 064.*

Xam Neua is one of the most intriguing provincial capitals in Laos and is buzzing with a colourful outdoor food market and the eclectic dry market. It is set against a picture-perfect mountain backdrop, amid forested hills and rice fields. The town itself was obliterated during the war and rebuilt after 1973, so it offers little in the way of sights. However, it has a bustling atmosphere, thanks to the many villagers who descend from the mountains to sell their wares here, and provides visitors with the increasingly rare chance to experience a culturally intact, unspoilt town. It is also a staging post for visiting the caves at Vieng Xai.

Sights

The **market** is a good place to see the province's mixture of cultures and peoples – Hmong, Yao, Tai Dam (Black Tai), Tai Khao (White Tai), Tai Neua (Northern Thai) and other ethnic groups – who can all be found buying and selling various commodities. In the adjoining dry market, examples of the distinctive weaving of Xam Neua and Xam Tai can be found at reasonable prices, along with goods trucked in from China and Vietnam. Loudspeakers in the market area often blast music and propaganda from 0600 in the morning and there is a strong military presence. Archways throughout the town. The province is known for its weaving and many houses in Xam Neua have looms on their verandas. There are also several workshops with four or five looms each; some of these still use traditional vegetable dyes rather than the aniline (chemical) dyes that are the norm in most other areas.

‼ *Walk 1 or 2 km back along Route 6 towards Muang Kham for excellent views of the town and an adjoining valley.*

South of Xam Neua

South of Xam Neua are the **Houiyad** falls, located amid undulating hills in a stunning river valley, and surrounded by fields, rice paddies and ethnic minority villages. The falls themselves don't rank highly in the Lao waterfall stakes but make a nice half-day picnic trip from Xam Neua. Nearby **Ban Houaiyad** is renowned for making belts from aluminium gathered from crashed aircrafts, although these days recycled cans are used instead. A few kilometres away are the **Nameuang hot springs** ① *17 km south of Xam Neua, off Route 6; at the junction follow the unpaved road for 3 km, 5000 kip,* which feature a small bathing pool and six washrooms, three of which have bathtubs. The site is currently managed by local villagers.

Continuing south on Route 6 towards Nam Nouan, the waterfall of **Nam Tok Dat Salari** is visible on the left, 3 km after the village of Ban Doan. The falls are difficult to miss as there are numerous empty houses and stalls by the road, used once a year by the people of Xam Neua for Pi Mai celebrations. A track on the right leads up through the jungle to the top of the falls, a very good swimming and picnic spot.

Sao Hintang

① *Off Route 6, 74 km south of Xam Neua and 36 km north of the junction with Route 1 at Phou Lao. For further information contact the tourist office in Xam Neua. Tours can also be organized from Phonsavanh through Mr Sousath Phetrasy of Maly Hotel (see Sleeping, page 173).*

The beguiling Hintang Archeological Park is about 130 km north of Phonsavanh and 56.5 km southwest of Xam Neua, on Route 6. At the billboard-sized sign in Ban Liang Sat, turn up the dirt road heading east. This road is quite rough in places so you'll need a 4WD car or all-terrain motorbike in order to reach the site in one piece. About 3 km up the road is a sign for the Kechintang Trail, a 90-minute walking trail that takes you to some of the sites. The first is visible from the road after a further 3 km, with Site two located another 3 km after that.

The park features hundreds of ancient upright stone pillars, menhirs and discs, gathered in Stonehenge-type patterns over a 10-km area, surrounded by jungle. The megoliths have been cut into narrow blades, up to 2 m tall, and stand one behind the other, with the tallest usually in the middle. According to local sources they are at least 1500 years old. Interspersed between the stone sites are burial chambers dug deep into the bedrock. These were originally covered with large stone discs, up to 7 m wide, and could only be accessed via a narrow vertical chimney.

The enigmatic stones are as mysterious as the Plain of Jars: no-one is quite sure who, or even which ethnic group, is responsible for erecting them and they have become steeped in legend. It is believed that the two sites are somehow linked, as they are fashioned from the same stone and share some archaeological similarities. In 1931, the sites were surveyed and partially excavated by an archaeological team, led by Madeleine Colani, although, by this time, the contents of the chambers had already been raided or simply washed away. The exploration uncovered a number of objects – funerary urns, ceremonial stones, bronze bracelets and ceramic pendants – that give credence to the theory that the stone park was an ancient burial site.

While travelling along Route 6 to the park keep your eyes peeled for the numerous roadside **fox-holes**. These small bolt-holes were used as air-raid shelters during the US bombardment of the area. A large number actually expand into large bunkers capable of accommodating 10 or 12 people.

East of Xam Neua

Xam Tai

Hua Phan is supposed to be a 'cradle' of traditional Lao weaving. The province's remoteness means that the diversity of designs produced here is second to none and techniques that have become rare elsewhere are still practised here. The premier centre for weaving is Xam Tai (local pronunciation, Xam Teua), 100 km southeast of Xam Neua, close to the Vietnamese border. You can try to charter a pickup to Xam Tai from the market, or hire a car at the **Lao Houng** hotel, but note that the road is bad and there is no guesthouse at Xam Tai.

Sop Hao

This town, 60 km east of Xam Neua on the Vietnam border, features a trade fair each Saturday but is pretty much a no-go zone for foreigners due to the presence of one of the country's last re-education centres. The border crossing here is only open to Lao and Vietnamese.

Vieng Xai (Viengsay) 🕖🖨🕔 ➠ *pp183-184. Colour map 1, B6.*

The village of Vieng Xai lies 31 km east of Xam Neua on a road that branches off Route 6 at Km 20. The trip from Xam Neua is possibly one of the country's most picturesque journeys, passing terraces of rice, pagodas, copper- and charcoal-coloured karst formations, dense jungle with misty peaks and friendly villages dotted among the mountains' curves. The area is characterized by lush tropical gardens, a couple of smallish lakes and spectacular limestone karsts, riddled with natural caves that proved crucial in the success of the left-wing insurgency in the 1960s and 1970s. Although it only takes one day to see the caves, it is worth spending some more time exploring the area. The valley contains many other poignant reminders of the struggle, although the war debris is less obvious here than in Xieng Khouang.

Ins and outs

There are seven caves open to visitors. Five were formerly occupied by senior Pathet Lao leaders (Prince Souphanouvong, Kaysone Phomvihan, Nouhak Phounsavanh, Khamtai Siphandon and Phoumi Vongvichit). All the caves are within walking distance of the village. Tickets are sold at the **Viengxay Caves Visitor Centre** ① *T064-314321, viengxaycavesvisitorcentre@yahoo.com, daily 0800-1200, 1300-1630; guided tours are conducted at 0900 and 1300, 30,000 kip with guide.* Tours are usually conducted on bikes which can be rented from the office (30,000 kip). If you want to take the tour outside of designated times you must pay extra. You will need to start early in the morning to see all the caves. If you plan on coming across from Xam Neua it is advisable to stay overnight. ➠ *For further information, see Sleeping, page 183.*

    The caves have a secretive atmosphere, with fruit trees and frangipani decorating the exteriors. Each one burrows deep into the mountainside and features 60-cm-thick concrete walls, encompassing living quarters, meeting rooms, offices, dining and storage areas. The caves are lit but you may find a torch useful.

Background

From 1964 onwards, Pathet Lao operations were directed from the cave systems at Vieng Xai, which provided an effective refuge from furious bombing attacks. The village of Vieng Xai grew from four small villages consisting of less than 10 families into a thriving hidden city concealing over 20,000 people in in the 100 plus caves in the area. The Pathet Lao leadership renamed the area Vieng Xai, meaning 'City of Victory' and it became the administrative and military hub of the revolutionary struggle.

A conservation survey of the area in 1982 identified over 95 caves of historical significance. Included in these was a former hospital complex approximately 15 km from Vieng Xai and a school for children of government officials at Ban Bac. A separate cave complex at Hang Long, 25 km from Xam Neua, housed the provincial government during the war years but is now completely abandoned. Other caves, called 'Embassy Caves', were intended for VIPs from other countries, with individual caves set aside for Russia, Vietnam, Cuba and China. Locals make unsubstantiated suggestions that King Sihanouk from Cambodia also spent a long time hiding out in Vieng Xai during the war.

Vieng Xai village

The village itself was built in 1973, when the bombing finally stopped and the short-lived Provisional Government of National Union was negotiated. Today the former capital of the liberated zone is an unlikely sight: surrounded by rice fields at the dead end of a potholed road, it features street lighting, power lines, sealed and kerbed streets and substantial public buildings – all in varying stages of decay. Nonetheless it is truly one of the most beautiful towns in Laos. The Garden of Eden-type village is dotted with fruit trees and hibiscus and is flanked by amazing karst formations and dotted with man-made lakes (reputedly formed from bomb craters). Vieng Xai is Vang Vieng without the backpackers and the river, though you can swim in the man-made lake, which is lined with thatched cabanas.

Just before the market and truck stop, a wonderful socialist-realist statue in gold-painted concrete pays tribute to those three pillars of the revolution: the farmer, the soldier and the worker; the worker has one boot firmly planted on a bomb inscribed 'USA'. Behind this statue is a **small museum**, which contains some interesting old photographs, many of them unlabelled. Few of the guides seem to know about the museum, so make a point of asking to visit it.

The main street divides as it reaches the top of the village to form a town 'square' which is in fact a triangle. At the apex is a war monument topped by a red star, while at the southern end is a yellow two-storey building housing government offices; the cave **tourist office** is next door. Follow the road past this building to the caves of Kaysone and Nouhak; go right to reach Khamtai's cave and what was once a recreation area; the road along the northern edge of the 'square' leads to the caves of Souphanouvong and Phoumi.

There is a fairly spectacular **waterfall**, 8 km before Vieng Xai. About 3 km after the turn-off from Route 6, a swift stream passes under a steel and concrete bridge. A path just before the bridge leads off to the left, following the river downstream. It takes just a few minutes to reach the top of the waterfall, but the path leads all the way to the bottom, about 20 minutes' walk. Swimming is not advised.

Tham Souphanouvong

A mossy path flanked by large grapefruit trees leads to Tham Souphanouvong. This cave was home to Prince Souphanouvong, the 'Red Prince' and son of the Queen of Luang Prabang. To the right of the path stands a pink stupa, the tomb of the prince's son, who beaten to death with a hammer by infiltrators a few kilometres away in 1967 at the age of 28. Souphanouvong's stunning garden, bursting with a rainbow of flowers and dripping with fruit, was planted in 1973-1974 and is a memorial to his son and metaphor for the war. An old bomb crater has been ingeniously concreted into a pool, referred to as the broken heart; a head, shoulders and neck have been landscaped around the heart. The whole area is surrounded by a sea of red plants, to symbolize all the blood lost during the war. Watch the far entrance of the cave as occasionally rocks have fallen. Souphanouvong and Phoumi's caves both feature a 'garage cave' at the base of the karst, a cavity in the limestone large enough to accommodate a car.

Kaysone's cave is reached by mossy steps cut into the cliff face and extends over 100 m. The cavern is surrounded by blossoming bushes and large frangipani trees. Like the others there is a suite of rooms including a bedroom, meeting room and library. A few of his books are on display; it's no surprise that the collection includes Lenin, Marx, Engels, Ho Chi Minh and an economic text from Vietnam. Also spotted around are a few gifts from foreign dignitories, such as a framed picture of Che Guevara courtesy of Fidel Castro, a lacquer-ware vase from Vietnam and a bust of Lenin. The cave's construction started some time prior to 1963 but Kaysone and Co moved in 1974. Kaysone rarely left the cave and only allowed the most important of visitors inside, mostly other Communist leaders. About 10 people lived in the cave, Kaysone, his children, a doctor, intelligence officer, cook and bodyguards. At the start of the war Kaysone's wife relocated to Yunnan, China where she was head of a school. These days she lives in Vientiane. The Americans knew of Kaysone's whereabouts but were unable to attack the cave directly or infiltrate it, due to its position and to the large number of Pathet Lao soldiers mounted on the summit. The cave remained Kaysone's official residence until 1973, when he relocated to the building in front of the cave. In 1975 he moved to Vientiane. An interesting feature of Kaysone's cave is a long, narrow passage which connects the living quarters to a large meeting area which includes emergency accommodation for dozens of guests.

Tham Than Khamtai

Khamtai Siphandone's cave and the Military Headquarters, is slightly different from the others. The first thing you'll notice is a set of three bomb craters within metres of the entrance to the cave. The craters, now overgrown, are so close together they almost touch. Possibly inspired by their arrival, the entrance is shielded by an enormous, tapering slab of concrete, 4.5 m high and nearly 2 m wide at the base. Inside, the cave is darker and more claustrophobic than the others, with no outside areas. The attendant may or may not lead you through a thick steel door at the bottom of some stairs well inside the cave. It gives access to a staircase which descends steeply before ending in a sheer drop of several metres, and connects to a number of military caves including the army administration. There is a long-ish tunnel which connects to Tham Xang Lot (Elephant Cave) but which is sometimes inaccessible.

Tham Xang Lot

A small distance from Khamtai's cave and included in its entry price, is the large and obvious entrance to what is known as Tham Xang Lot, or 'cave that an elephant can walk through'. Formerly used as an enclosure to keep animals such as elephants and monkies, during the war this natural cavern was used as a theatre, complete with stage, arch, orchestra pit and a concrete floor with space for an audience of several hundred. At the opposite end from the stage, a long passage featuring a number of stalactites and lit by daylight connects to the theatrette below Khamtai's cave. It is hard to imagine now, but this damp, dark area once entertained numerous of dancers, symphonies, circuses and foreign dignitaries from Romania, Bulgaria, Vietnam and China who would pop in for a boogie. As one local recalls: "I snuck in for a look and an orchestra was playing. I got so excited but was trying to contain myself because I was worried that the grenade in my pocket would go off." At times up to 2000 soldiers were hidden in the two caves.

Other caves

The **Artillery Cave**, set halfway up a hillside, offers phenomenal views. The cave was a military installation purposefully set up to conceal fighters who would return fire during US bombing raids. **Phoumi Vongvichid's Cave**, home to the former Minister of Education and Public Health, also houses the enclosure of **Sithon Kommadam**, of the Lao Theung minority, who was reputedly immune to bullets. **Nouhak Phoumsavan's**

Cave has been recently opened to the public. The cave was home to the former President of Laos.

West on Route 1 🚐🚌 ▶▶ *pp183-184.*

Nam Nouan

The junction of Routes 1 and 6 is known as **Phou Lao**; just to the south is the larger settlement of Nam Nouan, a staging post that travellers bound for Xam Neua or Nong Khiaw will invariably find themselves stopping at. The through traffic for Xam Neua is relatively frequent and most buses/*songthaew* from Phonsavanh stop on their way through. To get a connecting bus to Nong Khiaw is a little more complicated as Nam Noun is 7 km south of the junction between Routes 1 and 6, which is at a village called **Ban Sam Nyay**. You can get to the actual junction town by *songthaew* or by asking one of the locals for a lift on a motorbike. Most buses to/from Nong Khiaw stop at this junction town not Nam Nouan. It is a pleasant Khmu village with very little in the way of amenities. If you are coming from Nong Khiaw you will probably arrive disorientated and dishevelled at some ungodly hour. Locals may try to charge you an extortionate rate to get a pickup to Nam Nouan; if that is the case just see if you can grab a lift with someone on a motorbike for US$5-6.

Vieng Thong

Vieng Thong, also known as Muang Hiam, lies 158 km west of Xam Neua on Route 1 and is a reasonable stopover for those journeying to or from Nong Khiaw. The town itself has little to offer but the surrounding area is nothing short of spectacular and improved access in the near future should enable tourists to sample its attractions. The Nam Khan flows through the town, straight from Luang Prabang, so it's rather annoying that no tour operators have yet capitalized on what could be an amazing journey between the two areas.

❗ Surrounding Vieng Thong are numerous ethnic minority villages, mostly Hmong.

North of town are the Vieng Thong **hot springs** ⓘ *5000 kip*, which offer great respite from what can be quite a tiring journey. There's a decent bathing area and washrooms are available. To get there, cross the bridge, turn right and walk for 1 km; ask locals along the way.

Nam Et/Phou Loei NPA

Just 10 km beyond Vieng Thong is Laos' largest protected area, the Nam Et/Phou Loei National Protected Area. Camera trap studies conducted in recent years by the Wildlife Conservation Society have discovered a vast array of large mammals here, including tiger, guar, bear, leopard, macaque, wild pig and deer. The NPA also contains a couple of impressive caves that have piqued archaeologists' interests. The cavern of **Tham Han** is 20 km north of Vieng Thong, towards the Vietnamese border. A swift 20-minute stroll, following the road along the Nam Neun, will bring you to this river cave, which stretches a considerable distance into the hillside and leads to a village on the far side. It can also reportedly be accessed by boat (if there are any around).

❗ Don't venture into the caves without a guide who has good local knowledge.

Ban Secock, a small village 40 km west of Vieng Thong, is the place to go if you want to trek to the stunning Phou Loei waterfall, which should take around two hours. In the future it is hoped that there will be organized treks to Phou Loei, the second highest peak in Laos.

For the time being this area remains undeveloped, particularly from a tourism perspective. There aren't any major ecotourism operators running tours through the NPA yet although there are concerted efforts to get something up and running in the near future. The Nam Et/Phou Louei NPA is not yet setup for tourists however those

🛏 Sleeping

Xam Neua p177
C-E Lao Houng, next to the bridge over the Nam Xam facing the market, T064-312018. There are 28 fairly grotty rooms, some with en suite bathrooms, with Western toilet and hot shower. The communal bathrooms are dirty, with squat toilets and scoop baths. There is a pleasant view of the town and hills from upstairs, the staff are friendly and one of the girls speaks good English but there are much better deals around.

D Outhaithany Guesthouse, opposite the airport, a few kilometres out of town, T064-312121, F064-312414. Reasonably sized, rustic bungalows with hot water. Popular with tour groups. Great restaurant with fantastic views.

E Boun Home, in the lane around the corner from Shuliyo, T064-312223. Very clean rooms, private bathrooms and hot showers. One of the best deals going. Highly recommended.

E Shuliyo, about 100 m from the *songthaew* station. Comfortable, modern rooms with hot-water bath. Ask for the spacious 'hong har' (Room 5).

E-F Kheamxam Guesthouse, on the corner by the river, T064-312111. Wide range of fairly well-appointed rooms, with attached hot-water bathroom, some with a/c and TV.

Vieng Xai p179
Most visitors to Vieng Xai and the caves stay in Xam Neua and make a day trip out here. However, it is advisable to stay overnight as it is difficult to fit everything into one day unless you arrive very early.

E Naxay Guesthouse (there are 2 by this name), opposite Vieng Xai Cave Visitor Centre, T064-314330. The best option. 5 beautiful new bungalows with hot water, comfortable beds and Western toilet. Recommended.

F Naxay Guesthouse, between Kayson's Cave and the visitor centre, T064-314336. Very rustic accommodation in rattan house. Shared bathrooms. Beds as hard as a rock.

F Swampside Guesthouse, on the lake behind the statue. Basic and not very clean. Dorm rooms and outside toilet.

F Viengsay Guesthouse, follow the road that leads to Khamtai's Cave but turn left at the football field; the hotel is the first building on the left, T020-5881305. The hotel is the mouldering remnant of what were once comfortable quarters for visiting dignitaries. The big Communist edifice is extremely run down but still evokes past splendours and offers a few threadbare comforts. Doubles and triples available, ask for an upstairs room, shared bathroom. Electricity 24 hrs. The ramshackle building has a disturbing history as a re-education centre but its setting is superb, amid eucalyptus and Norfolk Island pines, with views of surrounding karsts.

Nam Nouan p182
This isn't the nicest place to stay but if you find yourself stuck here overnight, **Nam Nouan Guesthouse**, signposted with a small blue sign just near the row of restaurants, would suffice.

Vieng Thong p182
Vieng Thong has 3 below-average guesthouses, all with shared facilities, in the 20,000-30,000 kip range.

F Souksavan Guesthouse T064-314478. Probably the pick of the bunch. Rustic, basic rooms, with mosquito nets and attached bath.

🍴 Eating

Xam Neua p177
The colourful fresh food market has a wonderful selection of local dishes. There is also a good *feu*/coffee shop on the corner opposite the bus station. All the restaurants in Xam Neua display their menus in Lao script on white boards but they usually have an English menu tucked away somewhere, so ask to see it.

❦ **Dan Xam Muang**, a block back from the river, near the bridge, T064-314126. A good option. The fried fish is excellent as is the *feu*, *laap* and French fries. Good service.

❦ **Kittavanh Restaurant**, opposite the Nam Xam River near the end of the market.

Great Lao food, particularly *feu*, with a good English menu on a whiteboard.

Vieng Xai *p179*

There are a few noodle shops on the main street opposite the post office and in the market. There are restaurants at both **Naxay Guesthouses** (see Sleeping). The best bet for a good meal is the restaurant beside the large lake and **Vieng Xai Hotel**, which serves wonderful fish and has beautiful bungalows set up along the lake's edge. There are also several eating options at the market.

† **Nang Sang Jan Restaurant**, near the lake/swamp as you enter town, serves tasty *feu* and coffee. No English spoken but very helpful and friendly.

Vieng Thong *p182*

There are a few local restaurants and *feu* stalls.

⊙ Transport

Xam Neua *p177*
Air

The airport is 2 km from the centre of town. Lao Air, T061-312231, 020-5664106 (ask for Mr Pheng), laoair@laopdr.com, runs flights between **Vientiane** and Xam Neua, Sat and Mon, US$62 one way.

Bus/truck/songthaew

There are regular *songthaew* from Xam Neua to **Vieng Xai**, 60-90 mins, 20,000 kip, although there are virtually no services after 1500 in either direction. If you get stuck you can charter a vehicle for a whole day for US$30-40, 50 mins.

Xam Neua bus station is about 2 km from the centre of town and costs 5000 kip in a *songthaew*. Buses depart from Xam Neua to **Vieng Xai**, 4 times daily (in the morning), 20,000 kip; to **Nameo** (the Vietnam border), 0630, 25,000 kip; to **Nam Nouan**, 0700, 4 hrs, 27,000 kip; to **Vieng Thong**, 0720 40,000 kip; to **Phonsavanh**, 0800, 70,000 kip (10 hrs); to **Luang Prabang**, 0800, 16 hrs, 100,000 kip (the Luang Prabang bus goes via **Nong Khiaw**, 12 hrs, 70,000 kip); to **Vientiane**, 0800 and 1230, 24 hrs, 150,000 kip; to **Udomxai**, Sat 0900, 100,000 kip; to **Thanh Hoa** (Vietnam), Sat 0800, 100,000 kip.

Motorbike and minivan hire

Motorbikes, US$6 per day, can be rented from the **Thone motorbike shop**, 40 m and across the road from the **Xam Neua Provincial Tourism Office**, T064-312567, who can also organize minivan rental.

Tuk-tuk

A tuk-tuk to **Nameuang hot springs** should cost US$15 return; to **Vieng Xai**, 31 km, 50 min, 15,000-20,000 kip per person.

Vieng Xai *p179*

Pickups and passenger trucks run from in front of the market in Vieng Xai to **Xam Neua** regularly until 1500, 60-90 mins, around 10,000 kip. It will cost around 200,000 kip to charter a pickup if you miss the last truck back to Xam Neua. It's a better option to charter a vehicle in Xam Neua for a whole day trip to Vieng Xai.

Vieng Thong *p182*

The so-called public transport system is a bit hit and miss. The intersection near the market is the best place to catch a bus or truck east to **Xam Neua**, 158 km, 5-6 hrs, 30,000 kip, or west to **Nong Khiaw**, 175 km , 3-4 hrs, 20,000 kip, and **Luang Prabang**, 30,000 kip. Route 1 west from Vieng Thong is rough but was being upgraded in 2005. Some tourists have reported that this trip is impossible during the rainy season but this should change once the road has been completed.

⊙ Directory

Xam Neua *p177*

Banks The Lao Development Bank will change Thai ฿, US$ and Chinese ¥ into kip but will only accept TCs in US$. **Internet** Available from a house near the temple at 500 kip per min. **Post** Xam Neua has a post office, Mon-Fri 0800-1100 and 1300-1600, but it's best to wait until you are in either Phonsavanh or Luang Prabang. **Telephone** International phone calls can be made from Lao Telecom, behind the post office, daily 0800-1100 and 1300-1600.

Vieng Xai *p179*

Police The police station is behind the disused department store on the town square. **Post** There's a post office by the market but don't bother sending any mail from here.

Central Provinces

⁑ Footprint features

Introduction

Laos' central provinces, sandwiched between the Mekong (and Thailand) to the west and the Annamite Mountains (and Vietnam) to the east, are the least visited in the country. Travellers entering Laos from Vietnam cross the border via Lak Xao or Xepon but few choose to linger for long. This is a shame because the scenery here is stunning, with dramatic limestone karsts, enormous caves, beautiful rivers and forests. In particular, the upland areas to the east, off Route 8 and Route 12, are a veritable treasure trove of attractions, mottled with scores of caves, lagoons, rivers and unusual rock formations. Tourists will require some determination in these parts, as the infrastructure around here is still being developed. Also, the road network is likely to change once the nearly completed Nam Theun II Dam is finished. The Mekong towns of Thakhek and Savannakhet are also elegant and relaxed and, if you are short on time, Thakhek is the best stopover point for the central provinces.

★ Don't miss ...

1 **Travelling overland to Vietnam** Catch a bus across the Annamite Mountains on Route 8 via Lak Xao or Route 9 via Lao Bao, pages 188 and 210.

2 **Boat trip to Tham Kong Lor** Travel along the Nam Hinboun river through awe-inspiring Kong Lor cave, page 189.

3 **That Sikhot** Take a tuk-tuk to one of Laos' holiest sites, where Chao Sikhot is said to have come to a grisly end, page 196.

4 **The caves off Route 12** Head east from Thakhek to explore underground caverns in the limestone landscape, especially the stunningly beautiful Buddha Cave, page 197.

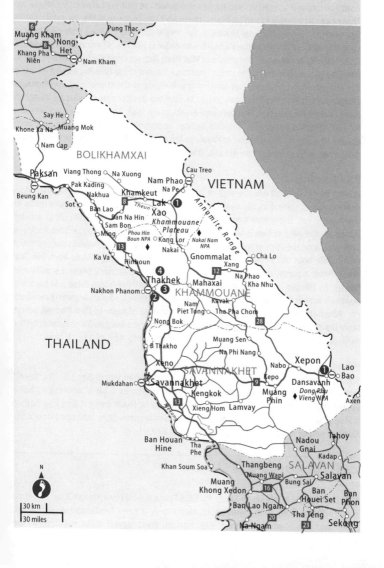

Paksan to Lak Xao → *Phone code: 054.*

East of Paksan the adventurous visitor can encounter some of the county's most stunning landscapes. This little-known region contains a maze of limestone karst peaks, studded with thousands of caves, a beautiful river and pristine jungle. Kong Lor cave, the principal tourist attraction in this area, smacks of Lord of the Rings, with the river cave running straight through the centre of a mountain. ⟫ *For Sleeping, Eating and other listings, see pages 193-195.*

Paksan and around 🏨🍴✳🚍 ⟫ *pp193-195. Colour map 2, B4.*

In the mid-1990s people used to stop in Paksan (Paxsan) to break the journey south (or north) but, now that road upgrading has shortened the journey between Vientiane and Thakhek to a bearable five to six hours, the town's one purpose in life, for most tourists, has been rendered obsolete. However, you might just find yourself stranded here on your way to Vientiane from the Vietnamese border at Lak Xao. There are other potential visitor draws, however, in the shape of **Wat Prah Bat**, an important pilgrimage site for Lowland Lao. Built in 1933, the stupa boasts a footprint of the Buddha as well as one of the largest drums in Laos. Overlooking the Mekong is the more modern **Phonsane Temple**, which isn't anything spectacular in itself but has become famous for its annual Naga Fireball Festival (see Festivals and events, page 194). And for those travellers who feel all 'templed out', there are also several opportunities to explore the province's natural heritage by boat, canoe or kayak 50 km east of Paksan, where the **Nam Kading** river, one of the most pristine in Laos, flows into the Mekong (see box, page 190).

Pak Kading

Pak Kading is a small whistle-stop of a town at the mouth of the Nam Kading. Many commentators slate it as the next major ecotourism centre but it's not quite ready for the hordes yet: there aren't really any tours set up and it's very difficult to arrange transport; the best option is to charter your own boat. The picturesque Nam Kading is known as a local fishery goldmine and is one of the most pristine rivers in the country. A worthwhile boat trip travels upstream through the Nam Kading NPA to **Nam Tok Taat Wang Fong**, a pretty, undulating set of small rapids spectacularly set in a small valley flanked by primary jungle and steep hills. The trip takes three hours there and back and boatmen wait at the boat landing at the south end of town, US$20, bargaining required.

Alternatively you can pick up a boat 15 km east of town to **Ban Phonsi**, where there are signposts advertising the boat trips. There are a few good restaurants on the main road through Ban Phonsi, as it has developed into a bit of a truck stop.

Ban Lao (Vieng Kham/Tham Beng)

Sitting at the junction of Route 13 and 8 is the small settlement of Ban Lao. The town's folk aren't quite sure of the official name, which creates a lot of confusion, but it seems Ban Lao is the safest bet (try Vieng Kham or Tham Beng if Ban Lao pulls a blank). The settlement is pretty nondescript and only noteworthy for its position at the western end of Route 8 to Kong Lor cave and Lak Xao.

East on Route 8 🚍🚏 ⟫ *pp193-195.*

After leaving the north-south Route 13, take Route 8 east towards Lak Xao. This road leads into the hills, with tremendous views over a karst landscape of pinnacles, cones and a patchwork of forest. Big charcoal grey, jagged rocks cut through the

Border essentials: Paksan-Beung Kan (Thailand)

This crossing is for the more intrepid travellers and is seldom used. Check information in advance. The Thai border is 2 km from Paksan on the Mekong, where there's a small port and immigration office, open daily 0800-1200 and 1330-1630. Visas are not available at the border and need to be arranged in advance. Boats to Beung Kan on the Thai side leave when they are full, usually every 30 minutes. You can charter a boat for around ฿300-400.

From Beung Kan there are irregular buses to Udon Thani and Bangkok.

surrounding jungle, conjuring a somewhat daunting, gothic fairytale images. Two-thirds of the way to Ban Na Hin on the right-hand side look out for **Phu Phu Man Limestone Forest**, a cluster of sharp limestone pillars, saw-toothing across the countryside. There is a a small lookout where you can stop; most *songthaew* passengers won't mind if you stop for a minute to take a picture.

Ban Na Hin (Khoun Kham)

Ban Na Hin is a real end-of-the-earth town, low on the charm front and redeemed only by the phenomenal landscapes surrounding it. Its two main *raisons d'être* are as a transit point for Nam Theun II dam operations and for Kong Lor cave to the south; the settlement is also known as Khoun Kham – the 'Gateway to Kong Lor'. Ban Na Hin has quite a big market where you can pick up fresh fruit and vegetables, bread and other supplies; if you haven't got a torch, it's a good idea to pick one up here. There are also a few cheap *feu* shops dotted around the market's periphery.

There isn't a whole lot more here but just outside of town is **Namsanam waterfall**. Take the signposted path on the left-hand side of Route 8, beside a colourful monastery. The trek to the falls is roughly 3 km through quite pleasant surroundings. The two-tiered, 70-m-tall falls are stunning and flow year round. There are reputed to be wild elephants in the area but the likelihood of seeing one is next to nil. The provincial tourism office has built an information centre on Route 8 just before the turn-off to Namsanam Falls for those needing further information. Apparently local guides do exist but you will probably find the waterfall before you find a guide.

Towards Tham Kong Lor

The first stage of the journey is by *songthaew* or tractor from Ban Na Hin to **Ban Napur**. (For details of this route by motorbike, see page 199.) From Ban Napur catch a boat along the Nam Hinboun to either **Ban Phonyang**, where eco-lodge **Sala Hin Boun** is located (see Sleeping, page 193), or to **Ban Kong Lor**, the closest village to the caves, where you can find a homestay for 50,000 kip, including food. The boat trip from Ban Napur to Ban Phonyang is fascinating, with excellent views of impressive limestone cliffs along the way and classic riverside scenes with people fishing and bathing. Take some padding as the wooden seats, even if they are cushioned, can be a bit uncomfortable. There are also reputed to be homestays at Ban Natan on the other side of Kong Lor.

It is almost impossible to do the 9- to 10-hour return trip from Ban Na Hin to Kong Lor in a day, as boat drivers won't travel in the dark.

Some people have reportedly trekked from Ban Na Hin to Ban Kong Lor (47 km) but there isn't much shade and you will need to bring loads of water, as there is nowhere to stock up until you reach Ban Phonyang. Some have suggested hitching a ride with a local tractor for the first 20 km as it is quite boring. The river trip is still undoubtedly the most scenic route. The journey varies from season to season so it is best to check on road conditions in advance. ▸▸ *For further details, see Transport, page 194.*

Hydropower: raid on resources

Major international scrutiny of the Nam Theun II hydropower project resulted in the World Bank's unprecedented investment in mitigating the environmental and social impacts of construction. Initially the World Bank said that if even one animal species was at risk, the project would be halted. Unfortunately these measures are not being carried over to the planning of other dams. The Lao government and foreign investors plan to further exploit the Mekong and its tributaries with over 30 dam projects in the coming decades. These dams do not have Nam Theun II's budget, safeguards or the international pressure required to reduce the environmental impact. The International River Network refers to this as the "hydropower gold rush" and predicts "grim consequences for Lao villagers and the Mekong River ecosystem".

The cumulative impact of the dam-building frenzy will have a major impact on the region's fisheries, which over 60 million people in the Lower Mekong depend on for food, income and transport. Worth an estimated US$2 billion annually, the Lower Mekong accounts for nearly 2% of the total world catch and 20% of all fish caught from inland waters of the world. More importantly, the annual catch accounts for 80% of the region's protein needs.

Dam building has a ripple out effect. Firstly, it has a direct environmental impact on the villages, animal and plant species surrounding the proposed dam site including the socioeconomic affect on the nearby villages. Secondly, there is a detrimental effect on the tributaries, the predominant breeding ground for the Mekong's fish. The dams will block migration routes and inundate the spawning grounds, poisoning tributaries with anoxic waters (water with reduced oxygen). Thirdly, there will be a negative cumulative effect on the Mekong River when scores of dams are built on the tributaries and the mainstream, particularly for those countries downstream.

One such example is the Nam Theun I project, co-owned by Malaysian, Gamuda Berhad, EGC of Thailand and the Lao Government. The dam is set to be built on the Nam Kading River, a Mekong tributary, in the Nam Kading National Protected Area in Bolikhamxay Province. This NPA is, ironically, one of the most remote and best-protected areas in Laos, home to countless endangered mammal and bird species. The NPA not only has regional significance as a refuge for some of Southeast Asia's most diverse plant and animal species, but it also has global significance. No less than five large and mid-sized animals have been discovered in this NPA since 1990, a number unmatched in the world. Nonetheless, the Lao Government, with its eye on the dollar and with scant regard for the environmental impact is set to storm ahead. Official assessments predict that the dam will have a dire environmental impact. Firstly, it will block fish migration routes to the upper reaches of the Nam Kading and its tributaries, having an irreversible consequence for fish biodiversity and numbers; it is estimated that the dam will wipe out 50% of the Nam Kading's fish species. Secondly, there will be a negative impact on the NPA's rare animal species. It is expected that the wildlife species that live in the NPA, much of it endangered, could be wiped out.

⫶ The Mlabri – spirits of the yellow leaves

The elusive Mlabri 'tribe', which occupies the forests around Lak Xao as well as parts of Thailand, represents one of the few remaining groups of hunter gatherers in Southeast Asia. They are also known as the Phi Tong Luang or 'Spirits of the Yellow Leaves'; when their shelters of rattan and banana leaves turn yellow they take this as a sign from the spirits that it is time to move on. Traditionally the Mlabri hunted using spears. If they were stalking larger game, they would brace the weapon against the ground, rather than throwing it, and allow the charging animal to impale itself on the point. In this way, the Mlabri were able to kill the great *saladang* wild buffalo (*Bos gaurus*), as well as bears and tigers. Smaller game was more common, however, and this was supplemented with tubers, nuts, honey and other forest products to provide a balanced diet.

Many of the Mlabri's traditions are already on the verge of extinction. The destruction of the forest means that the Mlabri have been forced to lead more sedentary lives, turning to settled agriculture in place of hunting and gathering, while inter-marriage with other tribes is reducing their number. Perhaps this is no bad thing: as recently as the 1980s, a Mlabri was displayed in a cage in a Bangkok department store. Today, many of the few Mlabri that remain have been forced to become cheap labourers for groups such as the Hmong.

Tham Kong Lor (Kong Lor cave) → *Do not miss this!*

ⓘ *Entrance fee at cave 5000 kip; US$15 for boat from Sala Kong Lor; US$10 to go through the cave.*

Tham Kong Lor cave can only be described as sensational. The Nam Hinboun River has tunnelled through the mountain, creating a giant rocky cavern, 6 km long, 90 m wide and 100 m high, which opens out into the blinding bright light at Ban Natan on the other side. The cave is apparently named after the drum makers who were believed to make their instruments here. Although very rare, it is also home to the largest living cave-dwelling spiders in the world, though it is unlikely you will have a run in with the massive arachnid. Fisherman will often come into the cave to try their luck as it is believed that 20-kg fish lurk below the surface.

At the start of the cave, you will have to scramble over some boulders while the boatmen carry the canoe over the rapids, so wear comfortable shoes with a good grip. A torch or, better, a head-lamp (2000 kip at Thakhek market), is also recommended. It is eerie travelling through the dark, cool cave, with water splashing and bats circulating. There are a few miniscule rapids inside and the cave's surface is bumped with nooks and crannies, crevices and holes. About two-thirds of the way through the cave is an impressive collection of stalagmites and stalactites.

The first stage of the journey is by *songthaew* or tractor from Ban Na Hin to Ban Napur. From Ban Napur catch a boat along the Nam Hinboun to either Ban Phonyang, where eco-lodge **Sala Hin Boun** is located (see Sleeping, page 193), or to Ban Kong Lor, the closest village to the caves, where you can find a homestay for 50,000 kip, including food. Beyond Ban Phonyang the river route to Tham Kong Lor is gorgeous, with small fish skipping out of the water, languid buffalo bathing, kids taking a dip and ducks floating by – all surrounded by a Lord of the Rings fantasyland of breathtaking cliffs and rocky outcrops. Don't expect the three- to four-hour boat trip to be cheap – it is around US$25 each way (if you are lucky). These prices will come down once the roads have improved and the boat drivers don't have a monopoly on transport.

⁝ Border essentials: Nam Phao-Cau Treo (Vietnam)

The border is 30 km east of Lak Xao at Nam Phao (Laos) and has been a legal crossing point since September 1997. There are buses to the border from Vientiane (via Paksan, see page 194). *Song-thaews* leave Lak Xao market every hour 20,000 kip and take about 50 minutes to the border (see also Transport, page 194). The border is open 0800-1700 and the official exit fee is 3000 kip, although the Lao border officials are quite lacksadaisical. Be prepared for slow service around lunchtime and an overtime fee at weekends. You need to organize Vietnamese visas in advance (ideally in Vientiane) as they aren't issued at the border. Crossing into Vietnam can induce culture shock as you will be descended upon by a gang of 'sharks', trying to extort ridiculous amounts for minivan/bus services to Vinh (reports of up to US$30!). Take your time to bargain for the right price (US$6-7 is reasonable), rather than rushing your travel arrangements. Arriving from Vietnam, 30-day Lao visas are issued at the border (prices vary for different nationalities but expect to pay around US$30-42).

It is possible to continue from Ban Natan, on the other side of Kong Lor, into the awesome Hinboun gorge. This is roughly 14 km long and, for much of the distance, vertical cliffs over 300 m high rise directly from the water on both sides. The discovery of some valuable religious documents indicates the historical significance of the gorge both during the Vietnamese War and much earlier. There is no white water but the river frequently flows quite fast. More impressive scenery then follows until the village of **Paktuk**, close to Route 13 where any journey can be continued. ▸▸ *For further information on getting to the Kong Lor cave, see Transport, page 194. The cave can also be visited as part of the 400-km 'loop' from Thakhek, see page 199.*

⁝ *Tham Natan is another enormous cave set in this remote countryside, requiring a 4WD and a good guide to find it.*

Lak Xao (Lac Sao) ⬛🚻🏨ℹ ▸▸ *pp193-195. Colour map 2, B5.*

Lak Xao is a relatively new town. It was established by the army's Bolisat Phathana Khet Phoudoi (BPKP or Mountainous Area Development Company) back in 1968 in a remote and sparsely populated area close to the border with Vietnam, and still retains a frontier atmosphere. It is sometimes called Muang Kham Keut, which is confusing because there is another Kham Keut, 30 km to the west of town. (This was the original settlement and is worth a visit as it is over 500 years old.) The surrounding countryside is beautiful but Lak Xao itself has little to recommend it, except that it provides a necessary break on the journey overland to Vietnam.

This part of Laos was once one of the richest in terms of wildlife. Unfortunately, you only have to look around the town to see that it's also a major logging centre, with big bulky timber trucks rumbling through to Vietnam. It is believed that Lak Xao was once a mini fiefdom controlled by an old, Lao general, who logged the town into oblivion. Another threat to the forests and fauna is the area's great hydropower potential. Many feared that the controversial **Nam Theun II** dam project would open up the region to yet more loggers and settlers. In reality, some dam pundits would suggest that logging in the surrounding region was reduced by the presence of the dam. Construction of the dam has been monitored by a hawk-eyed bunch of consultants and it was rumoured that, if even

⁝ *In the distance looms a line of cliffs, the last of which is known locally as Pa Pi Hai – the 'Ghost that Cries'.*

one fish species were to become extinct as a result of the dam-building efforts, then the World Bank and other financiers would pull the funds. The **Lak Xao Wildlife Centre** used to operate in the town, trying to protect animals displaced by the logging and dam construction. Unfortunately the centre has now closed and an assortment of wildlife is now to be found for sale at the market stalls: monkeys, reptiles, frogs and basically anything else the locals can lay their hands on.

The local army of tuk-tuk drivers is also worth mentioning as a breed apart. The town's Wild West atmosphere seems to have gone to their heads, so it's a question of holding on to your hats and your wallets, too, as they will probably do their level best to fleece you.

● Sleeping

Paksan *p188*
Accommodation seems insufficient, given the number of backpackers passing through the town.
C-D Paksan Hotel, T054-791333. Well appointed, Vietnamese-run hotel with clean, modern rooms.
E-F B&K Guesthouse, across the river, on the 1st road on the right, T054-212638. The friendly owners of this establishment speak very good English and, with clean rooms and en suite bathrooms, it's worth a try. There's a very good restaurant attached.

Ban Lao *p188*
If you get stuck en route there are 2 guesthouses on Route 13, just past the Route 8 intersection, which, by and large, are better than those found at Ban Na Hin.
E-F Bunthieng Guesthouse, on the right-hand side of Route 13. Reasonable accommodation, with basic furnishings.
F Vieng Thong, on the left-hand side of the road. Quite big rooms with fan.

Ban Na Hin *p189*
You may need to stay either here or in Ban Lao for 1 night if you are trying to make your way back quickly from Kong Lor cave. Accommodation is mostly of a 'rustic' nature.
D Mithuna Guesthouse, Route 8, T020-2240182. A surprise find, modern guesthouse with hot water, a/c, comfortable beds, internet and a fantastic restaurant attached. Great stop-off point for those wanting advice on getting to Kong Lor.
F SP Guesthouse, smack-bang in the centre of town. This wooden house is a little lacklustre, but the big verandas are quite nice.

Towards Tham Kong Lor *p189*
There are 2 guesthouses on Route 13 in **Ban Lao**, just past the Route 8 intersection, which are passable. Homestays are available in **Ban Kong Lor** and **Ban Natan**. The homestays charge about US$5 per person including breakfast.
B-C Sala Hin Boun, Ban Phonyang, 10 km from Kong Lor cave, T020-5614016, www.salalao.com. The best option. It enjoys a scenic location on the riverbank amongst karst rock formations and has 10 well-equipped and very pleasant rooms in 2 bungalows. Mr Kham, the manager, will arrange for a boat to pick you up in Napua for US$25, with advance notice. A tour to Kong Lor for 2-3 people is US$30 with picnic lunch. Discounts in low season.
D-E Sala Kong Lor Lodge, 6 km from Kong Lor cave, T051-214315. Lodge with 4 small huts with twin beds and a couple of rooms. There is also a campsite for US$2 per night.

Lak Xao *p192*
There are several reasonably pleasant places to stay in Lak Xao.
E Phoutthavong Guesthouse, T054-341074. Spotless rooms with a/c or fans, tiled floor, polished wooden furniture and wonderfully white paintwork that is at odds with the dusty atmosphere of the town. Recommended.
E Souriya Hotel , T054-341111. Another pleasant alternative with 20 spotlessly clean, simple rooms (some a/c) with TV and some baths (hot water). Friendly owner speaks quite good English.
E Vongsouda Guesthouse, T054-341035. Quite a nice guesthouse with a/c and en suite bathrooms with Western loos and hot water. Not the most comfortable mattresses

in the world but rooms are clean and serviceable. Clean and airy lobby but the real selling point is the large veranda outside the main entrance where you can sit and relax with a drink. Motorbike hire (US$15).

● Eating

Paksan p188
There are many small restaurants along the main drag. Few have English menus and most are of poor quality and not particularly cheap.
❢ **Saynamxam Restaurant**, at the north of the bridge. Has a fairly decent menu.

Ban Lao p188
There is a small market at the intersection, with several *feu* restaurants.

Lak Xao p192
❢ **Only One Restaurant**, 200 m from **Phoutthayong Guesthouse**, on the same side of the road. Plenty of tables in a pleasant, if unextraordinary, setting. Reasonable Vietnamese and Lao food, daily 0600-2200.

✹ Festivals and events

Paksan p188
Jul (movable) Every year **Wat Prah Bat** hosts a full moon festival.
Mid-Oct (movable) The famous **Naga Fireball Festival** (**Bang Fai Phayanuk**), at the Phonsane Temple, when small, colourful fireballs shoot out of the river.

◯ Transport

Paksan p188
Bus
The bus stop is next to the Morning Market. To **Vientiane**, 7 daily in the morning, 1-2 hrs, 25,000 kip. In the other direction, most buses from Vientiane to southern destinations ply through the town every couple of hours, so it's just a matter of waiting at the bus stop/market to pick up a lift: to **Thakhek**, 190 km, 4-5 hrs, 15,000 kip; to **Savannakhet**, 25,000 kip. To reach the Vietnam border at **Nam Phao** (see Border essentials, page 192), catch one of the border-bound buses that starts from the southern terminal in

Vientiane (see page 78) or travel by pickup to Lak Xao, 5-6 hrs, 50,000 kip, for onward transport (see below). These *songthaew* depart between 0500 and 0600.

Ban Lao p188
There is a small transport terminus at the intersection. If a bus/*songthaew* happens to dump you here, hop on one of the northbound buses to Vientiane or a southbound bus to Thakhek, Savannakhet and Pakse. *Songthaew* generally scurry through here from early in the morning to well into the afternoon, to **Ban Na Hin** (for Kong Lor cave, 15,000 kip), and **Lak Xao**, 25,000 kip.

Towards Tham Kong Lor p189
Getting to Kong Lor cave, for now, is not easy. The best way to get there is by road and boat. There is a small transport terminus at the Route 13/Route 8 intersection in **Ban Lao** (also known as Tham Beng or Vieng Kham) for north-south buses between Vientiane and Thakhek, Savannakhet or Pakse. *Songthaew* generally pass through here from early in the morning to well into the afternoon to **Ban Na Hin**, 20,000 kip. This trip along Route 8 is about 60 km. The drive between Ban La and Ban Na Hin is magical and passes through some truly amazing Gothic scenery; keep an eye out for the lookout at Km 54 from Route 13. Generally, a pick-up waits in Ban Na Hin to take passengers to Ban Kong Lor, 3 hrs, where you can pick up a cheap boat trip into the cave for US$10.

Alternatively, if the roads are in a state of decay, you can pick up a *songthaew*, tuk-tuk or tractor from the centre of Ban Na Hin (opposite the market) for the 10 km journey to **Ban Napur**, 30 mins, and then catch a boat to **Ban Phonyang**, 2-3 hrs US$25 one-way, or **Ban Kong Lor** (closer to the cave) US$30, and onto the cave, a further 1 hr, US$10-15.

A new road, scheduled to be completed in 2008, is in the works and will take visitors 50 km direct from Ban Na Hin (also known as Ban Khoun Kham) to Ban Kong Lor.

If you are staying at **Sala Hin Boun**, see Sleeping, they will send you a boat to Ban Napur to collect you, US$25.

Lak Xao *p192*
Songthaew depart for **Paksan**, every hr from 0700 daily, 5-6 hrs, 40,000 kip, and **Thakhek**, every hr 0730-noon daily, 40,000 kip. If you wish to leave after midday, go to Ban Lao and pick up a lift from there. Buses leave for **Vientiane** at 0500, 0600 and 0800, 6-8 hrs, 60,000 kip. These buses go via **Ban Lao** (Vieng Kham). There is a scheduled bus for **Thakhek** daily at 0730, 5-6 hrs, 50,000 kip.

The road up into the mountains is excellent, partly because there is a hydro-power dam here and also because of the need to establish and maintain good infra-structural links with neighbouring countries.

Pickups depart from the Lak Xao market throughout the day to the Vietnam border 32 km away, at **Nam Phao**, 1 hr, 10,000 kip each if you can fill a whole tuk-tuk but be prepared to barter hard. Often tour buses to Vietnam leave from the **Phou Doi Hotel**, so it is worth checking as it is an infinitely more comfortable mode of transport. There is also a minivan service from Lak Xao market to **Chung Thom**, near Vinh, daily 1100. Otherwise, it's sometimes cheaper to catch a ride in the mornings, as there's a better chance the drivers will be able to pick up passengers, but the chances deteriorate as the day goes on.

● Directory

Lak Xao *p192,*
Banks Lao Development Bank, open daily 0800-1500, with an hour's lunch break, quite a competitive exchange rate on major currencies. **Post** The post office is open daily 0800-1200 and 1300-1600.

Thakhek and around

➔ *Phone code: 052. Colour map 2, B5.*

Thakhek is sometimes translated as Indian (Khek or Khaek) Port (Tha), although it probably means Guest (Khaek) Port after the large number of people who settled here from the north. During the royalist period (through to the mid-1970s) it was a popular weekend destination for Thais who came here in droves to gamble. After the Communist victory, when Laos effectively shut up shop, everything went very quiet. But the recent recovery of commercial traffic has brought some life back to this small settlement, although Thakhek remains a quiet town, set in beautiful countryside.

The origins of Thakhek can be traced back to the Cambodia-based kingdoms of Chenla and Funan, which reached their heyday in the seventh century AD. But modern Thakhek was founded in 1911-1912, under the French, clearly evident in the architecture. Apart from Luang Prabang, this is probably the most outwardly French-looking town, particularly with the fading pastel hues of the villas around the town's fountain area.

Today Thakhek is the most popular stopover point in the central provinces, although it is still not considered a primary tourist destination. However, the region encompasses some of the most beautiful scenery in Laos: imposing jagged mountains, bottle green rivers and lakes and caves. Tourism infrastructure is still quite limited but a trip to this area will prove a highlight of most visitors' holidays to Laos, particularly the stunning karst scenery and impressive trip out to Buddha Cave, or the popular route known as 'the Loop' (see page 199). ➔➔ *For Sleeping, Eating and other listings, see pages 202-204.*

Ins and outs

Getting there and around Flights between Vientiane and Thakhek have been discontinued, as the improving quality of the road north to the capital makes flying unnecessary. There are two bus terminals: the main terminal, which is about 5 km from town and offers inter-provincial and international buses, and the small *songthaew* station, near Soksombook market, which services local regions.

Thakhek is small enough to negotiate on foot or by bicycle. A number of places organize motorbike hire, such as the **Thakhek Travel Lodge** and the Tourism

Information Centre, which acts as an agent for motorcycle dealers. ▸▸ *For further details, see Transport, page 203.*

Tourist information The **Tourism Information Centre** ① *Vientiane Rd, in a chalet-like building beside a derelict ferris wheel, T052-212512,* has particularly helpful staff who are champing at the bit to take tourists out on their ecotours and hikes. This is a good stop-off place for advice. Proceeds from the tours go to poor, local communities. The office is full of brochures and glossy displays of the surrounding sites.

Sights

There are few officially designated sights in Thakhek but many visitors consider it to be a gem of a settlement. Quiet and elegant, with some remaining Franco-Chinese architecture, including a simple fountain square, it has a fine collection of colonial-era shophouses, a breezy riverside position and a relaxed ambience.

‡ *Thakhek is also known as Muang Khammouan.*

What locals regard as the central business district at the river end of **Kouvoravong Road** is wonderful for its peeling buildings. Other visitors, in contrast, look more critically at the dusty streets, seeing pockets of squalor, dilapidated buildings and an uncharacteristic atmosphere of disinterest amongst the locals. ▸▸ *For details of the town's three markets, see Shopping, page 203.*

That Sikhot

① *6 km south of Thakhek, daily 0800-1800 (the gate is always open), admission 2000 kip, tuk-tuk 10,000 kip.*

That Sikhot or **Sikhotaboun** is one of Laos' holiest sites. It overlooks the Mekong and the journey downstream from Thakhek, along a quiet country road, reveals bucolic Laos at its best. The *that* was restored in 1956 but is thought to have been built by Chao Anou at the beginning of the 15th century, around the same time as That Ingheng in Savannakhet Province (see page 207). The *that* houses the relics of Chao Sikhot, a local hero, who founded the old town of Thakhek.

According to local legend, Sikhot was an ordinary man who once cooked some rice which he stirred with dirty – but as it turned out magic – sticks. When he ate the filthy rice he was bestowed with Herculean strength. At that time, the King of Vientiane had been having a major problem with elephants killing villagers and taking over the country (hard to believe now but Laos was once called Land of a Million Elephants). The king offered anyone who could save the region half his kingdom and his daughter's hand in marriage. Due to his new-found strength, Sikhot was able to take on the pachyderms and secure most of the surrounding area as well as Vientiane, whereupon he married the king of Vientiane's daughter. The king was unhappy about handing over his kingdom and daughter to this man, and

‡ *That Sikhot is yet another place that is said to contain some of the Buddha's bones.*

Thakhek

Passenger Boats to Nakhon Phanom
Choaanou
Customs **5**
Jetty
Vientiane Rd
Setthathirat Rd
Wat Nabo
Ounkham Rd
Nongbuakham
Kouvoravong Rd
Captain Bounkeut
Car Ferry to Nakhon Phanom
Mekong River
To Stadium
Public tuk-tuks to That Sikhot (6 km)
To ⑥ Post Office (200m), Market & Bus Terminal (2.5km)

N

400 metres
400 yards

Sleeping 🛏
Khammuan International **1**
Sooksomboon Guesthouse **4**
Southida Guesthouse **5**
Thakhek Travel Lodge **6**

Eating 🍴
Kaysone **1**
Lao-named Restaurant **2**
Noodle Stall **3**
Vanthiu **4**
Zukiyaki **5**

Central Provinces Thakhek & around

⁞ Border essentials: Thakhek-Nakhon Phanom (Thailand)

Thakhek is across the Mekong from Nakhon Phanom in Thailand. There's a customs and immmigration office by the pier in Thakhek, open daily 0800-1730, and boats cross between the two towns every hour or so (although this tends to slow down to an hourly service around lunchtime), 15,000 kip or ฿60, slightly cheaper in the other direction. There are usually 'overtime service fees' at weekends, when boats become less frequent and will generally ask for more money. From Nakhon Phanom, scheduled buses depart for Udon Thani and Bangkok. Arriving from Thailand, 30-day Lao visas are available at the border, US$30-42.

plotted with his daughter so as to to regain control. The king asked his daughter to discover whether Sikhot had any weakness. Her husband foolishly revealed to her that he could only be killed through his anus, so the King of Vientiane placed an archer at the bottom of Sikhot's pit latrine (a messy business that does not bear contemplating) and when the unfortunate Oriental Hercules came to relieve himself, he was killed by an arrow.

That Sikhot consists of a large gold stupa raised 29 m on a plinth, with a viharn upstream built in 1970 by the last King of Laos. The *that* is partly surrounded by a high wall. The tip of the stupa is said to be fashioned after a banana flower and there are reliefs of the Buddha in various *mudras* along the base. Stalls selling drinks and some food are to be found under the trees to the left. A major annual festival is held here in July and during February.

Kong Leng lake

ⓘ *33 km northeast of Thakhek.*

This site is usually incorporated into hikes as there isn't direct road access to the lake. This stunning lake is steeped in legend and locals believe an underground kingdom lies beneath the surface of the 100-m-deep lake. As a result, you must request permission to swim in this lake from the local village authority and you can only swim in the designated swimming zone. Fishing is not permitted. The beautiful green waters of the lake morph into different shades season to season due to the dissolved calcium from the surrounding limestone outcrops. It is very difficult to get to on your own and sometimes the track is completely inaccessible except on foot. The Tourism Information Office organizes excellent treks to the lake.

Excursions off Route 12 🚌🚲🚍 ›› *pp202-204.*

The caves along Route 12 can be visited on day trips from Thakhek, although some are difficult to find without a guide and access may be limited in the wet season. Many of the sights have no English signposts but locals will be more than obliging to confirm you are going in the right direction if you ask.

Tham Xang (Tham Pha Ban Tham)

This is the closest cave to Thakhek, around 9 km northeast of town. The cave is considered an important Buddhist shrine and contains a number of Buddhist artefacts, including some statues and a box containing religious scripts. The Buddhist component, however, pales into insignificance compared to the 'elephant head' that has formed from calcium deposits. Locals herald it as a miracle and in the Lao New Year they sprinkle water on it. Visitors will need a flashlight to find the formation along a small passage at the right-hand corner of the cave, behind the golden Buddha. To get to the cave, follow Route 12 for about 7 km until you pass the bridge, then turn right. Difficulties can arise reaching it in the wet season due to flooding. Of lesser interest but in the same general direction are a few **railway bridges**, part of a project, designed by the French in the early 1900s, to connect Laos and Vietnam, but abandoned in 1920. The best remnant is the bridge crossing the Nam Don river. To get there, turn north off Route 12 at Km 8 and follow the road for 1 km until you hit the old railway bed. Then turn right and continue along the dirt track for another 1 km until you cross the bridge.

Tham Pha (Buddha Cave)

ⓘ *Ban Na Khangxang, off Route 12, 18 km from Thakhek. A* songthaew *will cost US$15, use of boat 5000 kip and entrance to the cave 2000 kip. Women will need to hire a* sinh *(sarong) at the entrance, 2000 kip.*

A trip out here is highly recommended not for the cave itself, which is impressive in its own historical right, but for the surrounding villages, pristine waterways and wonderful karst scenery. A farmer hunting for bats accidentally stumbled across Buddha Cave (also knowns as Tham Pa Fa – Turtle Cave) in April 2004. On climbing up to the cave's mouth, he found 229 bronze Buddha statues, believed to be over 450 years old, and ancient palm leaf scripts. The Buddhas were part of the royal collection believed to have been hidden here when the Thais ransacked Vientiane. Since its discovery, the cave has become widely celebrated, attracting pilgrims from as far away as Thailand, particularly around Pi Mai (Lao New Year). In the wet season it is possible to bathe in the stunningly clear waters surrounding the cave, though women will need to bring a *sinh* (sarong). A wooden ladder and eysore concrete steps have been built to access the cave but it is still quite difficult to get to, as the road from Thakhek is in poor condition. It is recommended that you organize a guide through the Thakhek Information Office to escort you. In the wet season, it is necessary to catch a boat. The trip out to the cave is half the fun as it is surrounded by some truly stunning scenery of karst formations sprawling across the landscape like giant dinosaur teeth.

Tha Falang (Vang Santiphap – Peace Pool)

This lovely emerald billabong is surrounded by pristine wilderness and breathtaking cliffs. The swimming pool, created by the Nam Don river, was a favourite French picnic spot during the colonial period and it's a nice place to spend the afternoon or break your journey if you're doing 'the Loop' (see page 199). The water can become a bit stagnant in the dry season. To get there, follow Route 12 for 13 km and then turn north for 2 km. In the wet season it may be necessary to catch a boat from the Xieng Liab Bridge.

Tham Xiang Liab

Turn off Route 12 at Km 14 (1 km past the turn-off for Tham Xang) and follow the track south to reach Tham Xiang Liab, the first cave in the province to be officially opened to tourists. The 200-m-long cave sits at the foot of a 300-m-high limestone cliff, with a small swimming hole (in the dry season) at the far end. It is not easy to access the interior of the cavern on your own and, in the wet season, it can only be navigated by boat, as it usually floods. This cave, called 'sneaking around cave' derived its name from a legend of an old hermit who used to meditate here with his beautiful daughter. A novice monk fell in love with the hermit's daughter and the two love birds planned their trysts sneakily around this cave and Tham Nan Aen (see below). When the hermit found out he flew into a rage and did away with the novice monk; the daughter was banished to the cave for the rest of her life. There are limestone formations on the roof of the cave and experts have suggested that there may be some cave drawings hidden among the shadows.

This little-visited cave contains a small lake, reputed to be 75 m long, and a couple of interesting Buddhist shrines. Swimming in the lake is strictly prohibited as the auspicious waters are believed to have magical powers. To reach the cave, follow Route 12 to Km 17; beyond the narrow pass turn to the left (north) and follow the path for 400 m.

Tham Nan Aen

ⓘ *Admission 5000 kip.*

Follow Route 12 until you see a sign on the right (south) at Km 18, which reads '700 metres'; follow this path to the cave entrance. The giant of the local caverns, it is said to be 1.5 km long and stands over 100 m tall. It is worth a visit, if only to catch the cool breeze, which rushes from within the rock and emanates from the cave entrance. Outside the cave is a shady, wooded picnicking area and a rather motley collection of animals, a disgrace considering this is supposed to be a protected area. The large cave is accessed by a wooden platform, purpose-built in 1987, for the visiting Princess of Thailand. The breezy cave is like a labyrinth, with multiple chambers and entrances, and also contains a small underground freshwater pool. The cave has bizarre-looking stairs and fluorescent lighting.

Nam Don Resurgence

Close to Ban Na, off Route 12 at Km 14, 25 km northeast of Thakhek, is a beautiful lagoon, located within a cave and shaded by a sheer 300-m-tall cliff. The lagoon offers about 20 m of swimming then filters off into an underground waterway network, believed to extend for 3 km. In 1998 French surveyors found a rare species of blind cave fish 23 m below the surface. If you follow the cave wall round, there is another entrance which offers a good vista of the turquoise pool below. A trip to Nam Don Resurgence can be done in conjunction with the 'Loop' but requires a few hours. It is a bit tricky to find on your own so you might need to ask the locals or recruit a local guide. During the wet season, access is often only by boat. The Provincial Tourism Office runs some pretty good tours which include this sight.

Mahaxai

Mahaxai itself is a beautiful small town 50 km east of Thakhek on Route 12. The sunset here is quite extraordinary but even more stunning is the surrounding scenery of exquisite valleys and imposing limestone bluffs. A trip to Mahaxai should be combined with a visit to one or more of the spectacular caves along Route 12 and some river excursions to see the Xe Bang Fai gorges or run the rapids further downstream.

The Loop

Ins and outs

ⓘ *Contact Thakhek Travel Lodge (see Sleeping, page 202) for details of the route in their log book and for motorbike hire.*

A motorbike tour loops around Mahaxai, Lak Xao, the caves and other beautiful scenery along the way, and has become increasingly popular with the backpacker set. However, by doing the entire 'circuit' by motorbike you will miss some of the most beautiful landscapes in the country, many of which can only be accessed by boat, in particular the trip to Kong Lor cave (see page 189). The circuit – if done quickly – should take approximately three days but allow four or five, particularly if you want to sidetrack to Tham Kong Lor and the other caves along the way, and also to allow for the normal punctures and muddy shenanigans that are par for the course in this part of the world. The weather will have a major impact on the roads, which may in the wet season be impassable, it is imperative to check in advance.

The 'loop' is mostly for motorcyclists, who pick up a bike in Thakhek and travel by road. For those with patience steel it is possible to do the trip by public transport, although it is very difficult and time consuming. The whole loop covers an area over 400 km (without the side-trips). This includes 50 km from Thakhek to the Shell station before the turn-off to Mahaxai; 45 km between the Shell station and Nakai; 70 km between Nakai and Lak Xao; 66 km between Lak Xao and Ban Na Hin; 60 km between Ban Na Hin and Ban Lao and then 100 km between Ban Lao and Thakhek. The trip between Ban Lao and Ban Na Hin offers some spectacular views.

It is a wild ride in parts, so pack lightly: include a waterproof jacket, a torch, a few snacks, a long-sleeved shirt, sunglasses, sun block, closed-toe shoes, a *sinh* or sarong (to use as a towel, to stop dust and – for women – to bathe along the way), a phrase book and a good map. It is a bumpy, exhausting but enjoyable ride. Few of the sites are particularly well signposted in English so you will need to ask around. Most sites charge a parking fee for motorbikes.

Note that this whole region is very susceptible to change due to the Nam Theun II dam, a US$1.45 billion hydropower project (see page 202) and other developments in the area. It is imperative that you check for up-to-date information before travelling. Check on the status of the roads at the Tourism Information Office and in the log book at the **Thakhek Lodge**. This trip is difficult in the wet season and will probably only be possible for skilled riders on larger dirt-bikes. In the dry season it is very dusty.

The route
Thakhek to Mahaxai From Thakhek take Route 12 east. The 50-km trip to Mahaxai should take two to three hours, without stops. It can be a little bumpy, pot holed and particularly muddy during the rainy season. Most travellers will want to stop off

Around Thakhek: The Loop

at some of the caves, swimming holes or the railway line en route. Close to Mahaxai there is a small village, with a large, blue-coloured factory, and a good *feu* soup restaurant. After this, turn right at the T-junction to Mahaxai, where there are a few cheap guesthouses (see Sleeping, page 203).

Mahaxai to Nakai/Ban Tha Long Alternatively you can continue on to Nakai (an additional 1½ to two hours), where there are also basic guesthouses and fuel. There is a 5-km hilly section en route to Nakai, where the sandy roads can be difficult to navigate (although it's nothing compared to the hike into Kong Lor). There is a guesthouse in Nakai (40,000 kip, clean but with quite a few bugs) but this isn't the nicest of towns in which to stay so you might want to continue a further 20 km to Ban Tha Long, which has a lovely riverfront guesthouse, serving pretty good omelettes (40,000 kip).

Nakai/Ban Tha Long to Lak Xao Lak Xao is 70 km and four to five hours from Nakai or 50 km and three to four hours from Ban Tha Long. The road is relatively smooth due to the kindly efforts of the Nam Theun dam crew. Seventeen kilometres from Nakai you hit a junction. The left fork will take you to the Nam Theun II site; the most common route, though, is to take the right fork along the forested, paved road to Lak Xao. Lak Xao offers extraordinary scenery but doesn't emanate the kind of vibe which makes you want to stay for long.

Lak Xao to Kong Lor To get to Kong Lor from Lak Xao follow the road 62 km to **Ban Na Hin** (also known as **Khoun Kham**), the last town before Kong Lor. It has a couple of small guesthouses (see page 193). A new 50-km laterite road from Ban Na Hin to Kong Lor was being scheduled to open very soon after publication but at the time of publication getting to Kong Lor was tricky. Ask in advance at the tourism centre near the entrance to the falls. Follow the main road through town and turn south after the hydroelectric pro ject. Follow the hydroelectric waterway along the dusty road and after a few kilometres turn right at the intersection marked by red painted barrels. (You'll know you have the correct turning when you can see a settlement on the other side of the waterway.) Keep following the road until you hit a rusty bridge at **Namsanam**. Here you have two options, left or right. If you want it easy, turn right after the bridge and follow the mammoth power lines until you reach the crossroads, turn left and head for **Ban Napur** (also known as Naphouk Village). Here, there is a small enclosure where you can leave your bike or motorbike for a day or two, while you continue your journey to Kong Lor by boat. The boat trip is recommended over the final motorbike leg, as it takes in some absolutely stunning scenery (see page 189). In the wet season it is necessary to make this leg of the trip by boat (bike-minding fee 5000 kip). Eight kilometres from Kong Lor is **Sala Hin Boun**, which can make a pleasant stopover (see page 193). Alternatively, turn left at the bridge in Namsanam for a more adventurous ride, although this route can be impassable in the wet season, when you may have to carry your bike – not much fun. You'll drive through challenging but beautiful terrain for two hours – the first hour forest and the second hour farmland.

Ban Na Hin to Thakhek Once you get back to Ban Na Hin, check out **Namsanam waterfall** (see page 189), 3 km off the main road, then continue on Route 8 towards the intersection with Route 13. You will hit a little uphill stretch followed by a big downhill run; don't miss out on the stunning lookout point, well worth a break. At the intersection is the small village of Ban Lao (see page 188), from where it is 100 km back to Thakhek; this last stretch should take two hours and the scenery is pretty boring.

Nakai Nam Theun National Protected Area

The **Nakai Plateau** was once a royal hunting ground, but today it is part of a National Protected Area (NPA). Over 3700 sq km of stunning landscape have been designated for protection, making it the largest area of its type in Laos and some of the most pristine wilderness remaining in Southeast Asia. Gradually rising from the Nakai Plateau, the heavy jungle looms up into the Annamite Mountain range, bordering Vietnam. Although numbers are dwindling, there is a great wealth of rare and endangered flora and fauna in this region, including elephants, tigers, the giant muntjac, Asiatic black bears, Malayan sun bears, clouded leopards and the very rare saola (or spindlehorn).

During 2007 tourist access to the area was limited, almost certainly due to the **Nam Theun II Dam** project. Nam Theun NPA was thrown into the international spotlight over the controversial dam, which will supply electricity to nearby Thailand and will eventually be a major source of income for the Laos government. Many conservationists believe the project is an environmental minefield. The dam is expected to be flooded by 2008, with effects undoubtedly reverberating throughout the whole area. Visitors to the region should ask advice before travelling, as certain areas will be flooded, villages will be moved and new roads will replace the old ones.

● Sleeping

Thakhek *p195, map p196*
C-D Sooksomboon Guesthouse (formerly the Sikhot Hotel), Setthathirat Rd, T051-250777. An immensely attractive building that was once the provincial police station. It faces the Mekong and has the most character in Thakhek. The interior is 1970s kitsch, not to be cool but because it hasn't been renovated in the last 30 years. Once you get over the ghastly decor the place is actually very good value. The a/c rooms in the main house are best, with en suite bathrooms, bath tubs, fluffy chairs, some padded walls, fridge and TV. Also cheaper rooms in the motel-esque annexe. Prime location, with an excellent view across the river to Thailand. Run-down restaurant.
D Khammuan International (formerly the Chaleunxay Hotel), Kouvoravong Rd, T051-212171. Military-owned hotel that has a soulless penitentiary feel. Smallish rooms without windows but some have a/c and the en suite bathrooms are good with hot water showers. Cheaper single rooms with super-powerful ceiling fans are also available. Although the rooms are quite good value, you wouldn't put your mother up here as it may well double as a brothel.
D Mekong Hotel, Setthathirat Rd (or Mekong Rd), T051-250777. Prime location – hideous building. The putrid baby blue colour stands out like a psychedelic wart on what would otherwise be a pretty classic riverfront scene. Exterior aside, the large 1950s hotel has 60 or so a/c rooms overlooking the Mekong. No windows facing the river but the wide balconies are perfect for the sunset vista. Large, plain but clean, with TV, telephone, fridge and bathtub. Since you're not exposed to the exterior from your room, the US$10 asking price is one of the best deals in town. The Vietnamese management are friendly enough but don't speak much English.
D Southida Guesthouse, Chao Anou Rd (1 block back from the river), T051-212568. Very popular guesthouse in the centre of town. Clean comfortable rooms with a/c, TV, and hot water. Very helpful staff and small restaurant downstairs, offering an eccentric mixture of dishes, including sashimi. Often booked up.
D-E Thakhek Travel Lodge, 2 km from the centre of town, T030-5300145, travell@laotel.com. Popular guesthouse set in a beautifully restored and decorated house. Fantastic outdoor seating area and the furniture and embellishments are outstanding. The cheaper rooms are very basic. Good hotel restaurant particularly the Hawaii curry, and BBQ (which needs to be ordered in advance), espresso machine. The

Danish/Lao owners can provide travel advice, when they're around, and there's an excellent log-book for those intending to travel independently around the 'Loop'. Motorcycle hire, US$15 per day. Recommended for those planning adventure travel around the area. Ring them in advance if you're coming in on one of the midnight buses.

D-F Phoukanna, Vientiane Rd, T030-212092. Nice gardens and good value, homely rooms with TV and hot water. Mini-mart and excellent restaurant on site. The hotel itself is fantastic, and popular with the NGO crowd, if you can rouse the nonplussed staff from their sleep to organize a room.

Mahaxai *p199*
E-F Mahaxai Guesthouse. 10 large clean airy rooms, with en suite showers, upstairs rooms are brighter. There is an attractive balcony overlooking the river, ideal for sitting and watching the world go by. Around 40,000 kip.

🍴 Eating

Thakhek *p195, map p196*
Thakhek is not a place to come to for its cuisine. There is the usual array of noodle stalls – try the one in the town 'square' with good fruit shakes. Warmed baguettes are also sold at the square in the morning. The best place to eat is definitely at one of the riverside restaurants on either side of fountain square, where you can soak up the languid atmosphere, while knocking back a Beer Lao and tasty BBQ foods, and watching the spectacular river sunset morph through its various pinky tones. Otherwise, most restaurants are attached to hotels.

¶ **Kaysone Restaurant**, in the centre of town, T051-212563. Although from the outside this looks like someone's back yard, once inside you'll discover a sprawling restaurant compound. Very popular with the locals. *Sindat*, Korean BBQ, plus an à la carte menu comprising entrails and so forth. The ice cream here is fantastic. If you feel like belting out some tunes, there's karaoke on site. What more could one ask for?

¶ **Lao-named restaurant**, on the corner of Ounkham Rd and the east-west street leading to Wat Nabo. English menu with Lao

and some Western dishes, mainly centred around seafood. Popular with local expats.

¶ **Phoukanna**, see Sleeping. The best option, with good service and a large array of Western and Lao dishes.

¶ **Southida Guesthouse**, see Sleeping. Good value, does a reasonable Western breakfast and has a very eclectic menu including sashimi.

¶ **Sukiyaki**, Vientiane Rd, T020-5751533. A pokey but exceptionally friendly restaurant where a buffet of food is on offer which you can BBQ yourself on the tables.

¶ **Thakhek Travel Lodge**, see Sleeping. Recommended for their BBQs and Hawaiian curry.

¶ **Vanthiu Restaurant**. Walk through a wine shop to get to the Vietnamese restaurant out back. Friendly establishment, no English menu but some English dishes.

Mahaxai *p199*
Food is generally of a high quality in the local noodle shops and food stalls.

🛍 Shopping

Thakhek *p195, map p196*
A few duty-free shops at the pier stock Chinese 'champagne', French wines, spirits, perfume and cigarettes.

Markets
There are 3 markets in Thakhek, although the goods on sale are not geared to the weird predilections of visiting *falang*. The largest, **Talaat Souk Somboun** (Talaat Lak Saam), is at the bus terminal, 4 km east of town. It is a good place to pick up odds and ends, with tuk-tuks constantly ferrying market-goers to and fro (10,000 kip). **Talaat Lak Song** is at the eastern end of Kouvoravong Rd, about 1.5-2 km from the town centre. It is a mixed, largely dry goods market, although functional basketry and hand-crafted buffalo bells are also available. Finally, north on Chaoanou Rd is the **Talaat Nabo**.

🚌 Transport

Thakhek *p195, map p196*
There are no longer regular air or boat services to Vientiane. For boats to **Thailand**, see Border essentials, page 197.

Thakhek's **main bus station** is 4 km northeast of town. It is a large station with a mini-market and is open throughout the night. Frequent daily connections northbound to **Vientiane**, 346 km, 6-7 hrs, 40,000 kip; the VIP bus also dashes through town at 1300 daily, 60,000-80,000 kip. Frequent scheduled buses to **Paksan**, 190 km, 4-5 hrs; it is also possible to pick up a bus to Paksan en route to Vientiane. Get off at **Ban Lao**, 15,000 kip, for connections along Route 12.

Southbound buses to **Savannakhet**, every hr, 1100-2200 daily, 139 km, 2½ hrs, 20,000 kip; to **Pakse**, every hr until 2400 daily, 6-7 hrs; also to **Sekong**, 3 daily, 60,000 kip; to **Attapeu**, 1530 and 2200 daily, 65,000 kip; to **Don Khong**, 1600 daily, 15 hrs, 60,000 kip.

To **Dong Ha** (Vietnam), 0800 Sat, 80,000 kip; to **Thien Hué**, 2000 Mon, Tue and Thu, 80,000 kip.

Because of the irregular bus hours there is a small so-called 'guesthouse' at the bus station, where you can rent a bed for 25,000 kip. Best avoided.

The **local bus station** is at Talaat Lak Sarm and services towns and villages within the province. From here *songthaew* depart hourly between 0700 and 1400 to **Mahaxai**, 50 km, 2-3 hrs, 20,000 kip; to **Nakai**, 80 km, 2-4 hrs, 30,000 kip; **Na Phao** (Vietnam border) 142 km, 6-7 hrs, 40,000 kip; **Na Hin**, 45,000 kip. There is also a *songthaew* to **Kong Lor** village at 0730, 75,000 kip but this only runs when the road conditions are good (especially not in the wet season). Route 12 to the Vietnam border has been undergoing constant construction but is set to be complete in the next few years.

Motorbike hire
Bikes can be rented from **Thakhek Travel Lodge**, US$15 per day; and from the no-name rental shop, on the left-hand side, near the traffic lights, US$8 per day (ask for Mr Na). The Provincial Tourism Office can also organize motorbike rental.

Mahaxai *p199*
Songthaew leave from the station in the morning. The last bus back to **Thakhek** leaves Mahaxai at 1500.

❶ Directory

Thakhek *p195, map p196*
Banks BCEL, Vientiane Rd, just across from the post office, T051-212686, will change cash and TCs and does cash advances on Visa. **Lao Development Bank**, Kouvoravong Rd (eastern end), T052-212089, exchanges cash but doesn't do cash advances. There is also a second exchange counter at the immigration pier. **Internet** Available at the Thakhek Travel Lodge and stationery shop in the main street in town, 300 kip per min. **Post** Post office, Kouvoravong Rd (at crossroads with Nongbuakham Rd). **Telephone** International calls can be made from the post office.

Savannakhet Province → *Phone code: 041.*

Savannakhet Province has the highest provincial population in Laos. It consists of 15 districts, with 826,000 inhabitants dispersed within its boundaries. Like most other provinces in the country, Savannakhet is a kaleidoscope of ethnicities, including the Lao, Phouthai, Thaidam, Katang, Chali, Lava, Souai, Pako, Kaleng, Mangkong and Tai. The cultural diversity is even more visible in Savannakhet city, which has large Chinese and Vietnamese populations. Vietnamese and Thai merchants sell their products throughout the city, while the ubiquitous colonial houses and fading shopfronts are an ever-present reminder of French influence. According to official figures, this province records some of the highest tourist numbers in the country, although much of this is probably just transit traffic. Because of its proximity to both Thailand and Vietnam, Savannakhet is considered an important economic corridor. Savannakhet Province has several natural attractions, although the majority are a fair hike from the provincial capital. For those short on time in Laos, Pakse (see page 218) makes a better stopover than Savannakhet. ▸▸ *For Sleeping, Eating and other listings, see pages 211-214.*

Savannakhet 🚌🚲🏠❄️🏯▲🚌🎵 ▸▸ *pp211-214. Colour map 2, C5.*

Situated on the banks of the Mekong and at the start of the Route 9 to Danang in Vietnam, Savannakhet – or Savan as it is usually known – has a population of 124,000 and is an important river port and the gateway to the south. It is also an important trading centre with Thailand.

Across the Mekong, high-rise Mukdahan in Thailand may be cocking a snook at its poorer neighbour to the east, but Savannakhet has got a lot to offer that Mukdahan has bulldozed away in the name of modernization. It feels as though the country never left Savan: goats and chickens graze and wander around the urban area and a large portion of the town's French colonial roots still stand, moulding gently in the tropical climate. With a good lick of paint, Savannakhet could scrub up well and, although it's not quite Luang Prabang, it certainly shares many of the same characteristics. Whether this will last long is questionable. Construction of the Japanese-sponsored bridge across the Mekong to Mukdahan is finally complete and the bridge is now open.

Ins and outs

Getting there and around It is possible to cross into Vietnam by taking Route 9 east over the Annamite Mountains via Xepon. The border is at Dansavanh (Laos) and Lao Bao (Vietnam) (see Border essentials, page 210), 236 km east of Savannakhet, with bus connections direct from Savannakhet to Dong Ha, Hue and Danang. It is also possible to cross the border into Mukdahan via the new Friendship Bridge or by one of the more infrequent ferries. The government bus terminal on the northern edge of town, near the Savan Xai market, has connections with Vientiane, Thakhek, Pakse and Lao Bao; a tuk-tuk to the centre should cost about 10,000 kip. Just west of the bus station is the *songthaew* terminal, where vehicles depart to provincial destinations. Tuk-tuks, locally known as 'Sakaylab' (as in Skylab), criss-cross town. ▸▸ *For further details, see Transport, page 213.*

Tourist information The **Provincial Tourism Office** ① *Khanthabouli Rd, T052-214203,* is one of the best in the country and runs a number of excellent ecotours and treks to Dong Natad and Dong Phu Vieng National Protected Areas; these should be organized in advance. The office can also arrange guides and drivers for other trips. ▸▸ *For further details, see Activities and tours, page 212.*

Background

Savannakhet was established in 1642 by Prince Thao Keosimphali, the son of King Luang of Phonsim. The Prince relocated the majority of families from Ban Phonsim, 18 km east of Savannakhet, to the modern-day town, naming the new fiefdom Ban Thahae (Mineral Port Village). The name was later changed to Souvannaphoum and, in 1883, was adapted to Savannakhet by French colonizers. In 1989 US servicemen arrived in Savannakhet, searching for the remains of men missing in action (MIAs) and the whole town turned out to watch their arrival at the airport. Not realizing that the Lao bear absolutely no animosity towards Americans, the men kept their heads down and refused to disembark until the crowds dispersed. During the war against the Pathet Lao the Royal Lao Air Force operated out of Savannakhet and, towards the end of the conflict, even headquartered here.

Sights

Like any town of this size, Savan has quite a number of wats but none is particularly notable, unless 'watting' is a new and novel experience for you. **Wat Sounantha** on Nalao Road has a three-dimensional raised relief on the front of the *sim*, showing the Buddha in the *mudra* of bestowing peace, separating two warring armies. **Wat Sayaphum** on the Mekong is rather more attractive and has several early 20th-century monastery buildings. It is both the largest and oldest monastery in town, although it was only built at the end of the 19th century. Two of the monks at **Wat Sayamungkhun** speak some English and are pleased to talk about their 50-year-old monastery. There

Savannakhet

Sleeping
Hoong Thip **2**
Mekong **3**
Nanhai **4**
Nongsoda **5**
Phonepasut **6**
Saisouk **8**

Savanbanhao **10**
Savanpatthana
  Guesthouse **11**
Xayamoungkhun **12**

Eating
Lao-Paris **1**

Moonlight **7**
Nety's Food Garden **2**
Sakura (Khampa Café) **6**

Bar & clubs
Rose Bar **8**

N

200 metres
200 yards

is a large temple school here and, if you arrive during lessons, you may get roped into some impromptu English teaching.

Savan's **colonial heritage** can be seen throughout the central part of town. Perhaps the most attractive area is the square east of the Immigration office between Khanthabouli and Phetsalath roads. Simuang Road, near the Catholic church, is also rewarding in this regard. Evidence of Savan's diverse population is reflected in the **Chua Dieu Giac**, a Mahayana Buddhist pagoda at the intersection of Soutthanu and Phetsalath roads that serves the town's Vietnamese population. In deference to Theravada tradition, the *chua* has a *that* in the courtyard. There's also a Chinese school close to the Catholic church.

For those unable to get to the Ho Chi Minh Trail, there is some rusting war scrap in the grounds of the **Provincial Museum** ① *Khanthabouli Rd, Mon-Fri 0800-1130 and 1300-1600 (if it looks closed go across to the School of Medicine and knock on the curator's quarters, housed in the wooden building), 5000 kip*, and a tank just to the north. The museum (scruffy and dirty) has plenty of propaganda-style displays but little that is terribly enlightening, unless you are interested in the former revolutionary leader Kaysone Phomvihane.

Another attraction is the **Dinosaur Museum** ① *Khanthabouli Rd, south of the stadium, Mon-Fri 0800-1200 and 1400-1600, 5000 kip*, which houses a collection of four different dinosaur and early mammalian remains, and even some fragments of a meteorite that fell to earth over 100 million years ago. The first fossils in the region were unearthed in 1991 by a team of French and Lao scientists. All exhibits are accompanied by explanations in Lao and French; the staff speak good English and French and are happy to explain their work.

In the near future, the local tourism authority intends to open up a few more local sights to visitors, including Kaysone Phomvihane's former residence and the Thonglahasinh factory, where you can learn about the process of natural silk-dyeing (surprisingly interesting).

Around Savannakhet

That Inheng
This holy 16th-century *that* or stupa is 12 km northeast of Savannakhet. It was built during the reign of King Sikhottabong at the same time as That Luang in Vientiane, although local guides may try to convince you it was founded by the Indian emperor Asoka over 2000 years ago. Needless to say, there is no historical evidence to substantiate this claim. The wat is the site of an annual festival in February or March akin to the one celebrated at Wat Phou, Champasak (see page 223). The regular tuk-tuks that ferry people between Savannakhet and Xeno will usually take you to That Inheng (80,000 kip return). Otherwise, take a shared *songthaew* to Xeno and ask to hop off at That Inheng. They will usually take you all the way, but if they drop you at the turning it is only a 3-km walk from the road. Alternatively hire a bicycle in town and cycle out here.

Salt works
Located northeast of the city, the salt works make for a good excursion. About 90% of Lao salt is produced here, either in large open saltpans or in an interesting Heath-Robinson contraption where the saline solution is pumped into small metal trays over wood fires in open sheds.

Kengkok
Kengkok is 35 km south of Savan along Route 13 and then a further 25 km inland. The main reason to come to this village is to see the beautiful surrounding countryside.

⁝ Ho Chi Minh Trail

Throughout the Vietnam War, Hanoi denied the existence of the Ho Chi Minh Trail and, for most of it, Washington denied dropping 1.1 million tonnes of bombs on it – the biggest tonnage dropped per sq km in history. The North Vietnamese Army (NVA) used the Trail, really a 7000-km network of paths (trodden and cycled down by tens of thousands of men) and roads – some two-lane carriageways, capable of carrying tanks and truck convoys – to ferry food, fuel and ammunition to South Vietnam. Bunkers beneath the trail housed cavernous mechanical workshops and barracks. Washington tried everything in the book to stem the flow of supplies down the trail.

The Viet Minh had used it as far back as the 1950s in their war against the French. By 1966, 90,000 troops were pouring down the Trail each year, and four years later, 150,000 infiltrators were surging southwards using the jungle network. Between 1966 and 1971, the Trail was used by 630,000 communist troops; over the same period, it was also the conduit for 100,000 tonnes of provisions, 400,000 weapons and 50,000 tonnes of ordnance. At any given time, the Trail was guarded by 25,000 NVA troops and studded with artillery positions, anti-aircraft emplacements and SAM missiles.

The Trail wound its way through the Annamite mountains, entering Laos at the northeast end of the 'Panhandle', and heading southeast, with several access points into Cambodia and south Vietnam. Almost all roads running the north-south axis between southeastern and northeastern Laos were part of the Trail, and most towns sitting in these areas were obliterated by the US bombing campaign. The US airforce started bombing the Trail as early as 1964 in Operation Steel Tiger and B-52 first hit the Mu Gia pass on the Ho Chi Minh Trail in December 1965.

Carpet-bombing by B-52s was not admitted by Lao Prime Minister Prince Souvanna Phouma until 1969, by which time the US was dispatching 900 sorties a day to hit the Trail. It is estimated that it took 300 bombs for each NVA soldier killed on the Trail. The B-52 air strikes proved ineffective; they never succeeded in disrupting NVA supply lines for long.

In an effort to monitor NVA troop movements, the US wired the Trail with tiny electronic listening devices, infra-red scopes, heat- and smell-sensitive sensors, and locational

The only way to get here is to hire a car or tuk-tuk (200,000 kip return); make sure you remember to agree a pick-up time.

Champone District

An increasingly popular excursion, particularly for nature and wildlife enthusiasts, is a day trip to Champone District, location of Hai Suey Lake, the Monkey Forest and Don Deng Turtle Lake. A number of villages in the area provide an insight into the platitudes of local farming life. A tuk-tuk will do the round trip for US$40, divided amongst passengers. Otherwise contact the local tourist office, who should be able to hook you up with a guide/driver.

Take Route 13 south towards Pakse and turn left at Km 35; follow this road for approximately 20 km until you reach Ban Sokuan, a friendly village that's a great place to stop-off for a bite to eat to break the journey. **Hai Suey Lake**, the largest lake in Savannakhet Province, is located 4 km further on. Boats will generally do short trips on the lake for about 5000 kip. Another 7 km beyond Ban Sokuan is Ban Dong Meun, known as the **Monkey Forest**. If travelling independently ask locals along the way and beacons to guide fighter-bombers and B-52s to their target. The NVA carefully removed these devices to unused lengths of trail, urinated on them and retreated, while preparing to shoot down the bombers, which predictably arrived, on cue, from Clarke Field Air Base in the Philippines.

Creative US military technicians hatched countless schemes to disrupt life on the Trail: they bombed it with everything from Agent Orange (toxic defoliant) to Budweiser beer (an intoxicating inebriant) and washing up liquid (to make it into a frothing skid-track). In 1982 Washington finally admitted to dumping 200,000 gallons of chemical herbicides over the Trail between 1965 and 1966. The US also dropped chemical concoctions designed to turn soil into grease and plane-loads of Dragonseed – miniature bomblets which blew the feet off soldiers and the tyres off trucks. Nothing worked.

The US invasion of Cambodia in May 1970 forced Hanoi to further upgrade the Trail. This prompted the Pentagon to finally rubberstamp a ground assault on it, codenamed Lamson 719, in which south Vietnamese and US forces planned to capture the Trail-town of Tchepone, directly east of Savannakhet, inside Laos. The plans for the invasion were drawn up using maps without topographical features.

In February 1971, while traversing the Annamite range in heavy rain, the South Vietnamese forces were routed, despite massive air support. They retreated leaving the Trail intact, 5000 dead and millions of dollars-worth of equipment behind. Abandoned vehicles, bomb casings and sometimes, gutted choppers and bombers can still be seen along the Trail. There is more war debris here than on the Plain of Jars as trucks cannot easily enter the area and pick up the scrap metal. For a map of the Ho Chi Minh Trail, see page 279.

Despite the herbicides, the mountainous region around the trail is still blanketed in dense tropical forest – much of it remarkably undisturbed – and, because of its inaccessibility, the forest has not been raided by the timber merchants. However, many of the rare birds and animals found in the markets at Salavan are caught in this area. Many of the tribal groups (mainly Lao Theung) that populated the area before the war were forced to move onto the Boloven Plateau because of the heavy bombing of the Ho Chi Minh Trail.

they will point you in the right direction. The monkeys reign supreme from their forested habitat, not far from Champone River, and locals have attached many superstitions to their presence, such as imminent death if you hit a monkey. From Monkey Forest it is another 30 km south, via the Ban Nong Lan Chanh intersection, to Ban Dong Deng and **Turtle Lake** ① *admission 3000 kip*. There are fewer shelled creatures here than monkeys at Dong Meun, but they are still reasonably visible. Locals revere these soft-shelled turtles (*paa faa*) and it is believed that certain residents can summon the creatures from the waters with a special call.

Ban Houan Hine

Ban Houan Hine, or Stone House, was built between the sixth and the end of the seventh centuries. It does not begin to compare with the better known Wat Phou outside Champasak but a visit here can be combined with a visit to **That Phone**, a hilly Buddhist *that* en route. It was previously possible to travel by boat down the Mekong to this lesser known Khmer site, 75 km south of Savannakhet, but, again, improvements in road conditions coupled with the usual tourist's disposition to

⦂ Border essentials: Dansavanh-Lao Bao (Vietnam)

The Vietnam border is 236 km east of Savannakhet (45 km from Xepon). Getting through customs and dealing with potential obstacles on the other side means that it's impossible to state how long it may take to get into Vietnam itself.

Buses leave Savannakhhet for the border at 0630 and 0930 1200, four to five hours, 30,000 kip. There are buses that run from Savannakhet to Dong Ha, Hué and Danang, but you will need to change buses at the border.

The Lao border post is at Dansavanh, from where it is about 500 m to the Vietnamese immigration post and a further 3 km to Lao Bao, the first settlement across the border;

motorbike taxis are available to carry weary travellers. We have received reports of long delays at this border crossing, as paperwork is scrutinized and bags are checked and double checked. Don't be surprised if formalities take one hour – and keep smiling! The problem seems to be at the Vietnamese end but those with a Vietnamese visa should be OK. The closest Vietnamese consulate is in Savannakhet; see page 214 for visa application details and opening hours. Lao immigration can also issue 30-day tourist visas for US$30-42. Expect to pay 'overtime fees' on the Lao side if you come through on a Saturday or Sunday.

press on elsewhere, has meant this is no longer an option. Instead, buses take Route 13 south, 60 km from Savan, and then turn right onto a track for a further 15 km (signposted 'Stone House Pillars').

East on Route 9 ⬤🏍🚌 ⇢ pp211-214.

Xepon (Sepon) and around → Colour map 3, A3.

It is possible to cross into Vietnam by taking Route 9 east over the Annamite chain of mountains to **Lao Bao** (just over the border) and from there to the Vietnamese town of Dong Ha and the cities of Hué and Danang (see Border essentials, above). The largest place on the Lao side of the frontier is Xepon. At first glance it might seem that there's not much to see and do in Xepon but as there is a government guesthouse here, travellers very occasionally use it as a stopping place en route to Vietnam.

The waterfall of **That Salen** is 25 km north of Xepon. The owner of Vieng Xai Guesthouse will be able to get you there and extremely fit visitors have been known to hire bicycles. The other waterfall, **Sakoy**, is about 4 km away by river, or 15 km by main road towards Vietnam. Wide without being high, it's nevertheless a great place for a picnic, and some travellers have even pitched camp here, situated as it is by the small village of Ban Sakoy, surrounded by coconut trees. There is a tourist office in the town office in Xepon, where they can organize a boat trip to a traditional Lao village 2½ hours away. The area surrounding Xepon, particularly Ban Dong 20 km east of the town, intersected the Ho Chi Minh Trail and was devastated during the war. It remains littered with unexploded ordnance and war remnants.

Dong Phu Vieng National Protected Area

The Provincial Tourism Office (see Ins and outs, page 205) runs excellent treks through the Dong Phu Vieng National Protected Area, south of Route 9, which is home to wildlife such as Siamese crocodiles, Asian elephants, the endangered Eld's deer, langurs and wild bison (most of which you would be incredibly lucky to see). Located within the NPA is a **Song Sa Kae** (Sacred Forest and Cemetery), revered by the local Katang ethnic group, who are known for their buffalo sacrifices. The well-trained local guides show how traditional natural produce is gathered for medicinal, fuel or other purposes. The tours are exceptionally good value. Most will only run during the dry season.

Ho Chi Minh Trail

This is an enticing prospect for some visitors but getting here is not easy from Savannakhet and should only be attempted in the dry season, November to March being the ideal time. It is necessary to hire a Soviet jeep or 4WD in order to cross the rivers because many of the bridges are broken so your best bet is to organize a tour from Savan (see Activities and tours, page 212), although you could also travel with a guide on public buses, staying overnight in Xepon (see Sleeping, page 212), the nearest town to the Trail. A guide will charge US$20-30 per day, including meals and accommodation, if required. The easiest access point to the trail is **Ban Tapung**.

> ‡ Under no circumstances should you go anywhere near the Ho Chi Minh Trail without an experienced guide, as unexploded bombs abound.

● Sleeping

Savannakhet *p205, map p206*
Savannakhet has a good selection of places to stay for US$5 and upwards but real budget accommodation is scarce.
B Hoong Thip, Phetsalath Rd, T041-212262, F041-213230. A/c, satellite TV, dark rooms, big bathrooms en suite, breakfast included. Other services include sauna, and car hire with driver (US$25).
B-C Nanhai, Santisouk Rd, T041-212371, F041-212380. This 7-floor hotel is now considered one of the better places in town since the Auberge de Paris shut up shop. The 42 rooms, karaoke bars and dining hall are a prime example of a mainland Chinese hotel. Mainly used by Chinese businessmen, there is little atmosphere for the tourist. Rooms have a/c, TV, fridge, IDD telephones and en suite bathrooms but they smell musty and the single rooms are minuscule. The pool has no water. The hotel boasts the only lift in town. For enquiries, write to 313 RM Lasavong Rd. Decent restaurant.
B-C Phonepasut, Santisouk Rd, 1 km from town centre in quiet street, T041-212158. Motel-like place with 2 courtyards, restaurant and pool (US$1 for visitors). Rooms are clean, with hot water in the bathrooms, a/c and satellite TV. Friendly and well run with support services like fax and IDD telephones.
D Nongsoda, Tha He Rd, T041-212522. Oodles of white lace draped all over the house. Clean rooms with a/c and en suite bathrooms with wonderfully hot water. During the low season the hotel drops its room rate. Motorbike hire.

D-E Mekong, Tha He Rd, T041-212249. This place is housed in an attractive colonial villa on the Mekong, the rooms are large and generally clean, with good en suite bathrooms and some a/c. Mattresses vary hugely, so some spot-testing is a good idea. The hotel quite obviously operates as some kind of brothel and the Vietnamese management are diffident to the point of rudeness: if you can ignore these factors, then it's great.
D-F Savanbanhao, Senna Rd, T041-212202, sbtour@laotel.com. Centrally located hotel composed of 4 colonial-styles houses set around a quiet concrete courtyard, with a range of rooms. Most expensive have en suite showers and hot water. Beware the lethal Soviet water boiler. Some a/c. Large balcony. **Savanbanhao Tourism Co** is attached (see Activities and tours). Good for those who want to be in and out of Savannakhet, quickly, with relative ease.
E-F Savanpatthana Guesthouse, Senna Rd, next door to **Savanbanhao**, T041-213955. Ugly, grey building, bare and gloomy but with clean rooms. En suite bathrooms with squat toilet and rusty shower, no hot water. More expensive rooms upstairs are good value with a/c, although the 'VIP' rooms in the separate block are nothing to write home about, with tatty furniture and grubby albeit huge bathrooms. The predominantly male staff are helpful, when they are not too busy watching Thai boxing on TV.
E-F Xayamoungkhun (English sign just reads 'Guest House'), 85 Ratsavongseuk Rd, T041-212426. An excellent little hotel with

16 rooms in an airy colonial-era villa. Centrally positioned with a largish compound. Range of very clean rooms available, more expensive have hot water, a/c and fridge. Very friendly owners. Second-hand books and magazines are available. Recommended.
F Saisouk, Makhavenha Rd, T041-212207. A real gem. This breezy new guesthouse has good-sized twin and double rooms, immaculately furnished and spotlessly clean, some a/c, communal bathrooms. Beautifully decorated with interesting *objets d'art* and what look like dinosaur bones. Plenty of chairs and tables on the large verandas. Very friendly staff, reasonable English. Laundry service. Very friendly and homely.

Xepon *p210*
F Nangtoon Guesthouse, Route 9, 2 km from Xepon. Rooms with either fan or a/c and hot water in the bathrooms. Outstanding value. Recommended.
F Vieng Xai Guesthouse, T041-214895. A big house, wooden upstairs and concrete down, very clean, with shared bathroom. Friendly owners speak a little English.

🍴 Eating

Savannakhet *p205, map p206*
Several restaurants on the riverside serve good food and beer. The market also has stalls offering good, fresh food, including excellent Mekong River fish.
♥♥-♥ Nety's Food Garden, east of the immigration office. A mini hawker centre. Awnings shield diners from the sun and a handful of stalls serve good and cheap single-dish Lao, Vietnamese and Thai food.
♥ Lao-Paris, Simung St. A crumbling building with 4 tables on the grey veranda and a dingy interior. Tasty *falang* fare and Lao/Vietnamese dishes, opens at 0800 and serves a good breakfast. Cheap but definitely not haute cuisine.
♥ Moonlight Restaurant, Ratsavongseuk Rd T030-5315718. Cosy café serving a range of quite good Western dishes. Very popular with travellers and locals.
♥ Sakura, near the church (signs read Khampa Café), T041-212882. This is a bit

of a shock find – in a good way. A very atmospheric lantern-lit garden, with a country and western meets Oriental *sukiyaki* feel. Good sukiyaki fondue and basic Asian fare, like fried rice, but it's the atmosphere that makes it special. Recommended.

Xepon *p210*
On the west side of the market there is a reasonable restaurant called **Bouphan**, which does good eggs, *feu* and coffee.

🍸 Bars and clubs

Savannakhet *p205, map p206*
There are several large discos/beer gardens in town, most of which have live bands and are open 7 days a week. The reasonably surreal **Rose Bar** is popular, although it's not much of a bar, more a club-cum-beer garden, with lots of lights.

✹ Festivals and events

Savannakhet *p205, map p206*
Feb Than Ing Hang (movable) similar to the festival at Wat Phou, Champasak (see page 229).

🛍 Shopping

Savannakhet *p205, map p206*
Talaat Savan Sai Open 0700-1700 daily. The central market has moved from its former town location to a new site behind the government bus station, north of town. The brand spanking new building, built and managed by a Singaporean company, comes complete with parking spaces and one of the few escalators in Laos (although it doesn't work!). There is the usual selection of meat, vegetables, fruit, dry goods, fabrics and baskets, plus an abundance of gold and silversmiths.

There is a branch of **Lao Cotton** on Ratsavong Seuk Rd.

⛰ Activities and tours

Savannakhet *p205, map p206*
Savannakhet Provincial Tourism Authority, T041-214203. The tourism

🔴 *For an explanation of the eating and sleeping price codes used in this guide, see inside the*
🔴 *front cover. Other relevant information is found in Essentials, see pages 29-32.*

Border essentials: Savannakhet-Mukdahan (Thailand)

It is now possible to cross the border into Mukdahan via the new Friendship Bridge or by one of the more infrequent ferries. Lao visas (30 days) are available at the border.

authority runs excellent ecotours and treks to the national parks in the area. There are 14 keen English-speaking guides to take tourists out to see the local ethnic culture and sights. Highly worthwhile 1- to 3-day treks have been established, with proceeds filtering down to local communities to help ease poverty and encourage sustainable and culturally sensitive tourism practices. (It is rumoured that ethnic villagers are even given money for each wild animal that the tourists see, to ensure that rare and protected species aren't hunted into extinction.) Recommended.
Savanbanhao Tourism Co, at the Savanbanhao Hotel (see Sleeping), Mon-Sat 0800-1200, 1330-1630. Tours and trips to most sights in the area and sells bus tickets to Vietnam.

⊙ Transport

Savannakhet p205, map p206
Boat
Sadly boats no longer run to Vientiane, since the road has been improved. The only river services now are boats across the Mekong to **Mukdahan** (Thailand) See box, above.

Bus/truck
From the bus station on the northern edge of town, frequent northbound buses depart daily to **Vientiane**, 457 km on a good road, 8-9 hrs, 55,000 kip. Most of the Vientiane-bound buses also stop at **Thakhek**, 125 km, 2½-3 hrs, 25,000 kip; **Paksan**, 5-6 hrs, 55,000 kip, and **Pak Kading** 7-8 hrs, 55,000 kip. There are also specially scheduled morning buses to **Thakhek**.

Southbound buses to **Pakse** depart 6 times daily, 6-7 hrs, 30,000 kip; buses in transit from Vientiane to Pakse will also usually pick up passengers here. To **Don Khone**, 0700 daily, 9-10 hrs, 50,000 kip; to **Salavan**, 1200 and 1700 daily, 8-10 hrs, 45,000 kip; to **Attapeu**, 0900 daily, 9-12 hrs,

65,000 kip. This road is also in good condition.
Eastbound buses depart daily to **Xepon** and **Lao Bao** (Vietnam border, see page 210), 0630, 0930 and 1200 daily, 5-6 hrs, 30,000 kip. A bus also departs at 2200 daily for destinations within Vietnam, including **Hué**, 13 hrs, 110,000 kip; **Danang**, 508 km, 15 hrs, 110,000 kip, and **Hanoi**, 22 hrs, 200,000 kip; there are additional services at 0700 and 1800 Sat and 0700 Sun. Luxury Vietnam-bound buses can also be arranged through the **Savanbanhao Hotel** (see Sleeping), T041-212202, US$12. Although all of these buses claim to be direct, a bus change is required at the border.

Car, motorbike and bicycle hire
Car and driver can be hired from the **Savanbanhao Hotel** (see Sleeping). They also rent motorbikes, US$10 per day. **Lao-Paris Restaurant** (see Eating) rents bicycles for US$1 and motorbikes for US$10 per day.

Tuk-tuk
Most tuk-tuks charge around 10,000 kip per person for a local journey.

Xepon p210
Songthaew depart from the market to **Savannakhet** at 0800 daily, 30,000 kip. There are numerous *songthaew* from the market to **Lao Bao**, 45 km, 1 hr, 20,000 kip but you'll need to get there by 0700 to ensure a space. It's also possible to jump on the various buses from Savannakhet to Vietnam, which pass through Xepon, the cheapest option being the service to Lao Bao (see above).

⊙ Directory

Savannakhet p205, map p206
Banks Lao Development Bank, T041-212272, Oudomsinh Rd, open 0800-1200 and 1300-1530 Mon-Fri, will change most major currencies. Banque pour le Commerce Exterieur Lao (BCEL),

Chalmeaung Rd, T041-212226, will exchange currency as well. There are exchange counters around the market, any currency accepted, and at the pier (bad rate). The goldsmiths in the market regularly change money; all currencies bought and sold.

Customs and immigration Lao customs and immigration, Tha He Rd, at the passenger pier, for exit to Thailand and Lao visas, daily 0830-1200 and 1300-1600, overtime fees payable Sat and Sun.

Embassies and consulates Vietnam Consulate, Sisavangvong Rd, T041-212737, Mon-Fri 0730-1100, 1400-1630. Provides Vietnamese visas in 3 days on presentation of 2 photos and US$45. **Thai Consulate**, Kouvoravong Rd, open 0830-1200 for applications, 1400-1500, for visa collection, visas are issued on the same day if dropped off in the morning. **Internet** Phitsamay, Chalmeung Rd, is quite a decent internet café and shop in a convenient location. SPS Furniture Shop, Khantabuli Rd, 100 kip per min. **Medical services** Savannakhet Hospital, Khanthabouli Rd, T041-212051. Dr Kongsy, T041-212711. **Police** A block back from the river, near the Tourist Office, T041-212069. **Post** Post office Khanthabouli Rd, T041-212205, daily 0800-2200. **Telephone** Lao Telecom Office, next door to the post office, for domestic and international calls. There are also plenty of IDD call boxes scattered around town (including 1 next to the immigration office at the river).

� Footprint features

Introduction

Laos' southern provinces offer a varied array of enticements and a different character from the north of the country. Base yourself in the region's unofficial capital, Pakse, to explore the many attractions of Champasak Province, including the romantic, pre-Angkorian ruins of Wat Phou and Ban Kiet Ngong, with its elephants. Inland from Pakse is the Boloven Plateau, an area that was earmarked by the French for settlement and coffee production. The rivers running off the plateau have created a series of spectacular falls, including towering Tad Fan and stunning Tad Lo.

A highlight of any trip down south is Siphandon, where the Mekong divides into a myriad channels and 'Four Thousand Islands'. The idyllic, palm-fringed Don Khone, Don Deth and Don Khong provide perfect places to relax and absorb riverine life, as fisherman cast nets amongst lush green islets and children frolic on the sand bars.

★ Don't miss ...

1 **Don Daeng Island** Get a glimpse of truly bucolic Lao riverine life, page 223.
2 **Wat Phou** Take a day to discover Laos' own mini Angkor, page 223.
3 **Ban Kiet Ngong** Organize an elephant trek through the Xe Pian National Protected Area to spot the birdlife, page 226.
4 **Tad Lo** Base yourself at this Tahoy town in order to explore the Boloven Plateau; take a picnic at the enchanting Tad Yeung falls, pages 234 and 235.
5 **Don Khong** Hire a bicycle and cycle around the island for a glimpse of traditional riverside life in Laos, page 250.
6 **Khong Phapheng Falls** Listen to the 'voice of the Mekong' as it roars over these cascades, page 258.

Southern Laos

Pakse (Pakxe) and around

→ *Phone code: 031. Colour map 3, B2.*

Pakse is the largest town in the south and is strategically located at the junction of the Mekong and Xe Don rivers. Two bridges span the Xe Don here. The single-lane bridge downstream was built by the French in 1925, while the upstream structure was erected by the Soviet Union and was not completed until about 1990. Pakse is a busy commercial town, built by the French early in the 20th century as an administrative centre for the south. The town has seen better days but the tatty colonial buildings lend an air of old-world charm. Pakse is a major staging post for destinations further afield, such as the old royal capital of Champasak, famed for its pre-Angkor, seventh-century Khmer ruins of Wat Phou (see page 223). The town's old colonial ebb is quickly succumbing to Thai and Vietnamese influence. Regardless, it is still quite a charming spot. Champasak Province used to include Champasak, Sedon and Sitandon provinces. The governor's office was located in Ban Muang in Sedon prior to French settlement in the area. Pakse's appointment as a French administrative outpost in 1905 spurred the relocation of all major government offices and businesses across the three provinces to Pakse and an amalgamation of provincial authorities. Close to Pakse are ecotourism projects where elephant treks, birdwatching and homestays are possible. ►► *For Sleeping, Eating and other listings, see pages 227-232.*

Pakse

Sleeping	Lao Chaleun 4	Sang Aroun 9	Delta Coffee 1
Champasak Palace 1	Pakse 5		Dorn Sok Dee 2
Champa	Sabaidy 2	**Eating**	Jasmine 3
Residence 2	Guesthouse 7	Back Street Café 1	Ket Many 4
Lankham 3	Salachampa 8	Bakery 8	Korean Barbecue 5

Getting there Pakse is Southern Laos' transport hub: from here you can get to anywhere in the southern region, and travel between local centres often requires a connection through Pakse. Although it is not on the **border** with Thailand, Pakse is the largest Lao town close to the border crossing at Chongmek. From the Thai side, *songthaew* continue on to Ubon Ratchathani in Thailand. ▶▶ *For further details, see Border essentials, page 220.*

The **airport** is 2 km northwest of town; cross the bridge over the Xe Don next to Wat Luang and continue straight up No 13 Road; tuk-tuks will make the journey for around 20,000 kip. There is a small café and BCEL exchange in the terminal building. International flights from Bangkok and Siem Reap, as well as domestic flights to/from Vientiane, run several times a week.

A public passenger **boat** from Champasak to Pakse, 60,000 kip, leaves at 1500 and arrives in Pakse at 1700. But, do check on all times. Boats leave from Pakse to Champasak at 0830 and arrive at 1030.

There are three official bus terminals in Pakse: the **Northern terminal** (Km 7 on Route 13 north, T031-251508) is for buses to and from the north (a tuk-tuk from town costs 20,000 kip); the **Southern terminal** (Km 8 south on Route 13, T031-212981) is for buses to and from the south (a tuk-tuk from town costs 20,000 kip); and the **VIP bus terminal** (near the football stadium and Talaat Lak Song, T031-212228, just off Route 13) for VIP buses to **Ubon** (Thailand) and Vientiane. ▶▶ *For further details, see Transport, page 231.*

Getting around Tuk-tuks and **saamlors** are the main means of local transport and can be chartered for half a day for about US$5. The main tuk-tuk 'terminal' is at the Daoheung market. **Cars, motorbikes** and **bicycles** are available for hire from some hotels and tour companies. Note that the town's roads are numbered as if they were highways: No 1 Road through to No 46 Road. The result is that no-one knows where they live and tuk-tuk drivers are oblivious to road names. Even some hotel managers have no idea of the road outside their establishment.

Tourist information Champasak Provincial Tourism Office ① *No 11 Rd*, T031-212021, erratic hours but try Mon-Fri 0800-1200 and 1400-1600, have some fantastic ecotours on offer (some are offered in conjunction with local travel agents, such as **Green Discovery**, see Activities and tours, page 230). Mr Phouvanh, head of the information office, is very nice and knowledgeable.

Mengky Noodle Shop **7**
Nazim's **6**
Xuan Mai **12**

Sights 🏨🚺🅾️🔺🚌🅲

▶▶ *pp227-232.*

Pakse, by anyone's standards, is not a seething metropolis, which, of course, gives it much of its charm. But this is

Southern Laos Pakse & around

⁞ Border essentials: Vang Tao-Chongmek (Thailand)

This route is an important exit point for Lao traders; timber trucks rumble their way towards the sizeable timber yard at Chongmek (Thailand).

Lao visas (30 days) are also available at the border. There is a new bus service direct from Ubon Ratchathani bus station to Pakse. From Pakse the Thai-Lao international bus leaves from the VIP bus terminal 0700, 0830, 1430 and 1530, two-three hours, ฿200.

Travelling to Thailand, *songthaew* for the border at Vang Tao (Laos) depart from the Daoheung market in Pakse, daily 0800-1600 every hour, 45 km, one hour, US$1. The border is open daily 0500-2000 but allow yourself additional time to get there as the *songthaew* can be painfully slow. A faster alternative is one of the older taxis, 45 minutes, ฿300.

Once you've been dropped off at Vang Tao, walk 250 m to the building where you will receive an exit stamp; you may need to pay 'overtime fees' if you cross the border at the weekend. Walk another 50 m or so to the Thai border, where you will automatically be issued with a 30-day visa.

There is a post office and duty free shop at the border. Customs formalities are very relaxed.

From the Thai side, *songthaew* run to Phibun Mangsahan, one hour, ฿30, where you can pick up another *songthaew* (฿30) or a taxi-minibus (฿600 divided between all the passengers) to the city and airport of Ubon Ratchathani. Both airlines (Air Asia and Thai) and buses operate from Ubon Ratchathani direct to Bangkok (see page 26).

starting to change now that infrastructure has improved and Pakse is firmly linked into the Thai economy; it has become a major cross-roads between the two countries. A strong Vietnamese influence is also apparent.

There's not that much to see in Pakse, so far as official sights are concerned. Locals tend to mention the shopping centre-style market slap-bang in the centre of town and the Daoheung (morning) market as the most interesting places to visit; in fact, it may seem Pakse exists for little else (see page 229). However, although it does not offer an overwhelming amount of tourist attractions, it's a good place to base yourself to visit destinations further afield, including Tad Lo, Tad Fan and Wat Phou.

Champasak Museum

ⓘ *No 13 Rd (the main highway) running east out of town, close to the stadium. Daily 0800-1130 and 1300-1600 except public holidays. Admission 5000 kip.*

This museum opened in 1995 and displays pieces recovered from Wat Phou, handicrafts from the Lao Theung of the Boloven Plateau, weaponry, musical instruments and a seemingly endless array of photographs of plenums, congresses and assemblies and of prominent Lao dignitaries opening hydropower stations and widget factories. Visitors are shown around by charming Lao guides who speak only limited English, nor are the labels very informative. But it's still a treat for museum aficionados. Opposite the museum is a *that*-like **Heroes Monument**.

Wat Luang

There are 40 wats in town but none figures particularly high in the wat hall of fame. Wat Luang, in the centre of town, is the oldest. It was built in 1830, but was

⬤ *According to ML Manich in his* History of Laos, *the French decided to make Pakse the local administrative capital because they wanted to rule the country without interference from the royal house of Champasak.*

reconstructed and redecorated in 1990 at a cost of 27 million kip. The *sim* now sports
a kitsch pink and yellow exterior complete with gaudy relief work. Lots of monks can
be found loitering around the premises, as this is one of the main centres where they
practise English. The hefty doors were carved locally. The compound was originally
much larger but, in the 1940s, the chief of Champasak Province requisitioned the land
to accommodate a new road. To the right of the main entrance stands a stupa
containing the remains of Khatai Loun Sasothith, a former Prime Minister who died in
1959. To the right of the *sim* is the monks' dormitory, which dates from the 1930s; the
wooden building behind the *sim* is the monastic school, the biggest in southern Laos,
and on the left of the entrance is the library, built in 1943. These earlier structures are,
needless to say, the finest – at least for Western sensibilities. The compound backs
onto the Xe Don.

There are many more Lao monasteries in town. For those who desire a change
there is also a Vietnamese/Chinese Mahayana Buddhist **Linh Bao Tu Pagoda** on No
46 Road, and a church on No 1 Road.

Boun Oum Palace
Situated on the road north towards Paksong, the Boun Oum Palace is now the
Champasak Palace Hotel and by far the largest structure in town. Before Thai hotel
interests bought the place, it was the half-finished palace of the late Prince Boun Oum
of Champasak, the colourful overlord of southern Laos and a great collector of *objets
d'art*. He began constructing the house of his dreams in 1968, with the intention of
creating a monument with more than 1000 rooms. However, the Prince was exiled to
France before his dream was realized. Looking at the hotel it is hard not to conclude
that his exile was wholly for the best, at least architecturally.

Muang Khao
Muang Khao lies on the opposite bank of the Mekong to Pakse and, as the name
suggests (it means 'Old Town'), was established before its larger sibling across the
water. Once the French concentrated their attentions on Pakse, Muang Khao was
neglected and, consequently, has a quaintness largely absent from Pakse. Most
people come here en route to the Lao-Thai border at Chongmek but it does have some
attractive buildings. A tuk-tuk to Muang Khao would cost around US$1.

Ban Saphay
ⓘ *5 km off Route 13, 15 km northwest of Pakse. Public tuk-tuks (US$5) travel from the
'terminal' near Daoheung market, especially in the morning.* This specialist
silk-weaving village is 15 km north of town on the banks of the Mekong. Here about
200 women weave traditional Lao textiles on hand looms. The designs, like the
classic *lao mut mee*, show clear similarities with those of northeastern Thailand,
where the population is also Lao. However, there are also some unique designs.
Prices vary according to quality and intricacy but a sarong length (1.5 m) costs about
50,000-70,000 kip. There is also an unusual statue of Indra, Ganesh and Parvati at
the local wat.

Champasak and around 🚐🍴🚐 ▸▸ *pp227-232.*

The agricultural town of Champasak, which stretches along the right bank of the
Mekong for 4 km, is the nearest town to Wat Phou and, with enough comfortable
accommodation, is a good base from which to explore the site and the surrounding
area. It is about 40 km south of Pakse. The sleepy town is quaint and charming and a
fantastic place to spend the night in, though the trip can be done in a day from Pakse.

Getting there Most *songthaew* run from Pakse's Southern bus terminal on Route 13 to Ban Lak Sarm Sip (which translates as 'village 30 km'), where they take a right turn to Ban Muang (2-3 km). Here, people sell tickets for the ferry to Champasak (5000 kip; person and motorbike 8000 kip). The ferry runs from 0600 until 2000. At the time of publication public ferries were not running from Pakse to Champasak, though if you have enough cash and patience to scout around we have heard it is possible to charter a boat there (at quite a cost). ▶ *See also Transport, page 232.*

Tourist information Champasak District Visitor Information Centre ① *T020-2206215, Mon-Fri 0800-1600*, can arrange boats to Don Daeng, guides to Wat Phou and tours to surrounding sites. Guides charge US$10 per day or US$5 for half a day.

Sights

Champasak itself is dotted with simply stunning colonial buildings. The former residence of Champasak hereditary Prince Boun Oun and former leader of the right-wing opposition, who fled the country in 1975 after the Communist takeover, is quite possibly the most magnificent colonial building in Laos. His daughter-in-law now resides there and although it is not open to tourists it is certainly worth a look from the outside.

Champasak is known for its wood handicrafts and you'll find vases and other carved ornaments for sale near the jetty. About 15 km southwest of Champasak is **Don Talaat**, which is worth a visit for its weekly market (Saturday and Sunday). It's renowned for the number of snakes on show.

Um Muang (Tomo Temple)

① *Daily 0600-1630, admission 10,000 kip (but it is unclear who you are supposed to give this to); some of the local children may act as guides (7000 kip). It is possible to hire a car or tuk-tuk from Pakse. If you go by bus, you need to get off at Ban Huaytomo. There are no more boats from Pakse unless you charter one (which is expensive).*

Also known as Muang Tomo and Oup Moung, Um Muang is a lesser-known temple complex built at about the same time as Wat Phou on the opposite (left) bank of the Mekong. It lies 45 km south of Pakse off Route 13 and is accessible via the main road south from Pakse to Ban Thang Beng, Km 30, from where a track (vehicle access possible) leads 4 km to Ban Noi. From the village it is a 1-km walk to the temple. You can charter a boat from Don Daeng or Ban Muang, Champasak (30,000-100,000 kip, depending on which end of the island you are travelling from).

In colonial days, Um Muang was a stopping point for ships travelling upriver from Cambodia. Its main

Champasak

To ① & Ban Phapin (2 km)

Paddy Fields

Paddy Fields

Government Building

Unfinished Palace

UNESCO

Wat Thong

Ex-Royal Residences

Paddy Fields

To ⑦ , Wat Phou (8 km) & Don Talaat (15 km)

Lao Development

Boats

Mekong

100 metres
100 yards

Sleeping
Anouxa Guesthouse & Restaurant 1

Khamphouy Guesthouse 3
New Dokchampa 4
Saythong Guesthouse & Restaurant 5
Souchitra Guesthouse 6
Vong Pasued Guesthouse & Restaurant 7

treasure is a ninth-century Khmer-era temple complex built at roughly the same time as Wat Phou. The temple is thought to have been built by Yasarvoman I and is dedicated to Shiva's companion, Rudani. The site is an assortment of ruins, surrounded by jungle. A seven-headed sandstone *naga* greets you on arrival from the Mekong.

Like Wat Phou, the main temple is built of laterite and its carvings are in similar style to those of the bigger complex upriver. It is thought, in fact, that the laterite blocks used in the construction of Wat Phou were taken from Um Muang. There are also the ruins of a second building, more dilapidated and moss-covered, making it difficult to speculate about its function, and, hidden in the jungle, are the remains of two *baray*. Um Muang is not on the same scale and nowhere near as impressive as Wat Phou but stumbling across a sixth-century Khmer temple in the middle of the jungle is nonetheless a worthwhile experience. Despite the presence of seemingly abandoned tourist facilities, it's still an atmospheric spot. With great slabs of laterite protruding from the undergrowth and ancient sandstone carvings lying around the bushes, there is no doubt that a great deal about the site remains undiscovered.

Some of the best artefacts from the temple can be found in the museum in Pakse (see page 220).

Don Daeng Island

This idyllic river island sits right across from Champasak. It stretches for 8 km and is the perfect place for those wishing to see quintessential village life, with basket weaving, fishing and rice farming, and without the cars and hustle and bustle. There is a path around the island that can be traversed on foot or by bicycle. A crumbling ancient brick stupa, built in the same century as Wat Phu, is in the centre of the island and there are a few ancient remnants in **Sisak village** from the construction. The inhabitants of **Pouylao village** are known for their knife-making prowess. There is a lovely sandy beach on the Champasak side of the island, perfect for a dip. The way to get here is on an arranged ecotour which can include treks and explorations of local villages. The island has only recently opened up for tourism purposes, so it is important to tread lightly. Contact the Provincial Tourism Office in Pakse or the Tourism Office in Champasak for further information. A trip by boat from Champasak will cost around US$1.

Around Champasak

Hao Pa Kho island

One hour downriver from Pakse is this island, where Chao Boun Oum had his weekend house. It has lain abandoned since his exile to France.

Wat Phou ✪ ►► pp227-232.

Wat Phou lies at the foot of the Phou Pasak, 8 km southwest of Champasak and is the most significant Khmer archaeological site in Laos. With its teetering, weathered masonry, it conforms exactly to the Western ideal of the lost city. The mountain behind Wat Phou is called **Linga Parvata**, as the Hindu Khmers thought it resembled a lingam – albeit a strangely proportioned one. Although construction of the original Hindu temple complex was begun in the fifth and sixth centures, much of what remains today is believed to have been built in the 10th to 11th centuries. Wat Phou was a work in progress and was constructed and renovated over a period spanning several hundred years.

Ins and outs

Getting there The nearest town to Wat Phou is Champasak (see page 221), which also lies on the west (or right) bank of the Mekong River; the main road is on the east bank. Most *songthaew* run from Pakse's Southern bus terminal on Route 13 to **Ban Lak Sarm Sip** (which translates as 'village 30 km'), where they take a right turn to **Ban Muang** (2-3 km). Here, people sell tickets for the ferry to Champasak (or Ban Phaphin on the outskirts of Champasak (5000 kip; person and motorbike 8000 kip). From Champasak you can get a tuk-tuk to Wat Phou for around US$10 return. Most tourists prefer to cycle the 10 km from Champasak to the ruins. Bikes are available for hire (US$2) at the guesthouses in Champasak town. ▸▸ *For further details, see Transport, page 232.*

Tourist information The site is officially open daily 0800-1630 but the staff are happy to let you in if you get there for sunrise, even as early as 0530, and you won't get thrown out until 1800. Admission US$3 or around 30,000 kip goes towards restoration. There are foodstalls at the gate. There is also the Wat Phu Exhibition Centre at the entrance, a surprisingly good museum with a fantastic array of artefacts such as the garuda, nandi bull and explanations from Wat Phou. Entrance fee is included in admission to the temple. The centre closes at 1600.

Background

Linga Parvata provides an imposing backdrop to the crumbling temple ruins, many of which date from the fifth and sixth centuries, making them at least 200 years older than Angkor Wat. At that time, the Champasak area was the centre of power on the lower Mekong. The Hindu temple only became a Buddhist shrine in later centuries. The French explorer, Francis Garnier, discovered Wat Phou in 1866 and local villagers told him the temple had been built by 'another race'. Unfortunately, not much is known about Wat Phou's history. Ruins of a palace have been found next to the Mekong at Cesthapoura (halfway between Wat Phou and Champasak – now an army camp) and it is thought the sixth-century Chenla capital was based there.

Archaeologists and historians believe most of the building at Wat Phou was the work of the Khmer king, Suryavarman II (1131-1150), who was also responsible for starting work on Angkor Wat, Cambodia. The temple remained important for Khmer kings even after they had moved their capital to Angkor. They continued to appoint priests to serve at Wat Phou and sent money to maintain the temple until the last days of the Angkor Empire.

Exploring the site

1959 Palace and processional causeway The king and dignitaries would originally have sat on the platform above the 'tanks' or *baray* and presided over official ceremonies or watched aquatic games. In 1959 a palace was built on the platform so the king had somewhere to stay during the annual **Wat Phou Festival** (see page 229). The smaller house was for the king's entourage. A long avenue leads from the platform to the pavilions. The **processional causeway** was probably built by Khmer King Jayavarman VI (1080-1107), and may have been the inspiration for a similar causeway at Angkor Wat. The grand approach would originally have been flanked by statues of lions and mythical animals, but few traces remain.

● Local legend has it that the Emerald Buddha – now in Bangkok – is a fake and the
● authentic one is hidden in Wat Phou; archaeologists, however, are highly sceptical.

Pavilions The sandstone pavilions, on either side of the processional causeway, were added after the main temple and are thought to date from the 12th century (most likely from the reign of Suryavarman II). Although crumbling, with great slabs of laterite and collapsed lintels lying aesthetically around, both pavilions are remarkably intact and, as such, are the most photographed part of the temple complex. The pavilions were probably used for segregated worship by pilgrims, one for women (left) and the other for men (right). The porticoes of the two huge buildings face each other. The roofs were thought originally to have been poorly constructed with thin stone slabs on a wooden beam-frame and later replaced by Khmer tiles.

Only the outer walls now remain but there is enough still standing to fire the imagination: the detailed carving around the window frames and porticoes is well-preserved. The laterite used to build the complex was brought from **Um Muang**, also called Tomo Temple, another smaller Khmer temple complex a few kilometres downriver (see page 222), but the carving is in sandstone. The interiors were without permanent partitions, although it is thought that rush matting was used instead, and furniture was limited – reliefs only depict low stools and couches. At the rear of the women's pavilion are the remains of a brick construction, believed to have been the queen's quarters. Brick buildings were very costly at that time.

Nandi Pavilion and temple remains Above the pavilions is a small temple, the Nandi Pavilion, with entrances on two sides. It is dedicated to Nandi, the bull (Siva's vehicle), and is a common feature in Hindu temple complexes. There are three chambers, each of which would originally have contained statues – these have been stolen. As the hill begins to rise above the Nandi temple, the remains of six brick temples follow the contours, with three on each side of the pathway. All six are completely ruined and their function is unclear. Archaeologists and Khmer historians speculate that they may have been Trimurti temples. At the bottom of the steps is a portico and statue of the founder of Wat Phou, Pranga Khommatha. Many of the laterite paving stones and blocks used to build the steps have holes notched down each

Wat Phou

Holy Spring

Crocodile & Naga

Trimurti

Elephant Rock

Library

Main Sanctuary

Retaining walls

Portico

Statue of the founder of Wat Phou

N

Not to scale

Portico

Platform

Nandi Pavilion

Galleries

Portico

Women's Pavilion

Men's Pavilion

Baray

Baray

Processional Causeway - originally flanked with statues of lions & mythical animals

Platform

'1959 Palace'

Baray

Southern Laos Pakse & around

side; these would have been used to help transport the slabs to the site and drag them into position.

Main sanctuary The main sanctuary, 90 m up the hillside and orientated east-west, was originally dedicated to Siva. The rear section (behind the Buddha statue) is part of the original sixth-century brick building. Sacred spring water was channelled through the hole in the back wall of this section and used to wash the sacred linga. The water was then thrown out, down a shute in the right wall, where it was collected in a receptacle. Pilgrims would then wash in the holy water. The front of the temple was constructed later, probably in the eighth to ninth century, and has some fantastic carvings: apsaras, dancing Vishnu, Indra on a three-headed elephant (the former emblem of the kingdom of Lane Xang) and, above the portico of the left entrance, a carving of Siva, the destroyer, tearing a woman in two.

The Hindu temple was converted into a Buddhist shrine, either in the 13th century during the reign of the Khmer king Jayavarman VII or when the Lao conquered the area in the 14th century. A large Buddha statue now presides over its interior. There is also a modern Buddhist monastery complex on the site.

Around the sanctuary To the left of the sanctuary is what is thought to be the remains of a small library. To the right and to the rear of the main sanctuary is the **Trimurti**, the Hindu statues of Vishnu (right), Siva (central) and Brahma (left). Behind the Trimurti is the holy spring, believed by the Khmers to have possessed purificatory powers. Some of the rocks beyond the monks' quarters (to the right of the temple) have been carved with the figures of an elephant, a crocodile and a *naga*. They are likely to have been associated with human sacrifices carried out at the Wat Phou Festival; it is said the sacrifice took place on the crocodile and the blood was given to the *naga*. Present-day visitors to the festival in February (see page 229) should note that this practice has now stopped!

Around Wat Phou

For archeological enthusiasts who haven't had their fix from Wat Phou, there are several other ancient sites in close proximity, most in a state of disrepair. **Ho Nang Sida**, 1 km south of Wat Phou, is an understated ruined temple, overgrown with jungle and piles of rubble and rocks. The temple, called Lady Sida Hall, is believed to have sat on an ancient highway that linked Angkor Wat to Wat Phou; it was probably used as a hospital. One kilometre south of Ho Nang Sida is **Hong Nan Tao**, another set of ancient ruins, built under King Jayavarman VII and used as a shrine. Another 3 km along are three ancient stupas.

Xe Pian National Protected Area ⬤📄▲ ›› *pp227-232.*

The Xe Pian National Protected Area is rich in bird life and home to large water birds, as well as great hornbills, sun bears, Asiatic black bears and the yellow-cheeked crested gibbon.

North of Xe Pian, the village of **Ban Kiet Ngong** is at the **Kiet Ngong Wetland**, the largest wetland in Southern Laos. Here you'll find a community-based project which offers elephant trekking and homestay accommodation. The villagers have traditionally been dependent on elephants for agricultural work for centuries and their treks can be organized either through the Xe Pian National Protected Area or to the amazing fortress of **Phu Asa**. Located 2 km from Kiet Ngong at the summit of a small jungle-clad hill, this ancient ruined fortress is an enigmatic site that has left archaeologists puzzled. It consists of 20 stone columns, 2 m high, arranged in a semi-circle – they look a bit like a scaled-down version of Stonehenge.

To get to Ban Kiet Ngong from Pakse takes about 1½ hours. From Pakse follow Route 13 until you get to the Km 48 junction with Route 18 at **Thang Beng village** (the Xe Pian National Protected Area office is here). Follow Route 18 east for 7 km, turn right at the signpost for the last 1.5 km to Ban Kiet Ngong.

The provincial authorities are trying to promote ecotourism in this area, so please take this into consideration if you visit. To organize an elephant trek go to the **visitor centre** in Ban Kiet Ngong (T030-5346547), or contact **Kingfisher Eco-lodge** (see page 228). Several other two- to three-day trekking/homestay ecotours are offered in the area; contact the Provincial Tourism Information Office in Pakse. ▸▸ *For further details, see Activities and tours, page 230.*

● Sleeping

Pakse *p218, map p218*
A-B Champasak Palace, No 13 Rd, T031-212263, champasak_ palace_hotel@ yahoo.com. This is a massive chocolate box of a hotel with 55 rooms and lit up like a Christmas tree. It was conceived as a palace for a minor prince. There are some large rooms and 40 more modern, less elaborate rooms. It is quite bizarre to see bellhops in traditional uniforms. Recent renovations have resulted in a loss of original character in favour of modernity but some classic touches remain: wooden shutters, some art deco furniture and lovely tiles. The restaurant is one of the most atmospheric place to eat in town, set on a big veranda overlooking lovely frangipani trees. The friendly staff speak a smattering of English, there's a good terrace and the facilities are the best in town, including a massage centre. It's a great position above the Xe Don and the views from higher levels are stunning.
B-C Champa Residence (Residence du Champa), No 13 Rd, east of town near the stadium and museum, T031-212120, champare@laotel.com. Modern-style rooms, with a/c, minibar, hot water and satellite TV. Very clean and with some character. Attractive terrace and lush garden, visa accepted and tours arranged. Includes breakfast.
B-C Sang Aroun, Route 13, T031-252111. The most modern hotel in town, but lacks character. 58-rooms with cable TV and a/c. More expensive rooms have bathtub. Modern but lacks character.
B-D Pakse Hotel, No 5 Rd (facing the new market), T031-212131, www.hotelpakse.com. This is one of the nicest places to stay in town

with 65 rooms. The French owner, Mr Jérôme, has integrated local handicraft decorations and tasteful furnishings into this slick hotel which has 65 rooms. Breakfast included. Wi-Fi. Good rooftop restaurant with a perfect view over the city and river; the dimly lit eatery oozes ambience.
C-D Salachampa, No 10 Rd, T031-212273. The most characterful place in town. Choose a room in the main 1920s building: huge with wooden floors, large, en suite bath- rooms with warm-water showers; the upstairs rooms with balconies are best. There are also some additional, quaintly rustic rooms in a 'new' extension and a nice garden area between the two. Recommended for those wanting a touch of colonial elegance and friendly service. The rooms are exceptionally good value for money.
D Lao Chaleun Hotel, opposite Salachampa, corner of Roads 6 and 4, T031-251333, F031-251138. This place has 43 simply decorated a/c and fan rooms with TV and minibar. The name of the hotel means 'Modern Lao' but the façade of newness is starting to fade and the place is in need of some maintenance. A bit of an architectural eyebrow raiser: different areas of the hotel are separated by partitions under which you can duck to get to other corridors. The outer rooms have a communal veranda. Motorbike rental and other tour services offered.
E Lankham Hotel, No 13 Rd, T031-213314. Void of character with a slightly haphazard, casual atmosphere downstairs. The rooms themselves are very clean with comfortable beds but are the size of a shoe box.

● For an explanation of the eating and sleeping price codes used in this guide, see inside the
● front cover. Other relevant information is found in Essentials, see pages 29-32.

E-F **Sabaidy 2 Guesthouse**, No 24 Rd,
T031-212992,www.sabaidy2laos.com. A
wide range of rooms on offer, from dorms
through to rooms with private bathroom
and hot water. The rooms are quite basic but
the service is exceptional. The proprietor,
lively Mr Vong, offers tours. Mr Vong's
grandfather, Liam Douang Vongsaa, was the
first governor of Pakse and this building was
the governor's residence, where Mr Vong
was born in 1944. Very popular you may
need to book in advance. Basic food
available. Motorbike rental.

Champasak p221, map p222

C-D **Souchitra Guesthouse**, opposite former
royal residences. A selection of rooms ranging
from cheap cold-water rooms through to
tastefully decorated clean rooms with fan,
fridge and hot water. The ones in the newer
annex are better. Good restaurant downstairs.
D-F **Anouxa Guesthouse**, 1 km north of the
roundabout, T031-213272. A wide range of
accommodation from wooden bungalows
through to concrete rooms with hot water
and either a/c (pay extra) or fan. The
concrete villas are the best, with a serene
river vista from the balconies. Restaurant
is probably one of the best in town, over
looking the river plus a shady cabana. The
only drawback is that it is a little out of town.
Bikes for hire.
D-F **Vong Pasued Guesthouse**, 450 m
south of the roundabout, T020-2712402.
The grimy, dingy shop-front façade is
deceiving, as out the back, beside the river,
are a range of pleasant rooms for all budgets.
Strange resident parrot that squawks 'cow'
incessantly. The owners are very pleasant. A
firm favourite with the backpacker set, this
small family-run guesthouse offers pretty
reasonable rooms. The US$5 rooms by the
river are great value, clean with hot water,
The more basic US$3 rooms (mosquito nets,
thin walls and cold water) in an old longhouse are a bit run down. Good restaurant,
perfect for a natter with fellow travellers.
F **Khamphouy Guesthouse**, on the main
road southwest of the roundabout,
T031-252700. Delightful family-run place.
Fine bright but basic rooms in the main
house with shared facilities and 1 cottage
(in the garden) with 2 rooms and en suite
shower. Clean, comfortable, friendly, relaxed.

Bikes for hire. Good value for those on
a budget.
F **Saythong Guesthouse and Restaurant**,
on the main road southwest of the
roundabout, T020-2209215. Riverside
location. 5 basic rooms upstairs with shared
toilet; 6 more rooms with private showers
(3 with a/c) out the back. The rooms are
reasonable but the restaurant is better:
good food and ample portions.

Don Daeng p223

A **La Folie Lodge**, T030-5347603,
www.lafolie-laos.com. 24 rooms housed
in lovely wooden bungalows, each with its
own balcony. The lodge has a swimming
pool surrounded by landscaped tropical
gardens. Restaurant with good wine and
cocktail selection.
F **Homestays** are offered in a community-
lodge in Ban Hua Don Daeng for US$2. The
wooden lodge has 2 common rooms,
sleeping 5 people and has shared bathrooms
and dining area.

Xe Pian National Protected Area p226

B-C **Kingfisher Eco-lodge**, 700 m east of
Kiet Ngong, T030-5345016, www.kingfisher
ecolodge.com. Bonafide eco-lodge. In the
main lodge, wooden and thatched rooms
with shared bathroom. More expensive are
the glass-fronted bungalows. The restaurant,
set on the 2nd floor of the lodge affords
simply stunning views over the Pha Pho
wetlands.
F **Boun Home Guesthouse**, Ban Kiet Ngong,
T030-5346293. Very basic guesthouse with
wooden rooms and shared facilities.

🍴 Eating

Pakse p218, map p218

The town has numerous international
eateries. Most close at around 2100-2200;
Indian restaurants stay open latest.

There are a couple of fantastic *sindat*
(barbeque) places near the Da Heung market
that are extremely popular with the locals.

If the weather is fine, the **Pakse Hotel** has
a fantastic rooftop restaurant offering a
range of Lao dishes plus pretty good pizza.
Champasak Palace Hotel, see Sleeping.
Reasonable French interpretations in
sublime surroundings.

Ψ-Ψ Korean Barbecue, No 46 Rd (near corner with No 24 Rd), T031-212388. Classic Korean cook-it-yourself restaurant.

Ψ Back Street Café, Rd 46, almost directly behind **Delta Coffee** (look for signpost on main road). Open Tue-Sun 0900-2200. Great little intimate, Western-run restaurant. Brightly coloured walls and friendly atmosphere. Great coffee, hamburgers and fajitas with home-made tortillas, salsa and wraps.

Ψ Delta Coffee, Rd 13, opposite the **Champasak Palace Hotel**, T020-5345895. This place is a real find for those craving some Western comfort food. The extensive menu is tremendously varied and offers everything from pizza and lasagne to Thai noodles. Their coffee is brilliant and staff exceptionally friendly. They have an unusual ordering system in place where you write down orders by number.

Ψ Dorn Sok Dee Restaurant, near the new market. Justifiably popular for its Korean grilled meat dishes.

Ψ Jasmine Restaurant, No 13 Rd, T031-251002. This small place has outdoor seating and is a firm favourite with travellers. Offering the standard Indian fare and a few Malaysian dishes, it's reasonable value. The town's conglomerate of tuk-tuk drivers gather here and very subtly tout for business.

Ψ Ket Many Restaurant, 227 No 13 Rd, T031-212615. Chinese and Lao food from a limited menu in a/c restaurant. Deep-fried frog and Mekong River fish have both been recommended, or why not sample the spicy sour virgin pork uterus? Also serves European food (spaghetti, etc).

Ψ Mengky Noodle Shop, No 13 Rd. Serves bowls of tasty duck and beef noodle soup.

Ψ Nazim's Restaurant, nearly next door to the **Jasmine**, T020-5832792. Serving a very similar selection of Indian/Malaysian dishes, although the service is a little slower.

Ψ Xuan Mai, near Pakse Hotel, T031-213245, Vietnamese restaurant with outdoor kitchen and eating area. Good shakes and fresh spring rolls. Can be a bit hit and miss.

Bakeries

Crusty baguettes are available across town; great for breakfast with wild honey and fresh Boloven coffee.

Champasak *p221, map p222*

Most restaurants are in the guesthouses; all are cheap (Ψ).

Ψ Anouxa Guesthouse, see Sleeping. Has a small but delectable menu and lovely restaurant set over the river; opt for a fish dish. They also have a selection of wines.

Ψ Vong Paseud Guesthouse, see Sleeping. Has a cheap and extensive menu ranging from backpacker favourites like pancakes through to *tom yum* soup.

Xe Pian National Protected Area *p226*

Eating in Ban Kiet Ngong is very basic and you will have to rely on the local food. *Feu* and noodle soup can be made on the spot.

ΨΨ Kingfisher Eco-lodge, see Sleeping. A fantastic restaurant serving a range of Western and Lao dishes. Also stocks wine.

⊛ Festivals

Wat Phou *p223, map p225*

Wat Phou Festival lasts for 3 days around the full moon of the 3rd lunar month (usually Feb). Pilgrims come from far and wide to leave offerings at the temple. In the evening there are competitions – football, boat racing, bullfighting and cockfighting, Thai boxing, singing contests and the like. There is also some pretty extravagant imbibing of alcohol.

Phu Asa (**Ban Khiet Ngong**) Elephant festival usually held in **Mar or Apr**. Lots of elephants gather from all over the province and *mahouts* dressed in traditional costume. Procession to top of Phu Asa.

○ Shopping

Pakse *p218, map p218*

Film

There are a few shops on and around No 7 Rd and No 10 Rd where film can be developed, and a big Kodak shop on No 13 Rd.

Markets

Central market. The closest thing to a shopping centre in town remains half-filled with vendors mostly selling clothes. The initial plans were for it to be a pan-Asian centre, stocking Thai, Japanese, Vietnamese and Lao goods but this is yet to happen.

Daoheung market, opposite Champasak Museum. Even for Southeast Asia this is a major agglomeration of stalls and traders. It is best to get here between 0730 and 0800 when the place is in full swing; although it continues to function throughout the day, it does so in a rather semi-detached fashion. It's good for loads of unnecessary plastic and metal objects. Most people come here just to look but there are some fun things to buy: tin cans, clay pots, textiles and sarongs.

Textiles

Traditional handwoven silk cloth is available in the Daoheung Market (see above). There is a good handicraft shop opposite the small park near Wat Luang, which sells lovely woven baskets, wooden carvings and good-quality embroidery. Many people, however, prefer to visit **Ban Saphay** where the embroidery is actually produced and buy lengths there (see page 221). The *mut mee ikat* designs are similar to those produced across the border in the northeastern or Isan region of Thailand. However, here in Laos it is more likely that the cloth will be produced from home-produced silk (in Thailand, silk yarn is often interwoven with imported thread) and coloured using natural rather than aniline dyes.

▲▲ Activities and tours

Pakse *p218, map p218*
Massage and sauna
Keo Ou Don Physiotherapy, Ban Ta Ou Dome, T031-251895. Although this place is just out of the main town area, it is well worth the short trip. A wide range of massage options are offered, from oil through to foot massage, as well as the Lao favourite: the 'reduced fat massage' (be warned, this is like burning fat off). All treatments and the sauna cost under US$3.

There is also a small sauna and massage centre at the **Champasak Palace Hotel**, and a brilliant new massage place across the road from the **Pakse Hotel**.

Swimming
There is a public pool on the way to the Southern bus station, 5000 kip.

Tour operators
Most of the hotels in town arrange day tours to Wat Phou, Tad Lo and the Khong Phapheng Falls; of these the best is the **Pakse Hotel**. There are also a number of tour agencies in town, all of which will arrange tours to local sites like Wat Phou, Phu Asa, Khong Island and Champasak. They are also the best sources of information, although it is obviously in their interest to convince visitors that taking a tour is the best, possibly even the only, option.

Green Discovery, T031-252908, www.green discoverylaos.com, on the main road, offers a range of adventure tours and ecotourism treks around Champasak province including Ban Kiet Ngong, rafting, kayaking and cycling trips. Highly recommended.

Lane Xang Travel, opposite **Jasmine Restaurant** (also known as **Xplore Asia**), T020-2255176, www.xplore-asia.com. Offers a variety of tours and useful tour services (including a minivan service to Siphandon).

Sabaidy 2, see Sleeping, T031-212992. Mr Vong and crew offer a wide range of tours around a variety of top-notch provincial sites, very good value and recommended for visitors who are only around for 1-2 days (US$15 per person, 4 people min).

Xe Pian National Protected Area *p226*
Elephant treks and birdwatching
There are several 2- to 3-day trekking/ homestay trips offered in the area. These include elephant treks across the Xe Pian forests, wetlands and rocky outcrops; treks from Kiet Ngong Village to the top of **Phu Asa** (this one takes about 2 hrs, US$13; the elephant baskets can carry 2 people); and birdwatching trips. There is also a 2-day canoe/trekking trip called the **Ta Ong Trail** with guides trained in wildlife and the medicinal uses of plants. These tours are designed to ensure that local communities reap the rewards of tourism in a sustainable fashion and are highly recommended.

The **Kingfisher Eco-lodge** (see Sleeping), T030-5345016, can arrange for you to train to be a bona fide elephant rider with a traditional *mahout* (elephant keeper).

Tour operators in Pakse can also organize trips to the area. Contact the Provincial Tourism Office in Pakse, T031-212021.

If you wish to travel independently to this area, you need to allow enough time for the elephants to be organized by the *mahouts* once you arrive. Contact **Boun Hom**

Guesthouse, T030-5346293, in advance. Although only minimal English is spoken in the village, most of the locals will understand the purpose of your visit.

🚌 Transport

Pakse *p218, map p218*
For out-of-town journeys, hotels, such as the Souksamlam and Champasak Palace, and tour companies, such as Lane Xang, Champa May and Sodetour, charter cars and minibuses (with driver).

Air
The flight schedule changes frequently so it is best to check with a travel agent prior to making arrangements. There are currently flights to **Vientiane**, **Siem Reap**, and **Phnom Penh** with Lao Airlines, who have offices at the airport and by the river in town, T031-212252, Mon-Fri. Bangkok Airways also runs direct flights to/from Bangkok a couple of times a week US$140-one way.

Boat
Boats are much more irregular now that the roads have improved and there are ample public transport options. Boats to **Champasak** are on again-off again. Ask around to see what the latest status is. If you have enough people and money it is possible to charter a boat to **Don Khong** or Champasak, contact **Mr Boun My**, T020-5631008. See also Ins and outs, page 222.

Bus/songthaew
Buses/trucks travelling north (to **Savanna-khet, Thakhek and Vientiane**) leave from the Northern bus station, Km 7 on Route 13, across the Xe Don. The southern terminal is at Km 8 also on Route 13, heading south out of town. Lists of bus departures can be found in many of the hotels and guesthouses. There are regular morning departures to most destinations until 1600 and journey times are decreasing as the roads improve.

You can charter a tuk-tuk to the airport, northern bus station (8 km away), southern bus station (8 km away) for about 30,000 kip. To get to the VIP bus station, 2 km from the town centre, at *talaat lak song,* costs about 10,000 kip.

The Northern terminal 7 km north of town on Route 13. Hourly departures daily 0800-1500 to **Savannakhet**, 250 km, 5-6 hrs, 30,000 kip; to **Thakhek**, 8-9 hrs, 60,000 kip; to **Lak Sao**, 8-9 hrs, 75,000 kip; to **Paksan**, 10 hrs, 80,000 kip; to **Vientiane**, 16-18 hrs, 85,000 kip. These buses can be painfully slow due to the number of stops they make en route. For those heading to **Vientiane** it makes more sense to fork out a couple of extra dollars and pop on the much quicker and comfortable VIP bus at the VIP station.

The Southern terminal 8 km south of town on Route 13. There are regular bus connections with **Champasak**; stay on the bus if you are travelling to **Wat Phou** (see page 223). Ask for Ban Lak Sarm Sip (translates as 'village 30 km'); here there is a signpost and you turn right and travel 4 km towards Ban Muang (5 km). In the village there are people selling tickets for the ferry. (Dao Heung market, the morning market, has regular *songthaew* for Champasak in the morning, 15,000 kip.)

Local buses coming through from **Vientiane** provide the main means of transport to other destinations down south, so can be slightly off kilter. Buses depart for **Salavan**, 4 departures in the morning, 110 km, 2-3 hrs, 20,000 kip. This is a good alternative for those wishing to head to **Tad Lo**, 20,000 kip, just make sure that the bus is taking Route 20 (not Route 23) and that the driver understands you want to get off at the junction.

Songthaew to the **Bolaven Plateau**; **Paksong**, 50 km, 5 departures between 0800 and 1300, 20,000 kip. **Tad Fan**, 5 departures in the morning, 50 km, 1 hr, 15,000 kip; to **Tha Theng**, 5 departures in the morning, 20,000 kip; A *songthaew* leaves for **Ban Kiet Ngong** at 1300, 2-3 hrs, 20,000 kip.

Buses/*songthaew* leave for **Siphandon** between 0600 and 0900 (Muang Khong) 40,000 kip, 3-4 hrs; for **Ban Nakasang** (the closest port to Don Deth/Don Khon) several departures between 0730 and 1400, 40,000 kip 3-4 hrs. Several of the buses to Ban Nakasang also stop at **Ban Hat Xai Khoune** (the stop off for Don Khong). Make sure that you let the driver know whether you are going to Ban Nakasang or Ban Hat Xai Khoune rather than simply saying the name of the islands.

A more comfortable alternative to Siphandon is to take the minibus service to **Don Deth/Don Khong** which picks you up directly from your hotel and drops you off at either Ban Nakasang or Ban Hat Xai Khoune for 60,000 kip, 2 hrs. This actually works out to be much more cost-effective and time-effective. Most guesthouses can arrange for this minibus service in Pakse, as can **Lane Xang Travel** (see Tour operators, above), 60,000 kip, 2 hrs. This is highly recommended as, once you have paid all the fees involved with local transport, it costs about the same. It is also a shorter trip, so save yourself the headache.

VIP bus terminal See Ins and outs, page 219. Near the football stadium and Talaat Lak Song, T031-212228, just off Route 13. VIP buses to **Ubon** (Thailand) leave at 0800 and 0530 ₿200; VIP seat buses leave for **Vientiane** at 2000 arriving in Vientiane at 0600 (stopping in **Thakhek** en route) 150,000 kip. A VIP sleeping bus with comfy beds, duvet, cake, movies and milk thrown in (basically a mobile slumber party) leaves at 0830 arriving in Vientiane at 0600 (stopping en route to Thakhek), 150,000 kip. The beds are double, so unless you book 2 spaces you might end up sleeping next to a stranger. If you're tall ask for a bed towards the back of the bus. Make sure you secure your belongings on any of the overnight buses as some passengers can get sticky fingers.

Motorbike and bicycle hire
Sabaidy 2, see Sleeping, rents motorbikes with insurance for US$8 the 1st day and US$7 for subsequent days. The **Lankham Hotel** rents out bicycles (US$1 per day) standard small bikes (US$8 per day) and larger dirt bikes (US$20 per day).

Tuk-tuk/saamlor
These are the main forms of local transport. A tuk-tuk to the northern bus station should cost 30,000 kip. Shared tuk-tuks to local villages leave from the Daoheung market and from the stop on No 11 Rd near the jetty. Tuk-tuks can also be chartered by the hour. For services to the Thai border, see Border essentials, page 220.

Champasak *p221, map p222*
Boat
See Pakse Transport, above.

Bus/songthaew
To **Pakse** at 0630, 0730 and 0800, 15,000 kip 2 hrs (with wait for ferry). A shared *songthaew* to **Ban Thong Kop**, the village opposite Wat Phou, costs around 10,000 kip; direct to **Wat Phou** is US$8-10 return (chartered).

❶ Directory

Pakse *p218, map p218*
Banks BCEL Bank, No 11 Rd (beside the river), changes US$ and most currencies (cash) and offers a better commission rate on cash exchange than other banks, also Visa/MasterCard cash advances at 3% commission, Mon-Fri 0830-1530 (with 1 hr lunch break), they have a MasterCard only ATM; Lao Development Bank, No 13 Rd, T031-212168, cash and TCs exchanged; there is a branch of the Lao Viet Bank on the main road but it only changes TCs and cash, open Mon-Fri 0830-1530. **Embassies and consulates** Vietnam, No 24 Rd, Mon-Fri 0800-1300, 1400-1630, visas for Vietnam cost US$50 and take 3 days to process, so you are better off organizing your Vietnamese visa in Vientiane. **Internet** Expect to pay around 200 kip per min but discounts kick in usually after 1 hr: D@M's Internet & Email Service, No 13 Rd; **Medical services** There is a huge hospital between No 1 Rd and No 46 Rd, T031-212018, but neither their English skills nor medical service will suffice for complex cases; in case of emergencies you are better off going across to Ubon in Thailand; there is a pretty good pharmacy at the hospital which stocks most medications. **Police** T031-212145. **Post office** No 8 Rd, overseas telephone calls can also be made from here; express mail service available; note the ashtrays made from defused (one hopes) unexploded shells. **Telephone** Telecommunications office for fax and overseas calls on No 1 Rd, near No 13 Rd; all of the internet cafés have internet-call facilities which are by far the cheapest option.

Boloven Plateau

The French identified the Boloven Plateau, in the northeast of Champasak Province, as a prime location for settlement by hardy French farming stock. It is named after the Laven minority group that reside in the area. The soils are rich and the upland position affords some relief from the summer heat of the lowlands. Fortunately, their grand plans came to nought and, although some French families came to live here, they were few in number and all left between the 1950s and 1970s as conditions deteriorated. The area also suffered another setback during the war years, when the major surrounding towns were completely destroyed by US bombing campaigns. Even so, the area was developed as a coffee-, rubber-, tea- and cardamom-growing area. The cool breeze of the plateau, with an average altitude of 600 m, offers much respite from the stifling heat of surrounding lower lands, particularly in April and May. Today it is inhabited by a colourful mix of ethnic groups, such as the Laven, Alak, Tahoy and Suay, many of whom were displaced during the war. There are numerous villages dotted between the small settlement of Tha Teng and Salavan. The premier attraction in the area is the number of roaring falls plunging off the plateau. Today, Tad Lo and Tad Fan are particularly popular tourist destinations. While the grand Tad Yeung makes the perfect picnic destination, the plateau also affords excellent rafting and kayaking trips. A trip to a coffee or tea plantation also provides an interesting insight into the region. ❧ *For Sleeping, Eating and other listings, see pages 244-250.*

Ins and outs

As tourism expands in Laos, so areas like the Boloven are sure to become more accessible. For the moment though the tourist infrastructure is limited. Tour companies, especially in Pakse, 30 km away (see page 230), can organize trips. Alternatively, the best base is Tad Lo (see page 235). Other places near or on the Boloven are Salavan (see page 238), Sekong (see page 240) and Attapeu (see page 242); guesthouses in these towns can also offer assistance and information. Note that it is not always possible to drive across the Boloven Plateau from Salavan to Attapeu, as bad weather rapidly deteriorates the roads. In the wet season, parts of the new road recently constructed from Paksong can be washed away.

Background

The fertile farmland of the Boloven Plateau has given Salavan Province a strong agricultural base, supporting coffee, tea and cardamom plantations. The road from Paksong to Pakse is known as the Coffee Road. Coffee was introduced to the area by French settlers in the 1920s and 1930s, who then made a quick exit as the bombing escalated in the 1960s. It is mainly exported via Pakse to Thailand, Singapore and, formerly, the USSR. Fair Trade has also catapulted the coffee into the UK and US markets. Tea grown in this area, however, is for local use. The Boloven also has the perfect climate for durians; villages (particularly on the road from Paksong to Pakse) are liberally dotted with durian trees. The fruit is exceptionally rich and creamy and in the peak season, between May and July, can be bought from roadside stalls for just 1000 kip or so. Thanks to its fertility, the plateau is now rapidly repopulating and new farms are springing up. One can see evidence of the government's relocation policy everywhere on the plateau, where villages have been moved from higher lands to the lower lands, with the end goal of minimizing slash-and-burn agriculture and providing people better access to infrastructure, markets and other facilities. As a result, many new farming practices and produce have been steadily introduced. Towards Salavan, lots of banana plantations are cropping up and, between Paksong and Tha Teng, many small-time village operations are producing cabbage and corn crops, often sold roadside.

During the bombing of the Ho Chi Minh Trail (see page 208), to the east, many hilltribes and other ethnic minority groups also migrated to the Boloven, which consequently has become an ethnographic goldmine with more than 12 obscure minority groups living in the area, including the Katu, Alak, Tahoy, Suay, Ya Houne, Ngai and Suk. Most of the tribes are of Indonesian (or Proto-Malay) stock and have very different facial characteristics to the Lao; they are mainly animist (see page 301).

Paksong (Pakxong) and around 🛏️🚌 ➔ pp244-250.

Colour map 3, B3.
➔ *Phone code: 031.*

The main town on the Boloven Plateau is Paksong, a small market town 50 km east of Pakse. It was originally a French agricultural centre, popular during the colonial era for its cooler temperatures. Paksong was yet another casualty of the war and was virtually destroyed. The area is famous for its fruit and vegetables; even strawberries and raspberries can be cultivated here.

The town occupies a very scenic spot, however, the harsh weather in the rainy season changes rapidly, making it difficult to plan trips around the area. The town consists of little more than a couple of blocks of old shops and a big produce market, which acts as a trading centre for many of the outlying villages of the plateau.

Waterfalls around Paksong

Just 17 km from Paksong are the twin falls of **Tad Mone** and **Tad Meelook**. Once a popular picnic spot for locals, the area is now almost deserted and the swimming holes at the base of the falls are an idyllic place for a dip. To reach the falls take Route 23 northeast of Paksong towards Tha Teng and Salavan, until you reach a signposted turning; follow the road for about 3.5 km to reach the falls.

Not far from Paksong, 1 km off the road to Pakse, is **Tad Fan**, a dramatic 120-m-high waterfall, which is believed to be one of the tallest cascades in the country. The fall splits into two powerful streams roaring over the edge of the cliff and plummeting into the pool below, with mist and vapour shrouding views from above. The fall's name derives from the species of barking deer which formerly surrounded the area and local legends talk of large numbers of the species falling to their death down the mammoth falls. One of the best viewing spots for the falls is the **Tad Fan Resort**'s restaurant (see Sleeping, page 244), which offers an unobscured view of the magnificent site. Beware of the vendors aggressively hawking coffee, tea, orchids and other products on the entrance road.

> ✱ *Tad Jampapa, another stunning waterfall, can be found 42 km from Paksong on the way to Pakse; turn off at the sign on the north side of the road.*

Around 2 km from Tad Fan and 1 km from the main road is **Tad Yeung** (pronounced Tad N'Yeung) ① *entry 5000 kip*. Set amongst beautiful coffee plantations and sprinkled with wooden picnic huts, these falls are possibly the best on the plateau. Packing a picnic in Pakse and bringing it along for an afternoon trip is recommended. The cascades plummet 50 m to a pool at the bottom, which is possible to swim in, in the dry season. During the wet season the waterways create numerous little channels and islands around the cascades. Behind the main falls sits a cave – however it is best to get someone to guide you here. There is a slippery walk-way from the top of the falls to the bottom, where you can swim. The falls can be reached by taking local bus from Southern bus station in Pakse to Village Km 40 (ask to go to Lak See Sip). The turn-off is on the right from Pakse (and on the left from Paksong). There is a sign on the main road which indicates **Sihom Sabaidy Guesthouse**, follow this road about 700 m to the falls. These falls are a great option if you are trying to avoid the backpacker hoardes.

The falls sit on the edge of the **Dong Hua Sao National Protected Area** and access via the falls is one of the only ways to explore the area. Previously, it was inhabited by a number of rare species now dwindling in number. It is believed that a local population of tigers still resides in the protected area but the chances of spotting one are minimal. Trekking is offered around the waterfall but is quite difficult in the wet season due to slipperiness and leaches, so it's best to hire one of the guides at the **Tad Fan** resort. Take a track to the left off the main road at Ban Lak, Km 38; at the end of the track, a path leads down to a good viewpoint halfway down the horseshoe-shaped gorge. The magnificent falls offer stunning views but if you wish to swim you should trek further along to Tad Gniang, 2 km east of Tad Fan. **Tad Gniang,** named after the wild stags that populate the area, is only recommended for a dip during the dry season (October to the end of March). There is a charge of 2000 kip per person, plus an additional 3000 kip per motorbike. Tours to Tad Fan and Tad Gniang can be organized through most travel agents in Pakse (see page 230).

Thirty-six kilometres northeast of Pakse is **Paseum Waterfall** and **Utayan Bajiang Champasak** ① *T031-251294, 5000 kip entry fee,* a strange ethnic theme park popular with Thai tourists. The large compound features the small cascades, restaurant, model ethnic village, gardens and plenty of trails in between. They have bungalows, a tree house and rooms available for ₿1000. To get here from Pakse follow Route 13 towards Paksong and follow the left fork at Km 21 and turn off at the Km 30 mark.

Tha Teng and around 🚌🚍 ›› *pp244-250.*

On the Boloven Plateau, at the junction of Routes 23 and 16 between Salavan (45 km), Sekong (48 km) and Paksong (37 km), is Tha Teng, a village that was levelled during the war. Before that, it was the home of Jean Dauplay, the Frenchman who introduced coffee to Laos from Vietnam in 1920. Today the United Nations Development Programme (UNDP), in a joint venture with a private sector businessman, has set up a small wild honey-processing factory. Villagers are paid for the combs they collect from jungled hills around Tha Teng. The carefully labelled 'Wild honey from Laos' is exported to European health food shops. There are several ethnic minority villages in the area.

There isn't much to see in the town itself – essentially it's just a big roundabout, affording stunning views. There is, however, an excellent ethnic minority market starting at about 0600 daily, to which villagers come to sell produce from their plots. A convoy of tractors, horses and basket-carrying women puffing on pipes can be seen at day-break approaching the market.

Tad Lo and around 🚌🚲❄️⛺🚍 ›› *pp244-250. Colour map 3, B3.*

→ *Phone code: 031.*

Tad Lo is a popular 'resort' on the edge of the Boloven Plateau, 30 km from Salavan, and nestled alongside three rolling cascades. There are several places to stay in this idyllic retreat, good hiking, an exhilarating river to frolic in (especially in the wet season) and elephant trekking. In the vicinity of Tad Lo there are also several villages, which can be visited in the company of a local villager. The area has become particularly popular with the backpacker set, many of whom prefer to stay here rather than in Pakse.

The **Xe Xet** (or Houei Set) flows past Tad Lo, crashing over two sets of cascades nearby: **Tad Hang**, the lower series, is overlooked by the **Tad Lo Lodge** and **Saise Guesthouse** (see Sleeping, page 244), while **Tad Lo**, the upper, is a short hike away. The Xe Xet is yet another river being dammed in the area to produce hydropower for export to Thailand.

📍 *You are advised to hire a local guide on all treks to tribal villages as there have been reports of trouble arising between independent visitors and the Nay Ban (Village Chief).*

Getting there The turning for Tad Lo is at to Ban Houei Set on Route 20 between Pakse and Salavan. Catch a bus or *songthaew* from either town; most drivers know Tad Lo and will stop at Ban Houia Set (2½ hours from Pakse and under an hour from Salavan). There is a blue sign here indicating the way to Tad Lo – a 1.5-km walk along a dirt track and through the village of Ban Saen Wang. Usually you can get a tuk-tuk to Tad Lo for around 5000 kip. ▶ *For further details, see Transport, page 248.*

Tourist information A new **Community Guides** office has been established with a number of trained guides offering treks around the Tad Lo area and to nearby Ngai villages. Elephant treks can also be arranged from here for US$5 per elephant for a 90-minute trek through the jungle and river.

Each one of the guesthouses in Tad Lo can arrange guided treks to Ban Khian and Tad Soung. Before you set off, pop into **Tim's Restaurant** (see page 245) for a quick chat to Soulideth. A great source of free and friendly information, he is the foremost authority on all there is to do in the area and is unbelievably helpful. He can arrange tours and excursions – and anything else imaginable – with less hassle and more local involvement than anyone else. He'll also give you a map which you can copy. For more information, consult his website (www.tadlo.laopdr.com).

Tad Lo

To Salavan (31 km)
To Pakse (85 km)
20
Ban Houa Set
(1.5 km)
Path (3 km)
Ban Saen Wang
Tad Hang
Xe Xet
Tad Lo

N
Not to scale

Sleeping ●
Green House
 (Saise Guesthouse) 1
Sailomen Guesthouse 2

Saise Guesthouse 3
Sypaseuth Guesthouse
 & Restaurant 4
Tad Lo Lodge
 & Restaurant 5
Tim's Guesthouse
 & Restaurant 6

Around Tad Lo

There are two Alak villages, **Ban Khian** and **Tad Soung**, close to Tad Lo. Tad Soung is approximately 10 km away from the main resort area and are the most panoramic falls in the vicinity. The Alak are an Austro-Indonesian ethno-linguistic group. Their grass-thatched huts, with rounded roofs, are not at all Lao in style and are distinct from those in neighbouring Lao Theung villages. Most fascinating is the Alak's seeming obsession with death. The head of each household carves coffins out of logs for himself and his whole family (even babies), then stacks them, ready for use, under their rice storage huts. This tradition serves as a reminder that life expectancy in these remote rural areas is around 40 and infant mortality around 100 per 1000 live births; the number one killer is malaria.

Katou villages such as **Ban Houei Houne** (on the Salavan–Pakse road) are famous for their weaving of a bright cloth used locally as a *pha sinh* (sarong). This village also has an original contraption to pound rice: on the river below the village are several water-wheels which power the rice pounders. The idea originally came from Xam Neua and was brought to this village by a man who had fought with the

⁝ The fall of Tha Teng: a personal view

In 1968, I read about the fall of Tha Teng to the Pathet Lao. The small article was buried in a back page of the newspaper. Not many Americans really cared about this loss or even knew where Laos was, let alone Tha Teng. In 1969 I was flying over Tha Teng in my Bird Dog – a Cessna 170 – which was used in my work as a Forward Air Controller (Code name, Raven 58) for the United States Air Force. All that was left of this town was about 20 homes lining a road on the northern edge of the Boloven Plateau. The homes were gradually being overrun by heavy vegetation.

What was so important about this town that its loss would be reported in the United States? Tha Teng is strategically located on the northern edge of the Boloven Plateau. As a military outpost, it could be used to obtain intelligence about enemy activity. So, by occupying Tha Teng, the 'friendlies' – the Royal Lao Government – could, to a certain extent, control the gateway to the Boloven. With its loss, the Pathet Lao and North Vietnamese could move more easily in their efforts to control the plateau. The significance of the location of Tha Teng was well known to the Pathet Lao. It was rumoured that there was a cave northeast of Tha Teng which could hold a battalion of troops and whose entrance was large enough to walk an elephant through. Elephants were used to haul heavy equipment, ammunition and supplies into the cave. But, from the air, the terrain looked flat. Even the military topological maps did not indicate the possibility of a cave. However, on Thanksgiving Day 1969, I confirmed in fact the existence of that cave by

'clearing' away the 200-ft trees which protected its entrance. Further, it exposed a large permanent bivouac area in front of the cave entrance which provided facilities for at least a battalion-size unit. This staging area proved successful as the Pathet Lao captured the Boloven during their campaign of 1970.

The 'war-that-wasn't' in Laos was odd in more than just the sense that it wasn't a war. In Vientiane it was a common sight to see Pathet Lao soldiers coming down out of the mountains in full combat gear, including weapons, to obtain their daily rations. They could shop without concern of being captured and would then return to the mountains to join their combat units. These were the same soldiers that the Royal Lao army, who were also at the market, might be fighting later that same day. Three days each year, the war would stop in southern Laos. Officials from Salavan would get in a truck and head south toward the plateau. At the edge of the Bolovens they would stop to let armed Pathet Lao (PL) get on their truck so they could continue to each village on the plateau. These PL guards would make certain that the officials only went to the villages. As the officials visited each village, they would record the births, deaths and weddings which had taken place during the previous year. War or no war, official government records had to be maintained. Following the three-day yearly truce, the war would resume.

Source: Ken Thompson, Raven 58, who flew as a FAC over Laos and Vietnam from 1968 to 1970.

Pathet Lao. Tours to the village are run by **Saise Guesthouse**: at 150,000 kip per tour; it's best to set off in a group. **Tim's Restaurant** can also make arrangements for you.

Salavan (Saravan) and around 😑🎧🐷⛩️🚌🛈 ➤➤ pp244-250.

Colour map 3, B3.

→ *Phone code: 034.*

The capital of one of the most beautiful provinces in Laos, the old French town of Salavan (also Saravan and Saravane) lies at the northern edge of the Boloven Plateau and acts as a transport hub and trading centre for the agricultural commodities produced on the plateau. The Xe Don, which enters the Mekong at Pakse, flows along the edge of town. Salavan is a charming town with no pretensions. Pigs and buffalo wander along the roads, children play in the streets and shops sell such practical goods as anvils, bicycle tyres, lengths of wire, transmission parts and brightly coloured functional plastic objects. There are few handicrafts or postcards in sight. In the cool of the evening, when people are at rest, talking, cooking and playing, the town seems – despite the legacy of the war – to epitomize a more innocent past. If you happen to be walking past the market at 1700 or thereabouts, you may even find yourself invited to join the locals in a game of petang.

Ins and outs

Getting there Most buses from Pakse turn off Route 23 and travel to Salavan via Route 20, a new and comparatively fast road that goes past the turning to Tad Lo (see page 235). They often also stop for a while at the small market town of Ban Lao Ngam on the Houei Tapoung (46 km from Salavan, 79 km from Pakse). Some buses, though, take the longer and rougher route via Paksong (Route 23). ➤➤ *For further details, see Transport, page 249.*

History

This area was an important Champasak kingdom outpost called Muang Mam and populated by mostly Mon-Khmer ethnic groups. In 1828 the Siamese renamed the area Salawan, which has evolved into the current name.

Salavan changed hands several times during the American war in Indochina, as the Pathet Lao and forces of the Royal Lao Government fought for control of this critical town located on a strategic flank of the Ho Chi Minh Trail. The two sides, with the RLG supported by American air power, bombed and shelled the town in turn as they tried to dislodge one another and Salavan was all but obliterated. (There is a

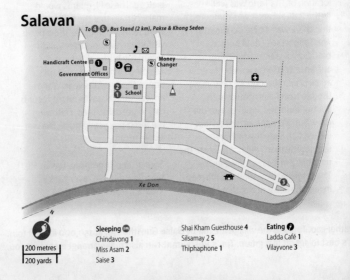

Salavan

To ④ ⑤, Bus Stand (2 km), Pakse & Khong Sedon

Handicraft Centre
Government Offices
Money Changer
School
Xe Don

Sleeping 😑		Eating 🍴
Chindavong **1**	Shai Kham Guesthouse **4**	Ladda Café **1**
Miss Asam **2**	Silsamay 2 **5**	Vilayvone **3**
Saise **3**	Thiphaphone **1**	

200 metres
200 yards

crude painting of the battle in the **Champasak Museum** in Pakse; see page 220.) Until a few years ago, there were still piles of war scrap, including unexploded bombs, shells and mortars in the streets. Now cleared away, reminders of the war are largely confined to the memories of older residents (most are under 30) and the pages of books. The consequences of the shelling and bombing today is that Salavan is a provincial capital with scarcely an ounce of physical beauty and almost no evidence of its French-era origins, except for the post office.

When US airforce pilots mounted bombing runs in Vietnam, their rules of engagement prohibited airstrikes within 500 m of a temple; in Cambodia, the margins were increased to 1 km. It has been said that in Laos such rules did not apply, but one retired US officer who was based there has written to us saying that "a complex web of rules [was] administered by levels of supervision stretching from the embassy in Vientiane, to Ho Chi Minh City, to Honolulu to the Pentagon, and included consultation with, and on the appropriate occasions approval by, the Lao government." Like Xieng Khouang, another critical town to the north, Salavan had one of the most beautiful temples in the country, **Wat Chom Keoh**, which was destroyed in an air raid in 1968. (The wat was commemorated on a postage stamp in the 1950s.)

Today all that remains of **Wat Chom Keoh** are two forlorn and shell-pocked corner-posts, one ruined chedi and a dilapidated wat building decaying still further in the grounds of the Salavan general hospital. The daily market in the centre of town is worth a visit, mainly, admittedly, because there is little else to see apart from the handicraft centre. In past years the market was an environmentalist's nightmare: all manner of wild creatures, some listed as endangered, would end up here, either for the cooking pot or for the trade in live wild animals (see Background, page 321). Today the frisson of such sights is, fortunately, no longer on offer. There's the usual array of frogs and fish, and perhaps a wild bird, squirrel or lizard, but not much else.

> ⁑ *Look carefully and you can still see evidence of the war: many of the awnings and umbrellas in the market are made from parachute silk.*

Ban Nong Boua

Ban Nong Boua, a beautiful lake near the source of the Xe Don, lies 18 km east of Salavan town. It is famed for its crocodiles (although apparently now only two remain), which move into the river in the dry season but usually stay out of sight. The locals have a number of cultural beliefs surrounding the crocodiles, so a donation – perhaps in order to offer a pig to the crocs, which the residents will actually consume themselves – is likely to be expected before they will escort you to the lake. The road to Ban Nong Boua is too rough to be negotiated by tuk-tuk, which means it is necessary to charter a jeep or other sturdy vehicle. There are two river crossings along the way, so any vehicle that won't fit in a small boat or brave the waters won't make it there. In the wet season it is advisable to travel by boat.

Ban Nong Boua is also rumoured to be a starting point for climbing **Phou Katae**, the 1588-m-high mountain that looms over Salavan from the south. However, *falangs* aren't welcome to climb it, either because of the American airstrip from the war that is supposedly up there, or because of the logging operations on the other side, which are not entirely legal nor public. Access to both Ban Nong Boua and Phou Katae is very difficult and is only recommended for the tougher independent traveller. There is nowhere to sleep near the mountain but it may be possible to sleep at the nearby temple if you have a mosquito net.

● *Salavan Province has a large hydroelectric power-generating capacity. The Xe Xet barrage, which emanates from the Nam Xe Xet, supplies power to Pakse; some electricity is also exported to Thailand.*

Tahoy, northeast of Salavan along Route 15, is a major centre of the Tahoy minority ethnic group. There are 30,000 Tahoy spread across the two adjoining provinces but the largest population lives here. Aside from being an interesting cultural insight into the Tahoy culture, the town is also renowned for war junk, as the Ho Chi Minh Trail dissected the area. Locals believe that there is a large tiger population in the area and tales are rife of this person or that person being eaten by a tiger. However, it would seem that the tigers aren't very forthcoming, as even tiger specialists have difficulty tracking the creatures.

Toum Lan is a Katong village 46 km north of Salavan, notable for its longhouse and traditional weaving techniques (ask Mr Bousasone at **Saise Guesthouse** for details). They also celebrate the Lapup festival, where buffaloes are usually sacrificed around the full moon in March. During the rainy season it is difficult to access the site. A bus leaves for Toum Lan at 1430 (15,000 kip) and returns at 0700. Accommodation may be possible in the village (10,000 kip).

The **Paseum** waterfall lies 81 km from Salavan on Route 20. It is a beautiful spot but is dominated by the resort that sits on the site. The proprietor has relocated a small ethnic village from their homes to the resort premises in order to make a distinctly dubious 'ethnic museum', where the villagers show tourists their 'traditional way of life'. As tourists approach, the villagers change out of their jeans and into traditional attire before running around, beating drums and playing traditional music.

Coffee Road

Heading south from Salavan, Route 20 reaches Ban Beng after 26 km (4 km from Tad Lo). Turn south (right if coming from Tad Lo or Pakse) on to Route 23 – the 'Coffee Road'.

> ❧ Ban Khan Nam Xiep on the Coffee Road is another Tahoy village.

From here the road climbs up to the lower slopes of the Boloven Plateau. From Ban Beng, the road is poor as far as Tha Teng, although there are indications that upgrading is in the pipeline. From Tha Teng to Sekong, however, the road is paved and very scenic. The area is still largely forested with a sparse population concentrated along the road and mainly cultivating coffee. Buses and trucks usually stop at the local market centre of Ban Tha Teng.

Towards Sekong the land is more intensively cultivated; there is even some irrigated rice. This is also an area of resettlement with a number of new villages carving out a small area of civilized space in the forest. The large logging yard and saw mill at Ban Phon, about 12 km north of Sekong, demonstrates the local economy's dependence on timber.

Sekong (Xekong, Muang Lamam) and around

🖼️🚻📷🍴🅲 ▸▸ *pages 244-250. Colour map 3, B4.*

→ *Phone code: 031.*

Sekong (or Xekong) is a new town and capital of the province of the same name. It is located on the Kong River at the eastern edge of the Boloven Plateau, about 100 km south of Salavan and a similar distance north of Attapeu, and was created comparatively recently from areas formerly part of Attapeu and Salavan. Much of Sekong's population voluntarily moved from Dakchung, close to the Vietnamese border, in the early 1980s, when the government created the new province and established better facilities.

For the moment, anyone travelling between Salavan and Attapeu (but probably not vice versa) must stay overnight here as the first bus from Salavan does not arrive until the last Pakse-bound bus for Attapeu has already departed (see Transport, page 248). As roads improve and journey times drop, however, it may become possible to make this trip without overnighting in Sekong.

Those hoping to chance upon an unknown gem of a town will be disappointed. In theory Sekong ought to be a good base to explore the people and scenery of the Boloven Plateau but there is simply no tourist infrastructure to make that possible. The only reason to come here, other than out of sheer perversity, is to take a boat down the Xe Kong to the much more attractive town of Attapeu (see Transport, page 249). The market, centered on the bus terminal, has some rather pathetic wild animals, such as giant flying squirrels, for sale – more, in fact, than Salavan which has an infamous reputation in this regard. There is a wat behind the market. A reminder of the war is the number of UXO that litter the area. The UXO office, near the Ministry of Finance, has set up a little exhibition and welcomes tourists.

Health warning Malaria is quite a serious problem in this area, particularly in the wet season, and precautions should be taken to avoid being bitten. Make sure you also take the correct prophylaxis (see page 38). The area is also littered with UXO, so stick to the well-worn path.

Towards Attapeu

The biggest draw-card in the area is the boat trip between Sekong and Attapeu down the stunning Xe Kong river. The four- to seven-hour journey through pristine wilderness, past riverside villages and the towering Boloven Plateau gives access to territory everyday tourists wouldn't get the opportunity to see. The trip should cost around US$60-70. Regular boats are not arranged so you will need to organize a baot in advance – ask at the Pha Thip restaurant or at the pier the day before; opt for a boatman who provides lifejackets as the trip crosses through some rapids. Although it can get hot, try to avoid taking a dip as a nasty piranha-like blow-fish called the *pa pao* lives in the waters and apparently has a voracious appetite for the human penis.

Travelling by road to Attapeu, about 25 km south of Sekong near the Alak village of Ban Mun Hua Mung, the Xe Nam Noi crashes over a series of waterfalls: 100 m east of the bridge is **Tad Houakone**, while signposted 4 km downstream is **Tad Phek**; in between are a number of smaller falls. Those tempted to swim in the falls, should dip in the higher pool as the Pa Pao (see above) is rumoured to live in the lower pools. A track leads from one to the other; during the dry season you can walk downriver between the two. A tuk-tuk can be hired for a day to see these sights (US$10-15), but you may be better off trying to hire a motorbike from one of the locals.

The road between Sekong and Attapeu, along the eastern edge of the imposing Boloven Plateau, has finally been completed, aside from a few tiny sections, despite being put on hold for many years while the bridge contractor was in jail. The spectacular 120-m-high **Tad Sekatamtok** tumbles from the Xe Nam Noi about 16 km from the junction (Km 52) with the new road towards Paksong and Pakse. Local sources call this the highest waterfall in the country, although it seems that every province will

Sekong

To Bus Station (2.5 km) & Tha Theng

Water Tower

Kaysone Monument

Victory That

Lake

Government Building

Boats to Attapeu

To Attapeu

Xe Kong

N

Not to scale

Sleeping
Koky Guesthouse 1
Sackda 2
Sekong Souksamlane & Restaurant 3

Somchany Guesthouse 4
Woman Fever Kosment Center Guesthouse 5

Eating
Khamting 1
Phathip 2
Saruya 3
Somview 4

Southern Laos Boloven Plateau

claim their waterfall is Laos' highest. Unlike its closest counterpart, Tad Fan, this fall is comprised of one giant surge burgeoning over the cliff-top, certainly securing its ranking as one of the country's most spectacular. Along the road to Attapeu are clearings where new villages have been created for the 'upland' Lao. In a bid to resettle these people, the government provided land, aid and resources for building and a space by the banks of the Xe Kong to grow vegetables and other crops to sell.

Attapeu Province 🛏️🍴🏔️🚌🍸 ⟫ pp244-250. Colour map 3, C4.

→ Phone code: 031.

Attapeu has an altogether different character from the Boloven Plateau, as the province is predominantly Lao Loum rather than comprised of ethnic minority groups. Attapeu Province was formerly administered under the Lane Xang Kingdom, King Saysetthathirath moved operations in 1571, later dying in the small town. Attapeu suffered greatly between 1964 and 1975, and evidence of this destruction is clear, particularly in the eastern corner along the Ho Chi Minh Trail, where the land is so cratered that some expats refer to it as 'moon-land'.

There are two National Protected Areas in Attapeu the **Dong Ampham Forest** and the eastern portion of the **Xe Pian** (see page 226), covering almost 250,000 ha in total. The NPAs (National Protected Areas) are home to numerous animal and plant species. You'll see giant logging trucks growling along the southern highway, transporting enormous trees, but visitor access to the sites is very difficult and tourism infrastructure is incredibly poor, rendering them almost impossible for a quick visit.

Ins and outs

Tourist information For information on the province, visit the **tourist office** in Attapeu town in the provincial hall, northwest of the town centre. It has large-scale relief maps of the area, good for hiking on or around the Boloven Plateau, and informative brochures on all there is to do in Attapeu. If intending to explore the countryside hereabouts, it is best to ask around for a guide.

Health warning Malaria is quite a serious problem in this area and precautions should be taken to avoid being bitten. Make sure you also take the correct prophylaxis (see page 38).

Attapeu town

Attapeu is an attractive, leafy town positioned on a bend in the Xe Kong, at the confluence of the Xe Kaman. Once referred to as the Golden Land for its gold deposits, Attapeu prides itself on the old provincial saying that "Attapeu people traded gold for chickens, while Salavan sold their own elephants to buy fire". According to ML Manich in his *History of Laos*, Attapeu should really be called Itkapü, which translates as 'buffalo dung', due to a misunderstanding between the original population and incoming Lao Loum people. The French, in their turn, transliterated Itkapü as Attapeu. For a pile of dung the town, however, is remarkably picturesque. For those in the ecotourism sector, Attapeu and its surrounding are heralded as the next up-and-coming place in Laos. For now, though, it is relatively free of the tourist hordes.

Apart from an unremarkable monastery, **Wat Luang**, dating from the 1930s, Attapeu is not over-endowed with obvious sights of interest. However, it is a pleasant place to walk around, with traditional wooden Lao houses with verandas and some French buildings. The people are friendly and traffic is limited. Vegetables are grown on the banks of the Xe Kong. Attapeu was fought over by the Pathet Lao and RLG, so it is a surprise that the town remains as attractive as it is. It was the only capital that was

Border essentials: Yalakhuntum-Bo Y (Vietnam)

The border crossing between Bo Y (Vietnam) and Yalakhuntum (Laos) on the newly opened route 18B (113 km from Attapeu) is now officially open. Although it is expected that Lao 30-day visas will be issued at the border, it is advisable to obtain a visa in advance until the border procedures have been fine-tuned. Vietnamese visas are not available at the border and will need to be obtained in advance. Buses leave Attapeu for Pleiku Mon, Wed and Fri at 0900 (US$10, 12 hours). More local buses from Attapeu were in the offing at the time of publication, so ask around.

never taken by the RLG and is consequently far more attached to the early years of the Lao PDR than the rest of the country; the local tourism authorities seem more intent on providing patriotic propaganda than real tourist information. Despite being one of the poorest provinces in Laos, Attapeu is developing fast due to improved infrastructure and the 2006 border opening at Bo Y, which has increased both trade and traffic to and from Vietnam.

Nongfa Lake

The real treasure of Attapeu is Nongfa Lake, which was 'discovered' in 1930. The crystal-clear blue lake shares many of its attributes with the beautiful volcanic lake of Yaek Loam in Cambodia. The shores are surrounded by pristine wilderness and mountains and the lake is considered an auspicious site by the local population. Although no conservationists have officially surveyed the lake, the government has done its own survey. Official tourist brochures proclaim, proudly, that the lake is so large that "a shot of an AK47 rifle from one edge of the lake never reaches the other". Most locals can't pinpoint exactly how to get to the enigmatic lake, so it's best to

Attapeu

Southern Laos Boloven Plateau

200 metres
200 yards

Sleeping
Aloon Sot Sai Guesthouse 1
Amphone Guesthouse 2 2
ATP Palace 3
Soksomphone Guesthouse 4

Eating
Darawan 1
Thi Thi 2

organize a tour with the tourism authorities. The lake is within the confines of the Dong Ampham National Protected Area, where the provincial tourism authorities sporadically run treks. It can also be reached via 4WD. Although several trails exist in the area much of the infrastructure remains undeveloped for tourist visits. It may take several days to find this little gem and the trip must not be undertaken without a well-informed guide.

East of Attapeu

The sleepy town of **Xaisetha** (Saisettha), which stretches along the north bank of the Xe Kaman, lies 12 km east of Attapeu along Route 18. There is regular transport from the east bank of the Xe Kong across from Attapeu. A further 18 km along Route 18, 30 km in all from Attapeu, is the Alak village of **Pa-am**, which sits directly on the Ho Chi Minh Trail. War memorabilia freaks might be interested in the Soviet surface-to-air missile launcher (still apparently live), abandoned there by the Vietnamese. It will cost you 5000 kip for a peek through the fence surrounding it.

West of Attapeu

The Lao Loum village of **Ban Mai** lies 50 km southwest of Attapeu. From Ban Mai it's 6 km to Ban Hinlat and, a further 6 km on, is the **Xe Pha** waterfall, which lies on the Se Pian. The falls are around 23 m high and 120 m wide. And another 9 km on from here, on the same river, are the **Xe Pang Lai** falls, the most stunning in the area.

From Ban Mai it is also possible to access 20-m-wide **Tad Samongphak** on a one-hour boat ride up the Se Pian. You may need a guide between the falls; ask locally, the tourism office is the best starting point. It should be possible to arrange accommodation in either village.

◉ Sleeping

Paksong and around p234
FBorlaven Guesthouse, Route 23 about 2 km north of the market, beyond Paksong town. The new brick and wood building has a cabin feel and is surrounded by coffee trees, corn fields and a flower garden. The simple rooms are bright (pink floral sheets) and clean with en suite bathrooms but no hot water. 50,000 kip. Very friendly owner speaks English.

Waterfalls around Paksong p234
B-CTad Fan Resort, T020-5531400, T020-5531400, Bangkok sales office T+66 (0)2-9686832, www.tadfane.com. Perched on the opposite side of the ravine from the falls is a series of wooden bungalows with nicely decorated rooms and en suite bathrooms, with hot showers. The 2nd floor of the excellent open-air restaurant offers the best view of the Tad Fane falls and serves a wide variety of Lao, Thai and Western food. Great service. Treks to the top of falls and the Dan-Sin-Xay Plain can be arranged.
ESihom Sabaidy Guesthouse. At the time of writing Mr Vong from **Sabaidy 2** in Pakse

(see page 228) was opening the new Sihom Sabaidy Guesthouse here. It is the only operational guesthouse in the vicinity of these falls. There are 8 basic rooms (US$5 per night) with shared hot-water bathrooms. There is an adjoining restaurant offering basic Lao meals, noodles, eggs and coffee. The guesthouse is on a coffee plantation and tours are available to the waterfall as well as to nearby orchid areas and to see how coffee is produced.

Tha Teng p235
EViphavahn Guesthouse, T034-211970, about 1 km east on Route 16 towards Sekong. This is by far the best option in the village. Decent, clean, simply decorated rooms with hot water, fan and Western toilet.

Tad Lo p235, map p236
B-ESaise Guesthouse (aka Sayse Guesthouse), T034-211886. The guesthouse comprises 2 sections: the lower part sits near the restaurant at the foot of Tad Hang and consists of rooms (US$12) and bungalows (US$6 or US$15 right next to the falls), all with

hot water and fans. The more attractive and peaceful option is the so-called **Green House** (the roof's a giveaway) above the falls. This is a wooden chalet with 6 huge rooms, 4 with en suite shower and toilet, and 2 of those with balconies overlooking the river. Breakfast included. The beautiful garden restaurant offers Lao and Thai food.

C Tad Lo Lodge, T034-211889, souriyavincent@yahoo.com. Reception on the east side of the falls with chalet-style accommodation (13 rooms) built right on top of the waterfalls on the opposite side; it's a bit of a hike from one to the other. Rates include breakfast and hot water. The location is attractive (during the wet season) and the accommodation is comfortable; cane rocking chairs on the balconies over-look the cascades on the left bank. Good restaurant serving plenty of Lao and Thai food.

There are now a number of small bungalow guesthouses near the bridge on the east side of the river, including:

E Tim's Guesthouse & Restaurant, down the bridge road, T020-564882, soulideth@gmail.com. Twin and double wooden bungalows with hot water, fans and lock boxes. Soulideth is full of local information and advice. Also internet access (expensive at 1000 kip per min), international calls, room service, laundry, book exchange, a substantial music collection. He runs a good range of sevices including bike rentals and just about anything else you could ask for. There is a laundry next door (10,000 kip per kilo).

E-F Sypaseuth Guesthouse & Restaurant, right next to the bridge. Wooden bungalows right on the riverbank are slightly run down but have fans and en suite bathrooms for only US$4. Also have 4 dingy concrete rooms set back from the river for US$6, and a couple of hovel-like triple rooms without a bathroom for US$2-3. Also a restaurant serving decent Lao food for US$1-2.

F Sailomen Guesthouse, next along the riverbank. Small, clean thatched bungalows with en suite bathrooms for US$2.50.

Salavan p238, map p238

E Silsamay 2 Guesthouse, just down the road from **Shai Kham**, T020-5548054. Bright, clean, well-furnished rooms with a/c or just a fan. Bathrooms have hot water and Western toilets. Recommended.

E-F Chindavong, T034-211065. There are 2 types of room on offer here. The cheaper rooms are basic, with fan but no en suite bathroom, the more expensive ones will be beautifully decorated, bamboo-clad, homely twin or double, with a/c, en suite bathroom, writing table, television, and 'chill out' area. Restaurant attached (no menu!). Recommended.

E-F Thiphaphone, T034-211063. Next to the **Chindavong** on the market side. Clean (but musty) basic rooms with wooden walls and decent mattresses. Some have a/c, TV and hot water, others only have fans. Spotless bathrooms, some en suite, some communal.

F Miss Asam, next to the Thiphaphone, T034-211062. This is a tiny little place, with very basic rooms. Not in the least bit customer focused.

F Saise Hotel, 2.5 km from the bus station on the other side of town near the river (get there by tuk-tuk), T034-211054/213775. Attractive guesthouse in large garden compound. The newer building has bright a/c rooms of a good standard with hot water; the older building has huge dank rooms with fans and large 'bathrooms' (tank of water and dipper, squat toilet). The management speak English and French – a useful source of information.

There are a couple of other establishments on the road to Pakse, about 1 km from the bus station.

Around Salavan p240

B-C Utayan Bajiang Champasak, T031-251294. This resort, beside the lovely Paseum waterfall, consists of ethnic-styled bungalows, a tree house and various other types of accommodation. There's also a restaurant by the water's edge. The resort caters predominantly to Thai package tourists and as a result there isn't much transport to get there. You will need to either travel independently or organize through a Pakse tour operator such as **Sabaidy 2**. There's a 5000 kip fee to enter the compound.

Sekong p240, map p241

E Koky Guesthouse, just off the main road towards the post office, T031-211401. A little house with rooms for rent. Service is very friendly but no English is spoken. Rooms have a/c and TV.

E Sackda, between the market and the water tower, T031-211086. Clean and very blue: blue sheets, blue walls, blue curtains, resulting in an overall blue glow. Basic rooms with a/c or a fan. Attached bathrooms have a shower and squat toilet.

E-F Sekong Souksamlane Hotel (aka Sekong Hotel), a block back from the post office, T031-211030, pholsena@laotel.com. Old, but apparently popular with the few local *falangs*, partly due to the attached restaurant, which will cook whatever you want, as long as the food is available at the local market (or just order from the English menu). 16 rooms, with a/c or fan, some with en suite bathrooms, cold shower, very functional and rather worn and dusty but OK for an overnight stop. Also 1 dorm room with 4 beds (**F**). The best rooms are upstairs; they have a balcony and get the mountain breeze. One of the rooms is reputedly haunted by some Malaysian UN officials who were drowned taking a boat downriver to Attapeu; they left their bags in their room and come back every so often to retrieve them.

F Woman Fever Kosment Center Guesthouse, the block behind the post office, T031-211046. Looks like a Lao government office or a large school with cement foundations and a wooden 2nd storey. The very spacious, very basic rooms go for 30,000 kip with a fan, and the shared bathroom has a *mundi* and squat toilet.

Attapeu *p242, map p243*
B-D ATP Palace (formerly the **Hotel Yingchokchay**), T031-212204, www.offroad.laotel.com. Renamed by the current owners, and a favourite with government officials and businessmen, this enormous and slightly decaying building offers rooms from US$6 (with fan) to US$25 (suites). The lovely rooms are plain, large and simple, with sweet dream-inducing mattresses and great en suite bathrooms. Breakfast is included. Internet access is available (when it's working) for 1000 kip per min.

F Aloon Sot Sai Guesthouse, 2 doors down from the **Soksomphone**, T031-211250. Small somewhat dingy rooms with fan, TV and en suite bathrooms for US$3-5. Rents motorbikes for US$10 per day.

F Soksomphone Guesthouse, T031-211046. 16 small but well-furnished

and airy rooms, some with en suites, some with TVs, others with enormous beds and clean shared bathrooms (*mundi* and squat toilet). Owners are slack but speak some English and French. Tours can be arranged to the surrounding area (but shop around first). Bicycles for hire.

⑤ Eating

Paksong and around *p234*
There are a small string of barbecue restaurants, past the market away from Route 23. The market also has a large restaurant section and there's a row of Vietnamese restaurants along Route 23 near the bank.

Borravan Plateau, Route 23 about 1 km from the market towards Tha Teng. Standard selection of Lao dishes in an indoor setting, safe from the weather. The owner is very friendly. Unfortunately there is no menu and no English spoken – so opt for something easy like *feu* or *laap*.

Cafés
Travellers Meeting Point Café, south of Route 23. Coffee tasting, good local advice.

Tad Lo *p235, map p236*
There are also a number of small Lao joints along the main road.
Jom, friendly with a good range of dishes.
Tad Lo Lodge, see Sleeping. A better albeit pricier option serving a variety of Thai Lao and Western dishes.
Tim's Guesthouse, see Sleeping. A popular restaurant serving good hearty breakfasts and some generic Western dishes.

Salavan *p238, map p238*
Most restaurants in Salavan serve much the same range of dishes. Along the road to Pakse near the handicraft centre are a number of barbecue joints offering whatever parts of a pig can be found, including just the fat. Between the handicraft centre and the market is the **Ladda Café**, a small shop set beneath a few large trees serving ice cream, etc. By the market towards the road to Pakse are a number of restaurants offering Korean grilled meat, the Lao buffet, *khao piak* and *feu*, among other things. The road into town makes a 90° turn to the left; just

Tahoy festival

There are several Tahoy settlements around the Boloven Plateau although the Tahoy population in Laos is only about 30,000. The village of Ban Paleng, not far from Tha Teng on Route 16, is a fascinating place to visit, especially in March (in accordance with the full-moon), when the animist Tahoy celebrate their annual three-day sacrificial festival. The village is built in a circle around the kuan (the house of sacrifice). A water buffalo is donated by each family in the village. The buffalo has its throat cut and the blood is collected and drunk.

The raw meat is divided among the families and surrounding villages are invited to come and feast on it. The head of each family throws a slab of meat into the lak khai – a basket hanging from a pole in front of the kuan – so that the spirits can partake too. The sacrifice is performed by the village shaman, then dancers throw spears at the buffalo until it dies. The villagers moved from the Vietnam border area to escape the war, but Ban Paleng was bombed repeatedly: the village is still littered with shells and unexploded bombs.

beyond is a small road on the right heading towards the Xe Don and Sekong. There are a few decent little restaurants here. The 2nd of the 3 is the best, and will make whatever you ask for, if they can understand your Lao.
♥ **Vilayvone**, on the airstrip side of the market. The only place in town with a written menu – and it's even in English. Offers MSG-laden Lao standards; the French fries are Salavan's sole attempt at Western food.

Sekong p240, map p241
All of the restaurants close relatively early, so last orders are no later than 2100. There are noodle shops in and around the market.
♥ **Khamting Restaurant**, next to Phathip. Popular with the locals, but no *falang* options and no English menu.
♥ **Phathip Restaurant**, opposite the Sekong Hotel. Owned by Nang Tu, a Vietnamese woman with considerable culinary expertise. The huge platters are a treat, especially the Vietnamese options. An amazing range of dishes on offer considering the location. The same *falangs* who have obviously helped with the menu must have also taught the chef a few things. The front of the menu boasts all sorts of information about the area, including dire warnings about both the contamination of Sekong Province with the residue from the Vietnam War, and 'the odd grumpy *falangs* that for one reason or the other seem to be more or less resident in this forgotten corner of South-east Asia'.
♥ **Somview Restaurant**, on the other side of the **Phathip**. Typical Lao food.
♥ **Souksamlane Restaurant**, attached to Sekong Hotel. Traditional Lao dishes and some European food. Tribal artefacts adorn the walls and are for sale. Not always open.

Attapeu p242, map p243
Attapeu is a small town and looking for an open restaurant after 2100 could prove quite difficult. Most establishments serve the local breakfast speciality *feu* 0700-0800. Just up from **Souksomphone Guesthouse** towards the wat and almost opposite each other are a few places selling ready-made Lao food in pots, cheap and good. There are also a number of noodle shops in the same area and near the boat jetty on the south side of town.
♥ **Sekong River Restaurant**, superb location down by the river. The speciality is goat, not fish as you might expect, prepared any way you can think of. Fish and other dishes are also available. It's also a good spot for a drink.
♥ **Thi Thi Restaurant**, between Wat Luang Muang Mai and the bridge, T031-211054. Vietnamese food, with lots of seafood, including eel and tortoise, cooked in a variety of imaginative ways; sometimes it's best not to ask!

✪ Entertainment

Salavan *p238, map p238*
Salavan lacks any sort of discos or bars but
most restaurants serve **Beer Lao**. The closest
thing to night-time entertainment is the
beer garden on the road to Pakse across
from the Shai Kham and Silsamay
Guesthouses. It's popular with locals from
about 1600 onwards, but beware that your
drink order might be doubled and come
complete with someone to drink it for you.

✺ Festivals and events

Tad Lo *p235, map p236*
Buffalo ceremony This traditional Tahoy
ceremony (page 247) takes place in a nearby
village on the first full moon in **Mar** and is
dedicated to the warrior spirit, whom the
local tribesmen ask for protection. Villagers
are happy for tourists to come and watch
(5000 kip per person). The spectacle kicks off
at about 2000, with dancing; the buffalo is
sacrificed the next morning at 0500.
Throughout the day, the entire village shares
the meat of the sacrificed animal, as well as
leaving some choice pieces for the spirits of
the dead warriors in the Ceremony House.
Tim's Guesthouse (see Sleeping) is the best
place to go for the low-down on this event.

◔ Shopping

Salavan *p238, map p238*
The **handicraft centre** near the market has a
decent selection of locally made textiles,
baskets and other locally made products. The
shop selling electrical goods also has some
allegedly tribal artefacts (probably overpriced
and being passed off as antiques). Basketry
items and traditional cloth pieces can be
found in and around the **market**; a craft shop
on the market square offers similar objects.

Sekong *p240, map p241*
Sekong Ethnic Store, a block back from the
Sekong Souksamlane Hotel, sells woven
basket 'backpacks' and other local products.
Alak and Katu woven textiles.

▲ Activities and tours

To organize **kayaking** and **rafting** trips
to the Boloven Plateau, contact **Green
Discovery**, in Pakse, see page 230.

Tad Lo *p235, map p236*
Elephant trekking
This is an excellent way to see the area
as there are few roads on the plateau and
elephants can go where jeeps cannot. It is
also a thrill being on the back of an elephant.
Contact any of the guesthouses (50,000 kip
per person, 1½ hrs; 2 people per elephant).

Attapeu *p242, map p243*
Attapeu Provincial Tourism Office,
northwest edge of town, has guides,
brochures and maps.
Attapeu Tours & Travel Co Ltd, ATP Palace
Hotel, T031-211204, offer trekking, ticketing
and car rental service. Aimed at the Viet/
Thai tourist crowds.

◉ Transport

Paksong and around *p234*
Bus
Regular connections to **Pakse**'s southern bus
terminal 0630-1600, 1½ hrs, 15,000 kip. For
onward journey to **Tad Fan** ask the *songthaew*
to stop at Km 38 and follow signs. Also buses to
Attapeu, daily 0830 and 1200, 3½-4½ hrs.

Tha Teng *p235*
Bus/songthaew
All transport departs from the market.
To **Salavan**, 0730 and 0830 daily, 1½ hrs,
10,000 kip; to **Sekong**, 0730, 1 hr, 10,000 kip;
to **Pakse**, 0530, 0630, 0730 and 0830 daily,
at least 2 hrs (87 km), 20,000 kip. Due to
its location many unscheduled buses pass
through Tha Teng between Pakse, Salavan
and Sekong, or Salavan, Paksong and
Attapeu. *Songthaew* leave intermittently
(most in the morning) for nearby destinations.

Tad Lo *p235, map p236*
Bus
There are buses from Ban Houei Set (1.5 km
north of Tad Lo) to **Pakse**, 5 daily, 20,000 kip;
also to **Salavan** (from either Pakse or Lao
Ngam), every hr daily 0730-1600, 40 mins,
7000 kip. You may also be able to catch the
daily service to **Vientiane** on its way north,
daily 0930 and 1430, 85,000 kip but don't
expect it to be on time.

Salavan *p238, map p238*
Bus/truck
The bus terminal is 2 km west of the town centre; a tuk-tuk either way costs about 10,000-15,000 kip. Salavan is by no means a tourist hub, which means the reliability of buses is dicey at best; scheduled connection times are as follows: to **Pakse**, 0630, 0730, 0830, 1000, 1215 and 1330 daily, 116 km, 3 hrs, 20,000 kip; to **Sekong**, 0730 and 1300 daily, 98 km, 4 hrs, 18,000 kip; to **Khong Xedon**, 1030 daily, 76 km, 3½ hrs, 17,000 kip, but most Savannakhet-bound buses will pass through as well; to **Lao Ngam** (via **Tad Lo**), 0600, 0815, 0945 and 1200 daily, 1 hr, 10,000 kip; to **Ta Oy**, 1100 daily but departure time varies wildly depending on the season, 84 km, 6 hrs, 28,000 kip; to **Savannakhet**, 0630 daily, 40,000 kip; to **Tha Teng**, 1000 daily, 10,000 kip; to **Vientiane**, 0830 daily, 85,000 kip. There are no buses further north than **Toum Lan**, 1430 daily, 15,000 kip.

Trickier destinations to get to from Salavan include **Attapeu** (you have to go by bus to Sekong, then find a bus to Attapeu) and **Lao Bao** (the best way is via Savannakhet and then along Route 9).

Sekong *p240, map p241*
Boat
To **Attapeu** down the Xe Kong, a beautiful and worthwhile trip, 5-7 hrs, US$50-60, check at the port or at the **Phathip Restaurant** (see Eating). Make sure you have a life jacket as at times the river can be hazardous. Boats take about 4 people and need to be chartered privately. This trip comes highly recommended.

Bus/truck
The bus station is 2.5 km out of town (tuk-tuk 5000 kip); some also stop on the highway near the hospital. To **Salavan**, 0600 and 1330 daily, 98 km, 3-4 hrs, 20,000 kip; to **Pakse** (via **Paksong**), 0530 and 0600 daily, 4-6 hrs, 25,000 kip. The lone bus to **Attapeu** leaves at 0800 daily, 2-3 hrs, 15,000 kip. This schedule is not set in concrete as buses are passing through.

Attapeu *p242, map p243*
Bicycle
Bikes can be hired from the **Souksomphone Guesthouse** for 20,000 kip.

Boat
An alternative way to get to **Ban Mai** is to charter a boat to Xe Nam Sai and pick up a connection from there.

It is possible to travel upriver from Attapeu to **Sekong**, but it would take much longer than downriver and be quite expensive.

Bus/truck
The main bus station is at the market 3 km northwest of town. Efficiency around the bus station is simply not on the agenda, and although there are daily connections with the main tourist hubs, departure times are a source of great argument and debate. Prices are more definite. A rough departure schedule follows, but you should check all onward connections on your arrival. To **Pa-am**, 30 km, 12,000 kip (or charter a tuk-tuk, US$15 return); to **Pakse**, from the market, 4 times daily, in the morning, 5-6 hrs, 35,000 kip; to **Sekong**, 1430 daily, 2-3 hrs, 20,000 kip (or you can take the Pakse or Savannakhet bus); to **Vientiane**, 0800 and 1100 daily, 20-24 hrs, 110,000 kip (take warm clothes as it can be chilly and uncomfortable); to **Savannakhet**, 0600 daily, 10-12 hrs, 65,000 kip. To get to **Salavan** you will have to transfer at Tha Teng. There are buses to **Ban Mai**, 0800, 1200 and 1400 daily, 1 hr (returning at 1600) but it is probably better to rent a tuk-tuk for around US$15 per day.

● Directory

Salavan *p238, map p238*
Banks Lao Development Bank, near the market, will exchange cash (US$ and Thai ฿) and TCs, open Mon-Fri. The shop selling electrical goods will also change money.
Post and telephone The post office is in a modern yellow building opposite the market; local calls only from telephone exchange in same building. For international calls, go to the **Telecoms centre**, Mon-Sat.

Sekong *p240, map p241*
Banks Lao Development Bank will exchange US$ and Thai ฿ only. **Post and telephone** Post office is in a yellow building not far from the Victory *That*; the telecommunications centre is next door, international calls possible.

Banks Lao Development Bank, Mon-Fri
0830-1630, reputed to change US$ and Thai
฿ only, despite what it says. Money changers
can be found around the market area;

try the gold/jewellery shops. **Post and
telephone** Post office, in town centre,
Mon-Fri 0800-1200 and 1300-1600. The
telephone office is next door, Mon-Sat
0700-1700, international calls.

Islands of the south

➔ *Phone code: 031. Colour map 3, C2/3.*

*This area, locally known as Siphandon, 'The 4000 Islands', is an idyllic picture-perfect
ending to any trip to Laos. The three main islands offer something for all tourists: the
larger Don Khong is great for exploring, take in the stunning vista and the traditional Lao
rural life; Don Deth is a backpacker haven and is good if you want to while away the days
with a good book in a hammock; and Don Khone is better for those wanting to take in
tourist sites such as the Li Phi falls or old colonial ruins. These are just three of the many
islands littered across the Mekong right at the southern tip of Laos near the border with
Cambodia. Half of the islands are submerged when the Mekong is in flood. Just before
the river enters Cambodia it divides into countless channels. The distance between the
most westerly and easterly streams is 14 km – the greatest width of the river in its whole
4200-km course. The river's volume is swelled by the Kong, San Srepok and Krieng
tributaries, which join just upstream from here. Pakha, or freshwater dolphins, can
sometimes be spotted in this area between December and May, when they come
upsteam to give birth to their young but they are increasingly endangered.* ➤➤ *For Sleeping,
Eating and other listings, see pages 258-265.*

Route 13 to Ban Hat Xai Khoune

The bus journey south from Pakse to Ban Hat Xai Khoune on Route 13 is 120 km and,
until recently, progress was excruciatingly slow. But now the whole road, including
the bridges, has been surfaced. The trip is worthwhile for the contrast it offers to
conditions in northeastern Thailand, just 20 km or so west. Much of the area is still
forested (large quantities of Lao timber are trucked to Thailand via Chongmek, west of
Pakse; see page 220) and villages are intermittent even on this road, the national
artery for north-south communications. Paddy fields sometimes appear to be fighting
a losing battle against the encroaching forest and most houses are roofed in thatch
rather than zinc. At **Ban Hat Xai Khoune** boats wait to transport passengers across the
Mekong to Don Khong and Muang Khong (see below). Further along, at Ban
Nakasang, boats shuffle tourists to Don Deth and Don Khone.

Don Khong ⬛🚻❀🚌🛈 ➤➤ *pp258-265.*

Don Khong is the largest of the Mekong islands at 16 km long and 8 km wide. It's a
tremendous place to relax or explore by bicycle. Visitors might be surprised by the
smooth asphalt roads, electricity and general standard of amenities that exist on the
island but two words explain it all – Khamtai Siphandone – Laos' former president,
who has a residence on the island. The island was electrified about five years before
the surrounding mainland areas and it is not unusual to see heavily armed personnel
cruising around the place. The former president spends much of his time on the
island, in his modest quarters near Ban Houa Khong, and ferries back and forth
between Vientiane and the island in his private helicopter. According to locals, he has
plans to establish some kind of resort on the island.

Ins and outs

Getting there The easiest way to get to all three major Siphandon islands from Pakse is by private minivan, 60,000 kip arranged by **Lane Xang Travel** and other operators in Pakse. The most luxurious way to get there is aboard the *Vat Phou* (departs Tuesdays, Thursdays and Saturdays from Pakse, www.asian-oasis.com), a beautiful boutique riverborne hotel that does a three-day/two-night cruise from Pakse to Champasak and Wat Phou to Don Khong and then back to Pakse.

In the high season *songthaew* depart Pakse's Southern bus terminal hourly between 0800 and 1200. The occasional bus will also ply the route but *songthaew* are the most common transport option. The journey to Ban Hat Xai Khoune (to catch a boat to Don Khong) should take between four and five hours and cost US$3; in most cases the bus/truck will board the **car ferry** (3000 kip) at

‡ *Make sure the bus or songthaew driver knows that you wish to go to Don Khong and not Don Khone; you need to indicate the ports closest to the islands not the islands themselves (ie Ban Hat Xai Khoune for Don Khong and Ban Nakasang for Don Deth or Don Khone).*

Mekong islands

Southern Laos Islands of the south

Ban Hat (1 km south of Ban Hat Xai Khoune) and take you right across to Ban Naa on Don Khong (1 km south of Muang Khong). There are also **motorboats** from Ban Hat Xai Khoune to Muang Khong (10,000 kip, dependent on the number of passengers). If there is not a bus directly to Don Khong, catch a bus bound for Ban Nakasang (the stop-off for Don Deth and Don Khon) and jump off at Ban Hat Xai Khoune. If by chance you get dumped at Ban Nakasang, you can arrange a boat to Don Khong from there; although this is a very pretty route it is time-consuming and costly (about US$20 and 1½ hours) and not the most efficient way to get to the island. ▶ *For further details, see Transport, page 263.*

Getting around All of the guesthouses can arrange bicycle hire for 10,000 kip per day. There are a few tuk-tuks in town but they are hardly required around tiny Muang Khong. It is, however, possible to charter a tuk-tuk, loaded with a bicycle or two, for the trip to the far side of the island and then cycle back. Some places hire motorbikes for US$10 a day.

Muang Khong

Don Khong's 'capital' is Muang Khong, a small former French settlement. 'Muang' means city but, although Muang Khong is the district's main settlement, it feels more like a village than a town, with only a few thousand inhabitants. Pigs and chickens scrabble for food under the houses and just 50 m inland the houses give way to paddy fields.

There are two wats in the town. **Wat Kan Khong**, also known as Wat Phuang Kaew, is visible from the jetty: a large gold Buddha in the *mudra* of subduing Mara garishly overlooks the Mekong. Much more attractive is **Wat Chom Thong** at the upstream extremity of the village, which may date from the early 19th century but which was much extended during the colonial period. The unusual Khmer-influenced *sim* may be gently decaying but it is doing so with style. The wat compound, with its carefully tended plants and elegant buildings, is very peaceful. The *naga* heads on the roof of the main *sim* are craftily designed to channel water, which issues from their mouths. The old *sim* to the left of the main entrance is also notable, although it is usually kept locked because of its poor condition.

For early risers the **morning market** in Muang Khong is also worthwhile – if only to see the fish before they are sold to the restaurants here and consigned to the cooking pot. Note that the market only really operates between 0530 and 0730. If you are getting up for the market,

Muang Khong

Sleeping
Auberge Sala Done Khong 1
Bounma Guesthouse 2
Mekong Guesthouse & Restaurant 4
Pon Hotel & Restaurant 5
Souksan 7
Villa Muang Khong & Restaurant 8

Eating
Souksan Chinese 2

it is worth setting the alarm clock even earlier to get onto the banks of the Mekong before 0600, when the sun rises over the hills to the east, picking out the silhouettes of fishermen in their canoes.

Exploring the island

Most people come to Muang Khong as a base for visiting the **Li Phi** and **Khong Phapheng Falls** (see pages 257 and 258) in the far south of Laos. However, these trips, alongside dolphin-watching trips are much easier to arrange from Don Deth or Don Khone. But the island is a destination in itself, and offers a great insight into Lao rural life without all the hustle and bustle found in more built-up areas. To a certain extent, save electricity, a sprinkling of cars and a couple of internet terminals, time stands still in Dong Khong.

The island is worth exploring by bicycle and deserves more time than most visitors give it. It is flat – except in the interior where there are approximately 99 hills – the roads are quiet, so there is less risk of being mown down by a timber truck, and the villages and countryside offer a glimpse of traditional Laos. Most people take the southern 'loop' around the island, via **Ban Muang Saen Nua**, a distance of about 25 km (two to three hours by bike). The villages south of Ban Muang Saen Nua are wonderfully picturesque with buffalos grazing and farmers tending to their rice crops. Unlike other parts of Laos the residents here are fiercely protective of their forests and logging incurs very severe penalties.

About 6 km north of Ban Muang Saen Nua is a hilltop wat which is arguably Don Khong's main claim to national fame. **Wat Phou Khao Kaew** (Glass Hill Monastery) is built on the spot where an entrance leads down to the underground lair of the *nagas*, known as **Muang Nak**. This underground town lies beneath the waters of the Mekong, with several tunnels leading to the surface – another is at That Luang in Vientiane. Lao legend has it that the *nagas* will come to the surface to protect the Lao whenever the country is in danger. (This means, to most Lao, whenever the Thais decide to attack.) Some people believe that the Thais tricked the Lao to build *thats* over the holes to prevent the *nagas* coming to their rescue – the hole at Wat Phou Khao Kaew is covered.

Tham Phou Khiaw is tucked away among the forests of the **Green Mountain** in the centre of the island. It's a small cave, containing earthenware pots. Buddha images and other relics and offerings litter the site. Every Lao New Year (April) townsfolk climb up to the cave to bathe the images. Although it's only 15 minutes' walk from the road, finding the cave is not particularly straightforward except during Lao New Year when it is possible to follow the crowds. Head 1.5 km north from Muang Khong on the road until you come to a banana plantation, with a couple of wooden houses. Take the pathway just before the houses through the banana plantation and at the top, just to the left, is a small gateway through the fence and a fairly well-defined path. Head up and along this path and, after 300 m or so, there is a rocky clearing. The path continues from the top right corner of the clearing for a further 200 m to a rocky mound that rolls up and to the left. Walk across the mound for about 20 m, until it levels out, and then head back to the forest. Keeping the rock immediately to your right, continue round and after 40 m there are two upturned tree trunks marking the entrance to the cave.

On the northern tip of the island is a sandy beach, though swimming is generally not advised due to parasites in the water and potentially strong currents. Word on the ground is that Lao's former President Siphandone will be building a resort here in the next few years. In nearby **Wat Houa Khong**, approximately 13 km north of Muang Khong, is the former President's modest abode set in traditional Lao style.

The Mekong: mother river of Southeast Asia

The Mekong River is the heart and soul of mainland Southeast Asia, a sinuous thread that binds Vietnam, Cambodia and Laos geographically, historically, culturally and economically.

The Mekong's source in eastern Tibet was only pin-pointed 1995. From here the giant river plies 4500 km through six countries, cutting through almost the entire length of Laos, dissecting Cambodia, and plunging into Vietnam's Mekong Delta before emptying into the South China Sea. The river is the 12th longest river in the world and is the 10th largest by volume of water dispersed into the ocean.

French explorer Francis Garnier commented that: "no other river, over such a length, has a more singular or remarkable character". The Mekong has indeed woven itself into the cultural fabric of the region and shaped its history, from the ancient Funan settlement in the Mekong Delta, through to the Khmer Empire, which established its capital at Angkor and relied on the river for transport and agriculture. After several expeditions the French, in the mid-19th century, developed grandiose plans to transform the Mekong into a river highway from China. (The plans were thwarted upon discovering that the Mekong could not be traversed.) The river later played an integral role in the Vietnam War for the running of Viet Cong supplies.

The river has been a major purveyor of culture, ushering in various religions, arts and customs and folklore, including enormous, colourful, boat races and annual water festivals, which celebrate the Mekong and its importance to agriculture. Nor is the river free from superstition or strange phenomena. In Laos thousands of people gather each year to witness naga fireballs rising from the river's surface.

Today, the Mekong is instrumental in the region's future prosperity, with more than 60 million people in Southeast Asia dependent on the river and its tributaries for their survival. Agriculture, particularly the farming of rice, relies on the river's annual flood-drought cycle. During the monsoon, the river swells to 30 times its original size, depositing rich fertilizing sediments along the floodplains and riverbanks.

Fish are an important part of the Lao diet constituting 80% of many people's protein requirement. The river is home to between 770 and 1300 species of freshwater fish, including the world's largest, a giant 300 kg catfish (the size of a grizzly bear). It also shelters the endangered Irrawaddy dolphin.

However, it is unclear how much longer the Mekong can be relied on to support millions of Vietnamese, Cambodian and Lao people. In the last decade, more than 100 large dam proposals have been tabled for the Mekong Basin, while China, the source of up to 45% of the lower Mekong's water, has embarked on a massive programme for the construction of eight new dams. Two of these have been completed and are already having a detrimental effect, altering the river's natural ebb and flow. Lao also has major dams planned including one mainstream one in the Siphandon region. Whether it goes ahead or not is undecided as opposition to it is massive. Chainarong Setthachua, director of South East Asia Rivers Network has said that: "Not only is the water the lowest in its history, it is also fluctuating; sometimes up, sometimes down. This comes from dam operations in China." The Mekong River Commission (MRC) agrees, pointing out that, in places, the river has reached rock-bottom levels.

▶▶ *pp258-265.*

The islands of Don Khone and Don Deth are the pot of gold at the end of the rainbow for most travellers who head to the southern tip of Laos, and it's not hard to see why. After the relative fever and bustle of Pakse, the transport headaches around the Boloven Plateau and the architectural wonder of Wat Phou, the bamboo huts that stretch along the banks of these two staggeringly beautiful islands are filled with contented travellers in no rush to move on. Don Deth is more of a backpacker haven, not dissimilar to the Koh Phangans and Vang

> ⚡ *Make sure the bus or songthaew driver knows that you wish to go to Don Khone (via Nakasong) rather than Don Khong.*

Viengs of the region, meanwhile Don Khone has been able to retain a more authentically Lao charm. Travelling by boat in this area is very picturesque: the islands are covered in coconut palms, flame trees, stands of bamboo, kapok trees and hardwoods; the river is riddled with eddies and rapids and it demands a skilled helmsman to negotiate them. In the distance, a few kilometres to the south, are the Khong Hai Mountains, which dominate the skyline and delineate the frontier between Laos and Cambodia.

Ins and outs

Getting there A number of companies run tours to this area, especially from Pakse (see Activities and tours, page 230). Private minivans from Pakse, 60,000 kip, are the most effective way to get there timewise and are worth the few extra dollars. To get to Don Deth or Don Khone independently from Pakse the bus/*songthaew* will need to drop you off at Ban Nakasang. The *songthaew* trip from Pakse can be mildy uncomfortable, particularly if it's raining; aim for a seat away from the sides of the vehicle. There is a toothless, charmless policeman who sits in Ban Nakasang bullying tourists off the bus and forcing them to walk to the boat dock. It's not a long haul – perhaps 500 m – but can be uncomfortable if you're laden with luggage. The 'ticket office' is located in a little restaurant to the right-hand side of the dock. But you can literally ask anyone that's jumping across to the islands for a lift, at a dramatically reduced rate. The boats take about 15 to 20 minutes to make the easy trip to the islands and cost around US$3 per person. Prices will be higher (US$5-6) if you are travelling solo.

Getting around A boat between Don Deth and Don Khone costs 30,000 kip; alternatively you can walk between the two islands, paying the 9000 kip charge to cross the bridge (also used as ticket to see Li Phi Falls). Both islands can easily be navigated by foot or bicycles can be rented from guesthouses for US$1 per day. ▶▶ *For further details, see Transport, page 264.*

Background

For those who have travelled on the slow, lazy upper reaches of the Mekong, huge roaring waterfalls might seem rather out of character. But here, near the Cambodian border, the underlying geology changes and the river is punctuated by rapids and the Khone Falls. The name Khone is used loosely and there are in fact two impressive cascades in the area: the Li Phi (or Somphamit) Falls and Khong Phapheng Falls – the latter are the largest in Southeast Asia and reputedly the widest in the world. Francis Garnier was suitably impressed when he ascended the Khone cataract in 1860, his boatmen hauling their vessels "through a labyrinth of rocks, submerged trees, and prostrate trunks still clinging to earth by their many roots".

The French envisaged Don Deth and Don Khone as strategic transit points in their grandiose masterplan to create a major Mekong highway from China. In the late 19th century, ports were built at the southern end of Don Khone and at the northern end of Don Deth and a narrow-gauge railway line was constructed across Don Khone in 1897 as an important bypass around the rapids for French cargo boats sailing upriver from Phnom Penh. In 1920, the French built a bridge across to Don Deth and extended the railway line to Don Deth port. This 5-km stretch of railway has the unique distinction of being the only line the French ever built in Laos. Although the lucrative Chinese supply line was never properly realized, the route remained operational until 1940.

A colonial-style customs house still stands in the shadow of the impressive railway bridge on Don Khone. On the southern side of the island lie the rusted corpses of the old locomotive and boiler car. Before pulling into Ban Khone Nua, the main settlement on Don Khone, Don Deth's original 'port' is on the right, with what remains of its steel rail jetty.

Ban Nakasang

Ban Nakasang, the jumping-off point for Don Khone and Don Deth, is not the most pleasant of Lao towns and several travellers have complained about being ripped off here. However, it has a thriving market, where most of the islanders stock up on their goods, so it's worth having a look around before you head off to the islands, particularly if you need to pick up necessities like torches or batteries.

Don Deth

This island has really woken up to tourism in the last couple of years and the riverbank is peppered with cheap-as-chips bamboo huts and restaurants geared to accommodate the growing wave of backpacker travellers that floods south to stop and recoup in this idyllic setting. A good book, hammock and icy beverage are the orders of the day here, but those with a bit more energy should explore the truly stunning surroundings. It's a great location for watching the sunrises and sunsets, for walking through shady palms and frangipani trees and for swimming off the beaches, which attract

Don Deth & Don Khone

N

600 metres
600 yards

Sleeping
Auberge Sala Don
  Khone 11
Boun Guesthouse 13
Bounhome 7
Deng Bungalows 18
King Kong Guesthouse
  & Restaurant 8
Lamphone Bungalows 25
Mama Leuah 9
Mama Mon & Papa 20
Mama Tan On 4
Miss Noy's 2
Mr Bounpath 14
Mr B's 3
Mr Oudomsouk 17

Mr Phao's 16
Mr Tho's 27
Pan's Guesthouse
  & Restaurant 26
Paradise Bungalows 19
Poonit Bungalows 22
Salaphae 10
Santiphab Guesthouse 5
Sompamit Guesthouse 12
Souksan Guesthouse
  & Restaurant 1
Xaymountry Residence 15

Eating
Khonsavanh 2
Pool Room 5
Riverside 1
Sengaroune 4

the hordes in the dry season. Away from the picturesque waterfront, the centre of the island comprises rice paddies and farms; you should take care not to harm crops when exploring the island.

The national tourism authorities have been coordinating with locals to ensure that the beautiful island doesn't become 'Vang Vieng-ified', so you'll find no *Friends* DVDs here ... although 'Happy' shakes have started to appear. The island has no electricity (except for a generator supply 1800-2200), no cars (except for the odd truck) and few other modern conveniences. Internet has amazingly made its way to the island, however, and it's still possible to get mobile phone coverage. Talk of electrification has been on the cards for many years but, so far, has not materialized. Most guesthouses run tours to the falls/dolphins. It costs around US$5 per person to charter a boat to see the dolphins from Don Khone (a bit more from Don Deth). The dwindling population of dolphins appears between December and May. If you do take a boat out make sure you keep your distance from them. A few entrepreneurial types are starting to promote adventure tourism here. Kayaking and rafting trips can be organized through **xplore-asia/Lang Xang Travel** (near the main port) for US$20 (minimum four people), T031-212893. Several guesthouses also have tubes for rent for 5000 kip. The river's current here is probably the strongest in all of Laos, so it is definitely inadvisable to go tubing in the wet season and probably not a good idea all year round. Swimming, visiting the falls and other activities all need to be undertaken with the utmost precaution as several tourists have drowned here.

Don Khone and Li Phi Falls

From the railway bridge, follow the southwest path through **Ban Khone Thai** and then wind through the paddy fields for 1.7 km (20 minutes' walk) to **Li Phi Falls** ① *aka Somphamit or Khone Yai falls, 9000 kip entry fee, paid at the bridge*. These are a succession of raging rapids, crashing through a narrow rocky gorge. In the wet season, when the rice is green, the area is beautiful; in the dry season, it is scorching. From the main vantage point on a jagged, rocky outcrop, the falls aren't that impressive, as a large stretch of them are obscured. 'Phi' means ghost, a reference, it is believed, to the bodies that floated down the river from the north during the war.

❗ *Do not be tempted to swim in the pools near Li Phi Falls. Several people have drowned here.*

It's best to visit Li Phi around June or July, when all the fishermen are putting out their bamboo fish traps. Every year Cambodia's Tonlé Sap lake reverses its flow sending millions of fish up the Mekong into Laos. During this time, each fish trap can catch 1000-2000 kg of fish in a day. In theory, enough fish are caught in these two short months to feed half the population of Laos, although most of the catch is exported to Thailand.

Dolphin spotting

The Mekong, south of Don Khone, is one of the few places in the world where it is possible to see freshwater dolphins. They can be spotted in the late afternoon from December to May, from the French pier at the end of the island, not far from the village of **Ban Hang Khon**. The walk across Don Khone from the railway bridge is some 4 km and bicycles can be hired by asking around. However the dolphins reside in deep-water pools and it is more likely to catch a glimpse of them if you're in a boat (from **Ban Kong Ngay** or Ban Hang Khon; a boat will cost US$5 to see the dolphins).

❗ *Try to organize your trip for the late afternoon, so you can enjoy sunset on the return trip.*

In 1996 there were thought to be 30 dolphins, after which the numbers seemed to decline and, according to local data, there were fears that only four or five were left, although a new calf has recently been spotted. The Lao-Cambodian border transects the dolphin pool and the Lao boatmen have to pay US$1 to the Cambodian authorities in order to access the waters in which the dolphins reside. Cambodia gets a bit tetchy about these 'border incursions' and may, on the odd occasion, deny access.

Khong Phapheng Falls

① *Ban Thatko, US$1 entry fee for foreigners; there are a number of food and drinks stalls. Guesthouses on Don Deth and Don Khone organize trips to the falls for around 60,000 kip per person (min 5 passengers) and will usually be booked in conjunction with a trip to see the dolphins. Boats can no longer go direct to the falls, so most tours will include a tuk-tuk ride from Ban Nakasang. Tour operators charge around 70,000 kip per person for the trip, depending on the number of people.*

About 36 km south of Ban Hat Xai Khoune at Ban Thatko, a road branches off Route 13 towards Khong Phapheng Falls, which roar around the eastern shore of the Mekong for 13 km. One fork of the road leads to a vantage point, where a large wooden structure, built up on stilts, overlooks the cascades for a fantastic head-on view of the falls. When you see the huge volume of white water boiling and surging over the jagged rocks below, it is hard to imagine that there is another 10 km width of river running through the other channels. A perilous path leads down from the viewpoint to the edge of the water. Be careful here. Unsurprisingly, the river is impassable at this juncture, as an 1860s French expedition led by adventurers Doudart de Lagrée and Francis Garnier discovered. Another road leads down to the bank of the Mekong, 200 m away, just above the lip of the falls; at this deceptively tranquil spot, the river is gathering momentum before it plunges over the edge. It was said that a tongue of rock once extended from the lip of the falls, and the noise of Khong Phapheng – literally 'the voice of the Mekong' – crashing over this outcrop could be heard many miles away. The rock apparently broke off during a flood surge but the cascades still make enough noise to justify their name. You can visit the falls by catching a *songthaew* from Ban Nakasang, US$10 return.

‼ *The principal settlement near Khone Phapheng falls, and the last Laotian town of any size before the Cambodian border, is Ban Khinak.*

● Sleeping

Don Khong (Muang Khong)
p250, map p252

Most of the guesthouses in Dong Khong have undergone name changes in recent years due to a change in legislation that requires any guesthouse with 14 or more rooms to be called a hotel and pay double the tax!

A-C Villa Muang Khong, T020-5515993, also in Vientiane on T021-261870, xbtrvlmk@laotel.com. A bungalow complex with 32 tidy a/c rooms and en suite Western bathrooms (hot water). Garden and pleasant restaurant serving Lao and European food. Bicycle, boat and minivan hire plus other tour services. Again, this place is a bit on the expensive side for what is on offer and service is a little on the slack side.

B Senesothxeune Hotel, Muang Khong, T031-5280577, www.ssxhotel.com. Tastefully designed, modern interpretation of colonial Lao architecture. Beautiful fittings, including carved wooden fish above each entrance and brass chandeliers. Rooms are fitted with mod cons like a/c, TV, hot water and minibar. Superior rooms have fantastic bathtubs. For those willing to splurge US$70 upgrade to the suite that comes with spa and living area. The hotel has a modern internet café and restaurant. The menu was quite limited when we visited but the proprietors assured us this was due to change in up-and-coming months. This is island's best accommodation by a long shot. This relative newcomer is run by the gentle, softly spoken Mr Senesavath and his wife, both former mathematics professors from Don Dok University in Vientiane. Both speak English and French. Recommended.

B Villa Muong Khong Hotel Guesthouse, T031-2130111, www.khongislandtravel.com. This hotel is part chalet, part mock Tudor, part Lao and part Thai – all amalgamated together by someone with a fetish for wagon wheels and concrete. Despite the identity crisis architecture, the place is in a perfect location and offers affordable rooms and is popular with tour groups. The rooms are large but a little on the spartan side. Kitch decorations but all the mod-cons hot water, bath and a/c. Internet available.

B-C Auberge Sala Done Khong, T031-212077, www.salalao.com. This traditional wooden house, the former holiday home of the previous regime's foreign minister, was once the best place to stay on Don Khong but, although the exterior is still stunning, the rooms just aren't worth the price. There are 12 large, tastefully decorated rooms with a/c, hot water and en suite bathrooms; the best are in the main building on the 1st floor where there is an attractive balcony overlooking the Mekong with comfortable deckchairs. Beautiful tile-work in shared areas but starting to get a little run down. Clean and professionally run, tours arranged, bicycles for hire, good food – very relaxing. Massages can be arranged. Slightly cheaper rate in the low season. Restaurant attached.

B-E Mekong Guesthouse, T031-213668. Simple, spotless rooms with fans, some overlooking the Mekong and all with comfortable mattresses. Some rooms have a/c and hot showers (US$20). There are also cheaper rooms with shared facilities (equally clean) in a wooden building.

B-E Souksan Hotel, northern end of town near Wat Chom Thong, T031-212071. The reception is in a homely building at the front, while the main accommodation area is in a block further back. Well-designed a/c rooms with en suite bathrooms and hot water set around a concrete garden. In a separate building, with bizarre river landscape paintings, the rooms are nicely decorated and comfortable with desk, cane chairs, tiled floorboards and hot water. For US$5 the fan rooms represent exceptional value. If you desire a/c the price is hiked up to US$30. They also run one of the most up-market guesthouses on Don Deth.

C-E Khang Kong Villa Guesthouse, back from the main road, town centre, T031-213539. Fantastic traditional Lao wooden building spruced up with some colourful paint. Spacious clean rooms, with or without a/c.

D-E Pon Hotel and Restaurant, T031-214037. The large, spotless rooms are very good value, with hot showers, mozzie nets and com-fortable beds for US$6. For US$10 you get a/c. Mr Pon, who speaks French and English, is perhaps the most helpful of all accommodation proprietors on the island and can offer an endless supply of tourist information and travel arrangements. Motorbike rental US$10 per day, US$5 per

½ day and bicycles US$1 per day. He can also arrange trips to the Cambodian border, to Don Deth and Don Khon and back to Pakse. In fact, Mr Pon should be your first point of contact for any needs. Massage can be organized in your room for 50,000 kip Recommended.

F Bounma Guesthouse, just off the main river road. Set in an old wooden building are a number of pungent but homely rustic rooms, decorated with interesting artefacts, and en suite cold-water bathrooms. There is a lovely communal area upstairs which looks over the grassy village area.

Ban Nakasang p256
Why anyone would want to stay in this town when the islands are 15 mins away is beyond comprehension but in case some kind of catastrophe strikes you can stay at the Nakasang Guesthouse (**F**), on the main road towards the river, a wooden house with very basic rooms and shared facilities.

Don Deth p256, map p256
Many people tend to make their choice of accommodation on the basis of word-of-mouth recommendations from other travellers; this is as good a way to choose as any, as the accommodation is all cheap and usually much of a muchness. It normally consists of spartan, thread-bare bungalows with bed, mosquito net and hammock, and shared squat toilets (unless otherwise stated). Always opt for a bungalow with a window, as the huts can get very hot. The wooden bungalows don't provide as much ventilation as the rattan equivalents but tend to attract fewer insects. Always check that the bungalow has a mosquito net. Other things to consider is the distance from the toilet to the bungalow (a midnight bolt across a rice paddy isn't much fun), the state of the hammock, whether there is a restaurant attached and whether generator power is provided. Note that there may be a small price-hike in accommodation in the near future to ensure that tourism benefits all of the island's inhabitants, including the farmers. Costs are likely to double once the island gets electricity.

The accommodation runs along both sides of the island, known as the **Sunset Side** and **Sunrise Side**. There is a large conglomeration of accommodation towards the northern tip, which is a good option for those wishing to socialize and hop between the various establishments' restaurants/bars; this is also the most common drop-off point. As a general rule, if you want peace and quiet, head for the bungalows towards the centre of each coast; ask the boat drivers to drop you off directly at the bungalows as it can be a difficult hike with baggage. There is really very little discernable difference between most lodgings on the Don Deth, so if you're looking for truly inspirational accommodation pop across to Don Khon.

Sunset Side

D-E Souksan Guesthouse and Restaurant, T031-212071, Houa Deth at the northern tip of the island, at the pinnacle of the Sunset and Sunrise sides. Convenient and very close to the dock, this place justifiably claims to offer the best view of the sunset. Mrs Khamsone cleared the area which now houses 20 or so twin and double rooms built from wood and bamboo with shared shower and toilets, not to mention a legendary Chinese restaurant. There are also a couple of concrete bungalows that are slightly more expensive. The beautiful garden is home to hundreds of butterflies, with little paths linking up to the restaurant. This place unfairly gets a bad wrap by those looking for ultra-budget accommodation; however, if you're looking for something a little more comfortable this is the island's only option; it is the hands-down winner on the island and more than worth the extra few bucks. That said, Don Khone still offers better accommodation at a more reasonable price.

F Miss Noy's, very close to the island tip and a small hike from the main drop-off dock, this place offers an excellent view of the sunset. Restaurant in a prime position with a good variety of dishes. The service here is exceptional. The owners are about to open several, clean, concrete bungalows which should be very comfortable and one of the island's more promising offerings.

F Mr B's, near the northern tip. The bungalows and grounds themselves are a bit lacklustre and there are chooks pecking around the back yard. However, the river views and the helpful staff make this an outstanding option.

Sunrise Side

F Bounhome, close to Bouasone towards the centre of the island. 5 bungalows in either rattan or wood. Small badminton court. The pigs tied to the huts don't improve the atmosphere.

F Deng Bungalows, next to Mr Oudomsouk's. Wooden bungalows on stilts. Very popular with those who want to hang on a hammock overlooking the water. Scenic position.

F King Kong Guesthouse and Restaurant, riverside, midway along the Sunrise Side. 3 spartan rattan bungalows and a smallish restaurant. Bike hire US$1. Tours and travel services.

F Lamphone Bungalows, mid-way down the island. 3 rattan bungalows, basic but lovely, and the restaurant here is good. An added bonus is the resident Australian baker who cooks up a mean foccacia and chocolate and banana donuts.

F Mama Leuah, on the south side of the former French concrete port towards the centre of the island. Several bungalows that have seen better days. Shared squat toilet facilities.

F Mama Mon and Papa, on the northern peninsula. Typical thatched bamboo bungalows with mozzie nets and shared facilities. Nice shady position. The restaurant has battery-powered lights for the night-time blackout and serves a pretty exceptional lentil curry.

F Mama Tan On, T020-5835699. This place changes its name every year but the atmosphere remains unchanged. One of the first bungalows on the island. If you are having trouble finding it also ask for some of its previous incarnations **Mama Rasta** or **Mama Tanon Rasta**. There is a beautiful view from the communal balcony and the effervescent Mama is good value with her jovial demeanour and back-slapping, cheeky quips. Small library. The place is somewhat down-trodden, with rattan huts and communal facilities but is popular for hanging out in the hammocks.

F Mr Oudomsouk, north of the old concrete French port. 4 spartan huts, with a couple of newish wooden bungalows. Small restaurant with a few board games and dominoes. Seems to be where the local monks like to chill out.

F Mr Phao's, riverfront. Brand spanking new wooden bungalows with lovely carved wooden furniture.

F Mr Tho's, T020-6567502. Wooden stilt bungalows with good hammocks and views of Don Khon. The staff are friendly. Rooms have unusual names, such as 'sticky rice bungalow', 'bamboo bungalow'. Advance booking necessary. Restaurant attached.

F Paradise Bungalows, north of the centre, next door to **Deng Guesthouse**. Wooden stilted bungalows in a very enchanting location. Note that the shared facilities are a long way from the bunglows, which makes for an annoying midnight dash to the loo.

F Poonit Bungalows, close to the dock. The big plus here is the sheer convenience of being close to the boats. However, the accommodation is very basic. Bike hire.

F Santiphab Guesthouse, far end of the island. 7 basic rattan bungalows right beside the bridge, most have the quintessential hammock. Idyllic setting, flanked by the Mekong on one side and rice paddies on the other – a friendly, timeless place. Good for those who want to be secluded and with quick access to Don Khone. Very cheap restaurant serves tasty fare along with buckets of atmosphere. Very little English spoken.

Don Khone *p257, map p256*
Although Don Deth attracts the vast majority of tourists, Don Khone holds its own by offering some very pleasant accommodation alternatives and close proximity to most of the attractions. In general, Don Khone evokes a much friendlier atmosphere.

B-C Salaphae, along from **Auberge Sala Don Khone**, T030-5256390, www.salalao.com. This is the most unusual accommodation in the whole Siphandon area. 3 rafts (and 6 rooms) are managed by ex-lawyer, Lesotho. Rooms have been decorated simply, with all the minor touches that can make accommo-dation outstanding. Hot water bathrooms. A wonderful deck, with seating overlooks the stunning river scenery. Fantastic restaurant. It's starting to get a little run down but is still a fantastic option. The proprietor also plans

to create a deluxe camping site and bunga-lows on another nearby island, Khon Pasoi which is 1.5 km from Don Khong. When these are completed they will be a great option for those tourists truly wanting to get away from it all. Check website for details.

B-D Auberge Sala Don Khone, Ban Khone Nua, T020-5633718, www.salalao.com. A former French hospital built in 1927, this is one of the nicest places to stay on the island. 2 traditional Luang Prabang-style houses have been built in the grounds, with 6 rooms, all with en suite hot shower and toilet, some with a/c. The restaurant, across from the guesthouse, is one of the best places to dine on any of the 3 islands, with an unobscured waterfront view from the comfy deckchairs and a good selection of food that offers great relief from the menus found in every other establishment. Generator 1800-2200. Reduced rate in low season. Tours and boat trips organized. The owner speaks excellent English.

C Pan's Guesthouse, opposite **Xaymountry**, T030-5346939. A relative newcomer to Don Khone, these wooden bungalows are exceptionally good value for money. The 6 riverside bungalows with hot water, fan and comfy mattresses are simple but comfortable and ultra clean. Mr Pan runs a small generator which means fans can stay on into the wee hours of the morning. He is truly one of the most helpful hosts in Siphandon and is at his guests' beck and call. Highly recommended for those on a limited budget.

F Boun Guesthouse, next door to **Auberge Sala Don Khone**. Mr Boun has built a couple of basic thatched bungalow with shared facilities and a few, newer wooden ones, with en suite bathrooms.

F Mr Bounpath, next door to **Sompamit**. Small thatched bungalows overlooking the river, very basic, shared facilities. Bike hire US$1 per day. Small restaurant attached.

F Sompamit Guesthouse, across from **Boun Guesthouse**, on the riverside, T020-5733145. Threadbare rattan thatched bungalows with mosquito nets and shared cold-water bathroom facilities. Also a couple of basic rooms with en suite bathrooms.

F Xaymountry Residence, towards the

bridge, T020-5735755. This absolutely splendid old wooden villa with polished floorboards does not live up to the potential grandeur of its exterior. Tacky linoleum floor covering but clean en suite bathrooms, some shared. No river views but magnificent old building.

🍴 Eating

Don Khong (Muang Khong)
p250, map p252

The majority of restaurants only serve fish and chicken: killing a pig or cow requires a lot of hungry diners. In the low season most restaurants will only be able to fulfill about half of the menu options. Special dishes such as a roast or *hor mok* will also need to be ordered at least a few hours, if not a day in advance to ensure the proprietors have the required produce in stock. Although many other towns and areas also make such a claim, Don Khong is renowned for the quality of its *la-lao* (rice liquor). Local fish with coconut milk cooked in banana leaves, *mok pa*, is a truly divine local speciality, which makes a trip to the islands worthwhile in itself.

†††-† Souksan Chinese Restaurant. Attractive place with a stunning, unobscured view of the river. Funnily enough there is an absence of Chinese food but there are other more generic Asian options including good local fish and tasty honeyed chicken. In recent years they have added a number of Western specialities, including the US$5 roast (beef, chicken or pork with potatoes and gravy), which needs to be ordered a day in advance.

† Mekong Restaurant, attached to the Mekong Hotel, see Sleeping. This restaurant is pleasantly positioned near the bank of the Mekong and provides legendary fare at seriously low prices. Good *feu*.

† Pon's Restaurant, see Sleeping, T031-214037. Good atmosphere, excellent food, try the fish soup. Also the *mok pa* here is excellent, order in advance. Very popular.

† Villa Muang Khong Hotel Restaurant, see Sleeping. Lao and European food – a limited but good selection of dishes.

Ban Nakasang *p256*

Two small thatched beachside restaurants serve good chicken *feu*. In the rainy season they move further up the bank. There are also food and drinks stalls on the right as you get off the boat.

Don Deth *p256, map p256*

Most people choose to eat at their guesthouses; they all have pretty much the same menu.

†††-† Mr B's, see Sleeping. Italian bruschetta, rice pudding and a famous selection of burgers including chicken and pumpkin. Good cocktails.

† Miss Noy's, see Sleeping. A large menu with some good Western offerings, a change from the rest of the places on the island.

† The Pool Room and Restaurant, near the main port. Has a pool table and fantastic Indian and Malay food. Good service.

† Souksan, see Sleeping. Excellent Chinese-inspired dishes in addition to well-cooked fish. The restaurant is in a prime location to take in the sunset. Will cook up a roast for US$5 with advanced notice.

There are also 2 cheap restaurants beside the dock: Riverside Restaurant and Khonsavanh Restaurant. They both offer outstanding river views but mediocre food and service. The Riverside is marginally better, predominantly due to the range of visa and travel services it can offer. Great places to watch the sun go down with an icy beverage but eat elsewhere.

Cafés and bakeries

Lamphone Bungalows, see Sleeping. For freshly baked goodies including foccacia.

Don Khone *p257, map p256*

Don Khone has better eateries and accommodation than Don Deth but remember that, in low season, most restaurants won't be able to provide many of their dishes due to the lack of supplies.

††† Auberge Sala Don Khone, see Sleeping. There's a beautiful view from the restaurant and some fine options on the menu, such as tuna and orange salad or steak salad. The service here is 5-star. Some of the more complicated options will need to be booked in advance.

††† Salaphae, see Sleeping. The best choice on the island, with a selection of scrumptious and creative dishes.

† Pan's Restaurant, across from his guesthouse (see Sleeping). A fantastic option on the island serving up brilliant home-made meals. The fish here is outstanding.

ⓨ **Sengaroune**, near the bridge, T020-5735009. Huge restaurant with large deck. Local Lao and Vietnamese-inspired cuisine. Good spring rolls. Very popular with the locals.

✹ Festivals

Don Khong *p250, map p252*
Dec A 5-day **Boat Racing** festival takes place early in the month, on the river opposite Muang Khong. It coincides with National Day on 2 Dec and is accompanied by a great deal of celebration, eating and drinking.

O Shopping

Don Deth *p256, map p256*
There isn't much to buy here. A small grocery store across from the port has a few essential items and snacks but is not very well stocked. If you're in desperate need of any items, make a quick trip to Ban Nakasang and pick up things from the market there. Most guesthouses go to Ban Nakasang on an almost daily basis and will usually buy things for you if you pay them 5000 kip or so.

▲ Activities and tours

Don Deth, Don Khone and around
p255, map p256
For boat trips, see page 264. Almost every guesthouse on the islands can arrange tours, transport and tickets. The best way to book yourself onto a tour on Don Deth is through the 'whiteboard' system. Whiteboards have been placed around the island (the most popular one is at the northern end, near the port); simply write your name down next to the tour or trip you wish to take. From Don Khone, it is possible to hire a boat for the day, to visit the islands and go fishing.

Fishing and dolphin watching
From **Don Khone**, it is possible to hire a boat for the day, to visit the islands and go fishing or dolphin watching. Boats depart from Kong Ngay, US$10, see Transport, page 264. On **Don Khone**, boats depart from Kong Ngay, US$5-10.

Boats from **Don Deth** depart when they have enough passengers and charge about US$6 per person; put your name on the noticeboard the day before. Rates are highly subject to change as they are based on petrol prices and the individual boatman's prerogative more than anything else. The best bet is to gather 4 or 5 people and then approach a boatman.

Khammunysai Bungalows organizes fishing trips, though most tour operators would be able to arrange a day out fishing if you asked. All tour operators offer trips to Khon Phapeng, 70,000 kip each, minimum 4 people.

Swimming
There is a sandy beach on **Don Khone** where many travellers like to take a dip. However, in the wet season this can be particularly dangerous as there is a nasty undercurrent and tourists have drowned here, so be careful. The other thing to consider is the parasite called schistosomiasis.

⊖ Transport

Don Khong *p250, map p252*
Boat
See also Ins and outs, page 252.

Pon's Hotel (reliable and recommended) can arrange boats to **Don Deth** or **Don Khone**. There are also several boatmen on the riverfront who are more than happy to take people for the right price. Fares tend to fluctuate according to international fuel prices but the going rate at the time of publication was US$15-20 for up to 10 people, one way. Expect to pay around 40,000 kip per person. Most leave around 0800-0830.

Bus/truck
A bus to **Pakse** departs from the intersection near Wat Kan Khong at around 0800 daily but it's worth asking the guesthouse owners for the most recent transport information; for earlier departures to **Pakse**, cross to Ban Hat Xai Khoune and try for transport south. *Songthaew* and buses head to Pakse at 0600, 0700, 0800, 0900, 3-4 hrs, US$4.

The minibus service back to Pakse can be organized by Mr Pon, it costs 70,000 kip (much more expensive than in the other direction) and includes ferry and drop off directly at your hotel in Pakse (2 hrs).

✷ Border essentials: Voen Kham-Don Kralor (Cambodia)

It is easy to get to Cambodia from the islands of Siphandon, although rules and regulations change regularly so it is better to check in advance. River transport has been superceded by road transport, making the crossing between Voen Kham (Laos) and Don Kralor (Cambodia) the most popular. It is still possible to cross at the river crossing at Voen Kham but hiring a boat will cost in excess of US$100 and is hardly worth it (though the trip is beautiful). The Cambodian post at Voen Kham is closed, so you will still have to get stamped in or out at Don Kralor anyway. Cambodian visas are available on the border and cost US$20 for 30 days. You will need two passport photographs; for a hefty fee, the Cambodian officials are happy to provide you with some. Lao visas are not available at the border and will need to be arranged in advance from

Phnom Penh. The Cambodian border is officially open daily 0800-1700, however border officials will process outside of these times for a overtime fee; expect to pay anywhere between US$3 and US$5 on the Cambodian side and a little less on the Lao side. On both sides of the border, officials will charge US$1 to stamp your passport.

Most tourism operators can arrange buses from Don Khong, Don Deth and Done Khone. From Don Khong, Mr Pon can organize transport by road to Don Kralor, Cambodia, US$18. You will need to change vehicles on the Cambodian side. Longer trips can be organized direct to Kratie US$25 (six hours) or direct to Phnom Penh US$31 (a massive 10- to 12-hour trip). Mr Pon can also organize transport for visitors from the Cambodian side back to Don Khong.

Ban Nakasang *p256*
Boat
To **Don Deth** and **Don Khone**, 15-20 mins, 30,000 kip per person. To **Don Khong**, 2 hrs, US$15-20 (divided between the passengers).

Bus/songthaew
Decent buses depart from Ban Nakasang's market, 3 daily in the morning – last one at 0800, northbound for **Pakse**, 40,000 kip; some continue onwards to **Vientiane**; get off at **Ban Hat Xai Khoune** for the crossing to **Don Khong**, US$1. To get to **Don Kralor** (on the Cambodian border) most guesthouses can organize the trip. Cambodian visas are available on the border but Lao visas weren't at the time of publication so these need to be organized in advance from the Cambodian side. Most guesthouses will sell tickets on a minivan to **Don Kralor**, the largest town on the other side of the Cambodian border, 130,000 kip, 2 hrs. Tickets can also be bought further to Kratie or Phnom Penh. Buses to Don Kralor (for the Cambodia border; see above) depart in the morning, 13 km, US$1; alternatively, you can charter a *songthaew*

for US$5, or hire a motorbike. To **Khong Phapheng**, take a tuk-tuk or motorcycle taxi for around US$6-7 return.

Don Deth, Don Khone and around
p255, map p256
Boat
Guesthouses organize boat trips around the area every day; rates are susceptible to change: to **Ban Nakasang**, 30,000 kip per person; to **Khong Phapheng Falls**, 60,000 kip, min 5 people.

There are 2 ways to get to **Don Khong**, from Ban Nakasang, either by boat, 2 hrs, US$15, or by bus (see above); motorbike taxis also make the trip for US$3. Although it's slower and more expensive, the boat trip is one of the loveliest in Laos. Boat hire for the day around the sites and islands costs US$15-20.

❶ Directory

Don Khong (Muang Khong)
p250, map p252
Banks There is a basic Lao Agriculture Promotion bank in town; hours are erratic and

it accepts only US$ or Thai ฿; guesthouses will also exchange cash at rates slightly poorer than market rate; a photocopy of your passport may be required. **Internet** Alpha Internet offers internet and internet telephone at 1000 kip per min; they also burn CDs, hire canoes and do laundry. **Post and telephone** The post office is opposite the jetty in the centre of town – unreliable and slow mail service; international dialling available here.

Don Deth *p256, map p256*
Banks There are no banks on the island; a foreign exchange service near the port will change most major currencies; Mr B of Mr B's guesthouse will also organize the cashing of TCs, but the commission here is quite hefty, so you are better off organizing your cash from Pakse. **Internet** There is a small internet café across from the port junction, 1000 kip per min; calls can also be made, min 10 mins. **Telephone** The best way to make a call is via the net, although most guest-houses will let you make calls from their mobiles, which can be incredibly expensive, up to US$4 a min. **Immigration** The Riverside Restaurant can organize Cambodian visas in 3 working days for US$55 or 5 working days for US$45.

Don Khone *p257*
Electricity No mains electricity but many places run generators daily 1800-2200. **Post and telephone** No post office and no telephones on the island; guesthouses may allow you to make international calls from their mobile phones, for up to US$4 per min.

⁂ Footprint features

History

Scholars of Lao history, before they even begin, need to decide whether they are writing a history of Laos; a history of the Lao ethnic group; or histories of the various kingdoms and principalities that have, through time, been encompassed by the present boundaries of the Lao People's Democratic Republic. Historians have tended to confront this problem in different ways without, often, acknowledging on what basis their 'history' is built. It is common to see 1365, the date of the foundation of the kingdom of Lane Xang, as marking the beginning of Lao history. But, as Martin Stuart-Fox points out, prior to Lane Xang the principality of Muang Swa, occupying the same geographical space, was headed by a Lao. The following account provides a brief overview of the histories of those peoples who have occupied what is now the territory of the Lao PDR.

Archaeological and historical evidence indicates that most Lao originally migrated south from China. This was followed by an influx of ideas and culture from the Indian subcontinent via Myanmar (Burma), Thailand and Cambodia – something which is reflected in the state religion, Theravada Buddhism.

Being surrounded by large, powerful neighbours, Laos has been repeatedly invaded over the centuries by the Thais (or Siamese) and the Vietnamese – who both thought of Laos as their buffer zone and backyard. They too have both left their mark on Lao culture. In recent history, Laos has been influenced by the French during the colonial era, the Japanese during the Second World War, the Americans during the Indochinese wars and, between 1975 and the early 1990s, by Marxism-Leninism.

It is also worth noting, in introduction, that historians and regimes have axes to grind. The French were anxious to justify their annexation of Laos and so used dubious Vietnamese documents to provide a thin legal gloss to their actions. Western historians, lumbered with the baggage of Western historiography, ignored indigenous histories. And the Lao People's Revolutionary Party uses history for its own ends too. The official three volume *History of Laos* is currently being written by Party-approved history hacks. The third volume (chronologically speaking) was published in 1989 and, working back in time, the first and second thereafter. As Martin Stuart-Fox remarks in his *A History of Laos*, "the communist regime is as anxious as was the previous Royal Lao government [pre-1975] to establish that Laos has a long and glorious past and that a continuity exists between the past and the present Lao state". In other words, Laos has not one history, but many. Take your pick.

First kingdom of Laos

Myth, archaeology and history all point to a number of early feudal Lao kingdoms in what is now South China and North Vietnam. External pressures from the Mongols under Kublai Khan and the Han Chinese forced the Tai tribes to migrate south into what had been part of the Khmer Empire. The mountains to the north and east served as a cultural barrier to Vietnam and China, leaving the Lao exposed to influences from India and the West. There are no documentary records of early Lao history (the first date in the Lao chronicles to which historians attach any real veracity is 1271) although it seems probable that parts of present-day Laos were annexed by Lannathai (Chiang Mai) in the 11th century and by the Khmer Empire during the 12th century. But neither of these states held sway over the entire area of Laos. Xieng Khouang, for example, was probably never under Khmer domination. This was followed by strong Siamese influence over the cities of Luang Prabang and Vientiane under the Siamese Sukhothai Dynasty. Laos (the country) in effect did not exist although the Laos (the people) certainly did.

⁞ Kings of Lane Xang

Fa Ngum	1353-1373	Pothisarath	1520-1548
Samsenthai	1373-1416	Setthathirat	1548-1571
Lan Kamdaeng	1417-1428	Saensurin	1572-1574
Phommathat	1428-1429	Mahaupahat (under	
Mun Sai	1429-1430	Burmese control)	1574-1580
Fa Khai	1430-1433	Saensurin	1580-1582
Khong Kham	1433-1434	Nakhon Noi (under	
Yukhon	1434-1435	Burmese control)	1582-1583
Kham Keut	1435-1441	Interregnum	1583-1591
Chaiyachakkapat-		Nokeo Koumone	1591-1596
Phaenphaeo		Thammikarath	1596-1622
(aka Sao Tiakaphat)	1441-1478	Upanyuvarat	1622-1623
Suvarna Banlang		Pothisarat	1623-1627
(aka Theng Kham)	1478-1485	Mon Keo	1627
Lahsaenthai Puvanart	1485-1495	Unstable period	1627-1637
Sompou	1497-1500	Sulinya Vongsa	1637-1694
Visunarat	1500-1520		

The downfall of the kingdom of Sukhothai in 1345 and its submission to the new Siamese Dynasty at Ayutthaya (founded in 1349) was the catalyst for the foundation of what is commonly regarded as the first truly independent Lao Kingdom – although there were smaller semi-independent Lao *muang* (city states, sometimes transliterated as *meuang*) existing prior to that date.

Fa Ngum and Lane Xang

The kingdom of Lane Xang (Lan Chang) emerged in 1353 under Fa Ngum, a Lao prince who had grown up in the Khmer court of Angkor. Fa Ngum is clearly an important man – that is, if the amount of space devoted to his exploits in the Lao chronicles is anything to go by. There is more written about him than there is about the following two centuries of Lao history. It is also safe to say that his life is more fiction than fact. Fa Ngum was reputedly born with 33 teeth and was banished to Angkor after his father, Prince Yakfah, was convicted of having an incestuous affair with a wife of King Suvarna Kamphong. In 1353 Fa Ngum led an army to Luang Prabang and confronted his grandfather, King Suvarna Kamphong. Unable to defeat his grandson on the battlefield, the aged king is said to have hanged himself and Fa Ngum was invited to take the throne. Three years later, in 1356, Fa Ngum marched on Vientiane – which he took with ease – and then on Vienkam, which proved more of a challenge. He is credited with piecing together Lang Xang – the Land of a Million Elephants (or, if not accented, the Valley of Elephants) – the golden age to which all histories of Laos refer to justify the existence (and greatness) of Laos.

In some accounts Lang Xang is portrayed as stretching from China to Cambodia and from the Khorat Plateau in present-day Northeast Thailand to the Annamite mountains in the east. But it would be entirely wrong to envisage the kingdom controlling all these regions. Lane Xang probably only had total control over a comparatively small area of present-day Laos and parts of Northeast Thailand; the bulk of this grand empire would have been contested with other surrounding kingdoms. In addition, the smaller *muang* and principalities would themselves have played competing powers off, one against another, in an attempt to maximize their own autonomy. It is this 'messiness' which led scholars of Southeast Asian history to suggest that territories as such did not exist, but rather zones of variable control. The historian OW Wolters coined the term *mandala* for "a particular and often unstable political situation in a vaguely defined geographical area without fixed boundaries and where smaller centres tended to look in all directions for security. *Mandalas* would expand and contract in concertina-like fashion. Each one contained several tributary rulers, some of whom would repudiate their vassal status when the opportunity arose and try to build up their own network of vassals".

Legend relates that Fa Ngum was a descendant of Khoum Borom, "a king who came out of the sky from South China". He is said to have succeeded to the throne of Nanchao in 729, aged 31, and died 20 years later, although this historical record is, as they say, exceedingly thin. Khoum Borom is credited with giving birth to the Lao people by slicing open a gourd in Muong Taeng (Dien Bien Phu, Vietnam) and his seven sons established the great Tai kingdoms. He returned to his country with a detachment of Khmer soldiers and united several scattered Lao fiefdoms. In those days, conquered lands were usually razed and the people taken as slaves to build up the population of the conquering group. (This largely explains why today there are far more Lao in northeastern Thailand than in Laos – they were forcibly settled there after King Anou was defeated by King Rama III of Siam in 1827 – see page 272.) The kings of Lane Xang were less philistine, demanding only subordination and allegiance as one part of a larger *mandala*.

Luang Prabang became the capital of the kingdom of Lane Xang. The unruly highland tribes of the northeast did not come under the kingdom's control at that time. Fa Ngum made Theravada Buddhism the official religion. He married the Cambodian king's daughter, Princess Keo Kaengkanya, and was given the Pra Bang (a golden statue, the most revered religious symbol of Laos), by the Khmer court.

It is common to read of Lane Xang as the first kingdom of Laos; as encompassing the territory of present-day Laos; and as marking the introduction of Theravada Buddhism to the country. On all counts this portrait is, if not false, then deeply flawed. As noted above, there were Lao states that predated Lane Xang; Lane Xang never controlled Laos as it currently exists; and Buddhism had made an impact on the Lao people before 1365. Fa Ngum did not create a kingdom; rather he brought together various pre-existing *muang* (city states) into a powerful *mandala*. As Martin Stuart-Fox writes, "From this derives his [Fa Ngum's] historical claim to hero status as the founder of the Lao Kingdom." But, as Stuart-Fox goes on to explain, there was no central authority and rulers of individual *muang* were permitted considerable autonomy. As a result the "potential for disintegration was always present".

After Fa Ngum's wife died in 1368, he became so debauched, it is said, that he was deposed in favour of his son, Samsenthai (1373-1416), who was barely 18 when he acceded the throne. He was named after the 1376 census, which concluded that he ruled over 300,000 Tais living in Laos; *samsen* means, literally, 300,000. He set up a new administrative system based on the existing *muang*, nominating governors to each that lasted until it was abolished by the Communist government in 1975. Samsenthai's death was followed by a period of unrest. Under King Chaiyachakkapat-Phaenphaeo (1441-1478), the kingdom came under increasing threat from the Vietnamese. How the Vietnamese came to be peeved with the Lao is another story which smacks of fable more than fact. King Chaiyachakkapat's eldest son, the Prince of Chienglaw, secured a holy white elephant. The emperor of Vietnam, learning of this momentous discovery, asked to be sent some of the beast's hairs. Disliking the Vietnamese, the Prince dispatched a box of its excrement instead, whereupon the Emperor formed an army of an improbably large 550,000 men. The Prince's army numbered 200,000 and 2000 elephants. (Considering that the population of Lane Xang under Samsenthai was said to be 300,000 this beggars statistical belief. Still, it is a good story.) The massive Vietnamese army finally prevailed – two Lao generals were so tired they fell off their elephants and were hacked to pieces – and entered and sacked Luang Prabang. But shortly thereafter they were driven out by Chaiyachakkapat-Phaenphaeo's son, King Suvarna Banlang (1478-1485). Peace was only fully restored under King Visunarat (1500-1520), who built Wat Visoun in Luang Prabang.

Increasing prominence and Burmese incursions Under King Pothisarath (1520-1548) Vientiane became prominent as a trading and religious centre. He married a Lanna (Chiang Mai) princess, Queen Yotkamtip, and when the Siamese King Ketklao was put to death in 1545, Pothisarath's son claimed the throne at Lanna. He returned to Lane Xang when his father died in 1548. Once again an elephant figured as a prime mover in the event: Pothisarath was demonstrating his prowess in the manly art of elephant lassoing when he was flung from his mount and fatally crushed. Asserting his right as successor to the throne, he was crowned Setthathirat in 1548 and ruled until 1571 – the last of the great kings of Lane Xang.

At the same time, the Burmese were expanding East and in 1556 Lanna fell into their hands. Setthathirat gave up his claim to that throne, to a Siamese prince, who ruled under Burmese authority. (He also took the Phra Kaeo – Thailand's famous 'Emerald' Buddha and its most sacred and revered image – with him to Luang Prabang and then to Vientiane. The residents of Chiang Mai are reputed to have pleaded that he leave it in the city, but these cries fell on deaf ears. The Phra Kaeo stayed in Vientiane until 1778 when the Thai general Phya Chakri 'repatriated' it to Thailand.) In 1563 Setthathirat pronounced Vieng Chan (Vientiane) the principal capital of Lane Xang. Seven years later, the Burmese King Bayinnaung launched an unsuccessful attack on Vieng Chan itself.

Setthathirat is revered as one of the great Lao kings, having protected the country from foreign domination. He built Wat Phra Kaeo (see page 57) in Vientiane, in which he placed the famous Emerald Buddha brought from Lanna. Setthathirat mysteriously disappeared during a campaign in the southern province of Attapeu in 1574, which threw the kingdom into crisis (see page 242). Vientiane fell to invading Burmese the following year and remained under Burmese control for seven years. Finally the anarchic kingdoms of Luang Prabang and Vientiane were reunified under Nokeo Koumane (1591-96) and Thammikarath (1596-1622).

Disputed territory

From the time of the formation of the kingdom of Lane Xang to the arrival of the French, the history of Laos was dominated by the struggle to retain the lands it had conquered. Following King Setthathirat's death, a series of kings came to the throne in quick succession. King Souligna Vongsa, crowned in 1633, brought long awaited peace to Laos. The 61 years he was on the throne are regarded as Lane Xang's golden age. Under him, the kingdom's influence spread to Yunnan in South China, the Burmese Shan States, Issan in Northeast Thailand and areas of Vietnam and Cambodia.

Souligna Vongsa was even on friendly terms with the Vietnamese: he married Emperor Le Thanh Ton's daughter and he and the Emperor agreed the borders between the two countries. The frontier was settled in a deterministic – but nonetheless amicable – fashion: those living in houses built on stilts with verandas were considered Lao subjects and those living in houses without piles and verandas owed allegiance to Vietnam.

During his reign, foreigners first visited the country – the Dutch merchant Gerrit van Wuysthoff arrived in 1641 to assess trading prospects – and Jesuit missionaries too. But other than a handful of adventurers, Laos remained on the outer periphery of European concerns and influence in the region.

The three kingdoms After Souligna Vongsa died in 1694, leaving no heir, dynastic quarrels and feudal rivalries once again erupted, undermining the kingdom's cohesion. In 1700 Lane Xang split into three: Luang Prabang under Souligna's grandson, Vientiane under Souligna's nephew and the new kingdom of Champasak was founded in the south 'panhandle'. This weakened the country and allowed the Siamese and Vietnamese to encroach on Lao lands. *Muang*, which previously owed clear allegiance to Lane Xang, began to look towards Vietnam or Siam. Isan muang in present day Northeast Thailand, for example, paid tribute to Bangkok; while Xieng Khouang did the same to Hanoi and, later, to Hué. The three main kingdoms that emerged with the disintegration of Lane Xang leant in different directions: Luang Prabang had close links with China, Vientiane with Vietnam's Hanoi/Hué and Champassak with Siam.

By the mid-1760s Burmese influence once again held sway in Vientiane and Luang Prabang and before the turn of the decade, they sacked Ayutthaya, the capital of Siam. Somehow the Siamese managed to pull themselves together and only two years later in 1778 successfully rampaged through Vientiane. The two sacred Buddhas, the Phra Bang and the Phra Kaeo (Emerald Buddha), were taken as booty back to Bangkok. The Emerald Buddha was never returned and now sits in Bangkok's Wat Phra Kaeo (see page 57).

King Anou (an abbreviation of Anurutha), was placed on the Vientiane throne by the Siamese. With the death of King Rama II of Siam, King Anou saw his chance of rebellion, asked Vietnam for assistance, formed an army and marched on Bangkok in 1827. In mounting this brave – some would say foolhardy – assault, Anou was apparently trying to emulate the great Fa Ngum. Unfortunately, he got no further than the Northeast Thai town of Korat where his forces suffered a defeat and were driven back. Nonetheless, Anou's rebellion is considered one of the most daring and ruthless rebellions in Siamese history and he was lauded as a war hero back home.

King Anou's brief stab at regional power was to result in catastrophe for Laos – and tragedy for King Anou. The first US arms shipment to Siam allowed the Siamese to sack Vientiane, a task to which they had grown accustomed over the years. (This marks America's first intervention in Southeast Asia.) Lao artisans were frogmarched to Bangkok and many of the inhabitants were resettled in Northeast Siam. Rama III had Chao Anou locked in a cage where he was taunted and abused by the population of Bangkok. He died soon afterwards, at the age of 62. The cause of his death has been variously linked to poison and shame. One of his supporters is said to have taken pity on the king and brought him poison. Other explanations simply say that he wished himself dead or that he choked to death. Whatever the cause, the disconsolate Anou, before he died, put a curse on Siam's monarchy, promising that the next time a Thai king set foot on Lao soil, he would die. To this day no Thai king has crossed the Mekong River. When the agreement for the supply of hydroelectric power was signed with Thailand in the 1970s, the Thai king was invited officially to open the Nam Ngum Dam, a feat he managed from a sandbank in the middle of the Mekong.

Disintegration of the kingdom Over the next 50 years, Anou's Kingdom was destroyed. By the time the French arrived in the late 19th century, the virtually unoccupied city was subsumed into the Siamese sphere of influence. Luang Prabang also became a Siamese vassal state, while Xieng Khouang province was invaded by Chinese rebels – to the chagrin of the Vietnamese, who had always considered the Hmong mountain kingdom (they called it Tran Ninh), to be their exclusive source of slaves. The Chinese had designs on Luang Prabang too and in order to quash their expansionist instincts, Bangkok dispatched an army there in 1885 to pacify the region and ensure the north remained firmly within the Siamese sphere of influence. This period was clearly one of confusion and rapidly shifting allegiances. In James McCarthy's book of his travels in Siam and Laos, *Surveying and Exploring in Siam* (1900), he states that an old chief of Luang Prabang remarked to him that the city had never been a tributary state of Annam (North Vietnam) but had formerly paid tribute to China. He writes:

"The tribute had consisted of four elephants, 41 mules, 533 lbs of nok (metal composed of gold and copper), 25 lbs of rhinoceros' horns, 100 lbs of ivory, 250 pieces of home-spun cloth, one horn, 150 bundles of areca palm nuts [for betel 'nut' chewing], 150 cocoanuts [sic] and 33 bags of roe of the fish pla buk [the giant Mekong cat fish, see page 321]."

The history of Laos during this period becomes, essentially, the history of only a small part of the current territory of the country: namely, the history of Luang Prabang. And because Luang Prabang was a suzerain state of Bangkok, the history of that kingdom is, in turn, sometimes relegated to a mere footnote in the history of Siam.

The French and independence

Following King Anou's death, Laos became the centre of Southeast Asian rivalry between Britain, expanding east from Burma and France, pushing west through Vietnam. In 1868, following the French annexation of South Vietnam and the formation of a protectorate in Cambodia, an expedition set out to explore the Mekong trade route to China. Once central and north Vietnam had come under the influence of the Quai d'Orsay in Paris, the French became increasingly curious about Vietnamese claims to chunks of Laos. Unlike the Siamese, the French – like the British – were concerned with demarcating borders and establishing explicit areas of sovereignty. This seemed extraordinary to most Southeast Asians at the time who could not see the point of spending so much time and effort mapping space when land was so abundant. However, it did not take long for the Siamese king to realize the importance of maintaining his claim to Siamese territories if the French in the east and the British in the south (Malaya) and west (Burma) were not to squeeze Siam to nothing.

However, King Chulalongkorn was not in a position to confront the French militarily and instead he had to play a clever diplomatic game if his kingdom was to survive. The French, for their part, were anxious to continue to press westwards from Vietnam into the Lao lands over which Siam held suzerainty. Martin Stuart-Fox argues that there were four main reasons underlying France's desire to expand West: the lingering hope that the Mekong might still offer a 'back door' into China; the consolidation of Vietnam against attack; the 'rounding out' of their Indochina possessions; and a means of further pressuring Bangkok. In 1886, the French received reluctant Siamese permission to post a vice consul to Luang Prabang and a year later he persuaded the Thais to leave. However, even greater humiliation was to come in 1893 when the French, through crude gunboat diplomacy – the so-called Paknam incident – forced King Chulalongkorn to give up all claim to Laos on the flimsiest of historical pretexts. Despite attempts by Prince Devawongse to manufacture a compromise, the French forced Siam to cede Laos to France and, what's more, to pay compensation. It is said that after this humiliation, King Chulalongkorn retired from public life, broken in spirit and health. So the French colonial era in Laos began.

What is notable about this spat between France and Siam is that Laos – the country over which they were fighting – scarcely figures. As was to happen again in Laos' history, the country was caught between two competing powers who used Laos as a stage on which to fight a wider and to them, more important, conflict.

Union of Indochina In 1893 France occupied the left bank of the Mekong and forced Thailand to recognize the river as the boundary. The French Union of Indochina denied Laos the area which is now Isan, northeast Thailand, and this was the start of 50 years of colonial rule. Laos became a protectorate with a *résident-superieur* in Vientiane and a vice-consul in Luang Prabang. However, as Martin Stuart-Fox points out, Laos could hardly be construed as a 'country' during the colonial period. "Laos existed again", he writes, "but not yet as a political entity in its own right, for no independent centre of Lao political power existed. Laos was but a territorial entity within French Indochina." The

French were not interested in establishing an identifiable Lao state; they saw Laos as a part and a subservient part at that, of Vietnam, serving as a resource-rich appendage to Vietnam. Though they had grand plans for the development of Laos, these were only expressed airily and none of them came to anything. "The French were never sure what to do with Laos", Stuart-Fox writes, "either the parts or the whole." Unlike Cambodia to the south, the French did not perceive Laos to have any historical unity or coherence and therefore it could be hacked about and developed or otherwise, according to their whim, as if it were a piece of brie.

In 1904 the Franco-British convention delimited respective zones of influence. Only a few hundred French civil servants were ever in Vientiane at any one time and their attitude to colonial administration – described as 'benign neglect' – was as relaxed as the people they governed. To the displeasure of the Lao, France brought in Vietnamese to run the civil service (in the way the British used Indian bureaucrats in Burma). But for the most part, the French colonial period was a 50-year siesta for Laos. The king was allowed to stay in Luang Prabang, but had little say in administration. Trade and commerce was left to the omnipresent Chinese and the Vietnamese. A small, French-educated Lao élite did grow up and by the 1940s they had become the core of a typically laid-back Lao nationalist movement.

Japanese coup Towards the end of the Second World War, Japan ousted the French administration in Laos in a coup in March 1945. The eventual surrender of the Japanese in August that year gave impetus to the Lao independence movement. Prince Phetsarath, hereditary viceroy and premier of the Luang Prabang Kingdom, took over the leadership of the Lao Issara, the Free Laos Movement (originally a resistance movement against the Japanese). They prevented the French from seizing power again and declared Lao independence on 1 September 1945. Two weeks later, the north and south provinces were reunified and in October, Phetsarath formed a Lao Issara government headed by Prince Phaya Khammao, the governor of Vientiane. France refused to recognize the new state and crushed the Lao resistance. King Sisavang Vong, unimpressed by Prince Phetsarath's move, sided with the French, who had their colony handed back by British forces. He was crowned the constitutional monarch of the new protectorate in 1946. The rebel government took refuge in Bangkok. Historians believe the Issara movement was aided in their resistance to the French by the Viet Minh – Hanoi's Communists.

Independence In response to nationalist pressures, France was obliged to grant Laos ever greater self government and, eventually, formal independence within the framework of the newly reconstructed French Union in July 1949. Meanwhile, in Bangkok, the Issara movement had formed a government-in-exile, headed by Phetsarath and his half-brothers: Prince Souvanna Phouma (see box opposite) and Prince Souphanouvong. Both were refined, French-educated men, with a taste for good wine and cigars. The Issara's military wing was led by Souphanouvong who, even at that stage, was known for his Communist sympathies. This was due to a temporary alliance between the Issara and the Viet Minh, who had the common cause of ridding their respective countries of the French. Within just a few months the so-called Red Prince had been ousted by his half-brothers and joined the Viet Minh where he is said to have been the moving force behind the declaration of the Democratic Republic of Laos by the newly-formed Lao National Assembly. The Lao People's Democratic Republic emerged – albeit in name only – somewhere inside Vietnam, in August 1949. Soon afterwards, the Pathet Lao (the Lao Nation) was born. The Issara movement quickly folded and Souvanna Phouma went back to Vientiane and joined the newly formed Royal Lao Government.

By 1953, Prince Souphanouvong had managed to move his Pathet Lao headquarters inside Laos and with the French losing their grip on the north provinces

Prince Souvanna Phouma: architect of independence and helmsman of catastrophe

Prince Souvanna Phouma was Laos' greatest statesman. He was prime minister on no less than eight occasions for a total of 20 years between 1951 and 1975. He dominated mainstream politics from independence until the victory of the Pathet Lao in 1975. But he was never able to preserve the integrity of Laos in the face of much stronger external forces. "Souvanna stands as a tragic figure in modern Lao history," Martin Stuart-Fox writes, a "stubborn symbol of an alternative, neutral, 'middle way'."

He was born in 1901 into a branch of the Luang Prabang royal family. Like many of the Lao elite he was educated abroad, in Hanoi, Paris and Grenoble, and when he returned to Laos he married a woman of mixed French-Lao blood. He was urbane, educated and, by all accounts, arrogant. He enjoyed fine wines and cigars, spoke French better than he spoke Lao, and was a Francophile – as well as a nationalist – to the end.

In 1950 Souvanna became a co-founder of the Progressive Party and in the elections of 1951 he headed his first government which negotiated and secured full independence from France.

Souvanna made two key errors of judgement during these early years. First, he ignored the need for nation building in Laos. And, second, he underestimated the threat that the Communists posed to the country. With regard to the first of these misjudgements, he seemed to believe – and it is perhaps no accident that he trained as an engineer and architect – that Laos just needed to be administered efficiently to become a modern state. He appeared either to reject, or to ignore the idea that the government first had to try and inculcate a sense of Lao nationhood.

The second misjudgement was his long-held belief that the Pathet Lao was a nationalist and not a Communist organization. He let the Pathet Lao grow in strength and this, in turn, brought the US into Lao affairs.

By the time the US began to intervene in Lao affairs in the late 1950s, the country already seemed to be heading for catastrophe. But in his struggle to maintain some semblance of independence for his tiny country, he ignored the degree to which Laos was being sucked into the quagmire of Indochina. As Martin Stuart-Fox writes: "He [Souvanna] knew he was being used, and that he had no power to protect his country from the war that increasingly engulfed it. But he was too proud meekly to submit to US demands – even as Laos was subjected to the heaviest bombing in the history of warfare. At least a form of independence had to be maintained."

When the Pathet Lao entered Vientiane in victory in 1975, Souvanna did not flee into exile. He remained to help in the transfer of power. The Pathet Lao, of course, gave him a title and then largely ignored him as they pursued their Communist manifesto. Again, Martin Stuart-Fox writes: "Souvanna ended his days beside the Mekong. He was to the end a Lao patriot, refusing to go into exile in France. The leaders of the new regime did consult him on occasions. Friends came to play bridge. Journalists continued to seek him out, although he said little and interviews were taped in the presence of Pathet Lao minions. When he died in January 1984, he was accorded a state funeral."

From Martin Stuart-Fox's *Buddhist Kingdom, Marxist State: the Making of Modern Laos* (White Lotus, 1996).

the weary colonizers granted the country full independence. Retreating honourably, France signed a treaty of friendship and association with the new royalist government and made the country a French protectorate.

The rise of Communism

French defeat While all this was going on, King Sisavang Vong sat tight in Luang Prabang instead of moving to Vientiane. But within a few months of independence, the ancient royal capital was under threat from the Communist Viet Minh and Pathet Lao. Honouring the terms of the new treaty, French commander General Henri Navarre determined in late 1953 to take the pressure off Luang Prabang by confronting the Viet Minh who controlled the strategic approach to the city at Dien Bien Phu. The French suffered a stunning defeat which presaged their withdrawal from Indochina. The subsequent occupation of two north Lao provinces by the Vietnam-backed Pathet Lao forces, meant the kingdom's days as a Western buffer state were numbered. The Vietnamese, not unlike their previous neighbours, did not respect Laos as a state, but as a extension of their own territory to be utilized for their own strategic purposes during the ensuing war.

With the Geneva Accord in July 1954, following the fall of Dien Bien Phu in May, Ho Chi Minh's government gained control of all territory north of the 17th parallel in neighbouring Vietnam. The Accord guaranteed Laos' freedom and neutrality, but with the Communists on the threshold, the US was not prepared to be a passive spectator: the demise of the French sparked an increasing US involvement. In an operation that was to mirror the much more famous war with Vietnam to the East, Washington soon found itself supplying and paying the salaries of 50,000 royalist troops and their corrupt officers. Clandestine military assistance grew, undercover special forces were mobilized and the CIA began meddling in Lao politics. In 1960 a consignment of weapons was dispatched by the CIA to a major in the Royal Lao Army called Vang Pao – or VP, as he became known – who was destined to become the leader of the Hmong.

US involvement: the domino effect Laos had become the dreaded first domino, which, using the scheme of US President Dwight D Eisenhower's famous analogy, would trigger the rapid spread of Communism if ever it fell. The time-trapped little kingdom rapidly became the focus of superpower brinkmanship. At a press conference in March 1961, President Kennedy is said to have been too abashed to announce to the American people that US forces might soon become embroiled in conflict in a far-away flashpoint that went by the inglorious name of 'Louse'. For three decades Americans have unwittingly mispronounced the country's name as Kennedy decided, euphemistically, to label it 'Lay-os' throughout his national television broadcast.

Coalitions, coups and counter-coups The US-backed Royal Lao Government of independent Laos – even though it was headed by the neutralist, Prince Souvanna Phouma – ruled over a divided country from 1951 to 1954. The US played havoc with Laos' domestic politics, running anti-communist campaigns, backing the royalist army and lending support to political figures on the right (even if they lacked experience or political qualifications). The Communist Pathet Lao, headed by Prince Souphanouvong and overseen and sponsored by North Vietnam's Lao Dong party since 1949, emerged as the only strong opposition. By the mid-1950s, Kaysone Phomvihane, later prime minister of the Lao PDR, began to make a name for himself in the Indochinese Communist Party. Indeed the close association between Laos and Vietnam went deeper than just ideology. Kaysone's father was Vietnamese, while Prince Souphanouvong and Nouhak Phounsavanh both married Vietnamese women.

Government of National Union Elections were held in Vientiane in July 1955 but were boycotted by the Pathet Lao. Souvanna Phouma became prime minister in

March 1956. He aimed to try to negotiate the integration of his half-brother's Pathet Lao provinces into a unified administration and coax the Communists into a coalition government. In 1957 the disputed provinces were returned to royal government control under the first coalition government. This coalition government, much to US discontent, contained two Pathet Lao ministers including Souphanouvong and Phoumi Vongvichit. This was one of Souvanna Phouma's achievements in trying to combine the two sides to ensure neutrality, although it was only short-lived. In May 1958 elections were held. This time the Communists' Lao Patriotic Front (Neo Lao Hak Xat) clinched thirteen of the 21 seats in the Government of National Union. The Red Prince, Souphanouvong and one of his aides were included in the cabinet and former Pathet Lao members were elected deputies of the National Assembly.

Almost immediately problems which had been beneath the surface emerged to plague the government. The rightists and their US supporters were shaken by the result and the much-vaunted coalition lasted just two months. Driven by Cold War prerogatives, the US could not abide by any government that contained Communist members and withdrew their aid, which the country had become much dependent upon. Between 1955 and 1958 the US had given four times more aid to Laos than the French had done in the prior eight years and it had become the backbone of the Lao economy. If Laos was not so dependent on this aid, it is quite plausible that the coalition government may have survived. The National Union fell apart in July 1958 and Souvanna Phouma was forced out of power. Pathet Lao leaders were jailed and the rightwing Phoui Sananikone came to power. With anti-Communists in control, Pathet Lao forces withdrew to the Plain of Jars in Xieng Khouang province. A three-way civil war ensued, between the rightists (backed by the US), the Communists (backed by North Vietnam) and the neutralists (led by Souvanna Phouma, who wanted to maintain independence from both the US and Communist countries).

Civil war CIA-backed strongman General Phoumi Nosavan thought Phoui's politics rather tame and with a nod from Washington he stepped into the breech in January 1959, eventually overthrowing Phoui in a coup in December and placing Prince Boun Oum in power. Pathet Lao leaders were imprisoned without trial. Confusion over Phoumas, Phouis and Phoumis led one American official to comment that it all "could have been a significant event or a typographical error".

Within a year, the rightist regime was overthrown by a neutralist *coup d'état* led by General Kong Lae and Prince Souvanna Phouma was recalled from exile in Cambodia to become prime minister of the first National Union. Souvanna Phouma incurred American wrath by inviting a Soviet ambassador to Vientiane in October. With US support, Nosavan staged yet another armed rebellion in December and sparked a new civil war. In the 1960 general elections, provincial authorities were threatened with military action if they did not support the rightwing groups and were rigged to ensure no Pathet Lao cadres could obtain a seat in office. In August 1960 paratroop neutralist Kong Le staged a successful coup d'état; however, with US funding, the rightists were able to assemble formidable troops in Savannakhet and marched to Vientiane, retaking the capital in mid-December. Kong Lae backed down, Souvanna Phouma shuffled back to Phnom Penh and a new rightwing government was set up under Boun Oum. By this stage, the Pathet Lao had consolidated considerable forces in the region surrounding the Plain of Jars and, with support from the Vietnamese, had been able to expand their territorial control in the north. This represented a major crisis to the incoming Kennedy administration that Stuart Martin-Fox (1996) describes as "second only to Cuba".

Zurich talks and the Geneva Accord The new prime minister, the old one and his Marxist half-brother finally sat down to talks in Zurich in June 1961, but any hope of an agreement was overshadowed by escalating tensions between the superpowers. In

1962, an international agreement on Laos was hammered out in Geneva by 14 participating nations and accords were signed, once again guaranteeing Lao neutrality.

By implication, the accords denied the Viet Minh access to the Ho Chi Minh Trail. But aware of the reality of constant North Vietnamese infiltration through Laos into South Vietnam, the head of the American mission concluded that the agreement was "a good bad deal".

Another coalition government of National Union was formed under the determined neutralist Prince Souvanna Phouma (as prime minister), with Prince Souphanouvong for the Pathet Lao and Prince Boun Oum representing the right. A number of political assassinations derailed the process of reconciliation. Moreover, antagonisms between the left and the right, both backed financially by their respective allies, made it impossible for the unfunded neutralists to balance the two sided into any form of neutrality. It was no surprise when the coalition government collapsed within a few months and fighting resumed. This time the international community just shrugged and watched Laos sink back into the vortex of civil war. Unbeknown to the outside world, the conflict was rapidly degenerating into a war between the CIA and North Vietnamese jungle guerrillas.

Secret War

The war that wasn't In the aftermath of the Geneva agreement, the North Vietnamese, rather than reducing their forces in Laos, continued to increase their manpower on the ground. With the Viet Minh denying the existence of the Ho Chi Minh Trail, while at the same time enlarging it, Kennedy dispatched an undercover force of CIA men, green berets and US-trained Thai mercenaries to command 9000 Lao soldiers. By 1963, these American forces had grown to 30,000 men. Historian Roger Warner believes that by 1965 "word spread among a select circle of congressmen and senators about this exotic program run by Lone Star rednecks and Asian hillbillies that was better and cheaper than anything the Pentagon was doing in South Vietnam." To the north, the US also supplied Vang Pao's force of Hmong guerrillas, dubbed 'Mobile Strike Forces'. With the cooperation of Prince Souvanna Phouma, the CIA's commercial airline, Air America, ferried men and equipment into Laos from Thailand (and opium out, it is believed). Caught between Cold War antagonisms it was impossible to maintain a modicum of neutrality as even the most staunch neutralist, Souvanna Phouma, began to become entangled. As Robbins argues, by the early 1960s, Sovanna Phouma – trying to reinforce the middle way – had given permission "for every clandestine manoeuvre the United States made to match the North Vietnamese. In turn Souvanna demanded that his complicity in such arrangements be kept secret, lest his position in the country become untenable." Owing to the clandestine nature of the military intervention in Laos, the rest of the world – believing that the Geneva settlement had solved the foreign interventionist problem – was oblivious as to what was happening on the ground. Right up until 1970, Washington never admitted to any activity in Laos beyond 'armed reconnaissance' flights over northern provinces. Richard Nixon, for example, claimed that "there are no American ground combat troops in Laos", which was stretching the truth to breaking point.

Meanwhile the North Vietnamese were fulfilling their two major strategic priorities in the country: continued use of the Ho Chi Minh trail (by this stage the majority of North Vietnamese munitions and personnel for the Viet Cong was being shuffled along the trail) and ensuring that the Plain of Jars did not fall under the control of the right, where the US could launch attacks on North Vietnam. This latter goal amounted to supporting the Pathet Lao in their aim to hold onto as much territory as possible in the north. The Pathet Lao, in turn, were dependent on the North Vietnamese for supplies – both material and manpower. As Martin Stuart-Fox (1996)

Background History

argues, "Pathet Lao leaders were not in a position after 1964 to reach any settlement that might have disadvantaged their Vietnamese mentors. Genuine Lao neutrality was out of the question for the Pathet Lao. It had to be subverted for the sake of the Vietnamese revolution." With both the US bankrolling the Royalist right and the Vietnamese puppeteering the Pathet Lao, within the country any pretence of maintaining a balance in the face of Cold War hostilities was shattered for neutralists like Souvanna Phouma.

Vietnam War

"Raven 58, crossing the fence"

'Raven' was the call sign used by Forward Air Controllers (FACs) in Laos. It came to designate, however, a special breed of FAC – someone who was highly motivated, aggressive, decisive, daring and exceptionally skilled and professional in their work. The mystique was heightened by the secrecy of the assignment. Pilots would leave Vietnam and seemingly disappear.

To understand the importance of a Raven's mission, it is first necessary to understand the mission of an FAC. A FAC had three responsibilities: to conduct air reconnaissance to obtain first-hand information concerning enemy locations, activity and threats; to control and direct Air Force or Navy aircraft bombers or Army artillery on enemy targets; and to control, direct and coordinate air strikes with ground troops for close air support.

As a Raven Forward Air Controller (Raven FAC), I had the privilege of belonging to an elite group of pilots who flew covert operations in Laos in support of the Royal Laotian Army or the CIA Special Guerrilla Units (SGUs).

SGUs were trained by CIA Country Team members. They were an elite fighting force designed to interdict movement of the North Vietnamese along the Ho Chi Minh Trail in the south or in areas around the Plain of Jars in the north. When they operated along the trail or in other forward locations, their supplies would be flown in by a Porter aircraft, piloted by Continental Air Service or Air America pilots. The advantage of this aircraft was that it could land and take off on a very short 'runway' – about 30.5 m long.

Normally, I would support the SGUs from the air, providing reconnaissance or fighter aircraft support. However, on one day they returned the favour. My airplane crashed in a rice paddy south of Attapeu. Nine North Vietnamese were across the paddy as I made a judicious move toward the opposite side. I knew that the SGUs were in the area near Attapeu, as I headed in that direction. As I came upon them, I recognized that they were friendly and shortly thereafter I was picked up by an Air America helicopter and flown to a nearby Lima Site (PS-38) for the night.

During the time of the Ravens, 1966 to 1975, there were only 191 pilots. Very few Americans actually ever went into Laos, except along the Ho Chi Minh Trail. My time in Laos was quite enjoyable. Officially, I was a forest ranger working for the Lao government. In fact, I worked for the American ambassador and provided visual reconnaissance and direct air support for the Royal Laotian Army and the CIA SGUs.

And there was much to discourage volunteers. The casualty rate was said to be 50%. The conditions were more harsh. And, then there were the drug dealers and gold dealers. (At that time it was illegal to trade in gold in the United States. One could only buy 'jewellery'. For that reason, contracted CIA pilots from Air America and Continental Air Service would be seen wearing heavy gold bracelets which were not much more than gold bars formed into a bracelet.)

But I had volunteered to join the Air Force for the specific purpose of going to Vietnam and Laos. I had been a student at Ohio State University and was exempt from the draft. I was 26 years old when I joined the Air

Souvanna Phouma appropriately referred to it as 'the forgotten war' and it is often termed now the 'non-attributable war'. The willingness on the part of the Americans to dump millions of tonnes of ordnance on a country which was ostensibly neutral may have been made easier by the fact that some people in the administration did not believe Laos to be a country at all. Bernard Fall wrote that Laos

Force – just under the 26½ age limit required of Air Force pilots. Having never flown before in my life I became a '90-day Wonder' as I received my commission as a second Lieutenant at Lackland Air Force Base in San Antonio, Texas. From Lackland I went to Laredo, Texas for Undergraduate Pilot Training. I completed my training in 1968, followed by 0-1 (Bird Dog) Special Operations Training, POW training and then on to the Philippines for Jungle Survival Training.

In Vietnam I was stationed at the Tuy Hoa MACV (Military Assistance Command Vietnam) compound where I flew in support of the Vietnamese Army. I volunteered for the Steve Canyon Program soon after arriving at Tuy Hoa. The Steve Canyon Program was named after Steve Canyon, the flamboyant adventurist comic strip character. As I departed Bien Hoa Air Force Base near Saigon for Laos, I learned why it was called Steve Canyon. The colonel who drove me to the airplane which would take me to my first stop in Thailand said: "Well, now all you have to look forward to is ... glory, money and medals!"

Ravens were a breed apart. They would wear what they wanted when flying – shorts and T-shirts, homemade flying suits or cowboy outfits. They would disregard the Air Force standards for flying time and clock as much as 150 to 200 hours a month.

The monetary rewards were appealing. While not the income a true 'mercenary' might receive – for example, US$50,000 or US$100,000 for flying certain cargo in Southeast Asia or the Middle East – the extra per diem income, free in addition to being paid for board and room, maids and cooks, and combat pay, was welcome. It could amount to an extra US$1000 per month.

Arriving at Udon Air Force Base in Northeast Thailand, I was directed to a remote area of the base called 'Det-1'. The commander didn't know much about what I would be doing, but he had to maintain my Air Force records, since when I went into Laos, I would be a 'civilian'. Flying into Laos was quite different from flying into other countries. To protect my destination, when I crossed the border I would radio: "Raven 58, crossing the fence." 'Laos' would never be mentioned.

Along with the AOC (Air Operations Center) commander, a radio operator, two airplane mechanics and a medic, I lived in the town of Pakse, in a large colonial villa. The living conditions were excellent. After flying out into the war zone each day and returning, I would go down town to a movie or to the Mekong Bar for dancing and music, or to an inviting sidewalk café for dinner.

I believed that the Lao knew who I was. But, I found out that many did not. While trying to make a call to Vietnam to speak with my future Vietnamese wife, Kim Chi, a new Air Force Lieutenant received the call and became inquisitive as to why I referred to myself as "Mister Thompson" rather than "Captain". Even military personnel in Vietnam, including Air Force Forward Air Controllers, did not know about the clandestine operations of the Ravens.

Adapted from text written by Ken Thompson, or Raven 58, who flew as a FAC in Vietnam and Laos for over 26 months between 1968 and 1970. He was awarded two Distinguished Flying Crosses and a Bronze Star for valour.

at the time was "neither a geographical nor an ethnic or social entity, but merely a political convenience", while a Rand Corporation report written in 1970 described Laos as "hardly a country except in the legal sense". More colourfully, Secretary of State Dean Rusk described it as a "wart on the hog of Vietnam". Perhaps those in Washington could feel a touch better about bombing the hell out of a country which, in their view, occupied a sort of political never never land – or which they could liken to an unfortunate skin complaint.

Not everyone agrees with this view that Laos never existed until the French wished it into existence. Scholar of Laos Arthur Dommen, for example, traces a true and coherent Lao identity back to Fa Ngum and his creation of the kingdom of Lane Xang in 1353, writing that it was "a state in the true sense of the term, delineated by borders clearly defined and consecrated by treaty" for 350 years. He goes on:

"Lao historians see a positive proof of the existence of a distinct Lao race (*sua sat Lao*), a Lao nation (*sat Lao*), a Lao country (*muong Lao*) and a Lao state (*pathet Lao*). In view of these facts, we may safely reject the notion, fashionable among apologists for a colonial enterprise of a later day, that Laos was a creation of French colonial policy and administration".

American bombing of the North Vietnamese Army's supply lines through Laos to South Vietnam along the Ho Chi Minh Trail in East Laos (see page 208) started in 1964 and fuelled the conflict between the Royalist Vientiane government and the Pathet Lao. The neutralists had been forced into alliance with the Royalists to avoid defeat in Xieng Kouang province. US bombers crossed Laos on bombing runs to Hanoi from air bases in Thailand and gradually the war in Laos escalated. In his book *The Ravens* (1987), Christopher Robbins sets the scene:

"Apparently, there was another war even nastier than the one in Vietnam and so secret that the location of the country in which it was being fought was classified. The cognoscenti simply referred to it as 'the Other Theater'. The men who chose to fight in it were hand-picked volunteers and anyone accepted for a tour seemed to disappear as if from the face of the earth."

America's side of the secret war was conducted from a one-room shack at the US base in Udon Thani, 'across the fence' in Thailand. This was the CIA's Air America operations room and in the same compound was stationed the 4802 Joint Liaison Detachment – or the CIA logistics office. In Vientiane, US pilots supporting Hmong General Vang Pao's rag-tag army, were given a new identity as rangers for the US Agency for International Development; they reported directly to the air attaché at the US embassy (see Raven 58 crossing the fence, page 280). Robbins writes that they "were military men, but flew into battle in civilian clothes – denim cutoffs, T-shirts, cowboy hats and dark glasses ... Their job was to fly as the winged artillery of some fearsome warlord, who led an army of stone age mercenaries in the pay of the CIA and they operated out of a secret city hidden in the mountains of a jungle kingdom ..." He adds that CIA station chiefs and field agents "behaved like warlords in their own private fiefdoms."

The most notorious of the CIA's unsavoury operatives was Anthony Posepny – known as Tony Poe, on whom the character of Kurtz, the crazy colonel played by Marlon Brando in the film *Apocalypse Now*, was based. Originally, Poe had worked as Vang Pao's case officer; he then moved to North Laos and operated for years, on his own, in Burmese and Chinese border territories, offering his tribal recruits one US dollar for each set of Communist ears they brought back. Many of the spies and pilots of this secret war have re-emerged in recent years in covert and illegal arms-smuggling rackets to Libya, Iran and the Nicaraguan Contras.

By contrast, the Royalist forces were reluctant warriors: despite the fact that civil war was a deeply ingrained tradition in Laos, the Lao themselves would go to great lengths to avoid fighting each other. One foreign journalist, reporting from Luang Prabang in the latter stages of the war, related how Royalist and Pathet Lao troops, encamped on opposite banks of the Nam Ou, agreed an informal ceasefire over Pi Mai (Lao New Year), to jointly celebrate the king's annual visit to the sacred Pak Ou Caves (see page 117). Most Lao did not want to fight. Correspondents who covered the war noted that without the constant goading of their respective US and North Vietnamese masters, many Lao soldiers would have happily gone home. Prior to the war, one military strategist described the Lao forces as one of the worst armies ever seen, adding that they made the [poorly regarded] "South Vietnamese Army look like Storm Troopers". "The troops lack the basic will to fight. They do not take initiative. A typical characteristic of the Laotian Army is to leave an escape route. US technicians attached to the various training institutions have not been able to overcome Lao apathy". (Ratnam, P, *Laos and the Superpowers*, 1980).

Air Force planes were often used to carry passengers for money – or to smuggle opium out of the Golden Triangle. In the field, soldiers of the Royal Lao Army regularly fled when faced with a frontal assault by the Vietnam People's Army (NVA). The officer corps was uncommitted, lazy and corrupt; many ran opium-smuggling rackets and saw the war as a ticket to get rich quick. In the south, the Americans considered Royal Lao Air Force pilots unreliable because they were loath to bomb their own people and cultural heritage.

The air war The clandestine bombing of the Ho Chi Minh Trail (see page 208) caused many civilian casualties – so-called collateral damage – and displaced much of the population in Laos' eastern provinces. A whole gamut of military devices and defoliants were used to destroy Lao territory and, although there are not really any official casualty figures in circulation, it is estimated that between a sixth and a tenth of the population were killed. By 1973, when the bombing stopped, the US had dropped over two million tonnes of bombs on Laos – equivalent to 700 kg of explosives for every man, woman and child in the country. It is reported that up to 70% of all B-52 strikes in Indochina were targeted at Laos. To pulverize the country to this degree 580,994 bombing sorties were flown. The bombing intensified during the Nixon administration: up to 1969 less than 500,000 tonnes of bombs had been dropped on Laos; from then on nearly that amount was dropped each year. In the 1960s and early 1970s, more bombs rained on Laos than were dropped during the Second World War – the equivalent of a plane load of bombs every eight minutes around the clock for nine years. This campaign cost American taxpayers more than US$2 million a day but the cost to Laos was incalculable. The activist Fred Branfman, quoted by Roger Warner in *Shooting at the Moon*, wrote: "Nine years of bombing, two million tons of bombs, whole rural societies wiped off the map, hundreds of thousands of peasants treated like herds of animals in a Clockwork Orange fantasy of an aerial African Hunting safari."

The war was not restricted to bombing missions – once potential Pathet Lao strongholds had been identified, fighters, using rockets, were sent to attempt to destroy them. Such was the intensity of the bombing campaign that villagers in Pathet Lao-controlled areas are said to have turned to planting and harvesting their rice at night. Few of those living in Xieng Khouang province, the Boloven Plateau or along the Ho Chi Minh Trail had any idea of who was bombing them or why. The consequences were often tragic, as in the case of Tham Phiu Cave (see page 171).

In *The Ravens*, Robbins tells of how a fighter pilot's inauspicious dream would lead the commander to cancel a mission; bomber pilots hated dropping bombs and when they did, aluminium canisters were carefully brought back and sold as scrap. After the war, the collection and sale of war debris turned into a valuable scrap metal industry for tribes' people in Xieng Khouang province and along the Ho Chi Minh Trail. Bomb casings, aircraft fuel tanks and other bits and pieces that were not sold to Thailand have been put to every conceivable use in rural Laos. They are used as cattle troughs, fence posts, flower pots, stilts for houses, water carriers, temple bells, knives and ploughs. The bomb craters are often turned into fish ponds.

But the bombing campaign has also left a more deadly legacy – of unexploded bombs and anti-personnel mines. Today, over 30 years after the air war ended, over 500,000 tonnes of deadly unexploded ordnance (UXO) is believed to still be scattered throughout nine of Laos' 13 provinces. Most casualties are caused by cluster bombs, or 'bombis' as they have become known. Cluster bombs are carried in large canisters called Cluster Bomb Units (CBUs), which open in mid-air, releasing around 670 tennis ball-sized bomblets. Upon detonation, the bombie propels around 200,000 pieces of shrapnel over an area the size of several football fields. This UXO contamination inhibits long-term development, especially in Xieng Khouang Province (see page 163), turning Laos' fertile fields, which are critical for agricultural production, into killing zones. Making farming in this part a Laos a highly dangerous occupation was simply one of those 'accidents' of war.

The land war Within Laos, the war largely focused on the strategic Plain of Jars in Xieng Khouang province (see page 163) and was co-ordinated from the town of Long Tien (the secret city), tucked into the limestone hills to the southwest of the plain. Known as the most secret spot on earth, it was not marked on maps and was populated by the CIA, the Ravens (the air controllers who flew spotter planes and called in air strikes) and the Hmong.

The Pathet Lao were headquartered in caves in Xam Neua province, to the north of the plain. Their base was equipped with a hotel cave (for visiting dignitaries), a hospital cave, embassy caves and even a theatre cave (see page 179).

The Plain of Jars (colloquially known as the PDJ, after the French Plaine de Jarres), was the scene of some of the heaviest fighting and changed hands countless times, the Royalist and Hmong forces occupying it during the wet season, the Pathet Lao in the dry. During this period in the conflict the town of Long Tien, known as one of the country's 'alternate' bases to keep nosy journalists away (the word 'alternate' was meant to indicate that it was unimportant), grew to such an extent that it became Laos' second city. James Parker in his book *Codename Mule* claims that the air base was so busy that at its peak it was handling more daily flights than Chicago's O'Hare airport. Others claim that it was the busiest airport in the world. There was also fighting around Luang Prabang and the Boloven Plateau to the south.

The end of the war Although the origins of the war in Laos were distinct from those which fuelled the conflict in Vietnam, the two wars had effectively merged by the early 1970s and it became inevitable that the fate of the Americans to the east would determine the outcome of the secret war on the other side of the Annamite Range. By 1970 it was no longer possible for the US administration to shroud the war in secrecy: a flood of refugees had arrived in Vientiane in an effort to escape the conflict.

During the dying days of the US-backed regime in Vientiane, CIA agents and Ravens lived in quarters south of the capital, known as KM-6 – because it was 6 km from town. Another compound in downtown Vientiane was known as 'Silver City' and reputedly also sometimes housed CIA agents. On the departure of the Americans and the arrival of the new regime in 1975, the Communists' secret police made Silver City their new home. Today, Lao people still call military intelligence officers 'Silvers' – and from time to time during the early 1990s, as Laos was opening up to international tourism, Silvers were even assigned as tour guides.

A ceasefire was agreed in February 1973, a month after Washington and Hanoi struck a similar deal in Paris. Power was transferred in April 1974 to yet another coalition government set up in Vientiane under the premiership of the ever-ready Souvanna Phouma. The neutralist prince once again had a Communist deputy and foreign affairs minister. The Red Prince, Souphanouvong, headed the Joint National Political Council. Foreign troops were given two months to leave the country. The North Vietnamese were allowed to remain along the Ho Chi Minh Trail, for although US forces had withdrawn from South Vietnam, the war there was not over.

The communists' final victories over Saigon (and Phnom Penh) in April 1975 were a catalyst for the Pathet Lao who advanced on the capital. Grant Evans in a *Short History of Laos* says that the most intriguing element of the communist takeover of

Laos was the slow pace in which it was executed. It is widely hailed as the 'bloodless' takeover. Due to the country's mixed loyalties the Pathet Lao government undertook a gradual process of eroding away existing loyalties to the Royalist government. As the end drew near and the Pathet Lao began to advance out of the mountains and towards the more populated areas of the Mekong valley – the heartland of the Royalist government – province after province fell with scarcely a shot being fired. The mere arrival of a small contingent of Pathet Lao soldiers was sufficient to secure victory – even though these soldiers arrived at Wattay Airport on Chinese transport planes to be greeted by representatives of the Royal Lao government. It is even possible that they were not even armed.

Administration of Vientiane by the People's Revolutionary Committee was secured on 18 August. The atmosphere was very different from that which accompanied the Communist's occupation of Saigon in Vietnam the same year. In Vientiane peaceful crowds of several hundred thousand turned out to hear speeches by Pathet Lao cadres. The King remained unharmed in his palace and while a coffin representing 'dead American imperialism' was ceremonially burned this was done in a 'carnival' atmosphere. Vientiane was declared 'officially liberated' on 23 August 1975. The coalition government was dismissed and Souvanna Phouma resigned for the last time. All communications with the outside world were cut.

While August 1975 represents a watershed in the history of Laos, scholars are left with something of a problem: explaining why the Pathet Lao prevailed. According to Martin Stuart-Fox, the Lao revolutionary movement "had not mobilized an exploited peasantry with promises of land reform, for most of the country was underpopulated and peasant families generally owned sufficient land for their subsistence needs. The appeal of the Pathet Lao to their lowland Lao compatriots was in terms of nationalism and independence and the preservation of Lao culture from the corrosive American influence; but no urban uprising occurred until the very last minute when effective government had virtually ceased to exist ... The small Lao intelligentsia, though critical of the Royal Lao government, did not desert it entirely and their recruitment to the Pathet Lao was minimal. Neither the monarchy, still less Buddhism, lost legitimacy." Stuart-Fox concludes that it was external factors, and in particular the intervention of outside powers, which led to the victory of the Pathet Lao. Without the Vietnamese and Americans, the Pathet Lao would not have won. For the great mass of Laos' population before 1975, Communism meant nothing. This was not a mass uprising but a victory secured by a small ideologically committed elite and forged in the furnace of the war in Indochina.

As the Pathet Lao seized power, rightist ministers, ranking civil servants, doctors, much of the intelligentsia and around 30,000 Hmong crossed the Mekong and escaped into Thailand, fearing that they would face persecution from the Pathet Lao. Although the initial exodus was large, the majority of refugees fled in the next few years up until 1980 as the Lao government introduced new reforms aimed at wiping out decadence and reforming the economic system.

The refugee camps By the late 1980s, a total of 340,000 people – 10% of the population and mostly middle class – had fled the country. At least half of the refugees were Hmong, the US's key allies during the war, who feared reprisals and persecution. From 1988, refugees who had made it across the border began to head back across the Mekong from camps in Thailand and to asylum in the US and France. More than 2000 refugees were also repatriated from Yunnan Province in China. For those prepared to return from exile overseas, the government offered to give them back confiscated property so long as they stayed for at least six months and become Lao citizens once again.

Nonetheless, many lived for years in squalid refugee camps, although the better connected and those with skills to sell secured US, Australian and French passports.

For Laos, a large proportion of its human capital drained westwards, creating a vacuum of skilled personnel that would hamper – and still does – efforts at reconstruction and development. But while many people fled across the Mekong, a significant number who had aligned themselves with the Royalists decided to stay and help build a new Laos. They saw themselves as Lao patriots and their patriotic duty was to stay.

Laos under Communism

The People's Democratic Republic of Laos was proclaimed in December 1975 with Prince Souphanouvong as president and Kaysone Phomvihane as secretary-general of the Lao People's Revolutionary Party (a post he had held since its formation in 1955). The king's abdication was accepted and the ancient Lao monarchy was abolished, together with King Samsenthai's 600-year-old system of village autonomy. But instead of executing their vanquished foes, the LPRP installed Souvanna and the ex-king, Savang Vatthana, as 'special advisers' to the politburo. On Souvanna's death in 1984, he was accorded a full state funeral. The king did not fare so well: he later died ignominiously while in detention after his alleged involvement in a counter-revolutionary plot (see below).

Surprisingly, the first actions of the new revolutionary government was not to build a new revolutionary economy and society, but to stamp out unsavoury behaviour. Dress and hairstyles, dancing and singing, even the food that was served at family celebrations, was all subject to rigorous official scrutiny by so-called 'Investigation Cadres'. If the person(s) concerned were found not to match up to the Party's scrupulous standards of good taste they were bundled off to re-education camps.

Relations with Thailand, which in the immediate wake of the revolution remained cordial, deteriorated in late 1976. A military coup in Bangkok led to rumours that the Thai military, backed by the CIA, was supporting Hmong and other right-wing Lao rebels. The regime feared that Thailand would be used as a spring-board for a royalist coup attempt by exiled reactionaries. This prompted the arrest of King Savang Vatthana, together with his family and Crown Prince Vongsavang, who were all dispatched to a Seminar re-education camp in Sam Neua province. They were never heard of again. In December 1989 Kaysone Phomvihane admitted in Paris, for the first time, that the king had died of malaria in 1984 and that the queen had also died "of natural causes" – no mention was made of Vongsavang. The Lao people have still to be officially informed of his demise. (Some commentators – like Christopher Kremmer in his book *Stalking the Elephant Kings* published in 1997 – have used the incarceration of the King to mount a stinging critique of the current regime in Vientiane. However, he does not adequately acknowledge the issue of the king's implication in a rightwing, counter-revolutionary plot.)

Re-education camps Between 30,000 and 40,000 reactionaries who had been unable to flee the country were interned in remote, disease-ridden camps for 're-education'. These camps referred to as Samanaya took their name from the Western word, seminar. The reluctant scholars were forced into slave labour in squalid jungle conditions and subjected to incessant political propaganda for anything from a few months up to 15 years. Historian Grant Evans suggests that many internees were duped into believing that the government wanted complete reconciliation and so went away for re-education willingly. Evans says the purpose of the camps was to "break the will of members of the old regime and instill in them fear of the new regime." Old men, released back into society after more than 15 years of re-education were cowed and subdued, although some were prepared to talk in paranoid whispers about their grim experiences in Xam Neua.

By 1978, the re-education policy starting to wind down, although, in 1986, Amnesty International released a report on the forgotten inhabitants of the re-education camps, claiming that 6000-7000 were still being held. By that time incarceration behind barbed wire had ended and instead the internees were 'arbitrarily restricted' rather than imprisoned. They were assigned to road construction teams and other public works projects. Nonetheless, conditions for these victims of the war in Indochina suffered from malnutrition, disease and many died prematurely in captivity. It is unclear how many died, but at least 15,000 have been freed. Officials of the old regime, ex-government ministers and former Royalist air force and army officers, together with thousands of others unlucky enough to have been on the wrong side, were released from the camps, largely during the mid to late 1980s. Most of the surviving political prisoners have now been reintegrated into society. Some work in the tourism industry and one, a former colonel in the Royal Lao Army, jointly owns the **Asian Pavilion Hotel** (formerly the **Vieng Vilai**) on Samsenthai Road in downtown Vientiane. After years of being force-fed Communist propaganda he now enjoys full government support as an ardent capitalist entrepreneur. The Lao, as scores of books like this one keep reminding their readers, are a gentle people and it is hard not to leave the country without that view being reinforced. Even the Lao People's Revolutionary Party seems quaintly inept and it is hard to equate it with its more brutal and sinister sister parties in Vietnam, Cambodia, China or the former Soviet Union. Yet five students who meekly called for greater political freedom in 1999 were whisked off by the police and have not been heard of since. So much for soggy ineptness.

Reflecting on 10 years of 'reconstruction' Laos' recent political and economic history is covered in more detail under Modern Laos (see below). But it is worth ending this short account of the country's history by noting the brevity of Laos' experiment with full-blown Communism. Just 10 years after the Pathet Lao took control of Vientiane, the leadership were on the brink of far-reaching economic reforms. By the mid-1980s it was widely acknowledged that Marxism-Leninism had failed the country and its people. The population were still dreadfully poor; the ideology of Communism had failed to entice more than a handful into serious and enthusiastic support for the party and its ways; and graft and nepotism were on the rise.

Modern Laos

Politics

President Kaysone Phomvihane died in November 1992, aged 71. (His right-hand man, Prince Souphanouvong – the so-called Red Prince – died just over two years later, on 9 January 1995.) As one obituary put it, Kaysone was older than he seemed, both historically and ideologically. He had been chairman of the LPRP since the mid-1950s and had been a protégé and comrade of Ho Chi Minh, who led the Vietnamese struggle for independence from the French. After leading the Lao Resistance Government – or Pathet Lao – from caves in Xam Neua province in the north, Kaysone assumed the premiership on the abolition of the monarchy in 1975. But under his leadership – and following the example of his mentors in Hanoi – Kaysone became the driving force behind the market-orientated reforms. The year before he died, he gave up the post of prime minister for that of president.

His death didn't change things much, as other members of the old guard stepped into the breach. Nouhak Phounsavanh – a sprightly 78-year-old former truck driver and hardline Communist – succeeded him as president. Nouhak didn't last terribly long in the position and in February 1998 he was replaced by 75-year-old General

Khamtai Siphandon – the outgoing prime minister and head of the LPRP. Khamtai represents the last of the revolutionary Pathet Lao leaders who fought the Royalists and the Americans. In April 2006, Siphandon, the last of the old guard from the caves in Vieng Xai, was replaced as president by Choummaly Sayasone.

Recent years

With the introduction of the New Economic Mechanism in 1986 so there were hopes, in some quarters at least, that economic liberalization would be matched by political *glasnost*. So far, however, the monolithic Party shows few signs of equating capitalism with democracy. While the Lao brand of Communism has always been seen as relatively tame, it remains a far cry from political pluralism. Laos' first constitution since the Communists came to power in 1975 was approved in 1991. The country's political system is referred to as a popular democracy, yet it has rejected any significant moves towards multi-party reforms.

Take the elections to the 108-seat National Assembly on 24 February 2002. All of the candidates standing for election had been approved by the LPRP's mass organization, the Lao Front for National Construction. While it is not necessary for a candidate to be a member of the LPRP to stand, they are closely vetted and have to demonstrate that they have a 'sufficient level of knowledge of party policy'. As with the previous elections to the National Assembly at the end of 1997, only one of the 108 deputies elected was not a member of the Lao People's Revolutionary Party. Who was this sole, brave symbol of political pluralism? The minister of justice. When President Khamtai Siphandone turned up to cast his ballot (voting is compulsory), one journalist asked him what the election would change. His answer: "There won't be any change." This pattern of party cadres maintaining political seats was repeated in the National Assembly elections held in April 2006, where LPRP members won 114 out of 115 parliamentary seats.

On the dreamy streets of Vientiane, the chances of a Tiananmen-style uprising are remote. But the events of the late 1980s and early 1990s in Eastern Europe and Moscow did alarm hardliners – just as they did in Beijing and Hanoi. They can be reasonably confident, however, that in their impoverished nation, most people are more worried about where their next meal is going to come from than they are about the allure of multi-party democracy. Day-to-day politics aren't on the radar of most Lao citizens and many would find it hard to name the president and prime minister.

The greatest concern for the Lao leadership (and in this sense the country mirrors developments in many other countries of Asia) is what effect westernization is having upon the population. The economic reforms, or so the authorities would seem to believe, have brought not only foreign investment and new consumer goods, but also greed, corruption, consumerism and various social ills from drugs to prostitution. This was starkly illustrated at the March 1996 party congress. Observers were expecting to find the congress reaffirm the policy of economic reform and rubber stamp it 'business as usual'. Instead one of the architects of the reform programme, Deputy Prime Minister Khamphoui Keoboualapha, was unceremoniously dumped. The reason? It was thought that he had become too close to Thailand and in particular to influential Thai investors. He was blamed more than most for the emergence of the various social ills that the leadership have been so desperate to stem. Khamphoui was rehabilitated in a leadership reshuffle in February 1998 but this was probably because the leadership reasoned that they needed people with some knowledge of economic policy to see the country through the Asian crisis. It would be surprising if the process of economic reform was reversed – although it will probably slow down from time to time reflecting domestic developments and concerns – largely because there is simply no alternative.

In 2007, the politburo still largely controlled the country and, for now, sweeping changes are unlikely. Most of the country's leaders are well into their 60s and were educated in communist countries like Russia and Vietnam. However, the younger Lao people (particularly those that have studied abroad in Japan, Australia, UK or the US) are starting to embrace new political and economic ideas. The government takes inspiration from Vietnam's success and is more likely to follow the lead of its neighbour rather than adopting any Western model of government.

Foreign relations

Laos is rapidly becoming a keystone in mainland Southeast Asia (see Economy, page 292) and sees its future in linking in with its more powerful and richer neighbours. To this end Laos joined the Association of Southeast Asian Nations (ASEAN) on 23 July 1997, becoming the group's second Communist member (Vietnam joined in July 1995). By joining, Vientiane hoped to be in a better position to trade off the interests of the various powers in the region, thereby giving it greater room for manoeuvre. It was also hoped that tiny Laos would be able to develop on the economic coat tails of Southeast Asia's fast-growing economic 'tigers' – a hope rudely dashed by the region's economic crisis which began with the collapse of the Thai baht on 3 July 1997.

One of Laos' strategies for further integration into the Asian economy is to establish itself as a regional transit point, with new highways dissecting the country at 100 km intervals. Construction of one major highway started in 2005, connecting Thailand's northernmost province of Chiang Rai to Kunming in China via the Lao provinces of Bokeo and Luang Namtha. The 700-km-long highway (of which 228 km is in Laos) could generate more income for the land-locked country. However, it also poses a major threat in terms of increased transmission of HIV from transient workers and truckers. To add insult to injury, China is opportunistically building a huge truck-stop near Boten in northwest Laos (see page 146), which is likely to wipe out a large proportion of the income Laos might have earned from transit vehicles.

Laos is the only landlocked country in Southeast Asia and Vientiane is keen to pursue a cooperative 'equilibrium policy' with its neighbours. There is a widely held view that Laos – a small, poor, weak and land-locked country – is best served by having multiple friends in international circles. It has often been referred to as a 'buffer' state, which exists to ensure that none of the surrounding countries have to border each other. The leadership in Vientiane is in the tricky situation of having to play off China's military might, Thailand's commercial aggressiveness and Vietnam's population pressures, while keeping everyone happy. The answer, in many people's minds, is to promote a policy of interdependence in mainland Southeast Asia.

Relations with Thailand From the 1980s the government took steps to improve its foreign relations – and Thailand has been the main beneficiary. Historically, Thailand has always been the main route for international access to landlocked Laos. Survival instincts told the Vientiane regime that reopening its front door was of paramount importance. The border disputes with Thailand have now been settled and the bloody clashes of 1987 and 1988, when thousands on both sides lost their lives, are history. Thailand is Laos' largest investor and the success of the market reforms depend more on Thailand than any other country (but see below on the economic crisis). Economic pragmatism, then, has forced the leadership in Vientiane to cosy up to Bangkok. This does not mean that relations are warm. Indeed, Vientiane is irredeemably suspicious of Thai intentions, a suspicion born of a history of conflict.

Thailand is Vientiane's lifeline to the outside world. The Thai Crown Princess Sirindhorn visited Laos in early 1990 – the first visit by a member of the Thai royal family for 15 years – and Thailand lifted a ban on the export of 200 'strategic goods' to Laos, which had been in place since 1975 and which covered everything from military equipment to food and bicycles. The two old foes agreed to build the Mittaphab – or Friendship – bridge across the Mekong linking Vientiane with Nong Khai in Northeast

Thailand. The bridge was built with Australian assistance and opened in 1994 (see page 82). However, fears of Laos becoming a Thai commercial colony has led the government to extend an extremely cautious welcome to Thai the recently completed bridge at Savannakhet in the southern panhandle, which provides a link west with the northeastern Thai town of Mukdahan and from there with southern Vietnam.

Historically, Thais have emerged as one of the biggest foreign investors in Laos. A number of Thai commercial banks have set up in Laos, along with businesspeople, consultants and loggers. Young Lao who previously attended universities in the Soviet bloc are now being dispatched to Thai universities. The warming of relations between Bangkok and Vientiane has raised some eyebrows: sceptics say Laos' wealth of unexploited natural resources is a tempting reward for patching things up. Thailand is also the most important player in the Nam Theun II hydropower project (see page 190). But to its credit, Thailand has prioritized aid to Laos and has signed joint ventures in almost every sector – from science and technology to trade, banking and agriculture. Thai businesspeople have partially taken over the state beer and brewery and the Thai conglomerate Shinawatra (owned by the former disgraced Thai prime minister) has been given telecommunications concessions. Nonetheless, Thai diplomats are only too aware of the poor reputation that their businessmen have in Vientiane. They are regarded as overbearing and superior in their attitude to the Lao and rapacious, predatory and mercenary in their business dealings. The Thai government has even run courses to try and improve business behaviour. But Thai perceptions of their neighbours are deeply entrenched. As one Thai critic once remarked: "Thai cultural diplomacy starts with the assumption that Thai culture is superior".

To understand Laos' fears of Thailand it is necessary to look back in history. Until the French absorbed Laos into Indochina, Laos came under Thai suzerainty and indeed the Siamese saw Laos as a junior, rather primitive, colony of theirs. When the foolhardy King Anou of Vientiane tried to recreate the great 14th-century Lao kingdom of Fa Ngum and invaded Siam he was soundly thrashed in a battle at Korat, in northeast Thailand, and then saw his capital Vientiane plundered, sacked and razed by Siamese forces – a fact which explains why today this ancient city is so devoid of architecture pre-dating the French period. Anou was captured and later died in captivity. Needless to say, Thai and Lao history is at odds on this period of history: Thai accounts paint Anou as a rebel; those written by Lao historians characterize him as a national hero.

It is only with this background in mind that Lao fears of Thai commercial hegemony can be fully appreciated. When, in 1988, former Thai Prime Minister Chatichai Choonhaven expressed a desire to turn Indochina "from a battlefield into a market place", this was viewed by many Lao – and some more thoughtful Thais – as tantamount to a threat of commercial invasion. (The theme was returned to in 1995 when a senior Thai diplomat, Suridhya Simaskul, remarked to the journalist Michael Vatikiotis, "We have passed the stage of turning battlefields into markets; now the market itself has become the battlefield.") Thailand, its own natural resources denuded through years of thoughtless exploitation, was hoping to pillage Laos' resource-rich larder. In July 1989, state-run Radio Vientiane broadcast a commentary, presumably officially sanctioned, stating: "Having failed to destroy our country through their military might [referring to the Ban Rom Klao border conflict of 1987-1988], the enemy has now employed a new strategy in attacking us through the so-called attempt to turn the Indochinese battlefield into a marketplace." It is this fear of Thailand and of over-dependence on Thailand, which has prompted the Lao government to do its utmost to try and diversify its commercial links. In a rather novel departure from the usual state of affairs, the Lao are also more scared of Thai cultural pollution than Western cultural pollution. The similarities between the two countries and the fact that many Lao households watch Thai television make Thailand seem more of a risk. In 1993, former president and Pathet Lao veteran Phoumi Vongvichi warned against the dangers of prostitution, 'depraved' dancing and gambling. The source of these threats to pristine Lao culture was Thailand. Newspaper reports even dubbed the Mittapheap Bridge the AIDS Bridge, because it was expected that the bridge would bring prostitution and AIDS to the country. Nonetheless, over the last few years, relations have grown from strength to strength, helped along as the traditional economic dependency on Thailand has been somewhat mitigated by Laos' ever-growing relations with China. Rather it is convenient to have Thailand as a partner to counterbalance and hedge China's growing domination of the region.

The sleeping giant awakens: relations with China In 1988 China and Laos normalized relations and this was followed by a defence co-operation agreement signed in 1993. Recently, Beijing has taken a particular interest in developing Laos' infrastructure, more out of self-interest than altruism. As China continues to develop at a breakneck speed, its interest in Laos' natural resources is expected to escalate substantially, particularly in the areas of timber, iron ore, copper, gold, and gemstones. China is now Laos' second largest trading partner and foreign investor. The Asian Development Bank (ADB) reported that Lao-China trade grew from US$33.1 million in 1990 to US$118.3 million in 2003, for the most part, in China's favour. Over the last few years the economic giant has secured a deal to build numerous roads in Laos pro bono, in exchange for logging the areas around the roads. In 2005, it seemed China had logged well beyond the limits that were initially agreed upon.

China's now gives more than US$280 million annually to Laos in development aid. It is also building the highway that will eventually link Yunnan province to Thailand via Laos, see page 289.

Between 2001 to August 2007, Chinese foreign direct investment amounted to US$1.1 billion. This is second only to Thailand's projects worth US$1.3 billion. Between 2006 and 2007, Chinese companies accounted for the majority of the US$1.1 billion worth of FDI approved. Of the 117 projects approved by the Committee of Planning and Investment, 45 were Chinese projects worth US$462 million. About a third of this investment was in hydropower.

Chinese companies are investing heavily in Lao's natural resources, including mining, rubber plantations and hydropower, alongside telecommunications, construction materials and hotels and restaurants.

Alongside this increased economic investment, there has been an increase in Chinese migration. The number of Chinese officially living in Laos is 30,000, though many believe the unofficial number is estimated to be 10 times that. Nonetheless, not a bad word is to be whispered about Beijing in the political corridors of Vientiane.

Laos' ever-tightening relationship with China could jeopardize ties with the country's closest ally, Vietnam, which shares a 1300-km-long border with Laos and historically has had poor relations with China.

Relations with Vietnam The Lao government has a special relationship with Vietnam, as it was Hanoi that helped the LPRP achieve power. Vietnam is also Laos' biggest trading partner. However, as Laos has turned to the West, Japan and Thailand for economic help, the government has become more critical of its closest Communist ally, Vietnam. Following Vietnam's invasion of Cambodia in December 1978, thousands of Vietnamese moved into northern Laos as permanent colonizers and by 1978 there were an estimated 40,000 Vietnamese regulars in Laos but, in 1987, 50,000 Vietnamese troops withdrew. In 1990 a Vientiane census found 15,000 Vietnamese living illegally in the capital, most of whom were promptly deported. With the death of President Kaysone Phomvihane in November 1992, another historical link with Vietnam was cut. He was half-Vietnamese and most of his cabinet owed their education and their posts to Hanoi's succour during the war years. As the old men of the Lao Communist Party, who owed so much to the Vietnamese, die off, so their replacements are looking elsewhere for investment and political support. They do not have such deep fraternal links with their brothers in Hanoi and are keen to diversify their international relations.

Relations with the USA Laos is the only country in Indochina to have maintained relations with the US since 1975, despite the fact that, thirty years since the illegal bombing campaign of Laos subsided, the US has neither offered a substantial sum of money for reparations nor helped to clear the tonnes of unexploded ordnance littering the eastern side of the country. Washington even expected the Lao government to allocate funds to help locate the bodies of US pilots shot down in the war. At a meeting between the Foreign Affairs Minister, General Phoune Sipaseuth, and the US Secretary of State, James Baker, in October 1990, Vientiane pledged to co-operate with the US over the narcotics trade and to step up the search for the 530 American MIAs still listed as missing in the Lao jungle. In mid-1993, tri-lateral talks between Laos, Vietnam and the US allowed for greater cooperation in the search for MIAs, many of whom are thought to have been airmen, shot down over the Ho Chi Minh Trail. The MIA charity, based in Vientiane, has since assumed quite a high profile. In October 1992, America's diplomatic presence in Laos was upgraded to ambassadorial status from chargé d'affaires and, at the end of 1997, a high-level US mission to Laos promised greater support in the country's bomb-defusing work. However, until 2004, Laos remained one of the few countries to be denied normal trade relations with the US, the others being North Korea, Cuba and Myanmar (Burma).

Furthermore, under duress from the US (a dangling carrot perhaps?) Laos has all but eradicated opium, at huge cost to the country socially and economically as it involved relocating many people with minimal assistance from the US. Since 1989, the US government has handed over US$38 million for drug control to the Lao government but this money hasn't stretched far enough to ensure that former opium producers aren't left starving. Relations between the two countries have improved. This is somewhat driven by the US desire to counterbalance growing Chinese influence in the region. Most mainland Southeast Asian countries are reaping the rewards by simultaneously playing off the two superpowers and securing as much aid and trade as possible from both. In February 2005, a Bilateral Trade Agreement between the US and Laos entered into force, leading to a rise in bilateral trade from US$15.7 million in 2006, from US$8.9 million in 2003.

Relations with other countries Fortunately Laos is unwilling to put all its eggs in one basket. Japan is now Laos' biggest aid donor and Vientiane has also courted other Western countries, particularly Sweden (a long-time ally), France, Germany and Australia, who have donated significant sums of aid. These days Washington and Tokyo offer more in the way of hope for the embattled regime than Moscow: in 1991, 100 Soviet economic and technical advisers were pulled out of the dilapidated flats they occupied on the outskirts of Vientiane; their withdrawal from the country signalled the end of the era of Soviet aid. While Russia gave Vientiane some leeway before it had to pay back its rouble debt, the country's former lifeline with Moscow has become of scant importance to Laos' economic future.

Economy

Until just over a decade ago, if the world's financial markets crashed and international trade and commerce collapsed overnight, Laos would have been blissfully immune from the catastrophe. It would be 'farming as usual' the next morning. Since the mid-1980s, though, the government has gradually begun cautiously to tread the free market path, veering off the old command system. Farms have been privatized and the state has to compete for produce with market traders at market prices. Many of the unprofitable state-owned businesses and factories have been leased or sold off.

Centuries of war and 15 years of Communism had little impact on the self-reliant villages of rural Laos. After the 1975 takeover, the Lao government, reliant on aid from Vietnam, decided to assuage this dependency by expanding on their existing economic base – agriculture. To this end, in March 1978 the government launched an agricultural cooperativization scheme – a plan to collectivize agriculture through the development of village-based cooperatives. The government's attempts at cooperativization proved unpopular and unworkable. Just before the cooperativization programme was abruptly suspended in mid-1979 there were 2800 cooperatives accounting for perhaps 25% of farming families. But even these figures overestimate the role of cooperatives at that time, for many were scarcely functioning. The little work that has been undertaken on agriculture during this period has shown that even when cooperatives were functioning, their members were reluctant participants and there was a good amount of foot-dragging and petty obstructionism. The reasons why cooperatives were such a failure are numerous. To begin with and unlike China and Vietnam, there were almost no large landlords, there was little tenancy and there was abundant land. The inequalities that were so obvious in neighbouring countries simply did not exist in Laos. Second, most farmers were subsistence cultivators; capitalism had barely made inroads into the Lao countryside and the forces of commercialization were largely absent. Further and third, the LPRP provided little support either of a technical or financial kind. As a result, farmers – largely uneducated and bound to their traditional methods of production – saw little incentive to change. In some areas it was not so much a lack of interest in cooperatives, but a positive dislike of them. There were reports of farmers slaughtering their cattle, burning their fields and eating their poultry, rather than handing their livestock or crops over to the Party. By mid-1979, when the policy was suspended, the leadership in Vientiane had concluded that their attempts at cooperativization had been a disaster.

Since the suspension of the policy, the government has returned to a free enterprise system in the countryside. Farmers now effectively own their land and, since a new land law was approved by the National Assembly in April 1997, they can pass it on to their children and use it as collateral to get a bank loan. They can produce whatever crops they like and can sell these on what has become virtually a free market. Lao farmers, though they may be poor and though technology may be antiquated, are in essence no different in terms of the ways they work than their kinsfolk over the Mekong in Thailand.

Laos made the jump from a sleepy agrarian economy hidden behind a facade of socialism to a reforming economy like China and Vietnam in the 1980s. In English this change is rather blandly named the New Economic Mechanism (NEM). Locally, the more evocative terms *chin thanakan mai* (new thinking) and *kanpatihup setthakit* (reform economy) are used. The origins of the NEM can be traced back to 1982 when the possibility of fundamental reform of the economy was first entertained by a small group within the leadership. The logic for economic reform and the integration of Laos into the regional – and world – economies was pretty compelling. During the decade of command planning from 1975 through to 1985 the economy grew at just 2.9% per year, barely sufficient to meet the needs of a growing population and not enough to fuel the desire for a better standard of living. The government's fear was that, like other communist countries, the failure to bring the Lao people a better standard of living might challenge the supremacy of the Lao People's Revolutionary Party. The decision to opt for reform seemed to be borne out as the economy picked up steam. For the next three or four years the debate continued within this small circle and it was not until 1985 that the NEM was actually pilot-tested in the Vientiane area, making Laos one of the very first countries to embrace 'perestroika'. As late General Secretary Kaysone Phomvihane stated at the Fourth Party Congress in 1986:

"In all economic activities, we must know how to apply objective laws and take into account socio-economic efficiency. At the present time, our country is still at the first stage of the transition period. Hence the system of economic laws now being applied to our country is very complicated. It includes not only the specific laws of socialism but also the laws of commodity production. Reality indicates that if we only apply the specific economic laws of socialism alone and defy the general laws pertaining to commodity production, or vice versa, we will make serious mistakes in our economic undertaking during this transition period" (General Secretary Kaysone Phomvihane, Fourth Party Congress 1986; quoted in Lao PDR 1989).

Under the horrified gaze of Marx and Lenin – their portraits still dominate the plenary hall – it was announced that the state motto had changed from "Peace, Independence, Unity and Socialism" to "Peace, Independence, Democracy, Unity and Prosperity". The last part is largely wishful thinking for one of the poorest countries in Southeast Asia, but it reflected the realization that unless Laos turned off the socialist road fast, it would have had great difficulty digging itself out of the economic quagmire that 15 years' adherence to Marxism had created.

The success of the reforms there led to the NEM being presented at – and adopted by – the critical Fourth Party Congress of 1986. The NEM encompasses a range of reformist policies, much like those adopted in other countries from Russia to Vietnam: a move to a market determination of prices and resource allocation; a shift away from central planning to 'guidance' planning; a decentralization of control to industries and lower levels of government and the encouragement of the private sector; the encouragement of foreign investment and the promulgation of a new investment law allowing more relaxed foreign ownership and 'tax holidays'; a lifting of barriers to internal and external trade.

What Laos was able to achieve by introducing the NEM was a very rapid reorientation of its economy. But the question to be asked is: 'what exactly was being reformed?' The assumption is that Laos, as a so-called transitional economy, was making – is making – the transition from communism to capitalism, from state to market. This, though, misses the point that in 1986 there was remarkably little in Laos to reform. The great majority of the population were poor farmers (and still are) and the country's industrial base was almost non-existent. There were almost no communes to break up and there was no large state industrial sector to dismember. It all meant that the task of the Lao leadership has been comparatively easy when compared with, say, Vietnam. In a sense, Laos was never socialist except in name and so the shift to a market economy involved not a move from socialism to capitalism, but from subsistence to capitalism.

This doesn't mean that reform has been a doddle, because although Laos may not have had to undo years of socialist reconstruction and development, there was also little that the leadership could build on to promote modernization. There were few skilled workers, low levels of infrastructure, large slices of the country are almost impossible to reach and few entrepreneurs and even fewer people with the money to invest in new ventures. In other words, Laos was short of most of the elements that constitute a modern economy.

To introduce the sweeping reforms former President Kaysone Phomvihane shouldered much of the blame for the miserable state of the economy, admitting that the Party had made mistakes. Laos underwent the political equivalent of an earth tremor in March 1991 at the Fifth Congress of the Lao People's Revolutionary Party (LPRP). Pro-market reforms were embraced and the politburo and central committee got a much-needed transfusion of new blood. At the same time, the hammer and sickle motif was quietly removed from the state emblem and enlightened sub-editors set to work on the national credo, which is emblazoned on all official documents. In August 1991, at the opening of the People's Supreme Assembly, Kaysone Phomvihane, the late President, said: "Socialism is still our objective, but it is a distant one. Very distant." With that statement, Kaysone embraced – somewhat reluctantly, it must be said – the country's market-orientated policy, Chin Thanakan Mai or 'New Thinking'.

At the Congress in 1991 he set the new national agenda: Laos had to step up its exports, encourage more foreign investment, promote tourism and rural development, entice its shifting cultivators into proper jobs and revamp the financial system. In doing so he prioritized the problems but offered no solutions bar the loosening of state control and the promotion of private enterprise.

The first task for the government was to stabilize the value of the local currency, the kip, and introduce market 'discipline' so as to eliminate a booming currency black market. So from 1986, when economic reforms were first introduced, Laos eliminated six of its seven official exchange rates to create a unified market-related rate. By the early 1990s the kip had stabilized at around 700 to the US dollar. The once-booming black market all but disappeared. Although still a non-convertible currency, the kip was as much in demand in Laos as the US dollar and Thai baht. This helped put Laos on a more competitive footing. Unfortunately for supporters of economic reform, the collapse of the Thai baht and the consequent fall in the value of the kip encouraged the Lao government to reintroduce currency controls (see the section below).

During the early years of reform, between 1986 and 1990, the economy grew and from 1991-1995 increased again to 6.5% per year. However economic liberalization also has its risks. The collapse of the Thai baht at the beginning of July 1997 also dragged down the Lao kip while Thailand's fall from economic grace caused Thai investment in Laos to evaporate (Thailand is Laos' largest foreign investor). 1998 saw zero growth and inflation escalated to nearly 100% as the government rather ineptly tried to control events. Since then the economy has stabilized.

Reform in a period of economic crisis

While Laos might be poor it was not insulated from the effects of Asia's economic crisis. Indeed, it is the reforms of the years since 1986 which has made the country vulnerable to developments beyond its borders. The Lao kip was dragged down by the depreciation of the Thai baht and lost value from US$1 = 978 kip in December 1996 to US$1 = 1780 kip in November 1997. Since then, it has sunk further and when this book went to press, there were 9385 kip to the US dollar. In fact there is no currency in Southeast Asia, with the exception of the Burmese kyat, which has lost more value.

As the currency lost value the government lost its nerve and slapped on currency controls and rounded up the private money changers who have been operating for years in Vientiane. The governor of the Lao central bank blamed "speculative attempts by opportunists" for the Kip's collapse. The trade deficit widened and eight state-owned banks became effectively insolvent. Inflation during 1997 rose and in 1998 continued to escalate to reach 100% by the end of the year. There was also a sharp downturn in investment (remember, Thailand is Laos' largest foreign investor).

The leadership held very different views on how to deal with the crisis. The so-styled conservatives in the politburo wanted the Lao government take a step back from the market and emphasize domestic resources. Reformists wanted further liberalization – à la IMF – and to extricate the country from the economic mess by integrating still more rapidly into the regional and world economies. The outcome of this debate, in typically Lao style, was a bit of both. The leadership took their foot off the pedal of economic reform but did not substantially reverse what was already in place. It also seems that they may have realized the futility of trying to rein back trade with neighbouring Thailand and China given their lack of economic control in many areas.

What was perhaps most surprising about Laos' economic malaise was the absence of any public disturbances. With the economy contracting, inflation running at more than 100%, banks broke, foreign investment evaporating and the government apparently clueless and helpless as to what to do, one might have expected just a little more public debate and criticism. After all, Thailand and South Korea both saw a change of government, Malaysia the trial and imprisonment of Deputy Prime Minister Anwar Ibrahim and Indonesia the violent dumping of Suharto, president of more than three decades. Laos may be renowned for the relaxed and forgiving ways of its people, but it is hard not to wonder, 'for how much longer?'

Building up the economy

Laos, as books constantly reiterate, is poor. While it is tempting to mouth those favourite words 'poor but happy', there can be little doubt that the major challenge facing the country is how to promote development. There are few people – whether government ministers or shifting cultivators, businessmen or hawkers – who do not fervently hope that their children will be better off than they. And 'better off' means richer. As Houmpheng Souralay of the Foreign Investment Management Committee said to Singapore's *Sunday Times*, "We want to catch up with our neighbours like Thailand, Cambodia and Vietnam." But, he significantly added, only if those "investments are wholesome and do not erode our cultural identity".

Traditionally, one of Laos' most important sources of foreign exchange was receipts from over-flight rights as the Boloven Plateau lies on the flight path from Bangkok to Hong Kong and Tokyo. Nearly 100 international flights traverse Lao airspace every day and in the mid-1990s the government was receiving payment for each one. But, today, most of the Laos' foreign exchange is reaped from their natural resources.

The country and its foreign strategists look to four distinct areas for future income. The first concentrates on mining and energy. Mining rights to some of Laos' huge lignite reserves have been sold to Thai investors, while hydropower projects are plentiful. Other untapped mineral resources include reserves of gold, gemstones and iron ore, while foreign companies have undertaken preliminary searches for oil. The second area of interest is agriculture and forestry. Investors are looking at growing feed grains like soya beans and maize for export to Thailand. Raw timber exports are being replaced by processed wood industries. More enlightened analysts also see Laos as a potential large exporter of organic agricultural products – after all, agriculture in the country has never had to rely on biochemical inputs or genetically engineered seeds. The third potential area for ongoing development is tourism, which continues to grow at the rate of knots but the government is wary of Laos going the same way as Thailand. The fourth and final strategy – and the most ambitious – is for Laos to become the service centre between China, Vietnam, Cambodia and Thailand.

In 2007 Lao was still amending policy and legislation in order to prepare for accession to the World Trade Organization. Laos' stated aim is to graduate from LDC (least developed country) status by 2020.

Major development constraints in Laos are the shortage of skilled workers and capital, an undeveloped communication system, poor educational and health resources, rugged terrain and low population density. Add to this a patchwork of cultures and different languages and it is easy to see why the country is difficult to manage. Even with large amounts of public expenditure going into infrastructure, the challenge of linking people to the market and the state remains supremely important. Without roads and transport farmers cannot obtain inputs for agriculture, market any surplus production or increase their incomes.

In an effort to make the business climate more attractive, the state bank now supplies credit to all sectors of the economy. Provincial banks have been told to operate as autonomous commercial banks. State enterprises have been warned that if their bottom line does not show a profit they are out of business. Provinces are free to conclude their own trading agreements with private companies and neighbouring countries – which generally means Thailand

Tens of thousands of people work for the government in a top-heavy and often corrupt bureaucracy. Working for the Laos government is considered a job for life. Civil servants are paid the equivalent of US$20-40 per month while domestic servants working for expatriate families receive double this figure, or more. No wonder official corruption and profiteering are on the increase. The main financial incentive available to civil servants are the perks offered by NGOs – such as use of a car, per diems for trips away and scholarships to foreign universities. Admirably, most people who work for the civil service in Laos do so for prestige and personal pride; there is little other incentive as the lure of long-term gains, in the form of corruption, usually take years to accrue.

Hydropower

The country's greatest economic potential lies in its natural resources – timber, gold, precious stones, coal and iron – and hydropower. Laos has been dubbed the 'battery' or 'Kuwait' of Southeast Asia and the government has signed various deals with Thailand, China and Vietnam to sell electricity.

It has been estimated that only 1% of the country's hydropower potential of some 18,000 MW has so far been exploited and myriad schemes are being discussed (see below). By far the largest of these is Nam Theun II (see page 190). The huge dam is expected to generate up to US$150 million revenue a year for Laos or approximately US$2 billion over a 25-year period. The hydropower project will involve exporting 95% of the electricity to Thailand; the rest will be used domestically.

A few years ago these grand hydropower plans all seemed eminently sensible: energy-hungry Thailand's economy was rapidly growing and Laos was well placed to meet its needs. But there were two issues that the Lao government and its international advisers failed to take sufficiently into account: the international environmental lobby and an economic slowdown. The Nam Theun II dam, for example, was delayed by the discoveries of rare bats and birds, with financial backing from agencies like the World Bank and the Asian Development Bank held up for years. The World Bank, now all too conscious that its environmental credentials have been tarnished by dam developments in India and elsewhere, has gone out of its way to ensure that all the required environmental and other studies are undertaken.

But the Nam Theun II dam is not quite the open-and-shut case it might appear, with the international environmental lobby on the side of local people and animals and the dastardly World Bank supporting shadowy businessmen and the interests of international capital. When local people were asked their views of the dam, many apparently welcomed it. Even some environmentalists argued that having the dam might be preferable to having the forests logged. For without the money that can be earned from selling electricity to Thailand one of the few alternatives is selling wood. As dam development nears an end, the results are yet to be determined. The majority of villagers seem happy with relocation efforts, while conservationists argue that the environmental damage is yet to be properly evaluated. Plans are underway to further exploit the potential of the Mekong and its tributaries, with over 60 projects slated for development over the next decade.

Mining and logging

Mining is also providing large revenue. In the years leading up to 2007, more than 140 mining concessions were allocated, many to Chinese looking for gold, copper, iron, potassium and bauxite. Australia's ORD Rivers Resources in collaboration with China's Nonferrous Metals International Mining Company (CNMIM) plans to develop a 727-sq-km concession on the Boloven Plateau in southern Laos into one of the world's largest bauxite mines.

The symbol of southern Laos should be the timber truck, garagantuan beasts loaded with decades-old trees dwarfing the small roads. Malaysian, Taiwanese, Chinese and Thai firms have been awarded timber concessions in the country, many of them working in collaboration with the Lao military which has become an important economic player.

Agriculture

This remains the mainstay of the Lao economy, accounting for just under half of the country's GDP. Around 80% of Lao citizens are employed in some kind of subsistence agriculture, which they depend on for their survival. Rice is the staple food crop, cultivated by the majority of the population, and nearly three-quarters of Laos' farmers grow enough to sell or barter some of their crop. It is believed that rice accounts for a quarter of the country's GDP. Other primary agricultural products include coffee, corn, sugarcane, vegetables, tobacco, ginger, water buffalo, pigs, cattle, poultry, sweet potatoes, cotton, tea and peanuts.

While Laos may be land rich, this does not mean that everyone necessarily has enough to eat, and the achievement of food security is one of the government's priority. National self-sufficiency does not equate with local food security. Food deficits are common, resulting in many households experiencing both chronic and acute malnutrition. There is also intra-regional variation. For example, Sekong in the south is traditionally a rice deficit province, as is Xieng Khouang in the centre. As we move down the scale, from national to regional, provincial, district and village, there are likely to be important variations in terms of food security. Even households that are in production surplus may face a consumption deficit due to their having to sell a portion of production to meet demands for cash or to pay off debts.

The growing population poses a challenge to rice farmers. Laos' population is increasing at 2.5% per annum – from 4.25 million in 1990 to 6.4 million in 2006. This means that in the last 15 years Laos has had to feed 50% more people. Luckily, during the same period the country increased rice production by 70% (one million tonnes a year). However, the challenge for Lao farmers is whether they will be able to increase the level of rice production as the population demand increases. As Laos' population is expected to grow to 8.8 million by the year 2020, the demand for rice is expected to exceed an additional million tons of rice.

The main agricultural areas are on the Mekong's floodplains, especially around Vientiane and Savannakhet. The government has been successful in expanding the area capable of producing two rice crops a year by upgrading and developing the country's irrigation infrastructure. Cotton, coffee, maize and tobacco are the other main crops and the production of these and other 'industrial' crops such as soya and mung beans has increased in recent years.

While shifting cultivators continue to pose a 'problem' to the government, their numbers have dropped substantially since 1985 as the land allocation programme has been enthusiastically implemented. This is reflected by the fact that they are now said to cut down 100,000 ha of forest a year now, compared with 300,000 in the early 1980s. The situation has improved dramatically since the mid-1970s when Hmong General Vang Pao complained to a *National Geographic* reporter that "In one year a single family will chop down and burn trees worth US$6000 and grow a rice crop worth US$240."

Dependency on aid and development aims

Laos depends heavily on imports – everything from agricultural machinery and cars to petrol products, textiles and pharmaceuticals – which are heavily financed by foreign aid. Western bilateral donors are enthusiastically filling the aid gap left by the Socialist bloc. In June 2003, Russia agreed to write off 70% of the loans from the Cold War period.

Countries and private donors are falling over each other to fund projects, particularly anything that involves government reform; NGOs are homing in and development banks are offering soft loans and structural adjustment programmes. As Laos' foreign debt is mostly on highly concessional terms, it is not crippled by repayment schedules, though there is a reasonably hefty bill awaiting them. But with development banks accelerating their project-funding, fears are mounting that Laos is teetering on the edge of a debt trap. Laos' annual debt service repayments, as a proportion of GDP is almost double the government's expenditure on health.

The share of foreign assistance to GDP has nearly tripled since the mid-1980s. In 2005, Laos' Foreign Minister Somsavat Lengsavat said that the country had received more than US$2.4 billion from foreign donors between 1991 and 2005. Economists based in Vientiane suggest that ODA (Official Development Assistance) accounts for roughly 60-70% of Laos' annual public expenditure budget. Official statistics put ODA at 11% of the country's annual GDP.

Poverty

As in neighbouring Vietnam, the economic reforms are beginning to widen inequalities in society. Most of those who are doing well live in towns or at least close to one of the country's main roads. This means that off-road communities, and especially those in remote rural areas, are finding that – at least in relative terms – they are becoming poorer. In addition, because it is mostly minority Lao Soung and Lao Theung who live in these marginal areas, the economic reforms are widening inequalities between ethnic groups. One foreign aid worker was quoted in the *Far Eastern Economic Review* saying: "When they come down to Vientiane, where the lowland Lao [the Lao Loum] live, it's like Hong Kong to them. Here's money, here's development. In their own villages, there's nothing." As in Vietnam, the need to ensure that the economic reforms bring benefits to all and not just a few, is a key political question. The leadership are acutely aware that widening inequalities could fuel political discontent and this is perhaps one reason why the government seems so intent on increasing the number of members of the National Assembly from ethnic minorities.

The average annual income in 2006 was US$572. Laos was ranked 133 out of 177 countries in the 2006 Human Development report and is the most underdeveloped countries in the Mekong region, ranking lower than Cambodia and Vietnam. Just over 1 in 5 students aged between 15-24 is illiterate. Around 15% of children still don't go to primary school and a further 60% are not enrolled in secondary school. Only 63% of students who started grade one were still in school by grade 5.

A fifth of the population is undernourished, 40% of children are underweight and only half the population has access to safe drinking water. Almost one in 10 children dies before the age of five, usually from communicable and preventable diseases such as acute respiratory infections, diarrhoea, malaria, measles, dengue fever and meningitis. Maternal mortality is also dangerously high, with around 530 maternal deaths per 100,000 births, probably due to the fact that only 17% of pregnant women have their baby delivered by a trained doctor.

The keystone of mainland Southeast Asia

In what sceptics might view as an ultimately futile effort, the leadership in Vientiane have chanced upon an economic future for their country: as the 'keystone' or 'crossroads' of Southeast Asia. Nor is it just Laos' leaders who are drumming up enthusiasm for this notion. The Asian Development Bank (the Asian arm of the World Bank) is at the forefront of developing – and funding – what has become known as the Greater Mekong Sub-region or GMS. This will link southwest China, Thailand, Myanmar (Burma), Cambodia, Vietnam and Laos. And within this scenario, Laos is the crucial pivotal country through which most road links will have to go. There is talk of a 'Golden Quadrangle' (as opposed to the infamous Golden Triangle) – even of a Golden Land. This reference draws on ancient Indian texts which talked of 'Suvarnaphum' – a Golden Land – which encompassed modern-day Thailand, Laos, Myanmar and probably Peninsular Malaysia and parts of Indonesia too.

Culture

People

Laos has a population of 6.2 million people, with an estimated annual growth rate of 2.4%, one of the highest in Southeast Asia. Savannakhet has the biggest population among provinces, with around 824,662 people. Vientiane is second with around 695,473 people, while Champasak province is in third place, with 603,880 people.

Ethnic groups

Laos is less a nation state than a collection of different tribes and languages. Its enormous ethnic diversity has long been an impediment to national integration. In total there are more than 60 ethnic groups which are often described as living in isolated, self-sufficient communities. Although communication and intercourse may have been difficult – and remains so – there has always been communication, trade and inter-marriage between the different Lao 'worlds' and today, with even greater interaction, the walls between them are becoming more permeable still.

Laos' ethnically diverse population is usually – and rather simplistically – divided by ecological zone into three groups: the wet rice cultivating, Buddhist Lao Loum of the lowlands, who are politically and numerically dominant, constituting just under half of the total population; the Lao Theung who occupy the mountain slopes and make up about a quarter of the population; and the Lao Soung, or upland Lao, who live in the high mountains and practise shifting cultivation and who represent less than a fifth of Laos' total population. Overall, in Laos the ethnic majority, Lao Loum, are in the minority. The terms were brought into general usage by the Pathet Lao who wished to emphasize that all of Laos' inhabitants were 'Lao' and to avoid the more derogatory terms that had been used in the past – such as the Thai word *kha*, (slave), to describe the Mon-Khmer Lao Theung like the Khmu and Lamet. Stereotypical representations of each category are depicted on the 1000 kip note.

The French viewed the Lao (not to put too fine a point on it) as if they were an exasperating child. But, as Virginia Thompson put it in the late 1930s, "For the rare Frenchman who sees in the Laotians a silly, lazy and naive people, there are hundreds who are charmed by their gentle affability". It was this affability which Henri Mouhout noted in the 1860s and which led some Frenchmen to express their concern as to what might happen to the Lao if the uncontrolled immigration and settlement of Siamese, Vietnamese and Chinese was permitted. (Norman Lewis in *A Dragon Apparent* said much the same about Frenchmen who had gone native: "Laos-ized Frenchmen are like the results of successful lobotomy operations – untroubled and mildly libidinous.").

Although the words have a geographical connotation, they should be viewed more as contrasting pairs of terms: *loum* and *theung* mean 'below' and 'above' (rather than hillsides and lowland), while *soung* is paired with *tam*, meaning 'high' and 'low'. These two pairs of oppositions were then brought together by the Pathet Lao into one three-fold division. Thus, the Lao Theung in one area may, in practice, occupy a higher location than Lao Soung in another area. In addition, economic change, greater interaction between the groups and the settlement of lowland peoples in hill areas means that it is possible to find Lao Loum villages in upland areas, where the inhabitants practise swidden, not wet rice, agriculture. So, although it is broadly possible to characterize the mountain slopes as inhabited by shifting cultivating Lao Theung of Mon-Khmer descent, in practice the neat delimitation of people into discrete spatial units breaks down and as the years go by is becoming increasingly untenable.

❗ Population by ethnic group

Group	Official category	% of total population
Tai	Lao Loum	55
Mon-Khmer	Lao Theung	35
Tibeto-Burman	Lao Soung	10

Lao Loum

It has been noted that the Lao who have reaped the rewards of reform are the Lao Loum of T'ai stock – not the Lao Theung who are of Mon-Khmer descent or the ethnic Lao Soung, such as the Hmong but also Akha and Lahu. Ing-Britt Trankell, in her book *On the Road in Laos: an Anthropological Study of Road Construction and Rural Communities* (1993), writes that the Lao Loum's "sense of [cultural and moral] superiority is often manifested in both a patronizing and contemptuous attitude toward the Lao Theung and Lao Sung, who are thought of as backward and less susceptible to socio-economic development because they are still governed by their archaic cultural traditions". This attitude is still prevalent today, where Lao Loum sneer at the cultural practices of other ethnic groups, such as the Akha, as being unmodern. As a result many of these groups are ashamed to wear their traditional clothes around as it has a stigma attached to it.

During the sixth and seventh centuries the Lao Loum arrived from the southern provinces of China. They occupied the valleys along the Mekong and its tributaries and drove the Lao Theung to more mountainous areas. The Lao Loum, who are ethnically almost indistinguishable from the Thais of the Isan region (the Northeast of Thailand), came under the influence of the Khmer and Indonesian cultures and sometime before the emergence of Lane Xang in the 14th century embraced Theravada Buddhism. The majority of Lao are Buddhist but retain many of their animist beliefs. Remote Lao Loum communities still usually have a *mor du* (a doctor who 'sees') or medium. The medium's job description is demanding: he must concoct love potions, heal the sick, devise and design protective charms and read the future.

Today, the Lao Loum are the principal ethnic group, accounting for nearly half the population, and Lao is their mother tongue. As the lowland Lao, they occupy the ricelands of the Mekong and its main tributary valleys. Their houses are traditionally made of wood and are built on stilts with thatched roofs – although tin roofs and Thai concrete houses are much more popular these days. The extended family is usually spread throughout several houses in one compound.

There are also several tribal sub-groups of this main Thai-Lao group; they are conveniently colour-coded and readily identifiable by their sartorial traits. There are, for example, the Red Tai, the White Tai and the Black Tai – who live in the upland valley areas in Xieng Khouang and Hua Phan provinces. That they live in the hills suggests they are Lao Theung, but ethnically and culturally they are closer to the Lao Loum.

Lao Theung

The Lao Theung, consisting of 45 different sub-groups, are the descendants of the oldest inhabitants of the country and are of Mon-Khmer descent. They are sometimes called *Kha* (slave), as they were used as labourers by the Thai and Lao kings and are still poorer than the Lao Loum. Traditionally, the Lao Theung were semi-nomadic and they still live mainly on the mountain slopes of the interior, along the whole length of the Annamite Chain from South China. There are concentrations of Akha, Alak and Ta-Oy on the Boloven Plateau in the south (see page 234) and Khmu in the north.

The Lao Theung's reliance on slash-and-burn, or shifting, agriculture is slowly being phased out. Traditionally, they would burn a small area of forest, cultivate it for

Background Culture

a few years and then, when the soil was exhausted, abandon the land until the vegetation had regenerated to replenish the soil. Some groups merely shifted fields in a 10-15 year rotation; others not only shifted fields but also their villages, relocating in a fresh area of forest when the land had become depleted of nutrients. To obtain salt, metal implements and other goods which could not be made or found in the hills, the tribal peoples would trade forest products such as resins and animal skins with the settled lowland Lao. Some groups, mainly those living closer to towns, have converted to Buddhism but many are still animist.

The social and religious beliefs of the Lao Theung and their general outlook on health and happiness are governed by their belief in spirits. The shaman is a key personality in any village. The Alak, from the Boloven Plateau (see page 233) test the prospects of a marriage by killing a chicken: the manner in which it bleeds will determine whether the marriage will be propitious. Buffalo sacrifices are also common in Lao Theung villages and it is not unusual for a community to slaughter all its livestock to appease the spirits.

Viet Minh guerrillas and American B-52s made life difficult for many of the Lao Theung tribes living in East Laos, who were forced to move away from the Ho Chi Minh Trail. By leaving their birth places the Lao Theung left their protecting spirits, forcing them to find new and unfamiliar ones.

Lao Soung
The Lao Soung began migrating to Laos from South China, Tibet and Burma, in the early 18th century, settling high in the mountains (some up to 2500 m). The Hmong (formerly known as the Meo) and Yao (also called the Mien) are the principal Lao Soung groups.

Yao (or Mien)
The Yao mainly live around Nam Tha – deep inside the Golden Triangle, near the borders with Thailand, Myanmar (Burma) and China. They are best known as craftspeople – the men make knives, crossbows, rifles and high-quality, elaborately designed silver jewellery, which is worn by the women. Silver is a symbol of wealth among the Yao and Hmong.

The Mien or Yao are unique among the hilltribes in that they have a tradition of writing based on Chinese characters. Mien legend has it that they came from 'across the sea' during the 14th century, although it is generally thought that their roots are in South China where they originated about 2000 years ago.

The Mien village is not enclosed and is usually found on sloping ground. The houses are large, wooden and need to accommodate an extended family of sometimes 20 or more. They are built on the ground, not on stilts and have one large living area and four or more bedrooms. As with other tribes, the construction of the house must be undertaken carefully. The house needs to be orientated appropriately, so that the spirits are not disturbed and the ancestral altar installed on an auspicious day.

The Mien combine two religious beliefs: on the one hand they recognize and pay their dues to spirits and ancestors (informing them of family developments); and on the other, they follow Taoism as it was practised in China in the 13th and 14th centuries. The Taoist rituals are expensive and the Mien appear to spend a great deal of their lives struggling to save enough money to afford the various life cycle ceremonies, such as weddings and death ceremonies. The Mien economy is based upon the shifting cultivation of dry rice, maize and small quantities of opium poppy.

Material culture The Mien women dress distinctively, with black turbans and red-ruffed tunics, making them easy to distinguish from the other hilltribes. All their clothes are made of black or indigo-dyed homespun cotton, which is then embroidered using distinctive cross-stitching. Their trousers are the most elaborate

Lao, Laos and Laotians

Most Lao are not Laotians. And not all Laotians are Lao. Lao tends to be used to describe people of Lao stock. There are, in fact, several times more Lao in neighbouring northeastern Thailand (Issan) – roughly 20 million – than there are in Laos, with a total population of some 5 million of whom perhaps a little over a half are ethnic Lao. At the same time not all Laotians – people who are nationals of Laos – are ethnic Lao. There are also significant minority populations including Chinese, Vietnamese, the Mon-Khmer Lao Theung and the many tribal groups that comprise the Lao Soung. After a few too many lau-lao it is easy to get confused.

garments. Unusually, they sew from the back of the cloth and cannot see the pattern they are making. The children wear embroidered caps with red pompoms on the top and by the ears. The men's dress is a simple indigo-dyed jacket and trousers, with little embroidery. They have been dubbed "the most elegantly dressed but worst-housed people in the world".

Akha (or Kaw)

The Akha, also called as the Ikho, Kho or Kha, have their origins in Yunnan, southern China, and from there spread into Burma (where there are nearly 200,000) and Laos and rather later into Thailand. There are three different Akha groups in northern Laos: the Akha Pouli, the Akha Pen and the Akha Jijaw. Around Muang Sing (see page 146) they constitute 22% of the population. They traditionally speak a Tibeto-Burmese language, which is believed to be represented in nine different written forms.

The Akha are shifting cultivators, growing primarily dry rice on mountainsides but also a wide variety of vegetables. The cultivation of rice is bound up with myths and rituals: the rice plant is regarded as a sentient being and the selection of the swidden, its clearance, the planting of the rice seed, the care of the growing plants and finally the harvest of the rice, must all be done according to the Akha Way. Any offence to the rice soul must be rectified by ceremonies. The Akha have no word for religion but believe in the 'Akha Way'. They are able to recite the names of all their male ancestors (60 names or more) and they keep an ancestral altar in their homes, at which food is offered up at important festivals and after the rice harvest. The two most important Akha festivals are the four-day Swinging Ceremony, celebrated during August, and New Year, when festivities also extend over four days. When someone dies they are wrapped in cloth, poor people in a white cloth, and rich people in a black cloth. They are kept in a wooden coffin, with a lid similar to a xylophone, for up to a month. A usual ritual *baci* will follow.

Akha villages are identified by their gates, a village swing and high-roofed houses on posts. At the upper and lower ends of the village are gates which are renewed every year. Visitors should walk through them in order to rid themselves of the spirit of the jungle. The gates are sacred and must not be defiled. Visitors must not touch the gates and should avoid going through them if they do not intend to enter a house in the village. A pair of wooden male and female carved figures are placed inside the entrance to signify that this is the realm of human beings. The female and male parts of the house are divided and two doorways enter the house, one which is entered through and the other which serves as the exit. ▶▶ *For information on how to behave in an Akha village, see Visiting an Akha village, page 142.*

The Akha are relatively sexually liberal. Each village usually has a small courting house, where young men and women can rendezvous privately. Women will generally have a number of partners before settling into marriage and pregnancy prior to marriage is not deemed as being shameful but rather as a sign of fecundity. Sexual abstinence is often used as punishment for those who commit offences. Marriage is monogamous; however, the rich and powerful are entitled to additional wives if their first wives can't conceive. Women adopt the husband's lineage upon marriage and usually move into or close to her partner's family home. Divorce exists but is not common, due to the financial pressures of raising children. A midwife generally delivers babies and men are not allowed in the house when the woman is in labour. Historically, twins born in villages were regarded as a very bad omen and were killed but this practice has now been outlawed and the children are put up for adoption.

Today the Akha are finding it increasingly difficult to follow the 'Akha Way'. Their complex rituals set them apart from both the lowland Lao and from the other hilltribes. The conflicts and pressures which the Akha currently face and their inability to reconcile the old with the new is claimed by some to explain why the incidence of opium addiction among the Akha is so high.

Material culture Akha clothing is made of homespun blue-black cloth (dyed from indigo), which is appliquéd for decoration. The basic clothing of an Akha woman is a head-dress, a jacket, a short skirt worn on the hips, with a sash and leggings worn from the ankle to below the knee, though many are starting to wear more mainstream clothing, as they are self-conscious of their traditional dress. They wear their jewellery as an integral part of their clothing, mostly sewn to their head dresses. This is the most characteristic item of Akha clothing and is adorned with jewellery and coins. The coins are made of pure silver and are used as currency (the small coins are worth about 15,000 kip and the large are worth about 50,000 kip). Girls wear similar clothing to the women, except that they sport caps rather than the elaborate head-dress of the mature women. The change from girl's clothes to women's clothes occurs through four stages during adolescence. Unmarried girls can be identified by the small gourds tied to their waist and head-dress. Men's clothing is much less elaborate. They wear loose-fitting Chinese-style black pants and a black jacket which may be embroidered. Both men and women use cloth shoulder bags.

Hmong

Origins The Hmong are probably the best-known tribe in Laos. In the 19th century, Chinese opium farmers drove many thousands of Hmong off their poppy fields and forced them south into the mountains of Laos. The Hmong did not have a written language before contact with Europeans and Americans and their heritage is mainly preserved through oral tradition. Hmong mythology relates how they flew in from South China on magic carpets. Village storytellers also like to propagate the notion that the Hmong are in fact werewolves, who happily devour the livers of their victims. This warrior tribe now mainly inhabits the mountain areas of Luang Prabang, Xieng Khouang and Xam Neua provinces where they practise shifting cultivation.

Economy and society Until a few years ago, other Lao and the rest of the world knew the Hmong as the Meo. Unbeknown to anyone except the Hmong, 'Meo' was a Chinese insult meaning 'barbarian' – conferred on them several millennia ago by Chinese who developed an intense disliking for the tribe. Returning from university in France in the mid-1970s, the Hmong's first highly qualified academic decided it was time to educate the world. Due to his prompting, the tribe was rechristened Hmong, their word for 'mankind'. This change in nomenclature has not stopped the Hmong from continuing to refer to the Chinese as 'sons of dogs'. Nor has it stopped the Lao Loum from regarding the Hmong as their cultural inferiors. But, again, the feelings are reciprocated: the Hmong have an inherent mistrust of the lowland Lao – exacerbated by years of war – and Lao Loum guides reluctantly enter Hmong villages.

The Hmong value their independence and tend to live at high altitudes, away from other tribes. This independence in addition to their former association with poppy cultivation and their siding with the US during the war has meant that of all the hilltribes, it is the Hmong who have been most severely persecuted. They have, in recent history, been perceived as a threat to the security of the state; a group that needs to be controlled and carefully watched.

Hmong villages tend not to be fenced, while their houses are built of wood or bamboo at ground level. Each house has a main living area and two or three sleeping rooms. The extended family is headed by the oldest male; he settles family disputes and has supreme authority over family affairs. Like the Karen, the Hmong too are spirit worshippers and believe in household spirits. Every house has an altar, where protection for the household is sought.

As animists, the Hmong believe everything from mountains and opium poppies to cluster bombs, has a spirit – or *phi* – some bad, some good. Shamans – or witchdoctors – play a central role in village life and decision making. The *phi* need to be placated incessantly to ward off sickness and catastrophe. It is the shaman's job to exorcise the bad *phi* from his patients. Until modern medicine arrived in Laos along with the Americans, opium was the Hmong's only palliative drug. Due to their lack of resistance to pharmaceuticals, the Hmong responded miraculously to the smallest doses of penicillin. Even plasters were revered as they were thought to contain magical powers which drew out bad *phi*.

Material culture The Hmong are the only tribe in Laos who make batik; indigo-dyed batik makes up the main panel of their skirts, with appliqué and embroidery added to it. The women traditionally wore black leggings from their knees to their ankles, black jackets (with embroidery) and a black panel or 'apron', held in place with a cummerbund. Even the youngest children wore clothes of intricate design with exquisite needlework. Traditionally the cloth would have been woven by hand on a foot-treddle/back-strap loom; today it is increasingly purchased from markets and often made of synthetic fabrics. Most Hmong today tend to wear Western-style clothes except for on auspicious occasions, such as Hmong New Year.

The White Hmong tend to wear less elaborate clothing from day to day, saving it for special occasions only. Hmong men wear loose-fitting black trousers, black jackets (sometimes embroidered) and coloured or embroidered sashes.

The Hmong particularly value silver jewellery; it signifies wealth and a good life. Men, women and children wear silver – tiers of neck rings, heavy silver chains with lock-shaped pendants, earrings and pointed rings on every finger. Through their life the Hmong will collect these heavy bands and lock them together with a spirit lock, which holds in their 32 souls. All the family jewellery is brought out at New Year and is an impressive sight, symbolizing the wealth of the family.

Hmong fighters in the 20th century In the dying days of the French colonial administration, thousands of Hmong were recruited to help fight the Vietnamese Communists. Vang Pao – known as VP – who would later command 30,000 Hmong mercenaries in the US-backed war against the Pathet Lao, was first picked out by a French colonel in charge of these *maquisards* (native movements). Later, the Hmong were recruited and paid by the CIA to fight the Pathet Lao. Under General VP, remote mountain villagers with no education were trained to fly T-28 fighter-bombers. It is said that when these US aircraft first started landing in remote villages, locals would carefully examine the undercarriage to see what sex they were.

At its peak, VP's army consisted of 250,000 fighters, the majority of whom were Hmong. Around 30,000 Hmong lost their life in the war, over a tenth of the Hmong population at the time. Even after the Pathet Lao's 'liberation' of Vientiane in 1975, Hmong refugees, encamped in hills to the south of the Plain of Jars, were attacked and flushed out by Vietnamese troops. The Hmong claimed that chemical weapons were being used against them, most notably 'yellow rain' (the biological agent, trichothecane mycotoxins), although biologists at Yale University suggested the substance was, in fact, faeces from swarms of over-flying bees.

When the war ended in 1975 there was a mass exodus of Hmong from Laos. Hmong refugees poured into Thailand, the exodus reaching a peak in 1979 when 3000 a month were fleeing across the Mekong. Many ended up in Thai refugee camps, where they lived in terrible conditions, for many years, sometimes decades. A temporary refugee camp called Ban Vinai was established by the Thai government in June 1975 solely to accommodate the Hmong. These camps are now part of history but one of the best accounts of this period can be read in Lynellyn D Long's *Ban Vinai: the Refugee Camp*. As a Jesuit priest who worked at the camp explained to the author: "Before, they [the refugees] had a life revolving around the seasons ... Here they cannot really work ... Here people make only dreams."

Thousands of Hmong also ended up in the US and France, fresh from the mountains of Laos: unsurprisingly they did not adapt easily. Various stress disorders were thought to have triggered heart attacks in many healthy young Hmong – a condition referred to as Sudden Unexplained Nocturnal Death Syndrome. In *The Ravens*, Robbins comments that "in a simpler age, it would have been said that the Hmong are dying of a broken heart". Today more than 100,000 Hmong live in the US – mostly on the west coast and in Minnesota – where they regularly lobby politicians. They are a very powerful pressure group but they are increasingly out of touch with the situation in Laos. Where the US-based Hmong remain important, however, is in the money they remit to their relatives in Laos.

Hmong insurgency A small group of Hmong, led by Vang Pao in the US, remained in Laos and continued to fight the Lao government through the 1980s and 1990s. There are probably still a small number of disaffected Hmong who cling to the cause but they have lost what credibility they may have had and, for the most part rely on leftover ammunition and guerilla tactics. The rebels' biggest public relations disaster came in 1989 when they shot dead several Buddhist monks while attacking a government convoy on the road to Luang Prabang.

Hmong insurgents have been staging reasonably regular attacks for years. A spate of bombings in Vientiane in 2000 was probably linked to the Hmong resistance and in 2004-2005 at least 15 civilians were killed by Hmong insurgents in the north of the country. The Hmong claim to be fighting for democracy and freedom but most are living in terrible conditions and starving, so robbery seems a more likely motivation behind their attacks.

The Lao government tends publicly to sidestep the issue, saying there is no official policy towards the Hmong. However, the eradication of opium and related resettlement programme has had a negative impact on the Hmong and there is undisputable evidence of human rights violations against the Hmong by the Lao government. In 2004, video footage was smuggled out of Laos showing the carnage of a military attack on a Hmong rebel group that had taken place in May 2004; the victims were children. On the other hand, the Lao government has appointed Hmong as governors of Phonsavanh, Xam Neua and Sayaboury provinces.

The donor community and international organizations continue keenly to watch the Lao government's response to the Hmong. Unfortunately, international pressure can destabilize important domestic policies. In 2005 it was reported that the government had requested groups involved in poverty alleviation in some provinces to prioritize the Hmong above all other ethnic groups when provincial budgets are allocated, regardless of their relative need.

Between 2004 and 2006 several groups of hundreds of Hmong insurgents surrendered. In December 2006 alone more than 400 members of the Hmong ethnic insurgents and their families came out of the jungle and surrendered to the authorities.

In 2007 American officials in the US arrested Vang Pao, the 77-year-old former CIA-backed general of the Royal Army in Laos, on a conspiracy to stage a coup in Vientiane. The criminal complaint said Vang Pao and the other Hmong defendants formed a committee "to evaluate the feasibility of conducting a military expedition or enterprise to engage in the overthrow of the existing government of Laos by violent means, including murder, assaults on both military and civilian officials of Laos and destruction of buildings and property." This included charges of inspecting shipments of military equipment that were to be purchased and shipped to Thailand. That equipment included machine guns, ammunition, rocket-propelled grenade launchers, anti-tank rockets, stinger missiles, mines and C-4 explosives.

Other communities

The largest non-Lao groups in Laos are the Chinese and Vietnamese communities in the main cities. Many of the Vietnamese were brought in by the French to run the country and stayed. In more recent years, Vietnam also tried to colonize parts of Laos. The Chinese have been migrating to Laos for centuries and are usually traders, restaurateurs and shop owners. Chinese immigration has increased greatly in recent years. With the relaxation in Communist policies in recent years, there has been a large influx of Thais; most are involved in business. In Vientiane there is also a small community of Indians running restaurants, jewellery and tailors' shops. The majority of the Europeans in Laos are NGO, embassy or mining company staff.

Architecture

The architecture of Laos reflects its turbulent history and has strong Siamese/Thai, Burmese and Khmer influences. Philip Rawson, in his book *The Art of Southeast Asia*, goes so far as to state that "The art of Laos is a provincial version of the art of Siam." This is unjustified in so far as art and architecture in Laos, though it may show many links with that of Siam/Thailand (unsurprisingly as over the centuries the two countries have, at various times, held sway over parts of each other's territory), also has elements and styles which are unique to it. Unfortunately, little has survived because many of the older structures were built of wood and were repeatedly ransacked by the Siamese/Thais, Chinese and Vietnamese and then bombed by the Americans. Religious buildings best exhibit the originality of Lao art and architecture.

Like Thailand and Myanmar (Burma), the stupa is the most dominant architectural form in Laos. In its classic Indian form, it is a voluptuous half round – a hemisphere – very like the upturned begging bowl that it is supposed to symbolize. This is surmounted by a shaft representing the Buddha's staff and a stepped pediment symbolizing his folded cloak. In Thailand the stupa has become elongated while in Laos it is also more angular, with four distinct sides. They are referred to as *that* (rather than *chedi*, as in Thailand).

In addition to the *that*, a Lao monastery or *wat* (*vat*) will also have a number of other buildings of which the most important is the *sim* or ordination hall (in Thai, *bot* or *ubosoth*). See box, page 308, for a short rundown on the main structures found in an orthodox Lao wat.

Architectural styles

Lao wats are generally less ornate and grand than those in Thailand, although the temples of Luang Prabang are stunning, with their layered roofs that sweep elegantly towards the ground. There are three main styles of temple architecture in Laos: Luang Prabang, Vientiane and Xieng Khouang. The last of these was almost lost forever because of the destruction wrought on the city of Xieng Khouang during the war (see page 169). Fortunately one or two examples exist in Luang Prabang.

The Lao wat

There is no English equivalent of the Lao word wat or vat. It is usually translated as either monastery or temple, although neither is correct. It is easiest to get around this problem by calling them wats. They were, and remain to some extent, the focus of the village or town; they serve as places of worship, education, meeting and healing. Without a wat, a village cannot be viewed as a 'complete' community. The wat is a relatively new innovation. Originally, there were no wats, as monks were wandering ascetics. It seems that although the word 'wat' was in use in the 14th century, these were probably just shrines, and were not monasteries. By the late 18th century, the wat had certainly metamorphosed into a monastery, so sometime in the intervening four centuries, shrine and monastery had united into a whole. Although wats vary a great deal in size and complexity, there is a traditional layout to which most of them conform.

Wats are usually separated from the secular world by two walls. Between these outer and inner walls are the monks' quarters or dormitories (kutis), perhaps a drum or bell tower (hor kong) that is used to toll the hours and to warn of danger and, in larger complexes, schools and other administrative buildings. Traditionally the kutis were placed on the south side of the wat. It was believed that if the monks slept directly in front of the principal Buddha image they would die young; if they slept to the left they would become ill;

Generalized plan of a wat

The Vientiane style is influenced by the central Thai style, with its high, pointed and layered roofs. Most of the main sanctuaries are rectangular and some, such as Wat Phra Kaeo in Vientiane, have a veranda around the entire building – a stylistic feature imported from Bangkok. Most of the larger sim have a veranda at the back as well as at the front. Vientiane's wats have higher roofs than those in Luang Prabang, the buildings are taller and the entrances are more prominent. The steps leading up to and if they slept behind it there would be discord in the community of monks.

The inner wall, which in bigger wats often takes the form of a gallery or cloister (*phra rabieng*) lined with Buddha images, represents the division between the worldly and the holy, the sacred and the profane. It is used as a quiet place for meditation. Within the inner courtyard, the holiest building is the ordination hall or *sim*, reserved for monks only. This is built on consecrated ground, and has a ring of eight stone tablets or boundary markers (*bai sema*), sometimes contained in mini-pavilions, arranged around it at the cardinal and subcardinal points and shaped like stylized leaves of the bodhi tree, often carved with representations of Vishnu, Siva, Brahma or Indra, or of nagas. Buried in the ground beneath the *bai sema* are stone spheres – and sometimes gold and jewellery. The *bai sema* mark the limit of earthly power. The ordination hall is characteristically a large, rectangular building with high walls and multiple sloping roofs (always odd in number) covered in glazed clay tiles (or wood tiles, in the north). At each end of the apex of the roof are *dok sofa*, or 'bunches of flowers', which represent garuda grasping two nagas (serpents) in its talons. *Chao faa*, flame-like protrusions are attached to the extreme edge of the downward slope of the roofs. Inside, often through elaborately carved and inlaid doors, is the main Buddha image. There may also be numerous subsidiary images. The inside walls of the *sim* may be decorated with murals depicting the Jataka tales or scenes from Buddhist and Hindu cosmology. Like the Buddha, these murals are meant to serve as meditation aids. It is customary for pilgrims to remove their shoes on entering any Buddhist building (or private house for that matter). Many complexes have secondary chapels, or *hor song phra* attached to the main sim.

Also found in the inner courtyard may be a number of other structures. Among the more common are that (chedis), tower-like relic chambers which in Laos and parts of northeastern Thailand (which is also Lao in terms of culture) take the distinctive lotus bud form. These can be built on a massive scale (such as That Luang in Vientiane, see page 53), and contain holy relics of the Buddha himself. More often, thats are smaller affairs containing the ashes of royalty, monks or pious lay people.

Another rarer feature is the library or scripture repository (*hau tai*), usually a small, tall-sided building where the Buddhist scriptures can be stored safely, high off the ground. *Salas* are open-sided rest pavilions which can be found anywhere in the wat compound; the *sala long tham* (study hall) is the largest and most impressive of these and is almost like a *sim* or *viharn* without walls. Here the monks say their prayers at noon. In villages wats often consist only of a sala, or meeting hall.

It seems that wats are often short-lived. Even great wats, if they lose their patronage, are deserted by their monks and fall into ruin. Unlike Christian churches, they depend on constant support from the laity; the wat owns no land or wealth, and must depend on gifts of food to feed the monks and money for repairs or

the main entrance are often guarded by *nagas* or *nyaks*, while the doorways themselves are usually flanked by pillars and topped with intricately carved porticoes. That Luang, in Vientiane, historically provided a template for most Lao stupas and its unique shape is found only in Laos and some areas of North and Northeast Thailand. As in other Buddhist countries, many of the stupas contain sacred relics – bones or hairs of the Buddha, or the ashes of kings.

The Luang Prabang architectural style has been influenced by North Thai temples. The roofs of the main sanctuaries are very low, almost touching the ground – best exemplified by the magnificent Wat Xieng Thong in Luang Prabang. The pillars tend to narrow towards the top, as tree trunks were originally used for columns and this form was copied when they started to be constructed of stuccoed brick. The wats often have a veranda at the back and the front. The most famous wats in Luang Prabang and Vientiane were built with royal patronage. But most wats in Laos were and are constructed piecemeal with donations from the local community. Royal wats can be identified by the number of *dok sofa*: more than 10 'flowers' signifies that the wat was built by a king.

The Xieng Khouang style appears to be an amalgam of Vientiane and Luang Prabang influences. The *sim* is raised on a multi-level pediment, as with Vientiane-style *sim*, while the low, sweeping roofs are similar to *sim* in Luang Prabang.

Arts and crafts

Lao art is well known for its wealth of ornamentation. As in other neighbouring Buddhist countries, the focus has been primarily religious in nature. Temple murals and bas-reliefs usually tell the story of the Buddha's life: the jataka tales. There has never been the range of art in Laos that there is in Thailand, as the country has been constantly dominated and influenced by foreign powers. Much of it has been destroyed over the centuries, as plundering neighbours ransacked towns and cities. The *Ramayana*, the Indian epic, has become part of the Lao cultural heritage and is known as the *Phra Lak Phra Lam*, see box page 312. Many of the doors and windows of temples are engraved with scenes from this story, depicting the struggle between good and evil. Prime examples are the huge teak shutters at Wat Xieng Thong in Luang Prabang.

Sculpture

Sculpture in Laos is more distinctive in style; the best pieces originate from the 16th to 18th centuries. Characteristic of Lao Buddha images is a nose like an eagle's beak, flat, extended earlobes and tightly curled hair. The best examples are in Wat Phra Kaeo and Wat Sisaket in Vientiane.

The 'Calling for Rain' mudra (the Buddha standing with hands pointing towards the ground, arms slightly away from the torso) is distinctively Lao (see page 61). The 'Contemplating the Tree of Enlightenment' mudra is also uniquely Lao – it depicts a standing Buddha with hands crossed in front of the body. There are many examples in the Pak Ou Caves, on the Mekong, 25 km upstream from Luang Prabang (see page 117).

Textiles

Of all Laos' artistic traditions, perhaps none is more varied and more vital than its handwoven textiles. These inevitably show some stylistic links with Thailand, but in many respects Laos' tradition is richer and certainly the cloth being produced in Laos today is far finer, more complex and more technically accomplished than any currently being woven in Thailand (although there are those in Thailand who would dispute this, assuming – wrongly – that Thailand is more advanced than Laos).

Weaving is a craft almost entirely performed by women and it has always been a mark of womanhood. Traditionally, a girl was not considered fit for marriage until she had mastered the art of weaving and the Lao Loum women were expected to weave a corsage for their wedding day. Today these traditions are inevitably less strictly adhered to and there are also a handful of fine male weavers. (Indeed, it has been suggested that these few male weavers produce better – or at least more adventurous – work than their female counterparts because they are less constrained by tradition and more willing to experiment with new designs.) Even so, a skilled weaver is held in high regard and enjoys a position of respect. Cloth is woven from silk, cotton, hemp and a variety of synthetic materials (mostly polyester) – or in some combination of these.

The finest weaving comes from the north. Around Xam Neua (and especially near Xam Tai), the Lao Neua produce some outstanding pieces. These were handed down through a family as heirlooms, stored in lidded stone jars to protect them from insects, moisture and sunlight and only worn on special occasions. But the recent history of this area forced people to sell their treasured textiles and few remain in situ. Indeed it was feared that the art of traditional weaving had been lost entirely in the area. Only the work of some NGOs and committed supporters has resuscitated high quality weaving in the area (and in Vientiane where some of the finest weavers now live and work). Lao Neua textiles are usually woven with a cotton warp and a silk weft and pieces include *pha sinh* (sarong), *pha baeng* (shawl) and blankets. Various methods are employed including *ikat* – where cotton is used as the Lao Neua consider that indigo dye does not take well on silk – and supplementary weft techniques. Pieces show bold bands of design and colour and the *pha sinh* is usually finished with a separate handwoven border. Among the designs are swastika motifs, *hong* (geese), diamond shapes, *nyak* (snake) heads, lions and elephants.

The Lao Loum of the Luang Prabang area also have a fine weaving tradition, different from that of the far north and northeast. *Pha sinh* produced here tend to have narrow vertical stripes, often alternating between dark and light. Silk tends to be used throughout on the finer pieces, although the yarn may be imported rather than locally produced and it is coloured using chemical dyes. Motifs include zigzags, flowers and some designs that are French in inspiration.

Around Pakse in the south and also in central Laos around Savannakhet and Thakhek designs are influenced by the Khmer and closest to those produced in the Isan region of northeast Thailand. *Matmii* ikat-woven cotton cloth is most characteristic. Designs are invariably geometric and today it is unusual to find a piece which has not been dyed using chemicals. Designs are handed down by mothers to their daughters and encompass a broad range from simple *sai fon* (falling rain) designs where random sections of weft are tied, to the more complex *mee gung* and *poom som*. The less common *pha kit* is a supplementary weft *ikat*, although designs are similar to those in *matmii*. *Pha fai* is a simple cotton cloth, in blue or white and sometimes simply decorated, for everyday use and also used as part of the burial ceremony, when a white length of *pha fai* is draped over the coffin.

Literature

Lao literature is similar to Thai and is likewise also influenced by the Indian epic the *Ramayana*, which in Laos is known as the *Phra Lak Phra Lam* (see box, page 312). Scenes from the Phra Lak Phram Lam can often be seen depicted in temple murals. The first 10 jataka tales, recounting the last 10 lives of the Gautama Buddha (the historic Buddha), have also been a major inspiration for Lao literature. The versions that are in use in Laos are thought to have been introduced from Lanna Thai (northern Thailand, Chiang Mai) in the 16th century, or perhaps from the Mon area of present day Myanmar and Thailand. In these 10 tales, known as the *Vesantara Jataka*, the Buddha renounces all his earthly possessions, even his wife and children. Although the jataka tales in Laos are clearly linked, in religious terms, with Buddhism and therefore with India, the stories have little in common with the Indian originals. They draw heavily on local legends and folklore and have merely been incorporated within a religious literary milieu. They are animist tales provided with a Buddhist gloss.

Traditionally, as in other parts of Southeast Asia, texts were recorded on palm leaves. The letters were inscribed with a stylus and the grooves darkened with oil. A

The Lao Ramayana: the Phra Lak Phra Lam

The *Phra Lak Phra Lam* is an adaptation of the Indian Hindu classic, the *Ramayana*, which was written by the poet Valmiki about 2000 years ago. This 48,000 line epic odyssey, often likened to the works of Homer, was introduced into mainland Southeast Asia in the early centuries of the first millennium. The heroes were transposed into a mythical, ancient, Southeast Asian landscape.

In Laos, as in Thailand, the *Phra Lak Phra Lam* quickly became highly influential. In Thailand this is reflected in the name of the former capital of Siam, Ayutthaya, taken from the legendary hero's city of Ayodhia. Unfortunately, these early Thai translations of the *Ramayana*, which also filtered into Laos, were destroyed following the sacking of Ayutthaya by the Burmese in 1767. The earliest extant version was written by Thai King Taksin around 1775.

The Lao, and Thai, versions of the *Ramayana* closely follow that of the original Indian story. They tell of the life of Ram (Rama), the King of Ayodhia. In the first part of the story, Ram renounces his throne following a long and convoluted court intrigue and flees into exile. With his wife Seeda (Sita) and trusted companion Hanuman (the monkey god), they undertake a long and arduous journey. In the second part, his wife Seeda is abducted by the evil king Ravana, forcing Ram to wage battle against the demons of Langka Island (Sri Lanka). He defeats the demons with the help of Hanuman and his monkey army and recovers his wife. In the third and final part of the story – and here it diverges sharply from the Indian original – Seeda and Ram are reunited and reconciled with the help of the gods (in the Indian version there is no such reconciliation). Another difference from the Indian version is the significant role played by Hanuman – here an amorous adventurer who dominates much of the third part of the epic.

There are also numerous sub-plots which are original to the *Phra Lak Phra Lam*, many building upon local myth and folklore. In tone and issues of morality, the Lao and Thai versions are less puritanical than the Indian original. There are also, of course, differences in dress, ecology, location and custom.

palm leaf manuscript kept under good conditions in a well-maintained *hau tai* or library can last 100 years or more.

With the incorporation of Laos into French Indochina in the late 19th century, the Lao elite renounced traditional Lao literature in favour of the French language and French artistic traditions. Many of the Lao elite were educated in France and those that were not still enjoyed a French-style education. Lao literature came to be looked down upon as primitive and simplistic and most scholars wrote instead in French.

As with traditional songs, much Lao poetry has been passed down the generations and remains popular. *Sin Xay* is one of the great Lao poems and has been written down (although many have not) and is found in many temples.

In 1778 the Thais plundered Laos and along with the two most sacred Buddha images – the Phra Bang and the Phra Kaeo (Emerald Buddha) – they pillaged a great deal of Lao religious literature and historical documents. Most Lao manuscripts – or *kampi* – are engraved on palm leaves and are 40-50 cm long, pierced with two holes and threaded together with cord. A bundle of 20 leaves forms a *phuk* and these are grouped together into *mat*, which are wrapped in a piece of cloth.

Language

The official language is Lao, the language of the ethnic majority. Lao is basically a monosyllabic, tonal language. It contains many polysyllabic words borrowed from Pali and Sanskrit (ancient Indian dialects) as well as words borrowed from Khmer. It has six tones, 33 consonants and 28 vowels. Lao is also spoken in Northeast Thailand and North Cambodia, which was originally part of the kingdom of Lane Xang. Lao and Thai, particularly the Northeast dialect, are mutually intelligible. Differences have mainly developed since French colonial days when Laos was insulated from developments of the Thai language. French is still spoken in towns – particularly by the older generation – and is often used in government but English is being increasingly used. Significant numbers of Lao have been to universities and colleges in the former Soviet Union and Eastern Europe, so Eastern European languages and Russian are also spoken, but not widely.

Many of the tribal groups have no system of writing and the Lao script is similar to Thai, to which it is closely related. One of the kings of the Sukhothai Dynasty, Ramkhamhaeng, devised the Thai alphabet in 1283 and introduced the Thai system of writing. Lao script is modelled on the early Thai script and is written from left to right with no spacing between the words.

Like many other newly independent countries, the leadership in the Lao PDR have attempted to make Lao the national language, in fact as well as in rhetoric. An oft-quoted phrase is 'Language reveals one's nationhood, manners reveals one's lineage'. Because Lao is so similar to Thai, there has also been a conscious attempt to maintain a sense of difference between the two countries' languages. Otherwise, some people believe, there exists the danger that Laos might simply become culturally absorbed within Greater Thailand. As scholars have pointed out, the cultural flows have essentially been one way: most people in Laos can understand Standard Thai, but few Thais (except in the Northeastern region) can understand Lao. Linguistically, Lao and Thai are both dialects of the same root language, but neither is the dialect of the other. (Many Thais view Lao as a linguistic offshoot of Thai and hence subordinate to Thai. Understandably, people in Laos take offence at this intimation.)

Because of this delicate intersection of nationality, identity and language, there has been a studied attempt to establish language principles for Lao that clearly separates it from Thai. To begin with it was necessary to establish an accepted, national version of spoken Lao (there are significant differences between areas). In other words, to produce Standard Lao which could be taught in schools, promoted in the media, and used in government. This effort at language engineering can be dated from the 1930s, and saw further refinements in the 1940s-1950s, 1970s and 1990s. (Note that these attempts to develop Standard Lao bridge the colonial, royalist and communist periods.) While this has been successful to the extent that Lao remains noticeably and significantly different from Thai, the major influence on the Lao language today remains that of Thai. ▸▸ *See also Language, page 39; and Useful words and phrases, page 326.*

Dance, drama and music

Lao music, songs and dances have much in common with those of the Thai. Instruments include bamboo flutes, drums, gongs, cymbals and pinched or bowed string instruments shaped like banjos. The national instrument is the *kaen*, a hand-held pipe organ. It is made from bamboo and is similar in appearance to the South American pan pipes. Percussion is an important part of a Lao orchestra and two of the most commonly used instruments are the *nang nat*, a xylophone and the *knong vony*, a series of bronze cymbals suspended from a wooden frame. The *seb noi* orchestra – a consortium of all these instruments – is used to introduce or conclude vocal recitals. The *seb gnai* orchestra includes two big drums and a Lao-style clarinet as well; it was used in royal processions and still accompanies certain religious ceremonies.

Despite the lack of written notation, many epic poems and legends have survived to the present day as songs, passed, with the composition itself, from generation to generation. Early minstrels took their inspiration from folklore, enriched by Indian myths. Traditional Lao music can now only be heard during performances of the *Phra Lak Phra Lam* (see box, page 312), the Lao version of the Indian epic the *Ramayana*. Many of the monasteries have experts on percussion who play every Buddhist sabbath. There is also a strong tradition of Lao folk music, which differs between tribal groups.

Secular songs, drawing largely on Lao literature for inspiration, are known as *mau lam* and can be heard at festival time not just in Laos but also in Northeast Thailand (where they are known as *mor lam*), which is also, culturally, 'Lao'. Indeed, there has been something of a Lao cultural revival in Northeast Thailand and some of the best performers are based there. It is also the best place to pick up cassette tapes of famous *mor lam/mau lam* singers.

In Vientiane and the provincial capitals, younger Lao tend to opt for Western-style pop. The Communist leadership have become increasingly concerned at this invasion of Western and Thai culture and there has been an attempt to limit the quantity of non-Lao music played in clubs and karaoke bars. The authorities have dictated that only a certain proportion of songs can be non-Lao and there are cultural police who occasionally check that these rules are being observed.

Classical Lao theatre and dance have Indian origins and were probably imported from the Cambodian royal courts in the 14th century. Thai influence has also crept in over the years.

Religion

Theravada Buddhism

Theravada Buddhism, from the Pali word *thera* (elders), means the 'way of the elders' and is distinct from the dominant Buddhism practised in India, Mahayana Buddhism or the 'Greater Vehicle'. The sacred language of Theravada Buddhism is Pali rather than Sanskrit, Bodhisattvas (future Buddhas) are not given much attention and emphasis is placed upon a precise and 'fundamental' interpretation of the Buddha's teachings, as they were originally recorded. By the 15th century, Theravada Buddhism was the dominant religion in Laos – as it was in neighbouring Siam (Thailand), Myanmar and Cambodia. Buddhism shares the belief, in common with Hinduism, in rebirth. A person goes through countless lives and the experience of one life is conditioned by the acts in a previous one. This is the Law of Karma (act or deed, from Pali *kamma*), the law of cause and effect. But, it is not, as commonly thought in the West, equivalent to fate.

For most people, nirvana is a distant goal and they merely aim to accumulate merit by living good lives and performing good deeds such as giving alms to monks. In this way the layman embarks on the Path to Heaven. It is also common for a layman to become ordained, at some point in his life (usually as a young man), for a three month period during the Buddhist Rains Retreat.

Monks should endeavour to lead stringently ascetic lives. They must refrain from murder, theft, sexual intercourse, untruths, eating after noon, alcohol, entertainment, ornament, comfortable beds and wealth. They are allowed to own only a begging bowl, three pieces of clothing, a razor, needle, belt and water filter. They can only eat food that they have received through begging. Anyone who is male, over 20 and not a criminal can become a monk.

The 'Way of the Elders', is believed to be closest to Buddhist as it originally developed in India. It is often referred to by the term 'Hinayana' (Lesser Vehicle), a disparaging name foisted onto Theravadans by Mahayanists. This form of Buddhism is the dominant contemporary religion in the mainland Southeast Asian countries of Laos, Thailand, Cambodia and Myanmar (Burma).

In Theravadan Buddhism, the historic Buddha, Sakyamuni, is revered above all else and most images of the Buddha are of Sakyamuni. Importantly and unlike Mahayana Buddhism, the Buddha image is only meant to serve as a meditation aid; it does not embody supernatural powers and is not supposed to be worshipped. However, the popular need for objects of veneration has meant that most images are worshipped. Pilgrims bring flowers and incense and prostrate themselves in front of the image. This is a Mahayanist influence which has been embraced by Theravadans.

Buddhism in Laos

The Lao often maintain that the Vientiane area converted to Buddhism at the time of the Moghul emperor Asoka. This seems suspiciously early and is probably untrue. The original stupa at That Luang, so it is claimed, was built to encase a piece of the Buddha's breastbone provided by Asoka. Buddhism was undoubtedly practised before Fa Ngum united Lane Xang and created a Buddhist Kingdom in the mid-14th century. He was known as the Great Protector of the Faith and brought the Phra Bang, the famous golden statue – the symbol of Buddhism in Laos – from Angkor in Cambodia to Laos.

Buddhism was gradually accepted among the lowland Lao but many of the highland tribes remain animist. Even where Buddhism has been practised for centuries, it is usually interwoven with the superstitions and rituals of animist beliefs. Appeasing the spirits and gaining merit are both integral features of life. Most highlanders are animists and the worship of *phi* or spirits has remained central to village life throughout the revolutionary years, despite the fact that it was officially banned by the government. Similarly, the *baci* ceremony – when strings representing guardian spirits are tied around the wrists of guests – is still practised in Laos.

In the late 1500s, King Setthathirat promoted Buddhism and built many monasteries or wats. Buddhism was first taught in schools in the 17th century and prospered until the Thai and Ho invasions of the 18th and 19th centuries when many of the wats were destroyed. With the introduction of socialism in 1975 Buddhism was banned from primary schools and people prohibited from giving alms to monks. With the increasing religious tolerance of the regime it is now undergoing a revival and many of the wats are being rebuilt and redecorated. Males are expected to become monks for three months or so before marriage, usually during Buddhist Lent. All members of the priesthood are placed under the authority of a superior – the *Phra Sangharaja* – whose seat was traditionally in the capital of the kingdom.

In line with Buddhist tradition, materialism and the accumulation of personal wealth is generally frowned on in Laos. Poverty is admired as a form of spirituality. This belief proved rather convenient for the Communist regime, when it was taken to extremes. Today, in the new capitalist climate, the traditional attributes of spirituality sit uncomfortably with Laos' increasingly bourgeois aspirations.

Buddhism, as it is practised in Laos, is not the 'other-worldly' religion of Western conception. Ultimate salvation – enlightenment, or *nirvana* – is a distant goal for most people. Lao Buddhists pursue the Law of Karma, the reduction of suffering. Meritorious acts are undertaken and demeritorious ones avoided so that life and more particularly future life, might be improved. Karma is often thought of in the West as fate. It is not. It is true that previous karma determines a person's position in society, but there is still room for individual action – and a person is ultimately responsible for that action. It is the law of cause and effect.

⁛ Mudras and the Buddha image

Artists producing images of the Buddha does not try to create an original piece of art; they are trying to be faithful to a tradition which can be traced back over centuries. It is important to appreciate that the Buddha image is not merely a work of art but an object of and for worship. Sanskrit poetry even sets down the characteristics of the Buddha – albeit in rather unlikely terms: legs like a deer, arms like an elephant's trunk, a chin like a mango stone and hair like the stings of scorpions. The Pali texts of Theravada Buddhism add the 108 auspicious signs, long toes and fingers of equal length, body like a banyan tree and eyelashes like a cow's. The Buddha can be represented either sitting, lying (indicating paranirvana), or standing, and (in Thailand) occasionally walking. He is often represented standing on an open lotus flower: the Buddha was born into an impure world, and likewise the lotus germinates in mud but rises above the filth to flower. Each image will be represented in a particular mudra or 'attitude', of which there are 40. The most common are:

Abhayamudra – dispelling fear or giving protection; right hand (sometimes both hands) raised, palm outwards, usually with the Buddha in a standing position.

Varamudra – giving blessing or charity; the right hand pointing downwards, the palm facing outwards, with the Buddha either seated or standing.

Vitarkamudra – preaching mudra; the ends of the thumb and index finger of the right hand touch to form a circle, symbolizing the Wheel of Law. The Buddha can either be seated or standing.

Dharmacakramudra – 'spinning the Wheel of Law'; a preaching mudra symbolizing the teaching of the first sermon. The hands are held in front of the chest, thumbs and index fingers of both joined, one facing inwards and one outwards.

Bhumisparcamudra – 'calling the earth goddess to witness' or 'touching the earth'; the right hand rests on the right knee with the tips of the fingers 'touching ground', thus calling the earth goddess Dharani/Thoranee to witness his enlightenment and victory over Mara, the king of demons. The Buddha is always seated.

Dhyanamudra – meditation; both hands resting open, palms upwards, in the lap, right over left.

Other points of note:
Vajrasana – yogic posture of meditation; cross-legged, both soles of the feet visible.

Virasana – yogic posture of meditation; cross-legged, but with the right leg on top of the left, covering the left foot (also known as paryankasana).

Buddha under Naga – the Buddha is shown in an attitude of meditation with a cobra rearing up over his head. This refers to an episode in the Buddha's life when he was meditating; a rain storm broke and Nagaraja, the king of the nagas (snakes), curled up under the Buddha (seven coils) and then used his seven-headed hood to protect the Holy One from the falling rain.

Buddha calling for rain – the Buddha is depicted standing, both arms held stiffly at the side of the body, fingers pointing downwards.

Bhumisparcamudra – calling the earth goddess to witness. Sukhothai period, 13th-14th century.

Dhyanamudra – meditation. Sukhothai period, 13th-14th century.

Abhayamudra – dispelling fear or giving protection. Lopburi Buddha, Khmer style 12th century.

Vitarkamudra – preaching,"spinning the Wheel of Law". Dvaravati Buddha, 7th-8th century, seated in the "European" manner.

Abhayamudra – dispelling fear or giving protection; subduing Mara position. Lopburi Buddha, Khmer style 13th century.

The Buddha 'Calling for rain'.

Background Religion

It is important to draw a distinction between 'academic' Buddhism, as it tends to be understood in the West and 'popular' Buddhism, as it is practised in Laos. In Laos, Buddhism is a syncretic religion: it incorporates elements of Brahmanism, animism and ancestor worship. Amulets are worn to protect against harm and are often sold in temple compounds. In the countryside, farmers have what they consider to be a healthy regard for the spirits (*phi*) and demons that inhabit the rivers, trees and forests. Astrologers are widely consulted by urban and rural dwellers alike. It is these aspects of Lao Buddhism which help to provide worldly assurance and they are perceived to be complementary, not in contradiction, with Buddhist teachings.

Most Lao villages will contain a temple, monastery or wat (the word does not translate accurately), see box page 308. The wat represents the mental heart of each community and most young men at some point in their lives will become ordained as monks, usually during the Buddhist Rains Retreat, which stretches from July to October. Previously this period represented the only opportunity for a young man to gain an education and to learn how to read. An equally important reason for a man to become ordained is so that he can accumulate merit for his family, particularly for his mother, who as a woman cannot become ordained.

As in Thailand, Laos has adopted the Indian epic *Ramayana*, which has been the inspiration for much Lao art and sculpture. Complete manuscripts of the Lao *Ramayana* – known as the *Phra Lak Phra Lam*; see box, page 312 – used to be kept at Wat Phra Kaeo and Wat Sisaket.

Buddhism under Communism

Buddhism's relationship with Communism has been complex and usually ambivalent. As the Pathet Lao began their revolutionary mission they saw in the country's monks a useful means by which to spread their message. Many monks, though they may themselves have renounced material possessions and all desires, were conscious of the inequalities in society and the impoverished conditions in which many people lived their lives. Indeed most of them came from poor rural backgrounds. In addition many monks saw themselves as the guardians of Lao culture and as the US became more closely involved in the country so they increasingly felt that it was their job to protect the people against the spread of an alien culture and mores. Therefore, right from the start, monks had a natural sympathy with the ideals of the Pathet Lao. Indeed, significant numbers renounced their vows and joined the revolution. Others stayed on in their monasteries, but used their positions and the teachings of the Buddha to further the revolutionary cause. The Pathet Lao, for their part, saw the monks as a legitimizing force which would assist in their revolutionary efforts. Monks were often the most respected individuals in society and if the Pathet Lao could somehow piggy-back on this respect then they too, it was reasoned, would gain in credibility and respect. The Rightist government also tried to do the same, but with notably less success.

With the victory of the Pathet Lao in 1975, their view of the *sangha* (monkhood) changed. No longer were monks a useful vehicle in building revolution; overnight they became a potential threat. Monks were forced to attend re-education seminars where they were instructed that they could no longer teach about merit or *karma*, two central pillars of Buddhism. Their sermons were taped by Pathet Lao cadres to be scrutinized for subversive propaganda and a stream of disillusioned monks began to flee to Thailand. So the *sangha* was emasculated as an independent force. Monks were forced to follow the directives of the Lao People's Revolutionary Party and the *sangha* came under strict Party control. Monasteries were expected to become mini-cooperatives so that they did not have to depend on the laity for alms and they were paid a small salary by the state for undertaking teaching and health work. In short, the LPDR seemed intent on undermining the *sangha* as an independent force in Lao society, making it dependent on the state for its survival and largely irrelevant to wider society. The success of the

Pathet Lao's policy of marginalization can be seen in the number of monks in the country. In 1975 there were 20,000 monks. By 1979 this had shrunk to just 1700.

However, before the *sangha* could sink into obscurity and irrelevance, the government eased its policy in 1979 and began to allow monks and the *sangha* greater latitude. In addition and perhaps more importantly, the leadership embraced certain aspects of Lao culture, one of which was Theravada Buddhism. The memorial to the revolutionary struggle in Vientiane, for example, was designed as a Buddhist that (stupa) and government ministers enthusiastically join in the celebration of Buddhist festivals.

Animism

While the majority of the population (about 60-65%) follow Theravada Buddhism, Animism is practised by about 30% of the population. The term Animism derives from the Latin word 'anima', meaning mind or soul. At a very basic level, Animism refers to a belief in spirits. Animism is particularly common among Lao Theung and Lao Soung groups minority groups but elements of Animism have also infiltrated or been grafted onto Buddhism and Lao culture at a broader level. Most people believe in *phi*, spirits, which are seen as fundamental to their relationship with nature and the community. The word *phi* has even been adopted into Lao language to mean ghost, while *phi-baa* means crazy. Many Lao people believe that spiritual forces need to be placated, usually through a *baci* ceremony (see page 33), as they can cause illness, disease or bad luck. Inexplicable events – including strange behaviour by foreign visitors – are often attributed to 'ghosts'. Buddhist monks are often called upon to exorcize bad spirits and most wats have a small spirit house built on the monastic grounds. Animists generally suffer little discrimination from the government; however, some practises are discouraged for health and security reasons.

Christianity in post-1975 Laos

The smallest religious group represented in Laos are Christians, including Roman Catholics, who account for around 2% of the population. There are around 30,000 to 40,000 Catholics in the country, many of whom are ethnic Vietnamese, concentrated in major urban centres along the Mekong River.

Following the revolution, many churches in provincial towns were turned into community centres and meeting halls. Vientiane's Evangelical Church has held a Sunday service ever since 1979 but it is only in recent years that Christians have felt free to worship openly and even this 'freedom' comes with qualifications. In 1989 the first consultation between the country's Christian leaders (Protestant and Roman Catholic) was authorized by the government; it was the first such meeting since 'liberation' and was also attended by government representatives and two Hmong leaders of the Buddhist Federation.

It's illegal for foreigners to proselytize in Laos; persons found guilty can be subject to arrest and deportation for 'creating social divisions'. Foreign missionaries were ejected from Laos in 1975 and, today, foreign NGOs affiliated with religious organizations are only allowed to work in the country on the condition that they don't try to spread their religion. Not many Buddhists have converted to Christianity but it seems to be growing among the animist hilltribes. The US Bible Society has recently published a modern translation of the Bible into Lao but tribal-language editions do not yet exist. The shortage of bibles and other literature has prompted Christian leaders to offer unsolicited gifts to the department of religious affairs to ease restrictions on the import of hymn books and bibles from Thailand.

While there is more freedom to worship today than during the pre-reform period, there is still a sense in the leadership that Christians are a political threat. In 1998 the authorities arrested 44 Christians, among them three Americans, for conducting unauthorized church services in people's private homes. The Americans were expelled but the Laotians were thrown in prison. This sort of knee-jerk reaction usually ends up being counter-productive. The US Congress responded to what they saw as religious persecution by blocking an economic agreement that was likely to significantly boost textile exports to the US. The fact that the leadership in Laos is hypersensitive to such issues was reinforced in November 1999 when six Christian leaders were reportedly arrested and imprisoned for planning a pro-democracy rally along with around 100 other activists.

Land and environment

Geography

Laos stretches about 1000 km from north to south, while distances from east to west range from 140 to 500 km. The country covers 236,800 sq km – less than half the size of France and just a third of the size of Texas. Only 24% of the population lives in towns. The country has the lowest population density in Asia, with 22 people per sq km.

Rugged mountains cover more than three-quarters of the country and with few all-weather roads (there are just 4000 km of sealed roads in the entire country), rivers remain important communication routes. Historically, the Mekong River has been the country's economic artery. On its banks nestle Laos' most important cities: in the north the small, colourful former royal capital of Luang Prabang, further south the administrative and political capital of Vientiane and farther south still the regional centres of Thakhek, Savannakhet and Pakse.

Laos is dominated by the Mekong River and the Annamite chain of mountains which both run southeast towards the East Sea (South China Sea). Flowing along the borders of Laos are 1865 km of the 4000 km-long Mekong River. The lowlands of the Mekong valley form the principal agricultural areas, especially around Vientiane and Savannakhet and these are home to the lowland Lao – sometimes argued to be the 'true' Lao. The Mekong has three main tributaries: the Nam Ou and Nam Tha from the north and the Nam Ngum, which flows into Vientiane province.

Much of the northern half of Laos is 1500 m or more above sea level and its karst limestone outcrops are deeply dissected by steep-sided river valleys. Further south, the Annamite chain has an average height of 1200 m. Heavily forested, rugged mountains form a natural barrier between Laos and Vietnam. Most of the country is a mixture of mountains and high plateau. There are four main plateau: the Xieng Khouang plateau, better known as the Plain of Jars, in the north, the Nakai and the limestone Khammuoane plateau in the centre and the 10,000 sq km Boloven Plateau to the south. The highest peak is the 2800 m Bia Mountain, which rises above the Xieng Khouang plateau to the northeast.

Climate

The rainy season is from May through to September-October; the tropical lowlands receive an annual average rainfall of 1250 mm a year. Temperatures during these months are between 30 and 40°C. In mountainous Xieng Khoung Province, it is cooler and temperatures can drop to freezing point in December and January. The first half of the dry season, from November to April, is cool, with temperatures between 10 and 20°C. This gives way to a hot, dry season from March to June when temperatures soar and are often in excess of 35°C. Average rainfall in Vientiane is 1700 mm, although in North Laos and the highlands it is much wetter, with more than 3000 mm each year.

Vegetation

Much of Laos is forested. The vegetation is rich and diverse: a mix of tropical and subtropical species. Grassy savannah predominates on plateau areas such as the Plain of Jars. In the forests, some hardwoods tower to over 30 m, while tropical palms and mango are found in the lowlands and large stands of pine in the remote northern hills.

Rural people rely heavily on the Mekong River and its watershed for everything from transport to rice production and fishing. It is estimated that 80% of the country is located near the Mekong, its tributaries or in the watershed. Over half of all vital protein consumed in rural areas comes from fish, frogs and other river creatures. Agriculture is of utmost importance to Lao people, with about 80% of the population engaged in subsistence farming.

In the mid-20th century over 70% of the country was covered with forest. Today, this number has been reduced to around 40% and of this only 17% remains old growth tropical forest. The rattan, cardamom, mushrooms, orchids and wild meat gathered from these forests are essential to rural livelihoods and in many cases generate over half of the income of a rural family. The Lao government has established 20 National Protected Areas or NPAs (formerly known as National Biodiversity Conservation Areas, NBCAs), plus two corridor areas, covering 14.3% of the country. Although this is a step forward, illegal hunting and logging is still rife in most areas.

Logging provides Laos with a large proportion of its export earnings. Officially, around 450,000 cu m of forest are felled each year for commercial purposes but this is probably an underestimate owing to the activities of illegal loggers, many of whom are Chinese, Vietnamese and Thai. A ban on the export of logs in 1988 caused official timber export earnings to slump 30% but environmentalists claim that the ban has had little impact on the number of logs being exported. Another ban was imposed in late 1991. In addition, shifting cultivators clear an estimated 100,000 ha of forest a year. The government sees shifting cultivators (most of whom are from one of Laos' ethnic minorities) as the primary cause of forest loss and the current five-year development plan has reiterated the government's commitment to 'totally eradicating' shifting cultivation. But if the situation is similar to neighbouring countries like Thailand and Vietnam then this will do little to preserve the forest because the primary culprits are commercial logging concerns. Government reforestation programmes far from compensate for the destruction. In October 1989 the Council of Ministers issued a decree on the preservation of forests of which the people appear to be blissfully unaware. There was a half-hearted propaganda campaign to 'teach every Lao citizen to love nature and develop a sense of responsibility for the preservation of forests'.

Wildlife

Mammals include everything from wildcats, leopards and tigers to bears, wild cattle and small barking deer. Laos is also home to the large Asian elk, rhinoceros, elephants, monkeys, gibbons and ubiquitous rabbits and squirrels. Ornithological life encompasses pheasants, partridges, many songbirds, ducks and some hawks and eagles – although in rural areas many birds (and other animals) have been killed for food. There is an abundant reptilian population, including cobras, kraits, crocodiles and lizards. The lower reaches of the Mekong River, marking the border between Cambodia and Laos, is the last place in Indochina where the rare Irrawaddy dolphin is to be found. However, dynamite fishing is decimating the population and today there are probably under 20 left. Another rare denizen of the Mekong, but one that stands a greater chance of survival, is the pa buk catfish (*Pangasianodon gigas*) which weighs up to 340 kg. This riverbed-dwelling fish was first described by Western science only in 1930, although Lao fishermen and their Thai counterparts had been catching it for many years – as James McCarthy notes in the account of his travels through Siam and Laos published in 1900. The fish is a delicacy and clearly has been for many years – its roe was paid as tribute to China in the late 19th century. Due to overfishing, by the 1980s the numbers of pa buk had become severely depleted. However, a breeding programme is having some success and young pa buk fingerlings are now being released into the Mekong.

There is an enormous problem of smuggling rare animals out of Laos, mainly to South Korea and China. In 1978, the gall bladder of a black bear from Laos was auctioned in Seoul for US$55,000. Teeth and bones of wild cats from Laos are in demand for Chinese medicine. The English-language daily, *Khao San Pathet Lao*, published a report estimating that in 1992 more than 10 tonnes of protected wild animals had been slaughtered for export in the northeastern province of Houa Phanh.

Laos' wildlife has taken a caning due to poachers peddling animals across the country's borders. In 2001 the authors of 'Wildlife Trade in Laos: the End of the Game' suspected that wildlife trade was the largest source of income in Lao villages after fishing and was worth a conservative estimate of US$35 million per year.

In 2004, the Lao government joined CITES, the world's foremost conservation treaty regulating the international trade in endangered species. Regardless, Laos is still home to a diverse range of wildlife will some 800 bird and 100 mammal species. New species are popping up on an almost annual basis.

The degree to which Laos' flora and fauna are under-researched was illustrated in August 1999 when it was announced that a previously unknown species of striped rabbit had been discovered quietly nibbling the grass in the mountains dividing Laos from Vietnam. This area of Indochina has proved a veritable cornucopia of unknown animals. During the 1990s scientists have discovered one antelope, several species of deer, an ox and even a remnant herd of Javan rhinoceros, a species which was previously thought to be confined to a small corner of West Java.

Books

Laos

Art and culture

Dakin, Brett (2003) *Another Quiet American*, Asia Books. Dakin's experiences of working in Laos, with some interesting cultural insights.

Evans, Grant (1999) *Laos: Culture and Society*, Chiang Mai, Thailand: Silkworm Books. Edited volume written by assorted scholars of Laos. Highly informed; for those who really want to know about the country.

Fay, Kim (2005) *To Asia with Love: A Connoisseur's Guide to Cambodia, Laos, Thailand Vietnam*, Global Directions Inc/ Things Asian Press. Great anthology of ideas, inspirations and experiences of Southeast Asia from the people who live there.

Phia Sing (1995) *Traditional Recipes of Laos*, Totnes, Devon, UK: Prospect Books. The best Lao cookbook available. The recipes were collected by the chief chef at the Royal Palace in Luang Prabang, Phia Sing, in the 1960s. They have been translated into English and made West-friendly by replacing some of the more esoteric ingredients.

Economics, politics and development

Dommen, Arthur J (1985) *Laos: Keystone of Indochina*, Boulder: Westview Press. Out of date but a reasonable overview.

Evans, Grant (1990) *Lao Peasants under Socialism*, New Haven: Yale University Press. The definitive account of farmers in modern Laos. A new edition published by Silkworm Books in Chiang Mai (Thailand) takes into account economic changes brought about by the New Economic Mechanism.

Stuart-Fox, Martin (1982) *Contemporary Laos*, St Lucia: Queensland University Press. A useful overview of Laos up to 1980.

Stuart-Fox, Martin (1986) *Laos – Politics, Economics and Society*, London: Francis Pinter. Out of date but a good single volume summary of the country providing historical and cultural background.

Stuart-Fox, Martin (1996) *Buddhist Kingdom, Marxist State: the Making of Modern Laos*, Bangkok: White Lotus. A collection of Stuart-Fox's various papers published over the years and brought up to date. Especially good on recent history.

Zasloff, J J and Unger, L (1991) (eds) *Laos: Beyond the Revolution*, Macmillan, Basingstoke. Edited volume with a mixed collection of papers; economics/politics chapters are already rather dated.

History
Kremmer, Christopher, *Bamboo Palace*, HarperCollins Australia. Traces Kremmer's attempts to unravel the mystery surrounding the Lao royal family.
Stuart-Fox, Martin and Kooyman, Mary (1992), *Historical Dictionary of Laos*, New York: the Scarecrow Press. Takes a dictionary approach to Laos' history which is fine if you are looking up a fact or two, but doesn't really lend itself to telling a narrative.
Stuart-Fox, Martin (1997), *A History of Laos*, CUP: Cambridge. Concentrates on the modern period.

Language
Higbie, James, *Lao-English/English-Lao Dictionary and Phrasebook*, Hippocrene Books, Inc.
Marcus, Russell (1983) *Lao-English/ English-Lao Dictionary*, Charles E Tuttle Co, USA. Perhaps the best dictionary available; US$16.95 from www.worldlanguage.com
Phone Bouaravong, *Learning Lao for Everyone*. Locally produced, with tapes.
Werner, Klaus *Learning and Speaking Lao*. Useful and cheaper than Marcus.

Laos and the Indochina War
Castle, Timothy (1993) *A War in the Shadow of Vietnam: US Military Aid to the Royal Lao Government 1955-1975*, New York: Columbia University Press.
Evans,Grant and Rowley, Kelvin (1990) *Red Brotherhood at War, Vietnam Cambodia & Laos since 1975*, Verso.
Evans, Grant (1983) *Yellow Rainmakers: Are Chemical Weapons Being Used in Southeast Asia*, Verso.
McCoy, Alfred W (1991) *The Politics of Heroin: CIA Complicity in the Global Drugs Trade*, Lawrence Hill/Chicago Review Press. Originally published at the beginning of the 1970s, the classic study of the politics of drugs in mainland Southeast Asia.
Parker, James (1995) *Codename Mule: Fighting the Secret War in Laos for the CIA*, Annapolis, Maryland: Naval Institute Press.

Personal story of Americans fighting in Laos. Much of it deals with fighting on the Plain of Jars.
Pyle and Faas (2003) *Lost Over Laos*, De Capo Press. The story of 4 photographers who died in Laos in 1971 and the search, years later, to recover the crash site.
Ratnam, P (1980) *Laos and the Superpowers*, Tulsi Publishing, India.
Robbins, Christopher (1979) *Air America: the Story of the CIS's Secret Airlines*, New York: Putnam Books. The earlier of Robbins' 2 books on the secret war. Made into a film of the same name with Mel Gibson in the starring role.
Robbins, Christopher (1989) *The Ravens: Pilots of the Secret War of Laos*, New York: Bantam Press. The best known of all the books on America's secret war in Laos. The story it tells seems almost too incredible to be true.
Warner, Roger (1995) *Back Fire: the CIA's Secret War in Laos and its Link to the War in Vietnam*, New York: Simon and Schuster. The best of the more recent books recounting the experiences of US servicemen in Laos. Excellent, engaging read. Also published as *Shooting at the Moon*.

Travel and geography
De Carne, Louis (1872) *Travels in Indochina and the Chinese Empire*, London: Chapman Hall. Recounts De Carne's experiences in Laos in 1872, some years before the country was colonized by the French.
Dooley, Tom (1958) *The Edge of Tomorrow*, Farrar, Strauss & Cudahy.
Du Pont De Bie, Natacha (2004) *Ant Egg Soup: The Adventures of a Food Tourist in Laos*, Sceptre. A wonderful portrait of Lao culture and food through the eyes of a food tourist.
Garstin, Crosbie (1928), *The Voyage from London to Indochina*, Heinemann. Hilarious, irreverent journey through Indochina.
Hoskins, John (1991), *The Mekong*, Bangkok: Post Publishing. A large format coffee table book with good photographs and a modest text. Widely available in Bangkok.
Lewis, Norman (1951), *A Dragon Apparent: Travels in Cambodia, Laos and Vietnam*. One of the finest travel books; reprinted by Eland Books but also available second-hand from many bookshops.

Maugham, Somerset (1930) *The Gentlemen in the Parlour: a Record of a Journey from Rangoon to Haiphong*, Heinemann: London. An account of Maugham's journey through Southeast Asia, in classic limpid prose.

McCarthy, James (1994) *Surveying and Exploring in Siam with Descriptions of Laos Dependencies and of Battles against the Chinese Haws*, White Lotus: Bangkok. First published in 1900. An interesting account by Englishman James McCarthy, who was employed by the government of Siam as a surveyor and adviser.

Mouhot, Henri (1986) *Travels in Indochina*, Bangkok: White Lotus. An account of Laos by France's most famous explorer of Southeast Asia. He tried to discover a 'back door' into China by travelling up the Mekong, but died of Malaria in Luang Prabang in 1860. The book has been republished by White Lotus and is easily available in Bangkok; there is also a more expensive reprint available from OUP (Kuala Lumpur).

Murphy, Dervla (1999) *One Foot in Laos*, John Murphy Publisher. An interesting, off-the-beaten-track travelogue of adventures and mishaps through Laos.

Stewart, Lucretia (1998), *Tiger Balm: Travels in Laos, Cambodia and Vietnam*, London: Chatto and Windus.

Southeast Asia

White Lotus, www.thailine.com/lotus, is a Bangkok-based publisher specializing in English language books (with many reprints of old books) on the region.

Dingwall, Alastair (1994) *Traveller's Literary Companion to Southeast Asia*, In Print: Brighton. Extracts from books by Western and regional writers on Southeast Asia. A good overview of what is available.

Dumareay, Jacques (1991) *The Palaces of South-East Asia: Architecture and Customs*, OUP: Singapore. A broad summary of palace art and architecture in Southeast Asia.

Fraser-Lu, Sylvia (1988) *Handwoven Textiles of South-East Asia*, OUP: Singapore. Large well-illustrated book with informative text.

Higham, Charles (1989) *The Archaeology of Mainland Southeast Asia from 10,000 BC to the Fall of Angkor*, CUP: Cambridge. Best summary of changing views of the archaeology of the mainland.

Reid, Anthony (1988) *Southeast Asia in the Age of Commerce 1450-1680: the Lands below the Winds*, Yale University Press: New Haven. Perhaps the best history of everyday life in Southeast Asia, looking at such themes as physical wellbeing, material culture and social organization. Also Volume 2 (1993) *Southeast Asia in the Age of Commerce 1450-1680: Expansion and Crisis*, Yale University Press: New Haven.

Rigg, Jonathan (1997) *Southeast Asia: the Human Landscape of Modernization and Development*, London: Routledge. Focuses on how people have responded to the challenges and tensions of modernization.

SarDesai, DR (1989) *Southeast Asia: Past and Present*, Macmillan: London. Skillful but at times frustratingly thin history of the region from the 1st century to the withdrawal of US forces from Vietnam.

Steinberg, DJ et al (1987) *In Search of Southeast Asia: a Modern History*, University of Hawaii Press: Honolulu. The best standard history of the region.

Tarling, Nicholars (1992) (edit) *Cambridge History of Southeast Asia*, CUP: Cambridge. 2-volume edited study by theme and region, with contributions from most of the leading historians of the region. The history is fairly conventional.

Footnotes

Useful words and phrases

Greetings

Yes/No	men/baw	A little, a bit	noi, hoi
Thank you/	kop jai/	Where?	you-sigh?
no thank you	baw, kop jai	How much is...?	Tow-dai?
Hello/goodbye	suh-bye-dee/lah-gohn	It doesn't matter,	baw penh yang
What is your name?	Chow seu yang?	never mind	
My name is...	koi seu....	Pardon?	kow toat?
Excuse me, sorry	ko toat	I don't understand	Kow baw cow-chi
Can/do you speak	Koy pahk pah-sah	How are you?	Chao suh-bye-dee-baw?
English?	Anhg-geet?	not very well	baw suh-bye

Getting around

Where is the	Sa ta ni lot	Is it far?	Kai baw?
train/bus station?	phai/mee yu sai?	Turn left/turn right	leo sai/leo qua
How much to go to...?	Khit la ka taw dai...?	Go straight on	pai leuy
That's expensive	pheng-lie	River	Xe/Se, Houei/Houai
Will you go for...kip?	Chow ja pai...kip?	Town	Muang/Mouang
What time does	Lot mea oak jay mong...?	Mountain	phou
the bus/train leave for...?			

Sleeping

What is the charge	Kit laka van nuang	Does the room	Hong me nam hawn baw?
each night?	taw dai?	have hot water?	
Is the room	Hong me ai yen baw?	Does the room	Me hang ap nam baw?
air conditioned?		have a bathroom?	
Can I see the room	Koi ko beunghong dea?	Can I have the bill	Koi ton han bai hap?
first please?		please?	

Eating

Can I see a menu?	Kho beung lay kan arhan?	Where is	Lahn ah hai you-sigh?
Can I have...?	Khoy tong kan...?	a restaurant?	
I am hungry	Koy heo kao	Breakfast	arhan sao
I am thirsty	Koy heo nahm	Lunch	arhan athieng
I want to eat	Koh yahk kin kao	It costs....kip	Lah-kah ahn-nee...kip

Time

in the morning	muh-sao	Monday	Van Chanh
in the afternoon	thon-by	Tuesday	Van Ang Khan
in the evening	muh-leng	Wednesday	Van Pud
today	muh-nee	Thursday	Van Pa Had
tomorrow	muh-ouhn	Friday	Van Sook
yesterday	muh van-nee	Saturday	Van Sao
		Sunday	Van Arthid

1	nung	20	sao
2	song	21	sao-et
3	sahm	22	sao-song
4	see	30	sahn-sip
5	hah	100	hoy
6	hoke	101	hoy-nung
7	chet	150	hoy-hah-sip
8	pet	200	song-hoy
9	cow	1000	phan
10	sip	10,000	sip-phan
11	sip-et	100,000	muun
12	sip-song	1,000,000	laan

Basic vocabulary

airport	deune yonh	hotel	hong
bank	had xay	island	koh (or) hath
bathroom	hong nam	market	ta lath
beach	heva	medicine	ya pua payad
beautiful	ngam	open	peud
bicycle	loht teep	petrol	nahm-mahn-eh-sahng
big	nyai	police	lam louad
boat	quoi loth bath	police station	poam lam louad
bus	loht-buht	post office	hong kana pai sa nee
bus station	hon kay ya	restaurant	han arhane
buy	sue	road	tha nonh
chemist	han kay ya	room	hong
clean	sa ard	shop	hanh
closed	arte	sick (ill)	bo sabay
cold	jenh	silk	mai
day	vanh (or) mua	small	noy
delicious	sehb	stop	yoot
dirty	soka pox	taxi	loht doy-sanh
doctor	than mah	that	nahn
eat	kinh	this	nee, ahn-nee
embassy	Satan Tood	ticket (air)	pee yonh
excellent	dee leuth	ticket (bus)	pee lot mea
expensive	pheng	toilet	hong nam
food	ah-han	town	nai mouang
fruit	mak-mai	very	lai-lai
hospital	hong moh	water	nam (or) nah
hot (temp)	hawn	what	men-nyung

Glossary

Amitabha the Buddha of the Past

Amulet protective medallion

Arhat one who has perfected himself

Avadana Buddhist narrative, telling of the deeds of saintly souls

Avalokitsvara also known as Amitabha and Lokeshvara, the name literally means 'World Lord'; he is the compassionate male Bodhisattva, the saviour of Mahayana Buddhism and represents the central force of creation in the universe

Bai sema boundary stones marking consecrated ground around a bot

Ban village; shortened from muban

Batik a form of resist dyeing

Bhikku Buddhist monk

Bodhi the tree under which the Buddha achieved enlightenment (*Ficus religiosa*)

Bodhisattva a future Buddha. In Mahayana Buddhism, someone who has attained enlightenment, but who postpones nirvana to help others reach it.

Boun Lao festival

Brahma the Creator, one of the gods of the Hindu trinity, usually represented with 4 faces, and often mounted on a hamsa

Brahmin a Hindu priest

Bun to make merit

Caryatid elephants, often used as buttressing decorations

Champa rival empire of the Khmers, of Hindu culture, based in present day Vietnam

Chao title for Lao kings

Charn animist priest who conducts the *basi* ceremony in Laos

Chat honorific umbrella or royal parasol

Chedi religious monument (often bell-shaped) containing relics of the Buddha or other holy remains

Chenla Chinese name for Cambodia before the Khmer era

Deva a Hindu-derived male god

Devata a Hindu-derived goddess

Dharma the Buddhist law

Dok sofa frond-like construction surmounting temple roofs in Laos. Over 10 flowers means the wat was built by a king

Dtin sin decorative border on a skirt

Dvarapala guardian figure, usually placed at the entrance to a temple

Funan the oldest Indianised state of Indochina and precursor to Chenla

Ganesh elephant-headed son of Siva

Garuda mythical divine bird, with predatory beak and claws, and human body; the king of birds, enemy of naga and mount of Vishnu

Gautama the historic Buddha

Geomancy divination by lines and figures

Gopura crowned or covered gate, entrance to a religious area

Hamsa sacred goose, Brahma's mount; in Buddhism it represents the flight of doctrine

Hinayana 'Lesser Vehicle', major Buddhist sect in Southeast Asia, usually termed Theravada Buddhism

Hor kong a pavilion built on stilts where the temple drum is kept

Hor latsalot temple chapel of the funeral cart

Hor song phra secondary chapel

Hor takang bell tower

Hor tray/trai library where manuscripts are stored in a Lao or Thai temple

Hor vay offering temple

Ikat tie-dye method of patterning cloth

Indra the Vedic god of the heavens, weather and war

Jataka(s) the birth stories of the Buddha; they normally number 547; the last 10 are the most important

Kala (makara) a demon ordered to consume itself; often sculpted with grinning face and bulging eyes over entranceways to act as a door guardian; also known as kirtamukha

Kathin/krathin a month period during the 8th lunar month when lay people present robes and gifts to monks

Ketumula flame-like motif above the Buddha head

Kinaree half-human, half-bird, usually depicted as a heavenly musician

Kirtamukha see kala

Koutdi see kuti

Krishna incarnation of Vishnu

Kuti living quarters of Buddhist monks in a temple complex

Laterite bright red tropical soil/stone commonly used in Khmer monuments

Linga phallic symbol and one of the forms of Siva. Embedded in a pedestal shaped to allow drainage of lustral water poured over it, the linga typically has a succession of cross sections: from square at the base through octagonal to round. These symbolize, in order, the trinity of Brahma, Vishnu and Siva

Lokeshvara see Avalokitsvara

Mahabharata a Hindu epic text

Mahayana 'Greater Vehicle', major Buddhist sect

Maitreya the future Buddha

Makara mythological aquatic reptile often found with the kala framing doorways

Mandala a focus for meditation; a representation of the cosmos

Mara personification of evil and tempter of the Buddha

Matmii Lao cotton ikat

Mat mi see matmii

Meru sacred or cosmic mountain at the centre of the world in Hindu-Buddhist cosmology; home of the gods

Mondop from the sanskrit, mandapa. A cube-shaped building, often topped with a cone-like structure, used to contain an object of worship like a footprint of the Buddha

Muang administrative unit

Muban village, usually shortened to ban

Mudra symbolic gesture of the hands of the Buddha

Nak Lao river dragon, a mythical guardian creature (see naga)

Naga benevolent mythical water serpent, enemy of Garuda

Naga makara fusion of naga and makara

Nalagiri the elephant let loose to attack the Buddha, who calmed him

Nandi/nandin bull, mount of Siva

Nirvana release from the cycle of suffering in Buddhist belief; 'enlightenment'

Nyak mythical water serpent (see naga)

Pa kama Lao men's all-purpose cloth

paddy/padi unhulled rice

Pali sacred language of Theravada Buddhism

Parvati consort of Siva

Pathet Lao Communist party based in the northeastern provinces of Laos until they came to power in 1975

Pha biang shawl worn by women in Laos

Pha sin piece of cloth, similar to sarong

Phi spirit

Phra sinh see pha sin

Pra Lam Lao version of the Ramayana

Pradaksina pilgrims' clockwise circumambulation of holy structure

Prah sacred

Prang form of stupa built in Khmer style, shaped like a corncob

Prasada stepped pyramid (see prasat)

Prasat residence of a king or of the gods (sanctuary tower), from the Indian prasada

Quan Am Chinese goddess of mercy

Rama incarnation of Vishnu, hero of the Indian epic, the Ramayana

Ramakien Lao version of the Ramayana

Ramayana Hindu romantic epic

Sakyamuni the historic Buddha

Sal the Indian sal tree (Shorea robusta), under which the historic Buddha was born

Sangha the Buddhist order of monks

Sim/sima main sanctuary and ordination hall in a Lao temple complex

Singha mythical guardian lion

Siva the Destroyer, one of the 3 gods of the Hindu trinity; the sacred linga was worshipped as a symbol of Siva

Sofa see dok sofa

Sravasti the miracle at Sravasti when the Buddha subdues the heretics

Stele inscribed stone panel

Stucco plaster, often heavily moulded

Stupa chedi

Tam bun see bun

Tavatimsa heaven of the 33 gods at the summit of Mount Meru

Thanon street

That shrine housing Buddhist relics, a spire or dome-like edifice commemorating the Buddha's life or a funerary temple for royalty

Theravada 'Way of the Elders'; major Buddhist sect also known as Hinayana Buddhism ('Lesser Vehicle')

Traiphum the 3 worlds of Buddhist cosmology – heaven, hell and earth

Trimurti the Hindu trinity of gods: Brahma, the Creator, Vishnu the Preserver and Siva the Destroyer

Tripitaka Theravada Buddhism's Pali canon

Ubosoth see bot

Urna the dot or curl on the Buddha's forehead, one of the distinctive physical marks of the Enlightened One

Usnisa the Buddha's top knot or 'wisdom bump'

Vahana 'vehicle', a mythical beast, upon which a deva or god rides

Viharn assembly hall in a Buddhist monastery

Vishnu the Protector, one of the gods of the Hindu trinity

Footnotes Glossary

Index → *bold refer to maps.*

Acknowledgements

Biggest *kop chai deu* to Stu and Dee Dee. Thanks to my excellent travelling companions Leigh McCormick, Samantha Porciello, David Hornsby and Morgan. In Luang Prabang eternal gratitude to Fabrice, Ivan, Caroline, Joanna and Karyn. In the south, thanks to Crazy Hat Paul. Lots of thanks to the mob in Vientiane – particularly for the late night *feu* runs and banter on punctuation through to politics.

Footprint would also like to thank Professor Larry Goodyer, Head of the Leicester School of Pharmacy and director of Nomad Medical, for providing the health section.

And finally, thanks to Joshua Eliot and Jane Bickersteth for their excellent work on earlier editions of *Footprint Laos*.

Map symbols

Administration

- ▢ Capital city
- ○ Other city, town
- ≈ International border
- ≈ Regional border

Roads and travel

- ═══ Motorway
- ──── Main road (National highway)
- ──── Minor road
- ---- Track
- ······ Footpath
- ──── Railway
- ⊣▬ Railway with station
- ✈ Airport
- 🚌 Bus station
- Ⓜ Metro station
- ---- Cable car
- ┼┼┼┼ Funicular
- ⛴ Ferry

Water features

- River, canal
- Lake, ocean
- Seasonal marshland
- Beach, sandbank
- Waterfall
- Reef

Topographical features

- Contours (approx)
- ▲ Mountain, volcano
- Mountain pass
- Escarpment
- Gorge
- Glacier
- Salt flat
- Rocks

Cities and towns

- Main through route
- Main street
- Minor street
- Pedestrianized street

(Other symbols — right column)

- Σ Ɔ Tunnel
- ---- Track
- ······· Footpath
- → One way-street
- ⅢⅢ Steps
- ⤨ Bridge
- Fortified wall
- Park, garden, stadium
- 😴 Sleeping
- 🍴 Eating
- 🎵 Bars & clubs
- Building
- ▪ Sight
- ✝ Cathedral, church
- Chinese temple
- Hindu temple
- Meru
- Mosque
- Stupa
- ✡ Synagogue
- ℹ Tourist office
- 🏛 Museum
- ✉ Post office
- Ⓟ Police
- Ⓢ Bank
- @ Internet
- ♪ Telephone
- Market
- Medical services
- Ⓟ Parking
- Petrol
- Golf
- A Detail map
- A Related map

Other symbols

- Archaeological site
- ♦ National park, wildlife reserve
- Viewing point
- Campsite
- Refuge, lodge
- Castle, fort
- Diving
- Deciduous, coniferous, palm trees
- Hide
- Vineyard, winery
- Distillery
- Shipwreck
- Historic battlefield

Laos

CHINA

(MAR
A)

VIETNAM

CHINA

Phongsali

Luang
Namtha

Udomxai

Houei Xai

Xam
Neua

Gulf of Tonkin

Mekong River
Luang
Prabang

Sayaboury   Phonsavanh
Plain of Jars

Vang Vieng

*Nam Ngum
Reservoir*   Paksan

VIENTIANE

Annamite Range

Mekong River

THAILAND

Thakhek

Savannakhet

Salavan

Sekong

Pakse   *Boloven
Plateau*

Attapeu

CAMBODIA

❶ ❷ ❸

Main road
Secondary road
Other road

Altitude in metres
3000
2000
1000
500
100
0

Neighbouring
country

N

100 km
100 miles

Map 1

CHINA

Lan Toui

Ou Neua · Xin Chai · Tao Phya

Khang

Xi Pha Ti · Den Xa

Muang Uthai · Ou · Muang Hat Him

Sien Loum · Sop Soum

Pay Cho

Ngay Neua · Phounot · La

Xing Py Kho · Hat Xa

Phongsali · Hu

Boua Neua · Xier

Nam Pung

PHONGS

Muang Sam Ph

Boun Tai · Kh

Ha

Long Nai Yang

Mok Quang

Pan Nam N

Mohan · Mua

Say

MYANMAR (BURMA)

Phaya Asa

Muang Sing · Yao · Boten

Mekong

Bo · Muang Nang · ◆ *Nam Ha NPA* · Nateui · Muang Hai

Muang Long · Xongta · Latxang

Ban Kha · Luang Namtha✈

Xieng Kok · Namo Tai · Lac

Pang · Muang La · Se

Pha · Vieng Phouka · Se

LUANG NAMTHA · Konoy · Se

Sen Po Mueng · Khas Khouis

Muang Moeng · ③ · Sop Ngin · Udomxai

Pia Sine · Na Houang · Pakmong · Lao

Ha Hen · Ta Hou · Ngeun · Pawi

BOKEO · Ban Sod · Na Lae · ②

Ta Fa · Nu · Muang Beng

Namngui · Poung · Houei Niete · **UDOMXAI** · Nam Ne

Chiang Khong · Houei Xai · Houei Nam · Kheun · Konpok · Donkton · Muang Inga · Coc N

Tha · Pha Udom · *Beng* · Lat Hane

Ham Lem · Thinkeo · **Muang Houn** · *Pak Ou Caves*

Pak Tha · Kham · Tu

Na Mao · Hat Teu

Pak Beng · Xeung Bo · Luang Pra✈

Hat Sah · Pak Kham · *Mekong* · Tanoun · Hou

Pang Hai · Meo · Pak Ngeun · Tha Suang · Phonxai Gnai

Muang Ngeun · Hongsa · Bouam Phay

Xieng Lom · Kiou Kacham

Xieng Hon · Muang Nan · Sen Cun

Mep · Na San · Tha Deua · P

Na Khoum

THAILAND · **Sayaboury** · La S

Kasi

Muang Phieng · Thieng

Lik

Na Sing · **VIENTIA**

Na Khem · Tam · Va

Map 2

Map 1

Ⓐ Ⓑ Ⓒ ① ② ③

Gulf of Tonkin

20 km
20 miles

Axen

Pahai

Chakeuy Tay   Ka Reen
Kaleum

Kong

SEKONG

Dak Chung
Phon
ong   Cha Van   Dak Klao   VIETNAM
Nam Hang

Thakkanat

Thac Kie   Kamone

Keng Say   Sala Tin Toc   Van Tat
Sala Tin Toc   Dong
Ampham
Sakke   Forest

peu   Xaisetha
Pa-am
Sau   18
TAPEU   Phya Ha   Yalakhuntum   Bo-Y
Tasseing

Chom
g My
Nieng

MBODIA

Credits

Editor: Felicity Laughton
Map editor: Sarah Sorensen
Picture editor: Kevin Feeney

Managing Director: Andy Riddle
Publisher: Patrick Dawson
Editorial: Alan Murphy, Sophie Blacksell, Nicola Jones, Jo Williams, Sara Chare
Cartography: Robert Lunn, Kevin Feeney
Cover design: Robert Lunn
Design: Mytton Williams
Sales and marketing: Zoë Jackson, Hannah Bonnell
Advertising sales manager: Renu Sibal
Finance and administration: Elizabeth Taylor

Photography credits

Front cover: Golden Temple, age fotostock/ Superstock
Back cover: Jock O'Tailan
Inside colour section: Jock O'Tailan, Claire Boobbyer; Amanda Ahn, Andrew McConnell, Atmotu Images, David South, dbimages, ImageState, Micah Hanson/Alamy; Jane Sweeney & Robert Harding Travel, JTB Photo, GIUZIOU Franck & hemis/Photolibrary; Carlos Arguelles, Alistair Michael Thomas/ Shutterstock; age fotostock/Superstock; age fotostock, Angelo Cavalli/Shutterstock

Print

Manufactured in India by Nutech. Pulp from sustainable forests.

Footprint feedback

We try as hard as we can to make each Footprint guide as up to date as possible but, of course, things always change. If you want to let us know about your experiences – good, bad or ugly – then don't delay, go to **www.footprintbooks.com** and send in your comments.

Publishing information

Footprint Laos
5th edition
© Footprint Handbooks Ltd
January 2008

ISBN 978 1 906098 18 6
CIP DATA: A catalogue record for this book is available from the British Library

® Footprint Handbooks and the Footprint mark are a registered trademark of Footprint Handbooks Ltd

Published by Footprint
6 Riverside Court
Lower Bristol Road
Bath BA2 3DZ, UK
T +44 (0)1225 469141
F +44 (0)1225 469461
discover@footprintbooks.com
www.footprintbooks.com

Neither the black and white nor coloured maps are intended to have any political significance.

Every effort has been made to ensure that the facts in this guidebook are accurate. However, travellers should still obtain advice about travel and visa requirements before travelling. Hotel and restaurant price codes should only be taken as a guide to the prices and facilities offered by the establishment. It is with the discretion of the owners to vary them from time to time. The authors and publishers cannot accept responsibility for any loss, injury or inconvenience however caused.